# READINGS IN THE WESTERN HUMANITIES

## VOLUME II
### REVISED PRINTING

Edited by

JULIE WILDHABER

KATHLEEN ENGELBERG

C. LANSING HAYS

Headnotes by

ROY T. MATTHEWS

F. DeWITT PLATT

Mayfield Publishing Company
Mountain View, California
London • Toronto

**Library of Congress Cataloging-in-Publication Data**

Readings in the Western Humanities / edited by Julie Wildhaber,
 Kathleen Engelberg, C. Lansing Hays ; headnotes by Roy T. Matthews,
 F. DeWitt Platt. — Rev. printing.
  p.    cm.
  "Designed to accompany Roy Matthews and DeWitt Platt's The Western
humanities"—Pref.
  ISBN 1-55934-456-3 (v. 1). — ISBN 1-55934-457-1 (v. 2)
  1. College readers.  2. Humanities—Problems, exercises, etc.
3. Readers—Humanities.  I. Wildhaber, Julie.  II. Engelberg,
Kathleen.  III. Hays, C. Lansing.  IV. Matthews, Roy T.  Western
humanities.
PE1122.G625   1994                            94-35337
                                                 CIP

International Standard Book Number information
*The Western Humanities*, 2/e                                    1-55934-412-1
*The Western Humanities*, 2/e, Volume 1                          1-55934-418-0
*The Western Humanities*, 2/e, Volume 2                          1-55934-421-0
*Readings in the Western Humanities*, Volume 1                   1-55934-456-3
*Readings in the Western Humanities*, Volume 2                   1-55934-457-1
*The Western Humanities*, 2/e, (#412-1)
  with *Readings* Volume 1 and *Readings* Volume 2               1-55934-463-6
*The Western Humanities*, 2/e, (#412-1)
  with *Readings* Volume 1 (#456-3)                              1-55934-464-4
*The Western Humanities*, 2/e, (#412-1)
  with *Readings* Volume 2 (#457-1)                              1-55934-465-2
*The Western Humanities*, 2/e, Volume 1 (#418-0)
  with *Readings* Volume 1 (#456-3)                              1-55934-466-0
*The Western Humanities*, 2/e, Volume 2 (#421-0)
  with *Readings* Volume 2 (#457-1)                              1-55934-467-9

Please call Mayfield Publishing Company at (800) 433-1279 to inquire about packaging
options not listed above.

Manufactured in the United States of America

10  9  8  7  6  5  4  3

Mayfield Publishing Company
1280 Villa Street
Mountain View, California 94041

Sponsoring editor, Holly J. Allen; production editor, Julianna Scott; text designer,
Wendy Calmenson; cover designer, Christine Zipparro; manufacturing manager,
Martha Branch. The text was set in 9/11 Palatino by ExecuStaff and printed on 50#
Butte des Morts by Banta Company.

Acknowledgments and copyrights continue at the back of the book on pages 253–255,
which constitute an extension of the copyright page.

 This book is printed on acid-free, recycled paper.

# Preface

This collection of literary and philosophical writings is designed to accompany Roy Matthews and DeWitt Platt's *The Western Humanities*, a textbook that surveys the artistic, cultural, and intellectual heritage of Western civilization from prehistory to the present. Volume I covers ancient Mesopotamia through the Renaissance; Volume II covers the Renaissance through the twentieth century.

Our principal goal in assembling this volume has been to bring the student into contact with as many diverse and representative voices as possible. Compiling an anthology is a quixotic process; the giants of Western thought stand before us, and we, armed with computers and liberal educations, cannot force them into a modest volume without compromises. Thus, we had to make choices.

Our first choice was to include certain voices and not others. The range of Western literature and philosophy is vast, and to keep these books within manageable length we had to exclude many worthwhile writers. Our second choice was to include particular selections and excerpts. Again, our desire for diversity and broad representation compelled us to reproduce relatively brief samples of many writers' work. We hope these samples will entice students into reading more of each of these writers.

We added headnotes to these readings to provide context for the student in order to gain a clearer picture of the importance of each selection. The headnotes were written by Roy T. Matthews and F. DeWitt Platt, the authors of the corresponding text, *The Western Humanities*, Second Edition.

We have been aided in selecting these writings by a number of experienced humanities faculties from around the country. We wish to thank them for their generous and thoughtful advice. Special thanks must go to Roy Matthews and DeWitt Platt for their counsel and for their superb work on *The Western Humanities*, which inspired the demand for this anthology.

# Contents

Chapter

# 11

# The Early Renaissance:
# Return to Classical Roots, 1400–1494

## LEON BATTISTA ALBERTI

## from *On Painting*

Book Two

Alberti's *On Painting* helped insure the triumph of the new Renaissance style over older medieval art. Published in Latin (1435) and Italian (1436), just as the Renaissance was picking up steam, this was the first modern treatise on the theory of painting; it became the era's authoritative guide for painters, both within and outside Florence, including Fra Angelico (about 1400–1455), Piero della Francesca (1420–1492), and perhaps Leonardo da Vinci (1452–1519). From 1600 until 1800, Alberti's treatise was invoked as an authority for painting practices approved by Europe's art academies. Today's historians still find this work invaluable, for it prepared the way for the art, the artist, and the patron of the Renaissance.

Alberti wrote his treatise "as a painter speaking to painters." The work is divided into three "books," or parts. Book I presents a mathematical method for creating perspective—the illusion of depth on a flat surface. Some perspectival ideas had long been used in Italy, but he was the first to codify them into an accessible work. Book II deals with painterly matters, such as color, drawing, and grace and beauty in poses and movements. Book III sets forth a type of humanist painting, by using Greco-Roman themes and depicting the soul's condition through bodily gestures and facial expressions.

Leon Battista Alberti (1404–1472) was the "universal man," the beau ideal of the age. His achievements rivaled those of the later Leonardo da Vinci. Besides painting, Alberti also mastered music, mathematics, engineering, architecture, sculpture, poetry, drama, and civil and canon law, and wrote books on most of these fields. He was a friend of Cosimo dè Medici (1389–1464), the merchant-banker who dominated Florence; Alberti was active in Cosimo's Platonic Academy,

1

the club of artists and thinkers who studied Plato (see *Phaedo* and *The Republic*) together. Alberti's spirit had such force that his friends called him the complete genius, hence the authority attributed to his works.

## Reading the Selection

This selection from Book II of *On Painting* shows Alberti as a Renaissance humanist, making the case for a radical new role for the age's painters. These painters are characterized by intellect, with the ascendancy of mind over hand visible in their art. Humanism is the theme: "[P]ainting contributes to the most honorable delights of the soul." This argument echoes the familiar rationale of humanists that studying and practicing grammar, rhetoric, logic, arithmetic, geometry, music, and astronomy—the seven liberal arts—are good exercises for the soul. What's radical in Alberti's claim is that never before had painting been ranked with the liberal arts. In fact, in the Middle Ages, painting was ranked low, on a par with crafts (shoemaking, weaving, and such). The favorable reception of this treatise encouraged the rise of independent artists, as evidenced around 1500 in the careers of Michelangelo, Leonardo da Vinci, and Raphael.

Alberti also argued that painting should be part of the core curriculum of the schools. To prove his case, he used examples from antiquity showing that the best families required that painting be taught to their sons and daughters. By 1513, Alberti's hope was realized in the well-rounded backgrounds of the idealized lady and gentleman of Castiglione's highly influential *The Book of the Courtier.*

Finally, Alberti was a pioneer in his claim for the sovereign power of paining: "Who can doubt that painting is the master art?" A generation later Leonardo gave voice to the identical claim.

---

Because this [process of] learning may perhaps appear a fatiguing thing to young people, I ought to prove here that painting is not unworthy of consuming all our time and study.

Painting contains a divine force which not only makes absent men present, as friendship is said to do, but moreover makes the dead seem almost alive. Even after many centuries they are recognized with great pleasure and with great admiration for the painter. Plutarch says that Cassander, one of the captains of Alexander, trembled through all his body because he saw a portrait of his King. Agesilaos, the Lacedaemonian, never permitted anyone to paint him or to represent him in sculpture; his own form so displeased him that he avoided being known by those who would come after him. Thus the face of a man who is already dead certainly lives a long life through painting. Some think that painting shaped the gods who were adored by the nations. It certainly was their greatest gift to mortals, for painting is most useful to that piety which joins us to the gods and keeps our souls full of religion. They say that Phidias made in Aulis a god Jove so beautiful that it considerably strengthened the religion then current.

The extent to which painting contributes to the most honourable delights of the soul and to the dignified beauty of things can be clearly seen not only from other things but especially from this: you can conceive of almost nothing so precious which is not made far richer and much more beautiful by association with painting. Ivory, gems and similar expensive things become more precious when worked by the hand of the painter. Gold worked by the art of painting outweighs an equal amount of unworked gold. If figures were made by the hand of Phidias or Praxiteles from lead itself— the lowest of metals—they would be valued more highly than

silver. The painter, Zeuxis, began to give away his things because, as he said, they could not be bought. He did not think it possible to come to a just price which would be satisfactory to the painter, for in painting animals he set himself up almost as a god.

Therefore, painting contains within itself this virture that any master painter who sees his works adored will feel himself considered another god. Who can doubt that painting is the master art or at least not a small ornament of things? The architect, if I am not mistaken, takes from the painter architraves, bases, capitals, columns, façades and other similar things. All the smiths, sculptors, shops and guilds are governed by the rules and art of the painter. It is scarcely possible to find any superior art which is not concerned with painting, so that whatever beauty is found can be said to be born of painting. *But also this, a dignified painting is held in high honour by many so that among all artists some smiths are named, only this is not the rule among smiths.* For this reason, I say among my friends that Narcissus who was changed into a flower, according to the poets, was the inventor of painting. Since painting is already the flower of every art, the story of Narcissus is most to the point. What else can you call painting but a similar embracing with art of what is presented on the surface of the water in the fountain?

Quintilian said that the ancient painters used to circumscribe shadows cast by the sun, and from this our art has grown. There are those who say that a certain Philocles, an Egyptian, and a Cleantes were among the first inventors of this art. The Egyptians affirm that painting was in use among them a good 6000 years before it was carried into Greece. They say that painting was brought to us from Greece after the victory of Marcellus over Sicily. But we are not interested in knowing who was the inventor of the art or the first painter, since we are not telling stories like Pliny. We are, however, building anew an art of painting about which nothing, as I see it, has been written in this age. They say that Euphranor of Isthmus wrote something about measure and about colours, that Antigonos and Xenocrates exchanged something in their letters about painting, and that Apelles wrote to Pelleus about painting. Diogenes Laertius recounts that Demetrius made commentaries on painting. Since all the other arts were recommended in letters by our great men, and since painting was not neglected by our Latin writers, I believe that our ancient Tuscan [ancestors] were already most expert masters in painting.

Trismegistus, an ancient writer, judged that painting and sculpture were born at the same time as religion, *for thus he answered Aesclepius: mankind portrays the gods in his own image from his memories of nature and his own origins.* Who can here deny that in all things public and private, profane and religious, painting has taken all the most honourable parts to itself so that nothing has ever been so esteemed by mortals?

The incredible prices of painted pictures have been recorded. Aristides the Theban sold a single picture for one hundred talents. They say that Rhodes was not burned by King Demetrius for fear that a painting of Protogenes' should perish. It could be said that the city of Rhodes was ransomed from the enemy by a single painting. Pliny collected many other such things in which you can see that good painters have always been greatly honoured by all. The most noble citizens, philosophers and quite a few kings not only enjoyed painted things but also painted with their own hands. Lucius Manilius, Roman citizen, and Fabius, a most noble man, were painters. Turpilius, a Roman knight, painted at Verona. Sitedius, praetor and proconsul, acquired renown as a painter. Pacuvius, tragic poet and nephew of the poet Ennius, painted Hercules in the Roman forum. Socrates, Plato, Metrodorus, Pyrrho were connoisseurs of painting. The emperors Nero, Valentinian, and Alexander Severus were most devoted to painting. It would be too long, however, to recount here how many princes and kings were pleased by painting. Nor does it seem necessary to me to recount all the throng of ancient painters. Their number is seen in the fact that 360 statues, part on horseback and part in chariots, were completed in four hundred days for Demetrius Phalerius, son of Phanostratus. In a land in which there was such a great number of sculptors, can you believe that painters were lacking? I am certain that both these arts are related and nurtured by the same genius, painting with sculpture. But I always give higher rank to the genius of the painter because he works with more difficult things.

However, let us return to our work. Certainly the number of sculptors and painters was great in those times when princes and plebeians, learned and unlearned enjoyed painting, and when painted panels and portraits, considered the choicest booty from the provinces, were set up in the theatres. Finally L. Paulus Aemilius and not a few other Roman citizens taught their sons painting along with the fine arts and the art of living piously and well. This excellent custom was frequently observed among the Greeks who, because they wished their sons to be well educated, taught them painting along with geometry and music. It was also an honour among women to know how to paint. Martia, daughter of Varro, is praised by the writers because she knew how to paint. Painting had such reputation and honour among the Greeks that laws and edicts were passed forbidding slaves to learn painting. It was certainly well that they did this, for the art of painting has always been most worthy of liberal minds and noble souls.

As for me, I certainly consider a great appreciation of painting to be the best indication of a most perfect mind, even though it happens that this art is pleasing to the uneducated as well as to the educated. It occurs rarely in any other art that what delights the experienced also moves the inexperienced. In the same way you will find that many greatly desire to be well versed in painting. Nature herself seems to delight in painting, for in the cut faces of marble she often paints centaurs and faces of bearded and curly headed kings. It is said, moreover, that in a gem from Pyrrhus all nine Muses, each with her symbol, are to be found clearly painted by nature. Add to this that in no other art does it happen that both the experienced and the inexperienced of every age apply themselves so voluntarily to the learning and exercising of it. Allow me to speak of myself here. Whenever I turn to painting for my recreation, which I frequently do when I am tired of more pressing affairs, I apply myself to it with so much pleasure that I am surprised that three or four hours have passed. Thus this art gives pleasure and praise to whoever is skilled in it; riches and perpetual fame to one who is master of it. Since these things are so, since painting is the best and most ancient ornament of things, worthy of free men, pleasing to learned and unlearned, I greatly encourage our studious youth to exert themselves as much as possible in painting.

Therefore, I recommend that he who is devoted to painting should learn this art. The first great care of one who seeks to obtain eminence in painting is to acquire the fame and renown of the ancients. It is useful to remember that avarice is always the enemy of virtue. Rarely can anyone given to acquisition of wealth acquire renown. I have seen many in the first flower of learning suddenly sink to money-making. As a result they acquire neither riches nor praise. However, if they had increased their talent with study, they would have easily soared into great renown. Then they would have acquired much riches and pleasure. . . .

# GIOVANNI PICO DELLA MIRANDOLA
# from *On the Dignity of Man*

The Latin oration *On the Dignity of Man* is a tour de force by Pico (1463–1494), a son of the noble house of Mirandola (Italy). Written when Pico was twenty-four, the oration is a mixture of Aristotelian, Hebraic, Arabic, Persian, and Aramaic notions, held together by Neo-Platonism—a blend of Plato's ideas and Christian beliefs. Its central Neo-Platonic motif is that love is the divine glue unifying the universe. Christian in structure, this heady synthesis of ideas breaks free of its frame to become a non-sectarian philosophy.

Pico's oration embodies the Renaissance spirit. In its appeal to wide-ranging sources, it expresses Renaissance zeal for the Classic texts of Greece and Rome as well as hitherto ignored ancient sources. Its theme is the Renaissance belief that the findings of reason and the truths of the Bible share a basic unity, which is reflected in the history of thought. Most of all, its view that human nature has no limits is the prototype of the Renaissance idea of unlimited possibility. Today this idea, with its corollary of free expression, is a defining trait of Western culture.

The oration was composed to introduce a debate Pico scheduled for Rome in 1487. In this debate, Pico proposed to defend nine hundred theses gleaned from his vast readings; he even offered to pay his potential opponents' travel expenses. The debate, however, did not take place because Pope Innocent VIII forbade it. The pope also appointed a commission to examine the debate topics, with the result that seven theses were condemned as heretical, and six more were suspect. Threatened by church officials, Pico subsequently settled in Florence where he was caught up in the anti-Renaissance crusade of the monk Savonarola. Pico's plan to wander as an evangelist was cut short, in 1494, when, at the age of thirty-one, he suddenly died.

## Reading the Selection

This selection from the oration *On the Dignity of Man* begins with a greeting—"Most venerable fathers"—thus establishing that the work was meant to be recited orally, ostensibly before a group of clergy. The major insights to be gained from this selection are Pico's concept of human nature and his style of reasoning.

Pico's concept of human nature is his major contribution to Western thought. For him, human nature is not fixed and the will is perfectly free. In a burst of lyricism he claimed that human beings are shape-shifting creatures who may be vegetative, bestial, rational, divine, or, even, co-equal with God: When humanity's quest ends, "we shall . . . not be ourselves, but He himself who made us" (omitted here). Brushing aside medieval ideas, Pico expresses the radiant faith of Renaissance humanism, that human beings are not flawed by original sin but are capable of becoming godlike.

Pico's style of reasoning reflects the Renaissance trend of treating old problems in new ways. To deal with the question of human nature, he takes the Platonic concept of the Great Chain of Being, which maintains that creation is a linked cord reaching step-by-step from the simplest life to God, and gives it a modern twist. Ancient thinkers had used the Great Chain of Being to argue that human potential is limited, since the place of human beings in the chain is fixed and change would destroy the whole creation. In contrast, Pico claimed that human beings may make of themselves anything they please, because, as hybrids of the whole creation, they exist both outside and above the Great Chain of Being.

Most venerable fathers, I have read in the records of the Arabians that Abdul the Saracen, on being asked what thing on, so to speak, the world's stage, he viewed as most greatly worthy of wonder, answered that he viewed nothing more wonderful than man. And Mercury's, "a great wonder, Asclepius, is man!" agrees with that opinion. On thinking over the reason for these sayings, I was not satisfied by the many assertions made by many men concerning the outstandingness of human nature: that man is the messenger between creatures, familiar with the upper and king of the lower; by the sharpsightedness of the senses, by the hunting-power of reason, and by the light of intelligence, the interpreter of nature; the part in between the standstill of eternity and the flow of time, and, as the Persians say, the bond tying the world together, nay, the nuptial bond; and, according to David, "a little lower than the angels." These reasons are great but not the chief ones, that is, they are not reasons for a lawful claim to the highest wonder as to a prerogative. Why should we not wonder more at the angels themselves and at the very blessed heavenly choirs?

Finally, it seemed to me that I understood why man is the animal that is most happy, and is therefore worthy of all wonder; and lastly, what the state is that is allotted to man in the succession of things, and that is capable of arousing envy not only in the brutes but also in the stars and even in minds beyond the world. It is wonderful and beyond belief. For this is the reason why man is rightly said and thought to be a great marvel and the animal really worthy of wonder. Now hear what it is, fathers; and with kindly ears and for the sake of your humanity, give me your close attention:

Now the highest Father, God the master-builder, had, by the laws of his secret wisdom, fabricated this house, this world which we see, a very superb temple of divinity. He had adorned the super-celestial region with minds. He had animated the celestial globes with eternal souls; he had filled with a diverse throng of animals the cast-off and residual parts of the lower world. But, with the work finished, the Artisan desired that there be someone to reckon up the reason of such a big work, to love its beauty, and to wonder at its greatness. Accordingly, now that all things had been completed, as Moses and Timaeus testify, He lastly considered creating man. But there was nothing in the archetypes from which He could mold a new sprout, nor anything in His storehouses which He could bestow as a heritage upon a new son, nor was there an empty judiciary seat where this contemplator of the universe could sit. Everything was filled up; all things had been laid out in the highest, the lowest, and the middle orders. But it did not belong to the paternal power to have failed in the final parturition, as though exhausted by child-bearing; it did not belong to wisdom, in a case of necessity, to have been tossed back and forth through want of a plan; it did not belong to the loving-kindness which was going to praise divine liberality in others to be forced to condemn itself. Finally, the best of workmen decided that that to which nothing of its very own could be given should be, in composite fashion, whatsoever had belonged individually to each and every thing. Therefore He took up man, a work of indeterminate form; and, placing him at the midpoint of the world, He spoke to him as follows:

"We have given to thee, Adam, no fixed seat, no form of thy very own, no gift peculiarly thine, that thou mayest feel as thine own, have as thine own, possess as thine own the seat, the form, the gifts which thou thyself shalt desire. A limited nature in other creatures is confined within the laws written down by Us. In conformity with thy free judgment, in whose hand We have placed thee, thou art confined by no bounds; and thou wilt fix limits of nature for thyself. I have placed thee at the center of the world, that from there thou mayest more conveniently look around and see whatsoever is in the world. Neither heavenly nor earthly, neither mortal nor immortal have We made thee. Thou, like a judge appointed for being honorable, art the molder and maker of thyself; thou mayest sculpt thyself into whatever shape thou dost prefer. Thou canst grow downward into the lower natures which are brutes. Thou canst again grow upward from thy soul's reason into the higher natures which are divine."

O great liberality of God the Father! O great and wonderful happiness of man. It is given him to have that which he chooses and to be that which he wills. As soon as brutes are born, they bring with them, "from their dam's bag," as Lucilius says, what they are going to possess. Highest spirits have been, either from the beginning or soon after, that which they are going to be throughout everlasting eternity. At man's birth the Father placed in him every sort of seed and sprouts of every kind of life. The seeds that each man cultivates will grow and bear their fruit in him. If he cultivates vegetable seeds, he will become a plant. If the seeds of sensation, he will grow into brute. If rational, he will come out a heavenly animal. If intellectual, he will be an angel, and a son of God. And if he is not contented with the lot of any creature but takes himself up into the center of his own unity, then, made one spirit with God and settled in the solitary darkness of the Father, who is above all things, he will stand ahead of all things. Who does not wonder at this chameleon which we are? Or who at all feels more wonder at anything else whatsoever? It was not unfittingly that Asclepius the Athenian said that man was symbolized by Prometheus in the secret rites, by reason of our nature sloughing its skin and transforming itself; hence metamorphoses were popular among the Jews and the Pythagoreans. For the more secret Hebrew theology at one time reshapes holy Enoch into an angel of divinity, whom they call *malach hashechina*, and at other times reshapes other men into other divinities. According to the Pythagoreans, wicked men are deformed into brutes and, if you believe Empedocles, into plants too. And copying them, Maumeth [Mohammed] often had it on his lips that he who draws back from divine law becomes a brute. And his saying so was reasonable: for it is not the rind which makes the plant, but a dull and non-sentient nature; not the hide which makes a beast of burden, but a brutal and sensual soul; not the spherical body which makes the heavens, but right reason; and not a separateness from the body but a spiritual intelligence which makes an angel. For example, if you see a man given over to his belly and crawling upon the ground, it is a bush not a man that you see. If you see anyone blinded by the illusions of his empty and Calypso-like imagination, seized by the desire of scratching, and delivered over to the senses, it is a brute not a man that you see. If you come upon a philosopher winnowing out all things by right reason, he is a heavenly not an earthly animal. If you come upon a pure contemplator, ignorant of the body, banished to the innermost places of the mind, he is not an earthly, not a heavenly animal; he more superbly is a divinity clothed with human flesh.

Who is there that does not wonder at man? And it is not unreasonable that in the mosaic and Christian holy writ man is sometimes denoted by the name "all flesh" and at other times by that of "every creature"; and man fashions, fabricates, transforms himself into the shape of all flesh, into the character of every creature. Accordingly, where Evantes the

Persian tells of the Chaldaean theology, he writes that man is not any inborn image of himself, but many images coming in from the outside: hence that saying of the Chaldaeans: *enosh hu shinuy vekamah tevaoth baal chayim*, that is, man is an animal of diverse, multiform, and destructible nature.

But why all this? In order for us to understand that, after having been born in this state so that we may be what we will to be, then, since we are held in honor, we ought to take particular care that no one may say against us that we do not know that we are made similar to brutes and mindless beasts of burden. But rather, as Asaph the prophet says: "Ye are all gods, and sons of the most high," unless by abusing the very indulgent liberality of the Father, we make the free choice, which he gave to us, harmful to ourselves instead of helpful toward salvation. Let a certain holy ambition invade the mind, so that we may not be content with mean things but may aspire to the highest things and strive with all our forces to attain them: for if we will to, we can. Let us spurn earthly things; let us struggle toward the heavenly. Let us put in last place whatever is of the world; and let us fly beyond the chambers of the world to the chamber nearest the most lofty divinity. There, as the sacred mysteries reveal, the seraphim, cherubim, and thrones occupy the first places. Ignorant of how to yield to them and unable to endure the second places, let us compete with the angels in dignity and glory. When we have willed it, we shall be not at all below them. . . .

Chapter

# 12

# The High Renaissance and Early Mannerism: 1494–1564

<hr>

## NICCOLÒ MACHIAVELLI

## from *The Prince*

### VIII. Those who come to power by crime

<hr>

*The Prince* is a short and strikingly honest handbook on how to win power and keep it. Based on Niccolò Machiavelli's (1469–1527) personal experiences as diplomat and government employee (in the service of his beloved Florence), the book has become the foundation of modern political theory. In his other works, in particular his histories of Italy and Florence, Machiavelli drew upon his Classical education and personal experiences to develop the message: Learn from the past what works and what does not. But nowhere else does Machiavelli express his thesis so boldly and succinctly as in *The Prince:* "The end justifies any means."

*The Prince*'s harsh and amoral attitude toward politics sparked controversies when first published. Many of Machiavelli's contemporaries, who were witnessing the end of the medieval Age of Faith and experiencing the dawn of a more secular time, were sharply divided over the meaning of his writings. Especially damaging to the book's reputation was its persistent low opinion of human nature. Succeeding generations have debated his analysis of human behavior and his consequent rationale for a strong government. In modern secular society, many readers have come to accept Machiavelli's view that political power, driven by personal or group interests, must be understood in utilitarian and practical terms.

*The Prince*, a treatise on the art of successful governing, is composed of three parts—a short first part, a long main section, and a conclusion. The first three chapters categorize and describe the various types of existing governments. The second part, which makes up most of the book, offers advice and examples on winning and maintaining political power. In these chapters, Machiavelli instructs the ruler on how to raise and organize armies, how to keep subjects loyal, and how to avoid the pitfalls of over-confidence and flattery. Throughout *The Prince*, the author compares and contrasts key terms that make a ruler a success or failure, such as practicing generosity rather than stinginess or exercising compassion instead of cruelty. Recognizing that princes cannot possess all the qualities of perfection, Machiavelli reasons that they often have to pretend to be what they are not in order to keep their subjects' loyalty. He also addresses the issue of fortune, what is now called opportunity, and emphasizes how often it affects a ruler. Machiavelli, in the concluding chapter, calls upon "the prince" to unite the Italians against foreign oppressors and drive them out of Italy.

### Reading the Selection

Chapter VIII, "Those who come to power by crime," constitutes a chapter in the second part of *The Prince* in which Machiavelli documents the various ways rulers found governments. The author employs the characteristic technique of comparing and contrasting a ruler from Classical times with one from his own era; using this device, he shows how cruelty, if employed swiftly and rarely, can be an effective weapon for gaining power. But princes, he argues in other chapters, should also strive to win their subjects' allegiance in more humane ways, for they must play many roles if they are to be successful rulers.

---

As there are also two ways of becoming a prince which cannot altogether be attributed either to fortune or to prowess, I do not think I ought to leave them out, even though one of them can be dealt with at greater length under the heading of republics. The two I have in mind are when a man becomes prince by some criminal and nefarious method, and when a private citizen becomes prince of his native city with the approval of his fellow citizens. In dealing with the first method, I shall give two examples, one from the ancient world, one from the modern, without otherwise discussing the rights and wrongs of this subject, because I imagine that these examples are enough for anyone who has to follow them.

Agathocles, the Sicilian, not only from the status of a private citizen but from the lowest, most abject condition of life, rose to become king of Syracuse. At every stage of his career this man, the son of a potter, behaved like a criminal; nonetheless he accompanied his crimes with so much audacity and physical courage that when he joined the militia he rose through the ranks to become praetor of Syracuse. After he had been appointed to this position, he determined to make himself prince and to possess by force and without obligation to others what had been voluntarily conceded to him. He reached an understanding about this ambition of his with Hamilcar the Carthaginian, who was campaigning with his armies in Sicily. Then one morning he assembled the people and Senate of Syracuse, as if he meant to raise matters which affected the republic; and at a prearranged signal he had all the senators, along with the richest citizens, killed by his soldiers; and when they were dead he seized and held the government of that city, without encountering any other internal opposition. Although he was twice routed and finally besieged by the Carthaginians, not only did he successfully defend the city, but, leaving some of his troops to defend it, he invaded Africa with the rest, and in a short time lifted the siege and reduced the Carthaginians to severe straits. They were compelled to make a pact with him, contenting themselves with the possession of Africa and leaving Sicily to Agathocles. So whoever studies that man's actions

will discover little or nothing that can be attributed to fortune, inasmuch as he rose through the ranks of the militia, as I said, and his progress was attended by countless difficulties and dangers; that was how he won his principality, and he maintained his position with many audacious and dangerous enterprises. Yet it cannot be called prowess to kill fellow citizens, to betray friends, to be treacherous, pitiless, irreligious. These ways can win a prince power but not glory. One can draw attention to the prowess of Agathocles in confronting and surviving danger, and his courageous spirit in enduring and overcoming adversity, and it appears that he should not be judged inferior to any eminent commander; nonetheless, his brutal cruelty and inhumanity, his countless crimes, forbid his being honoured among eminent men. One cannot attribute to fortune or prowess what was accomplished by him without the help of either.

In our own time, during the pontificate of Alexander VI, there was Oliverotto of Fermo. Years before, he had been left fatherless as a small boy and was brought up by a maternal uncle called Giovanni Fogliani. In his early youth he was sent to serve as a soldier under Paulo Vitelli so that he could win high command after being trained by him. When Paulo died, Oliverotto soldiered under Vitelozzo, his brother; and in a very short time, as he was intelligent, and a man of courage and audacity, he became Vitelozzo's chief commander. But he thought it was servile to take orders from others, and so he determined that, with the help of some citizens of Fermo to whom the enslavement of their native city was more attractive than its liberty, and with the favour and help of the Vitelli, he would seize Fermo for himself. He wrote to Giovanni Fogliano saying that, having been many years away from home he wanted to come and see him and his city and to make some investigation into his own estate. He had worked for nothing else except honour, he went on, and in order that his fellow citizens might see that he had not spent his time in vain, he wanted to come honourably, with a mounted escort of a hundred companions and servants. He begged Giovanni to arrange a reception which would bring honour to Giovanni as well as to himself, as he was Giovanni's foster child. Giovanni failed in no duty of hospitality towards his nephew. He had him honourably welcomed by the citizens of Fermo and lodged him in his own mansion. There, after a few days had passed during which he waited in order to complete the secret arrangements for his future crime, Oliverotto prepared a formal banquet to which he invited Giovanni Fogliani and the leading citizens of Fermo. After they had finished eating and all the other entertainment usual at such banquets was done with, Oliverotto artfully started to touch on subjects of grave importance, talking of the greatness of Pope Alexander and of Cesare his son, and of their enterprises. When Giovanni and the others began to discuss these subjects in turn, he got to his feet all of a sudden, saying that these were things to be spoken of somewhere more private, and he withdrew to another room, followed by Giovanni and all the other citizens. And no sooner were they seated than soldiers appeared from hidden recesses, and killed Giovanni and all the others. After this slaughter, Oliverotto mounted his horse, rode through the town, and laid siege to the palace of the governing council; consequently they were frightened into obeying him and into setting up a government of which he made himself the prince. And having put to death all who, because they would resent his rule, might injure him, he strengthened his position by founding new civil and military institutions. In this way, in the space of the year that he held the principality, he not only established himself in the city of Fermo but also made himself formidable to all the neighbouring states. His overthrow would have proved as difficult as that of Agathocles, if he had not let himself be tricked by Cesare Borgia when, at Sinigaglia, as was recounted above, Cesare trapped the Orsini and the Vitelli. Oliverotto was also trapped there, and a year after he committed parricide he was strangled along with Vitellozzo, the teacher as regards both his virtues and his crimes.

One might well wonder how it was that Agathocles, and others like him, after countless treacheries and cruelties, could live securely in his own country and hold foreign enemies at bay, with never a conspiracy against him by his countrymen, inasmuch as many others, because of their cruel behaviour, have not been able to maintain their rule even in peaceful times, let alone in the uncertain times of war. I believe that here it is a question of cruelty used well or badly. We can say that cruelty is used well (if it is permissible to talk in this way of what is evil) when it is employed once for all, and one's safety depends on it, and then it is not persisted in but as far as possible turned to the good of one's subjects. Cruelty badly used is that which, although infrequent to start with, as time goes on, rather than disappearing, grows in intensity. Those who use the first method can, with divine and human assistance, find some means of consolidating their position, as did Agathocles; the others cannot possibly stay in power.

So it should be noted that when he seizes a state the new ruler must determine all the injuries that he will need to inflict. He must inflict them once for all, and not have to renew them every day, and in that way he will be able to set men's minds at rest and win them over to him when he confers benefits. Whoever acts otherwise, either through timidity or bad advice, is always forced to have the knife ready in his hand and he can never depend on his subjects because they, suffering fresh and continuous violence, can never feel secure with regard to him. Violence must be inflicted once for all; people will then forget what it tastes like and so be less resentful. Benefits must be conferred gradually; and in that way they will taste better. Above all, a prince must live with his subjects in such a way that no development, either favourable or adverse, makes him vary his conduct. For, when adversity brings the need for it, there is no time to inflict harm; and the favours he may confer are profitless, because they are seen as being forced, and so they earn no thanks.

# BALDASSARE CASTIGLIONE
# from *The Book of the Courtier*

---

*The Book of the Courtier* (*courtier* being a "gentleman") belongs to the genre of etiquette books that flourished in Renaissance Europe, as a religious-based culture gave way to a more humanistic world. Books of this type were now much in demand, in response to this period's ideal that secular life in the upper levels of society should be marked by reserved grace, especially between the sexes. Court life, whether in the royal or aristocratic domain, already had well-established rules of behavior, derived from the medieval chivalric code; however, courts were still dominated by a male ethos, manifested in rough speech, crude manners, and general lack of refinement between men and women. Whereas most Renaissance etiquette books were meant to correct crude behavior and speech, *The Courtier* took a broader view by offering an idealized vision of court life, where courteous ladies became the arbiters of society. Published in 1528 and translated into most Western languages by 1600, this work became for Europe's upper classes the bible of politeness, its rules formalized into strict expectations. This Renaissance book is the source from which descend modern notions of "lady" and "gentlemen."

*The Courtier*'s author, Baldassare Castiglione (1478–1529), was himself a polished courtier, growing up among the Italian nobility and studying the Classics at the University of Milan. Later, he was attached to various north Italian ducal courts (Milan, Urbino, and Mantua), for whose rulers he performed military and diplomatic missions. While serving as the Duke of Mantua's ambassador to Rome, he was brought by his duties into the cultivated court of the Medici pope, Leo X; a later pope, Clement VII, made him the papal representative to Spain, a post he held until he died.

*The Courtier*, Castiglione's only publication, was his life's work. He was moved to write it during his eleven years at the ducal court of Urbino; the court was the center of an accomplished circle of artists, writers, and intellectuals, presided over by the old Duke and his young wife, Elisabetta. This Urbino circle, with its witty talk, integrity, and grace, came to embody, for Castiglione, his social ideal. Thus, when he wrote *The Courtier*, he tried to capture the conversational tone of this circle by making the work a dialogue, set during an evening in the ducal palace. In his book, as in life, Duchess Elisabetta is the playful leader of the group.

## Reading the Selection

This selection from *The Book of the Courtier* contains excerpts from Book I and Book III, dealing respectively with the qualities that define a courtier and a lady. Not based on real life, these attributes are ideals, meant as a guide for correct deportment and had been gleaned from Castiglione's readings in medieval and Classical literature. Of the ideal courtier, the participants agree that he should be both a soldier, trained in the bearing of arms, and a scholar, skilled in the liberal arts and social graces; however, they are of two minds as to which role should dominate.

No such dispute divides Castiglione's participants over the ideal lady: all concur that she should be the consummate hostess—charming, witty, graceful, physically attractive, and utterly feminine. An innovative aspect of this idealized model is the insistence that a lady be educated in the liberal arts in the same way as a gentleman. With this idea, the barrier is swept away that, since the Middle Ages, had excluded women from higher learning, though they remained barred from the universities until the nineteenth century.

• • •

'But to come to specific details, I judge that the first and true profession of the courtier must be that of arms; and this above everything else I wish him to pursue vigorously. Let him also stand out from the rest as enterprising, bold, and loyal to whomever he serves. And he will win a good reputation by demonstrating these qualities whenever and wherever possible, since failure to do so always incurs the gravest censure. Just as once a woman's reputation for purity has been sullied it can never be restored, so once the reputation of a gentleman-at-arms has been stained through cowardice or some other reproachful behaviour, even if only once, it always remains defiled in the eyes of the world and covered with ignominy. The more our courtier excels in this art, therefore, the more praise he will deserve, although I do not think he needs to have the professional knowledge of such things and the other qualities appropriate to a military commander. However, since the subject of what constitutes a great captain takes us into very deep waters, we shall be content, as we said, for the courtier to show complete loyalty and an undaunted spirit, and for these to be always in evidence. For men demonstrate their courage far more often in little things than in great. Very often in the face of appalling danger but where there are numerous witnesses one will find those who, though ready to drop dead with fear, driven on by shame or the presence of others, will press forward, with their eyes closed, and do their duty; and only God knows how. But in things of trifling importance, when they believe they can avoid danger without its being noticed, they are only too willing to play for safety. As for those who, even when they are sure they are not being observed or seen or recognized by anyone, are full of ardour and avoid doing anything, no matter how trivial, for which they would incur reproach, they possess the temper and quality we are looking for in our courtier. All the same, we do not wish the courtier to make a show of being so fierce that he is always blustering and bragging, declaring that he is married to his cuirass, and glowering with the haughty looks that we know only too well in Berto. To these may very fairly be said what a worthy lady once remarked jokingly, in polite company, to a certain man (I don't want just now to mention him by name) whom she had honoured by asking him to dance and who not only refused but would not listen to music or take part in the many other entertainments offered, protesting all the while that such frivolities were not his business. And when at length the lady asked what his business was, he answered with a scowl: "Fighting. . . ."

' "Well then," the lady retorted, "I should think that since you aren't at war at the moment and you are not engaged in fighting, it would be a good thing if you were to have yourself well greased and stowed away in a cupboard with all your fighting equipment, so that you avoid getting rustier than you are already."

'And of course everyone burst out laughing at the way she showed her contempt for his stupid presumption.

'Therefore,' Count Lodovico went on, 'the man we are seeking should be fierce, rough and always to the fore, in the presence of the enemy; but anywhere else he should be kind, modest, reticent and anxious above all to avoid ostentation or the kind of outrageous self-glorification by which a man always arouses loathing and disgust among those who have to listen to him.' . . .

'I should like our courtier to be a more than average scholar, at least in those studies which we call the humanities; and he should have a knowledge of Greek as well as Latin, because of the many different things that are so beautifully written in that language. He should be very well acquainted with the poets, and no less with the orators and historians, and also skilled at writing both verse and prose, especially in our own language; for in addition to the satisfaction this

will give him personally, it will enable him to provide constant entertainment for the ladies, who are usually very fond of such things. But if because of his other activities or through lack of study he fails to achieve a commendable standard in his writing, then he should take pains to suppress his work, to avoid ridicule, and he should show it only to a friend he can trust. And the exercise of writing will be profitable for him at least to the extent that it will teach him how to judge the work of others. For it is very unusual for someone who is not a practised writer, however erudite he may be, to understand completely the demanding work done by writers, or appreciate their stylistic accomplishments and triumphs and those subtle details characteristic of the writers of the ancient world. Moreover, these studies will make our courtier well informed and eloquent and (as Aristippus said to the tyrant) self-confident and assured no matter whom he is talking to. However, I should like our courtier to keep one precept firmly in mind: namely, that in what I have just discussed and in everything else he should always be diffident and reserved rather than forward, and he should be on his guard against assuming that he knows what he does not know. For we are instinctively all too greedy for praise, and there is no sound or song that comes sweeter to our ears; praise, like Sirens' voices, is the kind of music that causes shipwreck to the man who does not stop his ears to its deceptive harmony. Recognizing this danger, some of the philosophers of the ancient world wrote books giving advice on how a man can tell the difference between a true friend and a flatterer. Even so, we may well ask what use is this, seeing that there are so many who realize perfectly well that they are listening to flattery, and yet love the flatterer and detest the one who tells them the truth. Indeed, very often, deciding that the one who praises them is not being fulsome enough, they lend him a hand themselves and say such things that even the most outrageous flatterer feels ashamed. Let us leave these blind fools to their errors and decide that our courtier should possess such good judgement that he will not be told that black is white or presume anything of himself unless he is certain that it is true, and especially in regard to those flaws which, if you remember, when he was suggesting his game for the evening Cesare recalled we had often used to demonstrate the particular folly of this person or another. To make no mistake at all, the courtier should, on the contrary, when he knows the praises he receives are deserved, not assent to them too openly nor let them pass without some protest. Rather he should tend to disclaim them modestly, always giving the impression that arms are, as indeed they should be, his chief profession, and that all his other fine accomplishments serve merely as adornments; and this should especially be his attitude when he is in the company of soldiers, lest he behave like those who in the world of scholarship want to be taken for warriors and among warriors want to seem men of letters. In this way, as we have said, he will avoid affectation, and even his modest achievements will appear great.'

At this point, Pietro Bembo interrupted: 'I cannot see, my dear Count, why you wish this courtier, who is so literate and so well endowed with other worthy qualities, to regard everything as serving to adorn the profession of arms, and not arms and the rest as serving to adorn the profession of letters, which, taken by themselves, are as superior in dignity to arms as is the soul to the body, since letters are a function of the soul, just as arms are of the body.'

Then the Count answered: 'On the contrary, the profession of arms pertains both to the soul and to the body. But I should not want you to be the judge of this, Pietro, because by one of the parties concerned it would be assumed that you were prejudiced. And as this is a controversy that the wisest men have already thrashed out, there is no call to re-open it. As it is, I consider that it has been settled in favour of arms; and since I may form our courtier as I wish, I want him to be of the same opinion. If you think the contrary, wait until you hear of a contest in which the man who defends the cause of arms is allowed to use them, just as those who defend the cause of letters make use of letters in their defence; for if each one uses his own weapons, you will see that the men of letters will lose.

'Ah,' said Pietro Bembo, 'you were only too ready earlier on to damn the French for their scant appreciation of letters, and you mentioned the glory that they bring to men and the way they make a man immortal. And now you seem to have changed your mind. Do you not remember that:

> *Giunto Alessandro alla famosa tomba*
> *del fero Achille, sospirando disse:*
> *O fortunato, che sì chiara tromba*
> *trovasti, e chi di te sì alto scrisse!\**

\*The first quatrain of a sonnet by Petrarch, literally: 'When Alexander reached the famous tomb of fierce Achilles, he sighed and said: O happy man, who found so illustrious a trumpet, and one to write of you so nobly!'

And if Alexander was envious of Achilles not because of what he had done himself but because of the way he was blessed by fortune in having his deeds celebrated by Homer, we must conclude that he put a higher value on the writings of Homer than on the arms of Achilles. What other judge do you want, or what other verdict on the relative worth of arms and letters than the one delivered by one of the greatest commanders that has ever lived?'

The Count replied: 'I blame the French for believing that letters are harmful to the profession of arms, and I maintain myself that it is more fitting for a warrior to be educated than for anyone else; and I would have these two accomplishments, the one helping the other, as is most fitting, joined together in our courtier. I do not think that this means I have changed my opinion. But, as I said, I do not wish to argue which of them is more praiseworthy. Let it be enough that men of letters hardly ever choose to praise other than great men and glorious deeds, which deserve praise both on their own account and because, in addition, they provide writers with a truly noble theme. And this subject-matter embellishes what is written and, no doubt, is the reason why such writings endure, for otherwise, if they dealt not with noble deeds but with vain and trivial subjects, they would surely be read and appreciated less. And if Alexander was envious of Achilles because he was praised by Homer, it still does not necessarily follow that he thought more of letters than of arms; and if he had thought that he was as inferior to Achilles as a soldier as he believed that all those who would write

about him were inferior to Homer as writers, he would, I am sure, have far preferred brave exploits on his own part to brave talk from others. Therefore I believe that when he said what he did, Alexander was tacitly praising himself, and expressing a desire for what he thought he lacked, namely supreme ability as a writer, rather than for what he took for granted he already had, namely prowess as a warrior, in which he was far from acknowledging Achilles as his superior. So when he called Achilles fortunate he meant that if so far his own fame did not rival that of Achilles (which had been made bright and illustrious through so inspired a poem) this was not because his valour and merits were less notable or less deserving of the highest praise but because of the way fortune had granted Achilles a born genius to be his herald and to trumpet his deeds to the world. Moreover, perhaps Alexander wanted to encourage some gifted person to write about him, showing that his pleasure in this would be as great as his love and respect for the sacred monuments of literature. And now we have said enough about this subject.

'Indeed, far too much,' remarked signor Lodovico, 'for I don't think that one could discover anywhere in the world a vessel big enough to hold all the things you want to put into our courtier. . . .'

. . . Thus just as it is very fitting that a man should display a certain robust and sturdy manliness, so it is well for a woman to have a certain soft and delicate tenderness, with an air of feminine sweetness in her every movement, which, in her going and staying and whatsoever she does, always makes her appear a woman, without any resemblance to a man. If this precept be added to the rules that these gentlemen have taught the courtier, then I think that she ought to be able to make use of many of them, and adorn herself with the finest accomplishments, as signor Gaspare says. For I consider that many virtues of the mind are as necessary to a woman as to a man; as it is to be of good family; to shun affectation: to be naturally graceful; to be well mannered, clever and prudent; to be neither proud, envious or evil-tongued, nor vain, contentious or clumsy; to know how to gain and keep the favour of her mistress and of everyone else; to perform well and gracefully the sports suitable for women. It also seems to me that good looks are more important to her than to the courtier, for much is lacking to a woman who lacks beauty. She must also be more circumspect and at greater pains to avoid giving an excuse for someone to speak ill of her; she should not only be beyond reproach but also beyond even suspicion, for a woman lacks a man's resources when it comes to defending herself. And now, seeing that Count Lodovico has explained in great detail what should be the principal occupation of a courtier, namely, to his mind, the profession of arms, it seems right for me to say what I consider ought to be that of the lady at Court. And when I have done this, then I shall believe that most of my task has been carried out.

'Leaving aside, therefore, those virtues of the mind which she must have in common with the courtier, such as prudence, magnanimity, continence and many others besides, and also the qualities that are common to all kinds of women, such as goodness and discretion, the ability to take good care, if she is married, of her husband's belongings and house and children, and the virtues belonging to a good mother, I say that the lady who is at Court should properly have, before all else, a certain pleasing affability whereby she will know how to entertain graciously every kind of man with charming and honest conversation, suited to the time and the place and the rank of the person with whom she is talking. And her serene and modest behaviour, and the candour that ought to inform all her actions, should be accompanied by a quick and vivacious spirit by which she shows her freedom from boorishness; but with such a virtuous manner that she makes herself thought no less chaste, prudent and benign than she is pleasing, witty and discreet. Thus she must observe a certain difficult mean, composed as it were of contrasting qualities, and take care not to stray beyond certain fixed limits. . . .

'Now since signor Gaspare also asks what are the many things a lady at Court should know about, how she ought to converse, and whether her virtues should be such as to contribute to her conversation, I declare that I want her to understand what these gentlemen have said the courtier himself ought to know; and as for the activities we have said are unbecoming to her, I want her at least to have the understanding that people can have of things they do not practise themselves; and this so that she may know how to value and praise the gentlemen concerned in all fairness, according to their merits. And, to repeat in just a few words something of what has already been said, I want this lady to be knowledgeable about literature and painting, to know how to dance and play games, adding a discreet modesty and the ability to give a good impression of herself to the other principles that have been taught the courtier. And so when she is talking or laughing, playing or jesting, no matter what,

she will always be most graceful, and she will converse in a suitable manner with whomever she happens to meet, making use of agreeable witticisms and jokes. And although continence, magnanimity, temperance, fortitude of spirit, prudence and the other virtues may not appear to be relevant in her social encounters with others, I want her to be adorned with these as well, not so much for the sake of good company, though they play a part in this too, as to make her truly virtuous, and so that her virtues, shining through everything she does, make her worthy of honour.'

'I am quite surprised,' said signor Gaspare with a laugh, 'that since you endow women with letters, continence, magnanimity and temperance, you do not want them to govern cities as well, and to make laws and lead armies, while the men stay at home to cook and spin.'

The Magnifico replied, also laughing: 'Perhaps that would not be so bad, either.'

Then he added: 'Do you not know that Plato, who was certainly no great friend of women, put them in charge of the city and gave all the military duties to the men? Don't you think that we might find many women just as capable of governing cities and armies as men? But I have not imposed these duties on them, since I am fashioning a Court lady and not a queen. I'm fully aware that you would like by implication to repeat the slander that signor Ottaviano made against women yesterday, namely, that they are most imperfect creatures, incapable of any virtuous act, worth very little and quite without dignity compared with men. But truly both you and he would be very much in error if you really thought this. . . . '

Chapter

# 13

# The Religious Reformations, Northern Humanism, and Late Mannerism: 1500–1603

## DESIDERIUS ERASMUS

### from *The Praise of Folly*

Between 1470 and the onset of the Protestant Reformation, in the 1520s, the Renaissance spread from Italy north across the Alps where it fused with existing Christian thought to create Northern Humanism. As in Italy, humanists in the north looked to the Greco-Roman past for inspiration, thereby reviving widespread interest in Classicism. Unlike in Italy, however, scholars in northern Europe were Christians first and humanists second; they used Classical learning to shed light on perceived religious problems, namely corruption in the clergy, the church's emphasis on ritual to the neglect of moral order, and the general breakdown in spiritual life. In this way, the northern humanists pointed the way to the Protestant Reformation and helped shape Mannerism, the dominant cultural style between 1520 and 1600.

The most influential voice of Northern Humanism was the Dutch scholar Desiderius Erasmus (about 1466–1536), who was called by his colleagues the Prince of Humanists. Though educated in traditional Classical studies, he planned a career in the church, joining a monastery and also becoming a priest. But his love of learning and his distaste for monastic life combined to lead him to literature. His writings, beginning with the *Adagia* (1500), a collection of his commentaries on quotations from Classical authors, quickly made him a well-known scholar; he traveled across Europe as the guest of princes, kings, and church leaders. His gentle manner brought a calm to the period's religious debates; but as the Protestant revolt divided Europe, Erasmus's plea for tolerance was swept away by both sides. Still, Erasmus's treatises, letters, and, especially, his Greek edition of the New Testament (based on the then latest sources) insured his position as leader of Northern Humanism.

## Reading the Selection

Erasmus is best remembered for *The Praise of Folly* (1516), a biting satire on human vanity, which still rings true today. Written during one of his periodic visits to England and dedicated to his friend and fellow humanist, Sir Thomas More (see *Utopia*), it holds up to ridicule his period's leaders, such as scholars, lawyers, monks, and cardinals; it exposed their hypocrisy and worldly appetites. Though Erasmus thought his book had little lasting merit, deeming it an intellectual joke tossed off to amuse his friends, *The Praise of Folly* nonetheless echoed the thoughts of many contemporaries, and subsequent generations have enjoyed its wicked satire. Today, it is the one work by Erasmus most likely to be known to educated readers.

Erasmus, in *The Praise of Folly*, uses the literary device of personification, employed earlier by Boethius (see *The Consolation of Philosophy*) and Christine de Pizan (see *The Book of the City of Ladies*). Thus, he speaks through Dame Folly, a "goddess" who delights in her foolish followers. As this section opens, Dame Folly speaks, identifying herself, her parents, and her attendants: self-love, flattery, forgetfulness, pleasure, and sensuality. Ironically, she says human life would be unbearable without her (folly), for if people were always sensible, then everyone would be miserable.

Dame Folly then surveys the human comedy, laying out the foolish things in which each profession excels. Beneath the satire against the church, Erasmus's Christian humanism shines forth; for example, the work claims that points of theology and monkish pride have become more important than "mending a poor man's shoes"—a metaphor for the church's neglect of the needy.

---

[Folly is speaking.] In the same realm are those who are authors of books. All of them are highly indebted to me, especially those who blacken their pages with sheer triviality. For those who write learnedly to be criticized by a few scholars, not even ruling out a Persius or a Laelius as a judge, seem to be more pitiable than happy to me, simply because they are continuously torturing themselves. They add, they alter, they cross something out, they reinsert it, they recopy their work, they rearrange it, they show it to friends, and they keep it for nine years; yet they still are not satisfied with it. At such a price, they buy an empty reward, namely praise—and the praise of only a handful, at that. They buy this at the great expense of long hours, no sleep, so much sweat, and so many vexations. Add also the loss of health, the deterioration of their physical appearance, the possibility of blindness or partial loss of their sight, poverty, malice, premature old age, an early death, and if you can think of more, add them to this list. The scholar feels that he has been compensated for such ills when he wins the sanction of one or two other weak-eyed scholars. But my author is crazy in a far happier way for he, without any hesitation, rapidly writes down anything that comes to mind, his pen, or even his dreams. There is little or no waste of paper, since he knows that if the trifles are trivial enough the majority of the readers, that is, the fools and ignoramuses, will approve of them. What is the difference if one should ignore two or three scholars, even though he may have read them? Or what weight will the censure of a few scholars carry, so long as the multitudes give it acclaim?

Actually, the wiser writers are those who put out the work of someone else as their own. By a few alterations they transfer someone else's glory to themselves, disregarding the other person's long labor and comforting themselves with the thought that even though they might be publicly convicted of plagiarism, meanwhile they shall have enjoyed the fruits and glory of authorship. It is worth one's while to observe how pleased authors are with their own works when they are popular and pointed out in a crowd—as celebrities! Their work is on display in bookstores, with three cryptic words in large type on the title page, something like a magician's spell. Ye gods! After all, what are they but words? Few people will ever hear of them, compared to the total world population, and far fewer will admire them, since people's tastes vary so, even among the common people. And why is it that the very names of the authors are often false, or stolen from the books of the ancients? One calls himself Telemachus, another Stelenus or Laertes, still another Polycrates, and another Thrasymachus. As a result, nowadays it does not matter whether you dedicate your book to a chameleon or a gourd, or simply to alpha or beta, as the philosophers do.

The most touching event is when they compliment each other and turn around in an exchange of letters, verses, and superfluities. They are fools praising fools and dunces praising dunces. The first, in the opinion of the second, is an Alcaeus, and the second, in the opinion of the first, is a Callimachus. One holds another in higher esteem than Cicero, the other finds the one more learned than Plato. Or sometimes they will choose a competitor and increase their reputation by rivaling themselves with him. As a result the public is split with opposing viewpoints, until finally, when the dispute is over, each reigns as victor and has a triumphal parade. Wise men deride this as being absolute nonsense, which is just what it is. Who will deny it? Meanwhile, our authors are leading a luxurious life because of my excellence, and they would not exchange their accomplishments for even those of Scipius. And while the scholars most certainly derive a great deal of pleasure from laughing at them, relishing to the utmost the madnesses of others, they themselves owe me a great deal, which they cannot deny without being most ungrateful men.

Among men of the learned professions, a most self-satisfied group of men, the lawyers may hold themselves in the highest esteem. For while they laboriously roll up the stone of Sisyphus by the force of weaving six hundred laws together at the same time, by the stacking of commentary upon commentary and opinion upon opinion regardless of how far removed from the purpose, they contrive to make their profession seem to be most difficult of all. What is actually tedious they consider brilliant. Let us include with them the logicians and sophists, a breed of men more loquacious than the famed brass kettles of Dodona. Any one of them can outtalk any twenty women. They would be happier, though, if they were just talkative and not quarrelsome as well. In fact, they are so quarrelsome that they will argue and fight over a lock of a goat's wool, absurdly losing sight of the truth in the furor of their dispute. Their egotistical love keeps them happy, and manned with but three syllogisms, they will unflinchingly argue on any subject with any man. Their mere obstinacy affords them victory, even though you place Stentor against them.

Next in line are the scientists, revered for their beards and the fur on their gowns. They feel that they are the only men with any wisdom, and all other men float about as shadows. How senilely they daydream, while they construct their countless worlds and shoot the distance to the sun, the moon, the stars, and spheres, as with a thumb and line. They postulate causes for lightning, winds, eclipses, and other inexplicable things, never hesitating for a moment, as if they had exclusive knowledge about the secrets of nature, designer of elements, or as if they visited us directly from the council of the gods. Yet all this time nature is heartily laughing at them and their conjectures. It is a sufficient argument just proving that they have good intelligence for nothing. They can never explain why they always disagree with each other on every subject. In summation, knowing nothing in general they profess to know everything in particular. They are ignorant even to themselves, and at times they do not see the ditch or stone lying across their path, because many of them are day-dreamers and are absent-minded. Yet they proclaim that they perceive ideas, universals, forms without matter, primary substances, quiddities, entities, and things so tenuous that I'm afraid that Lynceus could not see them himself. The common people are especially disdained when they bring out their triangles, quadrangles, circles, and mathematical figures of the like. They place one on top of the other and arrange them into a maze. Then they deploy some letters precisely, as if in a battle formation, and finally they reverse them. And all of this is done only to confuse those who are ignorant of the field. These scientists do not like those who predict the future from the stars, and promise even more fantastic miracles. And these fortunate men find people who believe them.

Perhaps it would be better to pass silently over the theologians. Dealing with them, since they are hot-tempered, is like crossing Lake Camarina or eating poisonous beans. They may attack me with six hundred arguments and force me to retract what I hold; for if I refuse, they will immediately declare me a heretic. By this blitz action they show a desire to terrify anyone to whom they are ill-disposed. No other people are so adverse to acknowledge my favors to them, yet the divines are bound to me by extraordinary obligations. These theologians are happy in their self-love, and as if they

were presently inhabiting a third heaven, they look down on all men as though they were animals that crawled along the ground, coming near to pity them. They are protected by a wall of scholastic definitions, arguments, corollaries, and implicit and explicit propositions. They have so many hideouts that not even the net of Vulcan would be able to catch them; for they back down from their distinctions, by which they also cut through the knots of an argument, as if with a double-blade ax from Tenedos; and they come forth with newly invented terms and monstrous-sounding words. Furthermore, they explain the most mysterious matters to suit themselves, for instance, the method by which the world was set in order and began, through what channels original sin has come down to us through generations, by what means, in what measure, and how long the Omnipotent Christ was in the Virgin's womb, and how accidents subsist in the Eucharist without their substance.

But those have been beaten to death down through the ages. Here are some questions that are worthy of great (and some call them) illuminated theologians, questions that will really make them think, if they should ever encounter them. Did divine generation take place at a particular time? Are there several sonships in Christ? Whether this is a possible proposition: Does God the Father hate the Son? Could God the Father have taken upon Himself the likeness of a woman, a devil, an ass, a gourd, or a piece of flint? Then how would that gourd have preached, performed miracles, or been crucified? Also, what would Peter have consecrated, if he had administered the Eucharist, while Christ's body hung on the cross? Another thought: could Christ have been said to be a man at that very moment? Will we be forbidden to eat and drink after the resurrection? (Now, while there is time, they are providing against hunger and thirst!) These intricate subtleties are infinite, and there are others that are even more subtle, concerning instances of time, notions, relations, accidents, quiddities, and entities, which no one can perceive unless, like Lynceus, he can see in the blackest darkness things that aren't there.

We must insert those maxims, rather contradictions, that, compared to the Stoic paradoxes, appear to be the most common simplicity. For instance: it is a lesser crime to cut the throats of a thousand men than to sew a stitch on a poor man's shoe on the sabbath; it is better to want the earth to perish, body, boots, and breeches (as the saying goes), than to tell a single lie, however inconsequential. The methods that our scholastics follow only render more subtle the subtlest of subtleties; for you will more easily escape from a labyrinth than from the snares of the Realists, Nominalists, Thomists, Albertists, Occamists, and Scotists. I have not named them all, only a few of the major ones. But there is so much learning and difficulty in all of these sects that I should think the apostles themselves must have the need of some help from some other's spirit if they were to try to argue these topics with our new generation of theologians. . . .

Those who are the closest to these in happiness are generally called "the religious" or "monks," both of which are deceiving names, since for the most part they stay as far away from religion as possible and frequent every sort of place. I cannot, however, see how any life could be more gloomy than the life of these monks if I did not assist them in many ways. Though most people detest these men so much that accidentally meeting one is considered to be bad luck, the monks themselves believe that they are magnificent creatures. One of the chief beliefs is that to be illiterate is to be of a high state of sanctity, and so they make sure that they are not able to read. Another is that when braying out their gospels in church they are making themselves very pleasing and satisfying to God, when in fact they are uttering these psalms as a matter of repetition rather than from their hearts.

Indeed, some of these men make a good living through their uncleanliness and beggary by bellowing their petitions for food from door to door; there is not an inn, an announcement board, or a ship into which they are not accessible, here having a great advantage over other common beggars. According to them, though they are setting an apostolic example for us by their filthiness, their ignorance, their bawdiness, and their insolence. . . .

# SIR THOMAS MORE

## from *Utopia*

### Book II

Sir Thomas More's *Utopia* (1516) is the first work of utopian literature in modern times. It is also the source of this genre's name, *utopia* (from Greek, "not-place") being a pun on *eutopia* (from Greek, "well-place," or "place [where all is] well"). Written in Latin, it was printed both abroad and in England and soon became the talk of Europe. Since Thomas More (1478–1535) wrote, more than one hundred books have appeared on this idea.

The idea of a perfect place grew as Western history unfolded. It was first glimpsed by the immortal Utnapishtim, the Babylonian Noah, in *The Epic of Gilgamesh* (about 2500 B.C.). In the *Odyssey*, Homer named it the Elysian Fields. Another version was the Isles of the Blessed, as described by Horace. In Christianity it became paradise, called by St. Augustine (see *Confessions*) the Heavenly City. For the next thousand years, the celestial paradise (in contrast to the Earthly City) held sway in Europe. The Renaissance and the rise of secularism opened the way for More's earthly utopia.

More's *Utopia*, inspired by Plato's *The Republic*, was in tune with Christian Humanism (1500–1550), the literary movement (see Erasmus's *The Praise of Folly*) which used both Classical texts and the Bible as guides. To effect his goal—a critique of Europe—More presented an ideal society in the New World. This disguise was necessary, for rash opinions could and did lead to prison or death in this age. More, a Catholic, was eventually beheaded for his beliefs, at the command of Henry VIII, the founder of the Protestant sect called Anglicanism.

The inhabitants of More's Utopia are portrayed as having solved the problems plaguing Europe at the time. Utopia was a welfare state run on communistic lines, with no private property and no money. There was universal free education, six hours' labor daily, uniforms for citizens, free medical treatment, communal meals (with musical and reading accompaniment) in civic restaurants. Tolerance was granted to all religions. The penal code was simple and parties to legal suits were expected to plead their own cases as no lawyers were allowed. The law was harsh in sexual matters; adultery could result in slavery, repeated offenses in death. Divorce, however, was allowed by mutual consent. Gold was not to be used as currency but for useful objects such as chamberpots. Common storehouses of grains were maintained as reserves against famine. To complete More's dreamworld there was a Utopian alphabet and language.

When first published, this work was so convincing that some readers, unable to decode More's intellectual puzzles (such as his made-up Greek names), downgraded its literary value, thinking it merely a translation of a travel book to the New World.

Scholars now disagree over the meaning of More's playful work. One group labels it a Catholic allegory, whose purpose was to shame Christians into behaving better than the Utopians. Another group claims More as a Marxist before Marx, and the book as a political tract whose goal was to make Utopia's communism a model for Europe.

*Reading the Selection*

In this selection from Book II, Raphael Hythlodaeus (from Greek, "speaker of nonsense") describes Utopia's perfect society. In its communist system, all citizens worked to eat, except for thinkers and elected officials. The economy was run by syphogrants, controllers in charge of thirty households. In terms of war, the Utopians were peaceable, choosing violence only when all other methods failed.

---

## Their Economy and Occupations

All the Utopians, men and women alike, work at agriculture, and no one is inexperienced in it. They are trained in it from childhood, partly by school instruction and partly by practice. School children are often taken into the nearby fields as though for play, where they not only see men and women working, but get exercise by working themselves.

Besides sharing in the farm work, every person has some particular trade of his own, such as the manufacture of wool or linen, masonry, metal work, or carpentry. There is no other craft which is practiced by any considerable number of them. People wear the same sort of clothes throughout the island, except for the distinctions which mark the difference between the married and the unmarried. The fashion of clothing never changes. Their clothing looks well, does not hinder their movements, and is suitable both for summer and winter. Every household makes its own clothing, but each man and woman also learns one of the other trades I have mentioned. The women, being the weaker, practice the lighter crafts, such as working with wool or linen. The heavier crafts are left to the men. Generally the same trade passes down from father to son, often by natural inclination. But if anyone's interests lies elsewhere, he is adopted into a family practicing the trade he prefers. When anyone makes such a change, both his father and the magistrates see to it that he is transferred to a responsible and upright house-holder. After a man has learned one trade, if he desires to acquire another, it is managed in the same manner. When he has learned both, he follows whichever he likes better, unless the public has special need for the other.

The chief and almost the only business of the syphogrants is to see that no one sits around in idleness, and that everyone works hard at his trade. But no one has to wear himself out with endless toil from morning till night, as if he were a beast of burden. Such a life, though it is the common life of workmen in all other countries, is no better than a slave's. The Utopians work six hours out of the twenty-four. They work three hours before dinner. After dinner they rest two hours, and then go to work for another three hours. Then they have supper and at eight o'clock, counting from noon, they go to bed and sleep eight hours.

The other hours of the day, those that are not used for work, sleep, and meals, are left to their individual choice, on the understanding that they shall not waste them idly and wantonly. They use their free time busily on any pursuit that pleases them. Many of them fill these intervals with reading. They have the custom of giving public lectures daily before daybreak, which none are obliged to attend except such as are selected for pursuit of learning. Yet a great many from all ranks, both men and women, go to hear lectures of one sort or another, according to their interests. If anyone whose mind does not delight in intellectual pursuits prefers to spend his free time at his trade, as many do, this is not forbidden, but commended as beneficial to the commonwealth. After supper they spend an hour in some recreation, in summer gardening, in winter diverting themselves in their dining halls with music or talk. They know nothing about gambling with dice or other such foolish and ruinous games. They play two games not unlike our chess. One is a battle of numbers, in which one number plunders another. The other is a game in which the vices battle against the virtues. In this game the co-operation of the vices against the virtues and their opposition to each other is shown up very cleverly, as well as the special oppositions between particular virtues and vices, and the methods by which the vices openly assault or secretly undermine the virtues, and how the virtues break the strength of the vices and by what means finally one side or the other wins the victory.

To understand their way of life fully we must look at one point more carefully. They allot only six hours to labor, and you might think that a scarcity of essential goods would result. Actually their working hours are sufficient to provide not only an abundance, but even a superabundance of all the necessities and conveniences of life. You will easily understand this if you consider how large a part of the population in other countries is idle. In the first place, the women (and they are half the whole population) usually do no work, or if they do, their husbands lie snoring. Secondly, there is the multitude of priests and so-called religious men, as numerous as they are idle. Add to these all the rich men, especially great landlords, who are commonly called well-born and noble. Add their henchmen, the whole flock of swaggering bullies. Reckon in with these the strong and lusty beggars, who go about feigning some disease to excuse their laziness. You will find that the actual number of workers who supply the needs of mankind is much smaller than you would think. And now consider how few of these workers are employed in really necessary work. Because we measure values by money, we have to carry on many superfluous trades to support luxury and wantoness. If the multitude of our workers produced only what men need for good living, there would be such an abundance of goods that prices would go down and workmen could not subsist. You can easily imagine how little time would be enough to produce the goods that man's needs and convenience demand (and his pleasure too if it were true and natural pleasure), if only the workers in useless trades were placed in worthwhile occupations and all the idlers who languish in sloth but eat twice as much as laborers were put to work on useful tasks.

The truth of this supposition is very apparent in Utopia. Out of all the men and women whose age or health permit them to work, scarcely five hundred are exempted in each city and its surrounding area. Among these are the syphogrants, who are excused from labor by law. Yet they do not excuse themselves from it, because they incite others to work more easily by setting them an example. The Utopians grant the same exemption to some who apply themselves exclusively to learning, but only at the recommendation of the priests and in accordance with a secret vote of the syphogrants. If one of these persons disappoints their hopes, he is made a workman again. On the other hand it sometimes happens that a worker devotes his free time so zealously to learning and progresses so far through his diligence, that he is excused from his trade and is transferred to the class of the learned men. From this class are chosen ambassadors, priests, tranibors, and the prince himself (of old called the Barzanes, but later the Ademus). Since the rest of the entire population is neither idle nor engaged in useless occupations, it is easy to understand how they produce so much in so short a work day. . . .

### Their Warfare

They hate and detest war as a thing manifestly brutal, and yet practiced by man more constantly than by any kind of beast. Contrary to almost all other peoples they consider nothing so inglorious as the glory won in war. Nevertheless both the men and the women of Utopia regularly practice military exercises on certain days, so that they will be prepared when the need arises. They go to war cautiously and reluctantly, only to protect their own territory or that of their friends if an enemy has invaded it, or to free some wretched people from tyrannous oppression and servitude. They help their friends not only in defense, but also to avenge injuries. They do this only if they are consulted in the whole affair, if the facts are proved, and if the stolen plunder is not returned. Then they think they should wage war against the aggressor. They decide on this policy when booty is taken from their friends by force or when the merchants of one country are oppressed in another country by unjust laws or by twisting good laws. This they think is a greater evil than direct attack.

This was the sole cause of the war which the Utopians waged against the Alaopolitans for the sake of the Nephelogetes some time before our arrival, when a wrong seemed to have been done under pretext of right to Nephelogete merchants resident among the Alaopolitans. Whether or not an injustice was done, it was avenged by a terrible war, the strength of each side being augmented by the resources and the hatred of their neighbors. Some prosperous nations were ruined and others were greatly shaken. In the end after a series of misfortunes, the Alaopolitans, who had been a very thriving people compared to the Nephelogetes, were conquered and reduced to bondage by the Nephelogetes. Vigorously as the Utopians stood by their friends in the matter of reparations, they sought none for themselves.

If the Utopians themselves are cheated in this way, they carry their anger only to the point of cutting off trade with that country, provided no bodily injury is done. Not that they care less for their own citizens than for their neighbors, but they think it worse for their neighbors' property to be seized than their own. Their neighbors' merchants suffer a great injury because they lose their own property, but the Utopians think little of their loss, for only common goods have been lost. Besides whatever is exported must be in superfluous abundance at home, or it would not be shipped out. So they think it cruel to avenge a relatively unimportant loss by killing many men, whose death would only affect the lives and livelihood of others. But if any Utopian citizens are unjustly hurt or killed, whether by private or public policy, they send envoys demanding that the guilty persons be handed over to them. If that is refused, they declare war. If the guilty men are given up, their punishment is death or bondage.

The Utopians are troubled and ashamed when they gain a bloody victory, like merchants who have paid too high a price for what they have bought. If they overwhelm the enemy by skill and cunning, they exult and celebrate a public triumph, and erect a memorial for a victory efficiently won. When they win a victory by the strength of understanding (as only men can), they pride themselves on acting bravely and manfully. Bears, lions, boars, wolves, dogs, and other wild beasts fight with their bodies, and many of them surpass us in strength and ferocity as much as we surpass them in understanding and reason.

The Utopians have this one aim in war, to accomplish what they would gladly have achieved without war if just terms had been granted in time. Or if that cannot be done, they aim to exact so severe a revenge from those that have injured them that they will be afraid to do it again. Their policies are directed to these ends, which they strive toward in such a way as to avoid danger rather than to attain glory and fame.

As soon as war is declared, they at once arrange to have many small notices, which are marked with their official seal, set up by stealth in the most conspicuous places in the enemy's country. In these proclamations they promise great rewards to any one who will kill the enemy's king, and smaller rewards (but still very great) for killing those whom they regard as most responsible after the king for plotting aggression against them. They double the reward for anyone who brings in the proscribed man alive. Also they offer like rewards, as well as exemption from punishment, to any of the proscribed men who turn against their countrymen. As a result the proscribed men soon suspect everyone, distrust each other, and become distracted by their danger. It has often turned out that many of them, and even princes, have been betrayed by those whom they most trusted. The Utopians realize that rewards will spur men on to any sort of crime, and consequently they promise incredible gifts. Mindful of the danger which the assassins run, they see to it that the compensation is proportionate to the risk, and promise an immense amount of gold and also rich estates safely placed in neighboring countries. They keep these promises most faithfully. Though this manner of waging war by bidding for and buying enemies may seem like the cruel villainy of an ignoble mind, it is considered by the Utopians as a wise and praiseworthy policy, since it enables them to wage great wars without any battle at all. They even think themselves humane and merciful, because by the death of a few bad men they spare the lives of many innocent men who would otherwise die in battle, some fighting on their own side, some on the enemy's. Indeed they pity the mass of enemy soldiers no less than their own, for they know that they do not fight willingly, but are driven to it by the madness of their rulers.

If this method does not succeed, they sow the seeds of discord among the enemy by inciting the king's brother or some member of the nobility to plot for the crown. If these internal factions languish, then they arouse the neighboring people against the enemy and induce them to revive some old claims, such as kings never lack.

When they promise their resources to help in a war, they furnish money abundantly, but citizens very sparingly. They hold their own men most dear and of such account that they will not willingly exchange one of the citizens for an enemy's king. Since they keep their gold and silver for this single purpose, they spend it without reluctance, the more so as they will live no less well if they spend it all. Besides the wealth which they have at home, they have also boundless treasure abroad, many neighboring nations being in their debt, as I have said. So they hire mercenary soldiers from all sides, especially from the Zapoletes.

These people live five hundred miles from Utopia toward the east. They are a rude, fierce, wild people, who delight in the forests and mountains among which they are brought up. They are sturdy, well able to endure heat, cold, and hard work. They are unacquainted with luxuries or with agriculture, and are indifferent about housing and clothing. Their only productive occupation is taking care of cattle. For the most part they live by hunting and theft. It is as if they were born for war, and they watch carefully for any chance to engage in it. When they find such a chance they eagerly embrace it, great numbers of them going out and offering themselves at a low price to any one seeking soldiers. They know only one art for earning a living, the art of taking away life. They fight for their employers fiercely and with incorruptible fidelity. But they will not bind themselves to serve for any set time. They stipulate that they may fight next day for the enemy, if higher pay is offered, and come back on the day after that for still higher pay. There is seldom a war in which a considerable number of them are not fighting on both sides. So it commonly happens that men who are related to one another by blood and have served together in intimacy in the same campaigns are enlisted on opposite sides. Forgetful of their relationship and their friendship, they kill one another for no other reason than that they have been hired for a paltry wage by different kings. They think so much of money that they will change sides readily for an increase of only a penny a day. Thus they grow greedier and greedier for money, but money is of no use to them, for what they acquire with their blood, they soon waste profligately on contemptible pleasures.

This nation serves the Utopians against all people whatsoever, for they give higher pay than any others. Just as the Utopians seek out the best possible men to use at home, by the same principle they seek the worst men to misuse in war. When need requires, they induce the Zapoletes with promises of rich rewards to face hazards from which most of them never return. The Utopians pay the rewards in good faith to those who escape death, to incite them to similar deeds of daring later. And the Utopians have no concern over how many are killed, thinking they would deserve the thanks of the human race if they could purge the world of the whole of that disgusting and vicious people. . . .

# FRANÇOIS RABELAIS

# from *The Histories of Gargantua* and *Pantagruel*

Rabelais's *The Histories of Gargantua* and *Pantagruel* mark a fresh departure in Western letters. These robust satires, the first literary works to treat bodily functions and copulation graphically and without apology, gave the world the adjective *Rabelaisian*, meaning earthiness of speech. Because of their crudeness, the work became an underground classic—enjoyed in private but very little imitated with the notable exception of Swift (see *A Modest Proposal*). Only today, with the rise of freer public discourse, has Rabelais's legacy come into its own, as, for example, in the writings of Joyce (see *Ulysses*) and Ginsberg (see "A Supermarket in California").

Another reason these works represent a milestone in Western letters is that they signal the coming of the Renaissance to France. Lasting from 1515 until 1604, the French Renaissance was inspired by writers' and artists' "discovery" of Italy; literature and art clearly were altered by closer contact with ancient culture and Classical forms. It was at this time that the Classic ideal—the dominance of order over diversity, reason over passion—became a guiding force in French culture. François Rabelais (ca. 1494–1553) was a leader of this rebirth, though his sprawling books did not chime with Classicism's orderly ideal. More to the point, his works reflected this period's transitional nature. On one side he mocked the dying Middle Ages, with its tedious theological study; on the other side he praised the dawning Renaissance, with its love of Classical lore. In his works, he was also friendly to Protestantism, stressing simple piety just as its reformers did.

*The Histories of Gargantua* and *Pantagruel* are actually five books dealing with a legendary family of giants. Gargantua (1534), the second written, is now known as Book I, opening the series with the bawdy tale of Gargantua, focusing on his childhood and training for kingship. *Pantagruel* (1532), the first written, tells of Gargantua's giant son, Pantagruel, and is known as Book II. Basically a satire on scholastic education (see Aquinas's *Summa Theologica*), it also ridicules many timely topics—courtroom delays, lying lawyers, and pseudo-intellectuals. The other three books (the last published posthumously) contain further adventures of Pantagruel.

Rabelais's career mirrored this stormy age. Entered in a monastery as a youth, he abandoned the cloister and theology to study medicine. He later served as physician in a number of posts, mainly in France. To the disgust of critics, he spent his last years as a parish priest, delegating the duties but keeping the income. Because of his books, he was hounded by the authorities, but friends in church and state always came to his rescue.

### Reading the Selection

This selection contains probably the most famous passage from Book I on *Gargantua*. It features Gargantua's friend, the rascally Friar John ("the monk") and his "ideal" Abbey of Thélème, where "monks" and "nuns" were to live in accordance with the abbey's unchristian rule: "Do what you will." This abbey, with its pleasure-driven inmates, satirizes the faults that the Protestant reformers claimed against sixteenth-century monks. Beneath the broad satire the story seems to reinforce humanist morals: the best way to regulate one's life is "by the promptings of reason and good sense" and free people have a "natural spur and instinct" to seek virtue and avoid vice.

This passage also shows Rabelais's passion for words. For example, in the inscription over the Great Gate of Thélème, the words tumble down like a waterfall, offering an exaggerated list of those to be denied entry as well as those to be welcomed to the abbey.

---

### How Gargantua Had the Abbey of Thélème Built for the Monk

There only remained the monk to be provided for, and Gargantua wanted to make him abbot of Seuilly, but he refused the post. He next proposed to give him the abbey of Bourgueil or of Saint-Florant, whichever would suit him better, or both, if he fancied them. But the monk answered categorically that he wanted neither charge nor government of monks.

'For how should I be able to govern others,' he said, 'when I don't know how to govern myself? If it seems to you that I have done you, and may in the future do you welcome service, give me leave to found an abbey after my own devices.'

This request pleased Gargantua, and he offered him all his land of Thélème, beside the River Loire, to within six miles of the great forest of Port-Huault. The monk then requested Gargantua to institute his religious order in an exactly contrary way to all others.

'First of all, then,' said Gargantua, 'you mustn't build walls round it. For all other abbeys have lofty walls (murs).'

'Yes,' said the monk, 'and not without reason. Where there's a *mur* before and a *mur* behind, there are plenty of murmurs, envy, and mutual conspiracy.'

Moreover, seeing that in certain monasteries in this world it is the custom that if any woman enters—I speak of chaste and honest women—they wash the place where she trod, it was ordained that if any monk or nun happened to enter here, the spot where he or she had stood should be scrupulously washed likewise. And because in the religious foundations of this world everything is encompassed, limited, and regulated by hours, it was decreed that there should be no clock or dial at all, but that affairs should be conducted according to chance and opportunity. For Gargantua said that the greatest waste of time he knew was the counting of hours—what good does it do?—and the greatest nonsense in the world was to regulate one's life by the sound of a bell, instead of by the promptings of reason and good sense. Item, because at that time they put no women into religious houses unless they were one-eyed, lame, hunchbacked, ugly, malformed, lunatic, half-witted, bewitched, and blemished, or men that were not sickly, low-born, stupid, or a burden on their family. . . .

'By the way,' said the monk, 'if a woman is neither fair nor good, what can you do with her?'

'Make her a nun,' said Gargantua.

'Yes,' said the monk, 'and a sempstress of shirts.'

It was decreed that here no women should be admitted unless they were beautiful, well-built, and sweet-natured, nor any men who were not handsome, well-built, and of pleasant nature also.

Item, because men never entered nunneries except secretly and by stealth, it was decreed that here there should be no women when there were no men, and no men when there were no women.

Item, because both men and women, once accepted into a monastic order, after their novitiate year, were compelled and bound to remain for ever, so long as they lived, it was decreed that both men and women, once accepted, could depart from there whenever they pleased, without let or hindrance.

Item, because ordinarily monks and nuns made three vows, that is of chastity, poverty, and obedience, it was decreed that there anyone could be regularly married, could become rich, and could live at liberty.

With regard to the lawful age of entry, women were to be received at from ten to fifteen, and men at from twelve to eighteen. . . .

· · ·

*The Inscription Set Above the Great Gate of Thélème*

*Enter not here, vile hypocrites and bigots,*
*Pious old apes, and puffed-up snivellers,*
*Wry-necked creatures sawnier than the Goths,*
*Or Ostrogoths, precursors of Gog and Magog,*
*Woe-begone scoundrels, mock-godly sandal-wearers,*
*Beggars in blankets, flagellating canters,*
*Hooted at, pot-bellied, stirrers up of troubles,*
*Get along elsewhere to sell your dirty swindles.*
   *Your hideous deceits*
   *Would fill my fields and streets*
   *With villainy*
   *And with their falsity*
   *Would untune my song's notes,*
   *Your hideous deceits.*
*Enter not here, lawyers insatiable,*
*Ushers, lawyers' clerks, devourers of the people,*
*Holders of office, scribes, and pharisees,*
*Ancient judges who tie up good citizens*
*Like stray dogs with cord on their necks,*
*Your reward is earned now, and it is the gibbet.*
*So go and bray there. Here is done no violence,*
*Such as in your courts sets men fighting lawsuits.*
   *Lawsuits and wrangling*
   *Set us not jangling;*
   *We come here for pleasure.*
   *But may your leisure*
   *Be filled up with tangling*
   *Lawsuits and wrangling.*
*Enter not here, miserly usurers,*
*Gluttons and lechers, everlasting gatherers,*
*Tricksters and swindlers, mean pettifoggers,*
*Hunchbacked and snub-nosed, who in your lockers*
*Never have enough of gold coin and silver.*
*However much you pocket you're never satisfied.*
*You pile up still more, you mean-featured dastards,*
*May cruel death for this spoil your faces.*
   *Most hideous of faces,*
   *Take them and their grimaces,*
   *Shave them elsewhere, for here*
   *They're out of place, I fear.*
   *Shift them to other places,*
   *Most hideous of faces.*
*Enter not here, you rambling mastiff curs,*
*Morning nor evening, jealous, old and spiteful,*

*Nor you either, seditious mutineers,*
*Spirits, goblins, and fond husbands' familiars,*
*Greeks or Latins, more to be feared than wolves,*
*Nor you with your sores, gnawed to the bone by pox,*
*Take your ulcers elsewhere and show them to others,*
*Scabby from head to toe and brimful of dishonour,*
   *Grace, honour, praise, and light*
   *Are here our sole delight;*
   *Of them we make our song,*
   *Our limbs are sound and strong.*
   *This blessing fills us quite,*
   *Grace, honour, praise, and light.*
*Enter in here, and you shall be most welcome,*
*And having come, stay noble gentlemen!*
*Here is the place where income comes in well,*
*And having come affords good entertainment*
*For great and small, though thousands of them come.*
*Be then my cronies, my especial favourites,*
*Merry and nimble, jolly, gay, and sprightly,*
*And, in a word, the best of good companions.*
   *All worthy gentlemen,*
   *Keen witted and serene,*
   *From every coarseness free,*
   *Here find civility,*
   *Among your hosts will reign,*
   *All worthy gentlemen.*
*Enter in here, you who preach with vigour*
*Christ's Holy Gospel, never mind who scoffs,*
*Here you will find a refuge and a tower*
*Against the foeman's error, the picked arguments,*
*Which falsely seek to spread about their poison.*
*Enter, here let us found a faith profound,*
*And then let us confound by speech and writing,*
*All that are the foemen of the Holy Writ.*
   *Our Holy Writ and Word*
   *For ever shall be heard*
   *In this most holy spot.*
   *Each wears it on his heart,*
   *Each wears it as a sword,*
   *Our Holy Writ and Word.*
*Enter in here, you ladies of high lineage,*
*Here be frank and fearless, enter gaily in,*
*Flowers of all beauty, with heaven in your faces,*
*Upright in bearing, modest in behaviour,*
*Here you will find the dwelling-place of honour.*
*That noble gentleman who of this place was donor,*
*And gives rewards, has destined it for you.*
*He has provided gold sufficient for its upkeep.*
   *Gold freely given,*
   *A man's freely shriven,*
   *In exchange for awards.*
   *For it brings rewards*
   *To all mortal men,*
   *Gold freely given.*

· · ·

## The Rules According to Which the Thélèmites Lived

All their life was regulated not by laws, statutes, or rules, but according to their free will and pleasure. They rose from bed when they pleased, and drank, ate, worked, and slept when the fancy seized them. Nobody woke them; nobody compelled them either to eat or to drink, or to do anything else whatever. So it was that Gargantua had established it. In their rules there was only one clause:

*Do what you will*

because people who are free, well-born, well-bred, and easy in honest company have a natural spur and instinct which drives them to virtuous deeds and deflects them from vice; and this they called honour. When these same men are depressed and enslaved by vile constraint and subjection, they use this noble quality which once impelled them freely towards virtue, to throw off and break this yoke of slavery. For we always strive after things forbidden and covet what is denied us.

Making use of this liberty, they most laudably rivalled one another in all of them doing what they saw pleased one. If some man or woman said, 'Let us drink,' they all drank; if he or she said, 'Let us play,' they all played; if it was 'Let us go and amuse ourselves in the fields,' everyone went there. If it were for hawking or hunting, the ladies, mounted on fine mares, with their grand palfreys following, each carried on their daintily gloved wrists a sparrow-hawk, a lanneret, or a merlin, the men carrying the other birds.

So nobly were they instructed that there was not a man or woman among them who could not read, write, sing, play musical instruments, speak five or six languages, and compose in them both verse and prose. Never were seen such worthy knights, so valiant, so nimble both on foot and horse; knights more vigorous, more agile, handier with all weapons than they were. Never were seen ladies so good-looking, so dainty, less tiresome, more skilled with the fingers and the needle, and in every free and honest womanly pursuit than they were.

For that reason, when the time came that anyone in that abbey, either at his parents' request or for any other reason, wished to leave it, he took with him one of the ladies, the one who had accepted him as her admirer, and they were married to one another; and if at Thélème they had lived in devotion and friendship, they lived in still greater devotion and friendship when they were married. Indeed, they loved one another to the end of their days as much as they had done on their wedding day.

---

# MICHEL DE MONTAIGNE

# from *Essays*

## Book I, Chapter 31

---

The essay is ancient in form but the name is modern, coined by the French writer Montaigne in his *Essays* (from the French, *essai*, "attempt"), the first series published in 1580. Montaigne's personal essays were "attempts" at self-definition, to discover a sane and kindly way of living. With quiet authority, yet treating all truths as opinions, these essays impressed his readers, then and now. His works made the essay the West's most versatile literary form.

In form, Montaigne's essays are rambling, long (most run to several thousand words), and cover diverse topics (Smells, The Affection of Fathers for their Children, and The Length of Life). They are learned, yet jargon free; serious, yet marked by dry wit; and based on personal experience, while making points applicable to all. Widely read, Montaigne packed his pages with ideas from Plato (see *Phaedo* and *The Republic*), Plutarch, Cicero (see *On the Republic*), St. Augustine (see *Confessions*), and his own contemporaries, without always giving them credit. The result was a style linking pagan and Christian antiquity with the modern era.

Montaigne's constant subject is himself. Michel Eyquem de Montaigne (1533–1592) lived a divided life; he was a highly public figure (as counselor to the *Parlement* [law court] of Bordeaux, 1561–1570, and mayor of Bordeaux, 1581–1585); and he was a quiet philosopher, devoting himself to reading and writing. He worked on the *Essays* from 1572 until his death. With few references to career and family, the essays paint a "self-portrait" of his body, mind, and character. Driven by self-awareness—unique in this period but a commonplace today—he offers a running commentary on his kidney stones, eating habits, and vanity. He claimed he was "various and wavering," and the essays demonstrate these qualities in frequent digressions and shifting points of view.

What ultimately gives unity to the *Essays* is Montaigne's growing skepticism. He was repulsed by the fanatical wars between Protestants and Catholics which engulfed France and Europe at this time. In private, siding with Catholic tradition, he nevertheless, in his essays, attached little weight to Christian ethics. Nor did he find in the ancient philosophies a moral code able to control humanity. He concluded that humans were vain and doomed to doubts—a view often voiced in the Age of Mannerism (1520–1600), a period marked by anti-Renaissance norms and the belief in human depravity.

### Reading the Selection

"Of Cannibals" comprises Chapter 31 of Book I of the *Essays*. It reflected Montaigne's knowledge of the New World, gleaned from the works of historians, including those who detailed the horrors of the conquest or heard from American Indians themselves in France. Montaigne learned of the "cannibals" from Antarctic France (Brazil) in a work (1557) by Durand de Villegagnon, a French noble.

As horizons opened in the New World, old certainties gave way to doubts about European values. Montaigne, brought face-to-face with New World "cannibals," reacted with unusual (for his time) insight: "each man calls barbarism whatever is not his own practice"—one of the West's first instances of cultural relativism.

Montaigne's cultural relativism has been termed "primitivism," meaning respect for barbarous peoples and admiration for much of their culture based on an understanding of their motives. It resembles the "noble savage" belief of Rousseau (see *Confessions*), except that Montaigne accepted that savages can be as cruel as Europeans.

---

### Of Cannibals

When King Pyrrhus passed over into Italy, after he had reconnoitered the formation of the army that the Romans were sending to meet him, he said: "I do not know what barbarians these are" (for so the Greeks called all foreign nations), "but the formation of this army that I see is not at all barbarous." The Greeks said as much of the army that Flamininus brought into the country, and so did Philip, seeing from a knoll the order and distribution of the Roman camp, in his kingdom, under Publius Sulpicius Galba. Thus we should beware of clinging to vulgar opinions, and judge things by reason's way, not by popular say.

I had with me for a long time a man who had lived for ten or twelve years in that other world which has been discovered in our century, in the place where Villegaignon landed, and which he called Antarctic France. This discovery of a boundless country seems worthy of consideration. I don't know if I can guarantee that some other such discovery will not be made in the future, so many personages greater than ourselves having been mistaken about this one. I am afraid we have eyes bigger than our stomachs, and more curiosity than capacity. We embrace everything, but we clasp only wind.

Plato brings in Solon, telling how he had learned from the priests of the city of Saïs in Egypt that in days of old, before the Flood, there was a great island named Atlantis, right at the mouth of the Strait of Gibraltar, which contained more land than Africa and Asia put together, and that the kings of that country, who not only possessed that island but had stretched out so far on the mainland that they held the breadth of Africa as far as Egypt, and the length of Europe as far as Tuscany, undertook to step over into Asia and subjugate all the nations that border on the Mediterranean, as far as the Black Sea; and for this purpose crossed the Spains, Gaul, Italy, as far as Greece, where the Athenians checked them; but that some time after, both the Athenians and themselves and their island were swallowed up by the Flood.

It is quite likely that that extreme devastation of waters made amazing changes in the habitations of the earth, as people maintain that the sea cut off Sicily from Italy—

*'Tis said an earthquake once asunder tore*
*These lands with dreadful havoc, which before*
*Formed but one land, one coast*
                                        Virgil

—Cyprus from Syria, the island of Euboea from the mainland of Boeotia; and elsewhere joined lands that were divided, filling the channels between them with sand and mud:

*A sterile marsh, long fit for rowing, now*
*Feeds neighbor towns, and feels the heavy plow.*
                                        Horace

But there is no great likelihood that that island was the new world which we have just discovered; for it almost touched Spain, and it would be an incredible result of a flood to have forced it away as far as it is, more than twelve hundred leagues; besides, the travels of the moderns have already almost revealed that it is not an island, but a mainland connected with the East Indies on one side, and elsewhere with the lands under the two poles; or, if it is separated from them, it is by so narrow a strait and interval that it does not deserve to be called an island on that account.

It seems that there are movements, some natural, others feverish, in these great bodies, just as in our own. When I consider the inroads that my river, the Dordogne, is making in my lifetime into the right bank in its descent, and that in twenty years it has gained so much ground and stolen away the foundations of several buildings, I clearly see that this is an extraordinary disturbance; for if it had always gone at this rate, or was to do so in the future, the face of the world would be turned topsy-turvy. But rivers are subject to changes: now they overflow in one direction, now in another, now they keep to their course. I am not speaking of the sudden inundations whose causes are manifest. In Médoc, along the seashore, my brother, the sieur d'Arsac, can see an estate of his buried under the sands that the sea spews forth; the tops of some buildings are still visible; his farms and domains have changed into very thin pasturage. The inhabitants say that for some time the sea has been pushing toward them so hard that they have lost four leagues of land. These sands are its harbingers; and we see great dunes of moving sand that march half a league ahead of it and keep conquering land.

The other testimony of antiquity with which some would connect this discovery is in Aristotle, at least if that little book *Of Unheard-of Wonders* is by him. He there relates that certain Carthaginians, after setting out upon the Atlantic Ocean from the Strait of Gibraltar and sailing a long time, at last discovered a great fertile island, all clothed in woods and watered by great deep rivers, far remote from any mainland; and that they, and others since, attracted by the goodness and fertility of the soil, went there with their wives and children, and began to settle there. The lords of Carthage, seeing that their country was gradually becoming depopulated, expressly forbade anyone to go there any more, on pain of death, and drove out these new inhabitants, fearing, it is said, that in course of time they might come to multiply so greatly as to supplant their former masters and ruin their state. This story of Aristotle does not fit our new lands any better than the other.

This man I had was a simple, crude fellow—a character fit to bear true witness; for clever people observe more things and more curiously, but they interpret them; and to lend weight and conviction to their interpretation, they cannot help altering history a little. They never show you things as they are, but bend and disguise them according to the way they have seen them; and to give credence to their judgment and attract you to it, they are prone to add something to their matter, to stretch it out and amplify it. We need a man either very honest, or so simple that he has not the stuff to build up false inventions and give them plausibility; and wedded to no theory. Such was my man; and besides this, he at various times brought sailors and merchants, whom he had known on that trip, to see me. So I content myself with his information, without inquiring what the cosmographers say about it.

We ought to have topographers who would give us an exact account of the places where they have been. But because they have over us the advantage of having seen Palestine, they want to enjoy the privilege of telling us news about all the rest of the world. I would like everyone to write what he knows, and as much as he knows, not only in this, but in all other subjects; for a man may have some special knowledge and experience of the nature of a river or a fountain, who in other matters knows only what everybody knows. However, to circulate this little scrap of knowledge, he will undertake to write the whole of physics. From this vice spring many great abuses.

Now, to return to my subject, I think there is nothing barbarous and savage in that nation, from what I have been told, except that each man calls barbarism whatever is not his own practice; for indeed it seems we have no other test of truth and reason than the example and pattern of the opinions and customs of the country we live in. *There* is always the perfect religion, the perfect government, the perfect and accomplished manners in all things. Those people are wild, just as we call wild the fruits that Nature has produced by herself and in her normal course; whereas really it is those that we have changed artificially and led astray from the common order, that we should rather call wild. The former retain alive and vigorous their genuine, their most useful and natural, virtues and properties, which we have debased in the latter in adapting them to gratify our corrupted taste. And yet for all that, the savor and delicacy of some uncultivated fruits of those countries is quite as excellent, even to our taste, as that of our own. It is not reasonable that art should win the place of honor over our great and powerful mother Nature. We have so overloaded the beauty and richness of her works by our inventions that we have quite smothered her. Yet wherever her purity shines forth, she wonderfully puts to shame our vain and frivolous attempts:

*Ivy comes readier without our care;*
*In lonely caves the arbutus grows more fair;*
*No art with artless bird song can compare.*
　　　　　　　　　　Propertius

All our efforts cannot even succeed in reproducing the nest of the tiniest little bird, its contexture, its beauty and convenience; or even the web of the puny spider. All things, says Plato, are produced by nature, by fortune, or by art; the greatest and most beautiful by one or the other of the first two, the least and most imperfect by the last.

These nations, then, seem to me barbarous in this sense, that they have been fashioned very little by the human mind, and are still very close to their original naturalness. The laws of nature still rule them, very little corrupted by ours; and they are in such a state of purity that I am sometimes vexed that they were unknown earlier, in the days when there were men able to judge them better than we. I am sorry that Lycurgus and Plato did not know of them; for it seems to me that what we actually see in these nations surpasses not only all the pictures in which poets have idealized the golden age and all their inventions in imagining a happy state of man, but also the conceptions and the very desire of philosophy. They could not imagine a naturalness so pure and simple as we see by experience; nor could they believe that our society could be maintained with so little artifice and human solder. This is a nation, I should say to Plato, in which there is no sort of traffic, no knowledge of letters, no science of numbers, no name for magistrate or for political superiority, no custom of servitude, no riches or poverty, no contracts, no successions, no partitions, no occupations but leisure ones, no care for any but common kinship, no clothes, no agriculture, no metal, no use of wine or wheat. The very words that signify lying, treachery, dissimulation, avarice, envy, belittling, pardon—unheard of. How far from this perfection would he find the republic that he imagined: *Men fresh sprung from the gods* [Seneca].

*These manners nature first ordained.*
　　　　　　　　　　Virgil

For the rest, they live in a country with a very pleasant and temperate climate, so that according to my witnesses it is rare to see a sick man there; and they have assured me that they never saw one palsied, bleary-eyed, toothless, or bent with age. They are settled along the sea and shut in on the land side by great high mountains, with a stretch about a hundred leagues wide in between. They have a great abundance of fish and flesh which bear no resemblance to ours, and they eat them with no other artifice than cooking. The first man who rode a horse there, though he had had dealings with them on several other trips, so horrified them in this posture that they shot him dead with arrows before they could recognize him.

Their buildings are very long, with a capacity of two or three hundred souls; they are covered with the bark of great trees, the strips reaching to the ground at one end and supporting and leaning on one another at the top, in the manner of some of our barns, whose covering hangs down to the ground and acts as a side. They have wood so hard that they cut with it and make of it their swords and grills to cook their food. Their beds are of a cotton weave, hung from the roof like those in our ships, each man having his own; for the wives sleep apart from their husbands.

They get up with the sun, and eat immediately upon rising, to last them through the day; for they take no other meal than that one. Like some other Eastern peoples, of whom Suidas tells us, who drank apart from meals, they do not drink then; but they drink several times a day, and to capacity. Their drink is made of some root, and is of the color of our claret wines. They drink it only lukewarm. This beverage keeps only two or three days; it has a slightly sharp taste, is not at all heady, is good for the stomach, and has a laxative effect upon those who are not used to it; it is a very pleasant drink for anyone who is accustomed to it. In place of bread they use a certain white substance like preserved coriander. I have tried it; it tastes sweet and a little flat.

The whole day is spent in dancing. The younger men go to hunt animals with bows. Some of the women busy themselves meanwhile with warming their drink, which is their chief duty. Some one of the old men, in the morning before they begin to eat, preaches to the whole barnful in common, walking from one end to the other, and repeating one single sentence several times until he has completed the circuit (for the buildings are fully a hundred paces long). He recommends to them only two things: valor against the enemy and love for their wives. And they never fail to point out this obligation, as their refrain, that it is their wives who keep their drink warm and seasoned.

There may be seen in several places, including my own house, specimens of their beds, of their ropes, of their wooden swords and the bracelets with which they cover their wrists in combats, and of the big canes, open at one end, by whose sound they keep time in their dances. They are close shaven all over, and shave themselves much more cleanly than we, with nothing but a wooden or stone razor. They believe that souls are immortal, and that those who have deserved well of the gods are lodged in that part of heaven where the sun rises, and the damned in the west.

They have some sort of priests and prophets, but they rarely appear before the people, having their home in the mountains. On their arrival there is a great feast and solemn assembly of several villages—each barn, as I have described it, makes up a village, and they are about one French league from each other. The prophet speaks to them in public, exhorting them to virtue and their duty; but their whole ethical science contains only these two articles: resoluteness in war and affection for their wives. He prophesies to them things to come and the results they are to expect from their undertakings, and urges them to war or holds them back from it; but this is on the condition that when he fails to prophesy correctly, and if things turn out otherwise than he has predicted, he is cut into a thousand pieces if they catch him, and condemned as a false prophet. For this reason, the prophet who has once been mistaken is never seen again.

Divination is a gift of God; that is why its abuse should be punished as imposture. Among the Scythians, when the soothsayers failed to hit the mark, they were laid, chained hand and foot, on carts full of heather and drawn by oxen, on which they were burned. Those who handle matters subject to the control of human capacity are excusable if they do the best they can. But these others, who come and trick us with assurances of an extraordinary faculty that is beyond our ken, should they not be punished for not making good their promise, and for the temerity of their imposture?

They have their wars with the nations beyond the mountains, further inland, to which they go quite naked, with no other arms than bows or wooden swords ending in a sharp point, in the manner of the tongues of our boar spears. It is astonishing what firmness they show in their combats, which never end but in slaughter and bloodshed; for as to routs and terror, they know nothing of either.

Each man brings back as his trophy the head of the enemy he has killed, and sets it up at the entrance to his dwelling. After they have treated their prisoners well for a long time with all the hospitality they can think of, each man who has a prisoner calls a great assembly of his acquaintances. He ties a rope to one of the prisoner's arms, by the end of which he holds him, a few steps away, for fear of being hurt, and gives his dearest friend the other arm to hold in the same way; and these two, in the presence of the whole assembly, kill him with their swords. This done, they roast him and eat him in common and send some pieces to their absent friends. This is not, as people think, for nourishment, as of old the Scythians used to do; it is to betoken an extreme revenge. And the proof of this came when they saw the Portuguese, who had joined forces with their adversaries, inflict a different kind of death on them when they took them prisoner, which was to bury them up to the waist, shoot the rest of their body full of arrows, and afterward hang them. They thought that these people from the other world, being men who had sown the knowledge of many vices among their neighbors and were much greater masters than themselves in every sort of wickedness, did not adopt this sort of vengeance without some reason, and that it must be more painful than their own; so they began to give up their old method and to follow this one.

I am not sorry that we notice the barbarous horror of such acts, but I am heartily sorry that, judging their faults rightly, we should be so blind to our own. I think there is more barbarity in eating a man alive than in eating him dead; and in tearing by tortures and the rack a body still full of feeling, in roasting a man bit by bit, in having him bitten and mangled by dogs and swine (as we have not only read but seen within fresh memory, not among ancient enemies, but among neighbors and fellow citizens, and what is worse, on the pretext of piety and religion), than in roasting and eating him after he is dead.

Indeed, Chrysippus and Zeno, heads of the Stoic sect, thought there was nothing wrong in using our carcasses for any purpose in case of need, and getting nourishment from them; just as our ancestors, when besieged by Caesar in the city of Alésia, resolved to relieve their famine by eating old men, women, and other people useless for fighting.

*The Gascons once, 'tis said, their life renewed*
*By eating of such food.*
Juvenal

And physicians do not fear to use human flesh in all sorts of ways for our health, applying it either inwardly or outwardly. But there never was any opinion so disordered as to excuse treachery, disloyalty, tyranny, and cruelty, which are our ordinary vices.

So we may well call these people barbarians, in respect to the rules of reason, but not in respect to ourselves, who surpass them in every kind of barbarity.

Their warfare is wholly noble and generous, and as excusable and beautiful as this human disease can be; its only basis among them is their rivalry in valor. They are not fighting for the conquest of new lands, for they still enjoy that natural abundance that provides them without toil and trouble with all necessary things in such profusion that they have no wish to enlarge their boundaries. They are still in that happy state of desiring only as much as their natural needs demand; anything beyond that is superfluous to them.

They generally call those of the same age, brothers; those who are younger, children; and the old men are fathers to all the others. These leave to their heirs in common the full possession of their property, without division or any other title at all than just the one that Nature gives to her creatures in bringing them into the world.

If their neighbors cross the mountains to attack them and win a victory, the gain of the victor is glory, and the advantage of having proved the master in valor and virtue; for apart from this they have no use for the goods of the vanquished, and they return to their own country, where they lack neither anything necessary nor that great thing, the knowledge of how to enjoy their condition happily and be content with it. These men of ours do the same in their turn. They demand of their prisoners no other ransom than that they confess and acknowledge their defeat. But there is not one in a whole century who does not choose to die rather than to relax a single bit, by word or look, from the grandeur of an invincible courage; not one who would not rather be killed and eaten than so much as ask not to be. They treat them very freely, so that life may be all the dearer to them, and usually entertain them with threats of their coming death, of the torments they will have to suffer, the preparations that are being made for that purpose, the cutting up of their limbs,

and the feast that will be made at their expense. All this is done for the sole purpose of extorting from their lips some weak or base word, or making them want to flee, so as to gain the advantage of having terrified them and broken down their firmness. For indeed, if you take it the right way, it is in this point alone that true victory lies:

*It is no victory*
*Unless the vanquished foe admits your mastery.*
Claudian

The Hungarians, very bellicose fighters, did not in olden times pursue their advantage beyond putting the enemy at their mercy. For having wrung a confession from him to this effect, they let him go unharmed and unransomed, except, at most, for exacting his promise never again to take up arms against them.

We win enough advantages over our enemies that are borrowed advantages, not really our own. It is the quality of a porter, not of valor, to have sturdier arms and legs; agility is a dead and corporeal quality; it is a stroke of luck to make our enemy stumble, or dazzle his eyes by the sunlight; it is a trick of art and technique, which may be found in a worthless coward, to be an able fencer. The worth and value of a man is in his heart and his will; there lies his real honor. Valor is the strength, not of legs and arms, but of heart and soul; it consists not in the worth of our horse or our weapons, but in our own. He who falls obstinate in his courage, *if he has fallen, he fights on his knees* [Seneca]. He who relaxes none of his assurance, no matter how great the danger of imminent death; who, giving up his soul, still looks firmly and scornfully at his enemy—he is beaten not by us, but by fortune; he is killed, not conquered.

The most valiant are sometimes the most unfortunate. Thus there are triumphant defeats that rival victories. Nor did those four sister victories, the fairest that the sun ever set eyes on—Salamis, Plataea, Mycale, and Sicily—ever dare match all their combined glory against the glory of the annihilation of King Leonidas and his men at the pass of Thermopylae.

Who ever hastened with more glorious and ambitious desire to win a battle than Captain Ischolas to lose one? Who ever secured his safety more ingeniously and painstakingly than he did his destruction? He was charged to defend a certain pass in the Peloponnesus against the Arcadians. Finding himself wholly incapable of doing this, in view of the nature of the place and the inequality of the forces, he made up his mind that all who confronted the enemy would necessarily have to remain on the field. On the other hand, deeming it unworthy both of his own virtue and magnanimity and of the Lacedaemonian name to fail in his charge, he took a middle course between these two extremes, in this way. The youngest and fittest of his band he preserved for the defense and service of their country, and sent them home; and with those whose loss was less important, he determined to hold this pass, and by their death to make the enemy buy their entry as dearly as he could. And so it turned out. For he was presently surrounded on all sides by the Arcadians, and after slaughtering a large number of them, he and his men were all put to the sword. Is there a trophy dedicated to victors that would not be more due to these vanquished? The role of true victory is in fighting, not in coming off safely; and the honor of valor consists in combating, not in beating.

To return to our story. These prisoners are so far from giving in, in spite of all that is done to them, that on the contrary, during the two or three months that they are kept, they wear a gay expression; they urge their captors to hurry and put them to the test; they defy them, insult them, reproach them with their cowardice and the number of battles they have lost to the prisoners' own people.

I have a song composed by a prisoner which contains this challenge, that they should all come boldly and gather to dine off him, for they will be eating at the same time their own fathers and grandfathers, who have served to feed and nourish his body. "These muscles," he says, "this flesh and these veins are your own, poor fools that you are. You do not recognize that the substance of your ancestors' limbs is still contained in them. Savor them well; you will find in them the taste of your own flesh." An idea that certainly does not smack of barbarity. Those that paint these people dying, and who show the execution, portray the prisoner spitting in the face of his slayers and scowling at them. Indeed, to the last gasp they never stop braving and defying their enemies by word and look. Truly here are real savages by our standards; for either they must be thoroughly so, or we must be; there is an amazing distance between their character and ours.

The men there have several wives, and the higher their reputation for valor the more wives they have. It is a remarkably beautiful thing about their marriages that the same jealousy our wives have to keep us from the affection and kindness of other women, theirs have to win this for them. Being more concerned for their husbands' honor than for anything else, they strive and scheme to have as many companions as they can, since that is a sign of their husbands' valor.

Our wives will cry "Miracle!" but it is no miracle. It is a properly matrimonial virtue, but one of the highest order. In the Bible, Leah, Rachel, Sarah, and Jacob's wives gave their beautiful handmaids to their husbands; and Livia seconded the appetites of Augustus, to her own disadvantage; and Stratonice, the wife of King Deiotarus, not only lent her husband for his use a very beautiful young chambermaid in her service, but carefully brought up her children, and backed them up to succeed to their father's estates.

And lest it be thought that all this is done through a simple and servile bondage to usage and through the pressure of the authority of their ancient customs, without reasoning or judgment, and because their minds are so stupid that they cannot take any other course, I must cite some examples of their capacity. Besides the warlike song I have just quoted, I have another, a love song, which begins in this vein: "Adder, stay; stay, adder, that from the pattern of your coloring my sister may draw the fashion and the workmanship of a rich girdle that I may give to my love; so may your beauty and your pattern be forever preferred to all other serpents." This first couplet is the refrain of the song. Now I am familiar enough with poetry to be a judge of this: not only is there nothing barbarous in this fancy, but it is altogether Anacreontic. Their language, moreover, is a soft language, with an agreeable sound, somewhat like Greek in its endings.

Three of these men, ignorant of the price they will pay some day, in loss of repose and happiness, for gaining knowledge of the corruptions of this side of the ocean; ignorant also of the fact that of this intercourse will come their ruin (which I suppose is already well advanced: poor wretches, to let themselves be tricked by the desire for new things, and to have left the serenity of their own sky to come and see ours!)—three of these men were at Rouen, at the time the late King Charles IX was there. The king talked to them for a long time; they were shown our ways, our splendor, the aspect of a fine city. After that, someone asked their opinion, and wanted to know what they had found most amazing. They mentioned three things, of which I have forgotten the third, and I am very sorry for it; but I still remember two of them. They said that in the first place they thought it very strange that so many grown men, bearded, strong, and armed, who were around the king (it is likely that they were talking about the Swiss of his guard) should submit to obey a child, and that one of them was not chosen to command instead. Second (they have a way in their language of speaking of men as halves of one another), they had noticed that there were among us men full and gorged with all sorts of good things, and that their other halves were beggars at their doors, emaciated with hunger and poverty; and they thought it strange that these needy halves could endure such an injustice, and did not take the others by the throat, or set fire to their houses.

I had a very long talk with one of them; but I had an interpreter who followed my meaning so badly, and who was so hindered by his stupidity in taking in my ideas, that I could get hardly any satisfaction from the man. When I asked him what profit he gained from his superior position among his people (for he was a captain, and our sailors called him king), he told me that it was to march foremost in war. How many men followed him? He pointed to a piece of ground, to signify as many as such a space could hold; it might have been four or five thousand men. Did all his authority expire with the war? He said that this much remained, that when he visited the villages dependent on him, they made paths for him through the underbrush by which he might pass quite comfortably.

All this is not too bad—but what's the use? They don't wear breeches.

# QUEEN ELIZABETH I

The golden age of England coincided with the turbulent reign of Queen Elizabeth I (1533–1603), from 1558 to 1603. It was a period of momentous change in the political realm, as Protestant England was often under threat of invasion from Catholic forces on the continent. Anglicanism was establishing itself as England's state church, but this religious settlement provoked much unhappiness from English Puritans and Catholics. English sea power was beginning to make its presence felt around the globe. National consciousness was on the rise both in England and abroad, so that normal tensions between states were now heightened on the international stage. It was also a time of dramatic developments in the cultural domain, for this was the Age of Shakespeare, England's greatest writer.

Presiding ably over England's fortune during this momentous era was Elizabeth, a daughter of the Reformation. It was her imminent birth to King Henry VIII and Ann Boleyn, his second wife, which set into motion the events that culminated in England's becoming a Protestant state. That Elizabeth survived to become monarch at all was a tribute to her tact and her ability to keep her own counsel. Reared in the conspiratorial atmosphere at the royal court, she often was in personal danger, such as being imprisoned in the Tower of London. Nonetheless, she received a first-class humanist education which prepared her well to be queen. This education left its indelible marks on her nature, as she always appreciated music, poetry, Classical learning, and witty conversation. She also understood the power of language and could use it effectively, whether to persuade her advisers or Parliament itself, charm a court gathering, or inspire her armies on the eve of battle.

## Reading the Selection

Both these examples of Elizabeth's words, the poem entitled "The Doubt of Future Foes" and the "Speech to the Troops at Tilbury," convey, essentially, the same propagandistic message: No matter what threatens England, she, as Queen, will appeal to the best in her people, rally them around her leadership, and defeat her country's enemies. "The Doubt of Future Foes," written in rhyming couplets, was meant to be read in private and can be interpreted to mean threats to the Queen herself as well as to her country. The poem's military metaphors, such as "to poll their tops"—that is, to cut off enemies' heads—were carefully chosen to convey her readiness to resort to war, reflecting her awareness that some of her subjects might otherwise think that she, as a woman, might be a weak ruler.

When Elizabeth delivered the "Speech to the Troops at Tilbury," in 1588, English naval forces had just thwarted the invasion of the Spanish Armada, but it was not yet fully clear that the threat from Catholic Spain had gone away. Tilbury is east of London along the Thames river, and, there, Elizabeth addressed her army, speaking in the royal "we." From her first words, it is clear that some of the royal advisers cautioned against this appearance in open country; she was warned that her life might be at risk, presumably from dissident English Catholics who would welcome their coreligionists from Spain. The rest of the speech is a rousing call to arms, in the name of God, country, and the English people. She reassures her troops that she is ready "to live or die amongst you all." Such stirring words made Elizabeth into "Gloriana," the poetic name given this extraordinary woman by her admirers.

# The Doubt of Future Foes

The doubt of future foes exiles my present joy,
And wit me warns to shun such snares as threaten mine
annoy;
For falsehood now doth flow, and subjects' faith doth
ebb,
Which should not be if reason ruled or wisdom weaved
the web.
But clouds of joys untried do cloak aspiring minds,
Which turn to rain of late repent by changéd course of
winds.
The top of hope supposed the root upreared shall be,
And fruitless all their grafted guile, as shortly ye shall see.

The dazzled eyes with pride, which great ambition blinds,
Shall be unsealed by worthy wights whose foresight
falsehood finds.
The daughter of debate that discord aye doth sow
Shall reap no gain where former rule still peace hath
taught to know.
No foreign banished wight shall anchor in this port;
Our realm brooks not seditious sects, let them elsewhere
resort.
My rusty sword through rest shall first his edge employ
To poll their tops that seek such change or gape for
future joy.

# Speech to the Troops at Tilbury

My loving people,

We have been persuaded by some that are careful of our safety, to take heed how we commit our selves to armed multitudes, for fear of treachery; but I assure you I do not desire to live to distrust my faithful and loving people. Let tyrants fear, I have always so behaved myself that, under God, I have placed my chiefest strength and safeguard in the loyal hearts and good-will of my subjects; and therefore I am come amongst you, as you see, at this time, not for my recreation and disport, but being resolved, in the midst and heat of the battle, to live or die amongst you all; to lay down for my God, and for my kingdom, and my people, my honour and my blood, even in the dust. I know I have the body but of a weak and feeble woman; but I have the heart and stomach of a king, and of a king of England too, and think foul scorn that Parma or Spain, or any prince of Europe, should dare to invade the borders of my realm; to which rather than any dishonour shall grow by me, I myself will take up arms, I myself will be your general, judge, and rewarder of every one of your virtues in the field. I know already, for your forwardness you have deserved rewards and crowns; and We do assure you in the word of a prince, they shall be duly paid you. In the mean time, my lieutenant general shall be in my stead, than whom never prince commanded a more noble or worthy subject; not doubting but by your obedience to my general, by your concord in the camp, and your valour in the field, we shall shortly have a famous victory over those enemies of my God, of my kingdom, and of my people.

# MIGUEL DE CERVANTES
# from *Don Quixote*
## Part I

Cervantes' *Don Quixote,* arguably the greatest work in the Spanish language, has been one of the world's best-selling books since it appeared in the early seventeenth century. Over the centuries, this work has entertained millions with its satirical adventures of the dim-witted Don Quixote and his coarse side-kick, Sancho Panza. These unlikely heroes have been embraced by the world as lovable characters and have often been celebrated in other mediums (art, music, and films).

*Don Quixote* is essentially a satire on chivalry, the courtly code of the Middle Ages practiced by knights and ladies, especially in literature (see Chrètien de Troyes' *Arthurian Romances*). Chivalry was on the wane from 1400 onward, but chivalrous romances and love ballads retained their appeal in Spain throughout the 1500s. Spain's mania for the ballads and stories of chivalry led Cervantes to write this satire. More than half in love with the object of his satire, he in fact composed a book more romantically adventurous than the material he parodied.

In form, *Don Quixote* is one of the earliest novels. This should come as no surprise, since the novel form was more advanced in Spain than in the rest of Europe. This work, like early novels elsewhere (see Fielding's *The History of Tom Jones*), has a rambling structure, covering about one thousand pages. Its plot is rather planless, consisting of a string of episodes, enlivened with flashes of wit and happy phrases.

Carried along on Cervantes' river of words are the ridiculous heroes, the knight Don Quixote and the son of the soil Sancho Panza. Don Quixote is a hopeless romantic whose exploits come to nothing; he is forever either the butt of the jokes of others (for instance, when he is tricked by the priest disguised as a damsel in distress) or the victim of his own madness (for example, when he mistakes an ugly serving girl for Dulcinea, the beautiful lady of his dreams). In contrast, Sancho Panza is the soul of common sense who doggedly tries to save his master from misadventures. Together, they stand for Spain's divided soul: Quixote symbolizes the self-absorbed aristocratic spirit, consumed by honor and titles, and Panza, the enduring peasant eternally exploited by the nobility.

These characters also embody the novel's theme, the tension between dreams and reality. To live in dreams is to build castles in the air, like Don Quixote. But life without dreams leads to despair, like Sancho Panza. As Panza rides with Quixote through filthy ditches and over rampaging pigs, he comes to love and admire the Don's saintly nature, even though he considers him mad. Thus the moral is: Follow one's dreams, even though they come to naught.

For years, Miguel de Cervantes (1547–1615) led a swashbuckling life as a soldier, being wounded, captured, enslaved, and ransomed. After 1580 he tried to support his family through writing, and, often wound up in prison. His fortune was made when Part I of *Don Quixote* was published in 1605; Part II followed in 1615.

### Reading the Selection

This selection, Chapter VIII of Part I, contains the best-known episode in *Don Quixote.* In it, Quixote attacks forty windmills, mistaking them for giants. Deaf to Panza's pleas, Quixote winds up utterly defeated. This episode is the source of the English saying, "to tilt at windmills," meaning to fight with phantom enemies.

The second part of this selection deals with a Basque knight. It shows Cervantes resorting to an old literary device; he pretends that his "history" is actually a translation from an Arabic work.

### Chapter VIII. Of the valorous Don Quixote's success in the dreadful and never before imagined Adventure of the Windmills, with other events worthy of happy record.

At that moment they caught sight of some thirty or forty windmills, which stand on that plain, and as soon as Don Quixote saw them he said to his squire: 'Fortune is guiding our affairs better than we could have wished. Look over there, friend Sancho Panza, where more than thirty monstrous giants appear. I intend to do battle with them and take all their lives. With their spoils we will begin to get rich, for this is a fair war, and it is a great service to God to wipe such a wicked brood from the face of the earth.'

'What giants?' asked Sancho Panza.

'Those you see there,' replied his master, 'with their long arms. Some giants have them about six miles long.'

'Take care, your worship,' said Sancho; 'those things over there are not giants but windmills, and what seem to be their arms are the sails, which are whirled round in the wind and make the millstone turn.'

'It is quite clear,' replied Don Quixote, 'that you are not experienced in this matter of adventures. They are giants, and if you are afraid, go away and say your prayers, whilst I advance and engage them in fierce and unequal battle.'

As he spoke, he dug his spurs into his steed Rocinante, paying no attention to his squire's shouted warning that beyond all doubt they were windmills and no giants he was advancing to attack. But he went on, so positive that they were giants that he neither listened to Sancho's cries nor noticed what they were, even when he got near them. Instead he went on shouting in a loud voice: 'Do not fly, cowards, vile creatures, for it is one knight alone who assails you.'

At that moment a slight wind arose, and the great sails began to move. At the sight of which Don Quixote shouted: 'Though you wield more arms than the giant Briareus, you shall pay for it!' Saying this, he commended himself with all his soul to his Lady Dulcinea, beseeching her aid in his great peril. Then, covering himself with his shield and putting his lance in the rest, he urged Rocinante forward at a full gallop and attacked the nearest windmill, thrusting his lance into the sail. But the wind turned it with such violence that it shivered his weapon in pieces, dragging the horse and his rider with it, and sent the knight rolling badly injured across the plain. Sancho Panza rushed to his assistance as fast as his ass could trot, but when he came up he found that the knight could not stir. Such a shock had Rocinante given him in their fall.

'O my goodness!' cried Sancho. 'Didn't I tell your worship to look what you were doing, for they were only windmills? Nobody could mistake them, unless he had wind-mills on the brain.'

'Silence, friend Sancho,' replied Don Quixote. 'Matters of war are more subject than most to continual change. What is more, I think—and that is the truth—that the same sage Friston who robbed me of my room and my books has turned those giants into windmills, to cheat me of the glory of conquering them. Such is the enmity he bears me; but in the very end his black arts shall avail him little against the goodness of my sword.'

'God send it as He will,' replied Sancho Panza, helping the knight to get up and remount Rocinante, whose shoulders were half dislocated.

As they discussed this last adventure they followed the road to the pass of Lapice where, Don Quixote said, they could not fail to find many and various adventures, as many travellers passed that way. He was much concerned, however, at the loss of his lance, and, speaking of it to his squire, remarked: 'I remember reading that a certain Spanish knight called Diego Perez de Vargas, having broken his sword in battle, tore a great bough or limb from an oak, and performed such deeds with it that day, and pounded so many Moors, that he earned the surname of the Pounder, and thus he and his descendants from that day onwards have been called Vargas y Machuca. I mention this because I propose to tear down just such a limb from the first oak we meet, as big and as good as his; and I intend to do such deeds with it that you may consider yourself most fortunate to have won the right to see them. For you will witness things which will scarcely be credited.'

'With God's help,' replied Sancho, 'and I believe it all as your worship says. But sit a bit more upright, sir, for you seem to be riding lop-sided. It must be from the bruises you got when you fell.'

'That is the truth,' replied Don Quixote. 'And if I do not complain of the pain, it is because a knight errant is not allowed to complain of any wounds, even though his entrails may be dropping out through them.'

'If that's so, I have nothing more to say,' said Sancho, 'but God knows I should be glad if your worship would complain if anything hurt you. I must say, for my part, that I have to cry out at the slightest twinge, unless this business of not complaining extends to knights errants' squires as well.'

Don Quixote could not help smiling at his squire's simplicity, and told him that he could certainly complain how and when he pleased, whether he had any cause or no, for up to that time he had never read anything to the contrary in the law of chivalry.

Sancho reminded him that it was time for dinner, but his master replied that he had need of none, but that his squire might eat whenever he pleased. With this permission Sancho settled himself as comfortably as he could on his ass and, taking out what he had put into the saddle-bags, jogged very leisurely along behind his master, eating all the while; and from time to time he raised the bottle with such relish that the best-fed publican in Malaga might have envied him. Now, as he went along like this, taking repeated gulps, he entirely forgot the promise his master had made him, and reckoned that going in search of adventures, however danger-ous, was more like pleasure than hard work.

They passed that night under some trees, from one of which our knight tore down a dead branch to serve him as some sort of lance, and stuck into it the iron head of the one that had been broken. And all night Don Quixote did not sleep but thought about his Lady Dulcinea, to conform to what he had read in his books about knights errant spending many sleepless nights in woodland and desert dwelling on the memory of their ladies. Not so Sancho Panza; for, as his stomach was full, and not of chicory water, he slept right through till morning. And, if his master had not called him, neither the sunbeams, which struck him full on the face, nor the song of the birds, who in great number and very joyfully greeted the dawn of the new day, would have been enough to wake him. As he got up he made a trial of his bottle, and found it rather limper than the night before; whereat his heart sank, for he did not think they were taking the right road to remedy this defect very quickly. Don Quixote wanted no breakfast for, as we have said, he was determined to subsist on savoury memories. Then they turned back on to the road they had been on before, towards the pass of Lapice, which they sighted about three in the afternoon.

'Here,' exclaimed Don Quixote on seeing it, 'here, brother Sancho Panza, we can steep our arms to the elbows in what they call adventures. But take note that though you see me in the greatest danger in the world, you must not put your hand to your sword to defend me, unless you know that my assailants are rabble and common folk; in which case you may come to my aid. But should they be knights, on no account will it be legal or permissible, by the laws of chivalry, for you to assist me until you are yourself knighted.'

'You may be sure, sir,' replied Sancho, 'that I shall obey your worship perfectly there. Especially as I am very peaceable by nature and all against shoving myself into brawls and quarrels. But as to defending myself, sir, I shan't take much notice of those rules, because divine law and human law allow everyone to defend himself against anyone who tries to harm him.'

'I never said otherwise,' replied Don Quixote, 'but in the matter of aiding me against knights, you must restrain your natural impulses.'

'I promise you I will,' replied Sancho, 'and I will observe this rule as strictly as the Sabbath.'

In the middle of this conversation two monks of the order of St. Benedict appeared on the road, mounted on what looked like dromedaries; for the two mules they were riding were quite as big. They were wearing riding-masks against the dust and carrying sunshades. And behind them came a coach, with four or five horsemen escorting it, and two muleteers on foot.

In the coach, as it afterwards turned out, was a Basque lady travelling to Seville to join her husband, who was going out to take up a very important post in the Indies. The monks were not of her company, but merely journeying on the same road.

Now no sooner did Don Quixote see them in the distance than he said to his squire: 'Either I am much mistaken, or this will prove the most famous adventure ever seen. For those dark shapes looming over there must, beyond all doubt, be enchanters bearing off in that coach some princess they have stolen; and it is my duty to redress this wrong with all my might.'

'This will be a worse job than the windmills,' said Sancho. 'Look, sir, those are Benedictine monks, and the coach must belong to some travellers. Listen to me, sir. Be careful what you do, and don't let the Devil deceive you.'

'I have told you,' replied Don Quixote, 'that you know very little of this subject of adventures. What I say is true, and now you will see it.'

So saying, he rode forward and took up his position in the middle of the road along which the monks were coming; and when they got so near that he thought they could hear him, he called out in a loud voice: 'Monstrous and diabolical crew! Release immediately the noble princesses whom you are forcibly carrying off in that coach, or prepare to receive instant death as the just punishment for your misdeeds.'

The monks reined in their mules, and stopped in astonishment at Don Quixote's appearance and at his speech.

'Sir Knight,' they replied, 'we are neither monstrous nor diabolical, but two monks of St Benedict travelling about our business, nor do we know whether there are any princesses being carried off in that coach or not.'

'No fair speeches for me, for I know you, perfidious scoundrels!' cried Don Quixote. Then, without waiting for their reply, he spurred Rocinante and, with his lance lowered, charged at the foremost monk with such vigour and fury that, if he had not slid from his mule, he would have been thrown to the ground and badly hurt, if not killed outright. The second monk, on seeing his companion so treated, struck his heels into his stout mule's flanks and set her galloping over the plain fleeter than the wind itself. When Sancho Panza saw the monk on the ground, he got down lightly from his ass, ran up and started to strip him of his clothes. Upon this, two servants of the monks arrived and asked him why he was stripping their master. Sancho replied that the clothes fell rightly to his share as spoils of the battle which his master, Don Quixote, had won. The lads, who did not get the joke nor understand this talk of spoils and battles, saw that Don Quixote had gone off and was talking with the ladies in the coach, and so fell upon Sancho and knocked him down. And, pulling every hair from his beard, they kicked him mercilessly, and left him stretched on the ground, breathless and stunned. Then, without a moment's hesitation, the monk remounted his mule, trembling, terrified and as white as a sheet; and as soon as he was up he spurred after his comrade, who was waiting for him some distance off, watching to see the upshot of this sudden attack. But without caring to wait for the end of the adventure, they went on their way, crossing themselves more often than if they had had the Devil himself at their backs.

Don Quixote, as we have said, was talking with the lady in the coach: 'Your fair ladyship may now dispose of yourself as you desire, for now the pride of your ravishers lies in the dust, overthrown by this strong arm of mine. And lest you be racked with doubt as to the name of your deliverer, know that I am Don Quixote de la Mancha, knight errant, adventurer and captive to the peerless and beautiful lady, Dulcinea del Toboso. And in requital of the benefit you have received from me, I would ask no more of you than to go to El Toboso and present yourself on my behalf before that lady, telling her what I have done for your deliverance.'

All that Don Quixote said was overheard by one of the squires accompanying the coach, a Basque. And when he saw that the knight would not let them pass, but was talking of their turning back at once to El Toboso, he went up to Don Quixote and, grasping his lance, addressed him in bad Castilian and worse Basque.

'Get along, you ill-gotten knight. By God who made me, if you do not leave coach I kill you, sure as I be Basque.'

Don Quixote understood him very well, and replied with great calm: 'If you were a knight, as you are not, I should have punished your rash insolence by now, you slavish creature.'

'I not gentleman? I swear you liar, as I am a Christian. You throw down lance and draw sword, and you will see you are carrying the water to the cat. Basque on land, gentleman at sea. A gentleman, by the devil, and you lie if you say otherwise!'

' "Now you shall see," said Agrages,' quoted Don Quixote, and threw his lance down on the ground. Then, drawing his sword and grasping his shield, he rushed at his antagonist, determined to take his life. When the Basque saw him coming he would have liked to get down from his mule, as it was a poor sort of hired beast and not to be trusted, but there was nothing for it but to draw his sword. He was, however, lucky enough to be near the coach, from which he was able to snatch a cushion to serve as a shield; whereupon they immediately fell to, as if they had been two mortal enemies. The rest of the party tried to pacify them, but could not; for the Basque swore in his uncouth language that if they did not let him finish the battle, he would himself kill his mistress and all who hindered him.

The lady in the coach, amazed and terrified at the sight, made the coachman drive off a little way, and sat watching the deadly struggle from a distance. In the course of the fight the Basque dealt Don Quixote a mighty blow on one shoulder, thrusting above his shield, and had our knight been without

defence he would have been cleft to the waist. When Don Quixote felt the weight of that tremendous stroke he cried out aloud: 'O lady of my soul, Dulcinea, flower of beauty, come to the aid of this your knight, who for the sake of your great goodness is now in this dire peril!'

To speak, to raise his sword, to cover himself with his shield and attack the Basque: all this was the work of a moment. For he had resolved to risk everything upon a single stroke. The Basque, seeing him come on, judged Don Quixote's courage by his daring, and decided to do the same as he. So he covered himself well with his cushion and waited, unable to turn his mule in either direction, for the beast was now dead weary, and not being made for such games, could not budge a step.

Don Quixote, as we have said, rushed at the wary Basque with sword aloft, determined to cleave him to the waist; and the Basque watched, with his sword also raised and well guarded by his cushion; while all the by-standers trembled in terrified suspense, hanging upon the issue of the dreadful blows with which they threatened one another. And the lady of the coach and her waiting-women offered a thousand vows and prayers to all the images and places of devotion in Spain, that God might deliver their squire and them from the great peril they were in.

But the unfortunate thing is that the author of this history left the battle in suspense at this critical point, with the excuse that he could find no more records of Don Quixote's exploits than those related here. It is true that the second author of this work would not believe that such a curious history could have been consigned to oblivion, or that the learned of La Mancha could have been so incurious as not to have in their archives or in their registries some documents relating to this famous knight. So, strong in this opinion, he did not despair of finding the conclusion of this delightful story and, by the favour of Heaven, found it, as shall be told in our second part.

# WILLIAM SHAKESPEARE

## from *Hamlet*

### Act III: Scene I

---

Excepting the Bible, Shakespeare's *Hamlet* is perhaps the West's most famous literary work. Hardly a day passes without this play being acted, either on a commercial stage or in a school or college; and many versions of the play, on film and on tape, ensure its universal visibility. Hamlet's role is usually defined as the most difficult in the theater, and many actors, and a few actresses, often choose to play Hamlet as a crown to their careers. It is so well known that the world uses the term *Hamletlike* to describe people unable to make up their minds.

The hectic world in which *Hamlet* appeared gave no forecast of the play's future greatness. First staged in 1600, the play was one of a series that William Shakespeare (1564–1616) was turning out for the nearly insatiable demands of the commercial stage. He was fresh to London in 1590 from a middle-class youth in Stratford-upon-Avon. When Shakespeare retired to gentlemanly leisure in Stratford in 1610, he had written thirty-seven dramas—almost two plays a year.

The London audiences did not want masterpieces. Instead, they craved violence, ghosts, and murders galore; they wanted revenge tragedies, the most popular dramatic form in the Age of Elizabeth (1558–1603), England's golden age. This taste for blood is not surprising, for Elizabethan England made national heroes of pirate patriots like Francis Drake; it was accepted as normal that Protestants and Catholics should burn heretics alive. It is for this violence-filled age that Shakespeare wrote *Hamlet*, based on a bloody revenge tale, which had already inspired one play during the 1580s.

Shakespeare's *Hamlet* is set at the royal Danish court. Its revenge theme is activated by the murder of old King Hamlet. Prince Hamlet, depressed by his father's death, is plunged into a court seething with intrigue, carousing, ghosts, and spies; there are also wandering actors, an oath sworn on swords, a secret letter, a deadly duel, and a hasty funeral. Lest these devices be insufficiently entertaining, Hamlet himself veers from madman to scholar to prince to swordsman before he gets his revenge. At the end, the stage is littered with corpses and the major characters are all dead.

What rescues *Hamlet* from mere melodrama and pushes it into the stratosphere of great art are Shakespeare's majestic language and complete mastery of psychology. The theater, reborn in medieval productions like *Everyman*, with its simple morals and even simpler psychology, now came to maturity in Shakespeare's hands.

### Reading the Selection

This selection, from Act III, Scene I, depicts the growing suspicion in Elsinore Castle, as the revenge plot unfolds. King Claudius (the dead king's brother who assumed the throne) and Queen Gertrude question two courtiers, who are really spies, as to the motive of Hamlet's strange behavior ("dangerous lunacy"). The king rightly fears that Hamlet suspects him of murder; the queen is simply worried about her son. Disappointed in the news from his spies, the king sets a trap for Hamlet with Ophelia, Hamlet's girlfriend, as the bait. The king and his chief advisor, Polonius, secretly watch Hamlet's erratic treatment of Ophelia with the result that Claudius decides to exile Hamlet to England. This scene contains perhaps the play's most memorable passage, Hamlet's soliloquy (monologue) in which he considers taking his own life, beginning with the words: "To be or not to be. . . ."

———————

*Elsinore. A room in the Castle.*
*Enter* KING, QUEEN, POLONIUS, OPHELIA,
ROSENCRANTZ, GUILDENSTERN, *and* LORDS.

KING.  And can you by no drift of circumstance
Get from him why he puts on this confusion,
Grating so harshly all his days of quiet
With turbulent and dangerous lunacy?
ROS.  He does confess he feels himself distracted,
But from what cause he will by no means speak.
GUIL.  Nor do we find him forward to be sounded,
But with a crafty madness keeps aloof
When we would bring him on to some confession
Of his true state.
QUEEN.          Did he receive you well?
ROS.  Most like a gentleman.
GUIL.  But with much forcing of his disposition.
ROS.  Niggard of question, but of our demands
Most free in his reply.
QUEEN.          Did you assay him
To any pastime?
ROS.  Madam, it so fell out that certain players
We o'erraught on the way. Of these we told him,
And there did seem in him a kind of joy

To hear of it. They are here about the court,
And, as I think, they have already order
This night to play before him.
POL.                    'Tis most true;
And he beseech'd me to entreat your Majesties
To hear and see the matter.
KING.  With all my heart, and it doth much content me
To hear him so inclin'd.
Good gentlemen, give him a further edge
And drive his purpose on to these delights.
ROS.  We shall, my lord.

(*Exeunt* ROSENCRANTZ *and* GUILDENSTERN.)

KING.                    Sweet Gertrude, leave us too;
For we have closely sent for Hamlet hither,
That he, as 'twere by accident, may here
Affront Ophelia.
Her father and myself (lawful espials)
Will so bestow ourselves that, seeing unseen,
We may of their encounter frankly judge
And gather by him, as he is behav'd,
If't be th' affliction of his love, or no,
That thus he suffers for.

QUEEN.                              I shall obey you;
And for your part, Ophelia, I do wish
That your good beauties be the happy cause
Of Hamlet's wildness. So shall I hope your virtues
Will bring him to his wonted way again,
To both your honours.
OPH.                              Madam, I wish it may.

(*Exit* QUEEN.)

POL.   Ophelia, walk you here.—Gracious, so please you,
We will bestow ourselves.—(*To* OPHELIA) Read on this
book,
That show of such an exercise may colour
Your loneliness.—We are oft to blame in this,
'Tis too much prov'd, that with devotion's visage
And pious action we do sugar o'er
The devil himself.
KING. (*aside*)   O, 'tis too true!
How smart a lash that speech doth give my conscience!
The harlot's cheek, beautied with plast'ring art,
Is not more ugly to the thing that helps it
Than is my deed to my most painted word.
O heavy burthen!
POL.   I hear him coming. Let's withdraw, my lord.

(*Exeunt* KING *and* POLONIUS.)

(*Enter* HAMLET).

HAM.   To be, or not to be—that is the question:
Whether 'tis nobler in the mind to suffer
The slings and arrows of outrageous fortune
Or to take arms against a sea of troubles,
And by opposing end them. To die—to sleep—
No more; and by a sleep to say we end
The heartache, and the thousand natural shocks
That flesh is heir to. 'Tis a consummation
Devoutly to be wish'd. To die—to sleep.
To sleep—perchance to dream: ay, there's the rub!
For in that sleep of death what dreams may come
When we have shuffled off this mortal coil,
Must give us pause. There's the respect
That makes calamity of so long life.
For who would bear the whips and scorns of time,
Th' oppressor's wrong, the proud man's contumely,
The pangs of despis'd love, the law's delay,
The insolence of office, and the spurns
That patient merit of th' unworthy takes,
When he himself might his quietus make
With a bare bodkin? Who would these fardels bear,
To grunt and sweat under a weary life,
But that the dread of something after death—
The undiscover'd country, from whose bourn
No traveller returns—puzzles the will,
And makes us rather bear those ills we have
Than fly to others that we know not of?
Thus conscience does make cowards of us all,
And thus the native hue of resolution
Is sicklied o'er with the pale cast of thought,
And enterprises of great pith and moment
With this regard their currents turn awry
And lose the name of action.—Soft you now!

The fair Ophelia!—Nymph, in thy orisons
Be all my sins rememb'red.
OPH.                              Good my lord,
How does your honour for this many a day?
HAM.   I humbly thank you; well, well, well.
OPH.   My lord, I have remembrances of yours
That I have longed long to re-deliver.
I pray you, now receive them.
HAM.                              No, not I!
I never gave you aught.
OPH.   My honour'd lord, you know right well you did,
And with them words of so sweet breath compos'd
As made the things more rich. Their perfume lost,
Take these again; for to the noble mind
Rich gifts wax poor when givers prove unkind.
There, my lord.
HAM.   Ha, ha! Are you honest?
OPH.   My lord?
HAM.   Are you fair?
OPH.   What means your lordship?
HAM.   That if you be honest and fair, your honesty should
admit no discourse to your beauty.
OPH.   Could beauty, my lord, have better commerce than
with honesty?
HAM.   Ay, truly; for the power of beauty will sooner trans-
form honesty from what it is to a bawd than the force of
honesty can translate beauty into his likeness. This was some-
time a paradox, but now the time gives it proof. I did love
you once.
OPH.   Indeed, my lord, you made me believe so.
HAM.   You should not have believ'd me; for virtue cannot
so inoculate our old stock but we shall relish of it. I loved
you not.
OPH.   I was the more deceived.
HAM.   Get thee to a nunnery! Why wouldst thou be a
breeder of sinners? I am myself indifferent honest, but yet
I could accuse me of such things that it were better my mother
had not borne me. I am very proud, revengeful, ambitious;
with more offences at my beck than I have thoughts to put
them in, imagination to give them shape, or time to act them
in. What should such fellows as I do, crawling between earth
and heaven? We are arrant knaves all; believe none of us. Go
thy ways to a nunnery. Where's your father?
OPH.   At home, my lord.
HAM.   Let the doors be shut upon him, that he may play
the fool nowhere but in's own house. Farewell.
OPH.   O, help him, you sweet heavens!
HAM.   If thou dost marry, I'll give thee this plague for thy
dowry: be thou as chaste as ice, as pure as snow, thou shalt
not escape calumny. Get thee to a nunnery. Go, farewell. Or
if thou wilt needs marry, marry a fool; for wise men know
well enough what monsters you make of them. To a nunnery,
go; and quickly too. Farewell.
OPH.   O heavenly powers, restore him!
HAM.   I have heard of your paintings too, well enough.
God hath given you one face, and you make yourselves
another. You jig, you amble, and you lisp; you nickname
God's creatures and make your wantonness your ignorance.
Go to, I'll no more on't! it hath made me mad. I say, we will
have no more marriages. Those that are married already—

all but one—shall live; the rest shall keep as they are. To a
nunnery, go.

(*Exit.*)

OPH.   O, what a noble mind is here o'er-thrown!
The courtier's, scholar's, soldier's, eye, tongue, sword,
Th' expectancy and rose of the fair state,
The glass of fashion and the mould of form,
Th' observ'd of all observers—quite, quite down!
And I, of ladies most deject and wretched,
That suck'd the honey of his music vows,
Now see that noble and most sovereign reason,
Like sweet bells jangled, out of tune and harsh;
That unmatch'd form and feature of blown youth
Blasted with ecstasy. O, woe is me
T' have seen what I have seen, see what I see!

(*Enter* KING *and* POLONIUS.)

KING.   Love? his affections do not that way tend;
Nor what he spake, though it lack'd form a little,
Was not like madness. There's something in his soul
O'er which his melancholy sits on brood;
And I do doubt the hatch and the disclose
Will be some danger; which for to prevent,
I have in quick determination
Thus set it down: he shall with speed to England
For the demand of our neglected tribute.
Haply the seas, and countries different,
With variable objects, shall expel
This something-settled matter in his heart,
Whereupon his brains still beating puts him thus
From fashion of himself. What think you on't?
POL.   It shall do well. But yet do I believe
The origin and commencement of his grief
Sprung from neglected love.—How now, Ophelia?
You need not tell us what Lord Hamlet said.
We heard it all.—My lord, do as you please;
But if you hold it fit, after the play
Let his queen mother all alone entreat him
To show his grief. Let her be round with him;
And I'll be plac'd, so please you, in the ear
Of all their conference. If she find him not,
To England send him; or confine him where
Your wisdom best shall think.
KING.                                   It shall be so.
Madness in great ones must not unwatch'd go.

(*Exeunt.*)

# CHRISTOPHER MARLOWE
# from *Doctor Faustus*
## Scene I

Before Shakespeare (see *Hamlet*) came on the scene, London was being dazzled by Christopher
Marlowe (1564–1593), one of history's most brilliant and controversial authors. London watched,
in 1587, the premières of his first plays, Parts One and Two of *Tamburlaine the Great*, based on
the life of the Muslim conqueror Timur (about 1336–1405); they were acclaimed as the greatest
dramas of the day. During a meteoric career, he wrote five other plays, including *The Tragical
History of Doctor Faustus*, (about 1588), his masterpiece. In private life, he was dissolute, arrested
for fighting (twice) and for blasphemy. He was killed in a brawl over a bar bill.

Scholars have probed Marlowe's past, and it is clear that he lived in a world of lies and
secrets. While studying at Cambridge before coming to London, he seems to have been a spy,
hired by the government to sniff out secret Catholics. In London, reversing allegiances, he fell
in with a group of freethinkers, including the dramatist Thomas Kyd (ca. 1557–1595). It was Kyd
who, jailed and under torture, accused Marlowe of blasphemy. A government spy also linked
Marlowe, after his death, with atheism and homosexuality.

These sensational details color interpretations of Marlowe and his works. One school of
thought claims Marlowe as a rebel, either against religion (as an atheist) or gender roles (as a
homosexual), or both; these critics say he expressed his marginal status in manic depressive,
humorless works that oscillated between heady exuberance and dark despair. Another school,
ignoring biography altogether, either on principle or on the basis that the charges remain
unproved, judges his plays as reflections of a scholarly, Christian man and a moralist; these
critics cite him as a wielder of irony and a detached observer. Rather than resolve the debate,
the student is advised to read Marlowe with an open mind.

*Doctor Faustus*, based on a sixteenth-century German legend, has the theme of the
unbridled quest for knowledge, expressed through the scholar and magician, Doctor Faustus of

Wittenberg. Faustus, in despair over his limited learning, calls up Mephostopilis, servant to Lucifer, who offers him a contract: twenty-four years of unlimited power and pleasure in exchange for Faustus' soul. Faustus agrees. Along the way, he tricks the pope, overawes the Emperor, and woos Helen of Troy. When the contract is due, Faustus, begging for mercy, disappears at the stroke of midnight in a fury of clouds. As to the play's meaning, one school calls it a Christian morality fable, the other labels it a hymn to human ambition. The Faust legend was later renewed by Goethe (see *Faust*) who turned it into a powerful metaphor for the West's passion for destructive knowledge.

### Reading the Selection

This selection contains Act I, Scene I, of *Doctor Faustus*. In a prelude, the Chorus has called Faustus a man "swollen with cunning . . . and self-deceit." This is precisely the Faust of this soliloquy: "All things that move between the quiet poles [s]hall be at my command." Faustus' restless mind is revealed as, thumbing his books, he moves from Aristotle (philosophy), to Galen (medicine), to Justinian (law), to the Bible (Jerome's Vulgate); he then stops on occult books: "[T]hese are those that Faustus most desires."

The language is blank verse, a more flexible poetry than the "jiggling vein" (Marlowe's words) of rhymed couplets then being used by dramatists. The dignity and beauty of Marlowe's verses inspired other dramatists, most notably Shakespeare, to follow his lead.

———

(*Enter Faustus in his Study.*)
FAUSTUS.  Settle thy studies, Faustus, and begin
To sound the depth of that thou wilt profess.
Having commenced, be a divine in show,
Yet level at the end of every art
And live and die in Aristotle's works:
Sweet Analytics, 'tis thou hast ravished me! [*Reads.*]
*Bene disserere est finis logicis—*
Is to dispute well logic's chiefest end?
Affords this art no greater miracle?
Then read no more; thou hast attained the end.
A greater subject fitteth Faustus' wit:
Bid [being and not being] farewell, Galen come,
Seeing *ubi desinit philosophus, ibi incipit medicus;*[1]
Be a physician, Faustus, heap up gold
And be eternized for some wondrous cure. [*Reads.*]
*Summum bonum medicinae sanitas—*
The end of physic is our bodies' health:
Why, Faustus, hast thou not attained that end?
Is not thy common talk sound aphorisms?
Are not thy bills hung up as monuments
Whereby whole cities have escaped the plague
And thousand desperate maladies been eased?
Yet art thou still but Faustus, and a man.
Couldst thou make men to live eternally
Or, being dead, raise them to life again,
Then this profession were to be esteemed.
Physic, farewell. Where is Justinian? [*Reads.*]
*Si una eademque res legatur duobus,*[2]
*Alter rem, alter valorem rei, etc.—*
A pretty case of paltry legacies!

*Exhaereditare filium non potest pater nisi—*[3]
Such is the subject of the Institute
And universal body of the law.
His study fits a mercenary drudge
Who aims at nothing but external trash,
Too servile and illiberal for me.
When all is done, divinity is best.
Jerome's Bible, Faustus, view it well: [*Reads.*]
*Stipendium peccati mors est*—Ha! *Stipendium, etc.*
The reward of sin is death. That's hard.
*Si pecasse negamus, fallimur, et nulla est in nobis veritas—*
If we say that we have no sin
We deceive ourselves, and there's no truth in us.
Why then belike
We must sin and so consequently die,
Ay, we must die an everlasting death.
What doctrine call you this, *Che sera, sera:*
What will be, shall be? Divinity, adieu!
These metaphysics of magicians
And necromantic books are heavenly:
Lines, circles, signs, letters and characters—
Ay, these are those that Faustus most desires.
O what a world of profit and delight,
Of power, of honor, of omnipotence,
Is promised to the studious artisan!
All things that move between the quiet poles
Shall be at my command. Emperors and kings
Are but obeyed in their several provinces,
Nor can they raise the wind or rend the clouds;
But his dominion that exceeds in this
Stretcheth as far as doth the mind of man.
A sound magician is a mighty god:
Here, Faustus, try thy brains to gain a deity!

[1]"where the philosopher stops the physician begins"
[2]"If one and the same thing is bequeathed to two persons, one shall have the thing itself, the other its equivalent in value, etc."

[3]"A father cannot disinherit his son unless—"

Chapter

# 14

# The Baroque Age:
## Glamour and Grandiosity, 1600–1715

## JOHN DONNE

## Poems

John Donne led the Metaphysical Poets who flourished in England during the seventeenth century. Indebted to the anti-Classicism of late sixteenth-century Mannerism, these poets used Classical forms only to twist them into new patterns filled with paradox, metaphor, and varied "conceits," or literary devices of a fanciful kind meant to surprise by wit and ingenuity. A favorite conceit compared the macrocosm (the world) with the microcosm (the individual), as in these lines by John Cleveland (1613–1658), describing a courtship:

*With Drake I girdle in the world.*
*I hoop the firmament and make*
*This my embrace the zodiac.*

The chief mark of Metaphysical Poetry was its daring blend of opposites: the sacred with the profane, happiness with misery. Not true philosophers, these poets drew on the era's current of ideas—such as the sun-centered astronomy of Galileo and the circulation of the blood theory proposed by William Harvey—to illuminate eternal human themes, like the brevity of life and the transience of love. In their passion for learned allusions, they are a bridge between the Hellenistic poets (see Theocritus's *Idylls*) and Early Modern poets (see Eliot's "The Love Song of J. Alfred Prufrock").

The life of John Donne (1572–1631) reflects the clashing opposites beloved by the Metaphysical Poets. A sexual rake in his youth, Donne later repented and settled down to become, in 1621, one of England's most visible churchmen, the Dean of St. Paul's Cathedral, London. At dates unknown to scholars, he composed a body of poetry expressive of a divided soul: love poems mixed with sacred images and religious verses tinged with sexual symbols.

39

Some of Donne's love poems were nakedly sensual in their baring of the poet's heart. Reacting against the courtly tradition, which required the poet to humble himself before the beloved (see Marie de France's *The Lay of the Dolorous Knight*), he instead portrayed love as simply an amorous game to be enjoyed. Donne's divided nature nevertheless shines through, for some of his poems show him to be a Don Juan driven by love of conquest while others reveal a contented lover freed from passion's madness.

### Reading the Selection

"The Canonization" is a poem blending sacred and profane love. Its central conceit compares Donne and his mistress, who are ruining themselves for love, to religious martyrs; that is, they are to be "canonized" or made into saints. The conceit of the "love-martyr" is sustained throughout, as in line 3, "My five gray hairs, or ruined fortune, flout," which ironically anticipates those who object that the poet is too old or financially insecure for a sexual fling.

"A Valediction: Forbidding Mourning" mixes images of mortality and immortality. In the poem's inflated conceit, the routine pain felt at saying goodbye is equated with the sadness brought about by death. In another conceit, Donne reminds his mistress that their souls are one, just as two feet move as one. "Valediction" means leave-taking, and it may be that Donne wrote this poem for his wife when he left for France in 1611 for several months of travel.

Donne's best religious poems are sonnets, the fourteen line verse form imported from Italy in the late 1500s. "Holy Sonnet 10" expresses anguish at the death of a youth of promise ("soonest our best men with thee do go"), a reference perhaps to Donne's own son. The last line offers comfort based on *First Corinthians*, 25:xxvi: "The last enemy that shall be destroyed is death."

# *The Canonization*

For God's sake hold your tongue, and let me love,
  Or chide my palsy, or my gout,
My five gray hairs, or ruined fortune, flout,
  With wealth your state, your mind with arts improve,
    Take you a course, get you a place,
    Observe His Honor, or His Grace,
Or the King's real, or his stampèd face
  Contemplate; what you will, approve,
  So you will let me love.

Alas, alas, who's injured by my love?
  What merchant's ships have my sighs drowned?
Who says my tears have overflowed his ground?
  When did my colds a forward spring remove?
    When did the heats which my veins fill
    Add one man to the plaguy bill?
Soldiers find wars, and lawyers find out still
  Litigious men, which quarrels move,
  Though she and I do love.

Call us what you will, we are made such by love;
  Call her one, me another fly,
We're tapers too, and at our own cost die,
  And we in us find the eagle and the dove.
    The phoenix riddle hath more wit
    By us: we two being one, are it.

So, to one neutral thing both sexes fit.
  We die and rise the same, and prove
  Mysterious by this love.

We can die by it, if not live by love,
  And if unfit for tombs and hearse
Our legend be, it will be fit for verse;
  And if no piece of chronicle we prove,
    We'll build in sonnets pretty rooms;
    As well a well-wrought urn becomes
The greatest ashes, as half-acre tombs,
  And by these hymns, all shall approve
  Us canonized for love:

And thus invoke us: You whom reverend love
  Made one another's hermitage;
You, to whom love was peace, that now is rage;
  Who did the whole world's soul contract, and drove
    Into the glasses of your eyes
    (So made such mirrors, and such spies,
That they did all to you epitomize)
  Countries, towns, courts: Beg from above
  A pattern of your love!

# A Valediction: Forbidding Mourning

As virtuous men pass mildly away,
  And whisper to their souls to go,
Whilst some of their sad friends do say
  The breath goes now, and some say, No;

So let us melt, and make no noise,
  No tear-floods, nor sigh-tempests move,
'Twere profanation of our joys
  To tell the laity our love.

Moving of th' earth brings harms and fears,
  Men reckon what it did and meant;
But trepidation of the spheres,
  Though greater far, is innocent.

Dull sublunary lovers' love
  (Whose soul is sense) cannot admit
Absence, because it doth remove
  Those things which elemented it.

But we, by a love so much refined
  That our selves know not what it is,
Inter-assurèd of the mind,
  Care less, eyes, lips, and hands to miss.

Our two souls therefore, which are one,
  Though I must go, endure not yet
A breach, but an expansion,
  Like gold to airy thinness beat.

If they be two, they are two so
  As stiff twin compasses are two;
Thy soul, the fixed foot, make no show
  To move, but doth, if th' other do.

And though it in the center sit,
  Yet when the other far doth roam,
It leans and hearkens after it,
  And grows erect, as that comes home.

Such wilt thou be to me, who must
  Like th' other foot, obliquely run;
Thy firmness makes my circle just,
  And makes me end where I begun.

# Holy Sonnet 10

Death, be not proud, though some have callèd thee
Mighty and dreadful, for thou are not so;
For those whom thou think'st thou dost overthrow
Die not, poor Death, nor yet canst thou kill me.
From rest and sleep, which but thy pictures be,
Much pleasure; then from thee much more must flow,
And soonest our best men with thee do go,
Rest of their bones, and soul's delivery.
Thou art slave to fate, chance, kings, and desperate men,
And dost with poison, war, and sickness dwell,
And poppy or charms can make us sleep as well
And better than thy stroke; why swell'st thou then?
One short sleep past, we wake eternally
And death shall be no more; Death, thou shalt die.

# MOLIÈRE

# from *The Misanthrope*

## Act I

Following the fall of Rome, comic theater simply vanished for about one thousand years. During the Renaissance, theaters reappeared and again echoed with laughter. Comedy reemerged first in Italy (Machiavelli's *Mandragola,* 1520) and next in England (Shakespeare's comedies, 1590–1610) and Spain (Lope de Vega, comedies of intrigue, 1590–1635). Only after 1650 was it revived in France, by Molière, whom many claim as the greatest comic dramatist of the modern world.

Before Molière, French comedy was largely devoted to formula farces, often of Italian origin, which had improbable plots and stock characters who voiced predictable thoughts. Molière's genius enabled him to transform this low comedy into a great art. Most memorably, he sprinkled his comedy with ideas so that it rivaled tragedy—the West's premiere literary form since ancient Greece. Europe grew to love his thoughtful comedy, so that many consider it the standard for comic drama in the world today.

Molière's plays crackle with buffoonery, pratfalls, and sight gags, but, for the most part, his comedy is about character and human weakness. Taking the stock figures of farce, some as old as Menander (see *The Woman of Samos*), Molière breathed new life into them to create a gallery of modern social types. He delighted in the missteps of a social climber (*The Bourgeois Gentleman,* 1670) or the antics of a penny pincher (*The Miser,* 1668); and his "heroes" were never saved in the end. Compassionate but no social reformer, he was offended by hypocrisy, self-deception, and vanity. His moral distaste sprang not from religious scruples but from rationalism, for he thought that humans had better natures than their actions revealed.

Molière (Jean Baptiste Poquelin, 1622–1673) came to Paris with a theater troupe in 1658, after twelve years in the provinces; he soon established himself as a brilliant actor and a writer with a biting wit. In the 1660s, he wrote two plays, whose reception threatened his career: *Tartuffe* (1664), a satire on religious hypocrisy, and *Don Juan* (1665), a sympathetic portrait of the legendary lover. These controversial plays aroused a host of enemies, causing *Tartuffe* to be withdrawn (though a revised version appeared in 1669) and *Don Juan* to have only a limited run. These enemies would have driven Molière from the scene, too, had it not been for the unwavering patronage of King Louis XIV. It was in this context that Molière wrote *The Misanthrope* (1666), his masterpiece.

### Reading the Selection

*The Misanthrope* (Greek, "hater of mankind") is Molière's ironic portrait of Alceste, who deludes himself while trying to be honest with everyone else. The comic foil is Philinte, Alceste's opposite, who accepts that flattery and self-censorship are small prices to pay for social peace. The plot revolves around Alceste's doomed passion for the fickle Célimène. The play ends on a dark note as Alceste is "betrayed on all sides" by Célimène and Philinte.

This selection, Act I of the five-act play, reveals the basic natures of Alceste and Philinte. Alceste is a misanthrope: "All men are . . . detestable"; and Philinte is devoted to a golden mean: "Good sense views all extremes with detestation,/And bids us to be noble in moderation." Scholars believe that the Alceste-Philinte tension is a psychodrama reflecting an ongoing battle within Molière himself. Indeed, part of the play's popularity probably stems from the fact that there's a bit of misanthropy in the best of humankind.

### Scene I

PHILINTE, ALCESTE

PHILINTE

Now, what's got into you?

ALCESTE (*seated*)

Kindly leave me alone.

PHILINTE

Come, come, what is it? This lugubrious tone . . .

ALCESTE

Leave me, I said; you spoil my solitude.

PHILINTE

Oh, listen to me, now, and don't be rude.

ALCESTE

I choose to be rude, Sir, and to be hard of hearing.

PHILINTE

These ugly moods of yours are not endearing;
Friends though we are, I really must insist . . .

ALCESTE (*abruptly rising*)

Friends? Friends, you say? Well, cross me off your list.
I've been your friend till now, as you well know;
But after what I saw a moment ago
I tell you flatly that our ways must part.
I wish no place in a dishonest heart.

PHILINTE

Why, what have I done, Alceste? Is this quite just?

ALCESTE

My God, you ought to die of self-disgust.
I call your conduct inexcusable, Sir,
And every man of honor will concur.
I see you almost hug a man to death,
Exclaim for joy until you're out of breath,
And supplement these loving demonstrations
With endless offers, vows, and protestations;
Then when I ask you "Who was that?", I find
That you can barely bring his name to mind!
Once the man's back is turned, you cease to love him,
And speak with absolute indifference of him!
By God, I say it's base and scandalous
To falsify the heart's affections thus;
If I caught myself behaving in such a way,
I'd hang myself for shame, without delay.

PHILINTE

It hardly seems a hanging matter to me;
I hope that you will take it graciously

If I extend myself a slight reprieve,
And live a little longer, by your leave.

ALCESTE

How dare you joke about a crime so grave?

PHILINTE

What crime? How else are people to behave?

ALCESTE

I'd have them be sincere, and never part
With any word that isn't from the heart.

PHILINTE

When someone greets us with a show of pleasure,
It's but polite to give him equal measure,
Return his love the best that we know how,
And trade him offer for offer, vow for vow.

ALCESTE

No, no, this formula you'd have me follow,
However fashionable, is false and hollow,
And I despise the frenzied operations
Of all these barterers of protestations,
These lavishers of meaningless embraces,
These utterers of obliging commonplaces,
Who court and flatter everyone on earth
And praise the fool no less than the man of worth.
Should you rejoice that someone fondles you,
Offers his love and service, swears to be true,
And fills your ears with praises of your name,
When to the first damned fop he'll say the same?
No, no: no self-respecting heart would dream
Of prizing so promiscuous an esteem;
However high the praise, there's nothing worse
Than sharing honors with the universe.
Esteem is founded on comparison:
To honor all men is to honor none.
Since you embrace this indiscriminate vice,
Your friendship comes at far too cheap a price;
I spurn the easy tribute of a heart
Which will not set the worthy man apart:
I choose, Sir, to be chosen; and in fine,
The friend of mankind is no friend of mine.

PHILINTE

But in polite society, custom decrees
That we show certain outward courtesies. . . .

ALCESTE

Ah, no! we should condemn with all our force
Such false and artificial intercourse.
Let men behave like men; let them display
Their inmost hearts in everything they say;
Let the heart speak, and let our sentiments
Not mask themselves in silly compliments.

PHILINTE

In certain cases it would be uncouth
And most absurd to speak the naked truth;
With all respect for your exalted notions,
It's often best to veil one's true emotions.
Wouldn't the social fabric come undone
If we were wholly frank with everyone?
Suppose you met with someone you couldn't bear;
Would you inform him of it then and there?

ALCESTE

Yes.

PHILINTE

  Then you'd tell old Emilie it's pathetic
The way she daubs her features with cosmetic
And plays the gay coquette at sixty-four?

ALCESTE

I would.

PHILINTE

   And you'd call Dorilas a bore,
And tell him every ear at court is lame
From hearing him brag about his noble name?

ALCESTE

Precisely.

PHILINTE

  Ah, you're joking.

ALCESTE

      *Au contraire:*
In this regard there's none I'd choose to spare.
All are corrupt; there's nothing to be seen
In court or town but aggravates my spleen.
I fall into deep gloom and melancholy
When I survey the scene of human folly,
Finding on every hand base flattery,
Injustice, fraud, self-interest, treachery. . . .
Ah, it's too much; mankind has grown so base,
I mean to break with the whole human race.

PHILINTE

This philosophic rage is a bit extreme;
You've no idea how comical you seem;
Indeed, we're like those brothers in the play
Called *School for Husbands,* one of whom was
prey . . .

ALCESTE

Enough, now! None of your stupid similes.

PHILINTE

Then let's have no more tirades, if you please.
The world won't change, whatever you say or do;

And since plain speaking means so much to you,
I'll tell you plainly that by being frank
You've earned the reputation of a crank,
And that you're thought ridiculous when you rage
And rant against the manners of the age.

ALCESTE

So much the better; just what I wish to hear.
No news could be more grateful to my ear.
All men are so detestable in my eyes,
I should be sorry if they thought me wise.

PHILINTE

Your hatred's very sweeping, is it not?

ALCESTE

Quite right: I hate the whole degraded lot.

PHILINTE

Must all poor human creatures be embraced,
Without distinction, by your vast distaste?
Even in these bad times, there are surely a few . . .

ALCESTE

No, I include all men in one dim view:
Some men I hate for being rogues; the others
I hate because they treat the rogues like brothers,
And, lacking a virtuous scorn for what is vile,
Receive the villain with a complaisant smile.
Notice how tolerant people choose to be
Toward that bold rascal who's at law with me.
His social polish can't conceal his nature;
One sees at once that he's a treacherous creature;
No one could possible be taken in
By those soft speeches and that sugary grin.
The whole world knows the shady means by which
The low-brow's grown so powerful and rich,
And risen to a rank so bright and high
That virtue can but blush, and merit sigh.
Whenever his name comes up in conversation,
None will defend his wretched reputation;
Call him knave, liar, scoundrel, and all the rest,
Each head will nod, and no one will protest.
And yet his smirk is seen in every house,
He's greeted everywhere with smiles and bows,
And when there's any honor that can be got
By pulling strings, he'll get it, like as not.
My God! It chills my heart to see the ways
Men come to terms with evil nowadays;
Sometimes, I swear, I'm moved to flee and find
Some desert land unfouled by humankind.

PHILINTE

Come, let's forget the follies of the times
And pardon mankind for its petty crimes;
Let's have an end of rantings and of railings,
And show some leniency toward human failings.
This world requires a pliant rectitude;

Too stern a virtue makes one stiff and rude;
Good sense views all extremes with detestation,
And bids us to be noble in moderation.
The rigid virtues of the ancient days
Are not for us; they jar with all our ways
And ask of us too lofty a perfection.
Wise men accept their times without objection,
And there's no greater folly, if you ask me,
Than trying to reform society.
Like you, I see each day a hundred and one
Unhandsome deeds that might be better done,
But still, for all the faults that meet my view,
I'm never known to storm and rave like you.
I take men as they are, or let them be,
And teach my soul to bear their frailty;
And whether in court or town, whatever the scene,
My phlegm's as philosophic as your spleen.

ALCESTE

This phlegm which you so eloquently commend,
Does nothing ever rile it up, my friend?
Suppose some man you trust should treacherously
Conspire to rob you of your property,
And do his best to wreck your reputation?
Wouldn't you feel a certain indignation?

PHILINTE

Why, no. These faults of which you so complain
Are part of human nature, I maintain,
And it's no more a matter for disgust
That men are knavish, selfish and unjust,
Than that the vulture dines upon the dead,
And wolves are furious, and apes ill-bred.

ALCESTE

Shall I see myself betrayed, robbed, torn to bits,
And not . . . Oh, let's be still and rest our wits.
Enough of reasoning, now. I've had my fill.

PHILINTE

Indeed, you would do well, Sir, to be still.
Rage less at your opponent, and give some thought
To how you'll win this lawsuit that he's brought.

ALCESTE

I assure you I'll do nothing of the sort.

PHILINTE

Then who will plead your case before the court?

ALCESTE

Reason and right and justice will plead for me.

PHILINTE

Oh, Lord. What judges do you plan to see?

ALCESTE

Why, none. The justice of my cause is clear.

PHILINTE

Of course, man; but there's politics to fear. . . .

ALCESTE

No, I refuse to lift a hand. That's flat.
I'm either right, or wrong.

PHILINTE

                    Don't count on that.

ALCESTE

No, I'll do nothing.

PHILINTE

              Your enemy's influence
Is great, you know . . .

ALCESTE

                 That makes no difference.

PHILINTE

It will; you'll see.

ALCESTE

              Must honor bow to guile?
If so, I shall be proud to lose the trial.

PHILINTE

Oh, really . . .

ALCESTE

            I'll discover by this case
Whether or not men are sufficiently base
And impudent and villainous and perverse
To do me wrong before the universe.

PHILINTE

What a man!

ALCESTE

         Oh, I could wish, whatever the cost,
Just for the beauty of it, that my trial were lost.

PHILINTE

If people heard you talking so, Alceste,
They'd split their sides. You name would be a jest.

ALCESTE

So much the worse for jesters.

PHILINTE

               May I enquire
Whether this rectitude you so admire,
And these hard virtues you're enamored of
Are qualities of the lady whom you love?
It much surprises me that you, who seem

To view mankind with furious disesteem,
Have yet found something to enchant your eyes
Amidst a species which you so despise.
And what is more amazing, I'm afraid,
Is the most curious choice your heart has made.
The honest Eliante is fond of you,
Arsinoé, the prude, admires you too;
And yet your spirit's been perversely led
To choose the flighty Célimène instead,
Whose brittle malice and coquettish ways
So typify the manners of our days.
How is it that the traits you most abhor
Are bearable in this lady you adore?
Are you so blind with love that you can't find them?
Or do you contrive, in her case, not to mind them?

ALCESTE

My love for that young widow's not the kind
That can't perceive defects; no, I'm not blind.
I see her faults, despite my ardent love,
And all I see I fervently reprove.
And yet I'm weak; for all her falsity,
That woman knows the art of pleasing me,
And though I never cease complaining of her,
I swear I cannot manage not to love her.
Her charm outweighs her faults; I can but aim
To cleanse her spirit in my love's pure flame.

PHILINTE

That's no small task; I wish you all success.
You think then that she loves you?

ALCESTE

                              Heavens, yes!
I wouldn't love her did she not love me.

PHILINTE

Well, if her taste for you is plain to see,
Why do these rivals cause you such despair?

ALCESTE

True love, Sir, is possessive, and cannot bear
To share with all the world. I'm here today
To tell her she must send that mob away.

PHILINTE

If I were you, and had your choice to make,
Eliante, her cousin, would be the one I'd take;
That honest heart, which cares for you alone,
Would harmonize far better with your own.

ALCESTE

True, true: each day my reason tells me so;
But reason doesn't rule in love, you know.

PHILINTE

I fear some bitter sorrow is in store;
This love . . .

## Scene II

ORONTE, ALCESTE, PHILINTE

ORONTE (*to Alceste*)

                    The servants told me at the door
That Eliante and Célimène were out,
But when I heard, dear Sir, that you were about,
I came to say, without exaggeration,
That I hold you in the vastest admiration,
And that it's always been my dearest desire
To be the friend of one I so admire.
I hope to see my love of merit requited,
And you and me in friendship's bond united.
I'm sure you won't refuse—if I may be frank—
A friend of my devotedness—and rank.

(*During this speech of Oronte's, Alceste is abstracted, and seems unaware that he is being spoken to. He only breaks off his reverie when Oronte says:*)

It was for you, if you please, that my words were intended.

ALCESTE

For me, Sir?

ORONTE

                    Yes, for you. You're not offended?

ALCESTE

By no means. But this much surprises me. . . .
The honor comes most unexpectedly. . . .

ORONTE

My high regard should not astonish you;
The whole world feels the same. It is your due.

ALCESTE

Sir . . .

ORONTE

          Why, in all the State there isn't one
Can match your merits; they shine, Sir, like the sun.

ALCESTE

Sir . . .

ORONTE

          You are higher in my estimation
Than all that's most illustrious in the nation.

ALCESTE

Sir . . .

ORONTE

          If I lie, may heaven strike me dead!
To show you that I mean what I have said,
Permit me, Sir, to embrace you most sincerely,
And swear that I will prize our friendship dearly.

Give me your hand. And now, Sir, if you choose,
We'll make our vows.

ALCESTE

                    Sir . . .

ORONTE

                         What! You refuse?

ALCESTE

Sir, it's a very great honor you extend:
But friendship is a sacred thing, my friend;
It would be profanation to bestow
The name of friend on one you hardly know.
All parts are better played when well-rehearsed;
Let's put off friendship, and get acquainted first.
We may discover it would be unwise
To try to make our natures harmonize.

ORONTE

By heaven! You're sagacious to the core;
This speech has made me admire you even more.
Let time, then, bring us closer day by day;
Meanwhile, I shall be yours in every way.
If, for example, there should be anything
You wish at court, I'll mention it to the King.
I have his ear, of course; it's quite well known
That I am much in favor with the throne.
In short, I am your servant. And now, dear friend,
Since you have such fine judgment, I intend
To please you, if I can, with a small sonnet
I wrote not long ago. Please comment on it,
And tell me whether I ought to publish it.

ALCESTE

You must excuse me, Sir; I'm hardly fit
To judge such matters.

ORONTE

                    Why not?

ALCESTE

                         I am, I fear,
Inclined to be unfashionably sincere.

ORONTE

Just what I ask; I'd take no satisfaction
In anything but your sincere reaction.
I beg you not to dream of being kind.

ALCESTE

Since you desire it, Sir, I'll speak my mind.

ORONTE

*Sonnet.* It's a sonnet. . . . *Hope* . . . The poem's addressed
To a lady who wakened hopes within my breast.
*Hope* . . . this is not the pompous sort of thing,
Just modest little verses, with a tender ring.

ALCESTE

Well, we shall see.

ORONTE

                    *Hope* . . . I'm anxious to hear
Whether the style seems properly smooth and clear,
And whether the choice of words is good or bad.

ALCESTE

We'll see, we'll see.

ORONTE

                    Perhaps I ought to add
That it took me only a quarter-hour to write it.

ALCESTE

The time's irrelevant, Sir: kindly recite it.

ORONTE, (*reading*)

    *Hope comforts us awhile, t'is true,*
    *Lulling our cares with careless laughter,*
    *And yet such joy is full of rue,*
    *My Phyllis, if nothing follows after.*

PHILINTE

I'm charmed by this already; the style's delightful.

ALCESTE, (*sotto voce, to Philinte*)

How can you say that? Why, the thing is frightful.

ORONTE

    *Your fair face smiled on me awhile,*
    *But was it kindness so to enchant me?*
    *'Twould have been fairer not to smile,*
    *If hope was all you meant to grant me.*

PHILINTE

What a clever thought! How handsomely you phrase it!

ALCESTE (*sotto voce, to Philinte*)

You know the thing is trash. How dare you praise it?

ORONTE

    *If it's to be my passion's fate*
    *Thus everlasting to wait,*
    *Then death will come to set me free:*
    *For death is fairer than the fair;*
    *Phyllis, to hope is to despair*
    *When one must hope eternally.*

PHILINTE

The close is exquisite—full of feeling and grace.

ALCESTE (*sotto voce, aside*)

Oh, blast the close; you'd better close your face
Before you send your lying soul to hell.

PHILINTE

I can't remember a poem I've liked so well.

ALCESTE (*sotto voce, aside*)

Good Lord!

ORONTE (*to Philinte*)

        I fear you're flattering me a bit.

PHILINTE

Oh, no!

ALCESTE (*sotto voce, aside*)

      What else d'you call it, you hypocrite?

ORONTE (*to Alceste*)

But you, Sir, keep your promise now: don't shrink
From telling me sincerely what you think.

ALCESTE

Sir, these are delicate matters; we all desire
To be told that we've the true poetic fire.
But once, to one whose name I shall not mention,
I said, regarding some verse of his invention,
That gentlemen should rigorously control
That itch to write which often afflicts the soul;
That one should curb the heady inclination
To publicize one's little avocation;
And that in showing off one's works of art
One often plays a very clownish part.

ORONTE

Are you suggesting in a devious way
That I ought not . . .

ALCESTE

           Oh, that I do not say.
Further, I told him that no fault is worse
Than that of writing frigid, lifeless verse,
And that the merest whisper of such a shame
Suffices to destroy a man's good name.

ORONTE

D'you mean to say my sonnet's dull and trite?

ALCESTE

I don't say that. But I went on to cite
Numerous cases of once-respected men
Who came to grief by taking up the pen.

ORONTE

And am I like them? Do I write so poorly?

ALCESTE

I don't say that. But I told this person, "Surely
You're under no necessity to compose;
Why you should wish to publish, heaven knows.
There's no excuse for printing tedious rot
Unless one writes for bread, as you do not.
Resist temptation, then, I beg of you;

Conceal your pastimes from the public view;
And don't give up, on any provocation,
Your present high and courtly reputation,
To purchase at a greedy printer's shop
The name of silly author and scribbling fop."
These were the points I tried to make him see.

ORONTE

I sense that they are also aimed at me;
But now—about my sonnet—I'd like to be told . . .

ALCESTE

Frankly, that sonnet should be pigeonholed.
You've chosen the worst models to imitate.
The style's unnatural. Let me illustrate:

    For example, *Your fair face smiled on me awhile,*
    Followed by, *'Twould have been fairer not to smile!*
    Or this: *such joy is full of rue;*
    Or this: *For death is fairer than the fair;*
    Or, *Phyllis, to hope is to despair*
        *When one must hope eternally!*

This artificial style, that's all the fashion,
Has neither taste, nor honesty, nor passion;
It's nothing but a sort of wordy play,
And nature never spoke in such a way.
What, in this shallow age, is not debased?
Our fathers, though less refined, had better taste;
I'd barter all that men admire today
For one old love-song I shall try to say:

    *If the King had given me for my own*
    *Paris, his citadel,*
    *And I for that must leave alone*
    *Her whom I love so well,*
    *I'd say then to the Crown,*
    *Take back your glittering town;*
    *My darling is more fair, I swear,*
    *My darling is more fair.*

The rhyme's not rich, the style is rough and old,
But don't you see that it's the purest gold
Beside the tinsel nonsense now preferred,
And that there's passion in its every word?

    *If the King had given me for my own*
    *Paris, his citadel,*
    *And I for that must leave alone*
    *Her whom I love so well,*
    *I'd say then to the Crown,*
    *Take back your glittering town;*
    *My darling is more fair, I swear,*
    *My darling is more fair.*

There speaks a loving heart. (*To Philinte*) You're laughing, eh?
Laugh on, my precious wit. Whatever you say,
I hold that song's worth all the bibelots
That people hail today with ah's and oh's.

ORONTE

And I maintain my sonnet's very good.

ALCESTE

It's not at all surprising that you should.
You have your reasons; permit me to have mine
For thinking that you cannot write a line.

ORONTE

Others have praised my sonnet to the skies.

ALCESTE

I lack their art of telling pleasant lies.

ORONTE

You seem to think you've got no end of wit.

ALCESTE

To praise your verse, I'd need still more of it.

ORONTE

I'm not in need of your approval, Sir.

ALCESTE

That's good; you couldn't have it if you were.

ORONTE

Come now, I'll lend you the subject of my sonnet;
I'd like to see you try to improve upon it.

ALCESTE

I might, by chance, write something just as shoddy;
But then I wouldn't show it to everybody.

ORONTE

You're most opinionated and conceited.

ALCESTE

Go find your flatterers, and be better treated.

ORONTE

Look here, my little fellow, pray watch your tone.

ALCESTE

My great big fellow, you'd better watch your own.

PHILINTE (*stepping between them*)

Oh, please, please, gentlemen! This will never do.

ORONTE

The fault is mine, and I leave the field to you.
I am your servant, Sir, in every way.

ALCESTE

And I, Sir, am your most abject valet.

## Scene III

PHILINTE, ALCESTE

PHILINTE

Well, as you see, sincerity in excess
Can get you into a very pretty mess;
Oronte was hungry for appreciation. . . .

ALCESTE

Don't speak to me.

PHILINTE

What?

ALCESTE

No more conversation.

PHILINTE

Really, now . . .

ALCESTE

Leave me alone.

PHILINTE

If I . . .

ALCESTE

Out of my sight!

PHILINTE

But what . . .

ALCESTE

I won't listen.

PHILINTE

But . . .

ALCESTE

Silence!

PHILINTE

Now, is it polite . . .

ALCESTE

By heaven, I've had enough. Don't follow me.

PHILINTE

Ah, you're just joking. I'll keep you company.

# JOHN MILTON

# from *Paradise Lost*

## Book 1

Milton's *Paradise Lost* reflected the craze for epic which swept Europe in the 1600s. It towers above this period's other epics, which are largely unread today. Often called the Protestant epic, it was intended by Milton, who belonged to the Calvinist faith, as a response to Dante's *Divine Comedy.* While not the greatest poem in English, as some admirers claim, since its religious theme is out of tune with the pervasive secularism of the modern world, it most certainly is the most ambitious poem in the English language.

Milton's ambition is evident in his poem's great length—more than 10,000 lines divided into twelve books, or chapters—and grand theme—original sin, or the belief that all humans, male and female, are born evil. This Christian belief has few supporters today, being replaced by the secular belief of socially-created "evil"; but, when Milton wrote, original sin was a defining feature of Western culture. Milton thus tackled one of his period's basic beliefs in an effort to "justify the ways of God to men."

Milton's three major sources are the epics of Homer (see *Iliad, Odyssey*) and Vergil (see *Aeneid*) and the Book of Genesis (see *The New English Bible*). From Homer and Vergil come the full epic apparatus of invocations, digressions, similes, long speeches, history, folklore, perilous journeys, battles, and scenes in the underworld. The range is colossal, the sweep majestic, and the tone lofty. From Genesis comes the plot: the creation of Adam and Eve, their first sin, and expulsion from the Garden of Eden, or paradise. Milton's artistic purpose was to transform the Genesis story, along with related theological problems, into epic poetry.

*Paradise Lost* reflects the era of its birth, Restoration England (1661–1688), when the Stuarts once again ruled and the Puritan experiment was over. Milton now had leisure to write, since from 1639 to 1659, he lived for politics; first he was a propagandist for the Puritan cause and then an official in the Protectorate, Oliver Cromwell's dictatorship. Milton, though blind, composed this epic between 1660 and 1665, publishing it in 1665. The descriptions of Satan, "his horrid crew," and the construction of Hell may be interpreted as political allegory—Satan has been associated with both Charles I and Cromwell. The story, the loss of paradise, may express Milton's despair over the failure of the Protectorate, which had been regarded by its leaders as biblical doctrine in political and social practice, a kind of substitute for Eden before the Fall.

### Reading the Selection

This selection contains about one-fourth of Book I of *Paradise Lost.* "The Argument" gives a general overview and a summary of Book I. The poem is in blank verse, the verse form used by Marlowe (see *Doctor Faustus*) and Shakespeare (see *Hamlet*), but not heretofore adopted by poets. Milton's example blazed a path for later poets, such as Wordsworth (see "Tintern Abbey").

The opening lines announce Milton's theme: "man's first disobedience, and [its] fruit . . . death . . . and all our woe." As Homer invoked Calliope, the muse of epic poetry, so Milton prays that the Holy Ghost, the third person of the Christian Trinity, will act as a "Heavenly Muse." This passage also introduces Milton's glamorous anti-hero, Satan, the Prince of Darkness and fallen angel, who takes pleasure in his evil work: "[E]ver to do ill our sole delight." Pious readers of Milton have often complained that Satan steals the show with his fascinating villainy, as shown here in verbal exchanges with his second-in-command, Beelzebub.

## The Argument

This first book proposes, first in brief, the whole subject, man's disobedience, and the loss thereupon of Paradise, wherein he was placed: then touches the prime cause of his fall, the serpent, or rather Satan in the serpent; who, revolting from God, and drawing to his side many legions of angels, was, by the command of God, driven out of Heaven with all his crew, into the great deep. Which action passed over, the poem hastes into the midst of things; presenting Satan, with his angels, now fallen into Hell—described here not in the center (for heaven and earth may be supposed as yet not made, certainly not yet accursed), but in a place of utter darkness, fitliest called Chaos. Here Satan with his angels lying on the burning lake, thunderstruck and astonished, after a certain space recovers, as from confusion; calls up him who, next in order and dignity, lay by him; they confer of their miserable fall. Satan awakens all his legions, who lay till then in the same manner confounded. They rise: their numbers; array of battle; their chief leaders named, according to the idols known afterwards in Canaan and the countries adjoining. To these Satan directs his speech; comforts them with hope yet of regaining Heaven; but tells them, lastly, of a new world and new kind of creature to be created, according to an ancient prophecy or report in Heaven; for that angels were long before this visible creation was the opinion of many ancient fathers. To find out the truth of this prophecy, and what to determine thereon, he refers to a full council. What his associates thence attempt. Pandemonium, the palace of Satan, rises, suddenly built out of the deep: the infernal peers there sit in council.


Of man's first disobedience, and the fruit
Of that forbidden tree whose mortal taste
Brought death into the world, and all our woe,
With loss of Eden, till one greater Man
Restore us, and regain the blissful seat,
Sing, Heavenly Muse, that on the secret top
Of Oreb, or of Sinai, didst inspire
That shepherd who first taught the chosen seed
In the beginning how the heavens and earth
Rose out of Chaos: or, if Sion hill
Delight thee more, and Siloa's brook that flowed
Fast by the oracle of God, I thence
Invoke thy aid to my adventurous song,
That with no middle flight intends to soar
Above th' Aonian mount, while it pursues
Things unattempted yet in prose or rhyme.
And chiefly thou, O Spirit, that dost prefer
Before all temples th' upright heart and pure,
Instruct me, for thou know'st; thou from the first
Wast present, and, with mighty wings outspread,
Dovelike sat'st brooding on the vast abyss,
And mad'st it pregnant: what in me is dark
Illumine; what is low, raise and support;
That to the height of this great argument
I may assert Eternal Providence,
And justify the ways of God to men.
    Say first (for Heaven hides nothing from thy view,
Nor the deep tract of Hell), say first what cause
Moved our grandparents, in that happy state,
Favored of Heaven so highly, to fall off
From their Creator, and transgress his will
For one restraint, lords of the world besides?
Who first seduced them to that foul revolt?
    Th' infernal serpent; he it was, whose guile,
Stirred up with envy and revenge, deceived
The mother of mankind, what time his pride
Had cast him out from Heaven, with all his host
Of rebel angels, by whose aid aspiring
To set himself in glory above his peers,
He trusted to have equaled the Most High,
If he opposed; and with ambitious aim
Against the throne and monarchy of God
Raised impious war in Heaven and battle proud,
With vain attempt. Him the Almighty Power
Hurled headlong flaming from th' ethereal sky
With hideous ruin and combustion down
To bottomless perdition, there to dwell
In adamantine chains and penal fire,
Who durst defy th' Omnipotent to arms.
    Nine times the space that measures day and night
To mortal men, he with his horrid crew
Lay vanquished, rolling in the fiery gulf
Confounded though immortal. But his doom
Reserved him to more wrath; for now the thought
Both of lost happiness and lasting pain
Torments him; round he throws his baleful eyes,
That witnessed huge affliction and dismay,
Mixed with obdurate pride and steadfast hate.
At once, as far as angels ken, he views
The dismal situation waste and wild:
A dungeon horrible, on all sides round
As one great furnace flamed; yet from those flames
No light, but rather darkness visible
Served only to discover sights of woe,
Regions of sorrow, doleful shades, where peace
And rest can never dwell, hope never comes
That comes to all, but torture without end
Still urges, and a fiery deluge, fed
With ever-burning sulphur unconsumed:
Such place Eternal Justice had prepared
For those rebellious; here their prison ordained
In utter darkness and their portion set
As far removed from God and light of Heaven
As from the center thrice to th' utmost pole.
O how unlike the place from whence they fell!
There the companions of his fall, o'erwhelmed
With floods and whirlwinds of tempestuous fire,
He soon discerns; and, weltering by his side,
One next himself in power, and next in crime,
Long after known in Palestine, and named
Beëlzebub. To whom th' arch-enemy,

And thence in Heaven called Satan, with bold words
Breaking the horrid silence thus began:
  "If thou beëst he—but O how fallen! how changed
From him who in the happy realms of light
Clothed with transcendent brightness didst outshine
Myriads, though bright! if he whom mutual league,
United thoughts and counsels, equal hope
And hazard in the glorious enterprise,
Joined with me once, now misery hath joined
In equal ruin; into what pit thou seest
From what height fallen, so much the stronger proved
He with his thunder: and till then who knew
The force of those dire arms? Yet not for those,
Nor what the potent Victor in his rage
Can else inflict, do I repent or change,
Though changed in outward luster, that fixed mind
And high disdain, from sense of injured merit,
That with the Mightiest raised me to contend,
And to the fierce contention brought along
Innumerable force of spirits armed,
That durst dislike his reign, and me preferring,
His utmost power with adverse power opposed
In dubious battle on the plains of Heaven,
And shook his throne. What though the field be lost?
All is not lost: the unconquerable will,
And study of revenge, immortal hate,
And courage never to submit or yield:
And what is else not to be overcome?
That glory never shall his wrath or might
Extort from me. To bow and sue for grace
With suppliant knee, and deify his power
Who from the terror of this arm so late
Doubted his empire—that were low indeed;
That were an ignominy and shame beneath
This downfall; since, by fate, the strength of gods
And this empyreal substance cannot fail;
Since, through experience of this great event,
In arms not worse, in foresight much advanced,
We may with more successful hope resolve
To wage by force or guile eternal war,
Irreconcilable to our grand Foe,
Who now triùmphs, and in th' excess of joy
Sole reigning holds the tyranny of Heaven."
  So spake th' apostate angel, though in pain,
Vaunting aloud, but racked with deep despair;
And him thus answered soon his bold compeer:
  "O prince, O chief of many thronèd powers,
That led th' embattled seraphim to war
Under thy conduct, and in dreadful deeds
Fearless, endangered Heaven's perpetual King,
And put to proof his high supremacy,
Whether upheld by strength, or chance, or fate!
Too well I see and rue the dire event
That with sad overthrow and foul defeat
Hath lost us Heaven, and all this mighty host

In horrible destruction laid thus low,
As far as gods and heavenly essences
Can perish: for the mind and spirit remains
Invincible, and vigor soon returns,
Though all our glory extinct, and happy state
Here swallowed up in endless misery.
But what if he our Conqueror (whom I now
Of force believe almighty, since no less
Than such could have o'erpowered such force as ours)
Have left us this our spirit and strength entire,
Strongly to suffer and support our pains,
That we may so suffice his vengeful ire,
Or do him mightier service as his thralls
By right of war, whate'er his business be,
Here in the heart of Hell to work in fire,
Or do his errands in the gloomy deep?
What can it then avail though yet we feel
Strength undiminished, or eternal being
To undergo eternal punishment?"
  Whereto with speedy words th' arch-fiend replied:
  "Fallen cherub, to be weak is miserable,
Doing or suffering: but of this be sure,
To do aught good never will be our task,
But ever to do ill our sole delight,
As being the contrary to his high will
Whom we resist. If then his providence
Out of our evil seek to bring forth good,
Our labor must be to pervert that end,
And out of good still to find means of evil;
Which ofttimes may succeed, so as perhaps
Shall grieve him, if I fail not, and disturb
His inmost counsels from their destined aim.
But see! the angry Victor hath recalled
His ministers of vengeance and pursuit
Back to the gates of Heaven; the sulphurous hail,
Shot after us in storm, o'erblown hath laid
The fiery surge that from the precipice
Of Heaven received us falling; and the thunder,
Winged with red lightning and impetuous rage,
Perhaps hath spent his shafts, and ceases now
To bellow through the vast and boundless deep.
Let us not slip th' occasion, whether scorn
Or satiate fury yield it from our Foe.
Seest thou yon dreary plain, forlorn and wild,
The seat of desolation, void of light,
Save what the glimmering of these livid flames
Casts pale and dreadful? Thither let us tend
From off the tossing of these fiery waves;
There rest, if any rest can harbor there;
And reassembling our afflicted powers,
Consult how we may henceforth most offend
Our enemy, our own loss how repair,
How overcome this dire calamity,
What reinforcement we may gain from hope,
If not, what resolution from despair." . . .

# APHRA BEHN
## *The Willing Mistress*

———

Aphra Behn (1640–1689) was England's first professional woman of letters. She was not financially successful, though, for the literary world was still ruled by rich patrons. Ignored by would-be patrons, she was forced into debtors' prison for a time. Undaunted, she pressed on and left a distinguished literary legacy. She blamed her failure partly on being marginal in a male domain. In one play, for example, she railed against men who abused her for being a *woman* writer and she claimed instead that wit had no gender. Of Behn, Virginia Woolf (see *To the Lighthouse*) wrote in 1915: "All [English] women together ought to let flowers fall upon the tomb of Aphra Behn, for it was she who earned them the right to speak their minds."

Of obscure origins, Behn is thought to have spent two years in the then English colony of Surinam (modern Suriname) before settling in London. To some degree, this encounter with the world beyond Europe freed her of Eurocentrism, giving her a unique outlook for the time. She drew on this colonial world for *Oroonoko* (1688), a short story set in Surinam and focused on the doomed love of a black slave-prince and a slave woman. In this story she expressed, through the slave heroes, her fantasy of a golden age of social and sexual frankness—a type of primitivism similar to that of Montaigne (see "Of Cannibals"). Works like *Oroonoko* prepared the way for the next century's long romantic novels (see Fielding's *The History of Tom Jones*), often with non-European settings.

Behn also won renown as a comic dramatist. In form, her plays, almost twenty in number, belong to Restoration comedy, the comedy genre that flourished after the restoration of the monarchy (the later Stuart Dynasty) in 1661; it featured sexual and marital intrigue. Her works, such as *The Rover* (1677) and *The City Heiress* (1682), have been described as quite "as obscene and successful as" other plays of this period. One of her few serious dramas, *The Widow Ranter* (1690), about colonial rebellion, was the first English play set in the American colonies and may have reflected a visit to Virginia.

Behn also composed poetry and it, like her plays, chimed with the ruling artistic code in Restoration England. Behn wrote mainly love lyrics that catered to her audience's need to see themselves as members of an elegant and stylish society. The voice with which her poems spoke was some unnamed lady of fashion, and the situations generally involved sexual intrigue with a gentleman of fashion and often bordered on the licentious. Rather than breaking new ground, Behn's works typify this era's fashionable love lyrics.

### Reading the Selection

"The Willing Mistress" (1684), with its theme of a woman happily joining in her own seduction, is unusual only in that it was composed by a woman. Otherwise, it is typical of Restoration love verses in which male poets repeatedly portrayed women as willing partners. She sets this seduction in a kind of Classical, golden age where there is no realistic context to spoil the amorous play. This setting is indicated by the lover's name, Amyntas, a familiar name from pastoral poetry—a Classical genre that idealized rural life and that enjoyed a revival in the seventeenth century. The poem's sensual language is highly suggestive of sexual dalliance— "gently" (used twice), "yielding," "willing," "softening," and "easy." In form, the poem is an octave, a stanza of eight lines; the octave itself is a doubling of the quatrain, a four line stanza, which is the commonest stanza form in European poetry.

Amyntas led me to a grove,
  Where all the trees did shade us;
The sun itself, though it had strove,
  It could not have betrayed us.
The place secured from human eyes
  No other fear allows
But when the winds that gently rise
  Do kiss the yielding boughs.

Down there we sat upon the moss,
  And did begin to play
A thousand amorous tricks, to pass
  The heat of all the day.

A many kisses did he give
  And I returned the same,
Which made me willing to receive
  That which I dare not name.

His charming eyes no aid required
  To tell their softening tale;
On her that was already fired,
  'Twas easy to prevail.
He did but kiss and clasp me round,
  Whilst those his thoughts expressed:
And laid me gently on the ground;
  Ah who can guess the rest?

# JEAN RACINE

# from *Phaedra*

## Act II

Racine's *Phaedra* (1677) is considered by some to be the most famous tragedy in the French language. Written at the height of Racine's powers, when his plays were moving from triumph to triumph on the stage, this tragedy is thought to be his masterpiece; the role of Phaedra is the goal of all French actresses, as Hamlet is for English actors.

Racine's century was the Age of the Baroque; but, specifically in France, it was the Age of King Louis XIV, whose official court style was Classicism; he used his rich patronage, the most lavish toward writers in all history, to make this period the zenith of French literature. Racine, though a recipient of Louis XIV's patronage, did not write simply to please the king, for Classicism had been the dominant thread in French culture since being imported from Italy, in about 1500. Of all Racine's works, *Phaedra* most embodies the ideals of this style, which favored dignity, order, and good form.

The source for Racine's tragedy was the legend that the ancient Greek dramatist Euripides had told. In Euripides' story, Phaedra, wife of Theseus, King of Athens, became sexually obsessed with Hippolytus, son of Theseus from an earlier marriage; learning that he had cold feelings toward women, Phaedra hanged herself, but had her revenge by leaving a note accusing Hippolytus of attempted rape; Theseus then banished his innocent son, who was later killed while driving a chariot beside the sea. Racine altered this story, making Phaedra poison herself after hearing of Hippolytus's death. Racine also made Phaedra's love for her stepson Hippolytus incestuous, as would have been the case under seventeenth-century French law.

In retelling the tragedy of Phaedra, Racine was hemmed in by the strict rules of Classicism, which permitted no deviation in verse form (a twelve syllable line), number of acts (five), plot (simple), amount of scenery (minimal and unchanging), prohibition of certain topics (no criticism of French society), and ending (never happy). With little room to innovate or use his imagination, Racine turned his talents to depict human character and emotions. He rivaled the romantics in the emotionalism of Phaedra's love, and Hippolytus, contrary to the legend, lusts after another woman. So successful was *Phaedra* and Racine's other plays that French Classicism dominated European theater for the next century.

The plays of Jean Racine (1639–1699) reflected his tragic sense of life, probably acquired during his youth in Jansenist circles, the sect of French Catholics who shared Calvin's beliefs about predestination and original sin. Though a mainstream Catholic, Racine treated sin and destiny along Jansenist lines in his plays.

*Reading the Selection*

Act II, Scene Five, of *Phaedra* sets the scene for the unfolding of the tragedy. Here, Phaedra, first cautiously, then in an uncontrollable burst of passion, tells Hippolytus of her "insane" love for him. At this point, King Theseus is thought to be dead and thus the throne is vacant. Hippolytus is slow to recognize the meaning of her words, but then Phaedra admits, "'Twas no mistake." Having made this shameful admission, she asks him to kill her or she will take her own life. Phaedra's fate is now sealed. In later scenes, Theseus returns alive and events move inexorably to their tragic end. Hippolytus, banished because of Phaedra's lies, is dragged to his death by frightened horses; Phaedra, finally confessing her guilt, commits suicide.

---

## Scene V

PHAEDRA, HIPPOLYTUS, OENONE

PHAEDRA (*to Oenone, at stage rear*)

He's here. Blood rushes to my heart: I'm weak,
And can't recall the words I meant to speak.

OENONE

Think of your son, whose one hope rests with you.

PHAEDRA

My lord, they say you leave us. Before you do,
I've come to join your sorrows and my tears,
And tell you also of a mother's fears.
My son now lacks a father; and he will learn
Ere long that death has claimed me in my turn.
A thousand foes already seek to end
His hopes, which you, you only, can defend.
Yet I've a guilty fear that I have made
Your ears indifferent to his cries for aid.
I tremble lest you visit on my son
Your righteous wrath at what his mother's done.

HIPPOLYTUS

So base a thought I could not entertain.

PHAEDRA

Were you to hate me, I could not complain,
My lord. You've seen me bent on hurting you,
Though what was in my heart you never knew.
I sought your enmity. I would not stand
Your dwelling with me in the selfsame land.
I vilified you, and did not feel free
Till oceans separated you and me.
I went so far, indeed, as to proclaim
That none should, in my hearing, speak your name.
Yet if the crime prescribes the culprit's fate,
If I must hate you to have earned your hate,
Never did woman more deserve, my lord,
Your pity, or less deserve to be abhorred.

HIPPOLYTUS

It's common, Madam, that a mother spites
The stepson who might claim her children's rights.
I know that in a second marriage-bed
Anxiety and mistrust are often bred.

Another woman would have wished me ill
As you have, and perhaps been harsher still.

PHAEDRA

Ah, Prince! The Gods, by whom I swear it, saw
Fit to except me from that general law.
By what a different care am I beset!

HIPPOLYTUS

My lady, don't give way to anguish yet.
Your husband still may see the light of day;
Heaven may hear us, and guide his sail this way.
Neptune protects him, and that deity
Will never fail to heed my father's plea.

PHAEDRA

No one goes twice among the dead; and since
Theseus has seen those gloomy regions, Prince,
No god will bring him back, hope though you may,
Nor greedy Acheron yield up his prey.
But no! He is not dead; he breathes in you.
My husband still seems present to my view.
I see him, speak with him. . . . Ah, my lord, I feel
Crazed with a passion which I can't conceal.

HIPPOLYTUS

In your strong love, what wondrous power lies!
Theseus, though dead, appears before your eyes.
For love of him your soul is still on fire.

PHAEDRA

Yes, Prince, I burn for him with starved desire,
Though not as he was seen among the shades,
The fickle worshiper of a thousand maids,
Intent on cuckolding the King of Hell;
But constant, proud, a little shy as well,
Young, charming, irresistible, much as we
Depict our Gods, or as you look to me.
He had your eyes, your voice, your virile grace,
It was your noble blush that tinged his face
When, crossing on the waves, he came to Crete
And made the hearts of Minos' daughters beat.
Where were you then? Why no Hippolytus
Among the flower of Greece he chose for us?
Why were you yet too young to join that band
Of heroes whom he brought to Minos' land?

*You* would have slain the Cretan monster then,
Despite the endless windings of his den.
My sister would have armed you with a skein
Of thread, to lead you from that dark domain.
But no: I'd first have thought of that design,
Inspired by love; the plan would have been mine.
It's I who would have helped you solve the maze,
My Prince, and taught you all its twisting ways.
What I'd have done to save that charming head!
My love would not have trusted to a thread.
No, Phaedra would have wished to share with you
Your perils, would have wished to lead you through
The Labyrinth, and thence have side by side
Returned with you; or else, with you, have died.

HIPPOLYTUS

Gods! What are you saying, Madam? Is Theseus not
Your husband, and my sire? Have you forgot?

PHAEDRA

You think that I forgot those things? For shame,
My lord. Have I no care for my good name?

HIPPOLYTUS

Forgive me, Madam. I blush to have misread
The innocent intent of what you said.
I'm too abashed to face you; I shall take
My leave. . . .

PHAEDRA

        Ah, cruel Prince, 'twas no mistake.
You understood; my words were all too plain.
Behold then Phaedra as she is, insane
With love for you. Don't think that I'm content
To be so, that I think it innocent,
Or that by weak compliance I have fed

The baneful love that clouds my heart and head.
Poor victim that I am of Heaven's curse,
I loathe myself; you could not hate me worse.
The Gods could tell how in this breast of mine
They lit the flame that's tortured all my line,
Those cruel Gods for whom it is but play
To lead a feeble woman's heart astray.
You too could bear me out; remember, do,
How I not only shunned but banished you.
I wanted to be odious in your sight;
To balk my love, I sought to earn your spite.
But what was gained by all of that distress?
You hated me the more; I loved no less,
And what you suffered made you still more dear.
I pined, I withered, scorched by many a tear.
That what I say is true, your eyes could see
If for a moment they could look at me.
What have I said? Do you suppose I came
To tell, of my free will, this tale of shame?
No, anxious for a son I dared not fail,
I came to beg you not to hate him. Frail
Indeed the heart is that's consumed by love!
Alas, it's only you I've spoken of.
Avenge yourself, now; punish my foul desire.
Come, rid the world, like your heroic sire,
Of one more monster; do as he'd have done.
Shall Theseus' widow dare to love his son?
No, such a monster is too vile to spare.
Here is my heart. Your blade must pierce me there.
In haste to expiate its wicked lust,
My heart already leaps to meet your thrust.
Strike, then. Or if your hatred and disdain
Refuse me such a blow, so sweet a pain,
If you'll not stain your hand with my abhorred
And tainted blood, lend me at least your sword.
Give it to me! . . .

# 15

# The Baroque Age II:
## Revolutions in Scientific and Political Thought, 1600–1715

## FRANCIS BACON

### from *Essays*

#### Of Studies

Sir Francis Bacon (1561–1626), as the son of a high-ranking official under England's Queen Elizabeth I (see "The Doubt of Future Foes," etc.), seemed destined for a career as a courtier. He did indeed spend much of his life serving Elizabeth and her successor, James I, but he also found time to write extensively about the implications of the Scientific Revolution which, during the 1600s, was destroying the medieval world picture and establishing the scientific method as the basic way to understand the natural world. Inspired by the Renaissance, and in revolt against Aristotle and scholastic logic, Bacon proposed an inductive method of discovering truth; founded upon empirical observation, he proposed analysis of observed data resulting in hypotheses and verification of hypotheses through continued observation and experiment. The purpose of the Baconian method was to enable humanity to gain mastery over nature for humanity's own benefit.

Though he himself had no laboratory and made no discoveries, Bacon became the period's most persuasive champion of the "new learning." With his encouragement, science now became a movement as he gave it a sense of direction, wrote endlessly about its usefulness, and predicted that it would improve life. Both his enthusiasm for a better tomorrow built on the scientific method and his abiding faith in the capacity of humans to advance themselves inspired later generations to believe that they could make the world better. The zenith of Bacon's influence was in the eighteenth-century Enlightenment when Voltaire (see *Candide*), the age's leading thinker, called him, "the Secretary of Nature."

Bacon's scientific works included *The Advancement of Learning* and the *New Organon*, or "New Method" (1620). He also wrote a history of King Henry VII of England, legal works, and treatises on religious matters. Probably his most lasting impact was on English letters, as he made the essay genre a standard prose form. Borrowed from Montaigne (see *Essays*), the essay, in Bacon's hands, became a short composition, seldom exceeding a few hundred words, whose style was terse, moralistic, and aloof.

Despite outstanding achievements as a writer, his political career ended in scandal. Made Lord Chancellor, the highest position a commoner could then hold in the English government, under James I, Bacon quickly fell from power, charged with receiving bribes to which he confessed. He died five years later, in disgrace, his political reputation ruined.

### Reading the Selection

Much like Montaigne's, Bacon's essays embrace a miscellany of subjects, reflecting his restless intellect. Many of them appeal to the highest ideals, such as love, friendship, and truth, while others are incisive, sometimes cynical, observations on greed and riches, or on ambition and the struggle for power. As a rule, he omits his own experiences and, instead, distills what he has witnessed into political guidelines, advice, and aphorisms (pithy sayings).

"Of Studies," taken from Bacon's first group of *Essays* (1597), offers sound advice about learning, then and now. In it, he defines three goals of knowledge: studying for pleasure, for "ornament" (that is, to show off), and for useful knowledge. He recommends three paths to learning: reading, discussing, and writing. He also thinks that different subjects, such as history, mathematics, poetry, and natural philosophy (science), make humans more versatile.

---

Studies serve for delight, for ornament, and for ability. Their chief use for delight is in privateness and retiring; for ornament, is in discourse; and for ability, is in the judgment and disposition of business. For expert men can execute, and perhaps judge of particulars, one by one; but the general counsels, and the plots and marshaling of affairs, come best from those that are learned. To spend too much time in studies is sloth; to use them too much for ornament is affectation; to make judgment wholly by their rules is the humor of a scholar. They perfect nature, and are perfected by experience; for natural abilities are like natural plants, that need pruning by study; and studies themselves do give forth directions too much at large, except they be bounded in by experience. Crafty men condemn studies, simple men admire them, and wise men use them, for they teach not their own use; but that is a wisdom without them, and above them, won by observation. Read not to contradict and confute, nor to believe and take for granted, nor to find talk and discourse, but to weigh and consider. Some books are to be tasted, others to be swallowed, and some few to be chewed and digested; that is, some books are to be read only in parts; others to be read, but not curiously; and some few to be read wholly, and with diligence and attention. Some books also may be read by deputy and extracts made of them by others, but that would be only in the less important arguments and the meaner sort of books; else distilled books are like common distilled waters, flashy things. Reading maketh a full man, conference a ready man, and writing an exact man. And therefore, if a man write little, he had need have a great memory; if he confer little, he had need have a present wit; and if he read little, he had need have much cunning, to seem to know that he doth not. Histories make men wise; poets, witty; the mathematics, subtle; natural philosophy, deep; moral, grave; logic and rhetoric, able to contend. *Abeunt studia in mores.** Nay, there is no stond or impediment in the wit but may be wrought out by fit studies, like as diseases of the body may have appropriate exercises. Bowling is good for the stone and reins, shooting for the lungs and breast, gentle walking for the stomach, riding for the head, and the like. So if a man's wit be wandering, let him study the mathematics; for in demonstrations, if his wit be called away never so little, he must begin again. If his wit be not apt to distinguish or find differences, let him study the schoolmen, for they are *cumini sectores.* If he be not apt to beat over matters and to call up one thing to prove and illustrate another, let him study the laywer's cases. So every defect of the mind may have a special receipt.

---

* "Studies culminate in manners." (Ovid)

# RENÉ DESCARTES
# from *Discourse on Method*

The French thinker and mathematician René Descartes (1596–1650) is one of the intellectual founders of the modern world. He lived during the Age of Scientific Revolution, 1550–1700, when the earth-centered model of the universe was slowly giving way to the sun-centered model; medieval modes of reasoning were being replaced by mathematics and induction. He made important contributions to the new science, such as helping to establish the final form of the law of inertia and developing analytic geometry; however, it is for his rational (deductive) method that he is most remembered today.

Descartes's reasoning method first appeared in an introductory essay called *Discourse of the Method of Rightly Conducting the Reason and Seeking Truth in the Field of Science* (1637), which was attached to a treatise setting forth his discoveries in optics, meteorology, and geometry. The treatise is hardly read today, but the *Discourse on Method* (the essay's short title) has become a classic text of modern thought. Proposing a rational, deductive approach to all problems, his method had a double-edged effect: helping to end the reign of Aristotle and scholastic logic, while ensuring that deduction would play a major role in the new science. Cartesian deduction, with its mathematical emphasis, along with Baconian (see "Of Studies") induction, with its stress on experimentation, became the twin pillars of modern science. And Cartesian skepticism, as shown in the *Discourse*, became the starting point of modern philosophy.

Ironically, Descartes, the advocate of rationalism, became a philosopher because of a mystical experience. After completing his schooling, in 1612, at the Jesuit school at La Flèche, France, he spent the next nine years in travel and military service. Even though he profited from La Flèche, he was disillusioned by traditional studies with their crumbing worldview. Especially troubling was that in the sciences no new absolute criterion of truth seemed available to replace the old. During 1619, while on military duty, he had a series of dreams, which, according to his later accounts, pointed the way to certainty in the sciences, using mathematics. After 1621, he devoted the remainder of his life to study and writing, in fulfillment of this mystical mission.

## Reading the Selection

These two excerpts from Descartes's *Discourse on Method* contain the heart of the argument justifying his method. Part II lays out his four-step method of which step one is the most famous. Step one declares that he will accept as true only those ideas that register on his reason as clear, distinct, and free from internal contradiction—his standard of certainty in philosophy, which he thought would give results equivalent to those reached in science using geometry. The remaining steps of his method are: divide each problem into manageable parts; solve each part in an orderly fashion, moving from the simplest to the most complex; and, finally, check the results.

Part IV shows Descartes doubting everything as a necessary stage to clear the slate of philosophic confusion and to define those truths which can "clearly and distinctly" be affirmed without question. At the end of this process, he is left with the undeniable idea, "I think, therefore I am," meaning that he can doubt everything, except that *he himself is doubting*. From this first principle of self-awareness, Descartes deduces the existence of the physical world and, finally, God.

## Part II

• • •

Thus it is by custom and example that we are persuaded, much more than by any certain knowledge; at the same time, a majority of votes is worthless as a proof, in regard to truths that are even a little difficult of discovery; for it is much more likely that one man should have hit upon them for himself than that a whole nation should. Accordingly I could choose nobody whose opinions I thought preferable to other men's; and I was as it were forced to become by own guide.

But, like a man walking alone in the dark, I resolved to go so slowly, and use so much circumspection in all matters, as to be secured against falling, even if I made very little progress. In fact, I would not begin rejecting out of hand any of the opinions that might have previously crept into my belief without being introduced by reason, until I had first taken enough time to plan the work I was undertaking, and to look for the true method of attaining knowledge of everything that my mind could grasp.

The subjects I had studied a little when I was younger included, among the branches of philosophy, logic, and in mathematics, geometrical analysis and algebra. These three arts or sciences, it appeared, ought to make some contribution towards my design. But on examination I found that so far as logic is concerned, syllogisms and most of the other techniques serve for explaining to others what one knows; or even, like the art of Lully, for talking without judgment about matters one is ignorant of; rather than for learning anything. And although logic comprises many correct and excellent rules, there are mixed up with these so many others that are harmful or superfluous, that sorting them out is almost as difficult as extracting a Diana or Minerva from a block of rough marble. As for the analysis of the ancients, and the algebra of our time, besides their covering only a highly abstract and apparently useless range of subjects, the former is always so restricted to the consideration of figures, that it cannot exercise the understanding without greatly wearying the imagination; and in the latter, there is such a complete slavery to certain rules and symbols that there results a confused and obscure art that embarrasses the mind, instead of a science that develops it. That was why I thought I must seek for some other method, which would comprise the advantages of these three and be exempt from their defects. And as a multitude of laws often gives occasion for vices, so that a State is much better ruled when it has only a very few laws which are very strictly observed; in the same way, instead of the great number of rules that make up logic, I thought the following four would be enough, provided that I made a firm and constant resolution not to fail even once in the observance of them.

The first was never to accept anything as true if I had not evident knowledge of its being so; that is, carefully to avoid precipitancy and prejudice, and to embrace in my judgment only what presented itself to my mind so clearly and distinctly that I had no occasion to doubt it.

The second, to divide each problem I examined into as many parts as was feasible, and as was requisite for its better solution.

The third, to direct my thoughts in an orderly way; beginning with the simplest objects, those most apt to be known, and ascending little by little, in steps as it were, to the knowledge of the most complex; and establishing an order in thought even when the objects had no natural priority one to another.

And the last, to make throughout such complete enumerations and such general surveys that I might be sure of leaving nothing out.

Those long chains of perfectly simple and easy reasonings by means of which geometers are accustomed to carry out their most difficult demonstrations had led me to fancy that everything that can fall under human knowledge forms a similar sequence; and that so long as we avoid accepting as true what is not so, and always preserve the right order for deduction of one thing from another, there can be nothing too remote to be reached in the end, or too well hidden to be discovered. . . .

## Part IV

• • •

I had noticed long before, as I said just now, that in conduct one sometimes has to follow opinions that one knows to be most uncertain just as if they were indubitable; but since my present aim was to give myself up to the pursuit of truth alone, I thought I must do the very opposite, and reject as if absolutely false anything as to which I could imagine the least doubt, in order to see if I should not be left at the end believing something that was absolutely indubitable. So, because our senses sometimes deceive us, I chose to suppose that nothing was such as they lead us to imagine. Because there are men who make mistakes in reasoning even as regards the simplest points of geometry and perpetrate fallacies, and seeing that I was as liable to error as anyone else, I rejected as false all the arguments I had so far taken for demonstrations. Finally, considering that the very same experiences (*pensées*) as we have in waking life may occur also while we sleep, without there being at that time any truth in them, I decided to feign that everything that had entered my mind hitherto was no more true than the illusions of dreams. But immediately upon this I noticed that while I was trying to think everything false, it must needs be that I, who was thinking this (*qui le pensais*), was something. And observing that this truth 'I am thinking (*je pense*), therefore I exist' was so solid and secure that the most extravagant suppositions of the sceptics could not overthrow it, I judged that I need not scruple to accept it as the first principle of philosophy that I was seeking. . . .

# THOMAS HOBBES
# from *Leviathan*
## Part I

The English philosopher Thomas Hobbes (1588–1679) was probably the most radical thinker to be spawned by the Scientific Revolution of the 1600s. He was a scandalous figure to his contemporaries, for he was thought to be an atheist, and possibly was, though he denied it. Well-placed friends, including King Charles II, who forgave Hobbes's religious doubts and welcomed his defense of monarchy, intervened to save him from prison or burning at the stake. Hobbes developed a philosophy of mechanistic materialism; characterized by lack of free will and identification of mind as a "motion in the head," it owed its method to the geometric reasoning of Descartes (see *Discourse on Method*), its empiricism to Bacon ("Of Studies"), and its atomistic structure of nature to the ancient Atomists (see Epicurus's *Letter to Menoecus*) and their modern followers, such as Galileo Galilei (1564–1642). Galileo, whom Hobbes met in Italy, especially impressed him with the idea that human matter is in constant motion, guided by natural laws—the notion that Hobbes later made the guiding principle in *Leviathan*, his pioneering work in modern political theory. It is for his political writings that he is known today, his scientific works having passed into oblivion.

Hobbes's *Leviathan* (1651), in which he advocated absolute monarchy, reflected his disgust at the English Civil War, 1642–1649, which resulted in the abolition of England's kingship and the setting up of a republic. Having sat out the war in France where he sought sanctuary, 1640–1651, he became convinced that only an absolute king could restore social order and maintain national unity. He found the word *Leviathan* in the Book of Job (chapter 41) where God used it as a term for a sea monster "king" who rules "over all the children of pride"—an image of divine power. In Hobbes's book, "Leviathan" refers to an all-encompassing state or commonwealth that absorbs and directs all human actions.

Hobbes's method in *Leviathan* was to try to found a science of politics, based on the idea that the world is a machine of matter, moving according to law. Like Descartes, he wanted to establish an undeniable truth from which to deduce the rest of his philosophy. He located his truth in his gloomy view of human nature, which held that, left to their own devices, human beings would fight with each other all the time. This is his notion of the "war of every man against every man," which he thought existed in a "state of nature," that is, in periods when rule by law had broken down or else had never been established. It is to escape this anarchy that humanity gives up all its rights and its claims to self-government to a powerful state—Leviathan—which will protect them from themselves.

### Reading the Selection

"Of Man," taken from Chapter XIII of Part I of *Leviathan*, sets forth Hobbes's theory of human nature, as imagined in the state of nature. It is not that human beings are naturally evil, for there are no laws at first to prescribe what is good and bad; rather, it is that humans are by nature more selfish than social. They are created equal—"Nature hath made men . . . equal in the faculties of body and mind"—but they are driven by their passions, or desires, and all want the same things: "gain," "safety," and "reputation." Since "there is no power able to overawe them all," the result is a "time of war, where every man is enemy to every man." Thus, given free rein in the state of nature, humans create a form of life which is "solitary, poor, nasty, brutish, and short."

## Chapter XIII
## Of the Natural Condition of Mankind, as Concerning Their Felicity and Misery

Nature hath made men so equal in the faculties of body and mind as that though there be found one man sometimes manifestly stronger in body, or of quicker mind than another, yet when all is reckoned together, the difference between man and man is not so considerable as that one man can thereupon claim to himself any benefit to which another may not pretend as well as he. For as to the strength of body, the weakest has strength enough to kill the strongest, either by secret machination, or by confederacy with others that are in the same danger with himself.

And as to the faculties of the mind, setting aside the arts grounded upon words, and especially that skill of proceeding upon general and infallible rules, called science, which very few have, and but in few things as being not a native faculty, born with us, nor attained, as prudence, while we look after somewhat else, I find yet a greater equality amongst men than that of strength. For prudence is but experience; which equal time equally bestows on all men, in those things they equally apply themselves unto. That which may perhaps make such equality incredible is but a vain conceit of one's own wisdom, which almost all men think they have in a greater degree than the vulgar; that is, than all men but themselves and a few others, whom by fame or for concurring with themselves they approve. For such is the nature of men, that howsoever they may acknowledge many others to be more witty or more eloquent or more learned, yet they will hardly believe there be many so wise as themselves. For they see their own wit at hand, and other men's at a distance. But this proveth rather that men are in that point equal, than unequal. For there is not ordinarily a greater sign of the equal distribution of anything than that every man is contented with his share.

From this equality of ability ariseth equality of hope in the attaining of our ends. And therefore if any two men desire the same thing, which nevertheless they cannot both enjoy, they become enemies; and in the way to their end (which is principally their own conservation, and sometimes their delectation only), endeavor to destroy or subdue one another. And from hence it comes to pass, that where an invader hath no more to fear than another man's single power, if one plant, sow, build or possess a convenient seat, others may probably be expected to come prepared with forces united to dispossess and deprive him, not only of the fruit of his labor, but also of his life or liberty. And the invader again is in the like danger of another.

And from this difference of one another, there is no way for any man to secure himself so reasonable as anticipation; that is, by force or wiles to master the persons of all men he can, so long till he see no other power great enough to endanger him; and this is no more than his own conservation requireth, and is generally allowed. Also because there be some, that taking pleasure in contemplating their own power in the acts of conquest, which they pursue farther than their security requires; if others, that otherwise would be glad to be at ease within modest bounds, should not by invasion increase their power, they would not be able, long time, by standing only on their defense, to subsist. And by consequence, such augmentation of dominion over men, being necessary to a man's conservation, it ought to be allowed him.

Again, men have no pleasure, but on the contrary a great deal of grief, in keeping company, where there is no power able to overawe them all. For every man looketh that his companion should value him at the same rate he sets upon himself; and upon all signs of contempt or undervaluing, naturally endeavors, as far as he dares (which amongst them that have no common power to keep them in quiet, is far enough to make them destroy each other), to extort a greater value from his contemners, by damage; and from others, by the example.

So that in the nature of man, we find three principal causes of quarrel. First, competition; secondly, diffidence; thirdly, glory.

The first maketh men invade for gain; the second, for safety; and the third, for reputation. The first use violence, to make themselves masters of other men's persons, wives, children, and cattle; the second, to defend them; the third, for trifles, as a word, a smile, a different opinion, and any other sign of undervalue, either direct in their persons, or by reflection in their kindred, their friends, their nation, their profession, or their name.

Hereby it is manifest, that during the time men live without a common power to keep them all in awe, they are in that condition which is called war; and such a war as is of every man, against every man. For war consisteth not in battle only or the act of fighting; but in a tract of time, wherein the will to contend by battle is sufficiently known; and therefore the notion of time is to be considered in the nature of war, as it is in the nature of weather. For as the nature of foul weather lieth not in a shower or two of rain, but in an inclination thereto of many days together; so the nature of war consisteth not in actual fighting, but in the known disposition thereto during all the time there is no assurance of the contrary. All other time is peace.

Whatsoever therefore is consequent to a time of war, where every man is enemy to every man, the same is consequent to the time wherein men live without other security than what their own strength and their own invention shall furnish them withal. In such condition there is no place for industry, because the fruit thereof is uncertain; and consequently no culture of the earth; no navigation, nor use of the commodities that may be imported by sea; no commodious building; no instruments of moving and removing such things as require much force; no knowledge of the face of the earth; no account of time; no arts; no letters; no society; and, which is worst of all, continual fear, and danger of violent death; and the life of man, solitary, poor, nasty, brutish, and short.

It may seem strange to some man that has not well weighed these things, that nature should thus dissociate and render men apt to invade and destroy one another; and he may therefore, not trusting to this inference made from the passions, desire perhaps to have the same confirmed by experience. Let him therefore consider with himself; when taking a journey, he arms himself, and seeks to go well accompanied; when going to sleep, he locks his doors; when even in his house he locks his chests; and then when he knows there be laws and public officers, armed, to revenge all injuries shall be done him; what opinion he has of his fellow-subjects, when he rides armed; of his fellow-citizens, when he locks his doors; and of his children and servants, when he locks his chests. Does he not there as much accuse mankind by his actions as I do by my words? But neither of us accuse man's nature in it. The desires and other passions of man are in themselves no sin. No more are the actions that proceed from those passions, till they know a law that forbids them; which till laws be made they cannot know; nor can any law be made till they have agreed upon the person that shall make it.

It may peradventure be thought there was never such a time nor condition of war as this; and I believe it was never generally so over all the world; but there are many places where they live so now. For the savage people in many places of America, except the government of small families, the concord whereof dependeth on natural lust, have no government at all, and live at this day in that brutish manner, as I said before. Howsoever, it may be perceived what manner of life there would be, where there were no common power to fear, by the manner of life which men that have formerly lived under a peaceful government use to degenerate into in a civil war.

But though there had never been any time wherein particular men were in a condition of war one against another, yet in all times, kings and persons of sovereign authority, because of their independency, are in continual jealousies, and in the state and posture of gladiators; having their weapons pointing, and their eyes fixed on one another; that is, their forts, garrisons, and guns, upon the frontiers of their kingdoms; and continual spies upon their neighbors; which is a posture of war. But because they uphold thereby the industry of their subjects, there does not follow from it that misery which accompanies the liberty of particular men.

To this war of every man against every man, this also is consequent, that nothing can be unjust. The notions of right and wrong, justice and injustice, have there no place. Where there is no common power, there is no law; where no law, no injustice. Force and fraud are in war the two cardinal virtues. Justice and injustice are none of the faculties neither of the body nor mind. If they were, they might be in a man that were alone in the world, as well as his senses and passions. They are qualities that relate to men in society, not in solitude. It is consequent also to the same condition that there be no propriety, no dominion, no "mine" and "thine" distinct; but only that to be every man's that he can get; and for so long as he can keep it. And thus much for the ill condition which every man by mere nature is actually placed in; though with a possibility to come out of it, consisting partly in the passions, partly in his reason.

The passions that incline men to peace are fear of death, desire of such things as are necessary to commodious living, and a hope by their industry to obtain them. And reason suggesteth convenient articles of peace, upon which men may be drawn to agreement. These articles are they which otherwise are called the laws of nature. . . .

# JOHN LOCKE
## from *The Second Treatise of Civil Government*

No other modern thinker has influenced Western political thought as much as the English philosopher John Locke (1632–1704). He lived during an age of political upheaval, called the Glorious (or Bloodless) Revolution (1688): the Tories and the Whigs, England's first two political parties, joined together to rid their country of the tyrannical James II and welcomed as their new co-rulers his daughter, Mary, and her Dutch husband, William (William III and Mary II). Locke witnessed these events from the Netherlands, where he had fled in 1683 because he foresaw the accession of the absolutist and Catholic-leaning James II. When the entourage of William sailed to England in 1689 to claim the throne, Locke was on the ship that carried the future Queen Mary.

Locke's political theory is set forth in *Two Treatises of Government* (1690), which were published in the shadow of England's change in its ruling dynasty. The *First Treatise*, directed against Sir Robert Filmer's *Patriarcha* (1680), was an attack on the theory of absolute monarchy as based on the father's role in the family. In the more famous *Second Treatise of Civil Government*, Locke explained his own views in opposition to Filmer and (indirectly) Hobbes. Advocating the right to revolution and calling for government by consent of the governed, the *Second Treatise* seems to be simply a justification for the Glorious Revolution. But Locke had been working on both treatises since the 1680s, so they represent his mature political views.

Although Hobbes is never mentioned by name in the *Second Treatise,* it is clear that *Leviathan* is very much on Locke's mind when he wrote this little work. In contrast to Hobbe's centralized government with its claim to absolute power, Locke proposed a weak centralized government, its powers limited by a set of clearly defined personal rights: life, liberty, and, most especially, property. Locke also took a more optimistic view of human nature than Hobbes, seeing human beings as basically rational and capable of both controlling their passions on an individual level and ruling themselves in society. In the long run, Locke's *Second Treatise* laid the foundations for liberalism—a political theory that advocated natural rights and representative government.

The son of a lawyer, Locke graduated from Oxford where he was disillusioned with its outdated curriculum. He practiced medicine off and on during his life, tutored the sons of the wealthy, and served as private secretary for several prominent nobles. He held high government positions under William and Mary, until his death.

## Reading the Selection

The selection, from Chapter IX of Locke's *Second Treatise,* shows Locke giving a point-by-point refutation of Hobbe's political theory. Like Hobbes, Locke sees life as violent in the state of nature, but, unlike Hobbes, he attributes this violence to the lack of an "established, settled, known law," "an indifferent judge," and an independent executive (the germ of "the separation of powers" idea). These three things, while lacking in the state of nature, are acquired by humans when they enter into a social contract, thus enabling natural rights to be enjoyed in civil society.

The selection from Chapter XIX lays out Locke's argument in support of the right to revolution, pointing out that the innate conservatism of human beings will prevent its abuse.

---

### Chapter IX
### Of the Ends of Political Society and Government

123. If man in the state of Nature be so free as has been said, if he be absolute lord of his own person and possessions, equal to the greatest and subject to nobody, why will he part with his freedom, this empire, and subject himself to the dominion and control of any other power? To which it is obvious to answer, that though in the state of Nature he hath such a right, yet the enjoyment of it is very uncertain and constantly exposed to the invasion of others; for all being kings as much as he, every man his equal, and the greater part no strict observers of equity and justice, the enjoyment of the property he has in this state is very unsafe, very insecure. This makes him willing to quit this condition which, however free, is full of fears and continual dangers; and it is not without reason that he seeks out and is willing to join in society with others who are already united, or have a mind to unite for the mutual preservation of their lives, liberties and estates, which I call by the general name—property.

124. The great and chief end, therefore, of men uniting into commonwealths, and putting themselves under government, is the preservation of their property; to which in the state of Nature there are many things wanting.

Firstly, there wants an established, settled, known law, received and allowed by common consent to be the standard of right and wrong, and the common measure to decide all controversies between them. For though the law of Nature be plain and intelligible to all rational creatures, yet men, being biased by their interest, as well as ignorant for want of study of it, are not apt to allow of it as a law binding to them in the application of it to their particular cases.

125. Secondly, in the state of Nature there wants a known and indifferent judge, with authority to determine all differences according to the established law. For every one in that state being both judge and executioner of the law of Nature, men being partial to themselves, passion and revenge is very apt to carry them too far, and with too much heat in their own cases, as well as negligence and unconcernedness, make them too remiss in other men's.

126. Thirdly, in the state of Nature there often wants power to back and support the sentence when right, and to give it due execution. They who by any injustice offended will seldom fail where they are able by force to make good their injustice. Such resistance many times makes the punishment dangerous, and frequently destructive to those who attempt it.

127. Thus mankind, notwithstanding all the privileges of the state of Nature, being but in an ill condition while they remain in it are quickly driven into society. Hence it comes to pass, that we seldom find any number of men live any time together in this state. The inconveniences that they are therein exposed to by the irregular and uncertain exercise of the power every man has of punishing the transgressions of others, make them take sanctuary under the established laws of government, and therein seek the preservation of their property. It is this makes them so willingly give up every one

his single power of punishing to be exercised by such alone as shall be appointed to it amongst them, and by such rules as the community, or those authorised by them to that purpose, shall agree on. And in this we have the original right and rise of both the legislative and executive power as well as of the governments and societies themselves.

128. For in the state of Nature to omit the liberty he has of innocent delights, a man has two powers. The first is to do whatsoever he thinks fit for the preservation of himself and others within the permission of the law of Nature; by which law, common to them all, he and all the rest of mankind are one community, make up one society distinct from all other creatures, and were it not for the corruption and viciousness of degenerate men, there would be no need of any other, no necessity that men should separate from this great and natural community, and associate into lesser combinations. The other power a man has in the state of Nature is the power to punish the crimes committed against that law. Both these he gives up when he joins in a private, if I may so call it, or particular political society, and incorporates into any commonwealth separate from the rest of mankind.

129. The first power—viz., of doing whatsoever he thought fit for the preservation of himself and the rest of mankind, he gives up to be regulated by laws made by the society, so far forth as the preservation of himself and the rest of that society shall require; which laws of the society in many things confine the liberty he had by the law of Nature.

130. Secondly, the power of punishing he wholly gives up, and engages his natural force, which he might before employ in the execution of the law of Nature, by his own single authority, as he thought fit, to assist the executive power of the society as the law thereof shall require. For being now in a new state, wherein he is to enjoy many conveniences from the labour, assistance, and society of others in the same community, as well as protection from its whole strength, he is to part also with as much of his natural liberty, in providing for himself, as the good, prosperity, and safety of the society shall require, which is not only necessary but just, since the other members of the society do the like.

131. But though men when they enter into society give up the equality, liberty, and executive power they had in the state of Nature in the hands of the society, to be so far disposed of by the legislative as the good of the society shall require, yet it being only with an intention in every one the better to preserve himself, his liberty and property (for no rational creature can be supposed to change his condition with an intention to be worse), the power of the society or legislative constituted by them can never be supposed to extend farther than the common good, but is obliged to secure every one's property by providing against those three defects above mentioned that made the state of Nature so unsafe and uneasy. And so, whoever has the legislative or supreme power of any commonwealth, is bound to govern by established standing laws, promulgated and known to the people, and not by extemporary decrees, by indifferent and upright judges, who are to decide controversies by those laws; and to employ the force of the community at home only in the execution of such laws, or abroad to prevent or redress foreign injuries and secure the community from inroads and invasion.

And all this to be directed to no other end but the peace, safety, and public good of the people. . . .

• • •

## Chapter XIX
## Of the Dissolution of Government

223. To this, perhaps, it will be said that the people being ignorant and always discontented, to lay the foundation of government in the unsteady opinion and uncertain humour of the people, is to expose it to certain ruin; and no government will be able long to subsist if the people may set up a new legislative whenever they take offence at the old one. To this I answer, quite the contrary. People are not so easily got out of their old forms as some are apt to suggest. They are hardly to be prevailed with to amend the acknowledged faults in the frame they have been accustomed to. And if there be any original defects, or adventitious ones introduced by time or corruption, it is not an easy thing to get them changed, even when all the world sees there is an opportunity for it. This slowness and aversion in the people to quit their old constitutions has in the many revolutions have been seen in this kingdom, in this and former ages, still kept us to, or after some interval of fruitless attempts, still brought us back again to our old legislative of king, lords and commons; and whatever provocations have made the crown be taken from some of our princes' heads, they never carried the people so far as to place it in another line.

224. But it will be said this hypothesis lays a ferment for frequent rebellion. To which I answer:

First: no more than any other hypothesis. For when the people are made miserable, and find themselves exposed to the ill usage of arbitrary power, cry up their governors as much as you will for sons of Jupiter, let them be sacred and divine, descended or authorised from Heaven; give them out for whom or what you please, the same will happen. The people generally ill treated, and contrary to right, will be ready upon any occasion to ease themselves of a burden that sits heavy upon them. They will wish and seek for the opportunity, which in the change, weakness, and accidents of human affairs, seldom delays long to offer itself. He must have lived but a little while in the world, who has not seen examples of this in his time; and he must have read very little who cannot produce examples of it in all sorts of governments in the world.

225. Secondly: I answer, such revolutions happen not upon every little mismanagement in public affairs. Great mistakes in the ruling part, many wrong and inconvenient laws, and all the slips of human frailty will be borne by the people without mutiny or murmur. But if a long train of abuses, prevarications, and artifices, all tending the same way, make the design visible to the people, and they cannot but feel what they lie under, and see whither they are going, it is not to be wondered that they should then rouse themselves, and endeavour to put the rule into such hands which may secure to them the ends for which government was at first erected, and without which, ancient names and specious forms are so far from being better, that they are much worse

than the state of Nature or pure anarchy; the inconveniencies being all as great and as near, but the remedy farther off and more difficult.

226. Thirdly: I answer, that this power in the people of providing for their safety anew by a new legislative when their legislators have acted contrary to their trust by invading their property, is the best fence against rebellion, and the probablest means to hinder it. For rebellion being an opposition, not to persons, but authority, which is founded only in the constitutions and laws of the government: those, whoever they be, who, by force, break through, and, by force, justify their violation of them, are truly and properly rebels.

For when men, by entering into society and civil government, have excluded force, and introduced laws for the preservation of property, peace, and unity amongst themselves, those who set up force again in opposition to the laws, do *rebellare*—that is, bring back again the state of war, and are properly rebels, which they who are in power, by the pretence they have to authority, the temptation of force they have in their hands, and the flattery of those about them being likeliest to do, the properest way to prevent the evil is to show them the danger and injustice of it who are under the greatest temptation to run into it. . . .

Chapter

# 16

# The Age of Reason:
## 1700–1789

JONATHAN SWIFT

*A Modest Proposal*

Swift's *A Modest Proposal for preventing the children of poor people in Ireland from being a burden to their parents or country, and for making them beneficial to the public* is one of the bitterest works in world literature. It belongs to the satire genre founded by Juvenal (see *Satires*), but no other satirist, ancient or modern, has shown such moral indignation as Swift does in this political tract.

Its author, Jonathan Swift (1667–1745), was a moralist of a conservative and angry outlook, who was deeply devoted to Christian ideals. Though involved with women ("Stella" and "Varina") during his life, he was a misanthrope, partly because of innate crankiness and partly as revenge for dashed hopes. It often seemed as if the world were bent on crushing him. Ambitious for a post in either the government or the Anglican church, he was held back by his Irish birth, even though he was of English stock. His biting wit attracted England's leaders who hired him to write propaganda, but, for years, they failed to advance him. Eventually rewarded, he was made Dean of St. Patrick's (Anglican) cathedral in Dublin, a rich living but, to him, a place of exile. As Dean Swift, from 1713 until mentally incapacitated in 1742, he continued to write political tracts and other works, notably *Gulliver's Travels* (1726)—a satire describing four alternatives to the society he so hated.

### Reading the Selection

*A Modest Proposal* (1729) dates from the Dublin years. Swift's earlier anger against the Irish [a "nation of slaves, who sell themselves for nothing"] was past; in this tract, he defended Irish resistance to English oppression, as reflected in poverty and child beggary. For these ills, he proposed the ironic cure of cannibalism, "buying the children alive, and dressing them hot from the knife as we do roasting pigs." To Swift, an insane problem merited an insane remedy: better death than Ireland's living hell.

Swift enlivened his satire with parodies of contemporary social thought. Its pseudo-scientific jargon, for instance, was inspired by political arithmetic, the then new social science which taught that political decisions should be based on statistics. Parody of this science's methods is evident in the calculation of census data, the use of cost-benefit analysis, and the satire's ruling metaphor that equates human life with fattening animals for the market. Swift also stands on its head the age's belief that a nation's wealth is measured by population size; he points out instead the dangers of overpopulation, especially when the poor outnumber the rich. Finally, Swift ridicules existing religious opinion when he differentiates between the deserving and undeserving poor.

Beneath the bitterness, Swift's political goal was clear: a new Ireland, freed from poverty and beggary. His true aims, though utopian and dismissed in the satire as "other expedients," included taxing Ireland's absentee English landlords, supporting Irish manufacture and prohibiting imports of clothing and furniture, introducing thrift and patriotism, and healing internal divisions.

Swift's style often has a bawdy aspect, as in the reference to Rabelais (see *The Histories of Gargantua and Pantagruel*), termed "a grave author, an eminent French physician." Swift repeats Rabelais's comment that "more children [are] born in Roman Catholic countries about nine months after Lent, than at any other season," referring to increased sexual activity as a result of a Lenten-imposed fish diet, fish being considered an aphrodisiac.

---

It is a melancholy object to those who walk through this great town or travel in the country, when they see the streets, the roads, and cabin doors, crowded with beggars of the female sex, followed by three, four, or six children, all in rags and importuning every passenger for an alms. These mothers, instead of being able to work for their honest livelihood, are forced to employ all their time in strolling to beg sustenance for their helpless infants, who, as they grow up, either turn thieves for want of work, or leave their dear native country to fight for the Pretender in Spain, or sell themselves to the Barbadoes.

I think it is agreed by all parties that this prodigious number of children in the arms, or on the backs, or at the heels of their mothers, and frequently of their fathers, is in the present deplorable state of the kingdom a very great additional grievance; and therefore whoever could find out a fair, cheap, and easy method of making these children sound, useful members of the commonwealth would deserve so well of the public as to have his statue set up for a preserver of the nation.

But my intention is very far from being confined to provide only for the children of professed beggars; it is of a much greater extent, and shall take in the whole number of infants at a certain age who are born of parents in effect as little able to support them as those who demand our charity in the streets.

As to my own part, having turned my thoughts for many years upon this important subject, and maturely weighed the several schemes of other projectors, I have always found them grossly mistaken in their computation. It is true, a child just dropped from its dam may be supported by her milk for a solar year, with little other nourishment; at most not above the value of two shillings, which the mother may certainly get, or the value in scraps, by her lawful occupation of begging; and it is exactly at one year old that I propose to provide for them in such a manner as instead of being a charge upon their parents or the parish, or wanting food and raiment for the rest of their lives, they shall on the contrary contribute to the feeding, and partly to the clothing, of many thousands.

There is likewise another great advantage in my scheme, that it will prevent those involuntary abortions, and that horrid practice of women murdering their bastard children, alas, too frequent among us, sacrificing the poor innocent babes, I doubt, more to avoid the expense than the shame, which would move tears and pity in the most savage and inhuman breast.

The number of souls in this kingdom being usually reckoned one million and a half, of these I calculate there may be about two hundred thousand couples whose wives are breeders, from which number I subtract thirty thousand couples who are able to maintain their own children, although I apprehend there cannot be so many under the present distress of the kingdom; but this being granted, there will remain an hundred and seventy thousand breeders. I again subtract fifty thousand for those women who miscarry, or whose children die by accident or disease within the year. There only remain an hundred and twenty thousand children of poor parents annually born. The question therefore is, how this number shall be reared and provided for, which, as I have already said, under the present situation of affairs, is utterly impossible by all the methods hitherto proposed. For we can neither employ them in handicraft nor agriculture; we neither build houses (I mean in the country) nor cultivate land. They can very seldom pick up livelihood by stealing till they arrive at six years old, except where they are of towardly parts, although I confess they learn the rudiments much earlier, during which time they can however be looked upon only as probationers, as I have been informed by a principal gentleman in the country of Cavan, who protested to me that he never knew above one or two instances under the age of six, even in a part of the kingdom so renowned for the quickest proficiency in that art.

I am assured by our merchants that a boy or a girl before twelve years old is no salable commodity; and even when they come to this age, they will not yield above three pounds, or three pounds and half a crown at most on the Exchange; which cannot turn to account either to the parents or the kingdom, the charge of nutriment and rags having been at least four times that value.

I shall now therefore humbly propose my own thoughts, which I hope will not be liable to the least objection.

I have been assured by a very knowing American of my acquaintance in London, that a young healthy child well nursed is at a year old a most delicious, nourishing, and wholesome food, whether stewed, roasted, baked, or boiled; and I make no doubt that it will equally serve in fricassee or a ragout.

I do therefore humbly offer it to public consideration that of the hundred and twenty thousand children, already computed, twenty thousand may be reserved for breed, whereof only one fourth part to be males, which is more than we allow to sheep, black cattle, or swine; and my reason is that these children are seldom the fruits of marriage, a circumstance not much regarded by our savages, therefore one male will be sufficient to serve four females. That the remaining hundred thousand may at a year old be offered in sale to the persons of quality and fortune through the kingdom, always advising the mother to let them suck plentifully in the last month, so as to render them plump and fat for a good table. A child will make two dishes at an entertainment for friends; and when the family dines alone, the fore or hind quarter will make a reasonable dish, and seasoned with a little pepper or salt will be very good boiled on the fourth day, especially in winter.

I have reckoned upon a medium that a child just born will weigh twelve pounds, and in a solar year if tolerably nursed increaseth to twenty-eight pounds.

I grant this food will be somewhat dear, and therefore very proper for landlords, who, as they have already devoured most of the parents, seem to have the best title to the children.

Infant's flesh will be in season throughout the year, but more plentiful in March, and a little before and after. For we are told by a grave author, an eminent French physician, that fish being a prolific diet, there are more children born in Roman Catholic countries about nine months after Lent, than at any other season; therefore, reckoning a year after Lent, the markets will be more glutted than usual, because the number of popish infants is at least three to one in this kingdom; and therefore it will have one other collateral advantage, by lessening the number of Papists among us.

I have already computed the charge of nursing a beggar's child (in which list I reckon all cottagers, laborers, and four fifths of the farmers) to be about two shillings per annum, rags included; and I believe no gentleman would repine to give ten shillings for the carcass of a good fat child, which, as I have said, will make four dishes of excellent nutritive meat, when he hath only some particular friend or his own family to dine with him. Thus the squire will learn to be a good landlord, and grow popular among the tenants; the mother will have eight shillings net profit, and be fit for work till she produces another child.

Those who are more thrifty (as I must confess the times require) may flay the carcass; the skin of which artificially dressed will make admirable gloves for ladies, and summer boots for fine gentlemen.

As to our city of Dublin, shambles may be appointed for this purpose in the most convenient parts of it, and butchers we may be assured will not be wanting; although I rather recommend buying the children alive, and dressing them hot from the knife as we do roasting pigs.

A very worthy person, a true lover of his country, and whose virtues I highly esteem, was lately pleased in discoursing on this matter to offer a refinement upon my scheme. He said that many gentlemen of his kingdom, having of late destroyed their deer, he conceived that the want of venison might be well supplied by the bodies of young lads and maidens, not exceeding fourteen years of age nor under twelve, so great a number of both sexes in every country being now ready to starve for want of work and service; and these to be disposed of by their parents, if alive, or otherwise by their nearest relations. But with due deference to so excellent a friend and so deserving a patriot, I cannot be altogether in his sentiments; for as to the males, my American acquaintance assured me from frequent experience that their flesh was generally tough and lean, like that of our schoolboys, by continual exercise, and their taste disagreeable; and to fatten them would not answer the charge. Then as to the females, it would, I think with humble submission, be a loss to the public, because they soon would become breeders themselves; and besides, it is not improbable that some scrupulous people might be apt to censure such a practice (although indeed very unjustly) as a little bordering upon cruelty; which, I confess, hath always been with me the strongest objection against any project, how well soever intended.

But in order to justify my friend, he confessed that this expedient was put into his head by the famous Psalmanazar, a native of the island Formosa, who came from thence to London about twenty years ago, and in conversation told my friend that in his country when any young person happened to be put to death, the executioner sold the carcass to the persons of quality as a prime dainty; and that in his time the body of a plump girl of fifteen, who was crucified for an attempt to poison the emperor, was sold to his Imperial Majesty's prime minister of state, and other great mandarins of the court, in joints from the gibbet, at four hundred crowns. Neither indeed can I deny that if the same use were made of several plump young girls in this town, who without one single groat to their fortunes cannot stir abroad without a chair, and appear at the playhouse and assemblies in foreign fineries which they never will pay for, the kingdom would not be the worse.

Some persons of a desponding spirit are in great concern about that vast number of poor people who are aged, diseased, or maimed, and I have been desired to employ my thoughts what course may be taken to ease the nature of so grievous an encumbrance. But I am not in the least pain upon that matter, because it is very well known that they are every day dying and rotting by cold and famine, and filth and vermin, as fast as can be reasonably expected. And as to the younger laborers, they are now in almost as hopeful a condition. They cannot get work, and consequently pine away for want of nourishment to a degree that if any time they are accidentally hired to common labor, they have not strength to perform it; and thus the country and themselves are happily delivered from the evils to come.

I have too long digressed, and therefore shall return to my subject. I think the advantages by the proposal which I have made are obvious and many, as well as of the highest importance.

For first, as I have already observed, it would greatly lessen the number of Papists, with whom we are yearly over-run, being the principal breeders of the nation as well as our most dangerous enemies; and who stay at home on purpose to deliver the kingdom to the Pretender, hoping to take their advantage by the absence of so many good Protestants, who have chosen rather to leave their country than to stay at home and pay tithes against their conscience to an Episcopal curate.

Secondly, the poorer tenants will have something valuable of their own, which by law may be made liable to distress, and help to pay their landlord's rent, their corn and cattle being already seized and money a thing unknown.

Thirdly, whereas the maintenance of an hundred thousand children, from two years old and upwards, cannot be computed at less than ten shillings a piece per annum, the nation's stock will be thereby increased fifty thousand pounds per annum, besides the profit of a new dish introduced to the tables of all gentlemen of fortune in the kingdom who have any refinement in taste. And the money will circulate among ourselves, the goods being entirely of our own growth and manufacture.

Fourthly, the constant breeders, besides the gain of eight shillings per annum by the sale of their children, will be rid of the charge for maintaining them after the first year.

Fifthly, this food would likewise bring great custom to taverns, where the vintners will certainly be so prudent as to procure the best receipts for dressing it to perfection, and consequently have their houses frequented by all the fine gentlemen, who justly value themselves upon their knowledge in good eating; and a skillful cook, who understands how to oblige his guests, will contrive to make it as expensive as they please.

Sixthly, this would be a great inducement to marriage, which all wise nations have either encouraged by rewards or enforced by laws and penalties. It would increase the care and tenderness of mothers toward their children, when they were sure of a settlement for life to the poor babes, provided in some sort by the public, to their annual profit instead of expense. We should see an honest emulation among the married women, which of them could bring the fattest child to the market. Men would become as fond of their wives during the time of pregnancy as they are now of their mares in foal, their cows in calf, or sows when they are ready to farrow; nor offer to beat or kick them (as is too frequent a practice) for fear of a miscarriage.

Many other advantages might be enumerated. For instance, the addition of some thousand carcasses in our exportation of barreled beef, the propagation of swine's flesh, and improvements in the art of making good bacon, so much wanted among us by the great destruction of pigs, too frequent at our tables, which are no way comparable in taste or magnificence to a well-grown, fat, yearling child, which roasted whole will make a considerable figure at a lord mayor's feast or any other public entertainment. But this and many others I omit, being studious of brevity.

Supposing that one thousand families in this city would be constant customers for infants' flesh, besides others who might have it at merry meetings, particularly weddings and christenings, I compute that Dublin would take off annually about twenty thousand carcasses, and the rest of the kingdom (where probably they will be sold somewhat cheaper) the remaining eighty thousand.

I can think of no one objection that will possibly be raised against this proposal, unless it should be urged that the number of people will be thereby much lessened in the kingdom. This I freely own, and it was indeed one principal design in offering it to the world. I desire the reader will observe; that I calculate my remedy for this one individual kingdom of Ireland and for no other that ever was, is, or I think ever can be upon earth. Therefore, let no man talk to me of other expedients: of taxing our absentees at five shillings a pound: of using neither clothes nor household furniture except what is of our own growth and manufacture: of utterly rejecting the materials and instruments that promote foreign luxury: of curing the expensiveness of pride, vanity, idleness, and gaming in our women: of introducing a vein of parsimony, prudence, and temperance: of learning to love our country, in the want of which we differ even from Laplanders and the inhabitants of Topinamboo: of quitting our animosities and factions, nor acting any longer like the Jews, who were murdering one another at the very moment their city was taken: of being a little cautious not to sell our country and conscience for nothing: of teaching landlords to have at least one degree of mercy toward their tenants: lastly, of putting a spirit of honesty, industry, and skill into our shopkeepers; who, if a resolution could now be taken to buy only our native goods, would immediately unite to cheat and exact upon us in the price, the measure, and the goodness, nor could ever yet be brought to make one fair proposal of just dealing, though often and earnestly invited to it.

Therefore, I repeat, let no man talk to me of these and the like expedients, till he hath at least some glimpse of hope that there will ever be some hearty and sincere attempt to put them in practice.

But as to myself, having been wearied out for many years with offering vain, idle, visionary thoughts, and at length utterly despairing of success, I fortunately fell upon this proposal, which, as it is wholly new, so it hath something solid and real, of no expense and little trouble, full in our own power, and whereby we can incur no danger in disobliging England. For this kind of commodity will not bear exportation, the flesh being of too tender a consistence to admit a long continuance in salt, although perhaps I could name a country which would be glad to eat up our whole nation without it.

After all, I am not so violently bent upon my own opinion as to reject any offer proposed by wise men, which shall be found equally innocent, cheap, easy, and effectual. But before something of that kind shall be advanced in contradiction to my scheme, and offering a better, I desire the author or authors will be pleased maturely to consider two points. First, as things now stand, how they will be able to find food and raiment for an hundred thousand useless mouths and backs. And secondly, there being a round million of creatures in human figure throughout this kingdom, whose sole subsistence put into a common stock would leave them in debt two millions of pounds sterling, adding those who are beggars by profession to the bulk of farmers, cottagers, and laborers, with their wives and children who are beggars in effect; I desire those politicians who dislike my overture, and may perhaps be so bold to attempt an answer, that they will first ask the parents of these mortals whether they would not at this day think it a great happiness to have been sold for food at a year old in this manner I prescribe, and thereby have avoided such a perpetual scene of misfortunes as they have since gone through by the oppression of landlords, the impossibility of paying rent without money or trade, the want of common sustenance, with neither house nor clothes to cover them from the inclemencies of the weather, and the most inevitable prospect of entailing the like or greater miseries upon their breed forever.

I profess, in the sincerity of my heart, that I have not the least personal interest in endeavoring to promote this necessary work, having no other motive than the public good of my country, by advancing our trade, providing for infants, relieving the poor, and giving some pleasure to the rich. I have no children by which I can propose to get a single penny; the youngest being nine years old, and my wife past childbearing.

# ALEXANDER POPE
# from *An Essay on Man*

*To Henry St. John, Lord Bolingbroke*

The poet and essayist Alexander Pope (1688–1744) lived during one of the great eras in English letters, the Augustan Age (ca. 1660–1760). This period's authors drew inspiration from the first Augustan Age, that is, the reign of Emperor Augustus (27 B.C.–A.D. 14) when many fine writers flourished, notably Vergil, Horace, and Ovid. Imitating the style of the Roman heritage, Pope and the rest of these latter-day Augustans, including Swift (see *A Modest Proposal*), transformed their period into a time of harmony, decorum ("good taste"), and proportion. The Augustan ideal was correctness, and writers were under some moral and aesthetic obligation to instruct as well as to please. From the vantage of European letters, the Augustan Age was part of the Neoclassical movement, then sweeping across the West, whose writers (see Racine's *Phaedra*) believed that the Classical authors had set the literary standards for all time.

Early in his career, Alexander Pope, ever sensitive to the spirit of Classicism, developed a European-wide reputation and made himself financially secure with his translation of Homer's *Iliad* and *Odyssey*. He cemented his high literary position with his later works, such as poems, satires, epistles (letters in verse), and collected prose letters. Nowhere was his devotion to Classicism so evident as in his poetry where he wrote in heroic couplets—a verse form, nearly always in iambic pentameter rhymed in pairs, aa, bb, cc, dd, etc., with ten syllables in each line; it began perhaps with Chaucer (see *The Canterbury Tales*) but was perfected by the Augustan poets.

Pope's life was beset with misfortune. A Roman Catholic at a time when Protestantism, under King William and Queen Mary, reached new heights of popularity, he as a youth was barred from England's best educational institutions, its public (meaning "private") schools. Thus, he was tutored by several Catholic priests, studied at two private schools, and, after age thirteen, taught himself at home. Pope was never physically strong, being subject to a tubercular infection that left him small in stature and with curvature of the spine. He also was forced to endure his critics' bitter attacks on his writings, though he gave as good as he got, as, for example, in *The Dunciad*, a satire against the bad poets ("dunces") of his period. Nonetheless, he persevered to become a dominant voice of the Augustan Age.

*Reading the Selection*

Pope considered *An Essay on Man* as one of his most important works. To thwart his critics and gain the best possible reception for this long work, he published two poems that his enemies attacked while he then anonymously issued the *Essay on Man* which was highly praised. Typically, the *Essay* is composed in heroic couplets.

Addressed to Pope's patron, Henry St. John Bolingbroke ("St. John," line 1), the *Essay* comprises four epistles, on the favorite topic of Neoclassical writers, man and his activities: "The proper study of mankind is man." Epistle 1 deals with man in the cosmos; Epistle 2 analyzes man as an individual; Epistle 3 examines man in society; and Epistle 4 explores the theme of happiness, concluding that personal and social happiness are the same.

Pope's basic conservatism, though not in a negative sense, is shown in the excerpts from the *Essay* included here. In Epistle 1, he advocates the seemingly fatalistic principle that "Whatever is, is right," but, in Epistle 2, he encourages the study of man and his environment, with the end goal of fitting into the moral order.

----

## Epistle 1. Of the Nature and State of Man, With Respect to the Universe

Awake, my St. John! leave all meaner things
To low ambition, and the pride of kings.
Let us (since life can little more supply
Than just to look about us and to die)
Expatiate free o'er all this scene of man;
A mightly maze! but not without a plan;
A wild, where weeds and flowers promiscuous shoot,
Or garden, tempting with forbidden fruit.
Together let us beat this ample field,
Try what the open, what the covert yield;
The latent tracts, the giddy heights, explore
Of all who blindly creep, or sightless soar;
Eye Nature's walks, shoot folly as it flies,
And catch the manners living as they rise;
Laugh where we must, be candid where we can;
But vindicate the ways of God to man.

1. Say first, of God above, or man below,
What can we reason, but from what we know?
Of man, what see we but his station here,
From which to reason, or to which refer?
Through worlds unnumbered though the God be known,
'Tis ours to trace him only in our own.
He, who through vast immensity can pierce,
See worlds on worlds compose one universe,
Observe how system into system runs,
What other planets circle other suns,
What varied being peoples every star,
May tell why Heaven has made us as we are.
But of this frame the bearings, and the ties,
The strong connections, nice dependencies,
Gradations just, has thy pervading soul
Looked through? or can a part contain the whole?
Is the great chain, that draws all to agree,
And drawn supports, upheld by God, or thee?

2. Presumptuous man! the reason wouldst thou find,
Why formed so weak, so little, and so blind?
First, if thou canst, the harder reason guess,
Why formed no weaker, blinder, and no less!
Ask of thy mother earth, why oaks are made
Taller or stronger than the weeds they shade?
Or ask of yonder argent fields above,
Why Jove's satellites are less than Jove?
    Of systems possible, if 'tis confessed
That Wisdom Infinite must form the best,
Where all must full or not coherent be,
And all that rises, rise in due degree;
Then, in the scale of reasoning life, 'tis plain,
There must be, somewhere, such a rank as man:
And all the question (wrangle e'er so long)
Is only this, if God has placed him wrong?
    Respecting man, whatever wrong we call,
May, must be right, as relative to all.
In human works, though labored on with pain,
A thousand movements scare one purpose gain;
In God's, one single can its end produce;
Yet serves to second too some other use.
So man, who here seems principal alone,
Perhaps acts second to some sphere unknown,
Touches some wheel, or verges to some goal;
'Tis but a part we see, and not a whole.
    When the proud steed shall know why man restrains
His fiery course, or drives him o'er the plains;
When the dull ox, why now he breaks the clod,
Is now a victim, and now Egypt's god:
Then shall man's pride and dullness comprehend
His actions', passions', being's use and end;
Why doing, suffering, checked, impelled; and why
This hour a slave, the next a deity.
    Then say not man's imperfect, Heaven in fault;
Say rather, man's as perfect as he ought;
His knowledge measured to his state and place,
His time a moment, and a point his space.
If to be perfect in a certain sphere,
What matter, soon or late, or here or there?
The blest today is as completely so,
As who began a thousand years ago.

3. Heaven from all creatures hides the book of Fate,
All but the page prescribed, their present state:

From brutes what men, from men what spirits know:
Or who could suffer being here below?
The lamb thy riot dooms to bleed today,
Had he thy reason, would he skip and play?
Pleased to the last, he crops the flowery food,
And licks the hand just raised to shed his blood.
O blindness to the future! kindly given,
That each may fill the circle marked by Heaven:
Who sees with equal eye, as God of all,
A hero perish, or a sparrow fall,
Atoms or systems into ruin hurled,
And know a bubble burst, and now a world.

  Hope humbly then; with trembling pinions soar;
Wait the great teacher Death, and God adore!
What future bliss, he gives not thee to know,
But gives that hope to be thy blessing now.
Hope springs eternal in the human breast:
Man never is, but always to be blest:
The soul, uneasy and confined from home,
Rests and expatiates in a life to come.

  Lo! the poor Indian, whose untutored mind
Sees God in clouds, or hears him in the wind;
His soul proud Science never taught to stray
Far as the solar walk, or milky way;
Yet simple Nature to his hope has given,
Behind the cloud-topped hill, an humbler heaven;
Some safer world in depth of woods embraced,
Some happier island in the watery waste,
Where slaves once more their native land behold,
No fiends torment, no Christians thirst for gold!
To be, contents his natural desire,
He asks no angel's wing, no seraph's fire;
But thinks, admitted to that equal sky,
His faithful dog shall bear him company.

4. Go, wiser thou! and, in thy scale of sense,
Weigh thy opinion against Providence;
Call imperfection what thou fancy'st such,
Say, here he gives too little, there too much;
Destroy all creatures for thy sport or gust,
Yet cry, if man's unhappy, God's unjust;
If man alone engross not Heaven's high care,
Alone made perfect here, immortal there:
Snatch from his hand the balance and the rod,
Rejudge his justice, be the God of God!
In pride, in reasoning pride, our error lies;
All quit their sphere, and rush into the skies.
Pride still is aiming at the blest abodes,
Men would be angels, angels would be gods.
Aspiring to be gods, if angels fell,
Aspiring to be angels, men rebel:
And who but wishes to invert the laws
Of order, sins against the Eternal Cause.

5. Ask for what end the heavenly bodies shine,
Earth for whose use? Pride answers, "'Tis for mine:
For me kind Nature wakes her genial power,
Suckles each herb, and spreads out every flower;
Annual for me, the grape, the rose renew
The juice nectareous, and the balmy dew;

For me, the mine a thousand treasures brings;
For me, health gushes from a thousand springs;
Seas roll to waft me, suns to light me rise;
My footstool earth, my canopy the skies."

  But errs not Nature from this gracious end,
From burning suns when livid deaths descend,
When earthquakes swallow, or when tempests sweep
Towns to one grave, whole nations to the deep?
"No," 'tis replied, "the first Almighty Cause
Acts not by partial, but by general laws;
The exceptions few; some change since all began,
And what created perfect?"—Why then man?
If the great end be human happiness,
Then Nature deviates; and can man do less?
As much that end a constant course requires
Of showers and sunshine, as of man's desires;
As much eternal springs and cloudless skies,
As men forever temperate, calm, and wise.
If plagues or earthquakes break not Heaven's design,
Why then a Borgia, or a Catiline?
Who knows but he whose hand the lightning forms,
Who heaves old ocean, and who wings the storms,
Pours fierce ambition in a Caesar's mind,
Or turns young Ammon loose to scourge mankind?
From pride, from pride, our very reasoning springs;
Account for moral, as for natural things:
Why charge we Heaven in those, in these acquit?
In both, to reason right is to submit.

  Better for us, perhaps, it might appear,
Were there all harmony, all virtue here;
That never air or ocean felt the wind;
That never passion discomposed the mind:
But ALL subsists by elemental strife;
And passions are the elements of life.
The general ORDER, since the whole began,
Is kept in Nature, and is kept in man.

6. What would this man? Now upward will he soar,
And little less than angel, would be more;
Now looking downwards, just as grieved appears
To want the strength of bulls, the fur of bears.
Made for his use all creatures if he call,
Say what their use, had he the powers of all?
Nature to these, without profusion, kind,
The proper organs, proper powers assigned;
Each seeming want compènsated of course,
Here with degrees of swiftness, there of force;
All in exact proportion to the state;
Nothing to add, and nothing to abate.
Each beast, each insect, happy in its own;
Is Heaven unkind to man, and man alone?
Shall he alone, whom rational we call,
Be pleased with nothing, if not blessed with all?

  The bliss of man (could pride that blessing find)
Is not to act or think beyond mankind;
No powers of body or of soul to share,
But what his nature and his state can bear.
Why has not man a microscopic eye?
For this plain reason, man is not a fly.
Say what the use, were finer optics given,

To inspect a mite, not comprehend the heaven?
Or touch, if tremblingly alive all o'er,
To smart and agonize at every pore?
Or quick effluvia darting through the brain,
Die of a rose in aromatic pain?
If nature thundered in his opening ears,
And stunned him with the music of the spheres,
How would he wish that Heaven had left him still
The whispering zephyr, and the purling rill?
Who finds not Providence all good and wise,
Alike in what it gives, and what denies?

7. Far as creation's ample range extends,
The scale of sensual, mental powers ascends:
Mark how it mounts, to man's imperial race,
From the green myriads in the peopled grass:
What modes of sight betwixt each wide extreme,
The mole's dim curtain, and the lynx's beam:
Of smell, the headlong lioness between,
And hound sagacious on the tainted green:
Of hearing, from the life that fills the flood,
To that which warbles through the vernal wood:
The spider's touch, how exquisitely fine!
Feels at each thread, and lives along the line:
In the nice bee, what sense so subtly true
From poisonous herbs extracts the healing dew:
How instinct varies in the groveling swine,
Compared, half-reasoning elephant, with thine!
'Twixt that, and reason, what a nice barrier,
Forever separate, yet forever near!
Remembrance and reflection how allied;
What thin partitions sense from thought divide:
And middle natures, how they long to join,
Yet never pass the insuperable line!
Without this just gradation, could they be
Subjected, these to those, or all to thee?
The powers of all subdued by thee alone,
Is not thy reason all these powers in one?

8. See, through this air, this ocean, and this earth,
All matter quick, and bursting into birth.
Above, how high progressive life may go!
Around, how wide! how deep extend below!
Vast Chain of Being! which from God began,
Natures ethereal, human, angel, man,
Beast, bird, fish, insect, what no eye can see,
No glass can reach! from Infinite to thee,
From thee to nothing.—On superior powers
Were we to press, inferior might on ours:
Or in the full creation leave a void,
Where, one step broken, the great scale's destroyed:
From Nature's chain whatever link you strike,
Tenth or ten thousandth, breaks the chain alike.
   And, if each system in gradation roll
Alike essential to the amazing Whole,
The least confusion but in one, not all
That system only, but the Whole must fall.
Let earth unbalanced from her orbit fly,
Planets and suns run lawless through the sky,

Let ruling angels from their spheres be hurled,
Being on being wrecked, and world on world,
Heaven's whole foundations to their center nod,
And Nature tremble to the throne of God:
All this dread ORDER break—for whom? for thee?
Vile worm!—oh, madness, pride, impiety!

9. What if the foot, ordained the dust to tread,
Or hand, to toil, aspired to be the head?
What if the head, the eye, or ear repined
To serve mere engines to the ruling Mind?
Just as absurd, to mourn the tasks or pains,
The great directing MIND of ALL ordains.
   All are but parts of one stupendous whole,
Whose body Nature is, and God the soul;
That, changed through all, and yet in all the same,
Great in the earth, as in the ethereal frame,
Warms in the sun, refreshes in the breeze,
Glows in the stars, and blossoms in the trees,
Lives through all life, extends through all extent,
Spreads undivided, operates unspent,
Breathes in our soul, informs our mortal part,
As full, as perfect, in a hair as heart;
As full, as perfect, in vile man that mourns,
As the rapt seraph that adores and burns;
To him no high, no low, no great, no small;
He fills, he bounds, connects, and equals all.

10. Cease then, nor ORDER imperfection name:
Our proper bliss depends on what we blame.
Know thy own point: this kind, this due degree
Of blindness, weakness, Heaven bestows on thee.
Submit—In this, or any other sphere,
Secure to be as blest as thou canst bear:
Safe in the hand of one disposing Power,
Or in the natal, or the mortal hour.
All Nature is but art, unknown to thee;
All chance, direction, which thou canst not see;
All discord, harmony not understood;
All partial evil, universal good:
And, spite of pride, in erring reason's spite,
One truth is clear: Whatever IS, is RIGHT.

### Epistle 2. Of the Nature and State of Man With Respect to Himself, as an Individual

1. Know then thyself, presume not God to scan;
The proper study of mankind is Man.
Placed on this isthmus of a middle state,
A being darkly wise, and rudely great:
With too much knowledge for the skeptic side,
With too much weakness for the Stoic's pride,
He hangs between; in doubt to act, or rest,
In doubt to deem himself a god, or beast;
In doubt his mind or body to prefer,
Born but to die, and reasoning but to err;
Alike in ignorance, his reason such,
Whether he thinks too little, or too much:

Chaos of thought and passion, all confused;
Still by himself abused, or disabused;
Created half to rise, and half to fall;
Great lord of all things, yet a prey to all;

Sole judge of truth, in endless error hurled:
The glory, jest, and riddle of the world!

• • •

# DAVID HUME

## from *A Treatise of Human Nature*

### Book I

*A Treatise of Human Nature* is a classic text of Western thought, but it was not recognized as such when first published in 1738–1740. Its author, David Hume, lamented that it "fell stillborn from the press." He later revised and republished its two themes, the first on knowledge, in *Enquiries: Concerning Human Understanding* (1748), and the second on ethics, in *Concerning Principles of Morals* (1751). These works helped make Hume the greatest philosophical mind of his day. His skepticism, however, soon led to the defeat of the Enlightenment's optimistic rationalism and thus opened the door to Romanticism (see Rousseau's *Confessions*). Today, *A Treatise on Human Nature* is recognized as a revolutionary work of ideas.

Hume's argument in this treatise is subversive; he undermines that which he claims to defend. He begins in the critical spirit of the Age of Reason and ends up advocating skepticism. He follows the empirical ("knowledge comes from experience") method of the English thinker John Locke. Revising Locke's dictum that all "ideas" in the mind are first in the senses, he denies the existence of "the mind," holding that it is simply a grabbag of mental images. He then shows that Locke's dictum leads, not to certainty, but to solipsism, the belief that all that can be known is one's own mental world. Hume reached this conclusion by breaking "ideas" down into (a) sense impressions and (b) mental images formed as a result of these impressions. Thus, two worlds exist: the subjective world, which can be known and worked with but which contains no guarantee of its objective truth, and the external world which is perceived, if at all, through a screen of "ideas."

Hume also applied his empirical-skeptical method to causality, the idea that one event in the world "causes" another. He knew that such reasoning was typical of human thinking on empirical matters. In the end, he concluded that cause and effect is not communicated to the mind through the senses; it is merely an assumption made about the world. In reality, the notion of causality rests on habit. Later thinkers have found it difficult to refute Hume's skepticism.

David Hume (1711–1776) was controversial for his religious views. His known skepticism kept him from a professor's chair at Edinburgh University. To live in peace, he arranged to have printed after his death the *Dialogues concerning Natural Religion* (1779), an atheistic work which called God "an empty hypothesis."

### Reading the Selection

This selection from Book I of *A Treatise of Human Nature* deals with the topic of reason and shows Hume's empirical/skeptical method in action. Like other thinkers of the day, he wanted philosophy to achieve the same level of truth as was done in the sciences, namely, "rules [that] are certain and infallible." He then demonstrated the uncertainty of reason, and claimed "all knowledge degenerates into probability." Thus there is no truth, only skepticism.

Skepticism did not lead Hume to despair. Rather, he claimed to live in ignorance of his theory: "[N]either I, nor any other person was ever sincerely and constantly of that opinion." Elsewhere, Hume makes it plain that his theorizing did not interfere with his own happiness: "I dine, I play a game of back-gammon, I converse, and am merry with my friends; and when . . . I wou'd return to these speculations, they appear so cold, and strain'd, and ridiculous, that I cannot find in my heart to enter into them any further."

---

## Part IV
## Of the Sceptical and Other Systems of Philosophy.

### SECTION I.
### OF SCEPTICISM WITH REGARD TO REASON.

In all demonstrative sciences the rules are certain and infallible; but when we apply them, our fallible and uncertain faculties are very apt to depart from them, and fall into error. We must, therefore, in every reasoning form a new judgment, as a check or controul on our first judgment or belief; and must enlarge our view to comprehend a kind of history of all the instances, wherein our understanding has deceiv'd us, compar'd with those, wherein its testimony was just and true. Our reason must be consider'd as a kind of cause, of which truth is the natural effect; but such-a-one as by the irruption of other causes, and by the inconstancy of our mental powers, may frequently be prevented. By this means all knowledge degenerates into probability; and this probability is greater or less, according to our experience of the veracity or deceitfulness of our understanding, and according to the simplicity or intricacy of the question.

There is no Algebraist nor Mathematician so expert in his science, as to place entire confidence in any truth immediately upon his discovery of it, or regard it as any thing, but a mere probability. Every time he runs over his proofs, his confidence encreases; but still more by the approbation of his friends; and is rais'd to its utmost perfection by the universal assent and applauses of the learned world. Now 'tis evident, that this gradual encrease of assurance is nothing but the addition of new probabilities, and is deriv'd from the constant union of causes and effects, according to past experience and observation.

In accompts of any length or importance, Merchants seldom trust to the infallible certainty of numbers for their security; but by the artificial structure of the accompts, produce a probability beyond what is deriv'd from the skill and experience of the accomptant. For that is plainly of itself some degree of probability; tho' uncertain and variable, according to the degrees of his experience and length of the accompt. Now as none will maintain, that our assurance in a long numeration exceeds probability, I may safely affirm, that there scarce is any proposition concerning numbers, of which we can have a fuller security. For 'tis easily possible, by gradually diminishing the numbers, to reduce the longest series of addition to the most simple question, which can be form'd, to an addition of two single numbers; and upon this supposition we shall find it impracticable to shew the precise limits of knowledge and of probability, or discover that particular number, at which the one ends and the other begins. But knowledge and probability are of such contrary and disagreeing natures, that they cannot well run insensibly into each other, and that because they will not divide, but

must be either entirely present, or entirely absent. Besides, if any single addition were certain, every one wou'd be so, and consequently the whole or total sum; unless the whole can be different from all its parts. I had almost said, that this was certain; but I reflect, that it must reduce *itself,* as well as every other reasoning, and from knowledge degenerate into probability.

Since therefore all knowledge resolves itself into probability, and becomes at last of the same nature with that evidence, which we employ in common life, we must now examine this latter species of reasoning, and see on what foundation it stands.

In every judgment, which we can form concerning probability, as well as concerning knowledge, we ought always to correct the first judgment, deriv'd from the nature of the object, by another judgment, deriv'd from the nature of the understanding. 'Tis certain a man of solid sense and long experience ought to have, and usually has, a greater assurance in his opinions, than one that is foolish and ignorant, and that our sentiments have different degrees of authority, even with ourselves, in proportion to the degrees of our reason and experience. In the man of the best sense and longest experience, this authority is never entire; since even such-a-one must be conscious of many errors in the past, and must still dread the like for the future. Here then arises a new species of probability to correct and regulate the first, and fix its just standard and proportion. As demonstration is subject to the controul of probability, so is probability liable to a new correction by a reflex act of the mind, wherein the nature of our understanding, and our reasoning from the first probability become our objects.

Having thus found in every probability, beside the original uncertainty inherent in the subject, a new uncertainty deriv'd from the weakness of that faculty, which judges, and having adjusted these two together, we are oblig'd by our reason to add a new doubt deriv'd from the possibility of error in the estimation we make of the truth and fidelity of our faculties. This is a doubt, which immediately occurs to us, and of which, if we wou'd closely pursue our reason, we cannot avoid giving a decision. But this decision, tho' it shou'd be favourable to our preceeding judgment, being founded only on probability, must weaken still further our first evidence, and must itself be weaken'd by a fourth doubt of the same kind, and so on *in infinitum;* till at last there remain nothing of the original probability, however great we may suppose it to have been, and however small the diminution by every new uncertainty. No finite object can subsist under a decrease repeated *in infinitum;* and even the vastest quantity, which can enter into human imagination, must in this manner be reduc'd to nothing. Let our first belief be never so strong, it must infallibly perish by passing thro' so many new examinations, of which each diminishes somewhat of its force and vigour. When I reflect on the natural fallibility of my judgment, I have less confidence in my opinions, than when I only consider the objects concerning which I reason; and when I proceed still farther, to turn the scrutiny against every successive estimation I make of my faculties, all the rules of logic require a continual diminution, and at last a total extinction of belief and evidence.

Shou'd it here be ask'd me, whether I sincerely assent to this argument, which I seem to take such pains to inculcate, and whether I be really one of those sceptics, who hold that all is uncertain, and that our judgment is not in *any* thing possest of *any* measures of truth and falshood; I shou'd reply, that this question is entirely superfluous, and that neither I, nor any other person was ever sincerely and constantly of that opinion. Nature, by an absolute and uncontroulable necessity has determin'd us to judge as well as to breathe and feel; nor can we any more forbear viewing certain objects in a stronger and fuller light, upon account of their customary connexion with a present impression, than we can hinder ourselves from thinking as long as we are awake, or seeing the surrounding bodies, when we turn our eyes towards them in broad sunshine. Whoever has taken the pains to refute the cavils of this *total* scepticism, has really disputed without an antagonist, and endeavour'd by arguments to establish a faculty, which nature has antecedently implanted in the mind, and render'd unavoidable.

My intention then in displaying so carefully the arguments of that fantastic sect, is only to make the reader sensible of the truth of my hypothesis, *that all our reasonings concerning causes and effects are deriv'd from nothing but custom; and that belief is more properly an act of the sensitive, than of the cogitative part of our natures.* . . . .

---

# HENRY FIELDING

## from *The History of Tom Jones*

### Book 9

---

Henry Fielding (1707–1754) did not invent the modern novel—that honor belongs to Cervantes (see *Don Quixote*). Fielding's works, however, were so far advanced in form over their predecessors, such as Defoe's *Robinson Crusoe* (1719) and Richardson's *Pamela* (1740), that he must count as one of its founders. His most innovative work, *The History of Tom Jones, a Foundling* has been called the finest English novel.

Fielding's works were noted for their realism, the hallmark of novels ever since. Modern in spirit, he abhorred the medieval past, the "centuries of monkish dullness when the whole world seems to have been asleep." In his never dull novels, he used real life characters rather than universal types, and he chose historically accurate settings instead of scenes dictated by literary custom. He enhanced his plots' vividness by rooting them in minutely observed time. Rounding out the realism, he narrated his novels in a unique voice which convinced many readers they must be true. Innovations like these helped rid literature of aristocratic heroes and heroines, the West's dominant mode since *The Epic of Gilgamesh*, and allowed the novel to focus on ordinary men and women.

Fielding's novels also reflected the growing power of England's Protestant middle class, who made literature into a marketplace. Only fairly well-off readers, however, could afford to own his novels; *Tom Jones* (1749), for example, cost eighteen shillings, enough money to feed a family for a week. Though an aristocrat, Fielding knew his audience well, having already won success with his plays. In his novels, he gave this public what they wanted: high-spirited entertainments that were basically moralistic and religious in tone.

*Tom Jones* is an eight hundred-page novel of the comic and bawdy exploits of its robust hero. It concerns Jones, a foundling who loses and then regains the respect of those he loves, and, at the same time, uncovers his true identity. Its moral core is Christian—reflected in hatred of liars and hypocrites—but blended with tolerance for sexual sins. Jones, for instance, who is hotblooded, suffers penalties for his indiscretions, but virtue wins in the end. In form, this many-layered novel has characters popping in and out to create surprises as they reappear. This plotting reflects Fielding's dramatic instinct, honed by his years in the theater.

*Reading the Selection*

Book 9, Chapter 3 of *Tom Jones* describes the events at the Upton village inn. Located exactly halfway through the novel—there are eighteen books total—this episode marks a turning point in Jones's career. Jones, after rescuing Mrs. Waters (whose identity will not be revealed until the last book) from attempted rape by Northerton, takes her to safety. A battle takes place, of which the end result is to keep Jones's friend Partridge from seeing Mrs. Waters whom he could identify (wrongly) as Jones's mother. Thus this scene serves to prolong the plot and set up a later (false) recognition scene, when Jones will be identified as Mrs. Waters's abandoned son.

Book 9, Chapter 5 thickens the plot with its hint of incest, as love heats up between Jones and Mrs. Waters. As pointed out above, Partridge (wrongly) thinks that Mrs. Waters is Jones's mother and will make this claim in the last book, before it is disproved. Chapter 5, with its dining/seduction scene, shows also the wordly, teasing, and learned tone of the narrator. This episode was memorably filmed in Stanley Kubrick's *Tom Jones*.

---

### Chapter 3
### The Arrival of Mr Jones, with his Lady, at the Inn; with a very full Description of the Battle of Upton

Tho' the reader, we doubt not, is very eager to know who this lady was, and how she fell into the hands of Mr Northerton; we must beg him to suspend his curiosity for a short time, as we are obliged, for some very good reasons, which hereafter perhaps he may guess, to delay his satisfaction a little longer.

Mr Jones and his fair companion no sooner entered the town, than they went directly to that inn which, in their eyes, presented the fairest appearance to the street. Here Jones, having ordered a servant to shew a room above stairs, was ascending, when the dishevelled fair hastily following, was laid hold on by the master of the house, who cried, 'Hey day, where is that beggar wench going? Stay below stairs, I desire you;' but Jones at that instant thundered from above, 'Let the lady come up,' in so authoritative a voice, that the good man instantly withdrew his hands, and the lady made the best of her way to the chamber.

Here Jones wished her joy of her safe arrival, and then departed, in order, as he promised, to send the landlady up with some cloaths. The poor woman thanked him heartily for all his kindness, and said, she hoped she should see him again soon, to thank him a thousand times more. During this short conversation, she covered her white bosom as well as she could possibly with her arms: for Jones could not avoid stealing a sly peep or two, tho' he took all imaginable care to avoid giving any offence.

Our travellers had happened to take up their residence at a house of exceedingly good repute, whither Irish ladies of strict virtue, and many northern lasses of the same predicament, were accustomed to resort in their way to Bath. The landlady therefore would by no means have admitted any conversation of a disreputable kind to pass under her roof. Indeed so foul and contagious are all such proceedings, that they contaminate the very innocent scenes where they are committed, and give the name of a bad house, or of a house of ill repute, to all those where they are suffered to be carried on.

Not that I would intimate, that such strict chastity as was preserved in the temple of Vesta can possibly be maintained at a public inn. My good landlady did not hope for such a blessing, nor would any of the ladies I have spoken of, or indeed any others of the most rigid note, have expected or insisted on any such thing. But to exclude all vulgar concubinage, and to drive all whores in rags from within the walls, is within the power of everyone. This my landlady very strictly adhered to, and this her virtuous guests, who did not travel in rags, would very reasonably have expected of her.

Now it required no very blameable degree of suspicion, to imagine that Mr Jones and his ragged companion had certain purposes in their intention, which, tho' tolerated in some Christian countries, connived at in others, and practised in all; are however as expressly forbidden as murder, or any other horrid vice, by that religion which is universally believed in those countries. The landlady therefore had no sooner received an intimation of the entrance of the abovesaid persons, than she began to meditate the most expeditious means for their expulsion. In order to do this, she had provided herself with a long and deadly instrument, with which, in times of peace, the chambermaid was wont to demolish the labours of the industrious spider. In vulgar phrase, she had taken up the broomstick, and was just about to sally from the kitchen, when Jones accosted her with a demand of a gown, and other vestments, to cover the half-naked woman above stairs.

Nothing can be more provoking to the human temper, nor more dangerous to that cardinal virtue, patience, than solicitations of extraordinary offices of kindness, on behalf of those very persons with whom we are highly incensed. For this reason Shakespear hath artfully introduced his Desdemona soliciting favours for Cassio of her husband, as the means of enflaming not only his jealousy, but his rage, to the highest pitch of madness; and we find the unfortunate Moor less able to command his passion on this occasion, than even when he beheld his valued present to his wife in the hands of his supposed rival. In fact, we regard these efforts as insults on our understanding, and to such the pride of man is very difficulty brought to submit.

My landlady, though a very good-tempered woman, had, I suppose, some of this pride in her composition; for Jones had scarce ended his request, when she fell upon him with a certain weapon, which, tho' it be neither long, nor sharp, nor hard, nor indeed threatens from its appearance with either death or wound, hath been however held in great dread and abhorrence by many wise men; nay, by many brave ones; insomuch that some who have dared to look into the mouth of a loaded cannon, have not dared to look into a mouth where this weapon was brandished; and rather than run the hazard of its execution, have contented themselves with making a most pitiful and sneaking figure in the eyes of all their acquaintance.

To confess the truth, I am afraid Mr Jones was one of these; for tho' he was attacked and violently belaboured with the aforesaid weapon, he could not be provoked to make any resistance; but in a most cowardly manner applied, with many entreaties, to his antagonist to desist from pursuing her blows: in plain English, he only begged her with the utmost earnestness to hear him; but before he could obtain his request, my landlord himself entered into the fray, and embraced that side of the cause which seemed to stand very little in need of assistance.

There are a sort of heroes who are supposed to be determined in their chusing or avoiding a conflict, by the character and behaviour of the person whom they are to engage. These are said to know their man, and Jones, I believe, knew his woman; for tho' he had been so submissive to her, he was no sooner attacked by her husband, than he demonstrated an immediate spirit of resentment, and enjoined him silence under a very severe penalty; no less than that, I think, of being converted into fuel for his own fire.

The husband, with great indignation, but with a mixture of pity, answered, 'You must pray first to be made able; I believe I am a better man than yourself; ay, every way, that I am;' and presently proceeded to discharge half a dozen whores at the lady above stairs, the last of which had scarce issued from his lips, when a swinging blow from the cudgel that Jones carried in his hand assaulted him over the shoulders.

It is a question whether the landlord or the landlady was the most expeditious in returning this blow. My landlord, whose hands were empty, fell to with his fist, and the good wife, uplifting her broom, and aiming at the head of Jones, had probably put an immediate end to the fray, and to Jones likewise, had not the descent of this broom been prevented,— not by the miraculous intervention of any heathen deity, but by a very natural, tho' fortunate accident; *viz.* by the arrival of Partridge; who entered the house at that instant (for fear had caused him to run every step from the hill) and who, seeing the danger which threatned his master, or companion, (which you chuse to call him) prevented so sad a catastrophe, by catching hold of the landlady's arm, as it was brandished aloft in the air.

The landlady soon perceived the impediment which prevented her blow; and being unable to rescue her arm from the hands of Partridge, she let fall the broom; and then leaving Jones to the discipline of her husband, she fell with the utmost fury on that poor fellow, who had already given some intimation of himself, by crying, 'Zounds! do you intend to kill my friend?'

Partridge, though not much addicted to battle, would not however stand still when his friend was attacked; nor was he much displeased with that part of the combat which fell

to his share: he therefore returned my landlady's blows as soon as he received them; and now the fight was obstinately maintained on all parts, and it seemed doubtful to which side Fortune would incline, when the naked lady, who had listened at the top of the stairs to the dialogue which preceded the engagement, descended suddenly from above, and without weighing the unfair inequality of two to one, fell upon the poor woman who was boxing with Partridge; nor did that great champion desist, but rather redoubled his fury, when he found fresh succours were arrived to his assistance.

Victory must now have fallen to the side of the travellers (for the bravest troops must yield to numbers) had not Susan the chambermaid come luckily to support her mistress. This Susan was as two-handed a wench (according to the phrase) as any in the country, and would, I believe, have beat the famed Thalestris herself, or any of her subject Amazons; for her form was robust and manlike, and every way made for such encounters. As her hands and arms were formed to give blows with great mischief to an enemy, so was her face as well contrived to receive blows without any great injury to herself: her nose being already flat to her face; her lips were so large, that no swelling could be perceived in them, and moreover they were so hard, that a fist could hardly make any impression on them. Lastly, her cheekbones stood out, as if nature had intended them for two bastions to defend her eyes in those encounters for which she seemed so well calculated, and to which she was most wonderfully well inclined.

This fair creature entering the field of battle, immediately filed to that wing where her mistress maintained so unequal a fight with one of either sex. Here she presently challenged Partridge to single combat. He accepted the challenge, and a most desperate fight began between them.

Now the dogs of war being let loose, began to lick their bloody lips; now Victory with golden wings hung hovering in the air. Now Fortune taking her scales from her shelf, began to weight the fates of Tom Jones, his female companion, and Partridge, against the landlord, his wife, and maid; all which hung in exact balance before her; when a good-natured accident put suddenly an end to the bloody fray, with which half of the combatants had already sufficiently feasted. This accident was the arrival of a coach and four; upon which my landlord and landlady immediately desisted from fighting, and at their entreaty obtained the same favour of their antagonists; but Susan was not so kind to Partridge; for that Amazonian fair having overthrown and bestrid her enemy, was now cuffing him lustily with both her hands, without any regard to his request of a cessation of arms, or to those loud exclamations of murder which he roared forth.

No sooner, however, had Jones quitted the landlord, than he flew to the rescue of his defeated companion, from whom he with much difficulty drew off the enraged chambermaid; but Partridge was not immediately sensible of his deliverance; for he still lay flat on the floor, guarding his face with his hands, nor did he cease roaring till Jones had forced him to look up, and to perceive that the battle was at an end.

The landlord who had no visible hurt, and the landlady hiding her well scratched face with her handkerchief, ran both hastily to the door to attend the coach, from which a young lady and her maid now alighted. These the landlady presently ushered into that room, where Mr Jones had at first deposited his fair prize, as it was the best apartment in the house. Hither they were obliged to pass through the field of battle, which they did with the utmost haste, covering their faces with their handkerchiefs, as desirous to avoid the notice of anyone. Indeed their caution was quite unnecessary: for the poor unfortunate Helen, the fatal cause of all the bloodshed, was entirely taken up in endeavouring to conceal her own face, and Jones was no less occupied in rescuing Partridge from the fury of Susan; which being happily effected, the poor fellow immediately departed to the pump to wash his face, and to stop that bloody torrent which Susan had plentifully set a flowing from his nostrils.

• • •

## Chapter 5
### An Apology for all Heroes who have good Stomachs, with a Description of a Battle of the amorous Kind

Heroes, notwithstanding the high ideas, which by the means of flatterers they may entertain of themselves, or the world may conceive of them, have certainly more of mortal than divine about them. However elevated their minds may be, their bodies at least (which is much the major part of most) are liable to the worst infirmities, and subject to the vilest offices of human nature. Among these latter the act of eating, which hath by several wise men been considered as extremely mean and derogatory from the philosophic dignity, must be in some measure performed by the greatest prince, hero, or philosopher upon earth; nay, sometimes nature hath been so frolicksome as to exact of these dignified characters, a much more exorbitant share of this office, than she hath obliged those of the lowest order to perform.

To say the truth, as no known inhabitant of this globe is really more than man, so none need be ashamed of submitting to what the necessities of man demand; but when those great personages I have just mentioned, condescend to aim at confining such low offices to themselves; as when by hoarding or destroying, they seem desirous to prevent any others from eating, they then surely become very low and despicable.

Now after this short preface, we think it no disparagement to our heroe to mention the immoderate ardour with which he laid about him at this season. Indeed it may be doubted, whether Ulysses, who by the way seems to have had the best stomach of all the heroes in that eating poem of the Odyssey, ever made a better meal. Three pounds at least of that flesh which formerly had contributed to the composition of an ox, was now honoured with becoming part of the individual Mr Jones.

This particular we thought ourselves obliged to mention, as it may account for our heroe's temporary neglect of his fair companion; who eat but very little, and was indeed employed in considerations of a very different nature, which passed unobserved by Jones, till he had entirely satisfied that appetite which a fast of twenty-four hours had procured him; but his dinner was no sooner ended, than his attention to other matters revived; with these matters therefore we shall now proceed to acquaint the reader.

Mr Jones, of whose personal accomplishments we have hitherto said very little, was in reality, one of the handsomest young fellows in the world. His face, besides being the picture of health, had in it the most apparent marks of sweetness and good-nature. These qualities were indeed so characteristical in his countenance, that while the spirit and sensibility in his eyes, tho' they must have been perceived by an accurate observer, might have escaped the notice of the less discerning, so strongly was this good-nature painted in his look, that it was remarked by almost everyone who saw him.

It was, perhaps, as much owing to this, as to a very fine complection, that his face had a delicacy in it almost inexpressible, and which might have given him an air rather too effeminate, had it not been joined to a most masculine person and mien; which latter had as much in them of the Hercules, as the former had of the Adonis. He was besides active, genteel, gay, and good-humoured, and had a flow of animal spirits, which enlivened every conversation where he was present.

When the reader hath duly reflected on these many charms which all centered in our heroe, and considers at the same time the fresh obligations which Mrs Waters had to him, it will be a mark of more prudery than candour to entertain a bad opinion of her, because she conceived a very good opinion of him.

But whatever censures may be passed upon her, it is my business to relate matters of fact with veracity. Mrs Waters had, in truth, not only a good opinion of our heroe, but a very great affection for him. To speak out boldly at once, she was in love, according to the present universally received sense of that phrase, by which love is applied indiscriminately to the desirable objects of all our passions, appetites, and senses, and is understood to be that preference which we give to one kind of food rather than to another.

But tho' the love to these several objects may possibly be one and the same in all cases, its operations however must be allowed to be different; for how much soever we may be in love with an excellent surloin of beef, or bottle of Burgundy; with a damask rose, or Cremona fiddle; yet do we never smile, nor ogle, nor dress, nor flatter, nor endeavour by any other arts or tricks to gain the affection of the said beef, &c. Sigh indeed we sometimes may; but it is generally in the absence, not in the presence of the beloved object. For otherwise we might possibly complain of their ingratitude and deafness, with the same reason as Pasiphae doth of her bull, whom she endeavoured to engage by all the coquetry practised with good success in the drawing-room, on the much more sensible, as well as tender, hearts of the fine gentlemen there.

The contrary happens, in that love which operates between persons of the same species, but of different sexes. Here we are no sooner in love, than it becomes our principal care to engage the affection of the object beloved. For what other purpose indeed are our youth instructed in all the arts of rendering themselves agreeable? If it was not with a view to this love, I question whether any of those trades which deal in setting off and adorning the human person would procure a livelihood. Nay, those great polishers of our manners, who are by some thought to teach what principally distinguishes us from the brute creation, even dancing-masters themselves, might possibly find no place in society.

In short, all the graces which young ladies and young gentlemen too learn from others; and the many improvements which, by the help of a looking-glass, they add of their own, are in reality those very *spicula & faces amoris,* so often mentioned by Ovid; or, as they are sometimes called in our own language, *the whole artillery of love.*

Now Mrs Waters and our heroe had no sooner sat down together, than the former began to play this artillery upon the latter. But here, as we are about to attempt a description hitherto unessayed either in prose or verse, we think proper to invoke the assistance of certain aerial beings, who will, we doubt not, come kindly to our aid on this occasion.

'Say then, you Graces, you that inhabit the heavenly mansions of Seraphina's countenance; for you are truly divine, are always in her presence, and well know all the arts of charming; say, what were the weapons now used to captivate the heart of Mr Jones.'

'First, from two lovely blue eyes, whose bright orbs flashed lightning at their discharge, flew forth two pointed ogles. But happily for our heroe, hit only a vast piece of beef which he was then conveying into his plate, and harmless spent their force. The fair warrior perceived their miscarriage, and immediately from her fair bosom drew forth a deadly sigh. A sigh, which none could have heard unmoved, and which was sufficient at once to have swept off a dozen beaus; so soft, so sweet, so tender, that the insinuating air must have found its subtle way to the heart of our heroe, had it not luckily been driven from his ears by the coarse bubbling of some bottled ale, which at that time he was pouring forth. Many other weapons did she assay; but the God of Eating (if there be any such deity; for I do not confidently assert it) preserved his votary; or perhaps it may not be *dignus vindice nodus,* and the present security of Jones may be accounted for by natural means: for as love frequently preserves from the attacks of hunger, so may hunger possibly, in some cases, defend us against love.

'The fair one, enraged at her frequent disappointments, determined on a short cessation of arms. Which interval she employed in making ready every engine of amorous warfare for the renewing of the attack, when dinner should be over.

'No sooner then was the cloth removed, than she again began her operations. First, having planted her right eye sideways against Mr Jones, she shot from its corner a most penetrating glance; which, tho' great part of its force was spent before it reached our heroe, did not vent itself absolutely without effect. This the fair one perceiving, hastily withdrew her eyes, and leveled them downwards as if she was concerned for what she had done: tho' by this means she designed only to draw him from his guard, and indeed to open his eyes, through which she intended to surprize his heart. And now, gently lifting up those two bright orbs which had already begun to make an impression on poor Jones, she discharged a volley of small charms at once from her whole countenance in a smile. Not a smile of mirth, nor of joy; but a smile of affection, which most ladies have always ready at their command, and which serves them to show at once their good-humour, their pretty dimples, and their white teeth.

'This smile our heroe received full in his eyes, and was immediately staggered with its force. He then began to see the designs of the enemy, and indeed to feel their success. A parley now was set on foot between the parties; during which the artful fair so slily and imperceptibly carried on her attack, that she had almost subdued the heart of our heroe, before she again repaired to acts of hostility. To confess the truth, I am afraid Mr Jones maintained a kind of Dutch defence, and treacherously delivered up the garrison, without duly weighing his allegiance to the fair Sophia. In short, no sooner had the amorous parley ended, and the lady had unmasked the royal battery, by carelessly letting her handkerchief drop from her neck, than the heart of Mr Jones was entirely taken, and the fair conqueror enjoyed the usual fruits of her victory.'

Here the Graces think proper to end their description, and here we think proper to end the chapter.

---

# VOLTAIRE

## from *Candide*

---

Voltaire's *Candide* was the most popular novel of the Age of Reason. It is a delightful, sometimes bawdy tale which satirizes the follies of the Western world of the time. Presumably because of fear that the sharp satire might give offense in certain quarters, Voltaire is nowhere identified as the book's author. Instead, its title page says simply, "Translated from the German by Dr. Ralph''—a disguise which fooled no one, as readers recognized Voltaire's biting wit and deft touch. After two hundred years, *Candide* survives as one of the best loved fictional works in the world.

That Voltaire's novel survives is surprising, since it is a satire on topical events, and such satires are thought to grow stale as quickly as today's newspaper. What saves it from the dustbin of history is its glowing style—lighthearted, worldly, and sly—and the fact that most modern Westerners see the world much as Voltaire did. Who today does not share Voltaire's hatred of slavery, war, snobbery, religious persecution, and crooked clergy, or his skepticism about divine kings and utopian societies? Of course, not all of the satire works today, as in the anti-Semitic jokes and the portrayal of women as fickle. Still, the novel charms most readers as it pays homage to humanity's unsinkable spirit.

*Candide* is the story of the education of its naive hero, Candide, as he moves from Westphalia, a province in Prussia, across much of the Western world, including South America. What drives Candide's odyssey is the hope of marrying the lovely Cunegonde, a Westphalian baroness, who keeps slipping from his grasp. Despite Candide's love for Cunegonde, the novel is not a love story, since their troubles are treated as comedy. Instead, it is a novel of ideas whose characters, except for Candide, show little or no growth and simply express Voltaire's point of view.

The novel is subtitled *Optimism,* and it was facile optimism that aroused Voltaire's anger. Facile optimism, derived from the German thinker Leibniz, denies that evil exists and insists that the world is basically good. In the novel, Leibniz is represented by Pangloss [from Greek, "all tongue"], who, faced with constant trials, offers this advice: "This is the best of all possible worlds." Pangloss's opposite is Martin, a facile pessimist who thinks all happens for the worst. In the end, Candide rejects both rival philosophies, opting instead for pragmatism: "We must cultivate our gardens."

Voltaire (1694–1778) (born Francois Marie Arouet) dominated his age unlike any writer before or since. A universal genius, he wrote tragedies, poems, essays, novels, histories, dictionaries, letters, memoirs, philosophical treatises, and a work popularizing science. Of this vast work, very little is widely read today, except for *Candide.* Voltaire's spirit survives in the term *Voltarean,* meaning a skeptic yet one who tolerates all religious points of view.

### Reading the Selection

This selection, consisting of the novel's first six chapters, covers Candide's travel from Westphalia to Lisbon, where he barely survives an auto da fé—an "act of faith" in which heretics are persecuted. As calamities rain down on Candide, faithful Pangloss offers his optimistic bromides. Pangloss's litany quickly becomes absurd, though not to Candide. Voltaire's moral is the radiant belief that, faced with all of life's miseries, Candide and the other characters may fall into despair but never for long.

----

### Chapter I
### How Candide was brought up in a beautiful country house, and how he was driven away

There lived in Westphalia, at the country seat of Baron Thunder-ten-tronckh, a young lad blessed by nature with the most agreeable manners. You could read his character in his face. He combined sound judgment with unaffected simplicity; and that, I suppose, was why he was called Candide. The old family servants suspected that he was the son of the Baron's sister by a worthy gentleman of that neighbourhood, whom the young lady would never agree to marry because he could only claim seventy-one quarterings, the rest of his family tree having suffered from the ravages of time.

The Baron was one of the most influential noblemen in Westphalia, for his house had a door and several windows and his hall was actually draped with tapestry. Every dog in the courtyard was pressed into service when he went hunting, and his grooms acted as whips. The village curate was his private chaplain. They all called him Your Lordship, and laughed at his jokes.

The Baroness, whose weight of about twenty-five stone made her a person of great importance, entertained with a dignity which won her still more respect. Her daughter, Cunégonde, was a buxom girl of seventeen with a fresh, rosy complexion; altogether seductive. The Baron's son was in every way worthy of his father. His tutor, Pangloss, was the recognised authority in the household on all matters of learning, and young Candide listened to his teaching with that unhesitating faith which marked his age and character.

Pangloss taught metaphysico-theologo-cosmolo-nigology. He proved incontestably that there is no effect without a cause, and that in this best of all possible worlds, his lordship's country seat was the most beautiful of mansions and her ladyship the best of all possible ladyships.

'It is proved,' he used to say, 'that things cannot be other than they are, for since everything was made for a purpose, it follows that everything is made for the best purpose. Observe: our noses were made to carry spectacles, so we have spectacles. Legs were clearly intended for breeches, and we wear them. Stones were meant for carving and for building houses, and that is why my lord has a most beautiful house; for the greatest baron in Westphalia ought to have the noblest residence. And since pigs were made to be eaten, we eat pork all the year round. It follows that those who maintain that all is right talk nonsense; they ought to say that all is for the best.'

Candide listened attentively, and with implicit belief; for he found Lady Cunégonde extremely beautiful, though he never had the courage to tell her so. He decided that the height of good fortune was to have been born Baron Thunder-ten-tronckh and after that to be Lady Cunégonde. The next was to see her every day, and failing that to listen to his master Pangloss, the greatest philosopher in Westphalia, and consequently the greatest in all the world.

One Day Cunégonde was walking near the house in a little coppice, called 'the park', when she saw Dr. Pangloss behind some bushes giving a lesson in experimental physics to her mother's waiting-woman, a pretty little brunette who seemed eminently teachable. Since Lady Cunégonde took a great interest in science, she watched the experiments being repeated with breathless fascination. She saw clearly the Doctor's 'sufficient reason', and took note of cause and effect. Then, in a disturbed and thoughtful state of mind, she returned home filled with a desire for learning, and fancied that she could reason equally well with young Candide and he with her.

On her way home she met Candide, and blushed. Candide blushed too. Her voice was choked with emotion as she greeted him, and Candide spoke to her without knowing what he said. The following day, as they were leaving the dinner table, Cunégonde and Candide happened to meet behind a screen. Cunégonde dropped her handkerchief, and Candide picked it up. She quite innocently took his hand, he as innocently kissed hers with singular grace and ardour. Their lips met, their eyes flashed, their knees trembled, and their hands would not keep still. Baron Thunder-ten-tronckh, happening to pass the screen at that moment, noticed both cause and effect, and drove Candide from the house with powerful kicks on the backside. Cunégonde fainted, and on recovering her senses was boxed on the ears by the Baroness. Thus consternation reigned in the most beautiful and delightful of all possible mansions.

## Chapter II
## What happened to Candide amongst the Bulgars

After being turned out of this earthly paradise, Candide wandered off without thinking which way he was going. As he plodded along he wept, glancing sometimes towards heaven, but more often in the direction of the most beautiful of houses, which contained the loveliest of barons' daughters. He lay down for the night in the furrow of a ploughed field with snow falling in thick flakes; and, to make matters worse, he had nothing to eat. Next day, perished with cold and hunger, and without a penny in his pocket, he dragged his weary limbs to a neighboring town called Waldberghoff-trarbk-dikdorff, where he stopped at an inn and cast a pathetic glance towards the door.

Two men in blue noticed him.

'There's a well-made young fellow, chum,' said one to the other, 'and just the height we want.'

They went up to Candide and politely asked him to dine with them.

'Gentlemen,' said Candide modestly, 'I deeply appreciate the honour, but I haven't enough money to pay my share.'

'People of your appearance and merit, Sir, never pay anything,' said one of the men in blue; 'aren't you five feet five inches tall?'

'Yes, gentlemen, that is my height,' said Candide, with a bow.

'Very well, Sir, sit down; we'll pay your share, and what's more we shall not allow a man like you to go short of money. That's what men are for, to help each other.'

'You are quite right,' said Candide; 'for that is what Mr. Pangloss used to tell me. I am convinced by your courteous behaviour that all is for the best.'

His new companions then asked him to accept a few shillings. Candide took them gratefully and wanted to give a receipt; but his offer was brushed aside, and they all sat down to table.

'Are you not a devoted admirer . . . ?' began one of the men in blue.

'Indeed I am,' said Candide earnestly, 'I am a devoted admirer of Lady Cunégonde.'

'No doubt,' replied the man; 'but what we want to know is whether you are a devoted admirer of the King of the Bulgars.'

'Good Heavens, no!' said Candide; 'I've never seen him.'

'Oh, but he is the most amiable of kings and we must drink his health.'

'By all means, gentlemen,' replied Candide, and emptied his glass.

'That's enough,' they cried. 'You are now his support and defender, and a Bulgar hero into the bargain. Your fortune is made. Go where glory waits you.'

And with that they clapped him into irons and hauled him off to the barracks. There he was taught 'right turn', 'left turn', and 'quick march', 'slope arms' and 'order arms', how to aim and how to fire, and was given thirty strokes of the 'cat'. Next day his performance on parade was a little better, and he was given only twenty strokes. The following day he received a mere ten and was thought a prodigy by his comrades.

The bewildered Candide was still rather in the dark about his heroism. One fine spring morning he took it into his head to decamp and walked straight off, thinking it a privilege common to man and beast to use his legs when he wanted. But he had not gone six miles before he was caught, bound, and thrown into a dungeon by four other six-foot heroes. At the court martial he was graciously permitted to choose between being flogged thirty-six times by the whole regiment or having twelve bullets in his brain. It was useless to declare his belief in Free Will and say he wanted neither; he had to make his choice. So, exercising that divine gift called Liberty, he decided to run the gauntlet thirty-six times, and survived two floggings. The regiment being two thousand strong, he received four thousand strokes, which exposed every nerve and muscle from the nape of his neck to his backside. The course had been set for the third heat, but Candide could endure no more and begged them to do him the kindness of beheading him instead. The favour was granted, his eyes were bandaged, and he was made to kneel down. The King of the Bulgars passed by at that moment and asked what crime the culprit had committed. Since the King was a man of great insight, he recognised from what he was told about

Candide that here was a young philosopher utterly ignorant of the way of the world, and granted him a pardon, an exercise of mercy which will be praised in every newspaper and in every age. Candide was cured in three weeks by a worthy surgeon with ointments originally prescribed by Dioscorides; and he had just enough skin on his feet to walk, when the King of the Bulgars joined battle with the King of the Abars.

### Chapter III
### How Candide escaped from the Bulgars, and what happened to him afterwards

Those who have never seen two well-trained armies drawn up for battle, can have no idea of the beauty and brilliance of the display. Bugles, fifes, oboes, drums, and salvoes of artillery produced such a harmony as Hell itself could not rival. The opening barrage destroyed about six thousand men on each side. Rifle-fire which followed rid this best of worlds of about nine or ten thousand villains who infested its surface. Finally, the bayonet provided 'sufficient reason' for the death of several thousand more. The total casualties amounted to about thirty thousand. Candide trembled like a philosopher, and hid himself as best he could during this heroic butchery.

When all was over and the rival kings were celebrating their victory with Te Deums in their respective camps, Candide decided to find somewhere else to pursue his reasoning into cause and effect. He picked his way over piles of dead and dying, and reached a neighbouring village on the Abar side of the border. It was now no more than a smoking ruin, for the Bulgars had burned it to the ground in accordance with the terms of international law. Old men, crippled with wounds, watched helplessly the death-throes of their butchered women-folk, who still clasped their children to their bloodstained breasts. Girls who had satisfied the appetites of several heroes lay disembowelled in their last agonies. Others, whose bodies were badly scorched, begged to be put out of their misery. Whichever way he looked, the ground was strewn with the legs, arms, and brains of dead villagers.

Candide made off as quickly as he could to another village. This was in Bulgar territory, and had been treated in the same way by Abar heroes. Candide walked through the ruins over heaps of writhing bodies and at last left the theatre of war behind him. He had some food in his knapsack, and his thoughts still ran upon Lady Cunégonde. His provisions were exhausted by the time he reached Holland, but as he had heard that everyone in that country was rich and all were Christians, he had no doubt that he would be treated as kindly as he had been at Castle Thunder-ten-tronckh before Lady Cunégonde's amorous glances caused his banishment.

He appealed for alms from several important-looking people, who all told him that if he persisted in begging he would be sent to a reformatory to be taught how to earn his daily bread.

At last he approached a man who had just been addressing a big audience for a whole hour on the subject of charity. The orator peered at him, and said:

'What is your business here? Do you support the Good Old Cause?'

'There is no effect without a cause,' replied Candide modestly. 'All things are necessarily connected and arranged for the best. It was my fate to be driven from Lady Cunégonde's presence and made to run the gauntlet, and now I have to beg my bread until I can earn it. Things could not have happened otherwise.'

'Do you believe that the Pope is Antichrist, my friend?' said the minister.

'I have never heard anyone say so,' replied Candide; 'but whether he is or he isn't I want some food.'

'You don't deserve to eat,' said the other. 'Be off with you, you villain, you wretch! Don't come near me again or you'll suffer for it.'

The minister's wife looked out the window at that moment, and seeing a man who was not sure that the Pope was Antichrist, emptied over his head a pot full of . . . , which shows to what lengths ladies are driven by religious zeal.

A man who had never been christened, a worthy Anabaptist called James, had seen the cruel and humiliating treatment of his brother man, a creature without wings but with two legs and a soul; he brought him home and washed him, gave him some bread and beer and a couple of florins, and even offered to apprentice him to his business of manufacturing those Persian silks that are made in Holland. Candide almost fell at his feet.

'My tutor, Pangloss, was quite right,' he exclaimed, 'when he told me that all is for the best in this world of ours, for your generosity moves me much more than the harshness of that gentleman in the black gown and his wife.'

While taking a walk the next day, Candide met a beggar covered with sores. His eyes were lifeless, the end of his nose had rotted away, his mouth was all askew and his teeth were black. His voice was sepulchral, and a violent cough tormented him, at every bout of which he spat out a tooth.

### Chapter IV
### How Candide met his old tutor, Dr. Pangloss, and what came of it

Candide was moved more by compassion than by horror at the sight of this ghastly scarecrow, and gave him the two florins he had received from James, the honest Anabaptist. The apparition looked at him intently and, with tears starting to his eyes, fell on the young man's neck. Candide drew back in terror.

'Does this mean,' said one wretch to the other, 'that you don't recognize your dear Pangloss any more?'

'Pangloss!' cried Candide. 'Can this be my beloved master in such a shocking state! What misfortune has befallen you? What has driven you from the most lovely of mansions? What has happened to Lady Cunégonde, that pearl among women, the masterpiece of nature?'

'My breath fails me,' murmured Pangloss.

At this Candide quickly led him to the Anabaptist's stable, where he made him eat some bread, and as soon as he had revived, said to him:

'You mentioned Cunégonde?'

'She is dead,' replied the other.

At these words Candide fainted, but his friend restored him to his senses with a little sour vinegar which happened to be in the stable. Candide opened his eyes.

'Cunégonde is dead!' said he. 'Oh, what has become of the best of worlds? . . . But what did she die of? No doubt it was grief at seeing me sent flying from her father's lovely mansion at the point of a jack-boot?'

'No,' said Pangloss. 'She was disembowelled by Bulgar soldiers after being ravished as much as a poor woman could bear. When my lord tried to defend her, they broke his head. Her ladyship was cut into small pieces, and my poor pupil treated in precisely the same way as his sister. As for the house, not one stone was left standing on another; not a barn was left, not a sheep, not a duck, not a tree. But we have been amply avenged, for the Abars did just the same in a neighbouring estate which belonged to a Bulgar nobleman.'

At this tale Candide fainted once more. When he recovered his senses, he first said all that was called for, and then enquired into cause and effect, and into the 'sufficient reason' that had reduced Pangloss to such a pitiable state.

'I fear it is love,' said his companion; 'love, the comforter of humanity, the preserver of the universe, the soul of all living beings; tender love!'

'I know what this love is,' said Candide, with a shake of his head, 'this sovereign of hearts and quintessence of our souls: my entire reward has been a kiss and twenty kicks on the backside. But how could such a beautiful cause produce so hideous an effect upon you?'

'My dear Candide,' replied Pangloss, 'you remember Paquette, that pretty girl who used to wait on our noble lady. In her arms I tasted the delights of Paradise, and they produced these hellish torments by which you see me devoured. She was infected, and now perhaps she is dead. Paquette was given this present by a learned Franciscan, who had traced it back to its source. He had had it from an old countess, who had had it from a cavalry officer, who was indebted for it to a marchioness. She took it from her page, and he had received it from a Jesuit who, while still a novice, had had it in direct line from one of the companions of Christopher Columbus. As for me, I shall not give it to anyone, for I am a dying man.'

'What a strange genealogy, Pangloss!' exclaimed Candide. 'Isn't the devil at the root of it?'

'Certainly not,' replied the great man. 'It is indispensable in this best of worlds. It is a necessary ingredient. For if Columbus, when visiting the West Indies, had not caught this disease, which poisons the source of generation, which frequently even hinders generation, and is clearly opposed to the great end of Nature, we should have neither chocolate nor cochineal. We see, too, that to this very day the disease, like religious controversy, is peculiar to us Europeans. The Turks, the Indians, the Persians, the Chinese, the Siamese, the Japanese as yet have no knowledge of it; but there is a 'sufficient reason' for their experiencing it in turn in the course of a few centuries. Meanwhile, it has made remarkable progess amongst us, and most of all in these huge armies of honest, well-trained mercenaries, who decide the destinies of nations. It can safely be said that when thirty thousand men are ranged against an army of equal numbers, there will be about twenty thousand infected with pox on each side.'

'I could listen to you for ever,' said Candide; 'but you must be cured.'

'How can I be cured?' said Pangloss. 'I haven't a penny, my dear friend, and there is not a doctor in all this wide world who will bleed you or purge you without a fee.'

This last remark decided Candide. He hurried to James, the charitable Anabaptist, and, falling at his feet, painted so moving a picture of the state to which his friend had been reduced that the good man did not hesitate to take Dr. Pangloss in and had him cured at his own expense. During treatment, Pangloss lost only an eye and an ear. He still wrote well and had a perfect command of arithmetic, so the Anabaptist appointed him his accountant. Two months later he was obliged to go to Lisbon on business and set sail in his own ship, taking the two philosophers with him. On the voyage Pangloss explained to him how all was designed for the best. James did not share this view.

'Men,' he said, 'must have somewhat altered the course of nature; for they were not born wolves, yet they have become wolves. God did not give them twenty-four-pounders or bayonets, yet they have made themselves bayonets and guns to destroy each other. In the same category I place not only bankruptcies, but the law which carries off the bankrupts' effects, so as to defraud their creditors.'

'More examples of the indispensable!' remarked the one-eyed doctor. 'Private misfortunes contribute to the general good, so that the more private misfortunes there are, the more we find that all is well.'

While he was pursuing his argument the sky became overcast, the winds blew from the four corners of the earth, and the ship was caught in a most terrible storm in sight of the port of Lisbon.

## Chapter V
### Describing tempest, shipwreck, and earthquake, and what happened to Dr. Pangloss, Candide, and James, the Anabaptist

Half the passengers were at the last gasp of nervous and physical exhaustion from the pitching and tossing of the vessel, and were so weak that they had no strength left to realise their danger. The other half uttered cries of alarm and said their prayers, for the sails were torn, the masts were broken, and the ship was splitting. Work as they might, all were sixes and sevens, for there was no one to take command. The Anabaptist gave what help he could in directing the ship's course, and was on the poop when a madly excited sailor struck him a violent blow, which laid him at full length on the deck. The force of his blow upset the sailor's own balance, and he fell head first overboard; but, in falling, he was caught on a piece of the broken mast and hung dangling over the ship's side. The worthy James ran to his assistance and helped him to climb on board again. The efforts he made were so strenuous, however, that he was pitched into the sea in full view of the sailor, who left him to perish without taking the slightest notice. Candide was in time to see his benefactor reappear above the surface for one moment before being swallowed up for ever. He wanted to throw himself into the sea after the Anabaptist, but the great philosopher, Pangloss, stopped him by proving that Lisbon harbour was made on purpose for this Anabaptist to drown there. Whilst he was proving this from first principles, the ship split in two and all perished except Pangloss, Candide, and the brutal sailor who had been the means of drowning the honest Anabapist. The villain swam successfully to shore; and Pangloss and Candide, clinging to a plank, were washed up after him.

When they had recovered a little of their strength, they set off towards Lisbon, hoping they had just enough money in their pockets to avoid starvation after escaping the storm.

Scarcely had they reached the town, and were still mourning their benefactor's death, when they felt the earth tremble beneath them. The sea boiled up in the harbour and broke the ships which lay at anchor. Whirlwinds of flame and ashes covered the streets and squares. Houses came crashing down. Roofs toppled on to their foundations, and the foundations crumbled. Thirty thousand men, women and children were crushed to death under the ruins.

The sailor chuckled:

'There'll be something worth picking up here,' he remarked with an oath.

'What can be the "sufficient reason" for this phenomenon?' said Pangloss.

'The Day of Judgment has come,' cried Candide.

The sailor rushed straight into the midst of the debris and risked his life searching for money. Having found some, he ran off with it to get drunk; and after sleeping off the effects of the wine, he bought the favours of the first girl of easy virtue he met amongst the ruined houses with the dead and dying all around. Pangloss pulled him by the sleeve and said:

'This will never do, my friend; you are not obeying the universal rule of Reason; you have misjudged the occasion.'

'Bloody hell,' replied the other. 'I am a sailor and was born in Batavia. I have had to trample on the crucifix four times in various trips I've been to Japan. I'm not the man for your Universal Reason!'

Candide had been wounded by splinters of flying masonry and lay helpless in the road, covered with rubble.

'For Heaven's sake,' he cried to Pangloss, 'fetch me some wine and oil! I am dying.'

'This earthquake is nothing new,' replied Pangloss; 'the town of Lima in America experienced the same shocks last year. The same causes produce the same effects. There is certainly a vein of sulphur running under the earth from Lima to Lisbon.'

'Nothing is more likely,' said Candide; 'but oil and wine, for pity's sake!'

'Likely!' exclaimed the philosopher. 'I maintain it's proved!'

Candide lost consciousness, and Pangloss brought him a little water from a fountain close by.

The following day, while creeping amongst the ruins, they found something to eat and recruited their strength. They then set to work with the rest to relieve those inhabitants who had escaped death. Some of the citizens whom they had helped gave them as good a dinner as could be managed after such a disaster. The meal was certainly a sad affair, and the guests wept as they ate; but Pangloss consoled them with the assurance that things could not be otherwise:

'For all this,' said he, 'is a manifestation of the rightness of things, since if there is a volcano at Lisbon it could not be anywhere else. For it is impossible for things not to be where they are, because everything is for the best.'

A little man in black, an officer of the Inquisition, who was sitting beside Pangloss, turned to him and politely said:

'It appears, Sir, that you do not believe in original sin; for if all is for the best, there can be no such thing as the fall of Man and eternal punishment.'

'I most humbly beg your Excellency's pardon,' replied Pangloss, still more politely, 'but I must point out that the fall of Man and eternal punishment enter, of Necessity, into the scheme of the best of all possible worlds.'

'Then you don't believe in Free Will, Sir?' said the officer.

'Your Excellency must excuse me,' said Pangloss; 'Free Will is consistent with Absolute Necessity, for it was ordained that we should be free. For the Will that is Determined . . . '

Pangloss was in the middle of his sentence when the officer nodded to his henchman, who was pouring him out a glass of port wine.

## Chapter VI
### How a magnificent auto-da-fé was staged to prevent further earthquakes, and how Candide was flogged

The University of Coimbra had pronounced that the sight of a few people ceremoniously burned alive before a slow fire was an infallible prescription for preventing earthquakes; so when the earthquake had subsided after destroying three-quarters of Lisbon, the authorities of that country could find no surer means of avoiding total ruin than by giving the people a magnificent auto-da-fé.

They therefore seized a Basque, convicted of marrying his godmother, and two Portuguese Jews who had refused to eat bacon with their chicken; and after dinner Dr. Pangloss and his pupil, Candide, were arrested as well, one for speaking and the other for listening with an air of approval. Pangloss and Candide were led off separately and closeted in exceedingly cool rooms, where they suffered no inconvenience from the sun, and were brought out a week later to be dressed in sacrificial cassocks and paper mitres. The decorations on Candide's mitre and cassock were penitential in character, inverted flames and devils without tails or claws; but Pangloss's devils had tails and claws, and his flames were upright. They were then marched in procession, clothed in these robes, to hear a moving sermon followed by beautiful music in counterpoint. Candide was flogged in time with the anthem; the Basque and the two men who refused to eat bacon were burnt; and Pangloss was hanged, though that was not the usual practice on those occasions. The same day another earthquake occurred and caused tremendous havoc.

The terrified Candide stood weltering in blood and trembling with fear and confusion.

'If this is the best of all possible worlds,' he said to himself, 'what can the rest be like? Had it only been a matter of flogging, I should not have questioned it, for I have had that before from the Bulgars. But when it comes to my dear Pangloss being hanged—the greatest of philosophers—I must know the reason why. And was it part of the scheme of things that my dear Anabaptist (the best of men!) should be drowned in sight of land? And Lady Cunégonde, that

pearl amongst women! Was it really necessary for her to be disembowelled?'

He had been preached at, flogged, absolved, and blessed, and was about to stagger away, when an old woman accosted him and said:

'Pull yourself together, young man, and follow me.'

---

# JEAN-JACQUES ROUSSEAU
## from *Confessions*

### Book One
### 1712–1719

---

Voltaire (see *Candide*) dominated the Age of Reason, but, from today's vantage point, he takes second place to the Swiss thinker Rousseau, whose literary works significantly reshaped the West. Rousseau's works were often greeted with cries for his exile or arrest but most of his causes are now familiar parts of the modern landscape. For example, he is often credited with the "discovery" of childhood; for, in *Emile* (1761), he was one of the first to urge school reform based on graded stages of child development. In *The New Heloise* (1762), he pioneered the idea that marriages should be based on love and not simply be arranged, and, in *The Social Contract* (1762), he established the principles of modern direct democracy. His spirit foreshadowed the Romantic cultural movement, notably in *The Reveries of the Solitary Walker* (1792), a veritable anthology of what later became Romantic clichés about God in Nature. Finally, he was a Marxist before Marx, calling property the root of social inequality (*The Second Discourse*, 1755).

Jean-Jacques Rousseau (1712–1778) seemed to have his finger on the pulse of Western culture, perhaps because he was guided by his inner voice. That voice, contradictory and passionate, may still be heard speaking from the pages of his autobiography, *Confessions* (1781). Like almost everything Rousseau touched, the autobiography left a revolution in its wake. Other writers had taken themselves as subjects, most notably Augustine (see *Confessions*) and Montaigne (see *Essays*), but no one before Rousseau had written with such uncensored frankness. Rousseau's work pointed the way for modern confessional writing, in both autobiography and fiction; it inspired writers to search their childhoods for patterns that shaped their maturity (see Wordsworth's "Tintern Abbey" and Thoreau's *Walden*).

### Reading the Selection

This selection from the *Confessions* covers Rousseau's life from birth to seven years of age. It is memorable for establishing Rousseau's unique voice. The voice is obsessive, as shown by seventeen instances of "I," "my," or "myself" in the first seven sentences; self-pitying, as in the story of his birth which "cost my mother her life"; and emotional in both language ("cry," "groan," "romantic") and behavior (his exaggerated love of novels). The voice is also self-dramatizing, convinced that the world is listening, as when he imagines the Last Judgment with "numberless . . . men gather[ed] round me, [to] hear my confessions."

Rousseau presents himself as a "judge-penitent"; that is, he confesses to a moral weakness and then turns around and judges himself better than others for having exposed his own failing. In effect, he aims at moral power by revealing his sins. This pattern is in the Last Judgment fantasy, when he admits to "depravities," and then says that no witness to his recital can say, " 'I was a better man than he.' " This behavior, an outgrowth of his Calvinist faith, is the central motif of the *Confessions*. It leads him to reveal sexual hang-ups, religious vacillation, and a decision to place his five offspring in an orphanage as soon as each was born. The "judge-penitent" motif is confirmed at the end when he warns that anyone who doubts his honor, "even if he has not read my writings . . . deserves to be stifled."

Rousseau was a superb prose stylist who was fond of pithy sayings, or aphorisms, which, when taken out of context, could lead to misunderstandings. Two aphorisms appear here: "I felt before I thought" and "I had grasped nothing; I had sensed everything."

---

I have resolved on an enterprise which has no precedent, and which, once complete, will have no imitator. My purpose is to display to my kind a portrait in every way true to nature, and the man I shall portray will be myself.

Simply myself. I know my own heart and understand my fellow man. But I am made unlike any one I have ever met; I will even venture to say that I am like no one in the whole world. I may be no better, but at least I am different. Whether Nature did well or ill in breaking the mould in which she formed me, is a question which can only be resolved after the reading of my book.

Let the last trump sound when it will, I shall come forward with this work in my hand, to present myself before my Sovereign Judge, and proclaim aloud: 'Here is what I have done, and if by chance I have used some immaterial embellishment it has been only to fill a void due to a defect of memory. I may have taken for fact what was no more than probability, but I have never put down as true what I knew to be false. I have displayed myself as I was, as vile and despicable when my behaviour was such, as good, generous, and noble when I was so. I have bared my secret soul as Thou thyself hast seen it, Eternal Being! So let the numberless legion of my fellow men gather round me, and hear my confessions. Let them groan at my depravities, and blush for my misdeeds. But let each one of them reveal his heart at the foot of Thy throne with equal sincerity, and may any man who dares, say "I was a better man than he." '

I was born at Geneva in 1712, the son of Isaac Rousseau, a citizen of that town, and Susanne Bernard, his wife. My father's inheritance, being a fifteenth part only of a very small property which had been divided among as many children, was almost nothing, and he relied for his living entirely on his trade of watchmaker, at which he was very highly skilled. My mother was the daughter of a minister of religion and rather better-off. She had besides both intelligence and beauty, and my father had not found it easy to win her. Their love had begun almost with their birth; at eight or nine they would walk together every evening along La Treille, and at ten they were inseparable. Sympathy and mental affinity strengthened in them a feeling first formed by habit. Both, being affectionate and sensitive by nature, were only waiting for the moment when they would find similar qualities in another; or rather the moment was waiting for them, and both threw their affections at the first heart that opened to receive them. Fate, by appearing to oppose their passion, only strengthened it. Unable to obtain his mistress, the young lover ate out his heart with grief, and she counselled him to travel and forget her. He travelled in vain, and returned more in love than ever, to find her he loved still faithful and fond. After such a proof, it was inevitable that they should love one another for all their lives. They swore to do so, and Heaven smiled on their vows.

Gabriel Bernard, one of my mother's brothers, fell in love with one of my father's sisters, and she refused to marry him unless her brother could marry my mother at the same time. Love overcame all obstacles, and the two pairs were wedded on the same day. So it was that my uncle married my aunt, and their children became my double first cousins. Within a year both couples had a child, but at the end of that time each of them was forced to separate.

My uncle Bernard, who was an engineer, went to serve in the Empire and Hungary under Prince Eugène, and distinguished himself at the siege and battle of Belgrade. My father, after the birth of my only brother, left for Constantinople, where he had been called to become watchmaker to the Sultan's Seraglio. While he was away my mother's beauty, wit, and talents brought her admirers, one of the most pressing of whom was M. de la Closure, the French Resident in the city. His feelings must have been very strong, for thirty years later I have seen him moved when merely speaking to me about her. But my mother had more than her virtue with which to defend herself; she deeply loved my father, and urged him to come back. He threw up everything to do so, and I was the unhappy fruit of his return. For ten months later I was born, a poor and sickly child, and cost my mother her life. So my birth was the first of my misfortunes.

I never knew how my father stood up to his loss, but I know that he never got over it. He seemed to see her again in me, but could never forget that I had robbed him of her; he never kissed me that I did not know by his sighs and his convulsive embrace that there was a bitter grief mingled with his affection, a grief which nevertheless intensified his feeling for me. When he said to me, 'Jean-Jacques, let us talk of your mother,' I would reply: 'Very well, father, but we are sure to cry.' 'Ah,' he would say with a groan; 'Give her back to me, console me for her, fill the void she has left in my heart! Should I love you so if you were not more to me than a son?' Forty years after he lost her he died in the arms of a second wife, but with his first wife's name on his lips, and her picture imprinted upon his heart.

Such were my parents. And of all the gifts with which Heaven endowed them, they left me but one, a sensitive heart. It had been the making of their happiness, but for me it has been the cause of all the misfortunes in my life.

I was almost born dead, and they had little hope of saving me. I brought with me the seed of a disorder which has grown stronger with the years, and now gives me only occasional intervals of relief in which to suffer more painfully in some other way. But one of my father's sisters, a nice sensible woman, bestowed such care on me that I survived; and now, as I write this, she is still alive at the age of eighty, nursing a husband rather younger than herself but ruined by drink. My dear aunt, I pardon you for causing me to live, and I deeply regret that I cannot repay you in the evening of your days all the care and affection you lavished on me at the dawn of mine. My nurse Jacqueline is still alive too, and healthy and strong. Indeed the fingers that opened my eyes at birth may well close them at my death.

I felt before I thought: which is the common lot of man, though more pronounced in my case than in another's. I know nothing of myself till I was five or six. I do not know how I learnt to read. I only remember my first books and their effect upon me; it is from my earliest reading that I date the unbroken consciousness of my own existence. My mother had possessed some novels, and my father and I began to read them after our supper. At first it was only to give me some practice in reading. But soon my interest in this entertaining literature became so strong that we read by turns continuously, and spent whole nights so engaged. For we could never leave off till the end of the book. Sometimes my father would say with shame as we heard the morning larks: 'Come, let us go to bed. I am more a child than you are.'

In a short time I acquired by this dangerous method, not only an extreme facility in reading and expressing myself, but a singular insight for my age into the passions. I had no idea of the facts, but I was already familiar with every feeling. I had grasped nothing; I had sensed everything. These confused emotions which I experienced one after another, did not warp my reasoning powers in any way, for as yet I had none. But they shaped them after a special pattern, giving me the strangest and most romantic notions about human life, which neither experience nor reflection has ever succeeded in curing me of.

---

# MARY WOLLSTONECRAFT

# from *A Vindication of the Rights of Woman*

## Introduction

---

*A Vindication of the Rights of Woman* (1792) is a key text of feminism. Its author, Mary Wollstonecraft, was not the first feminist, for this cause began with Christine de Pizan (see *The Book of the City of Ladies*) in the 1400s, when it was called the "Woman Question." Wollstonecraft, however, gave feminism its modern focus (see Beauvoir's *The Second Sex*) as she made women's rights part of the struggle for human rights in general.

Human rights was the defining issue of the Enlightenment, but, no thinker before Wollstonecraft, including Voltaire (see *Candide*), Rousseau (see *Confessions*), and Jefferson (see *The Declaration of Independence*), even considered applying the concept of rights to women. In her treatise, she forever changed the character of the debate on rights by arguing that men and women alike shared in the rights bestowed by nature. For her, the rights of liberty and equality applied to both men and women, and if fraternity made all men brothers, then men must accept that they had sisters as well.

Wollstonecraft stood in Rousseau's shadow, but she rejected his argument that the "duties" of women are "to please, to be useful to [men], to make [men] love and esteem them, to educate [men] when young, and take care of [men] when grown up, to advise, to console [men], and to render [men's] lives easy and agreeable." While admitting that Rousseau accurately reflected existing society, she found his view morally wrong. She argued that women, as rational creatures, should be treated like men; that is, educated for virtue; society's goal should be the full, free expression of both sexes.

The feminism of Mary Wollstonecraft (1759–1797) sprang from her marginal status. Born into genteel poverty in England, she made her way in the world only with great difficulty. A failed career in teaching taught her the pain of being female and poor, without respect or independence. With her intellectual gifts, she was drawn into progressive circles where Enlightenment ideas flourished. When revolution broke out in France, she traveled to Paris where she shared with French militants their hopes for a new society, free of oppression. Back in London, she joined the radicals grouped around William Godwin (1756-1836), an ex-minister and novelist. When she was made pregnant by Godwin, they secretly married, fearing to offend radical friends by the disclosure of their wedding. She died in childbirth in 1797, giving life to the child later known as Mary Wollstonecraft Shelley, the author of *Frankenstein*.

### Reading the Selection

This selection—the treatise's introduction—offers a summary of Wollstonecraft's views. Like Rousseau, she accepts that men are physically stronger than women; unlike Rousseau, however, she maintains that men use this fact as a pretext to impose a greater inequality than nature allows, thus keeping women in "perpetual childhood."

According to her, men keep women in their place by treating them as "alluring mistresses," or sex objects. To this end, men have created a vocabulary in praise of feminine virtues, such as "soft phrases . . . [and] delicacy of sentiments." These, rather than being words of praise, are in reality words of subjection to man's demands, from a love of power. She condemns women for going along with men, in thinking themselves the "weaker vessels." She thinks that women should cease to be men's toys and make their own moral choices. Only then, when women can freely choose between reason and the passions, just as men do, will they become "affectionate wives and rational mothers"—the goal of this early feminist tract.

---

After considering the historic page, and viewing the living world with anxious solicitude, the most melancholy emotions of sorrowful indignation have depressed my spirits, and I have sighed when obliged to confess, that either nature has made a great difference between man and man, or that the civilization which has hitherto taken place in the world has been very partial. I have turned over various books written on the subject of education, and patiently observed the conduct of parents and the management of schools; but what has been the result?—a profound conviction that the neglected education of my fellow-creatures is the grand source of the misery I deplore; and that women, in particular, are rendered weak and wretched by a variety of concurring causes, originating from one hasty conclusion. The conduct and manners of women, in fact, evidently prove that their minds are not in a healthy state; for, like flowers which are planted in too rich a soil, strength and usefulness are sacrificed to beauty; and the flaunting leaves, after having pleased a fastidious eye, fade, disregarded on the stalk, long before the season when they ought to have arrived at maturity.—One cause of this barren blooming I attribute to a false system of education, gathered from the books written on this subject by men who, considering females rather as women than human creatures, have been more anxious to make them alluring mistresses than affectionate wives and rational mothers; and the understanding of the sex has been so bubbled by this specious homage, that the civilized women of the present century, with a few exceptions, are only anxious to inspire love, when they ought to cherish a nobler ambition, and by their abilities and virtues exact respect.

In a treatise, therefore, on female rights and manners, the works which have been particularly written for their improvement must not be overlooked; especially when it is asserted, in direct terms, that the minds of women are enfeebled by false refinement; that the books of instruction, written by men of genius, have had the same tendency as more frivolous productions; and that, in the true style of Mahometanism, they are treated as a kind of subordinate beings, and not as a part of the human species, when improveable reason is allowed to be the dignified distinction which raises men above the brute creation, and puts a natural sceptre in a feeble hand.

Yet, because I am a woman, I would not lead my readers to suppose that I mean violently to agitate the contested question respecting the equality or inferiority of the sex; but as the subject lies in my way, and I cannot pass it over without subjecting the main tendency of my reasoning to misconstruction, I shall stop a moment to deliver, in a few words, my opinion.—In the government of the physical world it is observable that the female in point of strength is, in general, inferior to the male. This is the law of nature; and it does not appear to be suspended or abrogated in favour of women. A degree of physical superiority cannot, therefore, be denied—and it is a noble prerogative! But not content with this natural pre-eminence, men endeavour to sink us still lower, merely to render us alluring objects for a moment; and women, intoxicated by the adoration which men, under the influence of their senses, pay them, do not seek to obtain a durable interest in their hearts, or to become the friends of the fellow creatures who find amusement in their society.

I am aware of an obvious inference:—from every quarter have I heard exclamations against masculine women; but where are they to be found? If by this appellation men mean to inveigh against their ardour in hunting, shooting, and gaming, I shall most cordially join in the cry; but if it be against the imitation of manly virtues, or, more properly speaking, the attainment of those talents and virtues, the exercise of which ennobles the human character, and which raise females in the scale of animal being, when they are comprehensively termed mankind;—all those who view them with a philosophic eye must, I should think, wish with me, that they may every day grow more and more masculine.

This discussion naturally divides the subject. I shall first consider women in the grand light of human creatures, who, in common with men, are placed on this earth to unfold their faculties; and afterwards I shall more particularly point out their peculiar designation.

I wish also to steer clear of an error which many respectable writers have fallen into; for the instruction which has hitherto been addressed to women, has rather been applicable to *ladies*, if the little indirect advice, that is scattered through Sandford and Merton, be excepted; but, addressing my sex in a firmer tone, I pay particular attention to those in the middle class, because they appear to be in the most natural state. Perhaps the seeds of false-refinement, immorality, and vanity, have ever been shed by the great. Weak, artificial beings, raised above the common wants and affections of their race, in a premature unnatural manner, undermine the very foundation of virtue, and spread corruption through the whole mass of society! As a class of mankind they have the strongest claim to pity; the education of the rich tends to render them vain and helpless, and the unfolding mind is not strengthened by the practice of those duties which dignify the human character.—They only live to amuse themselves, and by the same law which in nature invariably produces certain effects, they soon only afford barren amusement.

But as I propose taking a separate view of the different ranks of society, and of the moral character of women, in each, this hint is, for the present, sufficient; and I have only alluded to the subject, because it appears to me to be the very essence of an introduction to give a cursory account of the contents of the work it introduces.

My own sex, I hope, will excuse me, if I treat them like rational creatures, instead of flattering their *fascinating* graces, and viewing them as if they were in a state of perpetual childhood, unable to stand alone. I earnestly wish to point out in what true dignity and human happiness consists—I wish to persuade women to endeavour to acquire strength, both of mind and body, and to convince them that the soft phrases, susceptibility of heart, delicacy of sentiment, and refinement of taste, are almost synonymous with epithets of weakness, and that those beings who are only the objects of pity and that kind of love, which has been termed its sister, will soon become objects of contempt.

Dismissing then those pretty feminine phrases, which the men condescendingly use to soften our slavish dependence, and despising that weak elegancy of mind, exquisite sensibility, and sweet docility of manners, supposed to be the sexual characteristics of the weaker vessel, I wish to shew that elegance is inferior to virtue, that the first object of laudable ambition is to obtain a character as a human being, regardless of the distinction of sex; and that secondary views should be brought to this simple touchstone.

This is a rough sketch of my plan; and should I express my conviction with the energetic emotions that I feel whenever I think of the subject, the dictates of experience and reflection will be felt by some of my readers. Animated by this important object, I shall disdain to cull my phrases or polish my style;—I aim at being useful, and sincerity will render me unaffected; for, wishing rather to persuade by the force of my arguments, than dazzle by the elegance of my language, I shall not waste my time in rounding periods, or in fabricating the turgid bombast of artificial feelings, which, coming from the head, never reach the heart.—I shall be employed about things, not words!—and, anxious to render my sex more respectable members of society, I shall try to avoid that flowery diction which has slided from essays into novels, and from novels into familiar letters and conversation.

These pretty superlatives, dropping glibly from the tongue, vitiate the taste, and create a kind of sickly delicacy that turns away from simple unadorned truth, and a deluge of false sentiments and overstretched feelings, stifling the natural emotions of the heart, render the domestic pleasures insipid, that ought to sweeten the exercise of those severe duties, which educate a rational and immortal being for a nobler field of action.

The education of women has, of late, been more attended to than formerly; yet they are still reckoned a frivolous sex, and ridiculed or pitied by the writers who endeavour by satire or instruction to improve them. It is acknowledged that they spend many of the first years of their lives in acquiring a smattering of accomplishments; meanwhile strength of body and mind are sacrificed to libertine notions of beauty, to the desire of establishing themselves,—the only way women can rise in the world,—by marriage. And this desire making mere animals of them, when they marry they act as such children may be expected to act:—they dress; they paint, and nickname God's creatures.—Surely these weak beings are only fit for a seraglio!—Can they be expected to govern a family with judgment, or take care of the poor babes whom they bring into the world?

If then it can be fairly deduced from the present conduct of the sex, from the prevalent fondness for pleasure which takes place of ambition and those nobler passions that open and enlarge the soul; that the instruction which women have hitherto received has only tended, with the constitution of civil society, to render them insignificant objects of desire— mere propagators of fools!—if it can be proved that in aiming to accomplish them, without cultivating their understandings, they are taken out of their sphere of duties, and made ridiculous and useless when the short-lived bloom of beauty is over, I presume that *rational* men will excuse me for endeavouring to persuade them to become more masculine and respectable.

Indeed the word masculine is only a bugbear: there is little reason to fear that women will acquire too much courage or fortitude; for their apparent inferiority with respect to bodily strength, must render them, in some degree, dependent on men in the various relations of life, but why should it be increased by prejudices that give a sex to virtue, and confound simple truths with sensual reveries?

Women are, in fact, so much degraded by mistaken notions of female excellence, that I do not mean to add a paradox when I assert, that this artificial weakness produces a propensity to tyrannize, and gives birth to cunning, the natural opponent of strength, which leads them to play off those contemptible infantine airs that undermine esteem even whilst they excite desire. Let men become more chaste and modest, and if women do not grow wiser in the same ratio, it will be clear that they have weaker understandings. It seems scarcely necessary to say, that I now speak of the sex in general. Many individuals have more sense than their male relatives; and, as nothing preponderates where there is a constant struggle for an equilibrium, without it has naturally more gravity, some women govern their husbands without degrading themselves, because intellect will always govern.

Chapter

# 17

# Revolution, Reaction, and Cultural Response:
# 1760–1830

---

## THOMAS JEFFERSON

### from *The Declaration of Independence*

---

The American writer and statesman Thomas Jefferson (1743–1826) personified the liberal and rational ideals of the Age of Reason. In *The Declaration of Independence,* the document which severed ties between the American colonies and Britain, which he chiefly wrote, he translated this age's values into ringing phrases still echoed around the world. In his distinguished career, he worked to bring to fruition this era's vision; he held many public offices, both appointive and elective, including member of the Virginia House of Burgesses, delegate to the Continental Congress, ambassador to France, secretary of state, vice-president, and, finally, president.

Jefferson, a plantation owner, was born into the gentry of colonial Virginia, which assured him a comfortable life, the best available education, and opportunities for leadership when war with Britain came. In college, he studied the Classics, Shakespeare, Milton, and, above all, three figures whose knowledge of science, human nature, and politics greatly influenced his thinking: Newton, Bacon (see *Essays*), and Locke (see *The Second Treatise*). A member of the third generation of Enlightenment thinkers, Jefferson developed a philosophy geared to the improvement of life for individuals and society; it was inspired by faith in education and natural law theory. In the debates leading up to the American Revolution, he was guided by this philosophy and made a name for himself as an outspoken defender of free speech, free thought, and liberty of religious conscience. Thus, it was perhaps inevitable that, in Philadelphia, in 1776, as the delegates to the Continental Congress inched their way toward making a break with the British crown, they should appoint a committee to draw up a declaration of independence, and the committee would select Jefferson to draft the document.

## Reading the Selection

*The Declaration of Independence* contains four sections. The first section echoed, in plain and firm terms, what Jefferson called "the harmonizing sentiments of the day." These ideas were part of a set of beliefs, shared by the members of the Continental Congress; they could be traced back to Locke and had found recent voice in the colonists' writings leveled against the British. The second part is a specific bill of twenty-seven accusations against King George III's policies toward the American colonies. In the third section, the delegates maintain that they have, in vain, petitioned the British government many times to redress their grievances. In the fourth part, they conclude that the Congress has no alternative but to declare the colonies "free and independent," calling on the "Protection of divine Providence" as they pledge their lives, fortunes, and honor to each other in support of the Declaration.

Jefferson, who spent the better part of a month drafting and polishing the document, later asserted that it was intended to be "an expression of the American mind." He drew on longstanding principles: equal rights for all citizens as based on the laws of nature, popular sovereignty, and limited, constitutional government. He chose his words with great care and, in particular, the phrase "life, liberty and the pursuit of happiness" which, unlike Locke's wording ("life, liberty and property") expressed Jefferson's own Enlightenment philosophy, that society has more noble goals than the protection of citizens' wordly possessions.

---

When in the course of human events, it becomes necessary for one people to dissolve the political bands which have connected them with another, and to assume among the powers of the earth, the separate and equal station to which the Law of Nature and of Nature's God entitle them, a decent respect to the opinions of mankind requires that they should declare the causes which impel them to the separation.

We hold these truths to be self-evident, that all men are created equal, that they are endowed by their Creator with certain unalienable rights, that among these are life, liberty and the pursuit of happiness. That to secure these rights, governments are instituted among men, deriving their just powers from the consent of the governed. That whenever any form of government becomes destructive of these ends, it is the right of the people to alter or to abolish it, and to institute new government, laying its foundation on such principles and organizing its powers in such form, as to them shall seem most likely to effect their safety and happiness. Prudence, indeed, will dictate that governments long established should not be changed for light and transient causes; and accordingly all experience hath shown, that mankind are more disposed to suffer, while evils are sufferable, than to right themselves by abolishing the forms to which they are accustomed. But when a long train of abuses and usurpations, pursuing invariably the same object, evinces a design to reduce them under absolute despotism, it is their right, it is their duty, to throw off such government, and to provide new guards for their future security. Such has been the patient sufferance of these Colonies; and such is now the necessity which constrains them to alter their former systems of government. This history of the present King of Great Britain is a history of repeated injuries and usurpations, all having in direct object the establishment of an absolute tyranny over these States. . . .

---

# Declaration of the Rights of Man and Citizen

---

Like the American *Declaration of Independence*, which it resembles in its call for an end to tyranny and the establishment of a new political order, the French *Declaration of the Rights of Man and Citizen* reflected the ideals of the Age of Reason. These included the natural rights theory of Locke (see *The Second Treatise of Civil Government*), and the constitutional principles of the English political settlement of 1688. But this French document was firmly rooted in French history, for it meant to wipe out centuries of feudal privilege founded on tradition, blood, and wealth; at the same time, it assured French citizens of their natural and inalienable rights of liberty, property, security, and resistance to oppression, denied under the Old Regime.

In contrast to the American document, which appeared at the start of a revolution to justify future events, the French document was drafted after the French Revolution began and became one of a number of important pieces of legislation approved by the National Assembly in the summer of 1789. By the time the National Assembly passed the *Declaration of the Rights of Man and Citizen* on August 27, 1789, the revolution was in full swing. The Bastille, the symbolic prison of royal tyranny, had fallen on July 14; on August 3, the French aristocrats representing their Estate in the Assembly had risen, noble by noble, to renounce their feudal rights. When the Declaration of August 27 was passed, the way was cleared to deal with suffrage, taxes, the Catholic church, and the drafting of a constitution setting up a limited monarchy.

### Reading the Selection

The founding document of the French Revolution has stood the test of time, outlasting the Reign of Terror (1793–1794), the Napoleonic emperorship, later revolutions, constitutional crises, and five republics. After a brief preamble in which the past is blamed for the ills of the present and a rationale is presented justifying the presentation of these natural and civil rights, there follows a list of seventeen "rights of man and citizen."

The concepts of rights and law are joined together in many ways in the document. Law is referred to in nine of the seventeen articles. The committee that drafted the Declaration felt that since French law had been abused so often under the Old Regime it must now specify how the law was to protect citizens from arbitrary arrests, unfair trials, and *ex post facto* legislation. Law, as explained by the thinker Rousseau, expressed the general will that was embodied in representative government. Thus, citizens became eligible for public office according to their talents and not, as with past practice, their class position. This is a revolutionary aspect of this revolutionary document, for it transforms people from subjects, to be acted on, into citizens, who are self-governing.

The Declaration proclaimed that all citizens would be taxed, a correction of an abuse from the Old Regime when the rich were exempt from paying taxes. A "public force," or army, was still deemed necessary; however, it was not to be operated by the privileged few—once more, a reference to the past when army officers were uniformly of the nobility. Finally, the Declaration asserted that the free circulation of ideas was a "precious" right—a provision meant to remove the censorship that had muzzled society in the past.

---------

The representatives of the French people, organized in National Assembly, considering that ignorance, forgetfulness, or contempt of the rights of man are the sole causes of public misfortunes and of the corruption of governments, have resolved to set forth in a solemn declaration the natural, inalienable, and sacred rights of man, in order that such declaration, continually before all members of the social body, may be a perpetual reminder of their rights and duties; in order that the acts of the legislative power and those of the executive power may constantly be compared with the aim of every political institution and may accordingly be more respected; in order that the demands of the citizens, founded henceforth upon simple and incontestable principles, may always be directed towards the maintenance of the Constitution and the welfare of all.

Accordingly, the National Assembly recognizes and proclaims, in the presence and under the auspices of the Supreme Being, the following rights of man and citizen.

1.  Men are born and remain free and equal in rights; social distinctions may be based only upon general usefulness.

2.  The aim of every political association is the preservation of the natural and inalienable rights of man; these rights are liberty, property, security, and resistance to oppression.

3.  The source of all sovereignty resides essentially in the nation; no group, no individual may exercise authority not emanating expressly therefrom.

4.  Liberty consists of the power to do whatever is not injurious to others; thus the enjoyment of the natural rights of every man has for its limits only those that assure other members of society the enjoyment of those same rights; such limits may be determined only by law.

5.  The law has the right to forbid only actions which are injurious to society. Whatever is not forbidden by law may not be prevented, and no one may be constrained to do what it does not prescribe.

6.  Law is the expression of the general will; all citizens have the right to concur personally, or through their representatives, in its formation; it must be the same for all, whether it protects or punishes. All citizens, being equal before it, are equally admissible to all public offices, positions, and employments, according to their capacity, and without other distinction than that of virtues and talents.

7.  No man may be accused, arrested, or detained except in the cases determined by law, and according to the forms prescribed thereby. Whoever solicit, expedite, or execute arbitrary orders, or have them executed, must be punished; but every citizen summoned or apprehended in pursuance of the law must obey immediately; he renders himself culpable by resistance.

8.  The law is to establish only penalties that are absolutely and obviously necessary; and no one may be punished except by virtue of a law established and promulgated prior to the offence and legally applied.

9.  Since every man is presumed innocent until declared guilty, if arrest be deemed indispensable, all unnecessary

severity for securing the person of the accused must be severely repressed by law.

*10.* No one is to be disquieted because of his opinions, even religious, provided their manifestation does not disturb the public order established by law.

*11.* Free communication of ideas and opinions is one of the most precious of the rights of man. Consequently, every citizen may speak, write, and print freely, subject to responsibility for the abuse of such liberty in the cases determined by law.

*12.* The guarantee of the rights of man and citizen necessitates a public force; such a force, therefore, is instituted for the advantage of all and not for the particular benefit of those to whom it is entrusted.

*13.* For the maintenance of the public force and for the expenses of administration a common tax is indispensable; it must be assessed equally on all citizens in proportion to their means.

*14.* Citizens have the right to ascertain, by themselves or through their representatives, the necessity of the public tax, to consent to it freely, to supervise its use, and to determine its quota, assessment, payment, and duration.

*15.* Society has the right to require of every public agent an accounting of his administration.

*16.* Every society in which the guarantee of rights is not assured or the separation of powers not determined has no constitution at all.

*17.* Since property is a sacred and inviolable right, no one may be deprived thereof unless a legally established public necessity obviously requires it, and upon condition of a just and previous indemnity.

---

# WILLIAM WORDSWORTH
## *Lines Composed a Few Miles above Tintern Abbey*

---

Wordsworth's poem, "Lines Composed a Few Miles Above Tintern Abbey," represents a turning point in English letters. Before it appeared, poetry was dominated by the Neoclassical style (1660-1798), which was characterized by correctness in language and moral sentiments supportive of the existing social order; Neoclassical poets revered the Classical authors, especially the Romans, using their literary genres as models and sources of rules (see Pope's *An Essay on Man*). With the appearance of Wordsworth's poem (1798), poetry fell under the sway of the Romantic style, which was marked by rejection of the ideals and rules of Classicism and Neoclassicism; Romantic poets advocated the free, subjective expression of passion and personal feelings.

"Tintern Abbey" was one of the poems in *Lyrical Ballads* by William Wordsworth (1770–1850) and Samuel Taylor Coleridge (1772–1834). The poems in this collection were revolutionary in form, replacing what the two poets termed the artificial style of the Neoclassicists with a more natural verse. For Coleridge, this meant ballad forms, and, for Wordsworth, simple lyrics, voiced in the common language of the "middle and lower classes." This desire to reproduce customary speech, a reflection of the age's democratic revolutions, became henceforth a prominent motif in Western letters, even after the formal end of the Romantic period in 1848 (see Hurston's "How It Feels to Be Colored Me").

Wordsworth may have been a rebel in aesthetics, but he was a conservative in his social and political views, except for a brief flirtation with liberal ideas at the dawn of the French Revolution. From *Lyrical Ballads* onward, he used his poetry to express fears of the emerging modern world, such as teeming cities, mass democracy, and lack of community. He made the unspoiled countryside his symbol for the disappearing world of village England, under siege by the Industrial Revolution. For him, rural equaled good, urban equaled evil. His love for rural values was, at bottom, an attempt to revive the structures and symbols of the Middle Ages.

### Reading the Selection

"Tintern Abbey" reflects Wordsworth's lifelong (religious) love affair with Nature, which he conceives in pantheistic terms. Indeed, it is a classic expression of pantheism [Greek, "all gods"], the doctrine which identifies God with the forces and workings of nature. To this end, he describes Nature in terms usually reserved for God, such as finding peace of mind in

Nature and calling the natural world "[t]he anchor of my purest thoughts, the nurse, [t]he guide, the guardian of my heart, and soul of all my moral being."

The poem is a conversation, albeit one-sided, in which the poet speaks directly to his sister Dorothy ["My dear, dear Sister!"]. Its conversational tone is established by the blank verse—a Renaissance verse form often used by Romantic poets—and the informal speech. Its theme is the cult of Nature, about which, Wordsworth explains to Dorothy, his feelings have changed since he, "like a roe [deer]," roamed this spot five years before. Sadder but wiser, he now finds himself less exalted in mood, "but hearing . . . the still, sad music of humanity." He tries to describe his younger self, but finally gives up: "I cannot paint what then I was." He however recognizes in his sister his old feelings ("in thy voice I catch [t]he language of my former heart"), hence his lecture on Nature's moral power. Sharing Nature in the company of a loved one, as seen in "Tintern Abbey," became a familiar theme in later Romantic poetry and art.

---

Five years have past; five summers, with the length
Of five long winters! and again I hear
These waters, rolling from their mountain-springs
With a soft inland murmur.—Once again
Do I behold these steep and lofty cliffs,
That on a wild secluded scene impress
Thoughts of more deep seclusion; and connect
The landscape with the quiet of the sky.
The day is come when I again repose
Here, under this dark sycamore, and view
These plots of cottage-ground, these orchard-tufts,
Which at this season, with their unripe fruits,
Are clad in one green hue, and lose themselves
'Mid groves and copses. Once again I see
These hedge-rows, hardly hedge-rows, little lines
Of sportive wood run wild: these pastoral farms,
Green to the very door; and wreaths of smoke
Sent up, in silence, from among the trees!
With some uncertain notice, as might seem
Of vagrant dwellers in the houseless woods,
Or of some Hermit's cave, where by his fire
The Hermit sits alone.

         These beauteous forms,
Through a long absence, have not been to me
As is a landscape to a blind man's eye:
But oft, in lonely rooms, and 'mid the din
Of towns and cities, I have owed to them
In hours of weariness, sensations sweet,
Felt in the blood, and felt along the heart;
And passing even into my purer mind,
With tranquil restoration:—feelings too
Of unremembered pleasure: such, perhaps,
As have no slight or trivial influence
On that best portion of a good man's life,
His little, nameless, unremembered, acts
Of kindness and of love. Nor less, I trust,
To them I may have owed another gift,
Of aspect more sublime; that blessed mood,
In which the burthen of the mystery,
In which the heavy and the weary weight
Of all this unintelligible world,
Is lightened:—that serene and blessed mood,
In which the affections gently lead us on,—

Until, the breath of this corporeal frame
And even the motion of our human blood
Almost suspended, we are laid asleep
In body, and become a living soul:
While with an eye made quiet by the power
Of harmony, and the deep power of joy,
We see into the life of things.

         If this
Be but a vain belief, yet, oh! how oft—
In darkness and amid the many shapes
Of joyless daylight; when the fretful stir
Unprofitable, and the fever of the world,
Have hung upon the beatings of my heart—
How oft, in spirit, have I turned to thee,
O sylvan Wye! thou wanderer thro' the woods,
How often has my spirit turned to thee!

And now, with gleams of half-extinguished thought,
With many recognitions dim and faint,
And somewhat of a sad perplexity,
The picture of the mind revives again:
While here I stand, not only with the sense
Of present pleasure, but with pleasing thoughts
That in this moment there is life and food
For future years. And so I dare to hope,
Though changed, no doubt, from what I was when first
I came among these hills; when like a roe
I bounded o'er the mountains, by the sides
Of the deep rivers, and the lonely streams,
Wherever nature led: more like a man
Flying from something that he dreads, than one
Who sought the thing he loved. For nature then
(The coarser pleasures of my boyish days,
And their glad animal movements all gone by)
To me was all in all.—I cannot paint
What then I was. The sounding cataract
Haunted me like a passion: the tall rock,
The mountain, and the deep and gloomy wood,
Their colours and their forms, were then to me
An appetite; a feeling and a love,
That had no need of a remoter charm,
By thought supplied, nor any interest
Unborrowed from the eye.—That time is past,

And all its aching joys are now no more,
And all its dizzy raptures. Not for this
Faint I, nor mourn nor murmur; other gifts
Have followed; for such loss, I would believe,
Abundant recompense. For I have learned
To look on nature, not as in the hour
Of thoughtless youth; but hearing oftentimes
The still, sad music of humanity,
Nor harsh nor grating, though of ample power
To chasten and subdue. And I have felt
A presence that disturbs me with the joy
Of elevated thoughts; a sense sublime
Of something far more deeply interfused,
Whose dwelling is the light of setting suns,
And the round ocean and the living air,
And the blue sky, and in the mind of man:
A motion and a spirit, that impels
All thinking things, all objects of all thought,
And rolls through all things. Therefore am I still
A lover of the meadows and the woods,
And mountains; and of all that we behold
From this green earth; of all the mighty world
Of eye, and ear,—both what they half create,
And what perceive; well pleased to recognise
In nature and the language of the sense,
The anchor of my purest thoughts, the nurse,
The guide, the guardian of my heart, and soul
Of all my moral being.

                    Nor perchance,
If I were not thus taught, should I the more
Suffer my genial spirits to decay:
For thou art with me here upon the banks
Of this fair river; thou my dearest Friend,
My dear, dear Friend; and in thy voice I catch
The language of my former heart, and read
My former pleasures in the shooting lights
Of thy wild eyes. Oh! yet a little while
May I behold in thee what I was once,

My dear, dear Sister! and this prayer I make,
Knowing that Nature never did betray
The heart that loved her; 'tis her privilege,
Through all the years of this our life, to lead
From joy to joy: for she can so inform
The mind that is within us, so impress
With quietness and beauty, and so feed
With lofty thoughts, that neither evil tongues,
Rash judgments, nor the sneers of selfish men,
Nor greetings where no kindness is, nor all
The dreary intercourse of daily life,
Shall e'er prevail against us, or disturb
Our cheerful faith, that all which we behold
Is full of blessings. Therefore let the moon
Shine on thee in thy solitary walk;
And let the misty mountain-winds be free
To blow against thee: and, in after years,
When these wild ecstasies shall be matured
Into a sober pleasure; when thy mind
Shall be a mansion for all lovely forms,
Thy memory be as a dwelling-place
For all sweet sounds and harmonies; oh! then,
If solitude, or fear, or pain, or grief,
Should be thy portion, with what healing thoughts
Of tender joy wilt thou remember me,
And these my exhortations! Nor, perchance—
If I should be where I no more can hear
Thy voice, nor catch from thy wild eyes these gleams
Of past existence—wilt thou then forget
That on the banks of this delightful stream
We stood together; and that I, so long
A worshipper of Nature, hither came
Unwearied in that service; rather say
With warmer love—oh! with far deeper zeal
Of holier love. Nor wilt thou then forget,
That after many wanderings, many years
Of absence, these steep woods and lofty cliffs,
And this green pastoral landscape, were to me
More dear, both for themselves and for thy sake!

---

# JOHANN WOLFGANG VON GOETHE

## from *Faust: Part I*

### The Tragedy

---

   Goethe is generally acknowledged as Germany's greatest author, and *Faust* is considered his masterpiece. A play in verse, *Faust* is the most popular drama in Germany, where hardly a day passes without its being performed on some stage. Outside Germany, it is better known as a work to be read. This play's appeal is in its portrait of Faust as archetypal rebel, ready to trade his soul for forbidden knowledge. Some read a more sinister meaning into its appeal, making the Faustian quest a metaphor for what they perceive to be the West's drive for world dominion and mastery of nature.

Goethe's play merits comparison with Marlowe's *Dr. Faustus,* since both were based on the same legend. Where Marlowe's ending is morally ambiguous—is his Faust a noble martyr who played God or a sinner meant to warn others?—Goethe's Faust, despite his mistakes, is ultimately saved by God. Notwithstanding the clarity of its ending, Goethe introduced a new dimension of ambiguity into this work: *why* God rescues the wayward hero is not made clear.

Goethe recognized the moral uncertainty of his approach; unable to finish the play, he first presented it to the world with the hero Faust left alive and in despair. Subtitled Part I, this portion of *Faust* was issued in 1808. For the rest of Goethe's life he wrestled with Part II, finishing it before he died in 1832.

Despite the unresolved ending, Part I is Goethe's finest work. Faust is presented in this era's Romantic language, which rejected historic religion but believed there was a mystery at the core of life. Thus, Faust is revealed as obsessed with human ignorance ["ignorance is our fate, [a]nd this I hate"]. Disappointed in science, he calls up the devil Mephistopheles to learn "what the universe engirds." Faust, joined by Mephistopheles, then goes through a series of adventures in quest of life's elusive meaning. At the end of Part I, Faust's quest, rather than bringing knowledge, has brought despair; he prays, "Would I had never been born."

In Part II Goethe further muddles the play's moral. It ends with Faust ironically yielding his soul to Mephistopheles, thinking he is doing it for the good of humanity. Faust's motive is pure, but his act rests on an illusion: Mephistopheles has tricked him into a meaningless death. And yet, by saving Faust from Hell, Goethe seems to say that, to God, dreams count more than deeds.

The middle class Johann Wolfgang von Goethe (1749–1832) was one of the West's last universal men. Besides being a dramatist, he was also an essayist, author of lyric verse, novelist, lawyer, and scientist, writing on botany, anatomy, and the theory of color. No ivory tower intellectual, he was, for many years, a bureaucrat in Weimar, capital of the petty duchy of Saxe-Weimar-Eisenach.

### Reading the Selection

This selection contains most of *Faust*'s first scene. Introduced here are the two scholars Wagner and Faust who symbolize rival paths to truth, sense or sensibility, Enlightenment or Romanticism. Wagner is sense, dedicated to reason and determined to make "books my drink and meat." Faust, bored with Wagner ["this lickspittle of learning"], is sensibility, so devoted to feeling that he is paradoxically prepared to commit suicide to calm his soul. During the rest of Part I, Faust's commitment to Romantic feeling brings destruction in its wake. Perhaps because of destruction's link with feeling, Goethe later condemned Romanticism as "unhealthy."

---

### Night, Faust's Study (i)

*In a high-vaulted, narrow, gothic chamber, Faust is discovered restless at his desk.*

FAUST

Philosophy have I digested,
The whole of Law and Medicine,
From each its secrets I have wrested,
Theology, alas, thrown in.
Poor fool, with all this sweated lore,
I stand no wiser than I was before.
Master and Doctor are my titles;
For ten years now, without repose,
I've held my erudite recitals
And led my pupils by the nose.
And round we go, on crooked ways or straight,
And well I know that ignorance is our fate,

And this I hate.
I have, I grant, outdistanced all the others,
Doctors, pedants, clergy and lay-brothers;
All plague of doubts and scruples I can quell,
And have no fear of devil or of hell,
And in return am destitute of pleasure,
Knowing that knowledge tricks us beyond measure,
That man's conversion is beyond my reach,
Knowing the emptiness of what I teach.
Meanwhile I live in penury,
No worldly honour falls to me.
No dog would linger on like this,
And so I turn to the abyss
Of necromancy, try if art
Can voice or power of spirits start,
To do me service and reveal
The things of Nature's secret seal,
And save me from the weary dance

Of holding forth in ignorance.
Then shall I see, with vision clear,
How secret elements cohere,
And what the universe engirds,
And give up huckstering with words.
  O silver majesty of night,
Moon, look no more upon my plight,
You whom my eyes at midnight oft
Have gazed upon, when slow and soft
You crossed my papers and my books
With friendly, melancholy looks.
Would that my soul could tranquil stray
On many a moonlit mountain way,
By cavernous haunts with ghostly shadows,
Or thread the silver of the meadows,
Released from learning's smoky stew
To lave me in the moonlit dew.
  But, ah, this prison has my soul,
Damnable, bricked-in, cabined hole,
Where even the heaven's dear light must pass
Saddened through the painted glass.
Hemmed in with stacks of books am I,
Where works the worm with dusty mange,
While to the vaulted roof on high
The smoky ranks of papers range;
Retorts and jars my crib encumber,
And crowded instruments and, worse,
Loads of hereditary lumber—
And this, ay this, is called my universe.
  And shall I wonder why my heart
Is lamed and frightened in my breast,
Why all the springs of life that start
Are strangely smothered and oppressed?
Instead of all that life can hold
Of Nature's free, god-given breath,
I take to me the smoke and mould
Of skeletons and dust and death.
Up and away! A distant land
Awaits me in this secret book
From Nostradamus' very hand,
Nor for a better guide I look.
Now shall I read the starry pole,
In Nature's wisdom shall I seek
And know, with rising power of soul,
How spirit doth to spirit speak.
No dusty logic can divine
The meaning of a sacred sign.
Mysterious spirits, hovering near,
Answer me, if now ye hear!

(*He opens the book and lights upon the Sign of the Macrocosm.*)

Ah, strangely comes an onset of delight,
Invading all my senses as I gaze:
Young, sacred bliss-of-life springs at the sight,
And fires my blood in all its branching ways.
Was it a god who made this mystic scroll,
To touch my spirit's tumult with its healing,
And fill my wretched heart with joyous feeling,
And bring the secret world before my soul,

The hidden drive of Nature's force revealing?
Myself a god?—With lightened vision's leap
I read the riddle of the symbols, hear
The looms of Nature's might, that never sleep,
And know at last things spoken of the seer:
' 'Tis not the spirit world is sealed;
Thy heart is dead, thy senses' curtain drawn.
But, scholar, bathe, rejoicing, healed,
Thy earthly breast in streams of roseate dawn.'

(*He studies the sign.*)

Lo, single things inwoven, made to blend,
To work in oneness with the whole, and live
Members one of another, while ascend
Celestial powers, who ever take and give
Vessels of gold on heaven's living stair,
Their pinions fragrant with the bliss they bear,
Pervading all, that heaven and earth agree,
Transfixing all the world with harmony.
  O endless pageant!—But a pageant still,
A show, that mocks my touch or grasp or will!
Where are the nipples, Nature's springs, ah where
The living source that feeds the universe?
You flow, you give to drink, mysterious nurse,
And yet my soul is withered in despair.

(*Disconsolately he turns the pages until his glance rests on the sign of the Spirit of Earth.*)

A curious change affects me in this sign:
You, kindred Sprite of Earth, come strangely nearer;
My spirits rise, my powers are stronger, clearer,
As from the glow of a refreshing wine.
I gather heart to risk the world's encounter,
To bear my human fate as fate's surmounter,
To front the storm, in joy or grief not palter,
Even in the gnash of shipwreck never falter.
  The clouds close in above me
And hidden is the moon;
The lamp dies down.
A vapour grows—red quiverings
Dart round my head—there creeps
A shuddering from the vaulted roof
And seizes me!
I know, dread spirit of my call, 'tis you.
Stand forth, disclosed!
Ah, how my heart is harrowed through!
In tumult of feeling
My mind is riven, my senses reeling.
To you I yield, nor care if I am lost.
This thing must be, though life should be the cost.

(*He seizes the book and pronounces the secret sign of the Spirit. A reddish flame shoots up and the Spirit appears in the flame.*)

SPIRIT.  Who calls on me?

FAUST (*turning away*). O fearful form!

SPIRIT.                              At length
You have compelled me here. Your strength

Has wrestled long about my sphere,
And now—

FAUST.     I tremble: come not near.

SPIRIT.   With bated breath you laboured to behold me,
To hear my voice, to see me face to face.
You prayed with might, with depth that has controlled me,
And here am I!—What horror now can chase
The colour from your lips, my superman?
Where the soul's cry? The courage that began
To shape a world, and bear and foster it?
The heart that glowed, with lofty ardour lit,
To claim ethereal spirits as your peers?
Are you that Faust whose challenge smote my ears,
Who beat his way to me, proclaimed his hour,
And trembles now in presence of my power,
Writhes from the breath of it, a frightened worm?

FAUST.   And shall I, thing of flame, flinch at the sequel?
My name is Faust, in everything your equal.

SPIRIT.   In flood of life, in action's storm
I ply on my wave
With weaving motion
Birth and the grave,
A boundless ocean,
Ceaselessly giving
Weft of living,
Forms unending,
Glowing and blending.
So work I on the whirring loom of time,
The life that clothes the deity sublime.

FAUST.   Swift Spirit, you whose projects have no end,
How near akin our natures seem to be!

SPIRIT.   You match the spirit that you comprehend,
Not me. (*He vanishes.*)

FAUST (*filled with dismay*). Not you!
Whom then?
I, made in God's own image,
And not with you compare! (*A knock.*)
Damnation, that will be my Servitor!
My richest hope is in confusion hurled:
He spoils my vision of the spirit world,
This lickspittle of learning at my door.

(*Wagner in dressing-gown and night-cap, carrying a lamp.
Faust turns reluctantly.*)

WAGNER.   Beg pardon, but I heard you, Sir, declaiming—
Some tragedy, I'll warrant, from the Greek?—
That's just the learned art at which I'm aiming,
For people are impressed when scholars speak.
Indeed, I've heard the stage can be a teacher,
So that the actor can inspire the preacher.

FAUST.   Past question, if the parson is a mummer—
A thing you may discover, now and then.

WAGNER.   But, Sir, if learning ties us, winter, summer,
With holiday so rare, that we see men
As through a glass, remote and ill-defined,
How shall our counsel serve to lead mankind?

FAUST.   If feeling fails you, vain will be your course,
And idle what you plan unless your art
Springs from the soul with elemental force
To hold its sway in every listening heart.
Well, well, keep at it: ply the shears and paste,
Concoct from feasts of other men your hashes,
And should the thing be wanting fire or taste,
Blow into flame your little heap of ashes:
You'll find some apes and children who'll admire,
If admiration is your chief desire;
But what is uttered from the heart alone
Will win the hearts of others to your own.

WAGNER.   Yet by his style a speaker stands to win;
That I know well, and that I'm backward in.

FAUST. Trust honesty, to win success,
Be not a noisy jingling fool.
Good sense, Sir, and rightmindedness
Have little need to speak by rule.
And if your mind on urgent truth is set,
Need you go hunting for an epithet?
Nay, these your polished speeches that you make,
Serving mankind your snipped-out pie-frill papers,
They nourish us no more than winds that shake
The withered leaves, or shred the autumnal vapours.

WAGNER.   Ah me, Sir, long indeed is art;
Our life is very short, however,
And often, in my studious endeavour
A fearful dread assails my head and heart.
How hard it is to master ways and means
By which a man may reach the fountain-head!
And, ere he's half-way there, fate intervenes:
Before he knows it, the poor devil's dead.

FAUST.   Is parchment, then, your well of living water,
Where whosoever drinks shall be made whole?
Look not to stem your craving in that quarter:
The spring is vain that flows not from the soul.

WAGNER.   The pleasure, by your leave, is great, to cast
The mind into the spirit of the past,
And scan the former notions of the wise,
And see what marvellous heights we've reached at last.

FAUST.   Most nobly have we, up to the starry skies!
My friend, for us the alluring times of old
Are like a book that's sealed-up sevenfold.
And what you call the Spirit of the Ages
Is but the spirit of your learned sages,
Whose mirror is a pitiful affair,
Shunned by mankind after a single stare,
A mouldy dustbin, or a lumber attic,
Or at the most a blood-and-thunder play

Stuffed full of wit sententious and pragmatic,
Fit for the sawdust puppetry to say.

WAGNER.  And yet the world, the human heart and
      mind—
To understand these things must be our aim.

FAUST.  To understand—and how is that defined?
Who dares to give that child its proper name?
The few of understanding, vision rare,
Who veiled not from the herd their hearts, but tried,
Poor generous fools, to lay their feelings bare,
Them have men always burnt and crucified.
Excuse me, friend, it grows deep into night,
And now is time to think about adjourning.

WAGNER.  I could have stayed up longer with delight,
To join in discourse with your lofty learning.
But, Sir, to-morrow comes our Easter Day,
When I shall ask more questions, if I may.
I've learnt a deal, made books my drink and meat,
But cannot rest till knowledge is complete. *(Exit.)*

FAUST.

How strange, that he who cleaves to shallow things
Can keep his hopes alive on empty terms,
And dig with greed for precious plunderings,
And find his happiness unearthing worms!
  How dared this voice to raise its human bleat
Where waits the spirit world in immanent power?
And yet the man, so barren and effete,
Deserves my thanks in this most perilous hour.
He snatched me from a desperate despite
Fit to unhinge my reason, or to slay.
The apparition towered to such a height
My soul was dwarfed within me, in dismay.
  I, God's own image, who have seemed, forsooth,
Near to the mirror of eternal truth,
Compassed the power to shed the mortal clay
And revel in the self's celestial day,
I, who presumed in puissance to out-soar
The cherubim, to flow in Nature's veins,
With god-like joy in my creative pains,
I rode too high, and deep must I deplore:
One thunder-word has robbed me of my reins.
  I dare not, Spirit, count me in your sphere:
For, though I had the power to call you here,
No force have I that binds you or retains.
And in that moment dread and wondrous,
When I, so puny, grew so great,
You thrust me with a verdict thund'rous
Back to uncertain mortal fate.
Who is my guide? What shall I shun?
Or what imperious urge obey?
Alas, not only woes, but actions done,
Walk by us still, to hedge us on our way.
  The spirit's splendour, in the soul unfurled,
Is ever stifled with a stranger stuff.
High values, matched with good things of this world,
Mocking recede, and seem an airy bluff.

Our nobler veins, the true, life-giving springs,
Are choked with all the dust of earthy things.
  What though imaginate spread her wings
In early hope towards the things eternal,
Shrunk is her spacious realm in the diurnal
Defeat that loss and disappointment brings.
Full soon in deepest hearts care finds a nest,
And builds her bed of pain, in secret still,
There rocks herself, disturbing joy and rest,
And ever takes new shapes to work her will,
With fluttering fears for home or wife or child,
A thought of poison, flood or perils wild;
For man must quail at bridges never crossed,
Lamenting even things he never lost.
  Shall I then rank with gods? Too well I feel
My kinship with the worm, who bores the soil,
Who feeds on dust until the wanderer's heel
Gives sepulture to all his care and toil.
  Is it not dust, that fills my hundred shelves,
And walls me in like any pedant hack?
Fellow of moth that flits and worm that delves,
I drag my life through learned bric-a-brac.
And shall I here discover what I lack,
And learn, by reading countless volumes through,
That mortals mostly live on misery's rack,
That happiness is known to just a few?
You hollow skull, what has your grin to say,
But that a mortal brain, with trouble tossed,
Sought once, like mine, the sweetness of the day,
And strove for truth, and in the gloam was lost.
You instruments, you mock me to my face,
With wheel and gimbal, cylinder and cog;
You were my key to unlock the secret place:
The wards are cunning, but the levers clog.
For Nature keeps her veil inviolate,
Mysterious still in open light of day,
And where the spirit cannot penetrate
Your screws and irons will never make a way.
Here stands the gear that I have never touched,
My father's stuff, bequeathed to be my prison,
With scrolls of vellum, blackened and besmutched,
Where still the desk-lamp's dismal smoke has risen.
Better have spent what little was my own,
Than sweat for petty gains by midnight oil.
The things that men inherit come alone
To true possession by the spirit's toil.
What can't be used is trash; what can, a prize
Begotten from the moment as it flies.
  But what magnetic thing compels my gaze?
This phial fascinates me, like the sight
Of soothing moon when, deep in forest ways,
Our very thoughts are silvered with the light.
  You I salute, you flask of virtue rare,
That now I hand me down with reverent care;
In you I honour human wit and art.
You very spirit of the opiate flowers,
You distillation of the deadly powers,
Show to your master now your gracious heart:
To see you, touch you, soothes my strife and pain.
I hear a call towards the open main,

My tide of soul is ebbing more and more,
Lies at my feet the shining, glassy plain,
A new day beckons to another shore.
    As if on wings, a chariot of fire
Draws near me. I am ready to be free.
Piercing the ether, new-born, I aspire
To rise to spheres of pure activity.
This soaring life, this bliss of godlike birth,
How shall we earn it, who from worms must rise?
Yet true the call: I spurn the sun of earth,
Leave, resolute, its loveliness. My eyes
I lift in daring to fling wide the gate
Whose threshold men have ever flinching trod.
The hour is come, as master of my fate
To prove in man the stature of a god,
Nor blench before the cavern black and fell,
Imagination's torment evermore,
But dare the narrow flaming pass of hell
And stride in strength towards the dreaded door.

This step I take in cheerful resolution,
Risk more than death, yea, dare my dissolution.
    Pure crystal bowl, I take you from your case,
Come down, to help me, from your waiting-place.
Long have I owned your worth with unconcern,
You who could charm, upon high holidays,
My father's guests, and shining win their praise,
As each received the loving-cup in turn.
The pride of art, the legends in the frieze,
The drinker's pledge, to tell them all in rhyme,
Then lift the cup and drain it to the lees—
All brings me back the nights of youthful prime.
I shall not hand you now to any friend,
No witty praise of art do I intend,
For here's a cordial quick to drown the sense,
A chalice with dark opiate to dispense:
I choose, clear-eyed, the draught of my preparing
And drink my last, with all my spirit daring
To pledge the morrow's awful imminence. . . .

---

# JANE AUSTEN

## from *Pride and Prejudice*

---

Jane Austen (1775–1817), England's first great woman novelist, published her first work *Sense and Sensibility* in 1811. A comic novel about middle-class, provincial life, this work staked out a part of the literary world that she soon made her own. She knew this terrain intimately, for she spent her life in small towns, far from London. When *Sense and Sensibility* found an admiring public, there followed five more novels: *Pride and Prejudice* (1813); *Mansfield Park* (1814); *Emma* (1816); *Northanger Abbey* and *Persuasion*, issued jointly (1818). Of these, *Pride and Prejudice* is the most well-known.

*Pride and Prejudice* was written during the Napoleonic Era (1799–1815), when England was nearly always fighting France; the novel, however, contains no hint of these wars, except that a solider like Mr. Wickham appears as an eligible bachelor. Nor is there mention of the Industrial Revolution, which was changing England for the worse. The novel's world is rustic towns and unspoiled countryside with well-kept estates and tidy farms. Austen focused on a vanishing society whose smallest unit was the family and whose major problems involved shifting social relationships.

*Pride and Prejudice* has a simple plot: the Bennets—a shabby, genteel family of the middle class—find suitable husbands for their five daughters. Austen turns this plot into an intriguing story through clear writing, subtle irony, and, most notably, precise dissection of the manners and rituals of middle-class life: the balls, the letters and gossip, the visits back and forth, and the unexpected calamities, such as a social snub, an elopement, a betrayed secret, or a broken engagement. She was especially aware of society's constraints on women, as in the depiction of the dilemma of Charlotte Lucas, who weighs her future husband's ugly character against the social position he offers.

Austen composed *Pride and Prejudice* in the Neoclassical style, which had dominated English writing in the 1700s (see Fielding's *Tom Jones*). This style's stress on decorum and orthodox morals suited Austen's purposes very well. In effect she treated society as a dance, with her characters going through the paces with grace, good cheer, and determination. Neither romantic nor sentimental but with great insight, she showed people of varied temperaments dealing with social conventions.

## Reading the Selection

*Pride and Prejudice's* first three chapters show Austen's skillful handling of the characters and her good ear for dialogue. Chapter 1 deftly lays out the dynamics in the Bennet family: Mrs. Bennet is a social climber, eager to provide rich husbands for her daughters; she is vulgar in comparison to Mr. Bennett, who is beleaguered by his wife's prattling, yet does not stop her scheming. Mr. Bennet is partial to daughter Lizzy—Elizabeth—the highspirited heroine, as it turns out, of this delightful novel.

In Chapter II, Mr. Bennet reveals his social call on Mr. Bingley, a potential suitor for his daughters. Four daughters are introduced, and they begin to assert their individual natures.

Chapter III presents the last Bennet daughter Jane; the wealthy Mr. Bingley; and the haughty Mr. Darcy. Thereafter Darcy and Elizabeth give the novel its focus: proud Darcy and equally proud Elizabeth must endure mutual slights and disagreements before love can dissolve their prejudices against one another.

---

## Chapter 1

It is a truth universally acknowledged, that a single man in possession of a good fortune, must be in want of a wife.

However little known the feelings or views of such a man may be on his first entering a neighbourhood, this truth is so well fixed in the minds of the surrounding families, that he is considered as the rightful property of some one or other of their daughters.

'My dear Mr Bennet,' said his lady to him one day, 'have you heard that Netherfield Park is let at last?'

Mr Bennet replied that he had not.

'But it is,' returned she; 'for Mrs Long has just been here, and she told me all about it.'

Mr Bennet made no answer.

'Do not you want to know who has taken it?' cried his wife impatiently.

'*You* want to tell me, and I have no objection to hearing it.'

This was invitation enough.

'Why, my dear, you must know, Mrs Long says that Netherfield is taken by a young man of large fortune from the north of England; that he came down on Monday in a chaise and four to see the place, and was so much delighted with it that he agreed with Mr Morris immediately; that he is to take possession before Michaelmas, and some of his servants are to be in the house by the end of next week.'

'What is his name?'

'Bingley.'

'Is he married or single?'

'Oh! single, my dear, to be sure! A single man of large fortune; four or five thousand a year. What a fine thing for our girls!'

'How so? how can it affect them?'

'My dear Mr Bennet,' replied his wife, 'how can you be so tiresome! You must know that I am thinking of his marrying one of them.'

'Is that his design in settling here?'

'Design! nonsense, how can you talk so! But it is very likely that he *may* fall in love with one of them, and therefore you must visit him as soon as he comes.'

'I see no occasion for that. You and the girls may go, or you may send them by themselves, which perhaps will be still better, for as you are as handsome as any of them, Mr Bingley might like you the best of the party.'

'My dear, you flatter me. I certainly *have* had my share of beauty, but I do not pretend to be any thing extraordinary now. When a woman has five grown up daughters, she ought to give over thinking of her own beauty.'

'In such cases, a woman has not often much beauty to think of.'

'But, my dear, you must indeed go and see Mr Bingley when he comes into the neighbourhood.'

'It is more than I engage for, I assure you.'

'But consider your daughters. Only think what an establishment it would be for one of them. Sir William and Lady Lucas are determined to go, merely on that account, for in general you know they visit no new comers. Indeed you must go, for it will be impossible for *us* to visit him, if you do not.'

'You are over scrupulous surely. I dare say Mr Bingley will be very glad to see you; and I will send a few lines by you to assure him of my hearty consent to his marrying which ever he chuses of the girls; though I must throw in a good word for my little Lizzy.'

'I desire you will do no such thing. Lizzy is not a bit better than the others; and I am sure she is not half so handsome as Jane, nor half so good humored as Lydia. But you are always giving *her* the preference.'

'They have none of them much to recommend them,' replied he; 'they are all silly and ignorant like other girls; but Lizzy has something more of quickness than her sisters.'

'Mr Bennet, how can you abuse your own children in such a way? You take delight in vexing me. You have no compassion on my poor nerves.'

'You mistake me, my dear. I have a high respect for your nerves. They are my old friends. I have heard you mention them with consideration these twenty years at least.'

'Ah! you do not know what I suffer.'

'But I hope you will get over it, and live to see many young men of four thousand a year come into the neighbourhood.'

'It will be no use to us, if twenty such should come since you will not visit them.'

'Depend upon it, my dear, that when there are twenty, I will visit them all.'

Mr Bennet was so odd a mixture of quick parts, sarcastic humour, reserve, and caprice, that the experience of three and twenty years had been sufficient to make his wife understand his character. *Her* mind was less difficult to develope. She was a woman of mean understanding, little information, and uncertain temper. When she was discontented she fancied herself nervous. The business of her life was to get her daughters married; its solace was visiting and news.

### Chapter 2

Mr Bennet was among the earliest of those who waited on Mr Bingley. He had always intended to visit him, though to the last always assuring his wife that he should not go; and till the evening after the visit was paid, she had no knowledge of it. It was then disclosed in the following manner. Observing his second daughter employed in trimming a hat, he suddenly addressed her with,

'I hope Mr Bingley will like it Lizzy.'

'We are not in a way to know *what* Mr Bingley likes,' said her mother resentfully, 'since we are not to visit.'

'But you forget, mama,' said Elizabeth, 'that we shall meet him at the assemblies, and that Mrs Long has promised to introduce him.'

'I do not believe Mrs Long will do any such thing. She has two nieces of her own. She is a selfish, hypocritical woman, and I have no opinion of her.'

'No more have I,' said Mr Bennet; 'and I am glad to find that you do not depend on her serving you.'

Mrs Bennet deigned not to make any reply; but unable to contain herself, began scolding one of her daughters.

'Don't keep coughing so, Kitty, for heaven's sake! Have a little compassion on my nerves. You tear them to pieces.'

'Kitty has no discretion in her coughs,' said her father; 'she times them ill.'

'I do not cough for my own amusement,' replied Kitty fretfully.

'When is your next ball to be, Lizzy?'

'To-morrow fortnight.'

'Aye, so it is,' cried her mother, 'and Mrs Long does not come back till the day before; so, it will be impossible for her to introduce him, for she will not know him herself.'

'Then, my dear, you may have the advantage of your friend, and introduce Mr Bingley to *her*.'

'Impossible, Mr Bennet, impossible, when I am not acquainted with him myself; how can you be so teazing?'

'I honour your circumspection. A fortnight's acquaintance is certainly very little. One cannot know what a man really is by the end of a fortnight. But if *we* do not venture, somebody else will; and after all, Mrs Long and her nieces must stand their chance; and therefore, as she will think it an act of kindness, if you decline the office, I will take it on myself.'

The girls stared at their father. Mrs Bennet said only, 'Nonsense, nonsense!'

'What can be the meaning of that emphatic exclamation?' cried he. 'Do you consider the forms of introduction, and the stress that is laid on them, as nonsense? I cannot quite agree with you *there*. What say you, Mary? for you are a young lady of deep reflection I know, and read great books, and make extracts.'

Mary wished to say something very sensible, but knew not how.

'While Mary is adjusting her ideas,' he continued, 'let us return to Mr Bingley.'

'I am sick of Mr Bingley,' cried his wife.

'I am sorry to hear *that*; but why did not you tell me so before? If I had known as much this morning, I certainly would not have called on him. It is very unlucky; but as I have actually paid the visit, we cannot escape the acquaintance now.'

The astonishment of the ladies was just what he wished; that of Mrs Bennet perhaps surpassing the rest; though when the first tumult of joy was over, she began to declare that it was what she had expected all the while.

'How good it was in you, my dear Mr Bennet! But I knew I should persuade you at last. I was sure you loved your girls too well to neglect such an acquaintance. Well, how pleased I am! and it is such a good joke, too, that you should have gone this morning, and never said a word about it till now.'

'Now, Kitty, you may cough as much as you chuse,' said Mr Bennet; and, as he spoke, he left the room, fatigued with the raptures of his wife.

'What an excellent father you have, girls,' said she, when the door was shut. 'I do not know how you will ever make him amends for his kindness; or me either, for that matter. At our time of life, it is not so pleasant I can tell you, to be making new acquaintance every day; but for your sakes, we would do any thing. Lydia, my love, though you *are* the youngest, I dare say Mr Bingley will dance with you at the next ball.'

'Oh!' said Lydia stoutly, 'I am not afraid; for though I *am* the youngest, I'm the tallest.'

The rest of the evening was spent in conjecturing how soon he would return Mr Bennet's visit, and determining when they should ask him to dinner.

### Chapter 3

Not all that Mrs Bennet, however, with the assistance of her five daughters, could ask on the subject was sufficient to draw from her husband any satisfactory description of Mr Bingley. They attacked him in various ways; with barefaced questions, ingenious suppositions, and distant surmises; but he eluded the skill of them all; and they were at last obliged to accept the second-hand intelligence of their neighbour Lady Lucas. Her report was highly favourable. Sir William had been delighted with him. He was quite young, wonderfully handsome, extremely agreeable, and to crown the whole, he meant to be at the next assembly with a large party. Nothing could be more delightful! To be fond of dancing was a certain step towards falling in love; and very lively hopes of Mr Bingley's heart were entertained.

'If I can but see one of my daughters happily settled at Netherfield,' said Mrs Bennet to her husband, 'and all the others equally well married, I shall have nothing to wish for.'

In a few days Mr Bingley returned Mr Bennet's visit, and sat about ten minutes with him in his library. He had entertained hopes of being admitted to a sight of the young ladies, of whose beauty he had heard much; but he saw only the father. The ladies were somewhat more fortunate, for they had the advantage of ascertaining from an upper window, that he wore a blue coat and rode a black horse.

An invitation to dinner was soon afterwards dispatched; and already had Mrs Bennet planned the courses that were to do credit to her housekeeping, when an answer arrived which deferred it all. Mr Bingley was obliged to be in town the following day, and consequently unable to accept the honour of their invitation, &c. Mrs Bennet was quite disconcerted. She could not imagine what business he could have in town so soon after his arrival in Hertfordshire; and she began to fear that he might be always flying about from one place to another, and never settled at Netherfield as he ought to be. Lady Lucas quieted her fears a little by starting the idea of his being gone to London only to get a large party for the ball; and a report soon followed that Mr Bingley was to bring twelve ladies and seven gentlemen with him to the assembly. The girls grieved over such a number of ladies; but were comforted the day before the ball by hearing, that instead of twelve, he had brought only six with him from London, his five sisters and a cousin. And when the party entered the assembly room, it consisted of only five altogether; Mr Bingley, his two sisters, the husband of the eldest, and another young man.

Mr Bingley was good looking and gentlemanlike; he had a pleasant countenance, and easy, unaffected manners. His sisters were fine women, with an air of decided fashion. His brother-in-law, Mr Hurst, merely looked the gentleman; but his friend Mr Darcy soon drew the attention of the room by his fine, tall person, handsome features, noble mien; and the report which was in general circulation within five minutes after his entrance, of his having ten thousand a year. The gentlemen pronounced him to be a fine figure of a man, the ladies declared he was much handsomer than Mr Bingley, and he was looked at with great admiration for about half the evening, till his manners gave a disgust which turned the tide of his popularity; for he was discovered to be proud, to be above his company, and above being pleased; and not all his large estate in Derbyshire could then save him from having a most forbidding, disagreeable countenance, and being unworthy to be compared with his friend.

Mr Bingley had soon made himself acquainted with all the principal people in the room; he was lively and unreserved, danced every dance, was angry that the ball closed so early, and talked of giving one himself at Netherfield. Such amiable qualities must speak for themselves. What a contrast between him and his friend! Mr Darcy danced only once with Mrs Hurst and once with Miss Bingley, declined being introduced to any other lady, and spent the rest of the evening in walking about the room, speaking occasionally to one of his own party. His character was decided. He was the proudest, most disagreeable man in the world, and every body hoped that he would never come there again. Amongst the most violent against him was Mrs Bennet, whose dislike of his general behaviour, was sharpened into particular resentment, by his having slighted one of her daughters.

Elizabeth Bennet had been obliged, by the scarcity of gentlemen, to sit down for two dances; and during part of that time, Mr Darcy had been standing near enough for her to overhear a conversation between him and Mr Bingley, who came from the dance for a few minutes, to press his friend to join it.

'Come, Darcy,' said he, 'I must have you dance. I hate to see you standing about by yourself in this stupid manner. You had much better dance.'

'I certainly shall not. You know how I detest it, unless I am particularly acquainted with my partner. At such an assembly as this, it would be insupportable. Your sisters are engaged, and there is not another woman in the room, whom it would not be a punishment to me to stand up with.'

'I would not be so fastidious as you are,' cried Bingley, 'for a kingdom! Upon my honour, I never met with so many pleasant girls in my life, as I have this evening; and there are several of them you see uncommonly pretty.'

'*You* are dancing with the only handsome girl in the room,' said Mr Darcy, looking at the eldest Miss Bennet.

'Oh! she is the most beautiful creature I ever beheld! But there is one of her sisters sitting down just behind you, who is very pretty, and I dare say, very agreeable. Do let me ask my partner to introduce you.'

'Which do you mean?' and turning round, he looked for a moment at Elizabeth, till catching her eye, he withdrew his own and coldly said, 'She is tolerable; but not handsome enough to tempt *me*; and I am in no humour at present to give consequence to young ladies who are slighted by other men. You had better return to your partner and enjoy her smiles, for you are wasting your time with me.'

Mr Bingley followed his advice. Mr Darcy walked off; and Elizabeth remained with no very cordial feelings towards him. She told the story however with great spirit among her friends; for she had a lively, playful disposition, which delighted in any thing ridiculous.

The evening altogether passed off pleasantly to the whole family. Mrs Bennet had seen her eldest daughter much admired by the Netherfield party. Mr Bingley had danced with her twice, and she had been distinguished by his sisters. Jane was as much gratified by this, as her mother could be, though in a quieter way. Elizabeth felt Jane's pleasure. Mary had heard herself mentioned to Miss Bingley as the most accomplished girl in the neighbourhood; and Catherine and Lydia had been fortunate enough to be never without partners, which was all that they had yet learnt to care for at a ball. They returned therefore in good spirits to Longbourn, the village where they lived, and of which they were the principal inhabitants. They found Mr Bennet still up. With a book he was regardless of time; and on the present occasion he had a good deal of curiosity as to the event of an evening which had raised such splendid expectations. He had rather hoped that all his wife's views on the stranger would be disappointed; but he soon found that he had a very different story to hear.

'Oh! my dear Mr Bennet,' as she entered the room, 'we have had a most delightful evening, a most excellent ball. I wish you had been there. Jane was so admired, nothing could be like it. Every body said how well she looked; and Mr Bingley thought her quite beautiful, and danced with her twice. Only think of *that* my dear; he actually danced with her twice; and she was the only creature in the room that he asked a second time. First of all, he asked Miss Lucas. I was so vexed to see him stand up with her; but, however, he did not admire her at all: indeed, nobody can, you know; and he seemed quite struck with Jane as she was going down the dance. So, he enquired who she was, and got introduced, and asked her for the two next. Then, the two third he danced with Miss King, and the two fourth with Maria Lucas, and the two fifth with Jane again, and the two sixth with Lizzy, and the Boulanger—'

'If he had had any compassion for *me*,' cried her husband impatiently, 'he would not have danced half so much! For God's sake, say no more of his partners. Oh! that he had sprained his ankle in the first dance!'

'Oh! my dear,' continued Mrs Bennet, 'I am quite delighted with him. He is so excessively handsome! and his sisters are charming women. I never in my life saw any thing more elegant than their dresses. I dare say the lace upon Mrs Hurst's gown—'

Here she was interrupted again. Mr Bennet protested against any description of finery. She was therefore obliged to seek another branch of the subject, and related, with much bitterness of spirit and some exaggeration, the shocking rudeness of Mr Darcy.

'But I can assure you,' she added, 'that Lizzy does not lose much by not suiting *his* fancy; for he is a most disagreeable, horrid man, not at all worth pleasing. So high and so conceited that there was no enduring him! He walked here, and he walked there, fancying himself so very great! Not handsome enough to dance with! I wish you had been there, my dear, to have given him one of your set downs. I quite detest the man.'

---

# MARY SHELLEY

# from *Frankenstein*

---

Shelley's *Frankenstein* (1818) is a neglected classic, for fewer people have read the novel than know the story. This neglect began soon after publication, when the novel became the basis of a popular drama. The story's appeal grew in this century, inspiring countless movies, television films, cartoons, and even a musical. Success transformed the basic story, in the Nuclear Age, into a myth of humanity's foolish attempts to unlock the secrets of nature.

Shelley's original work deserves to be read, for it is both richer and more complex than the popular tale. It belongs to the genre of epistolary novel, or novel in the form of letters and diary entries—a popular eighteenth-century form. At the core of her novel is the story of Victor Frankenstein, a Swiss scientist who discovers the secret of life and creates a being from raw materials salvaged from graves, butcher shops, and dissecting rooms.

This creature—with no name thus adding to his inhuman traits—is of such loathsome appearance that all who see him are filled with horror and disgust. Innately kind, the creature is transformed by personal loneliness and encounters with fearful humans into a monster whose rage is directed toward Frankenstein and his family. Pursuit becomes the novel's theme as the monster chases his creator across pitiless, ice-filled seas, to a grim conclusion.

Frankenstein's tale is framed within a second story which concerns Robert Walton, an English sailor who seeks fame by making "a voyage of discovery towards the north pole." It is during this voyage that Walton meets Frankenstein, takes him on board ship, and hears his strange story. Walton's letters report his own exploits and those of Frankenstein and the monster, each in his own words.

Shelley intended *Frankenstein* to be a morality fable about unbridled ambition, as indicated by the subtitle, *The Modern Prometheus*. In Greek myth, Prometheus was a Titan who created the first man and woman and brought them mixed gifts, fire and sorrows. The novel's Prometheus is both Frankenstein and Walton. Together they symbolize knowledge pursued regardless of cost. This moral reflected Europe's reactionary mood in post-Napoleonic times, a period marked by economic depression and political repression.

Mary Wollstonecraft Shelley (1797–1851) had excellent literary ties, and this may have inspired her to become a writer. The daughter of the novelist William Godwin and the feminist Mary Wollstonecraft, she eloped with the poet Percy Bysshe Shelley, causing a scandal. She began *Frankenstein* in Switzerland, in summer 1817, while recovering from the birth of her second child. The novel was sparked by an evening of ghost stories told by Shelley and the poet Lord Byron. Mary Shelley was then only eighteen years old.

### Reading the Selection

This selection from Chapters 4 and 5 of *Frankenstein* gives Frankenstein's story—as recorded by Walton—of the "birth" of the monster. In telling his story, the doctor knows it is too late for himself—he accepts his ultimate death at the hands of the monster—but he wants Walton to avoid a similar fate by adopting a new moral code: Stifle ambition if it weakens natural feelings. If ambition were to be controlled, he reasoned, then "America would have been discovered more gradually, and the empires of Mexico and Peru had not been destroyed." Frankenstein— and Shelley—thus make a plea for a global family united by mutual ties of affection.

---

## Chapter 4

• • •

One of the phaenomena which had peculiarly attracted my attention was the structure of the human frame, and, indeed, any animal endued with life. Whence, I often asked myself, did the principle of life proceed? It was a bold question, and one which has ever been considered as a mystery: yet with how many things are we upon the brink of becoming acquainted, if cowardice or carelessness did not restrain our enquiries. I revolved these circumstances in my mind and determined thenceforth to apply myself more particularly to those branches of natural philosophy which relate to physiology. Unless I had been animated by an almost supernatural enthusiasm, my application to this study would have been irksome and almost intolerable. To examine the causes of life, we must first have recourse to death. I became acquainted with the science of anatomy, but this was not sufficient; I must also observe the natural decay and corruption of the human body. In my education my father had taken the greatest precautions that my mind should be impressed with no supernatural horrors. I do not ever remember to have trembled at a tale of superstition or to have feared the apparition of a spirit. Darkness had no effect upon my fancy, and a churchyard was to me merely the receptacle of bodies deprived of life, which, from being the seat of beauty and strength, had become food for the worm. Now I was led to examine the cause and progress of this decay and forced to spend days and nights in vaults and charnel-houses. My attention was fixed upon every object the most insupportable to the delicacy of the human feelings. I saw how the fine form of man was degraded and wasted; I beheld the corruption of death succeed to the blooming cheek of life; I saw how the worm inherited the wonders of the eye and brain. I paused, examining and analysing all the minutiae of causation, as exemplified in the change from life to death, and death to life, until from the midst of this darkness a sudden light broke in upon me—a light so brilliant and wondrous, yet so simple, that while I became dizzy with the immensity of the prospect which it illustrated, I was surprised that among so many men of genius who had directed their enquiries towards the same science, that I alone should be reserved to discover so astonishing a secret.

Remember, I am not recording the vision of a madman. The sun does not more certainly shine in the heavens than that which I now affirm is true. Some miracle might have produced it, yet the stages of the discovery were distinct and probable. After days and nights of incredible labour and fatigue, I succeeded in discovering the cause of generation and life; nay, more, I became myself capable of bestowing animation upon lifeless matter.

The astonishment which I had at first experienced on this discovery soon gave place to delight and rapture. After so much time spent in painful labour, to arrive at once at the summit of my desires was the most gratifying consummation of my toils. But this discovery was so great and overwhelming that all the steps by which I had been progressively led to it were obliterated, and I beheld only the result. What had been the study and desire of the wisest men since the creation of the world was now within my grasp. Not that, like a magic scene, it all opened upon me at once: the information I had obtained was of a nature rather to direct my endeavours so soon as I should point them towards the object of my search than to exhibit that object already accomplished. I was like the Arabian who had been buried with the dead and found a passage to life, aided only by one glimmering and seemingly ineffectual light.

I see by your eagerness and the wonder and hope which your eyes express, my friend, that you expect to be informed of the secret with which I am acquainted; that cannot be; listen patiently until the end of my story, and you will easily perceive why I am reserved upon that subject. I will not lead you on, unguarded and ardent as I then was, to your destruction and infallible misery. Learn from me, if not by my precepts, at least by my example, how dangerous is the acquirement of knowledge and how much happier that man is who believes his native town to be the world, than he who aspires to become greater than his nature will allow.

When I found so astonishing a power placed within my hands, I hesitated a long time concerning the manner in which I should employ it. Although I possessed the capacity of bestowing animation, yet to prepare a frame for the reception of it, with all its intricacies of fibres, muscles, and veins, still remained a work of inconceivable difficulty and labour. I doubted at first whether I should attempt the creation of a being like myself, or one of simpler organization; but my imagination was too much exalted by my first success to permit me to doubt of my ability to give life to an animal as complex and wonderful as man. The materials at present within my command hardly appeared adequate to so arduous an undertaking, but I doubted not that I should ultimately succeed. I prepared myself for a multitude of reverses; my operations might be incessantly baffled, and at last my work be imperfect; yet when I considered the improvement which every day takes place in science and mechanics, I was encouraged to hope my present attempts would at least lay the foundations of future success. Nor could I consider the magnitude and complexity of my plan as any argument of its impracticability. It was with these feelings that I began the creation of a human being. As the minuteness of the parts formed a great hindrance to my speed, I resolved, contrary to my first intention, to make the being of a gigantic stature; that is to say, about eight feet in height, and proportionately large. After having formed this determination and having spent some months in successfully collecting and arranging my materials, I began.

No one can conceive the variety of feelings which bore me onwards, like a hurricane, in the first enthusiasm of success. Life and death appeared to me ideal bounds, which I should first break through, and pour a torrent of light into our dark world. A new species would bless me as its creator and source; many happy and excellent natures would owe their being to me. No father could claim the gratitude of his child so completely as I should deserve theirs. Pursuing these reflections, I thought that if I could bestow animation upon lifeless matter, I might in process of time (although I now found it impossible) renew life where death had apparently devoted the body to corruption.

These thoughts supported my spirits, while I pursued my undertaking with unremitting ardour. My cheek had grown pale with study, and my person had become emaciated with confinement. Sometimes, on the very brink of certainty, I failed; yet still I clung to the hope which the next day or the next hour might realize. One secret which I alone possessed was the hope to which I had dedicated myself; and the moon gazed on my midnight labours, while, with unrelaxed and breathless eagerness, I pursued nature to her hiding-places. Who shall conceive the horrors of my secret toil as I dabbled among the unhallowed damps of the grave or tortured the living animal to animate the lifeless clay? My limbs now tremble, and my eyes swim with the remembrance; but then a resistless and almost frantic impulse urged me forward; I seemed to have lost all soul or sensation but for this one pursuit. It was indeed but a passing trance, that only made me feel with renewed acuteness so soon as, the unnatural stimulus ceasing to operate, I had returned to my old habits. I collected bones from charnel-houses and disturbed, with profane fingers, the tremendous secrets of the human frame. In a solitary chamber, or rather cell, at the top of the house, and separated from all the other apartments by a gallery and staircase, I kept my workshop of filthy creation: my eyeballs were starting from their sockets in attending to the details of my employment. The dissecting room and the slaughter-house furnished many of my materials; and often did my human nature turn with loathing from my occupation, whilst, still urged on by an eagerness which perpetually increased, I brought my work near to a conclusion.

The summer months passed while I was thus engaged, heart and soul, in one pursuit. It was a most beautiful season; never did the fields bestow a more plentiful harvest or the vines yield a more luxuriant vintage: but my eyes were insensible to the charms of nature. And the same feelings which made me neglect the scenes around me caused me also to forget those friends who were so many miles absent, and whom I had not seen for so long a time. I knew my silence disquieted them, and I well remembered the words of my father: 'I know that while you are pleased with yourself you will think of us with affection, and we shall hear regularly from you. You must pardon me if I regard any interruption in your correspondence as a proof that your other duties are equally neglected.'

I knew well therefore what would be my father's feelings, but I could not tear my thoughts from my employment, loathsome in itself, but which had taken an irresistible hold of my imagination. I wished, as it were, to procrastinate all that related to my feelings of affection until the great object, which swallowed up every habit of my nature, should be completed.

I then thought that my father would be unjust if he ascribed my neglect to vice or faultiness on my part, but I am now convinced that he was justified in conceiving that I should not be altogether free from blame. A human being in perfection ought always to preserve a calm and peaceful mind and never to allow passion or a transitory desire to disturb his tranquillity. I do not think that the pursuit of knowledge is an exception to this rule. If the study to which you apply yourself has a tendency to weaken your affections and to destroy your taste for those simple pleasures in which no alloy can possibly mix, then that study is certainly unlawful, that is to say, not befitting the human mind. If this rule were always observed; if no man allowed any pursuit whatsoever to interfere with the tranquillity of his domestic affections, Greece had not been enslaved, Caesar would have spared his country, America would have been discovered more gradually, and the empires of Mexico and Peru had not been destroyed.

But I forget that I am moralizing in the most interesting part of my tale, and your looks remind me to proceed.

My father made no reproach in his letters and only took notice of my silence by enquiring into my occupations more particularly than before. Winter, spring, and summer passed away during my labours; but I did not watch the blossom or the expanding leaves—sights which before always yielded me supreme delight—so deeply was I engrossed in my occupation. The leaves of that year had withered before my work drew near to a close, and now every day showed me more plainly how well I had succeeded. But my enthusiasm was checked by my anxiety, and I appeared rather like one doomed by slavery to toil in the mines, or any other unwholesome trade than an artist occupied by his favourite employment. Every night I was oppressed by a slow fever, and I became nervous to a most painful degree; the fall of a leaf startled me, and I shunned my fellow creatures as if I had been guilty of a crime. Sometimes I grew alarmed at the wreck I perceived that I had become; the energy of my purpose alone sustained me: my labours would soon end, and I believed that exercise and amusement would then drive away incipient disease; and I promised myself both of these when my creation should be complete.

**Chapter 5**

It was on a dreary night of November that I beheld the accomplishment of my toils. With an anxiety that almost amounted to agony, I collected the instruments of life around me, that I might infuse a spark of being into the lifeless thing that lay at my feet. It was already one in the morning; the rain pattered dismally against the panes, and my candle was nearly burnt out, when, by the glimmer of the half-extinguished light, I saw the dull yellow eye of the creature open; it breathed hard, and a convulsive motion agitated its limbs.

How can I describe my emotions at this catastrophe, or how delineate the wretch whom with such infinite pains and care I had endeavoured to form? His limbs were in proportion, and I had selected his features as beautiful. Beautiful! Great God! His yellow skin scarcely covered the work of muscles and arteries beneath; his hair was of a lustrous black, and flowing; his teeth of pearly whiteness; but these luxuriances only formed a more horrid contrast with his watery eyes, that seemed almost of the same colour as the dun-white sockets in which they were set, his shrivelled complexion and straight black lips.

The different accidents of life are not so changeable as the feelings of human nature. I had worked hard for nearly two years, for the sole purpose of infusing life into an inanimate body. For this I had deprived myself of rest and health. I had desired it with an ardour that far exceeded moderation; but now that I had finished, the beauty of the dream vanished, and breathless horror and disgust filled my heart. Unable to endure the aspect of the being I had created, I rushed out of the room and continued a long time traversing my bedchamber, unable to compose my mind to sleep. At length lassitude succeeded to the tumult I had before endured, and I threw myself on the bed in my clothes, endeavouring to seek a few moments of forgetfulness. But it was in vain; I slept, indeed, but I was disturbed by the wildest dreams. I thought I saw Elizabeth, in the bloom of health, walking in the streets of Ingolstadt. Delighted and surprized, I embraced her, but as I imprinted the first kiss on her lips, they became livid with the hue of death; her features appeared to change, and I thought that I held the corpse of my dead mother in my arms; a shroud enveloped her form, and I saw the grave-worms crawling in the folds of the flannel. I started from my sleep with horror; a cold dew covered my forehead, my teeth chattered, and every limb became convulsed; when, by the dim and yellow light of the moon, as it forced its way through the window shutters, I beheld the wretch—the miserable monster whom I had created. He held up the curtain of the bed; and his eyes, if eyes they may be called, were fixed on me. His jaws opened, and he muttered some inarticulate sounds, while a grin wrinkled his cheeks. He might have spoken, but I did not hear; one hand was stretched out, seemingly to detain me, but I escaped and rushed downstairs. I took refuge in the courtyard belonging to the house which I inhabited, where I remained during the rest of the night, walking up and down in the greatest agitation, listening attentively, catching and fearing each sound as if it were to announce the approach of the daemoniacal corpse to which I had so miserably given life.

Oh! No mortal could support the horror of that countenance. A mummy again endued with animation could not be so hideous as that wretch. I had gazed on him while unfinished; he was ugly then, but when those muscles and joints were rendered capable of motion, it became a thing such as even Dante could not have conceived.

I passed the night wretchedly. Sometimes my pulse beat so quickly and hardly that I felt the palpitation of every artery; at others, I nearly sank to the ground through languor and extreme weakness. Mingled with this horror, I felt the bitterness of disappointment; dreams that had been my food and pleasant rest for so long a space were now become a hell to me; and the change was so rapid, the overthrow so complete! . . .

---

# GEORGE GORDON, LORD BYRON

# from *Don Juan*

## Canto I

---

George Gordon, Lord Byron (1788–1824) was a titanic figure who was regarded by his generation as the spirit of Romanticism. While his popularity has waned today, he remains an influential writer of the Romantic period. Unlike Wordsworth (see "Tintern Abbey"), who extolled the unity of the human and natural realms and avoided direct references to politics, Byron was a European poet who was actively engaged with the major people and issues of his time. Through his poems, he sought to identify patterns linking the present to the recent and distant past.

What made these poems memorable was that Byron made himself their center, speaking in either his own voice or through a heroic surrogate. From his first to his last works, he thought of himself as both a man and a poet with a mission, even if dimly understood. Thus he represented himself in his poems as a figure of destiny on whom both the broad sweep of history and the entire Western poetic tradition converged. Byron's pose as a world-historical figure ruled by his "star" became an enduring image of the Romantic era and influenced later artists and writers, most notably Nietzsche (see *The Gay Science*, etc.).

The crucial dates in Byron's life are 1812, when he soared to fame with *Childe Harold's Pilgrimage,* a poem about his travels on the continent; 1816, when his marriage failed amid scandal involving charges of incest (probably true) with his half-sister, causing him to flee England, never to return; and 1824, when he died in Greece, in pursuit of republican ideals and fighting for Greek independence.

## Reading the Selection

Byron's greatest poem, *Don Juan* (Cantos I and II, 1819; Cantos III–V, 1821; and Cantos VI–XXVI, 1823–1824), dates from his years of exile, when he declared himself "born for opposition." Reflecting despair over the future, the poem condemned the political reaction set in motion by England and its allies after Napoleon's defeat. It also reflected Byron's rejection of his earlier Romanticism, as well as the entire Romantic movement, especially the Lake Poets (see "Tintern Abbey"). *Don Juan,* with its colloquial voice, republicanism, and celebration of life outside existing moral and social codes, was meant to be an antidote to conservative Lake poetry.

This poem is ostensibly about the notorious Spanish seducer Don Juan, whom Byron transforms into a virtuous hero. Like Byron, the Don is a culturally and socially alienated aristocrat, an ideal alter ego for the poet's plan to expose English hypocrisy. In the poem, Don Juan's story forms only the first level, extending from 1789 until the Don's death on the guillotine in 1793; a second level ranges over the period 1789 to 1823, showing how Europe betrayed its best political ideals; and a third level covers Byron's meteoric years from *Childe Harold* until his disgrace. Using these levels to comment upon one another, Byron conveys both a sense of distance and immediacy, as if time were frozen and everything were known.

This selection constitutes 56 of the 222 verses in Canto I. The verse form is *ottava rima* (Italian, "eighth rhyme"), an eight-line stanza rhyming abababcc. (A word of advice: the pronunciation of Don Juan is English; that is, the second syllable rhymes with "new one" and "true one.") *Ottava rima* had earlier been used by English poets, such as Behn (see "The Willing Mistress"), but Byron followed Italian writers who employed it for serio-comic effect. In *Don Juan,* this form gave him the artistic freedom that the wide-ranging subject matter demanded.

———

### 1

I want a hero: an uncommon want,
  When every year and month sends forth a new one,
Till, after cloying the gazettes with cant,
  The age discovers he is not the true one;
Of such as these I should not care to vaunt,
  I'll therefore take our ancient friend Don Juan—
We all have seen him, in the pantomime,
Sent to the Devil somewhat ere his time.

• • •

### 6

Most epic poets plunge *"in media res"*
  (Horace makes this the heroic turnpike road),
And then your hero tells, when'er you please,
  What went before—by way of episode,
While seated after dinner at his ease,
  Beside his mistress in some soft abode,
Palace, or garden, paradise, or cavern,
Which serves the happy couple for a tavern.

### 7

That is the usual method, but not mine—
  My way is to begin with the beginning;
The regularity of my design
  Forbids all wandering as the worst of sinning,
And therefore I shall open with a line
  (Although it cost me half an hour in spinning),
Narrating somewhat of Don Juan's father,
And also of his mother, if you'd rather.

### 8

In Seville was he born, a pleasant city,
  Famous for oranges and women—he
Who has not seen it will be much to pity,
  So says the proverb—and I quite agree;
Of all the Spanish towns is none more pretty,
  Cadiz perhaps—but that you soon may see;
Don Juan's parents lived beside the river,
A noble stream, and called the Guadalquivir.

**9**

His father's name was José—*Don,* of course—
  A true Hidalgo, free from every stain
Of Moor or Hebrew blood, he traced his source
  Through the most Gothic gentlemen of Spain;
A better cavalier ne'er mounted horse,
  Or, being mounted, e'er got down again,
Than José, who begot our hero, who
Begot—but that's to come—Well, to renew:

**10**

His mother was a learnéd lady, famed
  For every branch of every science known—
In every Christian language ever named,
  With virtues equaled by her wit alone:
She made the cleverest people quite ashamed,
  And even the good with inward envy groan,
Finding themselves so very much exceeded,
In their own way, by all the things that she did.

**11**

Her memory was a mine: she knew by heart
  All Calderon and greater part of Lopé,
So, that if any actor missed his part,
  She could have served him for the prompter's copy;
For her Feinagle's were an useless art,
  And he himself obliged to shut up shop—he
Could never make a memory so fine as
That which adorned the brain of Donna Inez.

**12**

Her favorite science was the mathematical,
  Her noblest virtue was her magnanimity,
Her wit (she sometimes tried at wit) was Attic all,
  Her serious sayings darkened to sublimity;
In short, in all things she was fairly what I call
  A prodigy—her morning dress was dimity,
Her evening silk, or, in the summer, muslin,
And other stuffs, with which I won't stay puzzling.

**13**

She knew the Latin—that is, "the Lord's prayer,"
  And Greek—the alphabet—I'm nearly sure;
She read some French romances here and there,
  Although her mode of speaking was not pure;
For native Spanish she had no great care,
  At least her conversation was obscure;
Her thoughts were theorems, her words a problem,
As if she deemed that mystery would ennoble 'em.

• • •

**17**

Oh! she was perfect past all parallel—
  Of any modern female saint's comparison;
So far above the cunning powers of Hell,
  Her Guardian Angel had given up his garrison;
Even her minutest motions went as well
  As those of the best time-piece made by Harrison;
In virtues nothing earthly could surpass her,
Save thine "incomparable oil," Macassar!

• • •

**23**

Don José and his lady quarrelled—*why,*
  Not any of the many could divine,
Though several thousand people chose to try,
  'Twas surely no concern of theirs nor mine;
I loath that low vice—curiosity;
  But if there's anything in which I shine,
'Tis in arranging all my friends' affairs,
Not having, of my own, domestic cares.

**24**

And so I interfered, and with the best
  Intentions, but their treatment was not kind;
I think the foolish people were possessed,
  For neither of them could I ever find,
Although their porter afterwards confessed—
  But that's no matter, and the worst's behind,
For little Juan o'er me threw, down stairs,
A pail of housemaid's water unawares.

**25**

A little curly-headed, good-for-nothing,
  And mischief-making monkey from his birth;
His parents ne'er agreed except in doting
  Upon the most unquiet imp on earth;
Instead of quarrelling, had they been but both in
  Their senses, they'd have sent young master forth
To school, or had him soundly whipped at home,
To teach him manners for the time to come.

**26**

Don José and the Donna Inez led
  For some time an unhappy sort of life,
Wishing each other, not divorced, but dead;
  They lived respectably as man and wife,
Their conduct was exceedingly well-bred,
  And gave no outward signs of inward strife,
Until at length the smothered fire broke out,
And put the business past all kind of doubt.

### 27

For Inez called some druggists and physicians,
  And tried to prove her loving lord was *mad*,
But as he had some lucid intermissions,
  She next decided he was only *bad*;
Yet when they asked her for her depositions,
  No sort of explanation could be had,
Save that her duty both to man and God
Required this conduct—which seemed very odd.

### 28

She kept a journal, where his faults were noted,
  And opened certain trunks of books and letters,
All which might, if occasion served, be quoted;
  And then she had all Seville for abettors,
Besides her good old grandmother (who doted);
  The hearers of her case became repeaters,
Then advocates, inquisitors, and judges,
Some for amusement, others for old grudges.

### 29

And then this best and meekest woman bore
  With such serenity her husband's woes,
Just as the Spartan ladies did of yore,
  Who saw their spouses killed, and nobly chose
Never to say a word about them more—
  Calmly she heard each calumny that rose,
And saw *his* agonies with such sublimity,
That all the world exclaimed, "What magnanimity!"

• • •

### 32

Their friends had tried at reconciliation,
  Then their relations, who made matters worse.
('Twere hard to tell upon a like occasion
  To whom it may be best to have recourse—
I can't say much for friend or yet relation):
  The lawyers did their utmost for divorce,
But scarce a fee was paid on either side
Before, unluckily, Don José died.

• • •

### 38

Sagest of women, even of widows, she
  Resolved that Juan should be quite a paragon,
And worthy of the noblest pedigree,
  (His Sire was of Castile, his Dam from Aragon):
Then, for accomplishments of chivalry,
  In case our Lord the King should go to war again,
He learned the arts of riding, fencing, gunnery,
And how to scale a fortress—or a nunnery.

### 39

But that which Donna Inez most desired,
  And saw into herself each day before all
The learnéd tutors whom for him she hired,
  Was, that his breeding should be strictly moral:
Much into all his studies she inquired,
  And so they were submitted first to her, all,
Arts, sciences—no branch was made a mystery
To Juan's eyes, excepting natural history.

### 40

The languages, especially the dead,
  The sciences, and most of all the abstruse,
The arts, at least all such as could be said
  To be the most remote from common use,
In all these he was much and deeply read:
  But not a page of anything that's loose,
Or hints continuation of the species,
Was ever suffered, lest he should grow vicious.

### 41

His classic studies made a little puzzle,
  Because of filthy loves of gods and goddesses,
Who in the earlier ages raised a bustle,
  But never put on pantaloons or bodices;
His reverend tutors had at times a tussle,
  And for their Aeneids, Iliads, and Odysseys,
Were forced to make an odd sort of apology,
For Donna Inez dreaded the Mythology.

### 42

Ovid's a rake, as half his verses show him,
  Anacreon's morals are a still worse sample,
Catullus scarcely has a decent poem,
  I don't think Sappho's Ode a good example,
Although Longinus tells us there is no hymn
  Where the Sublime soars forth on wings more ample;
But Virgil's songs are pure, except that horrid one
Beginning with *"Formosum Pastor Corydon."*

### 43

Lucretius' irreligion is too strong
  For early stomachs, to prove wholesome food;
I can't help thinking Juvenal was wrong,
  Although no doubt his real intent was good,
For speaking out so plainly in his song,
  So much indeed as to be downright rude;
And then what proper person can be partial
To all those nauseous epigrams of Martial?

### 44

Juan was taught from out the best edition,
  Expurgated by learnéd men, who place,

Judiciously, from out the schoolboy's vision,
  The grosser parts; but, fearful to deface
Too much their modest bard by this omission,
  And pitying sore his mutilated case,
They only add them all in an appendix,
Which saves, in fact, the trouble of an index.

• • •

### 47

Sermons he read, and lectures he endured,
  And homilies, and lives of all the saints;
To Jerome and to Chrysostom inured,
  He did not take such studies for restraints;
But how Faith is acquired, and then insured,
  So well not one of the aforesaid paints
As Saint Augustine in his fine Confessions,
Which make the reader envy his transgressions.

• • •

### 54

Young Juan now was sixteen years of age,
  Tall, handsome, slender, but well knit: he seemed
Active, though not so sprightly, as a page;
  And everybody but his mother deemed
Him almost man; but she flew in a rage
  And bit her lips (for else she might have screamed)
If any said so—for to be precocious
Was in her eyes a thing the most atrocious.

### 55

Amongst her numerous acquaintance, all
  Selected for discretion and devotion,
There was the Donna Julia, whom to call
  Pretty were but to give a feeble notion
Of many charms in her as natural
  As sweetness to the flower, or salt to Ocean,
Her zone to Venus, or his bow to Cupid,
(But this last simile is trite and stupid.)

• • •

### 60

Her eye (I'm very fond of handsome eyes)
  Was large and dark, suppressing half its fire
Until she spoke, then through its soft disguise
  Flashed an expression more of pride than ire,
And love than either; and there would arise
  A something in them which was not desire,
But would have been, perhaps, but for the soul
Which struggled through and chastened down the
    whole.

### 61

Her glossy hair was clustered o'er a brow
  Bright with intelligence, and fair, and smooth;
Her eyebrow's shape was like the aërial bow,
  Her cheek all purple with the beam of youth,
Mounting, at times, to a transparent glow,
  As if her veins ran lightning; she, in sooth,
Possessed an air and grace by no means common:
Her stature tall—I hate a dumpy woman.

### 62

Wedded she was some years, and to a man
  Of fifty, and such husbands are in plenty;
And yet, I think, instead of such a ONE
  'Twere better to have TWO of five-and-twenty,
Especially in countries near the sun:
  And now I think on't, *"mi vien in mente,"*
Ladies even of the most uneasy virtue
Prefer a spouse whose age is short of thirty.

• • •

### 69

Juan she saw, and, as a pretty child,
  Caressed him often—such a thing might be
Quite innocently done, and harmless styled,
  When she had twenty years, and thirteen he;
But I am not so sure I should have smiled
  When he was sixteen, Julia twenty-three;
These few short years make wondrous alterations,
Particularly amongst sun-burnt nations.

### 70

Whate'er the cause might be, they had become
  Changed; for the dame grew distant, the youth shy,
Their looks cast down, their greetings almost dumb,
  And much embarrassment in either eye;
There surely will be little doubt with some
  That Donna Julia knew the reason why,
But as for Juan, he had no more notion
Than he who never saw the sea of Ocean.

### 71

Yet Julia's very coldness still was kind,
  And tremulously gentle her small hand
Withdrew itself from his, but left behind
  A little pressure, thrilling, and so bland
And slight, so very slight, that to the mind
  'Twas but a doubt; but ne'er magician's wand
Wrought change with all Armida's fairy art
Like what this light touch left on Juan's heart.

### 72

And if she met him, though she smiled no more,
  She looked a sadness sweeter than her smile,
As if her heart had deeper thoughts in store
  She must not own, but cherished more the while
For that compression in its burning core;
  Even Innocence itself has many a wile,
And will not dare to trust itself with truth,
And Love is taught hypocrisy from youth.

• • •

### 75

Poor Julia's heart was in an awkward state;
  She felt it going, and resolved to make
The noblest efforts for herself and mate,
  For Honor's, Pride's, Religion's, Virtue's sake:
Her resolutions were most truly great,
  And almost might have made a Tarquin quake:
She prayed the Virgin Mary for her grace,
As being the best judge of a lady's case.

### 76

She vowed she never would see Juan more,
  And next day paid a visit to his mother,
And looked extremely at the opening door,
  Which, by the Virgin's grace, let in another;
Grateful she was, and yet a little sore—
  Again it opens, it can be no other,
'Tis surely Juan now—No! I'm afraid
That night the Virgin was no further prayed.

### 77

She now determined that a virtuous woman
  Should rather face and overcome temptation,
That flight was base and dastardly, and no man
  Should ever give her heart the least sensation,
That is to say, a thought beyond the common
  Preference, that we must feel, upon occasion,
For people who are pleasanter than others,
But then they only seem so many brothers.

### 78

And even if by chance—and who can tell?
  The Devil's so very sly—she should discover
That all within was not so very well,
  And, if still free, that such or such a lover
Might please perhaps, a virtuous wife can quell
  Such thoughts, and be the better when they're over;
And if the man should ask, 'tis but denial:
I recommend young ladies to make trial.

### 79

And, then, there are such things as Love divine,
  Bright and immaculate, unmixed and pure,
Such as the angels think so very fine,
  And matrons, who would be no less secure,
Platonic, perfect, "just such love as mine;"
  Thus Julia said—and thought so, to be sure;
And so I'd have her think, were *I* the man
On whom her reveries celestial ran.

• • •

### 90

Young Juan wandered by the glassy brooks,
  Thinking unutterable things; he threw
Himself at length within the leafy nooks
  Where the wild branch of the cork forest grew;
There poets find materials for their books,
  And every now and then we read them through,
So that their plan and prosody are eligible,
Unless, like Wordsworth, they prove unintelligible.

### 91

He, Juan (and not Wordsworth), so pursued
  His self-communion with his own high soul,
Until his mighty heart, in its great mood,
  Had mitigated part, though not the whole
Of its disease; he did the best he could
  With things not very subject to control,
And turned, without perceiving his condition,
Like Coleridge, into a metaphysician.

### 92

He thought about himself, and the whole earth,
  Of man the wonderful, and of the stars,
And how the deuce they ever could have birth;
  And then he thought of earthquakes, and of wars,
How many miles the moon might have in girth,
  Of air-balloons, and of the many bars
To perfect knowledge of the boundless skies;—
And then he thought of Donna Julia's eyes.

### 93

In thoughts like these true Wisdom may discern
  Longings sublime, and aspirations high,
Which some are born with, but the most part learn
  To plague themselves withal, they know not why:
'Twas strange that one so young should thus concern
  His brain about the action of the sky;
If *you* think 'twas Philosophy that this did,
I can't help thinking puberty assisted.

### 94

He pored upon the leaves, and on the flowers,
  And heard a voice in all the winds; and then
He thought of wood-nymphs and immortal bowers,
  And how the goddesses came down to men:
He missed the pathway, he forgot the hours,
  And when he looked upon his watch again,
He found how much old Time had been a winner—
He also found that he had lost his dinner.

• • •

### 104

'Twas on the sixth of June, about the hour
  Of half-past six—perhaps still nearer seven—
When Julia sate within as pretty a bower
  As e'er held houri in that heathenish heaven
Described by Mahomet, and Anacreon Moore,
  To whom the lyre and laurels have been given,
With all the trophies of triumphant song—
He won them well, and may he wear them long!

### 105

She sate, but not alone; I know not well
  How this same interview had taken place,
And even if I knew, I should not tell—
  People should hold their tongues in any case;
No matter how or why the thing befell,
  But there were she and Juan, face to face—
When two such faces are so, 'twould be wise,
But very difficult, to shut their eyes.

### 106

How beautiful she looked! her conscious heart
  Glowed in her cheek, and yet she felt no wrong:
Oh Love! how perfect is thy mystic art,
  Strengthening the weak, and trampling on the strong!
How self-deceitful is the sagest part
  Of mortals whom thy lure hath led along!
The precipice she stood on was immense,
So was her creed in her own innocence.

### 107

She thought of her own strength, and Juan's youth,
  And of the folly of all prudish fears,
Victorious Virtue, and domestic Truth,
  And then of Don Alfonso's fifty years:
I wish these last had not occurred, in sooth,
  Because that number rarely much endears,
And through all climes, the snowy and the sunny,
Sounds ill in love, whate'er it may in money.

• • •

### 111

The hand which still held Juan's, by degrees
  Gently, but palpably confirmed its grasp,
As if it said, "Detain me, if you please";
  Yet there's no doubt she only meant to clasp
His fingers with a pure Platonic squeeze;
  She would have shrunk as from a toad, or asp,
Had she imagined such a thing could rouse
A feeling dangerous to a prudent spouse.

### 112

I cannot know what Juan thought of this,
  But what he did, is much what you would do;
His young lip thanked it with a grateful kiss,
  And then, abashed at its own joy, withdrew
In deep despair, lest he had done amiss—
  Love is so very timid when 'tis new:
She blushed, and frowned not, but she strove to
    speak,
And held her tongue, her voice was grown so weak.

### 113

The sun set, and up rose the yellow moon:
  The Devil's in the moon for mischief; they
Who called her CHASTE, methinks, began too soon
  Their nomenclature; there is not a day,
The longest, not the twenty-first of June,
  Sees half the business in a wicked way,
On which three single hours of moonshine smile—
And then she looks so modest all the while!

### 114

There is a dangerous silence in that hour,
  A stillness, which leaves room for the full soul
To open all itself, without the power
  Of calling wholly back its self-control;
The silver light which, hallowing tree and tower,
  Sheds beauty and deep softness o'er the whole,
Breathes also to the heart, and o'er it throws
A loving languor, which is not repose.

### 115

And Julia sate with Juan, half embraced
  And half retiring from the glowing arm,
Which trembled like the bosom where 'twas placed;
  Yet still she must have thought there was no harm,
Or else 'twere easy to withdraw her waist;
  But then the situation had its charm,
And then—God knows what next—I can't go on;
I'm almost sorry that I e'er begun.

Oh Plato! Plato! you have paved the way,
  With your confounded fantasies, to more
Immoral conduct by the fancied sway
  Your system feigns o'er the controlless core
Of human hearts, than all the long array
  Of poets and romancers:—You're a bore,
A charlatan, a coxcomb—and have been,
At best, no better than a go-between.

And Julia's voice was lost, except in sighs,
  Until too late for useful conversation;
The tears were gushing from her gentle eyes,
  I wish, indeed, they had not had occasion;
But who, alas! can love, and then be wise?
  Not that Remorse did not oppose Temptation;
A little still she strove, and much repented,
And whispering "I will ne'er consent"—consented.

. . .

# PERCY BYSSHE SHELLEY

# Poems

———

Today, Percy Bysshe Shelley (1792–1822) is regarded as a great Romantic poet; in his own day, however, his works were not widely known. Of about 450 poems, only 70 or so were in print when he died. Poems issued during his life, like *Queen Mab* (1813), gave him a reputation for atheism and radicalism. Moreover, his scandalous life cast a shadow over his poetry and obscured its true meaning.

When Shelley fled England in 1818, he left behind a legend of bohemianism and rebellion, dating from early youth. As a student at Oxford, he was expelled for refusing to disown an atheistical pamphlet he had written. This expulsion led to a break with his wealthy father, who later disinherited him. After university, he offended middle-class norms by sharing households with likeminded friends, including unattached women. Both of his marriages began as elopements. The second elopement hastened the suicide of his first wife; her family then obtained a court order denying him access to his own children. The second marriage to Mary Wollstonecraft Godwin was more stable; still, the Shelleys fled England for the continent because of debts, as well as the not unreasonable fear that their children might also be taken away.

Shelley's last four years, wandering in Italy, brought maturity and some of his best poems, including *Prometheus Unbound* (1820), the story of the Titan persecuted by divine forces for his efforts to help humanity—a work whose subtext was Shelley's own trials. Back home, the legend of "Shelley-the-Monster" grew so that few mourned Shelley's drowning in Italy a month before his thirtieth birthday.

This century's critics have discovered a Shelley much different from the one of legend. He is a Platonist, who advocated (a) the doctrine of Platonic love, which holds that Physical Beauty is secondary to Intellectual Beauty, and (b) the idea that the poet is an inspired person ("the unacknowledged legislator of the world"). He is also considered a reformer today and less of a revolutionary, because he was repelled by violence of all kinds; also, his causes, such as democracy and vegetarianism, have entered the mainstream.

## Reading the Selection

"Ozymandias" (1817) and "England in 1819" (1819) are Shelley's most splendid sonnets. "Ozymandias" grew out of Romantic Hellenism, which made Greece into an imaginary world where hearts troubled by the present sought nourishment from the glorious past. Shelley's inspiration was a Greek writer's record of an inscription honoring Ozymandias, another name for Egypt's Ramses II. Shelley used the inscription (lines 10–11) to underscore the Platonic theme that human achievement is illusory. In "England in 1819," written during this exile, he described his country in the grip of post-Napoleonic reaction, though he ended with the prediction of a new day.

"Ode to the West Wind" (1820) is one of Shelley's most famous poems. It marked a personal crisis, following the loss of a second child in Italy, and savage reviews of new poems in England. In form, it comprises five sonnets, each built of three *terza rima* verses in the style of Dante (see *The Divine Comedy*) plus an end-couplet. The ode builds in emotional power as it moves along. The images of the first three sonnets—the leaf, the cloud, and the wave—are folded into the fourth sonnet with the words "If I were. . . ." In the fifth sonnet, the mood changes to become a prayer. Typically, the poem ends on a hopeful note: "If Winter comes, can Spring be far behind?"

# Ozymandias

I met a traveler from an antique land
Who said: Two vast and trunkless legs of stone
Stand in the desert . . . Near them, on the sand,
Half sunk, a shattered visage lies, whose frown,
And wrinkled lip, and sneer of cold command,
Tell that its sculptor well those passions read
Which yet survive, stamped on these lifeless things,

The hand that mocked them, and the heart that fed:
And on the pedestal these words appear:
"My name is Ozymandias, king of kings:
Look on my works, ye Mighty, and despair!"
Nothing beside remains. Round the decay
Of that colossal wreck, boundless and bare
The lone and level sands stretch far away.

# England in 1819

An old, mad, blind, despised, and dying King;
Princes, the dregs of their dull race, who flow
Through public scorn,—mud from a muddy spring;
Rulers who neither see nor feel nor know,
But leechlike to their fainting country cling
Till they drop, blind in blood, without a blow.
A people starved and stabbed in th' untilled field;

An army, whom liberticide and prey
Makes as a two-edged sword to all who wield;
Golden and sanguine laws which tempt and slay;
Religion Christless, Godless—a book sealed;
A senate, Time's worst statute, unrepealed—
Are graves from which a glorious Phantom may
Burst, to illumine our tempestuous day.

# Ode to the West Wind

### I

O wild West Wind, thou breath of Autumn's being,
Thou, from whose unseen presence the leaves dead
Are driven, like ghosts from an enchanter fleeing,

Yellow, and black, and pale, and hectic red,
Pestilence-stricken multitudes: O thou,
Who chariotest to their dark wintry bed

The wingéd seeds, where they lie cold and low,
Each like a corpse within its grave, until
Thine azure sister of the Spring shall blow

Her clarion o'er the dreaming earth, and fill
(Driving sweet buds like flocks to feed in air)
With living hues and odors plain and hill:

Wild Spirit, which art moving everywhere;
Destroyer and preserver; hear, oh, hear!

### II

Thou on whose stream, mid the steep sky's commotion,
Loose clouds like earth's decaying leaves are shed,
Shook from the tangled boughs of Heaven and Ocean,

Angels of rain and lightning: there are spread
On the blue surface of thine aery surge,
Like the bright hair uplifted from the head

Of some fierce Maenad, even from the dim verge
Of the horizon to the zenith's height,
The locks of the approaching storm. Thou dirge

Of the dying year, to which this closing night
Will be the dome of a vast sepulcher,
Vaulted with all thy congregated might

Of vapors, from whose solid atmosphere
Black rain, and fire, and hail will burst: oh, hear!

### III

Thou who didst waken from his summer dreams
The blue Mediterranean, where he lay,
Lulled by the coil of his crystálline streams,

Beside a pumice isle in Baiae's bay
And saw in sleep old palaces and towers
Quivering within the wave's intenser day,

All overgrown with azure moss and flowers
So sweet, the sense faints picturing them! Thou
For whose path the Atlantic's level powers

Cleave themselves into chasms, while far below
The sea-blooms and the oozy woods which wear
The sapless foliage of the ocean, know

Thy voice, and suddenly grow gray with fear,
And tremble and despoil themselves; oh, hear!

### IV

If I were a dead leaf thou mightest bear;
If I were a swift cloud to fly with thee;
A wave to pant beneath thy power, and share

The impulse of thy strength, only less free
Than thou, O uncontrollable! If even
I were as in my boyhood, and could be

The comrade of thy wanderings over Heaven,
As then, when to outstrip thy skyey speed
Scarce seemed a vision; I would ne'er have striven

As thus with thee in prayer in my sore need.
Oh, lift me as a wave, a leaf, a cloud!
I fall upon the thorns of life! I bleed!

A heavy weight of hours has chained and bowed
One too like thee: tameless, and swift, and proud.

### V

Make me thy lyre, even as the forest is:
What if my leaves are falling like its own!
The tumult of thy mighty harmonies

Will take from both a deep, autumnal tone,
Sweet though in sadness. Be thou, Spirit fierce,
My spirit! Be thou me, impetuous one!

Drive my dead thoughts over the universe
Like withered leaves to quicken a new birth!
And, by the incantation of this verse,

Scatter, as from an unextinguished hearth
Ashes and sparks, my words among mankind!
Be through my lips to unawakened earth

The trumpet of a prophecy! O Wind,
If Winter comes, can Spring be far behind?

# JOHN KEATS

## Poems

----

     Keats was the third of the triumvirate of Romantic poets whose meteoric careers brightened the literary skies of Regency England. A dark period of political reaction and economic downturn, it lasted from 1812 to 1820, when the future George IV was regent for his mad father, King George III. All three poets' talents were abruptly extinguished by early deaths, thereby giving rise to the mystique which has surrounded this poetic trio ever since. Lord Byron was 36 when he died of fever in Greece, in 1824; Shelley was 29 when he drowned in the sea off northern

Italy, in 1822; and, saddest of all, Keats was 25 when he died of tuberculosis in Rome, where he had gone to escape the harsh English winter, in 1820. For the romantic imagination, the untimely deaths, in a sense, guaranteed the genius of the three poets.

Little known to his generation, John Keats (1795–1820) rocketed to fame after his death. The three books of poems issued during his life (comprising about one-third of the 150 poems he wrote) met with ridicule; snobbish reviewers mocked his low social status (he was born at London's Swan and Hoop Livery Stables and worked as an apothecary—a drug salesman) and his radical politics. Indeed, one conservative reviewer coined the pejorative label Cockney School—meaning London-born poets whose works supposedly reflected their working class backgrounds and subversive politics; it was used against Keats and fellow radical writers, such as Leigh Hunt (1773–1835) and William Hazlitt (1778–1830). Despite this label, Keats's poetry lacked the specifically political focus that often characterized the works of his fellow Romantics, Byron and Shelley, much less the Cockney poets; instead, Keats's works revealed radicalism only in dedications to his friends and quotations from their works. For the most part, his poetry was typical of the Romantic school in general, in that it grew out of his life. Keats's most distinctive trait was the stoic voice he used to speak calmly and often indirectly of his own approaching death. His poems were composed at an astonishing pace, effectively produced over two years, the bulk between September 1818 and September 1819.

### Reading the Selection

Keats's best-known poem, "Ode on a Grecian Urn" (1820), shows his Romantic Hellenism in form, inspiration, and theme. Its form is Greek—the private ode (a poem with a complex structure, which is characterized by formality and lofty thoughts) (see Horace's *Odes*)—and the poem itself was inspired by Greek vases and sculptures. Its theme, "life is short, art is long," is expressed in an imaginary vase's unchanging scene; the image is of Arcadia, the pastoral land, populated by shepherds and shepherdesses, which Classical poets used as a symbol of rural serenity, or the harmony of the legendary Golden Age. In this Arcadian scene, time stands still: "unravish'd bride of quietness," "boughs that cannot shed [y]our leaves," and "thy streets forevermore [w]ill silent be." Admitting human frailty ["old age shall this generation waste"], Keats accepted the eternity of art: " 'Beauty is truth, truth beauty,' "—that is all/Ye know on earth, and all ye need to know." This conclusion became a truism in the Romantic Age's religion of art.

"To Autumn" (1820) is another of Keats's great private odes, this one celebrating the changing season (it was composed the previous September). It is melancholy in tone, proper for the autumnal season but also emblematic of his mood as he faced death.

# Ode on a Grecian Urn

### I

Thou still unravish'd bride of quietness,
  Thou foster-child of silence and slow time,
Sylvan historian, who canst thus express
  A flowery tale more sweetly than our rhyme:
What leaf-fring'd legend haunts about thy shape
  Of deities or mortals, or of both,
    In Tempe or the dales of Arcady?
  What men or gods are these? What maidens loath?
What mad pursuit? What struggle to escape?
  What pipes and timbrels? What wild ecstasy?

### II

Heard melodies are sweet, but those unheard
  Are sweeter; therefore, ye soft pipes, play on;
Not to the sensual ear, but, more endear'd,
  Pipe to the spirit ditties of no tone:
Fair youth, beneath the trees, thou canst not leave
  Thy song, nor ever can those trees be bare;
    Bold Lover, never, never canst thou kiss,
Though winning near the goal—yet, do not grieve;
  She cannot fade, though thou hast not thy bliss,
Forever wilt thou love, and she be fair!

### III

Ah, happy, happy boughs! that cannot shed
  Your leaves, nor ever bid the Spring adieu;
And, happy melodist, unwearied,
  Forever piping songs forever new;
More happy love! more happy, happy love!
  Forever warm and still to be enjoy'd,
    Forever panting, and forever young;
All breathing human passion far above,
  That leaves a heart high-sorrowful and cloy'd,
    A burning forehead, and a parching tongue.

### IV

Who are these coming to the sacrifice?
  To what green altar, O mysterious priest,
Lead'st thou that heifer lowing at the skies,
  And all her silken flanks with garlands drest?

What little town by river or sea shore,
  Or mountain-built with peaceful citadel,
    Is emptied of this folk, this pious morn?
And, little town, thy streets forevermore
  Will silent be; and not a soul to tell
    Why thou art desolate, can e'er return.

### V

O Attic shape! Fair attitude! with brede
  Of marble men and maidens overwrought,
With forest branches and the trodden weed;
  Thou, silent form, dost tease us out of thought
As doth eternity: Cold Pastoral!
  When old age shall this generation waste,
    Thou shalt remain, in midst of other woe
  Than ours, a friend to man, to whom thou say'st,
"Beauty is truth, truth beauty,"—that is all
  Ye know on earth, and all ye need to know.

## To Autumn

### 1

Season of mists and mellow fruitfulness,
  Close bosom-friend of the maturing sun;
Conspiring with him how to load and bless
  With fruit the vines that round the thatch-eves run;
To bend with apples the moss'd cottage-trees,
  And fill all fruit with ripeness to the core;
    To swell the gourd, and plump the hazel shells
  With a sweet kernel; to set budding more,
And still more, later flowers for the bees,
Until they think warm days will never cease,
    For summer has o'er-brimm'd their clammy cells.

### 2

Who hath not seen thee oft amid thy store?
  Sometimes whoever seeks abroad may find
Thee sitting careless on a granary floor,
  Thy hair soft-lifted by the winnowing wind;
Or on a half-reap'd furrow sound asleep,

Drows'd with the fume of poppies, while thy hook
  Spares the next swath and all its twined flowers:
And sometimes like a gleaner thou dost keep
  Steady thy laden head across a brook;
  Or by a cyder-press, with patient look,
    Thou watchest the last oozings hours by hours.

### 3

Where are the songs of spring? Ay, where are they?
  Think not of them, thou hast thy music too,—
While barred clouds bloom the soft-dying day,
  And touch the stubble-plains with rosy hue;
Then in a wailful choir the small gnats mourn
  Among the river sallows, borne aloft
    Or sinking as the light wind lives or dies;
And full-grown lambs loud bleat from hilly bourn;
  Hedge-crickets sing; and now with treble soft
  The red-breast whistles from a garden-croft;
    And gathering swallows twitter in the skies.

Chapter

# 18

# The Triumph of the Bourgeoisie:
# 1830–1871

## ALFRED, LORD TENNYSON
### *Ulysses*

Alfred, Lord Tennyson (1809–1892) was the most representative poet of England's Victorian period, the era of Victoria's reign (1837–1901); it was marked by the effects of the continuing industrial revolution, the influence of the theory of evolution, and waves of political and social reform. In this period of dynamic change, Tennyson's unflagging optimism and moral earnestness—expressed in his books of verses, beginning with *Poems, Chiefly Lyrical,* in 1830—made him an obvious choice for England's Poet Laureate. Thus, in 1850, he succeeded to this post on the death of Wordsworth. Tennyson took his duties as Poet Laureate seriously and produced many less than memorable poems on state occasions, and, at the same time, composed his most popular works: *Maud* (1855), *Ballads and Other Poems* (1880), *Locksley Hall Sixty Years After* (1886), and *Idylls of the King* (in installments, 1859–1889).

Tennyson's poems, regardless of when written, reflected his staunch adherence to Victorian ideals. The tendency of Victorian culture was to concentrate on the politically dominant and wealthy strata of society, that is, the ruling middle class. Tennyson's poems speak to and for this class, giving voice to their ambitions, sense of duty, and belief that history holds the key to human problems. His poetic mission was to glorify the obvious, to put into simple words the common thoughts of everyday humanity—not for him the vulnerability of a Romantic Shelley (see "Ozymandias," etc.) nor the learnedness of a Modernist like Eliot (see "The Love Song of J. Alfred Prufrock"). Still, despite its obviousness, Tennyson's poetry is filled with glorious phrases—such as "after many a summer dies the swan" (in "Tithonus," 1833)—which stick in the mind and continue to reverberate down the years.

*Reading the Selection*

"Ulysses" (composed 1833, published 1842) grew out of the major crisis of Tennyson's life, the loss of his good friend, Arthur Hallam; they had met at Cambridge and had served briefly as volunteers in an army of Spanish guerrillas. Hallam's loss plunged Tennyson into despair and, according to his son, "blotted out all joy from his life, and made him long for death." *In Memoriam* (1850) is his best-known work inspired by this death, but Tennyson himself admitted that "'Ulysses' gave my feeling about the need of going forward, and braving the struggle of life perhaps more simply than . . . *In Memoriam.*" Thus, the theme of "Ulysses" is the need for moral strength to overcome overwhelming grief; its concluding line, "To strive, to seek, to find and not to yield," was meant to embolden his own courage. Tennyson's uplifting conclusion has often been cited as symbolic of the "stiff-upper lip tradition" of the middle-class world of industrialists, empire-builders, and liberally educated men and women who produced the poet and for whom he spoke.

"Ulysses" reflects Tennyson's Philhellenism, as the Victorian passion for Greek culture was called. It is about Ulysses, the Latin name for Odysseus, the hero of Homer's *Odyssey,* a fitting subject for a period steeped in the Classics. Tennyson himself was allowed to enter Cambridge only after he had satisfied his clergyman father by reciting from memory all the odes of Horace. Although this episode was unique, Latin and Greek were the chief staples of study in England's public (meaning "private") schools and universities until World War II. Tennyson thus could assume his audience's familiarity with his topic.

---

It little profits that an idle king,
By this still hearth, among these barren crags,
Matched with an aged wife, I mete and dole
Unequal laws unto a savage race,
That hoard, and sleep, and feed, and know not me.
I cannot rest from travel; I will drink
Life to the lees. All times I have enjoyed
Greatly, have suffered greatly, both with those
That loved me, and alone; on shore, and when
Through scudding drifts the rainy Hyades
Vext the dim sea. I am become a name;
For always roaming with a hungry heart
Much have I seen and known—cities of men
And manners, climates, councils, governments,
Myself not least, but honored of them all,—
And drunk delight of battle with my peers,
Far on the ringing plains of windy Troy.
I am a part of all that I have met;
Yet all experience is an arch wherethrough
Gleams that untraveled world whose margin fades
For ever and for ever when I move.
How dull it is to pause, to make an end,
To rust unburnished, not to shine in use!
As though to breathe were life! Life piled on life
Were all too little, and of one to me
Little remains; but every hour is saved
From that eternal silence, something more,
A bringer of new things; and vile it were
For some three suns to store and hoard myself,
And this gray spirit yearning in desire
To follow knowledge like a sinking star,
Beyond the utmost bound of human thought.
   This is my son, mine own Telemachus,
To whom I leave the scepter and the isle,
Well-loved of me, discerning to fulfill

This labor, by slow prudence to make mild
A rugged people, and through soft degrees
Subdue them to the useful and the good.
Most blameless is he, centered in the sphere
Of common duties, decent not to fail
In offices of tenderness, and pay
Meet adoration to my household gods,
When I am gone. He works his work, I mine.
   There lies the port; the vessel puffs her sail;
There gloom the dark, broad seas. My mariners,
Souls that have toiled, and wrought, and thought with me,
That ever with a frolic welcome took
The thunder and the sunshine, and opposed
Free hearts, free foreheads—you and I are old;
Old age hath yet his honor and his toil.
Death closes all; but something ere the end,
Some work of noble note, may yet be done,
Not unbecoming men that strove with gods.
The lights begin to twinkle from the rocks;
The long day wanes; the slow moon climbs; the deep
Moans round with many voices. Come, my friends,
'Tis not too late to seek a newer world.
Push off, and sitting well in order smite
The sounding furrows; for my purpose holds
To sail beyond the sunset, and the baths
Of all the western stars, until I die.
It may be that the gulfs will wash us down;
It may be we shall touch the Happy Isles,
And see the great Achilles, whom we knew.
Though much is taken, much abides; and though
We are not now that strength which in old days
Moved earth and heaven, that which we are, we are,
One equal temper of heroic hearts,
Made weak by time and fate, but strong in will
To strive, to seek, to find, and not to yield.

# FREDERICK DOUGLASS
## from *Narrative of the Life of Frederick Douglass*

———

Frederick Douglass's autobiography reflects the maturity of the trend toward globalization of the world's culture, which began in about 1500. From then on, Europe exported peoples, technology, religions, and ideas to colonies in Asia, Africa, and the Americas; in return Europe received slaves and servants, foodstuffs, raw materials, religions, and ideas. Central to this process in the New World was the uprooting and transportation of Africans to work as slaves. The faint contours of a global literary culture were first visible in the 1600s, when European writers began to draw on colonial life. Spanish and English America now gave birth to colonial literatures, though at first heavily indebted to Europe. Hence the appearance, in 1845, of *Narrative of the Life of Frederick Douglass, an American Slave,* was a literary milestone; it introduced a unique literary genre, the slave narrative, thus loosening America's dependency on European models. Also, it was one of the first great books in the West since the fall of Rome to be written by a person of color; thus it pointed toward a unified world literature freed from the racial segregation that had so far characterized the varied literatures of the world since the Middle Ages. Douglass's later life also furthered globalization, as he was America's first ambassador (1889–1895) to Haiti, the Western Hemisphere's first black-ruled state.

Douglass's slave narrative is only the most famous and the most superbly crafted of the thousands of representative examples of the slave experiences of African-Americans that were published between the founding of the United States of America and the outbreak of its Civil War. These works, many of which sold by the thousands and some of which were translated into Dutch, German, and Celtic, made converts for Abolitionism, the anti-slavery movement that began in the late eighteenth century; it was concentrated in New England and helped prepare the moral ground for the Civil War. By focusing on the psychic wounds of slavery, these writers forced readers, then and now, to recognize that attempts to forge an American national identity would have to come to grips with the country's slave past.

### Reading the Selection

Frederick Douglass (about 1818–1895) was born on a Maryland plantation, the son of a slave woman and a white man, perhaps his master. Caught in his first bid for freedom, he slipped slavery's chains, in 1838, when he rode the train (the "upperground" railroad [his term]) from Baltimore to New York. He married Anna Murray, a Baltimore freewoman who had helped him escape, and they moved to Massachusetts, living as respected members of the black community. Becoming an advocate of Abolitionism, he wrote his life story, in 1845, partly to satisfy a creative need and partly to silence critics who thought him too eloquent to have ever been a slave.

This selection covers Douglass's youth in the household of his then master, Hugh Auld, in Baltimore. In it, Douglass describes his efforts to learn to read and write and the sense of empowerment conveyed by being literate. It is a heroic story, as he moves from "mental darkness" to the light of knowledge; in the process, he overcame obstacles, private and social, erected by white society to keep slaves ignorant of their rights. Possessing literacy placed Douglass within the context of this period's reformers who made education the universal panacea—a legacy of the Age of Reason.

———

I lived in Master Hugh's family about seven years. During this time, I succeeded in learning to read and write. In accomplishing this, I was compelled to resort to various stratagems. I had no regular teacher. My mistress, who had kindly commenced to instruct me, had, in compliance with the advice and direction of her husband, not only ceased to instruct, but had set her face against my being instructed by any one else. It is due, however, to my mistress to say of her, that she did not adopt this course of treatment immediately. She at first lacked the depravity indispensable to shutting me up in mental darkness. It was at least necessary for her to have some training in the exercise of irresponsible power, to make her equal to the task of treating me as though I were a brute.

My mistress was, as I have said, a kind and tender-hearted woman; and in the simplicity of her soul she commenced, when I first went to live with her, to treat me as she supposed one human being ought to treat another. In entering upon the duties of a slaveholder, she did not seem to perceive that I sustained to her the relation of a mere chattel, and that for her to treat me as a human being was not only wrong, but dangerously so. Slavery proved as injurious to her as it did to me. When I went there, she was a pious, warm, and tender-hearted woman. There was no sorrow or suffering for which she had not a tear. She had bread for the hungry, clothes for the naked, and comfort for every mourner that came within her reach. Slavery soon proved its ability to divest her of these heavenly qualities. Under its influence, the tender heart became stone, and the lamblike disposition gave way to one of tiger-like fierceness. The first step in her downward course was in her ceasing to instruct me. She now commenced to practise her husband's precepts. She finally became even more violent in her opposition than her husband himself. She was not satisfied with simply doing as well as he had commanded; she seemed anxious to do better. Nothing seemed to make her more angry than to see me with a newspaper. She seemed to think that here lay the danger. I have had her rush at me with a face made all up of fury, and snatch from me a newspaper, in a manner that fully revealed her apprehension. She was an apt woman; and a little experience soon demonstrated, to her satisfaction, that education and slavery were incompatible with each other.

From this time I was most narrowly watched. If I was in a separate room any considerable length of time, I was sure to be suspected of having a book, and was at once called to give an account of myself. All this, however, was too late. The first step had been taken. Mistress, in teaching me the alphabet, had given me the *inch,* and no precaution could prevent me from taking the *ell.*

The plan which I adopted, and the one by which I was most successful, was that of making friends of all the little white boys whom I met in the street. As many of these as I could, I converted into teachers. With their kindly aid, obtained at different times and in different places, I finally succeeded in learning to read. When I was sent on errands, I always took my book with me, and by going one part of my errand quickly, I found time to get a lesson before my return. I used also to carry bread with me, enough of which was always in the house, and to which I was always welcome; for I was much better off in this regard than many of the poor white children in our neighborhood. This bread I used to bestow upon the hungry little urchins, who, in return, would give me that more valuable bread of knowledge. I am strongly tempted to give the names of two or three of those little boys, as a testimonial of the gratitude and affection I bear them; but prudence forbids;—not that it would injure me, but it might embarrass them; for it is almost an unpardonable offence to teach slaves to read in this Christian country. It is enough to say of the dear little fellows, that they lived on

Philpot Street, very near Durgin and Bailey's ship-yard. I used to talk this matter of slavery over with them. I would sometimes say to them, I wished I could be as free as they would be when they got to be men. "You will be free as soon as you are twenty-one, *but I am a slave for life!* Have not I as good a right to be free as you have?" These words used to trouble them; they would express for me the liveliest sympathy, and console me with the hope that something would occur by which I might be free.

I was now about twelve years old, and the thought of being *a slave for life* began to bear heavily upon my heart. Just about this time, I got hold of a book entitled "The Columbian Orator." Every opportunity I got, I used to read this book. Among much of other interesting matter, I found in it a dialogue between a master and his slave. The slave was represented as having run away from his master three times. The dialogue represented the conversation which took place between them, when the slave was retaken the third time. In this dialogue, the whole argument in behalf of slavery was brought forward by the master, all of which was disposed of by the slave. The slave was made to say some very smart as well as impressive things in reply to his master—things which had the desired though unexpected effect; for the conversation resulted in the voluntary emancipation of the slave on the part of the master.

In the same book, I met with one of Sheridan's mighty speeches on and in behalf of Catholic emancipation. These were choice documents to me. I read them over and over again with unabated interest. They gave tongue to interesting thoughts of my own soul, which had frequently flashed through my mind, and died away for want of utterance. The moral which I gained from the dialogue was the power of truth over the conscience of even a slaveholder. What I got from Sheridan was a bold denunciation of slavery, and a powerful vindication of human rights. The reading of these documents enabled me to utter my thoughts, and to meet the arguments brought forward to sustain slavery; but while they relieved me of one difficulty, they brought on another even more painful than the one of which I was relieved. The more I read, the more I was led to abhor and detest my enslavers. I could regard them in no other light than a band of successful robbers, who had left their homes, and gone to Africa, and stolen us from our homes, and in a strange land reduced us to slavery. I loathed them as being the meanest as well as the most wicked of men. As I read and contemplated the subject, behold! that very discontentment which Master Hugh had predicted would follow my learning to read had already come, to torment and sting my soul to unutterable anguish. As I writhed under it, I would at times feel that learning to read had been a curse rather than a blessing. It had given me a view of my wretched condition, without the remedy. It opened my eyes to the horrible pit, but to no ladder upon which to get out. In moments of agony, I envied my fellow-slaves for their stupidity. I have often wished myself a beast. I preferred the condition of the meanest reptile to my own. Any thing, no matter what, to get rid of thinking! It was this everlasting thinking of my condition that tormented me. There was no getting rid of it. It was pressed upon me by every object within sight or hearing, animate or inanimate. The silver trump of freedom had roused my soul to eternal wakefulness. Freedom now appeared, to disappear no more forever. It was heard in every sound, and seen in every thing. It was ever present to torment me with a sense of my wretched condition. I saw nothing without seeing it, I heard nothing without hearing it, and felt nothing without feeling it. It looked from every star, it smiled in every calm, breathed in every wind, and moved in every storm.

I often found myself regretting my own existence, and wishing myself dead; and but for the hope of being free, I have no doubt but that I should have killed myself, or done something for which I should have been killed. While in this state of mind, I was eager to hear any one speak of slavery. I was a ready listener. Every little while, I could hear something about the abolitionists. It was some time before I found what the word meant. It was always used in such connections as to make it an interesting word to me. If a slave ran away and succeeded in getting clear, or if a slave killed his master, set fire to a barn, or did any thing very wrong in the mind of a slaveholder, it was spoken of as the fruit of *abolition.* Hearing the word in this connection very often, I set about learning what it meant. The dictionary afforded me little or no help. I found it was "the act of abolishing"; but then I did not know what was to be abolished. Here I was perplexed. I did not dare to ask any one about its meaning, for I was satisfied that it was something they wanted me to know very little about. After a patient waiting, I got one of our city papers, containing an account of the number of petitions from the north, praying for the abolition of slavery in the District of Columbia, and of the slave trade between the States. From this time I understood the words *abolition* and *abolitionist,* and always drew near when that word was spoken, expecting to hear something of importance to myself and fellow-slaves. The light broke in upon me by degrees. I went one day down on the wharf of Mr. Waters; and seeing two Irishmen unloading a scow of stone, I went, unasked, and helped them. When we had finished, one of them came to me and asked me if I were a slave. I told him I was. He asked, "Are ye a slave for life?" I told him that I was. The good Irishman seemed to be deeply affected by the statement. He said to the other that it was a pity so fine a little fellow as myself should be a slave for life. He said it was a shame to hold me. They both advised me to run away to the north; that I should find friends there, and that I should be free. I pretended not to be interested in what they said, and treated them as if I did not understand them; for I feared they might be treacherous. White men have been known to encourage slaves to escape, and then, to get the reward, catch them and return them to their masters. I was afraid that these seemingly good men might use me so; but I nevertheless remembered their advice, and from that time I resolved to run away. I looked forward to a time at which it would be safe for me to escape. I was too young to think of doing so immediately; besides, I wished to learn how to write, as I might have occasion to write my own pass. I consoled myself with the hope that I should one day find a good chance. Meanwhile, I would learn to write.

The idea as to how I might learn to write was suggested to me by being in Durgin and Bailey's ship-yard, and frequently seeing the ship carpenters, after hewing, and getting a piece of timber ready to use, write on the timber the name of that part of the ship for which it was intended. When a piece of timber was intended for the larboard side, it would be marked thus—"L." When a piece was for the starboard side, it would be marked thus—"S." A piece for the larboard side forward, would be marked thus—"L. F." When a piece was for starboard side forward, it would be marked thus—"S. F." For larboard aft, it would be marked thus—"L. A." For starboard aft, it would be marked thus—"S. A." I soon learned the names of these letters, and for what they were intended when placed upon a piece of timber in the shipyard. I immediately commenced copying them, and in a short time was able to make the four letters named. After that, when I met with any boy who I knew could write, I would tell him I could write as well as he. The next word would be, "I don't believe you. Let me see you try it." I would then make the letters which I had been so fortunate as to learn, and ask him to beat that. In this way I got a good many lessons in writing, which it is quite possible I should never have gotten in any other way. During this time, my copy-book was the board fence, brick wall, and pavement; my pen and ink was a lump of chalk. With these, I learned mainly how to write. I then commenced and continued copying the Italics in Webster's Spelling Book, until I could make them all without looking on the book. By this time, my little Master Thomas had gone to school, and learned how to write, and had written over a number of copy-books. These had been brought home, and shown to some of our near neighbors, and then laid aside. My mistress used to go to class meeting at the Wilk Street meetinghouse every Monday afternoon, and leave me to take care of the house. When left thus, I used to spend time in writing in the spaces left in Master Thomas's copy-book, copying what he had written. I continued to do this until I could write a hand very similar to that of Master Thomas. Thus, after a long, tedious effort for years, I finally succeeded in learning how to write.

# CHARLOTTE BRONTË
# from *Jane Eyre*
## Chapter 23

———

Charlotte Brontë (1816–1855) was the oldest member of perhaps the West's most famous literary family, which also included her two younger sisters, Emily (1818–1848), and Anne (1820–1849). The offspring of an Anglican priest, the Brontë daughters spent most of their youth at Haworth, a parsonage deep in rural Yorkshire in northern England. Haworth was a gloomy dwelling—all that the poor parish could provide—and was next to the churchyard, which early claimed the Brontë mother. Isolated thus from urban culture, the Brontë children were educated mainly at home with some months at shabby boarding schools. As a result, the children turned to each other and fashioned fantasy kingdoms; these became the subject of their first juvenile works, including tales, poems, journals, serial stories, and a monthly magazine—some of which survive. Without fully realizing it, the Brontës spent their youth preparing for literary careers.

The Brontë sisters left an indelible mark on Western letters. They wrote novels in the Gothic style, with varied degrees of success; in order to be taken seriously by Victorian critics who often treated women writers with disdain, they published their works under masculine names. The youngest sister, Anne, writing as "Acton Bell," won modest acclaim with *The Tenant of Wildfell Hall* (1848), a novel still in print today; the middle sister Emily, writing as "Ellis Bell," achieved undying fame with *Wuthering Heights* (1847), one of the most popular novels ever written, though not at the time; and the eldest sister Charlotte, writing as "Currer Bell," was the most successful of the group with *Jane Eyre* (1847), *Shirley* (1849), and *Villette* (1852). Today, Charlotte's reputation remains high, mainly due to the popularity of *Jane Eyre*, in both its original form and as the source for movies, TV dramas, and, most recently, a novel, *Wide Sargasso Sea*, by Jean Rhys.

### Reading the Selection

*Jane Eyre* is the story of the sufferings of a young woman, without wealth and social connections, as she struggles to find a place for herself in the world. The novel traces Jane's life from an unloved childhood at Gateshead, to her schooling at Lowood, to her adolescence at Thornfield Hall, where she was a governess. Finally, we read of her fulfillment, as she marries her employer at Ferndean. *Jane Eyre* is a pioneering novel in its frank portrayal of a heroine who refuses to accept her appointed place in society.

*Jane Eyre* reflected Charlotte's reading and her experiences. Inspired by Romantic poets like Byron (see *Don Juan*), she wanted to capture the sense of "felt" life, "what throbs fast and full, though hidden, what the blood rushes through, what is the unseen seat of life and the sentient target of death." In part autobiographical, this novel drew on her inner life and aspirations. Charlotte also made Jane Eyre "as plain and as small as" herself, for she wanted to show that "a heroine could be interesting without being beautiful."

This selection—Chapter 23 of *Jane Eyre*—concerns Jane's life at Thornfield, where she is governess to Adèle, the daughter of Mr. Rochester. Thoroughly Romantic in style, this chapter juxtaposes stormy nature with Jane's wild emotions. It ends with Jane planning marriage to her employer Mr. Rochester, who later will be revealed as already married. The problems resulting from Jane's engagement to Mr. Rochester take up much of the rest of the novel.

A splendid Midsummer shone over England: skies so pure, suns so radiant as were then seen in long succession, seldom favour, even singly, our wave-girt land. It was as if a band of Italian days had come from the South, like a flock of glorious passenger birds, and lighted to rest them on the cliffs of Albion. The hay was all got in; the fields round Thornfield were green and shorn; the roads white and baked; the trees were in their dark prime; hedge and wood, full-leaved and deeply tinted, contrasted well with the sunny hue of the cleared meadows between.

On Midsummer-eve, Adèle, weary with gathering wild strawberries in Hay Lane half the day, had gone to bed with the sun. I watched her drop asleep, and when I left her, I sought the garden.

It was now the sweetest hour of the twenty-four: 'day its fervid fires had wasted', and dew fell cool on panting plain and scorched summit. Where the sun had gone down in simple state—pure of the pomp of clouds—spread a solemn purple, burning with the light of red jewel and furnace flame at one point, on one hill-peak, and extending high and wide, soft and still softer, over half heaven. The east had its own charm of fine, deep blue, and its own modest gem, a rising and solitary star: soon it would boast the moon; but she was yet beneath the horizon.

I walked a while on the pavement; but a subtle, well-known scent—that of a cigar—stole from some window; I saw the library casement open a hand-breadth; I knew I might be watched thence; so I went apart into the orchard. No nook in the grounds more sheltered and more Eden-like; a very high wall shut it out from the court on one side; on the other a beech avenue screened it from the lawn. At the bottom was a sunk fence, its sole separation from lonely fields: a winding walk, bordered with laurels and terminating in a giant horse-chestnut, circled at the base by a seat, led down to the fence. Here one could wander unseen. While such honeydew fell, such silence reigned, such gloaming gathered, I felt as if I could haunt such shade for ever; but in treading the flower and fruit parterres at the upper part of the enclosure, enticed there by the light the now rising moon cast on this more open quarter, my step is stayed—not by sound, not by sight, but once more by a warning fragrance.

Sweet-brier and southernwood, jasmine, pink, and rose have long been yielding their evening sacrifice of incense: this new scent is neither of shrub nor flower; it is—I know it well—it is Mr Rochester's cigar. I look round and listen. I see trees laden with ripening fruit. I hear a nightingale warbling in a wood half a mile off: no moving form is visible, no coming step audible; but that perfume increases: I must flee. I make for the wicket leading to the shrubbery, and I see Mr Rochester entering. I step aside into the ivy recess; he will not stay long: he will soon return whence he came, and if I sit still he will never see me.

But no—eventide is as pleasant to him as to me, and this antique garden as attractive; and he strolls on, now lifting the gooseberry-tree branches to look at the fruit, large as plums, with which they are laden; now taking a ripe cherry from the wall; now stooping towards a knot of flowers, either to inhale their fragrance or to admire the dew-beads on their petals. A great moth goes humming by me; it alights on a plant at Mr Rochester's foot: he sees it, and bends to examine it.

'Now he has his back towards me,' thought I, 'and he is occupied too; perhaps, if I walk softly, I can slip away unnoticed.'

I trod on an edging of turf that the crackle of the pebbly gravel might not betray me: he was standing among the beds at a yard or two distant from where I had to pass; the moth apparently engaged him. 'I shall get by very well,' I meditated. As I crossed his shadow, thrown long over the garden by the moon, not yet risen high, he said quietly, without turning—

'Jane, come and look at this fellow.'

I had made no noise: he had not eyes behind—could his shadow feel? I started at first, and then I approached him.

'Look at his wings,' said he; 'he reminds me rather of a West Indian insect; one does not often see so large and gay a night-rover in England; there! he is flown.'

The moth roamed away. I was sheepishly retreating also; but Mr Rochester followed me, and when we reached the wicket he said—

'Turn back: on so lovely a night it is a shame to sit in the house; and surely no one can wish to go to bed while sunset is thus at meeting with moonrise.'

It is one of my faults, that though my tongue is sometimes prompt enough at answer, there are times when it sadly fails me in framing an excuse; and always the lapse occurs at some crisis, when a facile word or plausible pretext is specially wanted to get me out of painful embarrassment. I did not like to walk at this hour alone with Mr Rochester in the shadowy orchard; but I could not find a reason to allege for leaving him. I followed with lagging step, and thoughts busily bent on discovering a means of extrication; but he himself looked so composed and so grave also, I became ashamed of feeling any confusion: the evil—if evil existent or prospective there was—seemed to lie with me only; his mind was unconscious and quiet.

'Jane,' he recommenced, as we entered the laurel walk and slowly strayed down in the direction of the sunk fence and the horse-chestnut, 'Thornfield is a pleasant place in summer, is it not?'

'Yes, sir.'

'You must have become in some degree attached to the house—you who have an eye for natural beauties, and a good deal of the organ of Adhesiveness?'

'I am attached to it, indeed.'

'And though I don't comprehend how it is, I perceive you have acquired a degree of regard for that foolish little child Adèle, too; and even for simple Dame Fairfax?'

'Yes, sir; in different ways, I have an affection for both.'

'And would be sorry to part with them?'

'Yes.'

'Pity!' he said, and sighed and paused.

'It is always the way of events in this life,' he continued presently: 'no sooner have you got settled in a pleasant resting-place, than a voice calls out to you to rise and move on, for the hour of repose is expired.'

'Must I move on, sir?' I asked. 'Must I leave Thornfield?'

'I believe you must, Jane. I am sorry, Janet, but I believe indeed you must.'

This was a blow: but I did not let it prostrate me.

'Well, sir, I shall be ready when the order to march comes.'

'It is come now—I must give it to-night.'

'Then you *are* going to be married, sir?'

'Ex-act-ly—pre-cise-ly: with your usual acuteness, you have hit the nail straight on the head.'

'Soon, sir?'

'Very soon, my—that is, Miss Eyre: and you'll remember, Jane, the first time I, or Rumour, plainly intimated to you that it was my intention to put my old bachelor's neck into the sacred noose, to enter into the holy state of matrimony—to take Miss Ingram to my bosom, in short (she's an extensive armful: but that's not to the point—one can't have too much of such a very excellent thing as my beautiful Blanche): well, as I was saying—listen to me, Jane! You're not turning your head to look after more moths, are you? That was only a lady-clock, child, "flying away home". I wish to remind you that it was you who first said to me, with that discretion I respect in you—with that foresight, prudence, and humility which befit your responsible and dependent position—that in case I married Miss Ingram, both you and little Adèle had better trot forthwith. I pass over the sort of slur conveyed in this suggestion on the character of my beloved; indeed, when you are far away, Janet, I'll try to forget it: I shall notice only its wisdom; which is such that I have made it my law of action. Adèle must go to school; and you, Miss Eyre, must get a new situation.'

'Yes, sir, I will advertise immediately: and meantime, I suppose—' I was going to say, 'I suppose I may stay here, till I find another shelter to betake myself to': but I stopped, feeling it would not do to risk a long sentence, for my voice was not quite under command.

'In about a month I hope to be a bridegroom,' continued Mr Rochester; 'and in the interim, I shall myself look out for employment and an asylum for you.'

'Thank you, sir; I am sorry to give—'

'Oh, no need to apologize! I consider that when a dependent does her duty as well as you have done yours, she has a sort of claim upon her employer for any little assistance he can conveniently render her; indeed, I have already, through my future mother-in-law, heard of a place that I think will suit: it is to undertake the education of the five daughters of Mrs Dionysius O'Gall of Bitternutt Lodge, Connaught, Ireland. You'll like Ireland, I think: they're such warm-hearted people there, they say.'

'It is a long way off, sir.'

'No matter—a girl of your sense will not object to the voyage or the distance.'

'Not the voyage but the distance: and then the sea is a barrier—'

'From what, Jane?'

'From England and from Thornfield; and—'

'Well?'

'From *you*, sir.'

I said this almost involuntarily, and with as little sanction of free will, my tears gushed out. I did not cry so as to be heard, however; I avoided sobbing. The thought of Mrs O'Gall and Bitternutt Lodge struck cold to my heart; and colder the thought of all the brine and foam destined, as it seemed, to rush between me and the master at whose side I now walked; and coldest the remembrance of the wider ocean—wealth, caste, custom—intervened between me and what I naturally and inevitably loved.

'It is a long way,' I again said.

'It is, to be sure; and when you get to Bitternutt Lodge, Connaught, Ireland, I shall never see you again, Jane: that's morally certain. I never go over to Ireland, not having myself much of a fancy for the country. We have been good friends, Jane; have we not?'

'Yes, sir.'

'And when friends are on the eve of separation, they like to spend the little time that remains to them close to each other. Come! we'll talk over the voyage and the parting quietly, half an hour or so, while the stars enter into their shining life up in heaven yonder: here is the chestnut-tree: here is the bench at its old roots. Come, we will sit there in peace to-night, though we should never more be destined to sit there together.'

He seated me and himself.

'It is a long way to Ireland, Janet, and I am sorry to send my little friend on such weary travels: but if I can't do better, how is it to be helped? Are you anything akin to me, do you think, Jane?'

I could risk no sort of answer by this time: my heart was still.

'Because,' he said, 'I sometimes have a queer feeling with regard to you—especially when you are near to me, as now: it is as if I had a string somewhere under my left ribs, tightly and inextricably knotted to a similar string situated in the corresponding quarter of your little frame. And if that boisterous Channel, and two hundred miles or so of land, come broad between us, I am afraid that cord of communion will be snapped; and then I've a nervous notion I should take to bleeding inwardly. As for you—you'd forget me.'

'That I *never* should, sir: you know—' Impossible to proceed.

'Jane, do you hear that nightingale singing in the wood? Listen!'

In listening, I sobbed convulsively; for I could repress what I endured no longer; I was obliged to yield, and I was shaken from head to foot with acute distress. When I did speak, it was only to express an impetuous wish that I had never been born, or never come to Thornfield.

'Because you are sorry to leave it?'

The vehemence of emotion, stirred by grief and love within me, was claiming mastery, and struggling for full sway, and asserting a right to predominate, to overcome, to live, rise, and reign at last: yes—and to speak.

'I grieve to leave Thornfield: I love Thornfield: I love it, because I have lived in it a full and delightful life—momentarily at least. I have not been trampled on. I have not been petrified. I have not been buried with inferior minds, and excluded from every glimpse of communion with what is bright and energetic and high. I have talked, face to face, with what I reverence, with what I delight in—with an original, a vigorous, an expanded mind. I have known you, Mr Rochester; and it strikes me with terror and anguish to feel I absolutely must be torn from you for ever. I see the necessity of departure; and it is like looking on the necessity of death.'

'Where do you see the necessity?' he asked suddenly.

'Where? You, sir, have placed it before me.'

'In what shape?'

'In the shape of Miss Ingram; a noble and beautiful woman—your bride.'

'My bride! What bride? I have no bride!'

'But you will have.'

'Yes—I will!—I will!' he set his teeth.

'Then I must go—you have said it yourself.'

'No: you must stay! I swear it—and the oath shall be kept.'

'I tell you I must go!' I retorted, roused to something like passion. 'Do you think I can stay to become nothing to you? Do you think I am an automaton?—a machine without feelings? and can bear to have my morsel of bread snatched from my lips, and my drop of living water dashed from my cup? Do you think, because I am poor, obscure, plain, and little, I am soulless and heartless? You think wrong!—I have as much soul as you—and full as much heart! And if God had gifted me with some beauty and much wealth, I should have made it as hard for you to leave me, as it is now for me to leave you. I am not talking to you now through the medium of custom, conventionalities, nor even of mortal flesh: it is my spirit that addresses your spirit; just as if both had passed through the grave, and we stood at God's feet, equal—as we are!'

'As we are!' repeated Mr Rochester—'so,' he added, enclosing me in his arms, gathering me to his breast, pressing his lips to my lips: 'so, Jane!'

'Yes, so, sir,' I rejoined: 'and yet not so: for you are a married man—or as good as a married man, and wed to one inferior to you—to one with whom you have no sympathy—whom I do not believe you truly love; for I have seen and heard you sneer at her. I would scorn such a union: therefore I am better than you—let me go!'

'Where, Jane? To Ireland?'

'Yes—to Ireland. I have spoken my mind, and can go anywhere now.'

'Jane, be still; don't struggle so, like a wild frantic bird that is rending its own plumage in its desperation.'

'I am no bird; and no net ensnares me; I am a free human being with an independent will, which I now exert to leave you.'

Another effort set me at liberty, and I stood erect before him.

'And your will shall decide your destiny,' he said. 'I offer you my heart, my hand, and a share of all my possessions.'

'You play a farce, which I merely laugh at.'

'I ask you to pass through life at my side—to be my second self, and best earthly companion.'

'For that fate you have already made your choice, and must abide by it.'

'Jane, be still a few moments: you are over-excited: I will be still too.'

A waft of wind came sweeping down the laurel-walk, and trembled through the boughs of the chestnut: it wandered away—away—to an indefinite distance—it died. The nightingale's song was then the only voice of the hour: in listening to it I again wept. Mr Rochester sat quiet, looking at me gently and seriously. Some time passed before he spoke; he at last said—

'Come to my side, Jane, and let us explain and understand one another.'

'I will never again come to your side: I am torn away now, and cannot return.'

'But, Jane, I summon you as my wife: it is you only I intend to marry.'

I was silent: I thought he mocked me.

'Come, Jane—come hither.'

'Your bride stands between us.'

He rose, and with a stride reached me.

'My bride is here,' he said, again drawing me to him, 'because my equal is here, and my likeness. Jane, will you marry me?'

Still I did not answer, and still I writhed myself from his grasp: for I was still incredulous.

'Do you doubt me, Jane?'

'Entirely.'

'You have no faith in me?'

'Not a whit.'

'Am I a liar in your eyes?' he asked passionately. 'Little sceptic, you *shall* be convinced. What love have I for Miss Ingram? None: and that you know. What love has she for me? None: as I have taken pains to prove: I caused a rumour to reach her that my fortune was not a third of what was supposed, and after that I presented myself to see the result; it was coldness both from her and her mother. I would not—I could not—marry Miss Ingram. You—you strange, you almost unearthly thing!—I love you as my own flesh. You—poor and obscure, and small and plain as you are—I entreat to accept me as a husband.'

'What, me!' I ejaculated, beginning in his earnestness—and especially in his incivility—to credit his sincerity: 'me who have not a friend in the world but you—if you are my friend: not a shilling but what you have given me?'

'You, Jane, I must have you for my own—entirely my own. Will you be mine? Say yes, quickly.'

'Mr Rochester, let me look at your face: turn to the moonlight.'

'Why?'

'Because I want to read your countenance—turn!'

'There! you will find it scarcely more legible than a crumpled, scratched page. Read on: only make haste, for I suffer.'

His face was very much agitated and very much flushed, and there were strong workings in the features, and strange gleams in the eyes.

'Oh, Jane, you torture me!' he exclaimed. 'With that searching and yet faithful and generous look, you torture me!'

'How can I do that? If you are true, and your offer real, my only feelings to you must be gratitude and devotion—they cannot torture.'

'Gratitude!' he ejaculated; and added wildly—'Jane, accept me quickly. Say, Edward—give me my name—Edward—I will marry you.'

'Are you in earnest? Do you truly love me? Do you sincerely wish me to be your wife?'

'I do; and if an oath is necessary to satisfy, I swear it.'

'Then, sir, I will marry you.'

'Edward—my little wife!'

'Dear Edward!'

'Come to me—come to me entirely now,' said he; and added in his deepest tone, speaking in my ear as his cheek was laid on mine, 'Make my happiness—I will make yours.'

'God pardon me!' he subjoined ere long; 'and man meddle not with me: I have her, and will hold her.'

'There is no one to meddle, sir. I have no kindred to interfere.'

'No—that is the best of it,' he said. And if I had loved him less I should have thought his accent and look of exultation savage; but, sitting by him, roused from the nightmare of parting—called to the paradise of union—I thought only of the bliss given me to drink in so abundant a flow. Again and again he said, 'Are you happy, Jane?' And again and again I answered, 'Yes.' After which he murmured, 'It will atone—it will atone. Have I not found her friendless, and cold, and comfortless? Will I not guard, and cherish, and solace her? Is there not love in my heart, and constancy in my resolves? It will expiate at God's tribunal. I know my Maker sanctions what I do. For the world's judgement—I wash my hands thereof. For man's opinion—I defy it.'

But what had befallen the night? The moon was not yet set, and we were all in shadow: I could scarcely see my master's face, near as I was. And what ailed the chestnut tree? it writhed and groaned; while wind roared in the laurel walk, and came sweeping over us.

'We must go in,' said Mr Rochester: 'the weather changes. I could have sat with thee till morning, Jane.'

'And so,' thought I, 'could I with you.' I should have said so, perhaps, but a livid, vivid spark leapt out of a cloud at which I was looking, and there was a crack, a crash, and a close rattling peal; and I thought only of hiding my dazzled eyes against Mr Rochester's shoulder.

The rain rushed down. He hurried me up the walk, through the grounds, and into the house; but we were quite wet before we could pass the threshold. He was taking off my shawl in the hall, and shaking the water out of my loosened hair, when Mrs Fairfax emerged from her room. I did not observe her at first, nor did Mr Rochester. The lamp was lit. The clock was on the stroke of twelve.

'Hasten to take off your wet things,' said he; 'and before you go, good-night—good-night, my darling.'

He kissed me repeatedly. When I looked up, on leaving his arms, there stood the widow, pale, grave, and amazed. I only smiled at her, and ran upstairs. 'Explanation will do for another time,' thought I. Still, when I reached my chamber, I felt a pang at the idea she should even temporarily misconstrue what she had seen. But joy soon effaced every other feeling; and loud as the wind blew, near and deep as the thunder crashed, fierce and frequent as the lightning gleamed, cataract-like as the rain fell during a storm of two hours' duration, I experienced no fear and little awe. Mr Rochester came thrice to my door in the course of it, to ask if I was safe and tranquil: and that was comfort, that was strength for anything.

Before I left my bed in the morning, little Adèle came running in to tell me that the great horse-chestnut at the bottom of the orchard had been struck by lightning in the night, and half of it split away.

---

# SOJOURNER TRUTH
## *Ain't I a Woman?*

---

The African-American woman Sojourner Truth (1795–1883) was an original voice who was a force for vital change in the nineteenth century. She made her mark both as a writer and as a supporter of progressive causes. As author of *Narrative of Sojourner Truth* (1850), the first classic by an African-American woman writer, she made it possible for other African-American women (see Hurston, Brooks, and Walker) to speak their minds in print; thus, she contributed to the ongoing process of redefining Western culture. She was an advocate of women's rights, spiritualism, temperance, hydrotherapy (the use of water in treating disease), perfectionism (the belief that humans can achieve moral perfection on earth), Grahamism (the ideas of Sylvester Graham [1794–1851], an American vegetarian who urged dietary reform), and, most especially, anti-slavery; she aligned herself with advanced thinkers who envisioned a utopian society in the New World, free of the corruption of old Europe. Relatively unknown between 1900 and 1950, she was restored to her rightful place in history with the civil rights movement.

Sojourner Truth was not her birth name but an adopted name meant to erase her slave origins. Born Isabella, or "Bell," she originally shared her master's last name, Hardenberg; when she was sold to a man named Dumont, she took his last name. In 1843, mystical "voices" instructed her to change her name and pursue the life of an itinerant preacher. Thereafter her mission was to "sojourn" America and speak God's "truth." She was active in New England in the 1840s; in 1850, she shifted headquarters to Salem, Ohio, operating out of the office of the *Anti-Slavery Bugle*; and in 1857, she moved permanently to Battle Creek, Michigan.

Sojourner Truth's career as an anti-slave advocate resembled that of Frederick Douglass (see *Narrative of the Life of Frederick Douglass*), for both were famous Abolitionists and both published widely-read slave narratives. She differed from Douglass in two major ways: she experienced slavery in the north, and she never learned to read or write. As an ex-slave from New York (she bolted to freedom in 1827, the year slavery was abolished there), she could bear witness to the evils of northern slavery, even in the case of "kindly" masters. As an illiterate, she spoke for the African-Americans of her day, most of whom also could not read or write. The literate Douglass, whom she met in 1844, termed her "a genuine specimen of the uncultured [N]egro." Scholars today regard Sojourner Truth in many ways as the more authentic African-American voice of the two; Douglass, by becoming literate, is seen by some as a black European. Faithful to her roots, Sojourner Truth's *Narrative*, dictated to Olive Gilbert, represents the collective memory and vision of previously disenfranchised black America.

### Reading the Selection

This selection—the "Ain't I A Woman?" speech—is the record of Sojourner Truth's address at the 1851 Women's Rights convention in Akron, Ohio. This version was written from memory by the feminist Frances Gage, but its accuracy is questionable. (A more accurate record of the speech is the on-the-scene report printed in the *Anti-Slavery Bugle*.) Gage's version nonetheless was widely read and contributed to the image of Sojourner Truth as a nimble-witted, gifted orator. The speech, homespun and rich in biblical allusions, blends the themes of racial equality and women's rights—the two causes to which Sojourner Truth was most devoted.

———

Well, children, where there is so much racket there must be something out of kilter. I think that 'twixt the negroes of the South and the women at the North, all talking about rights, the white men will be in a fix pretty soon. But what's all this here talking about?

That man over there says that women need to be helped into carriages, and lifted over ditches, and to have the best place everywhere. Nobody ever helps me into carriages, or over mud-puddles, or gives me any best place! And ain't I a woman? Look at me! Look at my arm! I have ploughed and planted, and gathered into barns, and no man could head me! And ain't I a woman? I could work as much and eat as much as a man—when I could get it—and bear the lash as well! And ain't I a woman? I have borne thirteen children, and seen them most all sold off to slavery, and when I cried out with my mother's grief, none but Jesus heard me! And ain't I a woman?

Then they talk about this thing in the head; what's this they call it? (Intellect, someone whispers.) That's it, honey. What's that got to do with women's rights or negro's rights? If my cup won't hold but a pint, and yours holds a quart, wouldn't you be mean not to let me have my little half-measure full?

Then that little man in black there, he says women can't have as much rights as men, 'cause Christ wasn't a woman! Where did your Christ come from? Where did your Christ come from? From God and a woman! Man had nothing to do with Him.

If the first woman God ever made was strong enough to turn the world upside down all alone, these women together ought to be able to turn it back, and get it right side up again! And now they is asking to do it, the men better let them.

Obliged to you for hearing me, and now old Sojourner ain't got nothing more to say.

# HENRY DAVID THOREAU

# from *Walden*

---

Henry David Thoreau (1817–1862) was a nineteenth-century nonconformist whose twin messages of self-communion and harmony with nature fell on deaf ears in his own day. Educated in Classical and English literature at Harvard College, and inspired by America's reigning philosopher Ralph Waldo Emerson (1803–1882), he gave up a teaching career to devote his life to lecturing and writing. Over a period of seventeen years, from 1845 to 1862, he published a small body of work, mainly essays and two books, namely *A Week on the Concord and Merrimack Rivers* (1849) and *Walden* (1854); these reflected his growing disenchantment with industrialization and America's cult of success. When he died in 1862, the literary world barely mourned, for he was considered, if thought about at all, as an inferior disciple of Emerson and a minor literary figure.

Today Thoreau's reputation has undergone a massive reevaluation; he is generally accepted as one of the greats of Western thought and literature. His 1848 essay, *On the Duty of Civil Disobedience*, originally entitled "Resistance to Civil Government," became the bible for Gandhi's passive resistance campaign in India; and through Gandhi's example, it influenced Martin Luther King, Jr. (see "I Have a Dream") and the civil rights movement of the 1950s and 1960s. Thoreau's *Walden* is now recognized both as a classic of English prose and as the textbook for environmental groups devoted to saving the earth and its wildlife. *Walden*'s current popularity led to the printing of Thoreau's *Journals*, a fourteen-volume diary of his daily jottings (some of which he borrowed for his books). Clearly, his visionary message was so in advance of his age that literary success had to await the public's catching up to his ideas.

Disgusted with his age's materialism and trend toward increased power of government over the individual, Thoreau became what today might be called a "drop-out" from society. He began his career as a "drop-out" in 1841, when he moved in with Emerson and became both a disciple and general handyman. He remained in this situation until 1843, when the two men parted amicably. Two years later, in March 1845, Thoreau took the most significant step of his life: He moved to Walden Pond, near Concord, Massachusetts, where he built himself a wooden hut and led a Robinson Crusoe existence until September 1847. *Walden; or, Life in the Woods* is an outgrowth of the writer's two years spent at the pond, though it was written and polished over many years, incorporating entries from wide-ranging dates in the *Journals*. In form, *Walden* follows one year's changing seasons, beginning with summer, progressing through autumn and winter, and concluding with the earth's rebirth in springtime. Thus, despite the swaggering tone, the book is optimistic and celebrates life.

## Reading the Selection

This selection from *Walden* is taken from Chapter 2, "Where I Lived, and What I Lived For." In it, he reveals himself to be a "morning person," one who feels genuinely alive in the early hours of each day. His love of the morning becomes a metaphor for living with full consciousness—the purpose of his quest at Walden Pond. Consciousness, in turn, leads him to try to simplify his life, to cast away material things and to do the bare minimum labor to survive. "Our life is frittered away by detail," he proclaims. Thoreau's hatred of civilized society and his preference for living close to nature echoes the Swiss Romantic thinker, Rousseau (see *Confessions*).

---

• • •

Every morning was a cheerful invitation to make my life of equal simplicity, and I may say innocence, with Nature herself. I have been as sincere a worshipper of Aurora as the Greeks. I got up early and bathed in the pond; that was a religious exercise, and one of the best things which I did. They say the characters were engraven on the bathing tub of king Tching-thang to this effect: "Renew thyself completely each day; do it again, and again, and forever again." I can understand that. Morning brings back the heroic ages. I was as much affected by the faint hum of a mosquito making its invisible and unimaginable tour through my apartment at earliest dawn, when I was sitting with door and windows open, as I could be by any trumpet that ever sang of fame. It was Homer's requiem; itself an Iliad and Odyssey in the air, singing its own wrath and wanderings. There was something cosmical about it; a standing advertisement, till forbidden, of the everlasting vigor and fertility of the world. The morning, which is the most memorable season of the day, is the awakening hour. Then there is least somnolence in us; and for an hour, at least, some part of us awakes which slumbers all the rest of the day and night. Little is to be expected of that day, if it can be called a day, to which we are not awakened by our Genius, but by the mechanical nudgings of some servitor, are not awakened by our own newly-acquired force and aspirations from within, accompanied by the undulations of celestial music, instead of factory bells, and a fragrance filling the air—to a higher life than we fell asleep from; and thus the darkness bear its fruit, and prove itself to be good, no less than the light. That man who does not believe that each day contains an earlier, more sacred, and auroral hour than he has yet profaned, has despaired of life, and is pursuing a descending and darkening way. After a partial cessation of his sensuous life, the soul of man, or its organs rather, are reinvigorated each day, and his Genius tries again what noble life it can make. All memorable events, I should say, transpire in morning time and in a morning atmosphere. The Vedas say, "All intelligences awake with the morning." Poetry and art, and the fairest and most memorable of the actions of men, date from such an hour. All poets and heroes, like Memnon, are the children of Aurora, and emit their music at sunrise. To him whose elastic and vigorous thought keeps pace with the sun, the day is a perpetual morning. It matters not what the clocks say or the attitudes and labors of men. Morning is when I am awake and there is a dawn in me. Moral reform is the effort to throw off sleep. Why is it that men give so poor an account of their day if they have not been slumbering? They are not such poor calculators. If they had not been overcome with drowsiness they would have performed something. The millions are awake enough for physical labor; but only one in a million is awake enough for effective intellectual exertion, only one in a hundred millions to a poetic or divine life. To be awake is to be alive. I have never yet met a man who was quite awake. How could I have looked him in the face?

We must learn to reawaken and keep ourselves awake, not by mechanical aids, but by an infinite expectation of the dawn, which does not forsake us in our soundest sleep. I know of no more encouraging fact than the unquestionable ability of man to elevate his life by a conscious endeavor. It is something to be able to paint a particular picture, or to carve a statue, and so to make a few objects beautiful; but it is far more glorious to carve and paint the very atmosphere and medium through which we look, which morally we can do. To affect the quality of the day, that is the highest of arts. Every man is tasked to make his life, even in its details, worthy of the contemplation of his most elevated and critical hour. If we refused, or rather used up, such paltry information as we get, the oracles would distinctly inform us how this might be done.

I went to the woods because I wished to live deliberately, to front only the essential facts of life, and see if I could not learn what it had to teach, and not, when I came to die, discover that I had not lived. I did not wish to live what was not life, living is so dear, nor did I wish to practise resignation, unless it was quite necessary. I wanted to live deep and suck out all the marrow of life, to live so sturdily and Spartan-like as to put to rout all that was not life, to cut a broad swath and shave close, to drive life into a corner, and reduce it to its lowest terms, and, if it proved to be mean, why then to get the whole and genuine meanness of it, and publish its meanness to the world; or if it were sublime, to know it by experience, and be able to give a true account of it in my next excursion. For most men, it appears to me, are in a strange uncertainty about it, whether it is of the devil or of God, and have *somewhat hastily* concluded that it is the chief end of man here to "glorify God and enjoy him forever."

Still we live meanly, like ants; though the fable tells us that we were long ago changed into men; like pygmies we fight with cranes; it is error upon error, and clout upon clout, and our best virtue has for its occasion a superfluous and evitable wretchedness. Our life is frittered away by detail. An honest man has hardly need to count more than his ten fingers, or in extreme cases he may add his ten toes, and lump the rest. Simplicity, simplicity, simplicity! I say, let your affairs be as two or three, and not a hundred or a thousand; instead of a million count half a dozen, and keep your accounts on your thumb nail. In the midst of this chopping sea of civilized life, such are the clouds and storms and quicksands and thousand-and-one items to be allowed for, that a man has to live, if he would not founder and go to the bottom and not make his port at all, by dead reckoning, and he must be a great calculator indeed who succeeds. Simplify, simplify. . . .

# CHARLES DICKENS

## from *Hard Times*

### Chapter 5: The Key-note

Charles Dickens's (1812–1870) prolific and frenetic career made him the most popular and most successful author of the Victorian Age, perhaps second only to Shakespeare in popularity in the whole of English letters. Discovering his literary gift, Dickens rose from poverty (his father and family were in debtors' prison at one time); he became, first, a court transcriber, next a reporter in Parliament, and then a recorder of the human comedy with his *Sketches by Boz,* serialized in popular magazines. His reputation grew with the *Pickwick Papers,* followed by a stream of novels and a lecture tour of America, where he was lionized as the greatest author of the age. In the 1850s, he founded his own magazine and embraced many social causes that became themes in his writings. By the mid-1860s, having written fourteen novels, operated a magazine, and acted in amateur plays, his strenuous life began to undermine his health. When he died in 1870, he received national honors and was buried in Westminster Abbey.

Dickens combined a keen eye and ear for detail and dialect with his personal experiences to produce novels that rank as some of the masterpieces of nineteenth-century Realism. He was England's leading exponent of Realism, which had risen, in part, as a reaction against both Classicism and Romanticism. Rejecting the elegant writing ideal of Classicism and the sentimentality of Romanticism, the Realists believed that literature should serve a purpose and not be judged alone on its aesthetic merits. They were concerned with the world around them, not only with daily events but also with political and social issues. Life should be portrayed as it was, neither idealized nor romanticized—a bold and honest treatment of the human condition with specific details came to define Realism.

### Reading the Selection

Dickens published *Hard Times* between 1851 and 1854, at the height of his social and political crusades, which he waged in his magazine and novels; in *Bleak House,* he attacked the corrupt legal system, and in *Little Dorrit,* he criticized the government's conduct of the Crimean War. In *Hard Times* he addressed three current topics: class struggle, education, and Utilitarianism (the doctrine set forth in the social theory of Jeremy Bentham that the goal of society is "the greatest good for the greatest number").

Through the characters representing management (Gradgrind) and labor (Sissy's father) in Coketown (probably based on the factory town of Preston), Dickens publicized the class struggle that was being called in the 1840s the "Condition of England question." In Chapter 5, "The Key-note," the central idea is caught in the vivid picture of Coketown, its ugly buildings, polluted river, and ill-dressed inhabitants; the middle class's contempt for workers is seen in Gradgrind and Bounderby's hasty opinions. Gradgrind and Bounderby's prejudices flare up in the exchange with the working class youths, Bitzer and Sissy, who are judged disrespectful; Sissy's father, the object of their excursion into this run-down section of Coketown, is assumed to be a lazy drunk.

Prior to Chapter 5, Dickens satirized the Utilitarian approach to schooling with its unrelenting emphasis on "facts, facts, facts." In this selection, the reference to M'Choakumchild's school further registers his contempt for the period's style of education, with its emphasis on corporal punishment as a necessary aid to learning.

Coketown, to which Messrs Bounderby and Gradgrind now walked, was a triumph of fact; it had no greater taint of fancy in it than Mrs Gradgrind herself. Let us strike the key-note, Coketown, before pursuing our tune.

It was a town of red brick, or of brick that would have been red if the smoke and ashes had allowed it; but, as matters stood it was a town of unnatural red and black like the painted face of a savage. It was a town of machinery and tall chimneys, out of which interminable serpents of smoke trailed themselves for ever and ever, and never got uncoiled. It had a black canal in it, and a river that ran purple with ill-smelling dye, and vast piles of building full of windows where there was a rattling and a trembling all day long, and where the piston of the steam-engine worked monotonously up and own, like the head of an elephant in a state of melancholy madness. It contained several large streets all very like one another, and many small streets still more like one another, inhabited by people equally like one another, who all went in and out at the same hours, with the same sound upon the same pavements, to do the same work, and to whom every day was the same as yesterday and tomorrow, and every year the counterpart of the last and the next.

These attributes of Coketown were in the main inseparable from the work by which it was sustained; against them were to be set off, comforts of life which found their way all over the world, and elegancies of life which made, we will not ask how much of the fine lady, who could scarcely bear to hear the place mentioned. The rest of its features were voluntary, and they were these.

You saw nothing in Coketown but what was severely workful. If the members of a religious persuasion built a chapel there—as the members of eighteen religious persuasions had done—they made it a pious warehouse of red brick, with sometimes (but this only in highly ornamented examples) a bell in a bird-cage on the top of it. The solitary exception was the New Church; a stuccoed edifice with a square steeple over the door, terminating in four short pinnacles like florid wooden legs. All the public inscriptions in the town were painted alike, in severe characters of black and white. The jail might have been the infirmary, the infirmary might have been the jail, the town-hall might have been either, or both, or anything else, for anything that appeared to the contrary in the graces of their construction. Fact, fact, fact, everywhere in the material aspect of the town; fact, fact, fact, everywhere in the immaterial. The M'Choakumchild school was all fact, and the school of design was all fact, and the relations between master and man were all fact, and everything was fact between the lying-in hospital and the cemetery, and what you coudn't state in figures, or show to be purchaseable in the cheapest market and saleable in the dearest, was not, and never should be, world without end, Amen.

A town so sacred to fact, and so triumphant in its assertion, of course got on well? Why no, not quite well. No? Dear me!

No. Coketown did not come out of its own furnaces, in all respects like gold that had stood the fire. First, the perplexing mystery of the place was, Who belonged to the eighteen denominations? Because, whoever did, the labouring people did not. It was very strange to walk through the streets on a Sunday morning, and note how few of *them* the barbarous jangling of bells that was driving the sick and nervous mad, called away from their own quarter, from their own close rooms, from the corners of their own streets, where they lounged listlessly, gazing at all the church and chapel going, as at a thing with which they had no manner of concern. Nor was it merely the stranger who noticed this, because there was a native organization in Coketown itself, whose members were to be heard of in the House of Commons every session, indignantly petitioning for acts of parliament that should make these people religious by main force. Then, came the Teetotal Society, who complained that these same people *would* get drunk, and showed in tabular statements that they did get drunk, and proved at tea parties that no inducement, human or Divine (except a medal), would induce them to forego their custom of getting drunk. Then, came the chemist and druggist, with other tabular statements, showing that when they didn't get drunk, they took opium. Then, came the experienced chaplain of the jail, with more tabular statements, outdoing all the previous tabular statements, and showing that the same people *would* resort to low haunts, hidden from the public eye, where they heard low singing and saw low dancing, and mayhap joined in it; and where A. B., aged twenty-four next birthday, and committed for eighteen months' solitary, had himself said (not that he had ever shown himself particularly worthy of belief) his ruin began, as he was perfectly sure and confident that otherwise he would have been a tip-top moral specimen. Then, came Mr Gradgrind and Mr Bounderby, the two gentlemen at this present moment walking through Coketown, and both eminently practical, who could, on occasion, furnish more tabular statements derived from their own personal experience, and illustrated by cases they had known and seen, from which it clearly appeared—in short it was the only clear thing in the case—that these same people were a bad lot altogether, gentlemen; that do what you would for them they were never thankful for it, gentlemen; that they were restless, gentlemen; that they never knew what they wanted; that they lived upon the best, and bought fresh butter, and insisted on Mocha coffee, and rejected all but prime parts of meat, and yet were eternally dissatisfied and unmanageable. In short it was the moral of the old nursery fable:

*There was an old woman, and what do you think?*
*She lived upon nothing but victuals and drink;*
*Victuals and drink were the whole of her diet,*
*And yet this old woman would NEVER be quiet.*

Is it possible, I wonder, that there was any analogy between the case of the Coketown population and the case of the little Gradgrinds? Surely, none of us in our sober senses and acquainted with figures, are to be told at this time of day, that one of the foremost elements in the existence of the Coketown working people had been for scores of years, deliberately set at nought? That there was any Fancy in them demanding to be brought into healthy existence instead of struggling on in convulsions? That exactly in the ratio as they worked long and monotonously, the craving grew within them for some physical relief—some relaxation, encouraging good humour and good spirits, and giving them a vent—some recognized holiday, though it were but for an honest dance to a stirring band of music—some occasional light pie in which even M'Choakumchild had no finger—which craving must and would be satisfied aright, or must and would inevitably go wrong, until the laws of the Creation were repealed?

'This man lives at Pod's End, and I don't quite know Pod's End,' said Mr Gradgrind. 'Which is it, Bounderby?'

Mr Bounderby knew it was somewhere down town, but knew no more respecting it. So they stopped for a moment, looking about.

Almost as they did so, there came running round the corner of the street at a quick pace and with a frightened look, a girl whom Mr Gradgrind recognized. 'Halloa!' said he. 'Stop! Where are you going? Stop!' Girl number twenty stopped then, palpitating, and made him a curtsey.

'Why are you tearing about the streets,' said Mr Gradgrind, 'in this improper manner?'

'I was—I was run after, sir,' the girl panted, 'and I wanted to get away.'

'Run after?' repeated Mr Gradgrind. 'Who would run after *you*?'

The question was unexpectedly and suddenly answered for her, by the colourless boy, Bitzer, who came round the corner with such blind speed and so little anticipating a stoppage on the pavement, that he brought himself up against Mr Gradgrind's waistcoat, and rebounded into the road.

'What do you mean, boy?' said Mr Gradgrind. 'What are you doing? How dare you dash against—everybody—in this manner?'

Bitzer picked up his cap, which the concussion had knocked off; and backing, and knuckling his forehead, pleaded that it was an accident.

'Was this boy running after you, Jupe?' asked Mr Gradgrind.

'Yes, sir,' said the girl reluctantly.

'No, I wasn't, sir!' cried Bitzer. 'Not till she run away from me. But the horse-riders never mind what they say, sir; they're famous for it. You know the horse-riders are famous for never minding what they say,' addressing Sissy. 'It's as well known in the town as—please, sir, as the multiplication table isn't known to the horse-riders.' Bitzer tried Mr Bounderby with this.

'He frightened me so,' said the girl, 'with his cruel faces!'

'Oh!' cried Bitzer. 'Oh! An't you one of the rest! An't you a horse-rider! I never looked at her, sir. I asked her if she would know how to define a horse tomorrow, and offered to tell her again, and she ran away, and I ran after her, sir, that she might know how to answer when she was asked. You wouldn't have thought of saying such mischief if you hadn't been a horse-rider!'

'Her calling seems to be pretty well known among 'em,' observed Mr Bounderby. 'You'd have had the whole school peeping in a row, in a week.'

'Truly, I think so,' returned his friend. 'Bitzer, turn you about and take yourself home. Jupe, stay here a moment. Let me hear of your running in this manner any more, boy, and you will hear of me through the master of the school. You understand what I mean. Go along.'

The boy stopped in his rapid blinking, knuckled his forehead again, glanced at Sissy, turned about, and retreated.

'Now, girl,' said Mr Gradgrind, 'take this gentleman and me to your father's; we are going there. What have you got in that bottle you are carrying?'

'Gin,' said Mr Bounderby.

'Dear, no sir! It's the nine oils.'

'The what?' cried Mr Bounderby.

'The nine oils, sir. To rub father with.' Then, said Mr Bounderby, with a loud, short laugh, 'what the devil do you rub your father with nine oils for?'

'It's what our people always use, sir, when they get any hurts in the ring,' replied the girl, looking over her shoulder, to assure herself that her pursuer was gone. 'They bruise themselves very bad sometimes.'

'Serve 'em right,' said Mr Bounderby, 'for being idle.' She glanced up at his face, with mingled astonishment and dread.

'By George!' said Mr Bounderby, 'when I was four or five years younger than you, I had worse bruises upon me than ten oils, twenty oils, forty oils, would have rubbed off. I didn't get 'em by posture-making, but by being banged about. There was no rope-dancing for me; I danced on the bare ground and was larruped with the rope.'

Mr Gradgrind, though hard enough, was by no means so rough a man as Mr Bounderby. His character was not unkind, all things considered; it might have been a very kind one indeed, if he had only made some round mistake in the arithmetic that balanced it, years ago. He said, in what he meant for a reassuring tone, as they turned down a narrow road, 'And this is Pod's End; is it, Jupe?'

'This is it, sir, and—if you wouldn't mind, sir—this is the house.'

She stopped, at twilight, at the door of a mean little public house, with dim red lights in it. As haggard and as shabby, as if, for want of custom, it had itself taken to drinking, and had gone the way all drunkards go, and was very near the end of it.

'It's only crossing the bar, sir, and up the stairs, if you wouldn't mind, and waiting there for a moment till I get a candle. If you should hear a dog, sir, it's only Merrylegs, and he only barks.'

'Merrylegs and nine oils, eh!' said Mr Bounderby, entering last with his metallic laugh. 'Pretty well this, for a self-made man!'

# GUSTAVE FLAUBERT
# from *Madame Bovary*
## Chapter 8

———

Flaubert's *Madame Bovary* (1857) is considered the greatest novel in the French language. Its heroine, Emma Bovary, is the first of a line of unhappy middle-class wives, such as the Russian writer Tolstoy's Anna Karenina, who appear in modern fiction. Flaubert's story of Emma's revolt against marriage led officials to prosecute him (unsuccessfully) for "immorality." Such a charge is ludicrous today, partly because morals are more relaxed, and partly because studies of sexuality (see Freud's *Civilization*, Beauvoir's *The Second Sex*) have made Emma's adultery more understandable. Hence Flaubert's novel is a pioneering work in the literature of female consciousness.

Although published in 1857, when France was undergoing rapid change fueled by the rise of the railroad, the telegraph, and the newspaper, *Madame Bovary* was set in a slightly earlier, more stable period, before new technologies destroyed old ways of life. The novel's general subject is provincial culture (the subtitle was *Moeurs de province*, "provincial life"), which Flaubert despised with a vehemence akin to Marx. Unlike Marx, he remained a loyal member of the middle class, but he used this novel to portray the narrowness, mediocrity, and hypocrisy of small-town culture. This culture he expressed in the imaginary towns of Tostes and Yonville, in cultural artifacts (a keepsake album, a medical journal, and a shop ledger), speech patterns (everyone speaks in clichés), and social events (a local ball and an opera performance).

The novel's specific subject is Emma Bovary, whose personal tragedy is inevitable, given Flaubert's dark vision of provincial life. Convent educated, innately sensual, and addicted to Romantic novels, Emma is also a stupid, vulgar, and cruel woman. She marries Charles Bovary, a physician, who is goodhearted but insensitive, and within weeks she says: "Oh, why, dear God, did I marry him?" Bored with her husband, she allows herself to be seduced by Rodolphe Boulanger, a wealthy landowner and sexual libertine. She plunges into a downward spiral of pleasure-seeking, all of which ends in further disappointment. Beset by debt and despair, she takes arsenic and dies. Charles, now penniless, dies soon after.

Gustave Flaubert (1821–1880) practically invented the Realistic-style novel with this work. Its setting and characters were true to his world near Rouen, where he, the son of a doctor, lived on a private income (he left Rouen for three years to study law in Paris and for eighteen months to tour the Near East). Its meticulously prosaic language reflected the banal speech that he heard in Rouen (he kept a *Dictionary of Received Ideas* to collect choice examples of overheard clichés). Emma Bovary, he claimed, was patterned after himself: "Madame Bovary, c'est moi!" (I am Madame Bovary!)

### Reading the Selection

This selection, from Chapter 8 of *Madame Bovary*, takes place on the day of Yonville's agricultural show. Flaubert's account is cinematic, shifting back and forth between fragments of Rodolphe's seduction of Emma, which takes place upstairs in the Town Hall, and fragments of the town official Lieuvain's speech, which occurs out-of-doors. Emma sits mesmerized by Rodolphe's smooth whisperings ("You know that I am yours!"), just as Yonville's citizens listen transfixed by Lieuvain's oratory ("Keep steadily ahead!"). Hence, in Flaubert's vision, there is no escape from this provincial world, either through love or material progress: both are illusions.

• • •

'Madame Bovary!' exclaimed Homais. 'I must run and pay her my respects. She might like to have a seat in the enclosure, under the peristyle.'

And turning a deaf ear to the rest of the Widow Lefrançois' story, the chemist hurried off, with a smile on his lips, a jaunty stride, and any number of bowings in all directions, taking up a great deal of space with the long tails of his dress-coat flapping in the breeze behind him.

Rodolphe had noticed him from a distance and quickened his pace, but as Madame Bovary got out of breath, he slowed up again, smiling at her as he explained brusquely:

'That was to escape from the heavy fellow—you know, the chemist.'

She gave him a nudge.

'What's the meaning of that?' he asked himself, and as he walked along he surveyed her out of the corner of his eye.

Her calm profile gave no hint. It showed clear in the light, framed in the oval of her bonnet, which was tied with pale reed-like ribbons. She was looking straight in front of her, beneath her long curving lashes, and though her eyes were fully open they appeared slightly narrowed because of the blood that pulsated gently beneath the fine skin that covered her cheek-bones. Where her nostrils met was a pale pink glow. Her head leaned a little to one side, and between her parted lips you saw the pearly tips of her white teeth.

'Is she laughing at me?' Rodolphe wondered.

Emma's nudge had been simply a warning, however. Monsieur Lheureux was walking along beside them. Every now and then he made some conversational remark, such as 'What a glorious day!' 'Everybody's out of doors!' 'The wind's in the east!'

Madame Bovary took as little notice of his advances as did Rodolphe, though the draper came sidling up to them at their least movement, touching his hat and saying, 'Beg pardon?'

Outside the blacksmith's, instead of keeping on up to the gate along the roadway, Rodolphe turned abruptly down a side-path, drawing Madame Bovary with him.

'Farewell, Monsieur Lheureux!' he called out. 'Till we meet again!'

'How you got rid of him!' she said with a laugh.

'Why let people hang on to one?' he answered. 'And today, when I'm fortunate enough to be with you . . .'

Emma blushed. He left the sentence unfinished, and started talking about the lovely weather, and the delight of walking on the grass.

Some daisies were growing there.

'What pretty daisies!' he said. 'Oracles in plenty for all the local girls in love! . . . Suppose I pick one,' he added. 'What do you say?'

'Are *you* in love?' she asked, with a little cough.

'Eh! eh! who knows?' answered Rodolphe.

The show-ground was beginning to fill up, and the women helpers kept bumping into you with their big umbrellas, their baskets and their babies. You had frequently to be getting out of the way of a long row of peasant-girls,

maidservants in blue stockings and flat shoes, with silver rings on their fingers, who smelt of milk when you came close to them. They spread out hand in hand all across the field, from the row of aspens up to the marquee. By now the judging was due to start, and one after another the farmers were filing into a kind of arena marked off by a long rope hung on stakes.

Inside were the animals, their muzzles towards the rope, their rumps jostling together in a rough line. Somnolent pigs sank their snouts in the ground, calves lowed, sheep bleated, cows sprawled their bellies out on the grass, with one leg bent beneath them, and chewed with deliberation, blinking their heavy eyelids as the midges buzzed round them. Shirt-sleeved wagoners were holding the restive stallions, which kept neighing vociferously in the direction of the mares. These stood quite quiet, stretching out their necks, their manes drooping, while their foals rested in their shadows, or came up from time to time to suck. Above the undulating line of massed beasts, you saw a white mane ruffling up like a wave in the breeze, a pair of sharp horns jutting out, or the heads of some men running. Outside the arena, a hundred yards farther on, a big black bull stood apart, muzzled, with an iron ring through its nostrils, moving no more than an animal of bronze. A ragged child held it by a rope.

Sundry gentlemen were now advancing with heavy tread between the two rows of animals, examining each in turn and then conferring together in low tones. One, who looked more important than the rest, made jottings in a notebook as he went. This was the chairman of the judges, Monsieur Derozerays de la Panville. The minute he recognized Rodolphe he stepped briskly towards him.

'What's this, Monsieur Boulanger?' he said, with a pleasant smile. 'Are you deserting us?'

Rodolphe assured him he was coming directly. But when the chairman was once more out of earshot he said, 'I think not! When I can be with you!'

While ridiculing the Show, Rodolphe nevertheless produced his blue ticket, so that they could move about wherever they pleased, and he even halted occasionally in front of one of the fine 'exhibits'. Noticing, however, that Madame Bovary was unimpressed by these, he started making fun of the Yonville ladies and the way they were turned out. He apologized for being so carelessly dressed himself. His clothes were an incongruous mixture of the workaday and the elegant, such as is taken by the vulgar to denote an eccentric way of life, an emotional disturbance, or a subservience to aesthetics, combined always with a certain contempt for convention, by which they are either fascinated or exasperated. Frilly at the cuffs, his cambric shirt fluttered out in front between the revers of his grey drill waistcoat wherever the breeze took it. His broad-striped trousers terminated at the ankle above a pair of nankeen boots vamped with patent leather. These were so highly polished that you could see the grass in them; and in them he went trampling over the horse-dung, with one hand in his jacket pocket, his straw hat tilted to the side of his head.

'But then, when you live in the country . . .' he added.

'. . . There's no point in bothering,' said Emma.

'Exactly!' Rodolphe replied. 'Just fancy, there's not one of all these good people who's capable of understanding so much as the cut of a coat.'

They spoke of the dullness of the country, the lives that were smothered by it, the illusions that perished there.

'That's why,' said Rodolphe, 'I'm sinking into such a state of gloom. . . .'

'You!' she exclaimed in surprise. 'Why, I thought you were a very cheerful person.'

'Oh, on the surface, yes. I wear my jester's mask in public. But how often I've looked at a graveyard in the moonlight and wondered whether I wouldn't be better off lying there asleep with the rest of them!'

'Oh! But what about your friends?' she said. 'Don't you think of them?'

'My friends? What friends? Have I got any? Is there anyone who cares about me?'—and he accompanied these last words with a little hissing sound.

However, they had to step aside for a man coming up behind them with an immense scaffolding of chairs. He was so loaded that you could see nothing of him but the toes of his sabots and the tips of his outstretched arms. It was Lestiboudois the sexton, carting round the church chairs among the crowd. Full of ideas where his own interests were concerned, he had hit upon this method of turning the Show to account; and his enterprise was rewarded, for he had more customers than he could cope with. The villagers, feeling the warmth, had actually started squabbling over those straw seats that reeked of incense; and against their stout backs, covered with blobs of candle-grease, they were leaning with a certain awe.

Madame Bovary took Rodolphe's arm again.

'Yes,' he went on as though to himself, 'I've missed a lot, always being alone. If only I'd had some aim in life. If I'd met with affection. If I'd found someone . . . Oh, I'd have used all the energy I possessed—conquered everything, smashed down every obstacle.'

'It doesn't seem to me you've got much to grumble about,' said Emma.

'You think not?'

'After all, you're free'—she hesitated—'and rich.'

'You're laughing at me!' he exclaimed.

She assured him she was not. As she spoke, they heard the boom of a cannon. Everybody at once started rushing back to the village.

It was a false alarm; there was no sign of the Prefect. The judges were in a quandary: should they wait, or open the proceedings?

At last, from the far end of the square, appeared a large hired landau drawn by a pair of skinny horses, which were being roundly lashed by a coachman in a white hat. Binet just had time to shout 'Fall in!' and the Colonel to follow suit. There was a dive for the piled rifles. In the commotion, some of the men forgot to fasten their collars. The official equipage seemed to divine their discomfiture, however, for the pair of hacks slowed up, tugging at their chain, and ambled to a halt outside the Town Hall, just as the militia and the fire-brigade were deploying to the beat of the drums.

'Mark time!' shouted Binet.

'Halt!' shouted the Colonel. 'Into line—left—turn!'

After a 'Present arms', in which the smacking of the bands came rattling out like a copper kettle rolling downstairs, all the rifles were lowered again.

Thereupon a gentleman in a short silver-trimmed jacket was seen to step out of the carriage. He was bald in front and tufted behind, sallow-complexioned, and with an appearance of the utmost benignity. He narrowed his large heavy-lidded eyes to scan the crowd, lifted his pointed nose in the air and set a smile on his sunken mouth. Recognizing the mayor by his sash, he explained that the Prefect had been prevented from coming. He himself was an official on the Prefect's staff. He added a few words of apology. Tuvache responded in complimentary terms. The visitor declared himself overwhelmed. So they stood there face to face, their foreheads almost touching, surrounded by the judges, the councillors, the important personages, the militia, and the crowd at large. Holding his little black three-cornered hat against his chest, the great man reiterated his greetings, while Tuvache, bent like a bow, smiled back at him, stuttering and stammering and making protestation of his loyalty to the throne and his appreciation of the honour that was being done to Yonville.

Hippolyte, the groom from the inn, came limping up on his club-foot to take the reins from the coachman, and led the horses off beneath the archway of the Golden Lion, where a crowd of peasants gathered round to inspect the carriage. There was a tattoo on the drums, the howitzer thundered, and the gentlemen filed up and took their places on the platform, in the easy-chairs of red Utrecht velvet lent by Madame Tuvache.

A homogeneous group they were, with their soft, fair, slightly tanned faces, the colour of new cider, and their bushy whiskers sticking out above tall stiff collars supported by white cravats tied in a floppy bow. Every one of the waistcoats had velvet revers, every watch carried an oval cornelian seal at the end of a long band. Hands all rested on thighs, carefully lifting the creases of their trousers, which were of unsponged cloth and shone more brilliantly than their stout leather boots.

The ladies of the party kept at the back, between the pillars in the vestibule, while the body of the crowd faced them, standing up, or seated on Lestiboudois' chairs. For he had brought a load along with him from the meadow, and was all the while running off to get more from the church, causing such congestion with his trade that one had great difficulty in reaching the platform steps.

'I think myself,' said Monsieur Lheureux to the chemist, as the latter passed along to take his seat, 'that they ought to have put up a couple of Venetian masts, with something rich and a bit severe in the way of draping. It would have made a fine sight.'

'Certainly it would,' answered Homais. 'But there, what can you expect? The mayor *would* do the whole thing on his own. Poor old Tuvache, he hasn't got much taste; in fact, he's completely lacking in any sort of artistic sense.'

Meanwhile Rodolphe and Madame Bovary had gone up to the Council Chamber on the first floor of the Town Hall. It was empty, and so he declared that they would be able to enjoy the spectacle in comfort up there. Fetching three stools from the oval table under the bust of the King, he placed them by one of the windows, and they sat down side by side.

There was a great commotion on the platform, much whispering and parleying, and at last the Prefect's deputy rose. His name, now known to be Lieuvain, was being passed round among the crowd. After collecting his papers together and holding them close up to his eyes to see them better, he began:

'Gentlemen,

'Let me first be permitted, before addressing you on the object of our gathering here today—and this sentiment will, I am sure, be shared by all of you—let me be permitted, I say, to pay a fitting tribute to the Authorities, to the Government and, gentlemen, to our beloved Monarch and Sovereign Lord the King, to whom no branch of public or private prosperity is indifferent, and who steers the chariot of state with a hand at once so firm and so wise, amid the ceaseless perils of a stormy sea—who knows, moreover, how to gain respect for peace no less than for war—for Trade and for Industry, for Agriculture and for the Arts.'

'I ought to get a bit farther back,' said Rodolphe.

'Why?' said Emma.

But at that moment the official's voice rose to a remarkable pitch as he declaimed:

'Those days are past, gentlemen, when civil discord stained our public places with blood, when landowner, merchant, and working-man alike, as they courted peaceful slumbers, would tremble lest they be awakened by the clang of the tocsin; when the most subversive slogans were aimed in all audacity at the very foundations—'

'They might see me from down there,' Rodolphe explained, 'and then I'd have to spend a fortnight apologizing. And with my bad reputation . . .'

'What a thing to say about yourself!'

'No, no, it's abominable, I assure you.'

'However, gentlemen,' the speaker proceeded, 'if, driving those sombre pictures from my mind, I turn my gaze now to the present state of our fair land, what do I see? Everywhere, trade and the arts flourish. Everywhere new paths of communication, new arteries within the body politic, are opening up new contacts. Our great manufacturing centres thrive once more. Religion finds new strength and smiles in every heart. Our ports are full. Confidence returns. At last France breathes again!'

'Though I dare say I deserve it by ordinary standards,' Rodolphe added.

'How is that?' she asked.

'Why, do you not know that there are souls for ever in turmoil? Souls that must have dream and action turn and turn about—a passion of utter purity, and an orgy of self-indulgence? It leads one into all kinds of adventures and escapades.'

She gazed at him then as one might gaze at a traveller who has journeyed through strange lands.

'We poor women haven't even that diversion,' she remarked.

'Sorry diversion, for it never brings happiness.'

'Does anything?'

'Yes,' he answered, 'it comes along one day.'

'And this,' the distinguished visitor was saying, 'this you have realized, you who cultivate the land and labour in the fields, peaceable pioneers in a true task of civilization! Progressive and high-minded men! You have realized, I say, that the storms of political strife are, in very truth, more devastating than the riot of the elements!'

'It comes along one day,' Rodolphe repeated, 'all of a sudden, just when you are despairing of it. Then, new vistas open. It's as if a voice cried out "Behold!" You feel you must reveal yourself, give everything, sacrifice everything, to that person. Nothing need be said. You know! You have seen each other in your dreams'—and his eyes rested on hers. 'There before you, shining, sparkling, is the treasure you have sought so long. Still you doubt. You dare not believe. You stand dazed as if you had stepped out of darkness into light.'

Here Rodolphe helped out his words with motions, passing his hand over his face like a man in a trance. Then he let it fall on Emma's. She withdrew hers. The official read on:

'And who can wonder at it, gentlemen? Only he who remains so blind, so immersed, so deeply immersed, I do not fear to say, in the prejudices of a past age, as still to misconceive the spirit of our agricultural communities. Where, indeed, can one find more patriotism than in the country, more devotion to the common weal, in a word, more intelligence? I do not mean, gentlemen, a superficial intelligence—that vain embellishment of idle minds—but a profound and balanced intelligence that applies itself first and foremost to the pursuit of useful ends, contributing thus to the good of each, to the general advancement, and to the upholding of the State—the fruit of respect for law and fulfillment of duty!'

'Duty again!' said Rodolphe. 'Always on about duty. I'm sick to death of the word. What a lot of flannel-waistcoated old fogeys they are, pious old women with beads and bedsocks, for ever twittering in our ears about "Duty, duty!" To feel nobly and to love what is beautiful—that's our duty. Not to accept all the conventions of society and the humiliations society imposes on us.'

'Still . . . all the same . . .' Madame Bovary demurred.

'No! Why inveigh against the passions? Are they not the one beautiful thing there is on earth; the source of all heroism and enthusiasm, poetry, music, art, everything?'

'All the same,' said Emma, 'we must take some notice of what the world thinks, and conform to its morality.'

'But you see, there are two moralities,' he replied. 'One is the petty, conventional morality of men, clamorous, ever-changing, that flounders about on the ground, of the earth earthy, like that mob of nincompoops down there. The other, the eternal morality, is all about and above us, like the countryside that surrounds us and the blue heavens that give us light.'

Monsieur Lieuvain had just wiped his mouth with his handkerchief. He resumed:

'Now what should I be doing here, gentlemen, demonstrating the usefulness of farming to *you*? Who supplies our wants, who provides us with the means of life, but the farmer? The farmer, gentlemen, who, sowing with laborious hand the fertile furrows of our countryside, brings forth the corn which, crushed and ground by ingenious machinery, issues thence in the guise of flour, to be conveyed to our cities and speedily delivered to the baker, who makes it into a food for rich and poor alike. Is it not the farmer, again, who fattens his rich flocks to give us clothes? How should we clothe, or feed, ourselves were it not for the farmer? Nay, gentlemen, need we go even so far afield for our examples? Who has not frequently pondered on the great importance to us of that homely animal, the adornment of our poultry-yards, that provides us with soft pillows to sleep on, succulent flesh for our tables, and eggs?—But I could go on for ever enumerating, one by one, the various products that the well-tended earth lavishes like a bountiful mother upon her children. Here the vine, there the cider apple, elsewhere colza, cheese, or flax—gentlemen, let us not forget flax!—which has made such strides in recent years, and to which I would more especially draw your attention.'

He had no need to draw it, for the multitude sat open-mouthed to drink in his words. Tuvache, next to him, listened with staring eyes. Monsieur Derozerays gently closed his now and then. Farther along, the chemist, with his son Napoléon between his knees, had his hand cupped behind his ear so as not to lose a single syllable. The rest of the judges nodded their chins slowly up and down in their waistcoats to signify assent. The fire-brigade leaned on their bayonet-scabbards at the foot of the platform, and Binet stood motionless, his elbow stuck out, the point of his sabre in the air. He may have heard, but he could not have seen anything for the visor of his helmet, which came right down over his nose. His lieutenant, Monsieur Tuvache's youngest son, had his visor at a still more exaggerated angle. He was wearing an enormous helmet that wobbled on top of his head and allowed one end of his calico handkerchief to slip down behind. He smiled beneath it with a perfectly child-like sweetness, and his little white face, running with sweat, wore an expression of enjoyment, exhaustion and somnolence.

The crowd stretched right across to the houses on the far side of the square. There were people leaning out of every window, standing in every doorway. Justin, outside the chemist's shop, seemed quite transfixed by the sight that met his eyes. In spite of the silence, Monsieur Lieuvain's voice failed to carry in the air, and reached you only in fragmentary phrases, drowned here and there by the scraping of chairs among the crowd. Then all of a sudden you heard the long lowing of a bullock behind you, or lambs bleating to each other at the corners of the streets. They had been driven down by the shepherds and cowherds, and gave voice from time to time as their tongues snatched at a morsel of foliage hanging above their muzzles.

Rodolphe had drawn closer to Emma and was talking rapidly in a low voice.

'Doesn't this conspiracy of society revolt you? Is there a single feeling it does not condemn? The noblest instincts, the purest sympathies, are reviled and persecuted, and if ever two poor souls do meet, then everything is organized to prevent their union. They'll attempt it all the same, they'll flap their wings and call to one another. And no matter what happens, sooner or later, in six months or ten years, they'll meet again and love—because Fate ordains it, because they were born for one another.'

He sat with his arms folded on his knees. Raising his eyes to Emma's, he gazed at her closely, fixedly. She saw little gleams of gold playing about his dark pupils. She was near

enough to him to smell the cream on his glossy hair. She felt limp, she remembered the Viscount who had waltzed with her at La Vaubyessard: his beard had exhaled that same perfume of lemon and vanilla. Mechanically her eyelids narrowed as she breathed in the scent. She straightened up in her chair, and as she did so she caught a glimpse, right away on the farthest horizon, of the ancient *Hirondelle* slowly descending Leux Hill, trailing a long plume of dust behind it. It was in that yellow coach that Léon had so often come back to her; and along that road that he had gone from her for ever. She had a vision of him at his window across the way. Then everything blurred, the sky clouded over, and it seemed to her that she was still circling in the waltz, in the glare of the chandeliers, on the Viscount's arm, and Léon was not far away, he was just coming. . . . But all the while she was conscious of Rodolphe's face beside her. Her old desires became imbued with the sweetness of the present sensation, and, on this subtle breath of perfume that was being shed upon her soul, they were tossed about like grains of sand in a gust of wind. Her nostrils dilated rapidly, vigorously, breathing in the freshness of the ivy round the tops of the columns. She took off her gloves, wiped her hands, fanned her face with her handkerchief, while through the throbbing at her temples she could hear the hum of the crowd below and the speaker still droning out his singsong.

'Keep steadily ahead!' he was saying. 'Listen neither to the voice of hidebound habit nor to the impulsive counsels of rash experiment! Work above all at the improvement of the soil, at producing rich fertilizers, at breeding fine horses and cattle, fine sheep and pigs! Let this Agricultural Show be a peaceful arena where victor extends the hand of brotherhood to vanquished and wishes him success next time! . . . And now, to all those venerable retainers, lowly servants whose laborious toils have never before been recognized by any Government, I say: Come forward and receive the meed of your silent virtues! Rest assured that from this day forth the State will never lose sight of you, that it will encourage and protect you, will satisfy your just demands, and lighten, so far as in it lies, the painful burden of your sacrifice!'

And Monsieur Lieuvain sat down.

Monsieur Derozerays rose and began his speech. This was far less ornate than the official's, and recommended itself by a more positive flavour—a matter of more specialized knowledge and more exalted reflections. Eulogistic reference to the Government had less place in it, farming and religion had more. The bond that existed between the two was made clear—they had always worked together for civilization . . . While Rodolphe was talking to Madame Bovary about dreams, presentiments and magnetic attraction, the speaker went back to the infancy of society, to those savage times when men lived on acorns in the heart of great forests; from which he passed on to the period at which they had given up animals' skins for a covering of cloth, had ploughed the land and planted the vine. Now was this an improvement? Were there not perhaps more disadvantages than advantages in these discoveries? Monsieur Derozerays asked himself the question. Rodolphe had led on gradually from magnetism to affinities; and while the Chairman alluded to Cincinnatus at his plough, to Diocletian among his cabbages, to the Chinese emperors ushering in the new year with the sowing of seed, the young man was explaining to the young woman that the cause of these irresistible attractions lay in some previous existence.

'We, now, why did we meet? What turn of fate decreed it? Was it not that, like two rivers gradually converging across the intervening distance, our own natures propelled us towards one another?'

He took her hand, and she did not withdraw it.

'General Prize!' cried the Chairman.

'Just now, for instance, when I came to call on you...'

'Monsieur Bizet of Quincampoix.'

'...how could I know that I should escort you here?'

'Seventy francs!'

'And I've stayed with you, because I couldn't tear myself away, though I've tried a hundred times.'

'Manure!'

'And so I'd stay tonight and tomorrow and every day for all the rest of my life.'

'To Monsieur Caron of Argueil, a Gold Medal!'

'For I have never been so utterly charmed with anyone before.'

'To Monsieur Bain of Givry St Martin.'

'And so I shall cherish the memory of you.'

'For a merino ram . . .'

'But you'll forget me. I shall have passed like a shadow . . .'

'To Monsieur Belot of Notre-Dame . . .'

'No, say I shan't! Tell me I shall count for something in your thoughts, in your life?'

'Pigs: Prize divided! Monsieur Lehérissé and Monsieur Cullembourg, sixty francs each!'

Rodolphe squeezed her hand. He felt it warm and vibrant in his, like a captive turtle-dove trying to take wing. Whether she was trying to withdraw it, or responding to his pressure, her fingers made a movement.

'Oh, thank you, you do not repulse me!' he said. 'How sweet you are! You know that I am yours! Only let me look at you, let me gaze upon you!'

A breeze from the window ruffled the cloth on the table, and down in the square the peasant women's big bonnets lifted up, fluttering like white butterflies' wings.

'Oil-cake,' the Chairman continued. He began to go faster; 'Flemish fertilizer—Flax—Drainage—Long Leases—Domestic Service.'

Rodolphe had stopped speaking. They looked at one another, and their dry lips quivered in a supreme desire. Gently, effortlessly, their fingers intertwined. . . .

---

# FYODOR DOSTOEVSKY
## from *Notes from Underground*
### Part One

---

The Russian novelist Fyodor Dostoevsky (1821–1881), a master of nineteenth-century Realism, is acclaimed today as both a giant of world literature and a prophet of this century's culture.

Much of Dostoevsky's fame stems from his uncanny insight into the motives of his tormented heroes—like Raskolnikov in *Crime and Punishment* (1864) and Ivan and Dmitri in *The Brothers Karamazov* (1879–1880); he lays bare their souls, thus prefiguring the findings of depth psychology. He is equally known for his political wisdom, for he predicted the ultimate failure of liberalism and socialism, the rival theories that claimed to hold the key to the West's future. In contrast to these godless theories, which saw humanity as good and rational, he thought instead that it was depraved, irrational, and rebellious—thus incapable of self-rule. He concluded that the whole point of life is to seek salvation through suffering and love, a belief based on his mystical Orthodox faith.

Dostoevsky did not always have such a gloomy outlook. When he began to write in 1844, after giving up a military career, he was a "Westernizer," as Russians were termed who thought that their country should model itself on France and England, then Europe's leading progressive states. As a Westernizer, he believed that socialism would help alleviate the suffering of Russia's masses; his novels, such as *Poor Folk* (1846), reflected this hope and were written in the sentimental Romantic style then popular in the West. Events in 1848–1849 changed his point of view forever. He was arrested by the police on a charge of subversion (he belonged to a young socialist cell). Jailed and taken out to be shot, he was reprieved at the last minute, as part of a carefully orchestrated plan, and was sentenced to prison in Siberia. In prison, he had his eyes opened to cruelty by the behavior of both jailers and inmates. When he returned from

Siberia in 1859, he was a Slavophile, as Russians were called who thought that their country should keep true to its Slavic roots; as a Slavophile, he claimed that Russians were God's chosen people, and his writings thereafter expressed his hatred of Europe and were written in a Realistic style, which dwelt on suffering, with no hope of redemption, except in heaven, if then.

### Reading the Selection

This selection, the first three episodes of Part I of *Notes from Underground* (1862) (there are only two parts), introduces the "Mousehole Man," the unnamed social "drop-out" who narrates the novel. In form, the novel is the Mousehole Man's monologue protesting his age's advanced ideas—liberalism, democracy, socialism, and science—each of which saw enlightened self-interest as the key to human happiness. His protest springs from his conviction that human whims and wishes are bound to clash with what is socially useful—an idea Freud later made popular (see *Civilization and Its Discontents*). The narrator calls himself an "anti-hero," the first mention of this concept so central to this century's literature (see Kafka's *The Metamorphosis*). Bitter, self-mocking, and ironic, he speaks with Dostoevsky's own "nasty" voice, a fact confirmed by those who knew the author. A mountain of hate, he cannot decide which to loathe more: the West's dream of a well-fed, happy society, symbolized by the Crystal Palace (the 1851 London exhibition, the first world's fair), or his fellow Russians' enthusiasm for French socialists like Charles Fourier (1772–1837), whose ideas Dostoevsky once shared and who now seemed foolish and shallow.

---

## Underground

### I

I am a sick man . . . I am a spiteful man. I am an unpleasant man. I think my liver is diseased. However, I don't know beans about my disease, and I am not sure what is bothering me. I don't treat it and never have, though I respect medicine and doctors. Besides, I am extremely superstitious, let's say sufficiently so to respect medicine. (I am educated enough not to be superstitious, but I am.) No, I refuse to treat it out of spite. You probably will not understand that. Well, but *I* understand it. Of course, I can't explain to you just whom I am annoying in this case by my spite. I am perfectly well aware that I cannot "get even" with the doctors by not consulting them. I know better than anyone that I thereby injure only myself and no one else. But still, if I don't treat it, it is out of spite. My liver is bad, well then—let it get even worse!

I have been living like that for a long time now—twenty years. I am forty now. I used to be in the civil service, but no longer am. I was a spiteful official. I was rude and took pleasure in being so. After all, I did not accept bribes, so I was bound to find a compensation in that, at least. (A bad joke but I will not cross it out. I wrote it thinking it would sound very witty; but now that I see myself that I only wanted to show off in a despicable way, I will purposely not cross it out!) When petitioners would come to my desk for information I would gnash my teeth at them, and feel intense enjoyment when I succeeded in distressing some one. I was almost always successful. For the most part they were all timid people—of course, they were petitioners. But among the fops there was one officer in particular I could not endure. He simply would not be humble, and clanked his sword in a disgusting way. I carried on a war with him for eighteen months over that sword. At last I got the better of him. He left off clanking it. However, that happened when I was still young. But do you know, gentlemen, what the real point of my spite was? Why, the whole trick, the real vileness of it lay in the fact that continually, even in moments of the worst spleen, I was inwardly conscious with shame that I was not only not spiteful but not even an embittered man, that I was simply frightening sparrows at random and amusing myself by it. I might foam at the mouth, but bring me some kind of toy, give me a cup of tea with sugar, and I would be appeased. My heart might even be touched, though probably I would gnash my teeth at myself afterward and lie awake at night with shame for months after. That is the way I am.

I was lying when I said just now that I was a spiteful official. I was lying out of spite. I was simply indulging myself with the petitioners and with the officer, but I could never really become spiteful. Every moment I was conscious in myself of many, very many elements completely opposite to that. I felt them positively teeming in me, these opposite elements. I knew that they had been teeming in me all my life, begging to be let out, but I would not let them, would not let them, purposely would not let them out. They tormented me till I was ashamed; they drove me to convulsions, and finally, they bored me, how they bored me! Well, are you not imagining, gentlemen, that I am repenting for something now, that I am asking your forgiveness for something? I am sure you are imagining that. However, I assure you it does not matter to me if you are.

Not only could I not become spiteful, I could not even become anything: neither spiteful nor kind, neither a rascal nor an honest man, neither a hero nor an insect. Now, I am living out my life in my corner, taunting myself with the spiteful and useless consolation that an intelligent man cannot seriously become anything and that only a fool can become something. Yes, an intelligent man in the nineteenth century must and morally ought to be pre-eminently a characterless creature; a man of character, an active man, is pre-eminently a limited creature. That is the conviction of my forty years. I am forty years old now, and forty years, after all, is a whole lifetime; after all, that is extreme old age. To live longer than forty years is bad manners; it is vulgar, immoral. Who does live beyond forty? Answer that, sincerely and honestly. I will tell you who do: fools and worthless people do. I tell all old men that to their face, all those respectable old men, all those silver-haired and reverend old men! I tell the whole world that to its face. I have a right to say so, for I'll go on living to sixty myself. I'll live till seventy! Till eighty! Wait, let me catch my breath.

No doubt you think, gentlemen, that I want to amuse you. You are mistaken in that, too. I am not at all such a merry person as you imagine, or as you may imagine; however, if irritated by all this babble (and I can feel that you are irritated) you decide to ask me just who I am—then my answer is, I am a certain low-ranked civil servant. I was in the service in order to have something to eat (but only for that reason), and when last year a distant relation left me six thousand roubles in his will I immediately retired from the service and settled down in my corner. I used to live in this corner before, but now I have settled down in it. My room is a wretched, horrid one on the outskirts of town. My servant is an old country-woman, spiteful out of stupidity, and, moreover, she always smells bad. I am told that the Petersburg climate is bad for me, and that with my paltry means it is very expensive to live in Petersburg. I know all that better than all these sage and experienced counsellors and monitors. But I am going to stay in Petersburg. I will not leave Petersburg! I will not leave because . . . Bah, after all it does not matter in the least whether I leave or stay.

But incidentally, what can a decent man speak about with the greatest pleasure?

Answer: About himself.

Well, then, I will talk about myself.

## II

Now I want to tell you, gentlemen, whether you care to hear it or not, why I could not even become an insect. I tell you solemnly that I wanted to become an insect many times. But I was not even worthy of that. I swear to you, gentlemen, that to be hyperconscious is a disease, a real positive disease. Ordinary human consciousness would be too much for man's everyday needs, that is, half or a quarter of the amount which falls to the lot of a cultivated man of our unfortunate nineteenth century, especially one who has the particular misfortune to inhabit Petersburg, the most abstract and intentional city in the whole world. (There are intentional and unintentional cities.) It would have been quite enough, for instance, to have the consciousness by which all so-called straightforward persons and men of action live. I'll bet you think I am writing all this to show off, to be witty at the expense of men of action; and what is more, that out of ill-bred showing-off, I am clanking a sword, like my officer. But, gentlemen, whoever can pride himself on his diseases and even show off with them?

However, what am I talking about? Everyone does that. They do pride themselves on their diseases, and I, perhaps, more than any one. There is no doubt about it: my objection was absurd. Yet just the same, I am firmly convinced not only that a great deal of consciousness, but that any consciousness is a disease. I insist on it. Let us drop that, too, for a minute. Tell me this: why did it happen that at the very, yes, at the very moment when I was most capable of recognizing every refinement of "all the sublime and beautiful," as we used to say at one time, I would, as though purposely, not only feel but do such hideous things, such that—well, in short, such as everyone probably does but which, as though purposely, occurred to me at the very time when I was most conscious that they ought not to be done. The more conscious I was of goodness, and of all that "sublime and beautiful," the more deeply I sank into my mire and the more capable I became of sinking into it completely. But the main thing was that all this did not seem to occur in me accidentally, but as though it had to be so. As though it were my most normal condition, and not in the least disease or depravity, so that finally I even lost the desire to struggle against this depravity. It ended by my almost believing (perhaps actually believing) that probably this was really my normal condition. But at first, in the beginning, that is, what agonies I suffered in that struggle! I did not believe that others went through the same things, and therefore I hid this fact about myself as a secret all my life. I was ashamed (perhaps I am even ashamed now). I reached the point of feeling a sort of secret abnormal, despicable enjoyment in returning home to my corner on some disgusting Petersburg night, and being acutely conscious that that day I had again done something loathsome, that what was done could never be undone, and secretly, inwardly gnaw, gnaw at myself for it, nagging and consuming myself till at last the bitterness turned into a sort of shameful accursed sweetness, and finally into real positive enjoyment! Yes, into enjoyment, into enjoyment! I insist upon that. And that is why I have started to speak, because I keep wanting to know for a fact whether other people feel such an enjoyment. Let me explain: the enjoyment here consisted precisely in the hyperconsciousness of one's own degradation; it was from feeling oneself that one had reached the last barrier, that it was nasty, but that it could not be otherwise; that you no longer had an escape; that you could never become a different person; that even if there remained enough time and faith for you to change into something else you probably would not want to change; or if you did want to, even then you would do nothing; because perhaps in reality there was nothing for you to change into. And the worst of it, and the root of it all, was that it all proceeded according to the normal and fundamental laws of hyperconsciousness, and with the inertia that was the direct result of those laws, and that consequently one could not only not change but one could do absolutely nothing. Thus it would follow, as the result of hyperconsciousness, that one is not to blame for being a scoundrel, as though that were any consolation to the scoundrel once he himself has come to realize that he actually is a scoundrel. But enough. Bah, I have talked a lot of nonsense, but what have I explained? Can this enjoyment be explained? But I will explain it! I will get to the bottom of it! That is why I have taken up my pen.

To take an instance, I am terribly vain. I am as suspicious and touchy as a hunchback or a dwarf. But to tell the truth, there have been moments when if someone had happened to slap my face I would, perhaps, have even been glad of that. I say, very seriously, that I would probably have been able to discover a peculiar sort of enjoyment even in that—the enjoyment, of course, of despair; but in despair occur the most intense enjoyments, especially when one is very acutely conscious of one's hopeless position. As for the slap in the face—why then the consciousness of being beaten to a pulp would positively overwhelm one. The worst of it is, no matter how I tried, it still turned out that I was always the most to blame in everything, and what is most humiliating of all, to blame for no fault of my own but, so to say, through the laws of nature. In the first place, to blame because I am cleverer than any of the people surrounding me. (I have always considered myself cleverer than any of the people surrounding me, and sometimes, would you believe it, I have even been ashamed of that. At any rate, all my life, I have, as it were, looked away and I could never look people straight in the eye.) To blame, finally, because even if I were magnanimous, I would only have suffered more from the consciousness of all its uselessness. After all, I would probably never have been able to do anything with my magnanimity—neither to forgive, for my assailant may have slapped me because of the laws of nature, and one cannot forgive the laws of nature; nor to forget, for even if it were the laws of nature, it is insulting all the same. Finally, even if I had wanted to be anything but magnanimous, had desired on the countrary to revenge myself on the man who insulted me, I could not have revenged myself on anyone nor anything because I would certainly never have made up my mind to do anything, even if I had been able to. Why would I not have made up my mind? I want to say a few words about that in particular.

### III

After all, people who know how to revenge themselves and to take care of themselves in general, how do they do it? After all, when they are possessed, let us suppose, by the feeling of revenge, then for the time there is nothing else but that feeling left in their whole being. Such a man simply rushes straight toward his object like an infuriated bull with its horns down, and nothing but a wall will stop him. (By the way: facing the wall, such people—that is, the straightforward persons and men of action—are genuinely nonplussed. For them a wall is not an evasion, as for example for us people who think and consequently do nothing; it is not an excuse for turning aside, an excuse for which our kind is always very glad, though we scarcely believe in it ourselves, usually. No, they are nonplussed in all sincerity. The wall has for them something tranquilizing, morally soothing, final—maybe even something mysterious . . . but of the wall later.) Well, such a direct person I regard as the real normal man, as his tender mother nature wished to see him when she graciously brought him into being on the earth. I envy such a man till I am green in the face. He is stupid. I am not disputing that, but perhaps the normal man should be stupid, how do you know? Perhaps it is very beautiful, in fact. And I am all the more convinced of that suspicion, if one can call it so, by the fact that if, for instance, you take the antithesis of the normal man, that is, the hyperconscious man, who has come, of course, not out of the lap of nature but out of a retort (this is almost mysticism, gentlemen, but I suspect this, too), this retort-made man is sometimes so nonplussed in the presence of his antithesis that with all his hyperconsciousness he genuinely thinks of himself as a mouse and not a man. It may be a hyperconscious mouse, yet it is a mouse, while the other is a man, and therefore, etc. And the worst is, he himself, his very own self, looks upon himself as a mouse. No one asks him to do so. And that is an important point. Now let us look at this mouse in action. Let us suppose, for instance, that it feels insulted, too (and it almost always does feel insulted), and wants to revenge itself too. There may even be a greater accumulation of spite in it than in *l'homme de la nature et de la vérité*. The base, nasty desire to repay with spite whoever has offended it, rankles perhaps even more nastily in it than in *l'homme de la nature et de la vérité*, because *l'homme de la nature et de la vérité* through his innate stupidity looks upon his revenge as justice pure and simple; while in consequence of his hyperconsciousness the mouse does not believe in the justice of it. To come at last to the deed itself, to the very act of revenge. Apart from the one fundamental nastiness the unfortunate mouse succeeds in creating around it so many other nastinesses in the form of doubts and questions, adds to the one question so many unsettled questions, that there inevitably works up around it a sort of fatal brew, a stinking mess, made up of its doubts, agitations and lastly of the contempt spat upon it by the straightforward men of action who stand solemnly about it as judges and arbitrators, laughing at it till their healthy sides ache. Of course the only thing left for it is to dismiss all that with a wave of its paw, and, with a smile of assumed contempt in which it does not even believe itself, creep ignominiously into its mouse-hole. There, in its nasty, stinking, underground home our insulted, crushed and ridiculed mouse promptly becomes absorbed in cold, malignant and, above all, everlasting spite. For forty years together it will remember its injury down to the smallest, most shameful detail, and every time will add, of itself, details still more shameful, spitefully teasing and irritating itself with its own imagination. It will be ashamed of its own fancies, but yet it will recall everything, it will go over it again and again, it will invent lies against itself pretending that those things might have happened, and will forgive nothing. Maybe it will begin to revenge itself, too, but, as it were, piecemeal, in trivial ways, from behind the stove, incognito, without believing either in its own right to vengeance, or in the success of its revenge, knowing beforehand that from all its efforts at revenge it will suffer a hundred times more than he on whom it revenges itself, while he, probably will not even feel it. On its deathbed it will recall it all over again, with interest accumulated over all the years. But it is just in that cold, abominable half-despair, half-belief, in that conscious burying oneself alive for grief in the underworld for forty years, in that hyperconsciousness and yet to some extent doubtful hopelessness of one's position, in that hell of unsatisfied desires turned inward, in that fever of oscillations, of resolutions taken for ever and regretted again a minute later—that the savor of that strange enjoyment of which I have spoken lies. It is so subtle, sometimes so difficult to analyze consciously, that somewhat limited people, or simply people with strong nerves, will not understand anything at all in it. "Possibly," you will add on your own account with a grin, "people who have never received a slap in the face will not understand it either," and in that way you will politely hint to me that I, too, perhaps, have been slapped in the face in my life, and so I speak as an expert. I'll bet that you are thinking that. But set your minds at rest, gentlemen, I have not received a slap in the face, though it doesn't matter to me at all what you may think about it. Possibly, I even myself regret that I have given so few slaps in the face during my life. But enough, not another word on the subject of such extreme interest to you.

I will continue calmly about people with strong nerves who do not understand a certain refinement of enjoyment. Though in certain circumstances these gentlemen bellow their loudest like bulls, though this, let us suppose, does them the greatest honor, yet, as I have already said, confronted with the impossible they at once resign themselves. Does the impossible mean the stone wall? What stone wall? Why, of course, the laws of nature, the conclusions of natural science, of mathematics. As soon as they prove to you, for instance, that you are descended from a monkey, then it is no use scowling, accept it as a fact. When they prove to you that in reality one drop of your own fat must be dearer to you than a hundred thousand of your fellow creatures, and that this conclusion is the final solution of all so-called virtues and duties and all such ravings and prejudices, then you might as well accept it, you can't do anything about it, because two times two is a law of mathematics. Just try refuting it.

"But really," they will shout at you, "there is no use protesting; it is a case of two times two makes four! Nature does not ask your permission, your wishes, and whether you like or dislike her laws does not concern her. You are bound to accept her as she is, and consequently also all her conclusions. A wall, you see, is a wall—etc. etc." Good God! but what do I care about the laws of nature and arithmetic, when, for some reason, I dislike those laws and the fact that two times two makes four? Of course I cannot break through a wall by battering my head against it if I really do not have the strength to break through it, but I am not going to resign myself to it simply because it is a stone wall and I am not strong enough.

As though such a stone wall really were a consolation, and really did contain some word of conciliation, if only because it is as true as two times two makes four. Oh, absurdity of absurdities! How much better it is to understand it all, to be conscious of it all, all the impossibilities and the stone walls, not to resign yourself to a single one of those impossibilities and stone walls if it disgusts you to resign yourself; to reach, through the most inevitable, logical combinations, the most revolting conclusions on the ever-lasting theme that you are yourself somehow to blame even for the stone wall, though again it is as clear as day you are not to blame in the least, and therefore grinding your teeth in silent impotence sensuously to sink into inertia, brooding on the fact that it turns out that there is even no one for you to feel vindictive against, that you have not, and perhaps never will have, an object for your spite, that it is a sleight-of-hand, a bit of juggling, a card-sharper's trick, that it is simply a mess, no knowing what and no knowing who, but in spite of all these uncertainties, and jugglings, still there is an ache in you, and the more you do not know, the worse the ache.

---

# WALT WHITMAN

## *When Lilacs Last in the Dooryard Bloom'd*

---

Walt Whitman (1819–1892), America's first world-class poet, was also America's most American poet. Unlike any poet before or after, he made his own country the subject of his lifelong project. The poem group entitled *Leaves of Grass* (first edition, 1855; ninth or Deathbed edition, 1891–1892) is a hymn celebrating the whole life of the nation, with the poet identifying himself with male and female, young and old, white and black, slave and free, healthy and handicapped—and animals too. Speaking in a mystical, biblical voice, he sang of the body and of the soul, of night, earth, and sea, of vice, and of virtue. *Leaves of Grass* was a living work that evolved in structure over thirty-seven years, with almost constant revision, reordering, additions, and subtractions, starting with 12 and expanding to 383 poems in the Deathbed edition; it was meant to represent the growth of his country, to give voice to "a composite, electric, democratic personality," to embody America's Soul—the mystical Reality of national consciousness. "When Lilacs Last in the Dooryard Bloom'd" is one of the collection's most famous poems.

*Leaves of Grass*, innovative in form, style, and subject, helped free American poetry from European tradition; at the same time, it opened up European writing to fresh voices in the ever-widening global culture. Whitman's work attracted admirers among England's writers, who charged that Americans did not fully appreciate him. Though Whitman was not neglected at home (the then dean of American Letters, Emerson, welcomed *Leaves of Grass* with these words: "I greet you at the beginning of a great career. . . ."), it is true that Whitman had to deal with the criticism that *Leaves of Grass* was an immoral book, because of sexual overtones in certain poems. Indeed, because of this work, he was fired from a government clerkship, after serving less than six months.

Whitman's reputation has grown since the late 1950s when he was rediscovered by America's Beat Generation—a group of writers who were repulsed by society's materialism and militarism. The leading Beat poet, Allen Ginsberg, found a brother spirit in Whitman; they shared a contempt for elegant writing, as well as homosexual feelings, beard, and unkempt appearance. Both, too, shared a decided preference for society's rejects, called "beats" by Ginsberg but "roughs" by Whitman (a poem in *Leaves of Grass* introduced "Walt Whitman, an American, one of the roughs, a kosmos"). The bohemian Whitman was only one phase of his life, the time prior to the Civil War; after working during the war as a nurse to Northern and Southern soldiers in army hospitals in Washington, D.C., he settled down into a new persona, which he kept to the end: that of the "good gray poet," living quietly and receiving visitors.

### Reading the Selection

"When Lilacs Last in the Dooryard Bloom'd" commemorates the assassination of President Lincoln (never mentioned by name) on April 15, 1865. Deeply moved by Lincoln, whom he thought the prototypical democratic man, the living symbol of his own message to America, Whitman wanted to convey both his own grief and the universal meaning of this death. In form, the poem interweaves three symbols reflective of the springtime, the season of the president's death—the lilacs (the poet's love), the fallen western star (Lincoln), and the hermit thrush (the chant of death). This poem, along with three others, was added to *Leaves of Grass* in the 1871 edition.

---

**1**

When lilacs last in the dooryard bloom'd,
And the great star early droop'd in the western sky in
    the night,
I mourn'd, and yet shall mourn with ever-returning
    spring.

Ever-returning spring, trinity sure to me you bring,
Lilac blooming perennial and drooping star in the west,
And thought of him I love.

**2**

O powerful western fallen star!
O shades of night—O moody, tearful night!
O great star disappear'd—O the black murk that hides
    the star!
O cruel hands that hold me powerless—O helpless soul
    of me!
O harsh surrounding cloud that will not free my soul.

**3**

In the dooryard fronting an old farm-house near the
    whitewash'd palings,
Stands the lilac-bush tall-growing with heart-shaped
    leaves of rich green,
With many a pointed blossom rising delicate, with the
    perfume strong I love,

With every leaf a miracle—and from this bush in the
    dooryard,
With delicate-color'd blossoms and heart-shaped leaves of
    rich green,
A sprig with its flower I break.

**4**

In the swamp in secluded recesses,
A shy and hidden bird is warbling a song.
Solitary the thrush,
The hermit withdrawn to himself, avoiding the settlements,
Sings by himself a song.

Song of the bleeding throat,
Death's outlet song of life, (for well dear brother I know,
If though wast not granted to sing thou would'st surely die.)

**5**

Over the breast of the spring, the land, amid cities,
Amid lanes and through old woods, where lately the
    violets peep'd from the ground, spotting the gray
    debris,
Amid the grass in the fields each side of the lanes,
    passing the endless grass,
Passing the yellow-spear'd wheat, every grain from its
    shroud in the dark-brown fields uprisen,
Passing the apple-tree blows of white and pink in the
    orchards,

Carrying a corpse to where it shall rest in the grave,
Night and day journeys a coffin.

### 6

Coffin that passes through lanes and streets,
Through day and night with the great cloud darkening
the land,
With the pomp of the inloop'd flags with the cities
draped in black,
With the show of the States themselves as of crape-veil'd
women standing,
With processions long and winding and the flambeaus of
the night,
With the countless torches lit, with the silent sea of faces
and the unbared heads,
With the waiting depot, the arriving coffin, and the
sombre faces,
With dirges through the night, with the thousand voices
rising strong and solemn,
With all the mournful voices of the dirges pour'd around
the coffin,
The dim-lit churches and the shuddering organs—where
amid these you journey,
With the tolling tolling bells' perpetual clang,
Here, coffin that slowly passes,
I give you my sprig of lilac.

### 7

(Nor for you, for one alone,
Blossoms and branches green to coffins all I bring,
For fresh as the morning, thus would I chant a song for
you O sane and sacred death.

All over bouquets of roses,
O death, I cover you over with roses and early lilies,
But mostly and now the lilac that blooms the first,
Copious I break, I break the sprigs from the bushes,
With loaded arms I come, pouring for you,
For you and the coffins all of you O death.)

### 8

O western orb sailing the heaven,
Now I know what you must have meant as a month
since I walk'd,
As I walk'd in silence the transparent shadowy night,
As I saw you had something to tell as you bent to me
night after night,
As you droop'd from the sky low down as if to my side,
(while the other stars all look'd on,)
As we wander'd together the solemn night, (for
something I know not what kept me from sleep,)
As the night advanced, and I saw on the rim of the west
how full you were of woe,
As I stood on the rising ground in the breeze in the cool
transparent night,

As I watch'd where you pass'd and was lost in the
netherward black of the night,
As my soul in its trouble dissatisfied sank, as where you
sad orb,
Concluded, dropt in the night, and was gone.

### 9

Sing on there in the swamp,
O singer bashful and tender, I hear your notes, I hear
your call,
I hear, I come presently, I understand you,
But a moment I linger, for the lustrous star has detain'd me,
The star my departing comrade holds and detains me.

### 10

O how shall I warble myself for the dead one there I loved?
And how shall I deck my song for the large sweet soul
that has gone?
And what shall my perfume be for the grave of him I love?
Sea-winds blown from east and west,
Blown from the Eastern sea and blown from the Western
sea, till there on the prairies meeting,
These and with these and the breath of my chant,
I'll perfume the grave of him I love.

### 11

O what shall I hang on the chamber walls?
And what shall the pictures be that I hang on the walls,
To adorn the burial-house of him I love?

Pictures of growing spring and farms and homes,
With the Fourth-month eve at sundown, and the gray
smoke lucid and bright,
With floods of the yellow gold of the gorgeous, indolent,
sinking sun, burning, expanding the air,
With the fresh sweet herbage under foot, and the pale
green leaves of the trees prolific,
In the distance the flowing glaze, the breast of the river,
with a wind-dapple here and there,
With ranging hills on the banks, with many a line against
the sky, and shadows,
And the city at hand with dwellings so dense, and stacks
of chimneys,
And all the scenes of life and the workshops, and the
workmen homeward returning.

### 12

Lo, body and soul—this land,
My own Manhattan with spires, and the sparkling and
hurrying tides, and the ships,
The varied and ample land, the South and the North in
the light, Ohio's shores and flashing Missouri,
And ever the far-spreading prairies cover'd with grass
and corn.

Lo, the most excellent sun so calm and haughty,
The violet and purple morn with just-felt breezes,
The gentle soft-born measureless light,
The miracle spreading bathing all, the fulfill'd noon,
The coming eve delicious, the welcome night and the stars,
Over my cities shining all, enveloping man and land.


## 13

Sing on, sing on you gray-brown bird,
Sing from the swamps, the recesses, pour your chant
    from the bushes,
Limitless out of the dusk, out of the cedars and pines.

Sing on dearest brother, warble your reedy song,
Loud human song, with voice of uttermost woe.

O liquid and free and tender!
O wild and loose to my soul—O wondrous singer!

You only I hear—yet the star holds me, (but will soon
    depart,)
Yet the lilac with mastering odor holds me.


## 14

Now while I sat in the day and look'd forth,
In the close of the day with its light and the fields of
    spring, and the farmers preparing their crops,
In the large unconscious scenery of my land with its
    lakes and forests,
In the heavenly aerial beauty, (after the perturb'd winds
    and the storms,)
Under the arching heavens of the afternoon swift
    passing, and the voices of children and women,
The many-moving sea-tides, and I saw the ships how
    they sail'd,
And the summer approaching with richness, and the
    fields all busy with labor,
And the infinite separate houses, how they all went on,
    each with its meals and minutia of daily usages,
And the streets how their throbbings throbb'd, and the
    cities pent—lo, then and there,
Falling upon them all and among them all, enveloping
    me with the rest,
Appear'd the cloud, appear'd the long black trail,
And I knew death, its thought, and the sacred
    knowledge of death.

Then with the knowledge of death as walking one side
    of me,
And the thought of death close-walking the other side of me,
And I in the middle as with companions, and as holding
    the hands of companions,
I fled forth to the hiding receiving night that talks not,
Down to the shores of the water, the path by the swamp
    in the dimness,
To the solemn shadowy cedars and ghostly pines so still.

And the singer so shy to the rest receiv'd me,
The gray-brown bird I know receiv'd us comrades three,
And he sang the carol of death, and a verse for him I love.

From deep secluded recesses,
From the fragrant cedars and the ghostly pines so still,
Came the carol of the bird.

And the charm of the carol rapt me,
As I held as if by their hands my comrades in the night,
And the voice of my spirit tallied the song of the bird.

*Come lovely and soothing death,*
*Undulate round the world, serenely arriving, arriving,*
*In the day, in the night, to all, to each,*
*Sooner or later delicate death.*

*Prais'd be the fathomless universe,*
*For life and joy, and for objects and knowledge curious,*
*And for love, sweet love—but praise! praise! praise!*
*For the sure-enwinding arms of cool-enfolding death.*

*Dark mother always gliding near with soft feet,*
*Have none chanted for thee a chant of fullest welcome?*
*Then I chant it for thee, I glorify thee above all,*
*I bring thee a song that when thou must indeed come, come*
    *unfalteringly.*

*Approach strong deliveress,*
*When it is so, when thou hast taken them I joyously sing the*
    *dead,*
*Lost in the loving floating ocean of thee,*
*Laved in the flood of thy bliss O death.*

*From me to thee glad serenades,*
*Dances for thee I propose saluting thee, adornments and*
    *feastings for thee,*
*And the sights of the open landscape and the high-spread sky*
    *are fitting,*
*And life and the fields, and the huge and thoughtful night.*
*The night in silence under many a star,*
*The ocean shore and the husky whispering wave whose voice I*
    *know,*
*And the soul turning to thee O vast and well-veil'd death,*
*And the body gratefully nestling close to thee.*

*Over the tree-tops I float thee a song,*
*Over the rising and sinking waves, over the myriad fields and*
    *the prairies wide,*
*Over the dense-pack'd cities all and the teeming wharves and*
    *ways,*
*I float this carol with joy, with joy to thee O death.*


## 15

To the tally of my soul,
Loud and strong kept up the gray-brown bird,
With pure deliberate notes spreading filling the night.

Loud in the pines and cedars dim,
Clear in the freshness moist and the swamp-perfume,
And I with my comrades there in the night.

While my sight that was bound in my eyes unclosed,
As to long panoramas of visions.

And I saw askant the armies,
I saw as in noiseless dreams hundreds of battle-flags,
Borne through the smoke of the battles and pierc'd with
    missiles I saw them,
And carried hither and yon through the smoke, and torn
    and bloody,
And at last but a few shreds left on the staffs, (and all in
    silence,)
And the staffs all splinter'd and broken.

I saw battle-corpses, myriads of them,
And the white skeletons of young men, I saw them,
I saw the debris and debris of all the slain soldiers of the
    war,
But I saw they were not as was thought,
They themselves were fully at rest, they suffer'd not,
The living remain'd and suffer'd, the mother suffer'd,
And the wife and the child and the musing comrade
    suffer'd,
And the armies that remain'd suffer'd.

### 16

Passing the visions, passing the night,
Passing, unloosing the hold of my comrades' hands,

Passing the song of the hermit bird and the tallying song
    of my soul,
Victorious song, death's outlet song, yet varying ever-
    altering song,
As low and wailing, yet clear the notes, rising and
    falling, flooding the night,
Sadly sinking and fainting, as warning and warning, and
    yet again bursting with joy,
Covering the earth and filling the spread of the heaven,
As that powerful psalm in the night I heard from recesses,
Passing, I leave thee lilac with heart-shaped leaves,
I leave thee there in the door-yard, blooming, returning
    with spring.

I cease from my song for thee,
From my gaze on thee in the west, fronting the west,
    communing with thee,
O comrade lustrous with silver face in the night.

Yet each to keep and all, retrievements out of the night,
The song, the wondrous chant of the gray-brown bird,
And the tallying chant, the echo arous'd in my soul,
With the lustrous and drooping star with the
    countenance full of woe,
With the holders holding my hand nearing the call of the
    bird,
Comrades mine and I in the midst, and their memory
    ever to keep, for the dead I loved so well,
For the sweetest, wisest soul of all my days and lands—
    and this for his dear sake,
Lilac and star and bird twined with the chant of my soul,
There in the fragrant pines and the cedars dusk and
    dim.

---

# CHARLES DARWIN

## from *The Descent of Man*

---

Darwin's *The Descent of Man* (1871) is one of the West's most explosive books. In two volumes, the first limited to man and the second given to the role of sexual selection in evolution, it is written in matter-of-fact prose and backed by masses of scientific data. Darwin argues that evolution—the idea that all life began with a common ancestor, an amoeba-like being—is not a hypothesis, as had been claimed when this notion first appeared in Greek thought; rather, it is a principle of biology operating throughout nature. In other words, viewed over the course of millennia, the plant, animal, and human worlds constitute a vast cousinhood. Thus, Darwin's book destroyed the biblical view of human genesis, or creationism—Adam and Eve were the first parents, having been created by God after he had made the plant and animal kingdoms; this idea had dominated Western thought since Christianity became the religion of Rome in about A.D. 400. Darwin replaced it with the principle of evolution. The full meaning of evolution, that humans are creatures without souls and that life is without purpose, is still being worked out today.

*The Descent of Man*, while controversial, did not raise the firestorm of criticism that had greeted his earlier work, *The Origin of Species* (1859). It was in the 1859 work that he first advanced the principle of evolution, but he had not included the human species in his discussion of animal species, though he hinted at it. *The Origin of Species* had sold out on the first day of publication, but it also made him and his ideas notorious; this was a distressing turn of events for one of the most staid men in the Victorian Age—a period obsessed with respectability (Darwin even became seriously ill when confronted with unpleasant ideas). At the same time, he was the quintessential expression of the period's realism, a pure scientist, totally disinterested in theory and devoted solely to facts. It was only after amassing uncontrovertible data, collected, between 1831 and 1836, on his voyage to South America with the British ship, the *Beagle*, and, in the 1850s, in his investigation of orchids, that he was prepared to publish his research. By 1871, the principle of evolution, proven by Darwin's documentation, had won over his fellow scientists, so that when *The Descent of Man* appeared, despite the explosive theme, it was soon adopted into the worldview of most educated people.

The blind force "guiding" Darwinian evolution is natural selection, the notion that favorable variations within a species tend to be preserved, while unfavorable variations are destroyed; the result is the formation of new species. The variations occur randomly, without design on the part of a divine creator or desire on the part of the organism. Darwin claimed that the idea of natural selection was inspired by his reading of Thomas Malthus's essay *On Population* (1797); the idea, however, was also explicitly stated in Herbert Spencer's *Population* (1852), where it was called "survival of the fittest." It was Spencer's term which Darwin appropriated and made his own.

### Reading the Selection

This passage is taken from the last chapter of *The Descent of Man*. Here, Darwin praises man's intellectual ("godlike intellect") and moral faculties ("sympathy . . . for the most debased," and "benevolence . . . to other men [and] living creature[s]"), claiming them to be the result of natural selection instead of divine origin.

⋯

The main conclusion arrived at in this work, and now held by many naturalists who are well competent to form a sound judgment, is that man is descended from some less highly organized form. The grounds upon which this conclusion rests will never be shaken, for the close similarity between man and the lower animals in embryonic development, as well as in innumerable points of structure and constitution, both of high and of the most trifling importance—the rudiments which he retains, and the abnormal reversions to which he is occasionally liable—are facts which cannot be disputed. They have long been known, but until recently they told us nothing with respect to the origin of man. Now when viewed by the light of our knowledge of the whole organic world, their meaning is unmistakable. The great principle of evolution stands up clear and firm, when these groups of facts are considered in connection with others, such as the mutual affinities of the members of the same group, their geographical distribution in past and present times, and their geological succession. It is incredible that all these facts should speak falsely. He who is not content to look, like a savage, at the phenomena of nature as disconnected cannot any longer believe that man is the work of a separate act of creation. He will be forced to admit that the close resemblance of the embryo of man to that, for instance, of a dog—the construction of his skull, limbs, and whole frame, independently of the uses to which the parts may be put, on the same plan with that of other mammals—the occasional reappearance of various structures, for instance of several distinct muscles, which man does not normally possess, but which are common to the Quadrumana—and a crowd of analogous facts—all point in the plainest manner to the conclusion that man is the codescendant with other mammals of a common progenitor.

⋯

The main conclusion arrived at in this work, namely that man is descended from some lowly-organized form, will, I regret to think, be highly distasteful to many persons. But there can hardly be a doubt that we are descended from barbarians. The astonishment which I felt on first seeing a party of Fuegians on a wild and broken shore will never be forgotten by me, for the reflection at once rushed into my mind—such were our ancestors. These men were absolutely naked and bedaubed with paint, their long hair was tangled, their mouths frothed with excitement, and their expression was wild, startled, and distrustful. They possessed hardly any arts, and like wild animals lived on what they could catch; they had no government, and were merciless to everyone not of their own small tribe. He who has seen a savage in his native land will not feel much shame, if forced to acknowledge that the blood of some more humble creature flows in his veins. For my own part I would as soon be descended from that heroic little monkey, who braved his dreaded enemy in order to save the life of his keeper; or from that old baboon, who, descending from the mountains, carried away in triumph his young comrade from a crowd of astonished dogs—as from a savage who delights to torture his enemies, offers up bloody sacrifices, practices infanticide without remorse, treats his wives like slaves, knows no decency, and is haunted by the grossest superstitions.

Man may be excused for feeling some pride at having risen, though not through his own exertions, to the very summit of the organic scale; and the fact of his having thus risen, instead of having been aboriginally placed there, may give him hopes for a still higher destiny in the distant future. But we are not here concerned with hopes or fears, only with the truth as far as our reason allows us to discover it. I have given the evidence to the best of my ability; and we must acknowledge, as it seems to me, that man with all his noble qualities, with sympathy which feels for the most debased, with benevolence which extends not only to other men but to the humblest living creature, with his godlike intellect which has penetrated into the movements and constitution of the solar system—with all these exalted powers—Man still bears in his bodily frame the indelible stamp of his lowly origin.

# MARK TWAIN

## from *The Adventures of Huckleberry Finn*

### Chapter 15

Mark Twain (1835–1910) was another of the nineteenth-century writers who helped free American letters from the grip of Europe and establish a distinctively American writing style. Reared in the frontier village of Hannibal, Missouri, educated in the "school of hard-knocks" (he stopped formal schooling at age twelve), and adult resident of many parts of the country, including Missouri, Nevada, California, and Connecticut, Twain had a broad view of life in America. He also experienced many occupations—printer, Mississippi riverboat pilot, miner, journalist, travel writer, and publisher. All of this contributed to his uniquely American voice— part colorful storyteller, part hardboiled cynic, but, above everything, a hater of hypocrisy. Even his pen name bespoke his uniquely American heritage; for, being born Samuel Clemens, he changed it to "Mark Twain," the words called out by the Mississippi river leadsman (the deckhand who measured the water depth to assist the pilot): a depth of two fathoms (twelve feet) or mark twain.

Twain's books, such as *A Connecticut Yankee at King Arthur's Court* (1889), earned him fortunes and are still in print today; his most enduring works, *The Adventures of Tom Sawyer* (1876) and *The Adventures of Huckleberry Finn* (1884), made him a literary immortal. The latter novels, filled with local color, drew on memories of the world, the people, and the language of his experiences in Hannibal and his days on the river. The books also shared many characters, but their heroes' outlooks were markedly different: Tom, despite lapses, stands for society's conventional values, while Huck, the boy nobody wants, is the eternal rebel against respectability. Together, Tom and Huck mirror the never resolved struggle in Twain's own soul, between respectable living and the traditionless frontier. Today, *Huck Finn* is considered the greater novel, a reflection perhaps of our age's preference for its moral complexity.

### Reading the Selection

Twain prefaced *Huck Finn* with this notice: "Persons attempting to find a motive in this narrative will be prosecuted; persons attempting to find a moral in it will be banished; persons attempting to find a plot in it will be shot." Despite the warning, this novel has a motive in its desire to entertain, a moral in its redemption of both Huck and Jim—the social outcasts, one a white runaway boy and the other a slave seeking freedom—and a plot in its devotion to the Mississippi as a means of escape, as a source of danger, joy, food, and self-communion.

*Huck Finn* reflects its pre-Civil War setting in Huck's belief that slaves, namely Jim, belong to their rightful owners. Huck nevertheless is moral, despite modern critics who fault him for his defense of slavery and, in particular, his use of racist slurs toward Jim. Huck's morality gradually emerges in the novel. For example, Chapter 15, "Huck Loses the Raft—In the Fog—Huck finds the Raft—Trash," shows Huck hurting Jim's feelings but coming to realize that he loves Jim more than white society. Huck learns this lesson and changes his life accordingly: "I didn't do him no more mean tricks. . . ." Later, Huck helps Jim escape from slavery. What unifies the novel is the voice of Huck, whose speaking style, though meant to represent white dialect, may have been inspired by an African-American youth, named Jimmy, whose glibness Twain admired.

---

We judged that three nights more would fetch us to Cairo, at the bottom of Illinois, were the Ohio River comes in, and that was what we was after. We would sell the raft and get on a steamboat and go way up the Ohio among the free States, and then be out of trouble.

Well, the second night a fog begun to come on, and we made for a tow-head to tie to, for it wouldn't do to try to run in fog; but when I paddled ahead in the canoe, with the line, to make fast, there warn't anything but little saplings to tie to. I passed the line around one of them right on the edge of the cut bank, but there was a stiff current, and the raft come booming down so lively she tore it out by the roots and away she went. I see the fog closing down, and it made me so sick and scared I couldn't budge for most a half a minute it seemed to me—and then there warn't no raft in sight; you couldn't see twenty yards. I jumped into the canoe and run back to the stern and grabbed the paddle and set her back a stroke. But she didn't come. I was in such a hurry I hadn't untied her. I got up and tried to untie her, but I was so excited my hands shook so I couldn't hardly do anything with them.

As soon as I got started I took out after the raft, hot and heavy, right down the tow-head. That was all right as far as it went, but the tow-head warn't sixty yards long, and the minute I flew by the foot of it I shot out into the solid white fog, and hadn't no more idea which way I was going than a dead man.

Thinks I, it won't do to paddle; first I know I'll run into the bank or a tow-head or something; I got to set still and float, and yet it's mighty fidgety business to have to hold your hands still at such a time. I whooped and listened. Away down there, somewheres, I hears a small whoop, and up comes my spirits. I went tearing after it, listening sharp to hear it again. The next time it come, I see I warn't heading for it but heading away to the right of it. And the next time, I was heading away to the left of it—and not gaining on it much, either, for I was flying around, this way and that and 'tother, but it was going straight ahead all the time.

I did wish the fool would think to beat a tin pan, and beat it all the time, but he never did, and it was the still places between the whoops that was making the trouble for me. Well, I fought along, and directly I hears the whoop *behind* me. I was tangled good, now. That was somebody else's whoop, or else I was turned around.

I throwed the paddle down. I heard the whoop again; it was behind me yet, but in a different place; it kept coming, and kept changing its place, and I kept answering, till by-and-by it was in front of me again and I knowed the current had swung the canoe's head down stream and I was all right,

if that was Jim and not some other raftsman hollering. I couldn't tell nothing about voices in a fog, for nothing don't look natural nor sound natural in a fog.

The whooping went on, and in about a minute I come a booming down on a cut bank with smoky ghosts of big trees on it, and the current throwed me off to the left and shot by, amongst a lot of snags that fairly roared, the current was tearing by them so swift.

In another second or two it was solid white and still again. I set perfectly still, then, listening to my heart thump, and I reckon I didn't draw a breath while it thumped a hundred.

I just give up, then. I knowed what the matter was. That cut bank was an island, and Jim had gone down 'tother side of it. It warn't no tow-head, that you could float by in ten minutes. It had the big timber of a regular island; it might be five or six mile long and more than half a mile wide.

I kept quiet, with my ears cocked, about fifteen minutes, I reckon. I was floating along, of course, four or five mile an hour; but you don't ever think of that. No, you *feel* like you are laying dead still on the water; and if a little glimpse of a snag slips by, you don't think to yourself how fast *you're* going, but you catch your breath and think, my! how that snag's tearing along. If you think it ain't dismal and lonesome out in a fog that way, by yourself, in the night, you try it once—you'll see.

Next, for about a half an hour, I whoops now and then; at last I hears the answer a long ways off, and tries to follow it, but I couldn't do it, and directly I judged I'd got into a nest of tow-heads, for I had little dim glimpses of them on both sides of me, sometimes just a narrow channel between; and some that I couldn't see, I knowed was there, because I'd hear the wash of the current against the old dead brush and trash that hung over the banks. Well, I warn't long losing the whoops, down amongst the tow-heads; and I only tried to chase them a little while, anyway, because it was worse than chasing a Jack-o-lantern. You never knowed a sound dodge around so, and swap places so quick and so much.

I had to claw away from the bank pretty lively, four or five times, to keep from knocking the islands out of the river; and so I judged the raft must be butting into the bank every now and then, or else it would get further ahead and clear out of hearing—it was floating a little faster than what I was.

Well, I seemed to be in the open river again, by-and-by, but I couldn't hear no sign of a whoop nowheres. I reckoned Jim had fetched up on a snag, maybe, and it was all up with him. I was good and tired, so I laid down in the canoe and said I wouldn't bother no more. I didn't want to go to sleep, of course; but I was so sleepy I couldn't help it; so I thought I would take just one little cat-nap.

But I reckon it was more than a cat-nap, for when I waked up the stars was shining bright, the fog was all gone, and I was spinning down a big bend stern first. First I didn't know where I was; I thought I was dreaming; and when things begun to come back to me, they seemed to come up dim out of last week.

It was a monstrous big river here, with the tallest and the thickest kind of timber on both banks; just a solid wall, as well as I could see, by the stars. I looked away down stream, and seen a black speck on the water. I took out after it; but when I got to it it warn't nothing but a couple of saw-logs made fast together. Then I see another speck, and chased that; then another, and this time I was right. It was the raft.

When I got to it Jim was setting there with his head down between his knees, asleep, with his right arm hanging over the steering oar. The other oar was smashed off, and the raft was littered up with leaves and branches and dirt. So she'd had a rough time.

I made fast and laid down under Jim's nose on the raft, and begun to gap, and stretch my fists out against Jim, and says:

'Hello, Jim, have I been asleep? Why didn't you stir me up?'

'Goodness gracious, is dat you, Huck? En you ain' dead—you ain' drownded—you's back agin? It's too good for true, honey, it's too good for true. Lemme look at you, chile, lemme feel o' you. No, you ain' dead! you's back agin, 'live en soun', jis de same ole Huck—de same ole Huck, thanks to goodness!'

'What's the matter with you, Jim? You been a drinking?'

'Drinkin'? Has I ben a drinkin'? Has I had a chance to be a drinkin'?'

'Well, then, what makes you talk so wild?'

'How does I talk wild?'

'*How*? why, hain't you been talking about my coming back, and all that stuff, as if I'd been gone away?'

'Huck—Huck Finn, you look me in de eye; look me in de eye. *Hain't* you ben gone away?'

'Gone away? Why, what in the nation do you mean? *I* hain't been gone anywheres. Where would I go to?'

'Well, looky here, boss, dey's sumf'n wrong, dey is. Is I *me*, or who *is* I? Is I heah, or whah *is* I? Now dat's what I wants to know.'

'Well, I think you're here, plain enough, but I think you're a tangle-headed old fool, Jim.'

'I is, is I? Well you answer me dis. Didn't you tote out de line in de canoe, fer to make fas' to de tow-head?'

'No, I didn't. What tow-head? I hain't seen no tow-head.'

'You hain't seen no tow-head? Looky here—didn't de line pull loose en de raf' go a hummin' down de river, en leave you en de canoe behine in de fog?'

'What fog?'

'Why *de* fog. De fog dat's ben aroun' all night. End didn't you whoop, en didn't I whoop, tell we got mix' up in de islands en one un us got los' en 'tother one was jis' as good as los', 'kase he didn't know whah he wuz? En didn't I bust up agin a lot er dem islands en have a turrible time en mos'

git drownded? Now ain' dat so, boss—ain' it so? You answer me dat.'

'Well, this is too many for me, Jim. I hain't seen no fog, nor no islands, nor no troubles, nor nothing. I been setting here talking with you all night till you went to sleep about ten minutes ago, and I reckon I done the same. You couldn't a got drunk in that time, so of course you've been dreaming.'

'Dad fetch it, how is gwyne to dream all dat in ten minutes?'

'Well, hang it all, you did dream it, because there didn't any of it happen.'

'But Huck, it's all jis' as plain to me as—'

'It don't make no difference how plain it is, there ain't nothing in it. I know, because I've been here all the time.'

Jim didn't say nothing for about five minutes, but set there studying over it. Then he says:

'Well, den, I reck'n I did dream it, Huck; but dog my cats ef it ain't de powerfullest dream I ever see. En I hain't ever had no dream b'fo' dat's tired me like dis one.'

'Oh, well, that's all right, because a dream does tire a body like everything, sometimes. But this one was a staving dream—tell me all about it, Jim.'

So Jim went to work and told me the whole thing right through, just as it happened, only he painted it up considerable. Then he said he must start in and ''terpret' it, because it was sent for a warning. He said the first tow-head stood for a man that would try to do us some good, but the current was another man that would get us away from him. The whoops was warnings that would come to us every now and then, and if we didn't try hard to make out to understand them they'd just take us into bad luck, 'stead of keeping us out of it. The lot of tow-heads was troubles we was going to get into with quarrelsome people and all kinds of mean folks, but if we minded our business and didn't talk back and aggravate them, we would pull through and get out of the fog and into the big clear river, which was the free States, and wouldn't have no more trouble.

It had clouded up pretty dark just after I got onto the raft, but it was clearing up again, now.

'Oh, well, that's all interpreted well enough, as far as it goes, Jim,' I says; 'but what does *these* things stand for?'

It was the leaves and rubbish on the raft, and the smashed oar. You could see them first rate, now.

Jim looked at the trash, and then looked at me, and back at the trash again. He had got the dream fixed so strong in his head that he couldn't seem to shake it loose and get the facts back into its place again, right away. But when he did get the thing straightened around, he looked at me steady, without ever smiling, and says:

'What do dey stan' for? I's gwyne to tell you. When I got all wore out wid work, en wid de callin' for you, en went to sleep, my heart wuz mos' broke bekase you wuz los', en I didn' k'yer no mo' what become er me en de raf'. En when I wake up en fine you back again', all safe en soun', de tears come en I could a got down on my knees en kiss' yo' foot I's so thankful. En all you wuz thinkin 'bout wuz how you could make a fool uv ole Jim wid a lie. Dat truck dah is *trash*; en trash is what people is dat puts dirt on de head er dey fren's en makes 'em ashamed.'

Then he got up slow, and walked to the wigwam, and went in there, without saying anything but that. But that was enough. It made me feel so mean I could almost kissed *his* foot to get him to take it back.

It was fifteen minutes before I could work myself up to go and humble myself to a nigger—but I done it, and I warn't ever sorry for it afterwards, neither. I didn't do him no more mean tricks, and I wouldn't done that one if I'd a knowed it would make him feel that way.

# EMILY DICKINSON
# Poems

---

Emily Dickinson (1830–1886) was America's first great woman poet, but she was virtually unknown when she died. She published only three poems while living, and their original style doomed her to obscurity. Her world was New England, and, though Puritan values were in decline, a literary career for a woman then was hard to manage. She nonetheless pioneered the way for other female writers.

For the most part, Dickinson lived in Amherst, Massachusetts, where her father, Edward Dickinson, was treasurer of Amherst College for forty years. She is known to have made only two forays from Amherst, the first, in 1847–1848, when she was a student at Mount Holyoke Female Seminary, and, the second, in 1854, when she visited her father in Washington, D.C., where he was a congressman. After 1862, she became a recluse in her father's house, devoting her time to writing a "letter to the world"—the 1775 poems which constitute her legacy. These poems, which she asked to be destroyed at her death, were saved for posterity by her sister Lavinia. Ignoring her sister's instructions, Lavinia, aided by Thomas Wentworth Higginson, a minor literary figure who had been Dickinson's sole tie with the wider literary world, and Mabel Todd Loomis, the gifted wife of an Amherst professor, produced the first selection of these poems in 1891. It was not until the 1920s, with the appearance of a rebellious generation, that Dickinson's works found a welcoming audience. Since World War II, especially with the rise of feminism, her reputation has grown exponentially. Today this literary star is deemed of the magnitude of Thoreau and Whitman, who, with Dickinson, helped to create a unique American style of writing. In recent years, her name has been kept before the public by the success of the stage production, *Belle of Amherst*, based on her life and works.

Dickinson's poems were characterized by discordant metaphors—drawn from flowers, village life, the Bible, the law, and, like the Metaphysical Poets of the 1600s (see Donne's "The Canonization"), the mechanical and domestic arts. Compressed and elusive, her works prefigure Modernism, the ruling style from 1870 to 1970, which used rich metaphors; yet, at the same time, they reflect Late Romanticism (see Brontë's *Jane Eyre*), with their claustrophobic images and sexual disturbance.

## Reading the Selection

As life passed her by, Dickinson became ever more eccentric. Dressed in white, she became a village legend; some thought her half-demented. Death became a near obsession, as reflected in four poems printed here. "There's a certain Slant of light" (about 1861) shows her thoughts wandering to death, inspired surprisingly by the normally optimistic images of sunlight and church hymns. "I felt a Funeral, in my Brain" (about 1861) presents the unusual metaphor of a parade of persons trampling up and down her brain as corresponding to her state of disillusion; the poem is unfinished, a typical feature. "I heard a Fly buzz—when I died—" (about 1862) calls up a disturbed sexual image of the poet seated, the air moved only by the buzz of a fly—perhaps a metaphor of Dickinson's fate of life in death. "Because I could not stop for Death—" (about 1863) speaks to her feeling that death too soon ends life's little pleasures, such as "the School, where Children strove at Recess."

The remaining poem, "Much Madness is divinest Sense—," reveals Dickinson as a rebel, as she joins the "mad" against the sensible majority; the word "Chain" evokes a sense of being imprisoned.

## There's a certain Slant of light

There's a certain Slant of light,
Winter Afternoons—
That oppresses, like the Heft
Of Cathedral Tunes—

Heavenly Hurt, it gives us—
We can find no scar,
But internal difference,
Where the Meanings, are—

None may teach it—Any—
'Tis the Seal Despair—
An imperial affliction
Sent us of the Air—

When it comes, the Landscape lister
Shadows—hold their breath—
When it goes, 'tis like the Distance
On the look of Death—

## I felt a Funeral, in my Brain

I felt a Funeral, in my Brain,
And Mourners to and fro
Kept treading—treading—till it seemed
That Sense was breaking through—

And when they all were seated,
A Service, like a Drum—
Kept beating—beating—till I thought
My Mind was going numb—

And then I heard them lift a Box
And creak across my Soul

With those same Boots of Lead, again,
Then Space—began to toll,

As all the Heavens were a Bell,
And Being, but an Ear,
And I, and Silence, some strange Race
Wrecked, solitary, here—

And then a Plank in Reason, broke,
And I dropped down, and down—
And hit a World, at every plunge,
And Finished knowing—then—

## Much Madness is divinest Sense—

Much Madness is divinest Sense—
To a discerning Eye—
Much Sense—the starkest Madness—
'Tis the Majority

In this, as All, prevail—
Assent—and you are sane—
Demur—you're straightway dangerous—
And handled with a Chain—

## *I heard a Fly buzz—when I died—*

I heard a Fly buzz—when I died—
The Stillness in the Room
Was like the Stillness in the Air—
Between the Heaves of Storm—

The Eyes around—had wrung them dry—
And Breaths were gathering firm
For that last Onset—when the King
Be witnessed—in the Room—

I willed my Keepsakes—Signed away
What portion of me be
Assignable—and then it was
There interposed a Fly—

With Blue—uncertain stumbling Buzz—
Between the light—and me—
And then the Windows failed—and then
I could not see to see—

## *Because I could not stop for Death—*

Because I could not stop for Death—
He kindly stopped for me—
The Carriage held but just Ourselves—
And Immortality.

We slowly drove—He knew no haste
And I had put away
My labor and my leisure too,
For His Civility—

We passed the School, where Children strove
At Recess—in the Ring—
We passed the Fields of Gazing Grain—
We passed the Setting Sun—

Or rather—He passed Us—
The Dews drew quivering and chill—
For only Gossamer, my Gown—
My Tippet—only Tulle—

We paused before a House that seemed
A Swelling of the Ground—
The Roof was scarcely visible—
The Cornice—in the Ground—

Since then—'tis Centuries—and yet
Feels shorter than the Day
I first surmised the Horses' Heads
Were toward Eternity—

# Chapter

# 19

# The Age of Early Modernism:
## 1871–1914

FRIEDRICH NIETZSCHE

## from *The Gay Science*

The German thinker Friedrich Nietzsche (1844–1900) is a key, though paradoxical, figure in Western thought. Supremely influential on the diverse minds of his own day and those of succeeding generations (see Freud, Yeats, Sartre, Beauvoir, and Camus), he nonetheless felt an extreme psychological isolation from European culture; eventually he slipped into a paralyzing madness (perhaps the result of syphilis) for the last eleven years of his life. Even so, in his writings, he registered his poignantly ambivalent vision of the emerging nihilism—belief in nothing—which has characterized the West since 1900. He was a prophet of Modernism, the century-long movement, 1870 to 1970, which sought to wipe the cultural slate clean of both the Judeo-Christian and Greco-Roman traditions, as well as a prophet of Post-Modernism, Modernism's successor starting around 1970; Post-Modernism aimed at an open-ended, indeterminate set of attitudes, democratically embracing the contributions, tastes, and ideas of many groups of people, of all races, of all countries, past and present.

Nietzsche is also one of the most passionate and misunderstood writers in the West, in part because German Nazis in the 1930s made him their favorite philosopher and linked him to their campaign against the Jews and in favor of Aryan superiority; he is also misunderstood through his own doing, for Nietzsche's thought is clouded by an excess of adolescent emotion and his writing style is filled with aphorisms, or pithy sayings, which are easily misinterpreted when quoted out of context. Today, Nietzsche's linkage to Nazism has been exposed as false, since his writings repeatedly ridicule anti-Semites and German nationalists. Nietzsche's linkage to Nazism is now viewed as a joint fabrication by Nazis who twisted his ideas to support their cause and by his sister, a Nazi sympathizer and his literary executor, who edited his works to make this connection. As to interpretive problems arising from his style, that remains a central concern for all readers of this challenging writer.

## Reading the Selection

These selections, from *The Gay Science* (1882) and *Thus Spake Zarathustra* (1883), offer examples of Nietzsche's striking, biblical-sounding prose. Two themes dominate here: uncompromising hostility to religion and emphatic support of the idea of the Will to Power. He was the first major Western thinker to break completely with religion ("God is dead") and deny the truth of all transcendent belief. Much of his thought, such as radical perspectivism and rejection of universal values, was simply an attempt to come to terms with the full meaning of a godless world.

Nietzsche's second central theme was that inorganic and organic nature is ruled by the Will to Power, the blind force that courses through all things—an idea derived from Darwin (see *The Descent of Man*). Nietzsche thought societies healthy in which the Will to Power dominated; there, a natural hierarchy emerged where the strong ("masters") ruled the weak ("slaves"). In contrast, he thought societies doomed that suppressed the Will to Power; in particular, he objected to Christianity and its secular cousin socialism; he classified them as faiths of "little people," who paraded weaknesses as moral principles. His intent was to prepare the way for the *Übermensch*, or Overman, a new human type who with his robber instincts would be able to manipulate the masses and who was a law unto himself.

---

### 4

*What preserves the species.* The strongest and most evil spirits have so far advanced humanity the most: they have always rekindled the drowsing passions—all ordered society puts the passions to sleep; they have always reawakened the sense of comparison, of contradiction, of joy in the new, the daring, and the untried; they force men to meet opinion with opinion, model with model. For the most part by arms, by the overthrow of boundary stones, and by offense to the pieties, but also by new religions and moralities. The same "malice" is to be found in every teacher and preacher of the new. . . . The new is always *the evil*, as that which wants to conquer, to overthrow the old boundary stones and the old pieties; and only the old is the good. The good men of every age are those who dig the old ideas deep down and bear fruit with them, the husbandmen of the spirit. But all land is finally exhausted, and the plow of evil must always return.

There is a fundamentally erroneous doctrine in contemporary morality, celebrated particularly in England: according to this, the judgments "good" and "evil" are condensations of the experiences concerning "expedient" and "inexpedient"; what is called good preserves the species, while what is called evil is harmful to the species. In truth, however, the evil urges are expedient and indispensable and preserve the species to as high a degree as the good ones—only their function is different.

• • •

### 125

*The Madman.* Have you not heard of that madman who lit a lantern in the bright morning hours, ran to the market place, and cried incessantly, "I seek God! I seek God!" As many of those do not believe in God were standing around just then, he provoked much laughter. Why, did he get lost? said one. Did he lose his way like a child? said another. Or is he hiding? Is he afraid of us? Has he gone on a voyage? or emigrated? Thus they yelled and laughed. The madman jumped into their midst and pierced them with his glances.

"Whither is God" he cried. "I shall tell you. *We have killed him*—you and I. All of us are his murderers. But how have we done this? How were we able to drink up the sea? Who gave us the sponge to wipe away the entire horizon? What did we do when we unchained this earth from its sun? Whither is it moving now? Whither are we moving now? Away from all suns? Are we not plunging continually? Backward, sideward, forward, in all directions? Is there any up or down left? Are we not straying as through an infinite nothing? Do we not feel the breath of empty space? Has it not become colder? Is not night and more night coming on all the while? Must not lanterns be lit in the morning? Do we not hear anything yet of the noise of the gravediggers who are burying God? Do we not smell anything yet of God's decomposition? Gods too decompose. God is dead. God remains dead. And we have killed him. How shall we, the murderers of all murderers, comfort ourselves? What was holiest and most powerful of all that the world has yet owned has bled to death under our knives. Who will wipe this blood off us? What water is there for us to clean ourselves? What festivals of atonement, what sacred games shall we have to invent? Is not the greatness of this deed too great for us? Must not we ourselves become gods simply to seem worthy of it? There has never been a greater deed; and whoever will be born after us—for the sake of this deed he will be part of a higher history than all history hitherto."

Here the madman fell silent and looked again at his listeners; and they too were silent and stared at him in astonishment. At last he threw his lantern on the ground, and it broke and went out. "I come too early," he said then; "my time has not come yet. This tremendous event is still on its way, still wandering—it has not yet reached the ears of man. Lightning and thunder require time, the light of the stars requires time, deeds require time even after they are done, before they can be seen and heard. This deed is still more distant from them than the most distant stars—*and yet they have done it themselves.*"

It has been related further that on that same day the madman entered divers churches and there sang his *requiem aeternam deo*. Led out and called to account, he is said to have replied each time, "What are these churches now if they are not the tombs and sepulchers of God?"

・・・

**341**

*The greatest stress.* How, if some day or night a demon were to sneak after you into your loneliest loneliness and say to you, "This life as you now live it and have lived it, you will have to live once more and innumerable times more; and there will be nothing new in it, but every pain and every joy and every thought and sigh and everything immeasurably small or great in your life must return to you—all in the same succession and sequence—even this spider and this moonlight between the trees, and even this moment and I myself. The eternal hourglass of existence is turned over and over, and you with it, a dust grain of dust." Would you not throw yourself down and gnash your teeth and curse the demon who spoke thus? Or did you once experience a tremendous moment when you would have answered him, "You are a god, and never have I heard anything more godly." If this thought were to gain possession of you, it would change you, as you are, or perhaps crush you. The question in each and every thing, "Do you want this once more and innumerable times more?" would weigh upon your actions as the greatest stress. Or how well disposed would you have to become to yourself and to life to *crave nothing more fervently* than this ultimate eternal confirmation and seal?

---

# from *Thus Spoke Zarathustra*

## Part I

---

### 3

When Zarathustra came into the next town, which lies on the edge of the forest, he found many people gathered together in the market place; for it had been promised that there would be a tightrope walker. And Zarathustra spoke thus to the people:

"*I teach you the overman.* Man is something that shall be overcome. What have you done to overcome him?

"All beings so far have created something beyond themselves; and do you want to be the ebb of this great flood and even go back to the beasts rather than overcome man? What is the ape to man? A laughingstock or a painful embarrassment. And man shall be just that for the overman: a laughingstock or a painful embarrassment. You have made your way from worm to man, and much in you is still worm. Once you were apes, and even now, too, man is more ape than any ape.

"Whoever is the wisest among you is also a mere conflict and cross between plant and ghost. But do I bid you become ghosts or plants?

"Behold, I teach you the overman. The overman is the meaning of the earth. Let your will say: the overman *shall be* the meaning of the earth! I beseech you, my brothers, *remain faithful to the earth,* and do not believe those who speak to you of otherworldly hopes! Poison-mixers are they, whether they know it or not. Despisers of life are they, decaying and poisoned themselves, of whom the earth is weary: so let them go.

"Once the sin against God was the greatest sin; but God died, and these sinners died with him. To sin against the earth is now the most dreadful thing, and to esteem the entrails of the unknowable higher than the meaning of the earth.

"Once the soul looked contemptuously upon the body, and then this contempt was the highest: she wanted the body meager, ghastly, and starved. Thus she hoped to escape it and the earth. Oh, this soul herself was still meager, ghastly, and starved: and cruelty was the lust of this soul. But you, too, my brothers, tell me: what does your body proclaim of your soul? Is not your soul poverty and filth and wretched contentment?

"Verily, a polluted stream is man. One must be a sea to be able to receive a polluted stream without becoming unclean. Behold, I teach you the overman: he is this sea; in him your great contempt can go under.

"What is the greatest experience you can have? It is the hour of the great contempt. The hour in which your happiness, too, arouses your disgust, and even your reason and your virtue.

"The hour when you say, 'What matters my happiness? It is poverty and filth and wretched contentment. But my happiness ought to justify existence itself.'

"The hour when you say, 'What matters my reason? Does it crave knowledge as the lion his food? It is poverty and filth and wretched contentment.'

"The hour when you say, 'What matters my virtue? As yet it has not made me rage. How weary I am of my good and my evil! All that is poverty and filth and wretched contentment.'

"The hour when you say, 'What matters my justice? I do not see that I am flames and fuel. But the just are flames and fuel.'

"The hour when you say, 'What matters my pity? Is not pity the cross on which he is nailed who loves man? But my pity is no crucifixion.'

"Have you yet spoken thus? Have you yet cried thus? Oh, that I might have heard you cry thus!

"Not your sin but your thrift cries to heaven; your meanness even in your sin cries to heaven.

"Where is the lightning to lick you with its tongue? Where is the frenzy with which you should be inoculated?

"Behold, I teach you the overman: he is this lightning, he is this frenzy."

When Zarathustra had spoken thus, one of the people cried: "Now we have heard enough about the tightrope walker; now let us see him too!" And all the people laughed at Zarathustra. But the tightrope walker, believing that the word concerned him, began his performance.

· · ·

### On Reading and Writing

Of all that is written I love only what a man has written with his blood. Write with blood, and you will experience that blood is spirit.

It is not easily possible to understand the blood of another: I hate reading idlers. Whoever knows the reader will henceforth do nothing for the reader. Another century of readers—and the spirit itself will stink.

That everyone may learn to read, in the long run corrupts not only writing but also thinking. Once the spirit was God, then he became man, and now he even becomes rabble.

Whoever writes in blood and aphorisms does not want to be read but to be learned by heart. In the mountains the shortest way is from peak to peak: but for that one must have long legs. Aphorisms should be peaks—and those who are addressed, tall and lofty. The air thin and pure, danger near, and the spirit full of gay sarcasm: these go well together. I want to have goblins around me, for I am courageous. Courage that puts ghosts to flight creates goblins for itself: courage wants to laugh.

I no longer feel as you do: this cloud which I see beneath me, this blackness and gravity at which I laugh—this is your thundercloud.

You look up when you feel the need for elevation. And I look down because I am elevated. Who among you can laugh and be elevated at the same time? Whoever climbs the highest mountains laughs at all tragic plays and tragic seriousness.

Brave, unconcerned, mocking, violent—thus wisdom wants us: she is a woman and always loves only a warrior.

You say to me, "Life is hard to bear." But why would you have your pride in the morning and your resignation in the evening? Life is hard to bear; but do not act so tenderly! We are all of us fair beasts of burden, male and female asses. What do we have in common with the rosebud, which trembles because a drop of dew lies on it?

True, we love life, not because we are used to living but because we are used to loving. There is always some madness in love. But there is also always some reason in madness.

And to me too, as I am well disposed toward life, butterflies and soap bubbles and whatever among men is of their kind seem to know most about happiness. Seeing these light, foolish, delicate, mobile little souls flutter—that seduces Zarathustra to tears and songs.

I would believe only in a god who could dance. And when I saw my devil I found him serious, thorough, profound, and solemn: it was the spirit of gravity—through him all things fall.

Not by wrath does one kill but by laughter. Come, let us kill the spirit of gravity!

I have learned to walk: ever since, I let myself run. I have learned to fly: ever since, I do not want to be pushed before moving along.

Now I am light, now I fly, now I see myself beneath myself, now a god dances through me.

Thus spoke Zarathustra.

---

# OSCAR WILDE

## from *The Picture of Dorian Gray*

### The Preface

---

The meteoric career of the Irish novelist, playwright, and poet Oscar Wilde (1845–1900) is without parallel in Western letters. In 1890, with the serialization of his novel *The Picture of Dorian Gray,* he was at the peak of his powers, the most popular writer in England and America; however, in 1895, though married and with children, he was tried and found guilty of homosexual acts and sentenced to two years in Reading Prison, which he later wrote about in the poem, *The Ballad of Reading Gaol.* In 1900, having exiled himself to France, he died penniless, abandoned by friends and family—a victim of his age's hypocrisy and puritanism. With the rise of more enlightened sexual attitudes, his name has been rescued from infamy; he is now celebrated as one of the great figures of his century, whose fame as a wit is legendary (Sample: "The most difficult pose in the world is to be natural"), and whose plays, such as *The Importance of Being Earnest* (1895), have become standards in the repertory of the English-speaking stage.

Wilde was the most visible member of the aesthetic movement that flourished in England during the waning years of the nineteenth century. Aestheticism describes the belief of an unorganized group of anti-establishment writers and artists who held to the principle of art for art's sake, rather than the moralistic goals which dominated late Victorian, mercantile culture. Against the prevailing materialism and vulgarity of the business classes, who held the arts in contempt, the aesthetes proposed the pursuit of the beautiful, even to the extent of making life itself into a work of art. Wilde seemed to personify this movement when, new to London in the 1880s, he sauntered down Picadilly (London's most fashionable street) dressed in a velvet suit and carrying a lily. With gusto, he played the role of an aesthete in society, but it was finally his literary genius that brought the world to his feet, however briefly.

## Reading the Selection

This selection—The Preface to *The Picture of Dorian Gray*—consists of a list of Wilde's epigrams (cleverly worded statements, making a pointed observation, and often concluding with a satirical thrust) and witticisms, expressive of his art for art's sake outlook, including his views on art, beauty, literature, and literary movements. He identifies the reading public with Caliban, the Savage in Shakespeare's *The Tempest* and thus a representation of misguided humanity.

There follows the novel, in which Wilde explores the art for art's sake philosophy, through the character of Dorian Gray, a handsome London man-about-town. Central to the plot is an artist's magical portrait of Gray, which, though safely out of sight, nevertheless ages, even gruesomely so, as it registers in its face all of the immoral acts of the hero; meanwhile, Gray, who is determined to experiment with forbidden pleasures, remains frozen in his timeless beauty. Gray's search for the unconventional is an updating of Goethe's *Faust*, for he betrays a woman who loves him and kills the artist who painted the portrait; at the novel's end, he mutilates the painting, and his youthful face suddenly turns "withered, wrinkled and loathesome." With the hindsight provided by the theories of Freud, *The Picture of Dorian Gray* may now be interpreted as a complex metaphor of Wilde's guilt over his secret sex life.

---

The artist is the creator of beautiful things.

To reveal art and conceal the artist is art's aim.

The critic is he who can translate into another manner or a new material his impression of beautiful things.

The highest, as the lowest, form of criticism is a mode of autobiography.

Those who find ugly meanings in beautiful things are corrupt without being charming. This is a fault.

Those who find beautiful meanings in beautiful things are the cultivated. For these there is hope.

They are the elect to whom beautiful things mean only Beauty.

There is no such thing as a moral or an immoral book. Books are well written, or badly written. That is all.

The nineteenth-century dislike of Realism is the rage of Caliban seeing his own face in a glass.

The nineteenth-century dislike of Romanticism is the rage of Caliban not seeing his own face in a glass.

The moral life of man forms part of the subject-matter of the artist, but the morality of art consists in the perfect use of an imperfect medium. No artist desires to prove anything. Even things that are true can be proved.

No artist has ethical sympathies. An ethical sympathy in an artist is an unpardonable mannerism of style.

No art is ever morbid. The artist can express everything.

Thought and language are to the artist instruments of an art.

Vice and virtue are to the artist materials for an art.

From the point of view of form, the type of all the arts is the art of the musician. From the point of view of feeling, the actor's craft is the type.

All art is at once surface and symbol.

Those who go beneath the surface do so at their peril.

Those who read the symbol do so at their peril.

It is the spectator, and not life, that art really mirrors.

Diversity of opinion about a work of art shows that the work is new, complex, and vital.

When critics disagree the artist is in accord with himself.

We can forgive a man for making a useful thing as long as he does not admire it. The only excuse for making a useless thing is that one admires it intensely.

All art is quite useless.

# KATE CHOPIN
## *The Story of an Hour*

Kate Chopin (born Catherine O'Flaherty, 1851–1904) was an important American writer around 1900, but she was neglected for most of this century. Famed as a local colorist, she wrote about Creole and Cajun life in Louisiana (in two collections of stories, *Bayou Folk* [1894] and *A Night in Acadie* [1897], and a novel, *At Fault* [1890]; it was a world she knew well from her twelve-year-long marriage to a Creole planter and merchant. Ultimately, she set in motion events that abruptly ended her literary career when she published *The Awakening* (1899), her masterpiece. A tale of adulterous passion, about a woman who awakens to find the man she loves is not her husband (inevitably called the American equivalent of Flaubert's *Madame Bovary*), this novel unleashed a firestorm of public criticism when it first appeared. Libraries across the nation banned it, and in her home town of St. Louis, the Fine Arts Club denied her membership, despite her obvious distinction. Sensitive to the cry raised against the novel, Chopin was stunned into silence and never wrote again. When she died, her name and works passed from memory until rediscovered in the sixties, prompted by the burgeoning feminist movement. Today her reputation has been restored to the literary pantheon, and she is regarded as a pioneer of Post-Modernism, with her keen interest in marginal people and feminist themes.

### Reading the Selection

Chopin's "The Story of an Hour" is, in actuality, little more than an anecdote. In the Middle Ages, it would have been a moral fable that delivered a religious message; in Chopin's hands, however, it became a story meant to surprise with its ironic twist at the end—a type of tale pioneered by the then popular writer, O. Henry (1862–1910), the pen name of William Sydney Porter. Chopin's story recounts the ironic fate of Louise Mallard, who secretly welcomes the news of her husband Brently's unexpected death in a railroad disaster; then she discovers that he is still very much alive, having "been far from the scene of the accident," at which point she falls down dead, the victim of "heart disease."

Chopin manages to make several points with this sad little tale. She has Louise condemn the institution of marriage, because it allows "men and women [to] believe that they have a right to impose a private will upon a fellow-creature." Indeed, Louise's initial joy, on hearing of Brently's death, is that she is finally free of him: "Free! Body and soul free!" Chopin also is a keen student of the world, for she has an exquisite grasp of the poignant disjuncture that the death of a loved one creates for a survivor—as in the way that Louise's grief is engulfed by the sounds of life ("a peddlar was crying his wares . . . some one was singing . . . sparrows were twittering"). Chopin also understands the human heart, as in her description of Louise's kaleidoscopic emotions: Paralyzed inability to understand gives way to weeping, to locking herself in her room, to listening to life in the square, to stifling a sob, and, ultimately, to accepting her true feelings.

What makes the story especially intriguing is that it has an autobiographical aspect, though to what degree is not clear. Chopin heard the news of her husband's unexpected death just as Louise did here; however, whereas Louise is "killed by joy," Chopin was left, at thirty-two years of age, with six children to support. One wonders if, given such a great material burden, Chopin's husband's death allowed her to "live for herself," Louise's wish.

Knowing that Mrs. Mallard was afflicted with a heart trouble, great care was taken to break to her as gently as possible the news of her husband's death.

It was her sister Josephine who told her, in broken sentences; veiled hints that revealed in half concealing. Her husband's friend Richards was there, too, near her. It was he who had been in the newspaper office when intelligence of the railroad disaster was received, with Brently Mallard's name leading the list of "killed." He had only taken the time to assure himself of its truth by a second telegram, and had hastened to forestall any less careful, less tender friend in bearing the sad message.

She did not hear the story as many women have heard the same, with a paralyzed inability to accept its significance. She wept at once, with sudden, wild abandonment, in her sister's arms. When the storm of grief had spent itself she went away to her room alone. She would have no one follow her.

There stood, facing the open window, a comfortable, roomy armchair. Into this she sank, pressed down by a physical exhaustion that haunted her body and seemed to reach into her soul.

She could see in the open square before her house the tops of trees that were all aquiver with the new spring life. The delicious breath of rain was in the air. In the street below a peddler was crying his wares. The notes of a distant song which some one was singing reached her faintly, and countless sparrows were twittering in the eaves.

There were patches of blue sky showing here and there through the clouds that had met and piled one above the other in the west facing her window.

She sat with her head thrown back upon the cushion of the chair, quite motionless, except when a sob came up into her throat and shook her, as a child who has cried itself to sleep continues to sob in its dreams.

She was young, with a fair, calm face, whose lines bespoke repression and even a certain strength. But now there was a dull stare in her eyes, whose gaze was fixed away off yonder on one of those patches of blue sky. It was not a glance of reflection, but rather indicated a suspension of intelligent thought.

There was something coming to her and she was waiting for it, fearfully. What was it? She did not know; it was too subtle and elusive to name. But she felt it, creeping out of the sky, reaching toward her through the sounds, the scents, the color that filled the air.

Now her bosom rose and fell tumultuously. She was beginning to recognize this thing that was approaching to possess her, and she was striving to beat it back with her will—as powerless as her two white slender hands would have been.

When she abandoned herself a little whispered word escaped her slightly parted lips. She said it over and over under her breath: "free, free, free!" The vacant stare and the look of terror that had followed it went from her eyes. They stayed keen and bright. Her pulses beat fast, and the coursing blood warmed and relaxed every inch of her body.

She did not stop to ask if it were or were not a monstrous joy that held her. A clear and exalted perception enabled her to dismiss the suggestion as trivial.

She knew that she would weep again when she saw the kind, tender hands folded in death; the face that had never looked save with love upon her, fixed and gray and dead. But she saw beyond that bitter moment a long procession of years to come that would belong to her absolutely. And she opened and spread her arms out to them in welcome.

There would be no one to live for her during those coming years; she would live for herself. There would be no powerful will bending hers in that blind persistence with which men and women believe they have a right to impose a private will upon a fellow-creature. A kind intention or a cruel intention made the act seem no less a crime as she looked upon it in that brief moment of illumination.

And yet she had loved him—sometimes. Often she had not. What did it matter! What could love, the unsolved mystery, count for in face of this possession of self-assertion which she suddenly recognized as the strongest impulse of her being!

"Free! Body and soul free!" she kept whispering.

Josephine was kneeling before the closed door with her lips to the keyhole, imploring for admission. "Louise, open the door! I beg; open the door—you will make yourself ill. What are you doing, Louise? For heaven's sake open the door."

"Go away. I am not making myself ill." No; she was drinking in a very elixir of life through that open window.

Her fancy was running riot along those days ahead of her. Spring days, and summer days, and all sorts of days that would be her own. She breathed a quick prayer that life might be long. It was only yesterday she had thought with a shudder that life might be long.

She arose at length and opened the door to her sister's importunities. There was a feverish triumph in her eyes, and she carried herself unwittingly like a goddess of Victory. She clasped her sister's waist, and together they descended the stairs. Richards stood waiting for them at the bottom.

Some one was opening the front door with a latchkey. It was Brently Mallard who entered, a little travel-stained, composedly carrying his gripsack and umbrella. He had been far from the scene of accident, and did not even know there had been one. He stood amazed at Josephine's piercing cry; at Richards' quick motion to screen him from the view of his wife.

But Richards was too late.

When the doctors came they said she had died of heart disease—of joy that kills.

# FRANZ KAFKA
# from *The Metamorphosis*
## I

The Austrian Franz Kafka (1883–1924) is generally described as one of the founders of Modernist fiction, but scholars are divided over the meaning of his life for twentieth-century culture.

One school of thought labels Kafka a prophet of modern life and emphasizes his triple alienation, as a German-speaking Jew from the Czech-speaking and Protestant section of largely Roman Catholic Austria. This school further claims that Kafka, a deeply self-aware writer, used his own plight to create literary heroes—each a modern Everyman often named "K."—who was a victim of forces beyond his control. Thus, in this view, Kafka's works may be interpreted variously, as existentialist parables about meaning in a godless age, or as religious allegories about the retreat of the divine in modern times, or as satires on modern bureaucracy and its oppression of the individual (Kafka was a lifelong civil servant).

Downplaying Kafka as a prophet, another school of thought stresses the autobiographical in his works. Impressed by the soul-searching revealed in his *Diaries* (2 vols., 1948–1949), this school claims that Kafka was tormented by his Oedipal situation: Kafka, the frail, sensitive, and intellectual son, was dominated by his physically fit, no-nonsense, businessman father. Indeed, Kafka once asserted that all his works were about his father. Thus, in this view, Kafka was always writing about his own condition.

As usual, the true meaning of Kafka probably lies between the two rival views, part visionary, part anguished son. Whatever the view, his works inspired the term *Kafkaesque*, a self-absorbed style marked by feelings of guilt and paranoid helplessness.

Despite present fame, Kafka in his own day doubted the worth of his literary efforts. When *Metamorphosis and Other Stories* (1915) and *The Penal Colony* (1919) met with little critical acclaim, he planned to have the rest of his work destroyed at his death. His literary executor frustrated this wish and (happily) arranged for these remaining works to be published: *The Trial* (1925), *The Castle* (1926), and *Amerika* (1927)—all classics of Modernist literature.

## Reading the Selection

"When Gregor Samsa woke up one morning from unsettling dreams, he found himself changed in his bed into a monstrous vermin [cockroach]." Kafka's opening line from *Metamorphosis* helped change Modernist literature, opening it to the theme of transformation, as in Philip Roth's *The Breast* (the hero is changed into a human breast); and, in general, Kafka enabled fiction to go beyond Realism and Naturalism. Probably inspired by Ovid's *Metamorphoses*, Kafka's story was unlike anything in Ovid's work. While Ovid concentrated on external effects, Kafka wrote from the inside, detailing the hero's feelings and reactions as he adapted to his changed form.

Interpretation of the symbolic story of Gregor Samsa, who is clearly Kafka's alter ego, leads to two different directions. On the one hand, Samsa's change into a cockroach is a sign of Kafka's inferiority toward his oppressive father; it is seen clearly by Samsa's father's forcing his cockroach-son back into the closed room—a concrete sign of Oedipal struggle as set forth by Freud, whose ideas were still new when Kafka wrote. On the other hand, Samsa's alienation, feeling cut off from human society, corresponds with the then current theory of Max Weber regarding the dehumanizing impact of bureaucratization on society.

When Gregor Samsa woke up one morning from unsettling dreams, he found himself changed in his bed into a monstrous vermin. He was lying on his back as hard as armor plate, and when he lifted his head a little, he saw his vaulted brown belly, sectioned by arch-shaped ribs, to whose dome the cover, about to slide off completely, could barely cling. His many legs, pitifully thin compared with the size of the rest of him, were waving helplessly before his eyes.

"What's happened to me?" he thought. It was no dream. His room, a regular human room, only a little on the small side lay quiet between the four familiar walls. Over the table, on which an unpacked line of fabric samples was all spread out—Samsa was a traveling salesman—hung the picture which he had recently cut out of a glossy magazine and lodged in a pretty gilt frame. It showed a lady done up in a fur hat and a fur boa, sitting upright and raising up against the viewer a heavy fur muff in which her whole forearm had disappeared.

Gregor's eyes then turned to the window, and the overcast weather—he could hear raindrops hitting against the metal window ledge—completely depressed him. "How about going back to sleep for a few minutes and forgetting all this nonsense," he thought, but that was completely impracticable, since he was used to sleeping on his right side and in his present state could not get into that position. No matter how hard he threw himself onto his right side, he always rocked onto his back again. He must have tried it a hundred times, closing his eyes so as not to have to see his squirming legs, and stopped only when he began to feel a slight, dull pain in his side, which he had never felt before.

"Oh God," he thought, "what a grueling job I've picked! Day in, day out—on the road. The upset of doing business is much worse than the actual business in the home office, and, besides, I've got the torture of traveling, worrying about changing trains, eating miserable food at all hours, constantly seeing new faces, no relationships that last or get more intimate. To the devil with it all!" He felt a slight itching up on top of his belly; shoved himself slowly on his back closer to the bedpost, so as to be able to lift his head better; found the itchy spot, studded with small white dots which he had no idea what to make of; and wanted to touch the spot with one of his legs but immediately pulled it back, for the contact sent a cold shiver through him.

He slid back again into his original position. "This getting up so early," he thought, "makes anyone a complete idiot. Human beings have to have their sleep. Other traveling salesmen live like harem women. For instance, when I go back to the hotel before lunch to write up the business I've done, these gentlemen are just having breakfast. That's all I'd have to try with my boss; I'd be fired on the spot. Anyway, who knows if that wouldn't be a very good thing for me. If I didn't hold back for my parents' sake, I would have quit long ago, I would have marched up to the boss and spoken my piece from the bottom of my heart. He would have fallen off the desk! It is funny, too, the way he sits on the desk and talks down from the heights to the employees, especially when they have to come right up close on account of the boss's being hard of hearing. Well, I haven't given up hope completely; once I've gotten the money together to pay off my parents' debt to him—that will probably take another five or six years—I'm going to do it without fail. Then I'm going to make the big break. But for the time being I'd better get up, since my train leaves at five."

And he looked over at the alarm clock, which was ticking on the chest of drawers. "God Almighty!" he thought. It was six-thirty, the hands were quietly moving forward, it was actually past the half-hour, it was already nearly a quarter to. Could it be that the alarm hadn't gone off? You could see from the bed that it was set correctly for four o'clock; it certainly had gone off, too. Yes, but was it possible to sleep quietly through a ringing that made the furniture shake? Well, he certainly hadn't slept quietly, but probably all the more soundly for that. But what should he do now? The next train left at seven o'clock; to make it, he would have to hurry like a madman, and the line of samples wasn't packed yet, and he himself didn't feel especially fresh and ready to march around. And even if he did make the train, he could not avoid getting it from the boss, because the messenger boy had been waiting at the five-o'clock train and would have long ago reported his not showing up. He was a tool of the boss, without brains or backbone. What if he were to say he was sick? But that would be extremely embarrassing and suspicious because during his five years with the firm Gregor had not been sick even once. The boss would be sure to come with the health-insurance doctor, blame his parents for their lazy son, and cut off all excuses by quoting the health-insurance doctor, for whom the world consisted of people who were completely healthy but afraid to work. And, besides, in this case would he be so very wrong? In fact, Gregor felt fine, with the exception of his drowsiness, which was really unnecessary after sleeping so late, and he even had a ravenous appetite.

Just as he was thinking all this over at top speed, without being able to decide to get out of bed—the alarm clock had just struck a quarter to seven—he heard a cautious knocking at the door next to the head of his bed. "Gregor," someone called—it was his mother—"it's a quarter to seven. Didn't you want to catch the train?" What a soft voice! Gregor was shocked to hear his own voice answering, unmistakably his own voice, true, but in which, as if from below, an insistent distressed chirping intruded, which left the clarity of his words intact only for a moment really, before so badly garbling them as they carried that no one could be sure if he had heard right. Gregor had wanted to answer in detail and to explain everything, but, given the circumstances, confined himself to saying, "Yes, yes, thanks, Mother, I'm just getting up." The wooden door must have prevented the change in Gregor's voice from being noticed outside, because his mother was satisfied with this explanation and shuffled off. But their little exchange had made the rest of the family aware that, contrary to expectations, Gregor was still in the house, and already his father was knocking on one of the side doors, feebly but with his fist. "Gregor, Gregor," he called, "what's going on?" And after a little while he called again in a deeper, warning voice, "Gregor! Gregor!" At the other side door, however, his sister moaned gently, "Gregor? Is something the matter with you? Do you want anything?" Toward both sides Gregor answered: "I'm all ready," and made an effort, by meticulous pronunciation and by inserting long pauses between individual words, to eliminate everything from his voice that might betray him. His father went back to his breakfast, but his sister whispered, "Gregor, open up, I'm pleading with you." But Gregor had absolutely no intention of opening the door and complimented himself instead on the precaution he had adopted from his business trips, of locking all the doors during the night even at home.

First of all he wanted to get up quietly, without any excitement; get dressed; and, the main thing, have breakfast, and only then think about what to do next, for he saw clearly that in bed he would never think things through to a rational conclusion. He remembered how even in the past he had often felt some kind of slight pain, possibly caused by lying in an uncomfortable position, which, when he got up, turned out to be purely imaginary, and he was eager to see how today's fantasy would gradually fade away. That the change in his voice was nothing more than the first sign of a bad cold, an occupational ailment of the traveling salesman, he had no doubt in the least.

It was very easy to throw off the cover; all he had to do was puff himself up a little, and it fell off by itself. But after this, things got difficult, especially since he was so unusually broad. He would have needed hands and arms to lift himself up, but instead of that he had only his numerous little legs, which were in every different kind of perpetual motion and which, besides, he could not control. If he wanted to bend one, the first thing that happened was that it stretched itself out; and if he finally succeeded in getting this leg to do what he wanted, all the others in the meantime, as if set free, began to work in the most intensely painful agitation. "Just don't stay in bed being useless," Gregor said to himself.

First he tried to get out of bed with the lower part of his body, but this lower part—which by the way he had not seen yet and which he could not form a clear picture of—proved too difficult to budge; it was taking so long; and when finally, almost out of his mind, he lunged forward with all his force, without caring, he had picked the wrong direction and slammed himself violently against the lower bedpost, and the searing pain he felt taught him that exactly the lower part of his body was, for the moment anyway, the most sensitive.

He therefore tried to get the upper part of his body out of bed first and warily turned his head toward the edge of the bed. This worked easily, and in spite of its width and weight, the mass of his body finally followed, slowly, the movement of his head. But when at last he stuck his head over the edge of the bed into the air, he got too scared to continue any further, since if he finally let himself fall in this position, it would be a miracle if he didn't injure his head. And just now he had better not for the life of him lose consciousness; he would rather stay in bed.

But when, once again, after the same exertion, he lay in his original position, sighing, and again watched his little legs struggling, if possible more fiercely, with each other and saw no way of bringing peace and order into this mindless motion, he again told himself that it was impossible for him to stay in bed and that the most rational thing was to make any sacrifice for even the smallest hope of freeing himself from the bed. But at the same time he did not forget to remind himself occasionally that thinking things over calmly—indeed, as calmly as possible—was much better than jumping to desperate decisions. At such moments he fixed his eyes as sharply as possible on the window, but unfortunately there was little confidence and cheer to be gotten from the view of the morning fog, which shrouded even the other side of the narrow street. "Seven o'clock already," he said to himself as the alarm clock struck again, "seven o'clock already and still such a fog." And for a little while he lay quietly, breathing shallowly, as if expecting, perhaps, from the complete silence the return of things to the way they really and naturally were.

But then he said to himself, "Before it strikes a quarter past seven, I must be completely out of bed without fail. Anyway, by that time someone from the firm will be here to find out where I am, since the office opens before seven." And now he started rocking the complete length of his body out of the bed with a smooth rhythm. If he let himself topple out of bed in this way, his head, which on falling he planned to lift up sharply, would presumably remain unharmed. His back seemed to be hard; nothing was likely to happen to it when it fell onto the carpet. His biggest misgiving came from his concern about the loud crash that was bound to occur and would probably create, if not terror, at least anxiety behind all the doors. But that would have to be risked.

When Gregor's body already projected halfway out of bed—the new method was more of a game than a struggle, he only had to keep on rocking and jerking himself along—he thought how simple everything would be if he could get some help. Two strong persons—he thought of his father and the maid—would have been completely sufficient; they would have had to shove their arms under his arched back, in this way scoop him off the bed, bend down with their burden, and then just be careful and patient while he managed to swing himself down onto the floor, where his little legs would hopefully acquire some purpose. Well, leaving out the fact that the doors were locked, should he really call for help? In spite of all his miseries, he could not repress a smile at this thought.

He was already so far along that when he rocked more strongly he could hardly keep his balance, and very soon he would have to commit himself, because in five minutes it would be a quarter past seven—when the doorbell rang. "It's someone from the firm," he said to himself and almost froze, while his little legs only danced more quickly. For a moment everything remained quiet. "They're not going to answer," Gregor said to himself, captivated by some senseless hope. But then, of course, the maid went to the door as usual with her firm stride and opened up. Gregor only had to hear the visitor's first word of greeting to know who it was—the office manager himself. Why was only Gregor condemned to work for a firm where at the slightest omission they immediately suspected the worst? Were all employees louts without exception, wasn't there a single loyal, dedicated worker among them who, when he had not fully utilized a few hours of the morning for the firm, was driven half-mad by pangs of conscience and was actually unable to get out of bed? Really, wouldn't it have been enough to send one of the apprentices to find out—if this prying were absolutely necessary—did the manager himself have to come, and did the whole innocent family have to be shown in this way that the investigation of this suspicious affair could be entrusted only to the intellect of the manager? And more as a result of the excitement produced in Gregor by these thoughts than as a result of any real decision, he swung himself out of bed with all his might. There was a loud thump, but it was not a real crash. The fall was broken a little by the carpet, and Gregor's back was more elastic than he had thought, which explained the not very noticeable muffled sound. Only he had not held his head carefully enough and hit it; he turned it and rubbed it on the carpet in anger and pain.

"Something fell in there," said the manager in the room on the left. Gregor tried to imagine whether something like what had happened to him today could one day happen even to the manager; you really had to grant the possibility. But, as if in rude reply to this question, the manager took a few decisive steps in the next room and made his patent leather boots creak. From the room on the right his sister whispered, to inform Gregor, "Gregor, the manager is here." "I know," Gregor said to himself; but he did not dare raise his voice enough for his sister to hear.

"Gregor," his father now said from the room on the left, "the manager has come and wants to be informed why you didn't catch the early train. We don't know what we should say to him. Besides, he wants to speak to you personally. So please open the door. He will certainly be so kind as to excuse the disorder of the room." "Good morning, Mr. Samsa," the manager called in a friendly voice. "There's something the matter with him," his mother said to the manager while his father was still at the door, talking. "Believe me, sir, there's something the matter with him. Otherwise how would Gregor have missed a train? That boy has nothing on his mind but the business. It's almost begun to rile me that he never goes out nights. He's been back in the city for eight days now, but every night he's been home. He sits there with us at the table, quietly reading the paper or studying timetables. It's already a distraction for him when he's busy working with his fretsaw. For instance, in the span of two or three evenings he carved a little frame. You'll be amazed how pretty it is; it's hanging inside his room. You'll see it right away when Gregor opens the door. You know, I'm glad that you've come, sir. We would never have gotten Gregor to open the door by ourselves; he's so stubborn. And there's certainly something wrong with him, even though he said this morning there wasn't." "I'm coming right away," said Gregor slowly and deliberately, not moving in order not to miss a word of the conversation. "I haven't any other explanation myself," said the manager. "I hope it's nothing serious. On the other hand, I must say that we businessmen—fortunately or unfortunately, whichever you prefer—very often simply have to overcome a slight indisposition for business reasons." "So can the manager come in now?" asked his father, impatient, and knocked on the door again. "No," said Gregor. In the room on the left there was an embarrassing silence; in the room on the right his sister began to sob.

Why didn't his sister go in to the others? She had probably just got out of bed and not even started to get dressed. Then what was she crying about? Because he didn't get up and didn't let the manager in, because he was in danger of losing his job, and because then the boss would start hounding his parents about the old debts? For the time being, certainly, her worries were unnecessary. Gregor was still here and hadn't the slightest intention of letting the family down. True, at the moment he was lying on the carpet, and no one knowing his condition could seriously have expected him to let the manager in. But just because of this slight discourtesy, for which an appropriate excuse would easily be found later on, Gregor could not simply be dismissed. And to Gregor it seemed much more sensible to leave him alone now than to bother him with crying and persuasion. But it was just the uncertainty that was tormenting the others and excused their behavior.

"Mr. Samsa," the manager now called, raising his voice, "what's the matter? You barricade yourself in your room, answer only 'yes' and 'no,' cause your parents serious, unnecessary worry, and you neglect—I mention this only in passing—your duties to the firm in a really shocking manner. I am speaking here in the name of your parents and of your employer and ask you in all seriousness for an immediate, clear explanation. I'm amazed, amazed. I thought I knew you to be a quiet, reasonable person, and now you suddenly seem to want to start strutting about, flaunting strange whims. The head of the firm did suggest to me this morning a possible explanation for your tardiness—it concerned the cash payments recently entrusted to you—but really, I practically gave my word of honor that this explanation could not be right. But now, seeing your incomprehensible obstinacy, I am about to lose even the slightest desire to stick up for you in any way at all. And your job is not the most secure. Originally I intended to tell you all this in private, but since you make me waste my time here for nothing, I don't see why your parents shouldn't hear too. Your performance of late has been very unsatisfactory; I know it is not the best season for doing business, we all recognize that; but a season for not doing any business, there is no such thing, Mr. Samsa, such a thing cannot be tolerated."

"But, sir," cried Gregor, beside himself, in his excitement forgetting everything else, "I'm just opening up, in a minute. A slight indisposition, a dizzy spell, prevented me from getting up. I'm still in bed. But I already feel fine again. I'm just getting out of bed. Just be patient for a minute! I'm not as well as I thought yet. But really I'm fine. How something like this could just take a person by surprise! Only last night I was fine, my parents can tell you, or wait, last night I already had a slight premonition. They must have been able to tell by looking at me. Why didn't I report it to the office! But you always think that you'll get over a sickness without staying home. Sir! Spare my parents! There's no basis for any of the accusations that you're making against me now; no one has ever said a word to me about them. Perhaps you haven't seen the last orders I sent in. Anyway, I'm still going on the road with the eight o'clock train; these few hours of rest have done me good. Don't let me keep you, sir. I'll be at the office myself right away, and be so kind as to tell them this, and give my respects to the head of the firm."

And while Gregor hastily blurted all this out, hardly knowing what he was saying, he had easily approached the chest of drawers, probably as a result of the practice he had already gotten in bed, and now he tried to raise himself up against it. He actually intended to open the door, actually present himself and speak to the manager; he was eager to find out what the others, who were now so anxious to see him, would say at the sight of him. If they were shocked, then Gregor had no further responsibility and could be calm. But if they took everything calmly, then he, too, had no reason to get excited and could, if he hurried, actually be at the station by eight o'clock. At first he slid off the polished chest of drawers a few times, but at last, giving himself a final push, he stood upright; he no longer paid any attention to the pains in his abdomen, no matter how much they were burning. Now he let himself fall against the back of a nearby chair, clinging to its slats with his little legs. But by doing this he had gotten control of himself and fell silent, since he could now listen to what the manager was saying.

"Did you understand a word?" the manager was asking his parents. "He isn't trying to make fools of us, is he?" "My God," cried his mother, already in tears, "maybe he's seriously ill, and here we are, torturing him. Grete! Grete!" she then cried. "Mother?" called his sister from the other side. They communicated by way of Gregor's room. "Go to the doctor's immediately. Gregor is sick. Hurry, get the doctor. Did you just hear Gregor talking?" "That was the voice of an animal," said the manager, in a tone conspicuously soft compared with the mother's yelling. "Anna!" "Anna!" the father called through the foyer into the kitchen, clapping his hands, "get a locksmith right away!" And already the two girls were running with rustling skirts through the foyer—how could his sister have gotten dressed so quickly?—and tearing open the door to the apartment. The door could not be heard slamming; they had probably left it open, as is the custom in homes where a great misfortune has occurred.

But Gregor had become much calmer. It was true that they no longer understood his words, though they had seemed clear enough to him, clearer than before, probably because his ear had grown accustomed to them. But still, the others now believed that there was something the matter with him and were ready to help him. The assurance and confidence with which the first measures had been taken did him good. He felt integrated into human society once again and hoped for marvelous, amazing feats from both the doctor and the locksmith, without really distinguishing sharply between them. In order to make his voice as clear as possible for the crucial discussions that were approaching, he cleared his throat a little—taking pains, of course, to do so in a very muffled manner, since this noise, too, might sound different from human coughing, a thing he no longer trusted himself to decide. In the next room, meanwhile, everything had become completely still. Perhaps his parents were sitting at the table with the manager, whispering; perhaps they were all leaning against the door and listening.

Gregor slowly lugged himself toward the door, pushing the chair in front of him, then let go of it, threw himself against the door, held himself upright against it—the pads on the bottom of his little legs exuded a little sticky substance—and for a moment rested there from the exertion. But then he got started turning the key in the lock with his mouth. Unfortunately it seemed that he had no real teeth—what was he supposed to grip the key with?—but in compensation his jaws, of course, were very strong; with their help he actually got the key moving and paid no attention to the fact that he was undoubtedly hurting himself in some way, for a brown liquid came out of his mouth, flowed over the key, and dripped onto the floor. "Listen," said the manager in the next room, "he's turning the key." This was great encouragement to Gregor; but everyone should have cheered him on, his father and mother too. "Go, Gregor," they should have called "keep going, at that lock, harder, harder!" And in the delusion that they were all following his efforts with suspense, he clamped his jaws madly on the key with all the strength he could muster. Depending on the progress of the key, he danced around the lock; holding himself upright only by his mouth, he clung to the key, as the situation demanded, or pressed it down again with the whole weight of his body. The clearer click of the lock as it finally snapped back literally woke Gregor up. With a sigh of relief he said to himself, "So I didn't need the locksmith after all," and laid his head down on the handle in order to open wide [one wing of the double doors.]

Since he had to use this method of opening the door, it was really opened very wide while he himself was still invisible. He first had to edge slowly around the one wing of the door, and do so very carefully if he was not to fall flat on his back just before entering. He was still busy with this difficult maneuver and had no time to pay attention to anything else when he heard the manager burst out with a loud "Oh!"—it sounded like a rush of wind—and now he could see him, standing closest to the door, his hand pressed over his open mouth, slowly backing away, as if repulsed by an invisible, unrelenting force. His mother—in spite of the manager's presence she stood with her hair still unbraided from the night, sticking out in all directions—first looked at his father with her hands clasped, then took two steps toward Gregor, and sank down in the midst of her skirts spreading out around her, her face completely hidden on her breast. With a hostile expression his father clenched his fist, as if to drive Gregor back into his room, then looked uncertainly around the living room, shielded his eyes with his hands, and sobbed with heaves of his powerful chest.

Now Gregor did not enter the room after all but leaned against the inside of the firmly bolted wing of the door, so that only half his body was visible and his head above it, cocked to one side and peeping out at the others. In the meantime it had grown much lighter; across the street one could see clearly a section of the endless, grayish-black building opposite—it was a hospital—with its regular windows starkly piercing the façade; the rain was still coming down, but only in large, separately visible drops that were also pelting the ground literally one at a time. The breakfast dishes were laid out lavishly on the table, since for his father breakfast was the most important meal of the day, which he would prolong for hours while reading various newspapers. On the wall directly opposite hung a photograph of Gregor from his army days, in a lieutenant's uniform, his hand on his sword, a carefree smile on his lips, demanding respect for his bearing and his rank. The door to the foyer was open, and since the front door was open too, it was possible to see out onto the landing and the top of the stairs going down.

"Well," said Gregor—and he was thoroughly aware of being the only one who had kept calm—"I'll get dressed right away, pack up my samples, and go. Will you, will you please let me go? Now, sir, you see, I'm not stubborn and I'm willing to work; traveling is a hardship, but without it I couldn't live. Where are you going, sir? To the office? Yes? Will you give an honest report of everything? A man might find for a moment that he was unable to work, but that's exactly the right time to remember his past accomplishments and to consider that later on, when the obstacle has been removed, he's bound to work all the harder and more efficiently. I'm under so many obligations to the head of the firm, as you know very well. Besides, I also have my parents and my sister to worry about. I'm in a tight spot, but I'll also work my way out again. Don't make things harder for me than they already are. Stick up for me in the office, please. Traveling salesmen aren't well liked there, I know. People think they make a fortune leading the gay life. No one has any particular reason to rectify this prejudice. But you, sir, you have a better perspective on things than the rest of the office, an even better perspective, just between the two of us, than the head of the firm himself, who in his capacity as owner easily lets his judgment be swayed against an employee. And you also know very well that the traveling salesman, who is out of the office practically the whole year round, can so easily become the victim of gossip, coincidences, and unfounded accusations, against which he's completely unable to defend himself, since in most cases he knows nothing at all about them except when he returns exhausted from a trip, and back home gets to suffer on his own person the grim consequences, which can no longer be traced back to their causes. Sir, don't go away without a word to tell me you think I'm at least partly right!"

But at Gregor's first words the manager had already turned away and with curled lips looked back at Gregor only over his twitching shoulder. And during Gregor's speech he did not stand still for a minute but, without letting Gregor out of his sight, backed toward the door, yet very gradually, as if there were some secret prohibition against leaving the room. He was already in the foyer, and from the sudden movement with which he took his last step from the living room, one might have thought he had just burned the sole of his foot. In the foyer, however, he stretched his right hand far out toward the staircase, as if nothing less than an unearthly deliverance were awaiting him there.

Gregor realized that he must on no account let the manager go away in this mood if his position in the firm were not to be jeopardized in the extreme. His parents did not understand this too well; in the course of the years they had formed the conviction that Gregor was set for life in this firm; and furthermore, they were so preoccupied with their immediate troubles that they had lost all consideration for the future. But Gregor had this forethought. The manager must be detained, calmed down, convinced, and finally won over; Gregor's and the family's future depended on it! If only his sister had been there! She was perceptive; she had already begun to cry when Gregor was still lying calmly on his back. And certainly the manager, this ladies' man, would have listened to her; she would have shut the front door and in the foyer talked him out of his scare. But his sister was not there, Gregor had to handle the situation himself. And without stopping to realize that he had no idea what his new faculties of movement were, and without stopping to realize

either that his speech had possibly—indeed, probably—not been understood again, he let go of the wing of the door; he shoved himself through the opening, intending to go to the manager, who was already on the landing, ridiculously holding onto the banisters with both hands; but groping for support, Gregor immediately fell down with a little cry onto his numerous little legs. This had hardly happened when for the first time that morning he had a feeling of physical well-being; his little legs were on firm ground; they obeyed him completely, as he noted to his joy; they even strained to carry him away wherever he wanted to go; and he already believed that final recovery from all his sufferings was imminent. But at that very moment, as he lay on the floor rocking with repressed motion, not far from his mother and just opposite her, she, who had seemed so completely self-absorbed, all at once jumped up, her arms stretched wide, her fingers spread, and cried, "Help, for God's sake, help!" held her head bent as if to see Gregor better, but inconsistently darted madly backward instead; had forgotten that the table laden with the breakfast dishes stood behind her; sat down on it hastily, as if her thoughts were elsewhere, when she reached it; and did not seem to notice at all that near her the big coffeepot had been knocked over and coffee was pouring in a steady stream onto the rug.

"Mother, Mother," said Gregor softly and looked up at her. For a minute the manager had completely slipped his mind; on the other hand at the sight of the spilling coffee he could not resist snapping his jaws several times in the air. At this his mother screamed once more, fled from the table, and fell into the arms of his father, who came rushing up to her. But Gregory had no time now for his parents; the manager was already on the stairs; with his chin on the banister, he was taking a last look back. Gregor was off to a running start, to be as sure as possible of catching up with him; the manager must have suspected something like this, for he leaped down several steps and disappeared; but still he shouted "Agh," and the sound carried through the whole staircase. Unfortunately the manager's flight now seemed to confuse his father completely, who had been relatively calm until now, for instead of running after the manager himself, or at least not hindering Gregor in his pursuit, he seized in his right hand the manager's cane, which had been left behind on a chair with his hat and overcoat, picked up in his left hand a heavy newspaper from the table, and stamping his feet, started brandishing the cane and the newspaper to drive Gregor back into his room. No plea of Gregor's helped, no plea was even understood; however humbly he might turn his head, his father merely stamped his feet more forcefully. Across the room his mother had thrown open a window in spite of the cool weather, and leaning out, she buried her face, far outside the window, in her hands. Between the alley and the staircase a strong draft was created, the window curtains blew in, the newspapers on the table rustled, single sheets fluttered across the floor. Pitilessly his father came on, hissing like a wild man. Now Gregor had not had any practice at all walking in reverse, it was really very slow going. If Gregor had only been allowed to turn around, he could have gotten into his room right away, but he was afraid to make his father impatient by this time-consuming gyration, and at any minute the cane in his father's hand threatened to come down on his back or his head with a deadly blow. Finally, however, Gregor had no choice, for he noticed with horror that in reverse he could not keep going in one direction; and so, incessantly throwing uneasy side-glances at his father, he began to turn around as quickly as possible, in reality turning only very slowly. Perhaps his father realized his good intentions, for he did not interfere with him; instead, he even now and then directed the maneuver from afar with the tip of his cane. If only his father did not keep making this intolerable hissing sound! It made Gregor lose his head completely. He had almost finished the turn when—his mind continually on this hissing—he made a mistake and even started turning back around to his original position. But when he had at last successfully managed to get his head in front of the opened door, it turned out that his body was too broad to get through as it was. Of course in his father's present state of mind it did not even remotely occur to him to open the other wing of the door in order to give Gregor enough room to pass

through. He had only the fixed idea that Gregor must return to his room as quickly as possible. He would never have allowed the complicated preliminaries Gregor needed to go through in order to stand up on one end and perhaps in this way fit through the door. Instead he drove Gregor on, as if there were no obstacle, with exceptional loudness; the voice behind Gregor did not sound like that of only a single father; now this was really no joke any more, and Gregor forced himself—come what may—into the doorway. One side of his body rose up, he lay lop-sided in the opening, one of his flanks was scraped raw, ugly blotches marred the white door, soon he got stuck and could not have budged any more by himself, his little legs on one side dangled tremblingly in midair, those on the other were painfully crushed against the floor—when from behind his father gave him a hard shove, which was truly his salvation, and bleeding profusely, he flew far into his room. The door was slammed shut with the cane, then at last everything was quiet.

# SIGMUND FREUD

## from *Civilization and Its Discontents*

### III

The Austrian physician and psychologist Sigmund Freud (1856–1939), like the English biologist Darwin, was a pioneer of twentieth-century thinking. Indeed, it may be said that Freud began where Darwin (see *The Descent of Man*) left off. Darwin claimed that life was not the result of a divine plan, set up at the dawn of time by a benevolent God; rather it was the outcome of millennia of purposeless and random changes, in an endless competition of survival of the fittest, so that the one thing which remains true for the human enterprise is the constancy of struggle. From this starting point, Freud argued that endless struggle, both within each individual and between the individual and society, is the basic nature of the human condition.

The founder of psychoanalysis—that is, the probing of the mind through the "free association" of ideas buried in it—Freud was one of the first to map out the subconscious, as he sought to prove that each person's self is a battle zone. The results of this probing into depth psychology led him to conclude that below the surface of human consciousness (ego) lurks a set of innate drives (id); the id is mainly sexual and aggressive, engaged in a continual war with the individual's socially acquired standards of right and wrong, called conscience (superego). Whether the ego can successfully negotiate the continual conflict between the id and the superego has dramatic meaning, resulting in either happiness or self-destructive behavior. With this reasoning, Freud insisted on the primacy of the unconscious mind in helping to shape the self and thereby laid to rest the psychology of Locke, which had claimed that human consciousness is molded exclusively by the environment.

Near the end of his life as he was suffering from cancer of the mouth, Freud wrote *Civilization and Its Discontents* (1929), in which he applied his new insights to the field of history. Written in the shadow of the rise of totalitarian states, of both the right and the left, across Europe, and perhaps tinged with a sense of his own impending death, this book offers a gloomy philosophy of history; Freud argues that humanity collectively is locked in a never-ending conflict between the aggressive drives of the collective id (Thanatos, the death instinct) and the sexual drives (Eros, the pleasure principle)—a macrocosmic version of the private war inside each person. The book ends with a question added in 1931 when the menace of the Nazi leader Hitler was becoming apparent; it is expressive of his ambiguous hopes—"Who can foresee [the] result?"

## Reading the Selection

This selection, taken from section III of *Civilization and Its Discontents,* demonstrates why Freud is called a prophet of Modernism, the anti-traditional movement which flourished between 1870 and 1970. In this section, he reasons that the eighteenth-century Enlightenment was wrong in its belief that human happiness is the goal of history. He instead tries to prove that happiness is fleeting (the "discontent" of the title of this book), perhaps only a dream to be pursued, but never fully achievable. To him, misery and suffering are encoded into each person, because of the unresolvable conflict between private sexual drives and the demands of civilization for cooperation. At best, he holds out hope for various strategies for coping with unhappiness, most notably, practicing sublimation, the channeling of libidinal (sexual) energies into socially beneficial activities.

---

Our enquiry concerning happiness has not so far taught us much that is not already common knowledge. And even if we proceed from it to the problem of why it is so hard for men to be happy, there seems no greater prospect of learning anything new. We have given the answer already by pointing to the three sources from which our suffering comes: the superior power of nature, the feebleness of our own bodies and the inadequacy of the regulations which adjust the mutual relationships of human beings in the family, the state and society. In regard to the first two sources, our judgement cannot hesitate long. It forces us to acknowledge those sources of suffering and to submit to the inevitable. We shall never completely master nature; and our bodily organism, itself a part of that nature, will always remain a transient structure with a limited capacity for adaptation and achievement. This recognition does not have a paralysing effect. On the contrary, it points the direction for our activity. If we cannot remove all suffering, we can remove some, and we can mitigate some: the experience of many thousands of years has convinced us of that. As regards the third source, the social source of suffering, our attitude is a different one. We do not admit it at all; we cannot see why the regulations made by ourselves should not, on the contrary, be a protection and a benefit for every one of us. And yet, when we consider how unsuccessful we have been in precisely this field of prevention of suffering, a suspicion dawns on us that here, too, a piece of unconquerable nature may lie behind—this time a piece of our own psychical constitution.

When we start considering this possibility, we come upon a contention which is so astonishing that we must dwell upon it. This contention holds that what we call our civilization is largely responsible for our misery, and that we should be much happier if we gave it up and returned to primitive conditions. I call this contention astonishing because, in whatever way we may define the concept of civilization, it is a certain fact that all the things with which we seek to protect ourselves against the threats that emanate from the sources of suffering are part of that very civilization.

How has it happened that so many people have come to take up this strange attitude of hostility to civilization? I believe that the basis of it was a deep and long-standing dissatisfaction with the then existing state of civilization and that on that basis a condemnation of it was built up, occasioned by certain specific historical events. I think I know what the last and the last but one of those occasions were. I am not learned enough to trace the chain of them far back enough in the history of the human species; but a factor of this kind hostile to civilization must already have been at work in the victory of Christendom over the heathen religions. For it was very closely related to the low estimation put upon earthly life by the Christian doctrine. The last but one of these occasions was when the progress of voyages of discovery led to contact with primitive peoples and races. In consequence of insufficient observation and a mistaken view of their manners and customs, they appeared to Europeans to be leading a simple, happy life with few wants, a life such as was unattainable by their visitors with their superior civilization. Later experience has corrected some of those judgements. In many cases the observers had wrongly attributed to the absence of complicated cultural demands what was in fact due to the bounty of nature and the ease with which the major human needs were satisfied. The last occasion is especially familiar to us. It arose when people came to know about the mechanism of the neuroses, which threaten to undermine the modicum of happiness enjoyed by civilized men. It was discovered that a person becomes neurotic because he cannot tolerate the amount of frustration which society imposes on him in the service of its cultural ideals, and it was inferred from this that the abolition or reduction of those demands would result in a return to possibilities of happiness.

There is also an added factor of disappointment. During the last few generations mankind has made an extraordinary advance in the natural sciences and in their technical application and has established his control over nature in a way never before imagined. The single steps of this advance are common knowledge and it is unnecessary to enumerate them. Men are proud of those achievements, and have a right to be. But they seem to have observed that this newly-won power over space and time, this subjugation of the forces of nature, which is the fulfillment of a longing that goes back thousands of years, has not increased the amount of pleasurable satisfaction which they may expect from life and has not made them feel happier. From the recognition of this fact we ought to be content to conclude that power over nature is not the *only* precondition of human happiness, just as it is not the *only* goal of cultural endeavour; we ought not to infer from it that technical progress is without value for the economics of our happiness. One would like to ask: is there, then, no positive gain in pleasure, no unequivocal increase in my feeling of happiness, if I can, as often as I please, hear the voice of a child of mine who is living hundreds of miles away or if I can learn in the shortest possible time after a friend has reached his destination that he has come through the long and difficult voyage unharmed? Does it mean nothing that medicine has succeeded in enormously reducing infant mortality and the danger of infection for women in childbirth, and, indeed, in considerably lengthening the average life of a civilized man? And there is a long list that might be added to benefits of this kind which we owe to the much-despised era of scientific and technical advances. But here the voice of pessimistic criticism makes itself heard and warns us that most of these satisfactions follow the model of the 'cheap enjoyment' extolled in the anecdote—the enjoyment obtained by putting a bare leg from under the bedclothes on a cold winter night and drawing it in again. If there had been no railway to conquer distances, my child would never have left his native town and I should need no telephone to hear his voice; if travelling across the ocean by ship had not been introduced, my friend would not have embarked on his sea-voyage and I should not need a cable to relieve my anxiety about him. What is the use of reducing infantile mortality when it is precisely that reduction which imposes the greatest restraint on us in the begetting of children, so that, taken all round, we nevertheless rear no more children than in the days before the reign of hygiene, while at the same time we have created difficult conditions for our sexual life in marriage, and have probably worked against the beneficial effects of natural selection? And, finally, what good to us is a long life if it is difficult and barren of joys, and if it is so full of misery that we can only welcome death as a deliverer? . . .

It is time for us to turn our attention to the nature of this civilization on whose value as a means to happiness doubts have been thrown. We shall not look for a formula in which to express that nature in a few words, until we have learned something by examining it. We shall therefore content ourselves with saying once more that the word 'civilization' describes the whole sum of the achievements and the regulations which distinguish our lives from those of our animal ancestors and which serve two purposes—namely to protect men against nature and to adjust their mutual relations. In order to learn more, we will bring together the various features of civilization individually, as they are exhibited in human communities. In doing so, we shall have no hesitation in letting ourselves be guided by linguistic usage or, as it is also called, linguistic feeling, in the conviction that we shall thus be doing justice to inner discernments which still defy expression in abstract terms.

The first stage is easy. We recognize as cultural all activities and resources which are useful to men for making the earth serviceable to them, for protecting them against the violence of the forces of nature, and so on. As regards this side of civilization, there can be scarcely any doubt. If we go back far enough, we find that the first acts of civilization were the use of tools, the gaining of control over fire and the construction of dwellings. Among these, the control over fire stands out as a quite extraordinary and unexampled achievement, while the others opened up paths which man has followed ever since, and the stimulus to which is easily guessed. With every tool man is perfecting his own organs, whether motor or sensory, or is removing the limits to their functioning. Motor power places gigantic forces at his disposal, which, like his muscles, he can employ in any direction; thanks to ships and aircraft neither water nor air can hinder his movements; by means of spectacles he corrects defects in the lens of his own eye; by means of the telescope he sees into the far distance; and by means of the microscope he overcomes the limits of visibility set by the structure of his retina. In the photographic camera he has created an instrument which retains the fleeting visual impressions, just as a gramophone disc retains the equally fleeting auditory ones; both are at bottom materializations of the power he possesses of recollection, his memory. With the help of the telephone he can hear at distances which would be respected as unattainable even in a fairy tale. Writing was in its origin the voice of an absent person; and the dwelling-house was a substitute for the mother's womb, the first lodging, for which in all likelihood man still longs, and in which he was safe and felt at ease.

These things that, by his science and technology, man has brought about on this earth, on which he first appeared as a feeble animal organism and on which each individual of his species must once more make its entry ('oh inch of nature!') as a helpless suckling—these things do not only sound like a fairy tale, they are an actual fulfillment of every—or of almost every—fairy-tale wish. All these assets he may lay claim to as his cultural acquisition. Long ago he formed an ideal conception of omnipotence and omniscience which he embodied in his gods. To these gods he attributed everything that seemed unattainable to his wishes, or that was forbidden to him. One may say, therefore, that these gods were cultural ideals. To-day he has come very close to the attainment of this ideal, he has almost become a god himself. Only, it is true, in the fashion in which ideals are usually attained according to the general judgement of humanity. Not completely; in some respects not at all, in others only half way. Man has, as it were, become a kind of prosthetic God. When he puts on all his auxiliary organs he is truly magnificent; but those organs have not grown on to him and they still give him much trouble at times. Nevertheless, he is entitled to console himself with the thought that this development will not come to an end precisely with the year 1930 A.D. Future ages will bring with them new and probably unimaginably great advances in this field of civilization and will increase man's likeness to God still more. But in the interests of our investigations, we will not forget that present-day man does not feel happy in his Godlike character.

We recognize, then, that countries have attained a high level of civilization if we find that in them everything which can assist in the exploitation of the earth by man and in his protection against the forces of nature—everything, in short, which is of use to him—is attended to and effectively carried out. . . .

No feature, however, seems better to characterize civilization than its esteem and encouragement of man's higher mental activities—his intellectual, scientific and artistic achievements—and the leading role that it assigns to ideas in human life. Foremost among those ideas are the religious systems, on whose complicated structure I have endeavoured to throw light elsewhere. Next come the speculations of philosophy; and finally what might be called man's 'ideals'—his ideas of a possible perfection of individuals, or of peoples or of the whole of humanity, and the demands he sets up on the basis of such ideas. The fact that these creations of his are not independent of one another, but are on the contrary closely interwoven, increases the difficulty not only of describing them but of tracing their psychological derivation. If we assume quite generally that the motive force of all human activities is a striving towards the two confluent goals of utility and a yield of pleasure, we must suppose that this is also true of the manifestations of civilization which we have been discussing here, although this is easily visible only in scientific and aesthetic activities. But it cannot be doubted that the other activities, too, correspond to strong needs in men—perhaps to needs which are only developed in a minority. Nor must we allow ourselves to be misled by judgements of value concerning any particular religion, or philosophic system, or ideal. Whether we think to find in them the highest achievements of the human spirit, or whether we deplore them as aberrations, we cannot but recognize that where they are present, and, in especial, where they are dominant, a high level of civilization is implied.

The last, but certainly not the least important, of the characteristic features of civilization remains to be assessed: the manner in which the relationships of men to one another, their social relationships, are regulated—relationships which affect a person as a neighbour, as a source of help, as another person's sexual object, as a member of a family and of a State. Here it is especially difficult to keep clear of particular ideal demands and to see what is civilized in general. Perhaps we may begin by explaining that the element of civilization enters on the scene with the first attempt to regulate these social relationships. If the attempt were not made, the relationships would be subject to the arbitrary will of the individual: that is to say, the physically stronger man would decide them in the sense of his own interests and instinctual impulses. Nothing would be changed in this if this stronger man should in turn meet someone even stronger than he. Human life in common is only made possible when a majority comes together which is stronger than any separate individual and which remains united against all separate individuals. The power of this community is then set up as 'right' in opposition to the power of the individual, which is condemned as 'brute force.' This replacement of the power of the individual by the power of a community constitutes the decisive step of civilization. The essence of it lies in the fact that the members of the community restrict themselves in their possibilities of satisfaction, whereas the individual knew no such restrictions. The first requisite of civilization, therefore, is that of justice—that is, the assurance that a law once made will not be broken in favour of an individual. This implies nothing as to the ethical value of such a law. The further course of cultural development seems to tend towards making the law no longer an expression of the will of a small community—a caste or a stratum of the population or a racial group—which, in its turn, behaves like a violent individual towards other, and perhaps more numerous, collections of people. The final outcome should be a rule of law to which all—except those who are not capable of entering a community—have contributed by a sacrifice of their instincts, and which leaves no one—again with the same exception—at the mercy of brute force.

The liberty of the individual is no gift of civilization. It was greatest before there was any civilization, though then, it is true, it had for the most part no value, since the individual was scarcely in a position to defend it. The development of civilization imposes restrictions on it, and justice demands that no one shall escape those restrictions. What makes itself felt in a human community as a desire for freedom may be their revolt against some existing injustice, and so may prove favourable to a further development of civilization; it may remain compatible with civilization. But it may also spring from the remains of their original personality, which is still untamed by civilization and may thus become the basis in them of hostility to civilization. The urge for freedom, therefore, is directed against particular forms and demands of civilization or against civilization altogether. It does not seem as though any influence could induce a man to change his nature into a termite's. No doubt he will always defend his claim to individual liberty against the will of the group. A good part of the struggles of mankind centre round the single task of finding an expedient accommodation—one, that is, that will bring happiness—between this claim of the individual and the cultural claims of the group; and one of the problems that touches the fate of humanity is whether such an accommodation can be reached by means of some particular form of civilization or whether this conflict is irreconcilable. . . .

Sublimation of instinct is an especially conspicuous feature of cultural development; it is what makes it possible for higher psychical activities, scientific, artistic or ideological, to play such an important part in civilized life. If one were to yield to a first impression, one would say that sublimation is a vicissitude which has been forced upon the instincts entirely by civilization. But it would be wiser to reflect upon this a little longer. In the third place, finally, and this seems the most important of all, it is impossible to overlook the extent to which civilization is built up upon a renunciation of instinct, how much it presupposes precisely the non-satisfaction (by suppression, repression or some other means?) of powerful instincts. This 'cultural frustration' dominates the large field of social relationships between human beings. As we already know, it is the cause of the hostility against which all civilizations have to struggle. It will also make severe demands on our scientific work, and we shall have much to explain here. It is not easy to understand how it can become possible to deprive an instinct of satisfaction. Nor is doing so without danger. If the loss is not compensated for economically, one can be certain that serious disorders will ensue.

Chapter

# 20

# The Age of the Masses and the Zenith of Modernism: 1914–1945

## T.S. ELIOT

### *The Love Song of J. Alfred Prufrock*

Eliot's "The Love Song of J. Alred Prufrock" (1915) is one of the first great works of Modernist poetry, which flourished from about 1904 until about 1939. Modernist poetry continued to be written after 1939, but its zenith was reached in the earlier time. Its aim is typical of Modernism in general, to make a radical break with the nineteenth century and establish a new style more in keeping with the kaleidoscopic changes taking place today.

Modernist poetry, first of all, is not Victorian, for it is opposed to the sentimentality of Romanticism, the fine writing of Neoclassicism, and the illustration of Realism—the leading styles of the Victorian Age. Modernist poetry also offers no moral lesson, nor a popular message, but, instead, is deliberately difficult. Its difficulty springs from its dense writing, its rich allusiveness (quotations from other literary works), and its high intellectual tone. Though anti-traditional, it is the heir of the Hellenistic (see Theocritus's *Idylls*) and the Metaphysical poets (see Donne's "The Canonization," etc.), both of whom specialized in difficult and learned works. Modernist poetry is often composed in free verse, which has no regular meter or line length and relies on natural speech and the variation of stressed and unstressed syllables, a type of poetry perfected by Whitman (see "When Lilacs Last in the Dooryard Bloom'd").

The Anglo-American T. S. Eliot (born, Thomas Stearns Eliot), the pioneer of Modernist poetry, grew up in a middle-class St. Louis family, studied at Harvard, and earned a Ph.D. in philosophy. He migrated to England on the eve of World War I, marrying a genteel English woman, who later became psychotic and whom he divorced and put in an insane asylum. Although he never held an academic post, choosing to support himself first as a banker, and later as a publisher—particularly of Modernist works—he became the dominant poet of his day and a powerbroker of Modernist literature. He was also one of this period's leading critics, helping to develop what came to be called the New Criticism, which was ideally suited for interpreting Modernist poetry; it advocated "close reading" and detailed textual analysis of the work rather than an interest in the mind and personality of the poet, sources, the history of ideas, and political and social implications.

### Reading the Selection

To read "The Love Song of J. Alfred Prufrock," in terms of new Criticism, is to read it not as the work of T.S. Eliot, but to study it as the expression of J. Alfred Prufrock, whoever he may be. He indeed may be Eliot's alter ego, but that is irrelevant here. The reader has, in effect, been given an intellectual puzzle, to figure out Prufrock and his loves. The epigraph, the opening quotation from Dante's *Inferno*, establishes that Prufrock is shy about revealing himself, just as is the character in Dante. Drawing the reader into the text, "Let us go then, you and I," Prufrock takes the reader on a walk through a seedy neighborhood where the image of yellow fog and smoke engulf everything. Shyly, Prufrock reveals himself, his lack of self-confidence, his hesitancy to do anything, his sad confession that his life is measured with coffee spoons. He lacks the courage to make an overture to a woman whose bare arms and perfume haunt his memory. Confused, he fears failure and the onset of age ("I grow old"), and wonders what he will be like as an old man. At the end, the imagery shifts to seductive mermaids who lure him ever onward into another world, or perhaps to his destruction.

———

*S'io credesse che mia risposta fosse
A persona che mai tornasse al mondo,
Questa fiamma staria senza più scosse.
Ma per ciò che giammai di questo fondo
Non tornò vivo alcun, s'i'odo il vero,
Senza tema d'infamia ti rispondo.*[1]

Let us go then, you and I,
When the evening is spread out against the sky
Like a patient etherized upon a table;
Let us go, through certain half-deserted streets,
The muttering retreats
Of restless nights in one-night cheap hotels
And sawdust restaurants with oyster-shells:
Streets that follow like a tedious argument
Of insidious intent
To lead you to an overwhelming question . . .
Oh, do not ask, "What is it?"
Let us go and make our visit.

In the room the women come and go
Talking of Michelangelo.

The yellow fog that rubs its back upon the window-panes
The yellow smoke that rubs its muzzle on the
　　window-panes
Licked its tongue into the corners of the evening,
Lingered upon the pools that stand in drains,
Let fall upon its back the soot that falls from chimneys,
Slipped by the terrace, made a sudden leap,
And seeing that it was a soft October night,
Curled once about the house, and fell asleep.

And indeed there will be time
For the yellow smoke that slides along the street,
Rubbing its back upon the window-panes;
There will be time, there will be time
To prepare a face to meet the faces that you meet;
There will be time to murder and create,
And time for all the works and days of hands
That lift and drop a question on your plate;
Time for you and time for me,
And time yet for a hundred indecisions,
And for a hundred visions and revisions,
Before the taking of a toast and tea.

In the room the women come and go
Talking of Michelangelo.

And indeed there will be time
To wonder, "Do I dare?" and, "Do I dare?"
Time to turn back and descend the stair,
With a bald spot in the middle of my hair—
[They will say: "How his hair is growing thin!"]
My morning coat, my collar mounting firmly to the chin,
My necktie rich and modest, but asserted by a simple pin—
[They will say: "But how his arms and legs are thin!"]
Do I dare

[1] Epigraph from Dante's *Inferno*, canto XXVII, 61–66: "If I thought my answer were given to anyone who could ever return to the world, this flame would shake no more; but since none ever did return above from this depth, if what I hear is true, without fear of infamy, I answer thee." This response is given by Guido da Montelfetro when he is asked who he is.

Disturb the universe?
In a minute there is time
For decisions and revisions which a minute will reverse.

For I have known them all already, known them all:
Have known the evenings, mornings, afternoons,
I have measured out my life with coffee spoons;
I know the voices dying with a dying fall
Beneath the music from a farther room.
 So how should I presume?

And I have known the eyes already, known them all—
The eyes that fix you in a formulated phrase,
And when I am formulated, sprawling on a pin,
When I am pinned and wriggling on the wall,
Then how should I begin
To spit out all the butt-ends of my days and ways?
 And how should I presume?

And I have known the arms already, known them all—
Arms that are braceleted and white and bare
[But in the lamplight, downed with light brown hair!]
Is it perfume from a dress
That makes me so digress?
Arms that lie along a table, or wrap about a shawl.
 And should I then presume?
 And how should I begin?
 . . . . .

Shall I say, I have gone at dusk through narrow streets
And watched the smoke that rises from the pipes
Of lonely men in shirt-sleeves, leaning out of windows? . . .

I should have been a pair of ragged claws
Scuttling across the floors of silent seas.
 . . . . .

And the afternoon, the evening, sleeps so peacefully!
Smoothered by long fingers,
Asleep . . . tired . . . or it malingers,
Stretched on the floor, here beside you and me.
Should I, after tea and cakes and ices,
Have the strength to force the moment to its crisis?
But though I have wept and fasted, wept and prayed,
Though I have seen my head [grown slightly bald]
 brought in upon a platter,
I am no prophet—and here's no great matter;
I have seen the moment of my greatness flicker,
And I have seen the eternal Footman hold my coat, and
 snicker,
And in short, I was afraid.

And would it have been worth it, after all,
After the cups, the marmalade, the tea,
Among the porcelain, among some talk of you and me,

Would it have been worth while,
To have bitten off the matter with a smile,
To have squeezed the universe into a ball
To roll it toward some overwhelming question,
To say: "I am Lazarus, come from the dead,
Come back to tell you all, I shall tell you all"—
If one, settling a pillow by her head,
 Should say: "That is not what I meant at all.
 That is not it, at all."

And would it have been worth it, after all,
Would it have been worth while,
After the sunsets and the dooryards and the sprinkled
 streets,
After the novels, after the teacups, after the skirts that
 trail along the floor—
And this, and so much more?—
It is impossible to say just what I mean!
But as if a magic lantern threw the nerves in patterns on
 a screen:
Would it have been worth while
If one, settling a pillow or throwing off a shawl,
And turning toward the window, should say:
 "That is not it at all,
 That is not what I meant, at all."
 . . . . .

No! I am not Prince Hamlet, nor was meant to be;
Am an attendant lord, one that will do
To swell a progress, start a scene or two,
Advise the prince; no doubt, an easy tool,
Deferential, glad to be of use,
Politic, cautious, and meticulous;
Full of high sentence, but a bit obtuse;
At times, indeed, almost ridiculous—
Almost, at times, the Fool.

I grow old . . . I grow old . . .
I shall wear the bottoms of my trousers rolled.

Shall I part my hair behind? Do I dare to eat a peach?
I shall wear white flannel trousers, and walk upon the beach.
I have heard the mermaids singing, each to each.

I do not think that they will sing to me.

I have seen them riding seaward on the waves
Combing the white hair of the waves blown back
When the wind blows the water white and black.

We have lingered in the chambers of the sea
By sea-girls wreathed with seaweed red and brown
Till human voices wake us, and we drown.

# JAMES JOYCE

# from *Ulysses*

## Proteus

---

Joyce's *Ulysses* is now recognized as perhaps the greatest Modernist novel, though it met stiff resistance, except in avant-garde circles, when it was published in Paris in 1922. Part of the resistance stemmed from the novelty of the Modernist novel's form itself, which, despite the best efforts of Woolf (see *To the Lighthouse*) and Stein (see *The Autobiography of Alice B. Toklas*), had not yet been fully accepted by middle-class readers. *Ulysses* was typical of Modernist innovation in that the telling of the story became secondary to the project of describing a "sensibility" (a term popularized by Eliot), meaning "creative faculty of a writer"); above all, the narrative voice was not omniscient but was fragmented among several characters who spoke their thoughts in a stream-of-consciousness way. Part of the resistance to *Ulysses* was also its difficulty, for it was a nearly-one-thousand-page modern version of Homer's *Odyssey*, contrasting the ancient author's twenty-four books of heroic deeds with an ordinary day in the lives of three middle-class Dubliners—Stephen Dedalus and Leopold and Molly Bloom. Most of all, *Ulysses* met resistance because of its explicit sexual language, which offended middle-class morals; the novel, which did not appear in America or England until the 1930s, became the age's test case for artistic freedom.

The Irish author James Joyce (1882–1941) came from a large Catholic family in Dublin, studied there at University College, the Catholic counterpart to Protestant Trinity College, and spent time in medical school. Unlike most of his fellow students, he was not attracted to the Irish Renaissance, which was then flourishing; indeed, he heaped scorn upon it and its leaders, notably Yeats. From the beginning, Joyce aligned himself with the world of European letters. He soon settled on the continent, living the rest of his life in Paris, Zurich, and Trieste. In Paris, he fell under the influence of Edouard Dujardin, a French Symbolist poet, who introduced him to "stream of consciousness" technique.

### Reading the Selection

This selection, from Chapter Three, "Proteus," of *Ulysses*, recounts, in a stream-of-consciousness style, the actions and thoughts of Stephen Dedalus, Joyce's alter ego and whose last name is taken from the Greek hero famed for his creativity. As Stephen walks along Sandymount Strand in Dublin, he thinks about his family, his rejected Catholic upbringing, his disappointments as a writer, Irish politics and literature, and the meaning of his life.

This passage shows the rich allusiveness (quotations from other works) of Joyce's style, weaving together Classical themes (Plato's "Demiurgos"), Christian theology ("wombed in sin"), especially with references to ancient heresies ("Arius"), foreign words and phrases (five different tongues), music (*aria de sortita*), various quotations, and memories of Stephen's (Joyce's) family and friends.

The stream-of-consciousness method may be seen clearly here: A reference is made to abortion, midwives or *frauenzimmer*, which leads to thoughts of navelcords, which, in turn, symbolize connections among humans; this line of thought results in speculation about Eve's smooth stomach since she had no navel, being born from Adam's rib.

Puns and plays on words abound, the hallmark of Joyce's mature style. The passage concludes with Stephen mocking his literary ambition, as he refers to the ancient library at Alexandria and to the Renaissance scholar, Pico della Mirandola.

Ineluctable modality of the visible: at least that if no more, thought through my eyes. Signatures of all things I am here to read, seaspawn and seawrack, the nearing tide, that rusty boot. Snotgreen, bluesilver, rust: coloured signs. Limits of the diaphane. But he adds: in bodies. Then he was aware of them bodies before of them coloured. How? By knocking his sconce against them, sure. Go easy. Bald he was and a millionaire, *maestro di color che sanno*. Limit of the diaphane in. Why in? Diaphane, adiaphane. If you can put your five fingers through it, it is a gate, if not a door. Shut your eyes and see.

Stephen closed his eyes to hear his boots crush crackling wrack and shells. You are walking through it howsomever. I am, a stride at a time. A very short space of time through very short times of space. Five, six: the *nacheinander*. Exactly: and that is the ineluctable modality of the audible. Open your eyes. No. Jesus! If I fell over a cliff that beetles o'er his base, fell through the *nebeneinander* ineluctably. I am getting on nicely in the dark. My ash sword hangs at my side. Tap with it: they do. My two feet in his boots are at the end of his legs, *nebeneinander*. Sounds solid: made by the mallet of *Los Demiurgos*. Am I walking into eternity along Sandymount strand? Crush, crack, crick, crick. Wild sea money. Dominie Deasy kens them a'.

*Won't you come to Sandymount,*
*Madeline the mare?*

Rhythm begins, you see. I hear. A catalectic tetrameter of iambs marching. No, agallop: *deline the mare*.

Open your eyes now. I will. One moment. Has all vanished since? If I open and am for ever in the black adiaphane. *Basta!* I will see if I can see.

See now. There all the time without you: and ever shall be, world without end.

They came down the steps from Leahy's terrace prudently, *Frauenzimmer*: and down the shelving shore flabbily their splayed feet sinking in the silted sand. Like me, like Algy, coming down to our mighty mother. Number one swung lourdily her midwife's bag, the other's gamp poked in the beach. From the liberties, out for the day. Mrs Florence MacCabe, relict of the late Patk MacCabe, deeply lamented, of Bride Street. One of her sisterhood lugged me squealing into life. Creation from nothing. What has she in the bag? A misbirth with a trailing navelcord, hushed in ruddy wool. The cords of all link back, strandentwining cable of all flesh. That is why mystic monks. Will you be as gods? Gaze in your omphalos. Hello. Kinch here. Put me on to Edenville. Aleph, alpha: nought, nought, one.

Spouse and helpmate of Adam Kadmon: Heva, naked Eve. She had no navel. Gaze. Belly without blemish, bulging big, a buckler of taut vellum, no; whiteheaped corn, orient and immortal, standing from everlasting to everlasting. Womb of sin.

Wombed in sin darkness I was too, made not begotten. By them, the man with my voice and my eyes and a ghost-woman with ashes on her breath. They clasped and sundered, did the coupler's will. From before the ages He willed me and now may not will me away or ever. A *lex eterna* stays about him. Is that then the divine substance wherein Father and Son are consubstantial? Where is poor dear Arius to try conclusions? Warring his life long on the contransmagnificand-jewbangtantiality. Illstarred heresiarch. In a Greek watercloset he breathed his last: euthanasia. With beaded mitre and with crozier, stalled upon his throne, widower of a widowed see, with upstiffed omophorion, with clotted hinderparts.

Airs romped around him, nipping and eager airs. They are coming, waves. The whitemaned seahorses, champing, brightwindbridled, the steeds of Mananaan.

I mustn't forget his letter for the press. And after? The Ship, half twelve. By the way go easy with that money like a good young imbecile. Yes, I must.

His pace slackened. Here. Am I going to Aunt Sara's or not? My consubstantial father's voice. Did you see anything of your artist brother Stephen lately? No? Sure he's not down in Strasburg terrace with his aunt Sally? Couldn't he fly a bit higher than that, eh? And and and and tell us Stephen, how is uncle Si? O weeping God, the things I married into. De boys up in de hayloft. The drunken little costdrawer and his brother, the cornet player. Highly respectable gondoliers. And skeweyed Walter sirring his father, no less. Sir. Yes, sir. No, sir. Jesus wept: and no wonder, by Christ.

I pull the wheezy bell of their shuttered cottage: and wait. They take me for a dun, peer out from a coign of vantage.

—It's Stephen, sir.

—Let him in. Let Stephen in.

A bolt drawn back and Walter welcomes me.

—We thought you were someone else.

In his broad bed nuncle Richie, pillowed and blanketed, extends over the hillock of his knees a sturdy forearm. Cleanchested. He has washed the upper moiety.

—Morrow, nephew.

He lays aside the lapboard whereon he drafts his bills of costs for the eyes of Master Goff and Master Shapland Tandy, filing consents and common searches and a writ of *Duces Tecum*. A bogoak frame over his bald head: Wilde's *Requiescat*. The drone of his misleading whistle brings Walter back.

—Yes, sir?

—Malt for Richie and Stephen, tell mother. Where is she?

—Bathing Crissie, sir.

Papa's little bedpal. Lump of love.

—No, uncle Richie . . .

—Call me Richie. Damn your lithia water. It lowers. Whusky!

—Uncle Richie, really . . .

—Sit down or by the law Harry I'll knock you down.

Walter squints vainly for a chair.

—He has nothing to sit down on, sir.

—He has nowhere to put it, you mug. Bring in our Chippendale chair. Would you like a bite of something? None of your damned lawdeedaw air here; the rich of a rasher fried with a herring? Sure? So much the better. We have nothing in the house but backache pills.

*All'erta!*

He drones bars of Ferrando's *aria de sortita*. The grandest number, Stephen, in the whole opera. Listen.

His tuneful whistle sounds again, finely shaded, with rushes of the air, his fists bigdrumming on his padded knees.

This wind is sweeter.

Houses of decay, mine, his and all. You told the Clongowes gentry you had an uncle a judge and an uncle a general in the army. Come out of them, Stephen. Beauty is not there. Nor in the stagnant bay of Marsh's library where you read the fading prophecies of Joachim Abbas. For whom? The hundred-headed rabble of the cathedral close. A hater of his kind ran from them to the wood of madness, his mane foaming in the moon, his eyeballs stars. Houyhnhnm, horse-nostrilled. The oval equine faces. Temple, Buck Mulligan, Foxy Campbell. Lantern jaws. Abbas father, furious dean, what offence laid fire to their brains? Paff! *Descende, calve, ut ne nimium decalveris.* A garland of grey hair on his comminated head see him me clambering down to the footpace (*descende*), clutching a monstrance, basiliskeyed. Get down, bald poll! A choir gives back menace and echo, assisting about the altar's horns, the snorted Latin of jackpriests moving burly in their albs, tonsured and oiled and gelded, fat with the fat of kidneys of wheat.

And at the same instant perhaps a priest round the corner is elevating it. Dringdring! And two streets off another locking it into a pyx. Dringadring! And in a ladychapel another taking housel all to his own cheek. Dringdring! Down, up, forward, back. Dan Occam thought of that, invincible doctor. A misty English morning the imp hypostasis tickled his brain. Bringing his host down and kneeling he heard twine with his second bell the first bell in the transept (he is lifting his) and, rising, heard (now I am lifting) their two bells (he is kneeling) twang in diphthong.

Cousin Stephen, you will never be a saint. Isle of saints. You were awfully holy, weren't you? You prayed to the Blessed Virgin that you might not have a red nose. You prayed to the devil in Serpentine avenue that the fubsy widow in front might lift her clothes still more from the wet street. *O si, certo!* Sell your soul for that, do, dyed rag pinned round a squaw. More tell me, more still! On the top of the Howth tram alone crying to the rain: *naked women!* What about that, eh?

What about what? What else were they invented for?

Reading two pages apiece of seven books every night, eh? I was young. You bowed to yourself in the mirror, stepping forward to applause earnestly, striking face. Hurray for the God-damned idiot! Hray! No-one saw: tell no-one. Books you were going to write with letters for titles. Have you read his F? O yes, but I prefer Q. Yes, but W is wonderful. O yes, W. Remember your epiphanies on green oval leaves, deeply deep, copies to be sent if you died to all the great libraries of the world, including Alexandria? Someone was to read them there after a few thousand years, a mahamanvantara. Pico della Mirandola like. Ay, very like a whale. When one reads these strange pages of one long gone one feels that one is at one with one who once . . .

The grainy sand had gone from under his feet. His boots trod again a damp crackling mast, razorshells, squeaking pebbles, that on the unnumbered pebbles beats, wood sieved by the shipworm, lost Armada. Unwholesome sandflats waited to suck his treading soles, breathing upward sewage breath. He coasted them, walking warily. A porter-bottle stood up, stogged to its waist, in the cakey sand dough. A sentinel: isle of dreadful thirst. Broken hoops on the shore; at the land a maze of dark cunning nets; farther away chalkscrawled backdoors and on the higher beach a drying-line with two crucified shirts. Ringsend: wigwams of brown steersmen and master mariners. Human shells. . . .

# WILLIAM BUTLER YEATS
# Poems

William Butler Yeats (1865–1939) is another in the line of gifted Irish writers, starting with Swift (see *A Modest Proposal*), and including Wilde (see *The Picture of Dorian Gray*) and Joyce (see *Ulysses*), who have contributed mightily to English letters. Yeats's fame is based mainly on his Modernist poetry, lyrical and passionate, but his achievements were varied and broad.

Born into a Protestant family in Dublin, Yeats early on fell in love with his country's myths and legends. As Ireland was still suffering under English rule, he wanted to reawaken the spirit of his people with poems on traditional and nationalist themes. Thus he joined the Irish literary Renaissance, the late-nineteenth-century movement that wanted to dispel the influence of English literature and revive Irish Celtic culture. Two of his works that influenced this movement were *The Wanderings of Oisin* (1889) and *The Celtic Twilight* (1893), the latter of which was dismissed by Joyce with the punning phrase "cultic twalette." Nevertheless, Yeats's impact was strong; "Celtic twilight" is the term now used to denote the Romantic atmosphere that was cultivated and admired by these Irish writers. Yeats also cofounded, in 1901, Dublin's now world-famous Abbey Theater, whose goal was to promote Irish drama. For it, Yeats wrote plays, rarely performed today, though writing for the stage pruned his style of the Romantic excesses that had earlier marred it.

After 1916, Yeats's poems took a political turn, in the wake of that year's Easter Rebellion, the uprising of the Irish against the English; it was brutally suppressed but became a legend in the drive for Irish independence—achieved in 1921 and finalized in 1922. He also continued to pare down his language, to make it more ironic and epigrammatic (a concise and cleverly worded statement, meant to suggest a truism). By 1920, he was at the top of his form, writing in a spare and colloquial style. It is the poems of these years, eloquent and based on myth, whether inherited or invented by himself, which earned him the 1925 Nobel Prize and are generally regarded as his crowning achievement.

## Reading the Selection

Yeats's "The Second Coming" (1921) has a Nietzschean theme, the end of the Christian era and the birth of a new age. Its ironic title refers, not to Jesus' second coming, but to the birth of a new religion, the offspring of a "rough beast, its hour come round at last." The sphinxlike beast, "a shape with lion body and the head of a man," is a horrifying symbol of this new faith.

Yeats's description of culture in collapse ("things fall apart"), as set forth in the poem's opening lines, was typical of the pessimism which seized intellectuals after World War I. The poem's primary metaphor is a "gyre," the whirling motion which Yeats made symbolic of life's periodic rise and fall, as last happened at the birth of Jesus. That the life gyre is "widening" points to a cultural crisis until the gyre begins to "narrow." Lost in the "widening gyre," "the falcon cannot hear the falconer": a telling symbol of social breakdown at all levels in the modern world.

In "Sailing to Byzantium" (1928), Yeats used Classical myth to reflect on growing old. Surprisingly, he welcomes the passing of youth and finds that age gives him a hunger for life. Thus, he contrasts "monuments of unageing intellect" with youth's "sensual music." Yeats's main metaphor is "Byzantium," the ancient city rebuilt as Constantinople—his symbol of artistic perfection.

# The Second Coming

Turning and turning in the widening gyre
The falcon cannot hear the falconer;
Things fall apart; the center cannot hold;
Mere anarchy is loosed upon the world,
The blood-dimmed tide is loosed, and everywhere
The ceremony of innocence is drowned;
The best lack all conviction, while the worst
Are full of passionate intensity.

Surely some revelation is at hand;
Surely the Second Coming is at hand.
The Second Coming! Hardly are those words out

When a vast image out of *Spirits Mundi*
Troubles my sight: somewhere in sands of the desert
A shape with lion body and the head of a man,
A gaze blank and pitiless as the sun,
Is moving its slow thighs, while all about it
Reel shadows of the indignant desert birds.
The darkness drops again; but now I know
That twenty centuries of stony sleep
Were vexed to nightmare by a rocking cradle,
And what rough beast, its hour come round at last,
Slouches towards Bethlehem to be born?

# Sailing to Byzantium

### 1

That is no country for old men. The young
In one another's arms, birds in the trees
—Those dying generations—at their song,
The salmon-falls, the mackerel-crowded seas,
Fish, flesh, or fowl, commend all summer long
Whatever is begotten, born, and dies.
Caught in that sensual music all neglect
Monuments of unageing intellect.

### 2

An aged man is but a paltry thing,
A tattered coat upon a stick, unless
Soul clap its hands and sing, and louder sing
For every tatter in its mortal dress,
Nor is there singing school but studying
Monuments of its own magnificence;
And therefore I have sailed the seas and come
To the holy city of Byzantium.

### 3

O sages standing in God's holy fire
As in the gold mosaic of a wall,
Come from the holy fire, perne in a gyre,*
And be the singing-masters of my soul.
Consume my heart away; sick with desire
And fastened to a dying animal
It knows not what it is; and gather me
Into the artifice of eternity.

### 4

Once out of nature I shall never take
My bodily form from any natural thing,
But such a form as Grecian goldsmiths make
Of hammered gold and gold enamelling
To keep a drowsy Emperor awake;
Or set upon a golden bough to sing
To lords and ladies of Byzantium
Of what is past, or passing, or to come.

*Spin round

# LANGSTON HUGHES
# Poems

———

Langston Hughes (1902–1967) is one of the first great African-American poets and the most published black writer of his era. Altogether he wrote sixteen books of poetry, two novels, seven books of short stories, two autobiographies, five works of nonfiction, and nine books for children; he also edited nine anthologies, translated several Haitian and Spanish writers, and wrote about thirty plays. Reviewed widely in mainstream journals by mainstream writers and acquainted with leading artists and writers at home and abroad, Hughes was sometimes described, during his lifetime, as the "poet laureate of the American Negro," or as "Shakespeare in Harlem."

Hughes was a web of paradoxes that largely reflected his anguish as a black man in a white world. The son of a black middle-class family in Joplin, Missouri (his father was a businessman and his mother was a schoolteacher), he came to speak for America's poor black masses. Passionate about writing, yet distant and difficult to know, Hughes was apparently a very lonely man who never seemed to have any deep or longstanding love affairs. Familiar with standard English, having studied at Columbia University, New York (1921–1922), and having graduated from Lincoln University, Pennsylvania (1929), he made his literary task the creation of a body of works based on vernacular speech of the black working and rural classes—an innovation which succeeded, since subsequent black writers (see Walker's "Everyday Use") followed his lead. A citizen of the world, fluent in French and Spanish, and widely traveled in Europe, Asia, Africa, and Mexico, he never wavered in his commitment to black vernacular culture.

Hughes, mainly through his poetry, soared to fame in the Harlem Renaissance, the 1920s cultural revival centered in the black area of New York City called Harlem. At this time, jazz, blues, and folk-ballads went mainstream; Hughes was one of the first black writers to recognize the genius of this music and incorporate it into his works. He appropriated the cadences of jazz and the moods and themes of blues and folk-ballads to create a soulful poetry.

Resisting the temptation encouraged by the period's growing and mobile black middle class to write in a Europeanized style, Hughes wrote primarily about blackness. His poems often concerned the struggle of black artists to be true to their race, and, at the same time, to be Americans. In 1927, he wrote: "American standardization [requires us] to be as little Negro and as much American as possible." He gradually came to see poetry as a kind of salvation, for it allowed him to speak in his African-American voice and yet identify with America's heritage; for example, he claimed kinship with the reclusive poet, Emily Dickinson.

## Reading the Selection

"The Negro Speaks of Rivers" (1921) is Hughes's best-known poem, written when he was nineteen and a student at Columbia. This poem was inspired by a quarrel with his father, who apparently hated his own race, but it is surprisingly free of rancor on Hughes's part. The poem celebrates black history, linking it to storied rivers—the Euphrates, the Congo, the Nile, and the Mississippi.

"Theme for English B" (1951) and "Harlem" (1951) continue Hughes's project of integrating the black experience into American letters. It should be noted that the latter poem contains the phrase, "a raisin in the sun," made even more memorable later when it became the title of a Pulitzer Prize play, written by Lorraine Hansberry.

# The Negro Speaks of Rivers

I've known rivers:
I've known rivers ancient as the world and older than the
    flow of human blood in human veins.

My soul has grown deep like the rivers.

I bathed in the Euphrates when dawns were young.
I built my hut near the Congo and it lulled me to sleep.
I looked upon the Nile and raised the pyramids above it.

I heard the singing of the Mississippi when Abe Lincoln
    went down to New Orleans, and I've seen its muddy
    bosom turn all golden in the sunset

I've known rivers:
Ancient, dusky rivers.

My soul has grown deep like the rivers.

# Theme for English B

The instructor said,

  Go home and write
  a page tonight.

  And let that page come out of you—
  Then, it will be true.

I wonder if it's that simple?

I am twenty-two, colored, born in Winston-Salem.
I went to school there, then Durham, then here
to this college on the hill above Harlem.
I am the only colored student in my class.
The steps from the hill lead down to Harlem,
through a park, then I cross St. Nicholas,
Eighth Avenue, Seventh, and I come to the Y,
the Harlem Branch Y, where I take the elevator
up to my room, sit down, and write this page:

It's not easy to know what is true for you or me
at twenty-two, my age. But I guess I'm what
I feel and see and hear. Harlem, I hear you:
hear you, hear me—we two—you, me talk on this page.
(I hear New York, too.) Me—who?

Well, I like to eat, sleep, drink, and be in love.
I like to work, read, learn, and understand life.
I like a pipe for a Christmas present,
or records—Bessie, bop, or Bach.

I guess being colored doesn't make me not like
the same things other folks like who are other races.
So will my page be colored that I write?
Being me, it will not be white.
But it will be
a part of you, instructor.
You are white—
yet a part of me, as I am a part of you.
That's American.
Sometimes perhaps you don't want to be a part of me.
Nor do I often want to be a part of you.
But we are, that's true!
As I learn from you,
I guess you learn from me—
although you're older—and white—
and somewhat more free.

This is my page for English B.

# Harlem

What happens to a dream deferred?

Does it dry up
like a raisin in the sun?
Or fester like a sore—
And then run?
Does it stink like rotten meat?

Or crust and sugar over—
like a syrupy sweet?

Maybe it just sags
like a heavy load.

*Or does it explode?*

# VIRGINIA WOOLF
# from *To the Lighthouse*
## Part II: Time Passes

Virginia Woolf (1882–1941) was a major force in the Modernist project of dethroning the past and establishing the reign of newness everywhere. Much of her power as a catalyst sprang from her role in the Bloomsbury group, the coterie of writers who lived between the wars in the Bloomsbury area of London and had a strong impact on letters, art, and philosophy. A founder of the Hogarth Press, she influenced what people of this period read, publishing writers like Eliot (see "The Love Song of J. Alfred Prufrock"), who shared her Modernist outlook. Through her essays, she assisted in the triumph of new art, as, for example, in her 1910 piece welcoming the first London exhibit of the Post-Impressionist school. When feminism slowed down after British women won the right to vote in 1918, she renewed the feminist cause with her essay, *A Room of One's Own* (1929), in which she advocated cultural freedom for women. A toughminded critic (*The Common Reader*, 2 vols., 1925, 1932), she interpreted and made popular the era's new writings. Beyond all this, she was a novelist, trying new narrative methods, and it was in this area that she made her greatest contribution.

Woolf's novels reflected distaste for Realism, the style favored by late-nineteenth-century writers who focused on the surface of life while ignoring the mind's intersection with the external world. Woolf thought such intersections crucial, for it was there that readers achieved insight by understanding not only facts but their symbolic import. To this end, she adopted the stream-of-consciousness method, pioneered by Joyce (see *Ulysses*), to explore how different characters in her novels reacted and felt about each other and their environment. For example, in *Mrs Dalloway* (1925) she skillfully showed her upper-class heroine's complexity beneath a conventional exterior by presenting in a single day all the lives that touched hers, near or far, even unseen. Partly modeled on herself (Woolf was the daughter of Leslie Stephen, a famous man of letters in nineteenth-century London), Mrs. Dalloway was the society woman Woolf might have become had she not pursued a literary career.

### Reading the Selection

*To the Lighthouse* (1927) is concerned with the nature of reality, as filtered through memory. It is set in the out-of-the-way Hebrides Islands, off Scotland, with a lighthouse nearby, in the Ramsay's summer house crammed with family and guests. Nothing much happens, except that life unfolds, revealing petty tensions and old wounds among the assembled household. In form, the novel is divided into three sections, resembling successive waves on the shore, each wave transcending its predecessor. Part I, "The Window," is filled with idle summer chatter, and a trip to the lighthouse is canceled when the weather turns foul; Part II, "Time Passes" (the selection here), describes the summer house over several years (Mrs. Ramsay is now dead) through an anonymous voice that moves freely backward and forward in time, describing a world of objects bereft of human meaning; and Part III, "The Lighthouse," presents the much delayed sailing trip to the Lighthouse, portraying it as a quietly healing event for those who make it—ancient hurts are set aside and new ties are forged among the Ramsay family. The section closes with the vision, partly moral, partly aesthetic, of the houseguest Lily Briscoe, who was in love with the Ramsay family. Woolf's work, growing out of childhood summers with the Stephen family, transforms a personal memory into a universal story of love and forgiveness.

## I

Well, we must wait for the future to show," said Mr. Bankes, coming in from the terrace.

"It's almost too dark to see," said Andrew, coming up from the beach.

"One can hardly tell which is the sea and which is the land," said Prue.

"Do we leave that light burning?" said Lily as they took their coats off indoors.

"No," said Prue, "not if every one's in."

"Andrew," she called back, "just put out the light in the hall."

One by one the lamps were all extinguished, except that Mr. Carmichael, who liked to lie awake a little reading Virgil, kept his candle burning rather longer than the rest.

## II

So with the lamps all put out, the moon sunk, and a thin rain drumming on the roof a downpouring of immense darkness began. Nothing, it seemed, could survive the flood, the profusion of darkness which, creeping in at keyholes and crevices, stole round window blinds, came into bedrooms, swallowed up here a jug and basin, there a bowl of red and yellow dahlias, there the sharp edges and firm bulk of a chest of drawers. Not only was furniture confounded; there was scarcely anything left of body or mind by which one could say, "This is he" or "This is she." Sometimes a hand was raised as if to clutch something or ward off something, or somebody groaned, or somebody laughed aloud as if sharing a joke with nothingness.

Nothing stirred in the drawing-room or in the dining-room or on the staircase. Only through the rusty hinges and swollen sea-moistened woodwork certain airs, detached from the body of the wind (the house was ramshackle after all) crept round corners and ventured indoors. Almost one might imagine them, as they entered the drawing-room questioning and wondering, toying with the flap of hanging wall-paper, asking, would it hang much longer, when would it fall? Then smoothly brushing the walls, they passed on musingly as if asking the red and yellow roses on the wall-paper whether they would fade, and questioning (gently, for there was time at their disposal) the torn letters in the waste-paper basket, the flowers, the books, all of which were now open to them and asking, Were they allies? Were they enemies? How long would they endure?

So some random light directing them with its pale footfall upon stair and mat, from some uncovered star, or wandering ship, or the Lighthouse even, the little airs mounted the staircase and nosed round bedroom doors. But here surely, they must cease. Whatever else may perish and disappear, what lies here is steadfast. Here one might say to those sliding lights, those fumbling airs that breathe and bend over the bed itself, here you can neither touch nor destroy. Upon which, wearily, ghostily, as if they had feather-light fingers and the light persistency of feathers, they would look, once, on the shut eyes, and the loosely clasping fingers, and fold their garments wearily and disappear. And so, nosing, rubbing, they went to the window on the staircase, to the servants' bedrooms, to the boxes in the attics; descending, blanched the apples on the dining-room table, fumbled the petals of roses, tried the picture on the easel, brushed the mat and blew a little sand along the floor. At length, desisting, all ceased together, gathered together, all sighed together; all together gave off an aimless gust of lamentation to which some door in the kitchen replied; swung wide; admitted nothing; and slammed to.

[Here Mr. Carmichael, who was reading Virgil, blew out his candle. It was midnight.]

## III

But what after all is one night? A short space, especially when the darkness dims so soon, and so soon a bird sings, a cock crows, or a faint green quickens, like a turning leaf, in the hollow of the wave. Night, however, succeeds to night. The winter holds a pack of them in store and deals them equally, evenly, with indefatigable fingers. They lengthen; they darken. Some of them hold aloft clear planets, plates of brightness. The autumn trees, ravaged as they are, take on the flash of tattered flags kindling in the gloom of cool cathedral caves where gold letters on marble pages describe death in battle and how bones bleach and burn far away in Indian sands. The autumn trees gleam in the yellow moonlight, in the light of harvest moons, the light which mellows the energy of labour, and smooths the stubble, and brings the wave lapping blue to the shore.

It seemed now as if, touched by human penitence and all its toil, divine goodness had parted the curtain and displayed behind it, single, distinct, the hare erect; the wave falling; the boat rocking, which, did we deserve them, should be ours always. But alas, divine goodness, twitching the cord, draws the curtain; it does not please him; he covers his treasures in a drench of hail, and so breaks them, so confuses them that it seems impossible that their calm should ever return or that we should ever compose from their fragments a perfect whole or read in the littered pieces the clear words of truth. For our penitence deserves a glimpse only; our toil respite only.

The nights now are full of wind and destruction; the trees plunge and bend and their leaves fly helter skelter until the lawn is plastered with them and they lie packed in gutters and choke rain-pipes and scatter damp paths. Also the sea tosses itself and breaks itself, and should any sleeper fancying that he might find on the beach an answer to his doubts, a sharer of his solitude, throw off his bedclothes and go down by himself to walk on the sand, no image with semblance of serving and divine promptitude comes readily to hand bringing the night to order and making the world reflect the compass of the soul. The hand dwindles in his hand; the voice bellows in his ear. Almost it would appear that it is useless in such confusion to ask the night those questions as to what, and why, and wherefore, which tempt the sleeper from his bed to seek an answer.

[Mr. Ramsay, stumbling along a passage one dark morning, stretched his arms out, but Mrs. Ramsay having died rather suddenly the night before, his arms, though stretched out, remained empty.]

### IV

So with the house empty and the doors locked and the mattresses rolled round, those stray airs, advance guards of great armies, blustered in, brushed bare boards, nibbled and fanned, met nothing in bedroom or drawing-room that wholly resisted them but only hangings that flapped, wood that creaked, the bare legs of tables, saucepans and china already furred, tarnished, cracked. What people had shed and left—a pair of shoes, a shooting cap, some faded skirts and coats in wardrobes—those alone kept the human shape and in the emptiness indicated how once they were filled and animated; how once hands were busy with hooks and buttons; how once the looking-glass had held a face; had held a world hollowed out in which a figure turned, a hand flashed, the door opened, in came children rushing and tumbling; and went out again. Now, day after day, light turned, like a flower reflected in water, its sharp image on the wall opposite. Only the shadows of the trees, flourishing in the wind, made obeisance on the wall, and for a moment darkened the pool in which light reflected itself; or birds, flying, made a soft spot flutter slowly across the bedroom floor.

So loveliness reigned and stillness, and together made the shape of loveliness itself, a form from which life had parted; solitary like a pool at evening, far distant, seen from a train window, vanishing so quickly that the pool, pale in the evening, is scarcely robbed of its solitude, though once seen. Loveliness and stillness clasped hands in the bedroom, and among the shrouded jugs and sheeted chairs even the prying of the wind, and the soft nose of the clammy sea airs, rubbing, snuffling, iterating, and reiterating their questions—"Will you fade? Will you perish?"—scarcely disturbed the peace, the indifference, the air of pure integrity, as if the question they asked scarcely needed that they should answer: we remain.

Nothing it seemed could break that image, corrupt that innocence, or disturb the swaying mantle of silence which, week after week, in the empty room, wove into itself the falling cries of birds, ships hooting, the drone and hum of the fields, a dog's bark, a man's shout, and folded them round the house in silence. Once only a board sprang on the landing; once in the middle of the night with a roar, with a rupture, as after centuries of quiescence, a rock rends itself from the mountain and hurtles crashing into the valley, one fold of the shawl loosened and swung to and fro. Then again peace descended; and the shadow wavered; light bent to its own image in adoration on the bedroom wall; and Mrs. McNab, tearing the veil of silence with hands that had stood in the wash-tub, grinding it with boots that had crunched the shingle, came as directed to open all windows, and dust the bedrooms.

### V

As she lurched (for she rolled like a ship at sea) and leered (for her eyes fell on nothing directly, but with a sidelong glance that deprecated the scorn and anger of the world—she was witless, she knew it), as she clutched the banisters and hauled herself upstairs and rolled from room to room, she sang. Rubbing the glass of the long looking-glass and leering sideways at her swinging figure a sound issued from her lips—something that had been gay twenty years before on the stage perhaps, had been hummed and danced to, but now, coming from the toothless, bonneted, care-taking woman, was robbed of meaning, was like the voice of witlessness, humour, persistency itself, trodden down but springing up again, so that as she lurched, dusting, wiping, she seemed to say how it was one long sorrow and trouble, how it was getting up and going to bed again, and bringing things out and putting them away again. It was not easy or snug this world she had known for close on seventy years. Bowed down she was with weariness. How long, she asked, creaking and groaning on her knees under the bed, dusting the boards, how long shall it endure? but hobbled to her feet again, pulled herself up, and again with her sidelong leer which slipped and turned aside even from her own face, and her own sorrows, stood and gaped in the glass, aimlessly smiling, and began again the old amble and hobble, taking up mats, putting down china, looking sideways in the glass, as if, after all, she had her consolations, as if indeed there twined about her dirge some incorrigible hope. Visions of joy there must have been at the wash-tub, say with her children (yet two had been base-born and one had deserted her), at the public-house, drinking; turning over scraps in her drawers. Some cleavage of the dark there must have been, some channel in the depths of obscurity through which light enough issued to twist her face grinning in the glass and make her, turning to her job again, mumble out the old music hall song. The mystic, the visionary, walking the beach on a fine night, stirring a puddle, looking at a stone, asking themselves "What am I," "What is this?" had suddenly an answer vouchsafed them: (they could not say what it was) so that they were warm in the frost and had comfort in the desert. But Mrs. McNab continued to drink and gossip as before.

### VI

The spring without a leaf to toss, bare and bright like a virgin fierce in her chastity, scornful in her purity, was laid out on fields wide-eyed and watchful and entirely careless of what was done or thought by the beholders. [Prue Ramsay, leaning on her father's arm, was given in marriage. What, people said, could have been more fitting? And, they added, how beautiful she looked!]

As summer neared, as the evenings lengthened, there came to the wakeful, the hopeful, walking the beach, stirring the pool, imaginations of the strangest kind—of flesh turned to atoms which drove before the wind, of stars flashing in their hearts, of cliff, sea, cloud, and sky brought purposely together to assemble outwardly the scattered parts of the vision within. In those mirrors, the minds of men, in those pools of uneasy water, in which clouds for ever turn and shadows form, dreams persisted, and it was impossible to resist the strange intimation which every gull, flower, tree, man and woman, and the white earth itself seemed to declare (but if questioned at once to withdraw) that good triumphs, happiness prevails, order rules; or to resist the extraordinary stimulus to range hither and thither in search of some absolute good, some crystal of intensity, remote from the known pleasures and familiar virtues, something alien to the processes of domestic life, single, hard, bright, like a diamond in the sand, which would render the possessor secure. Moreover, softened and acquiescent, the spring with her bees humming and gnats dancing threw her cloak about her, veiled her eyes, averted her head, and among passing shadows and flights of small rain seemed to have taken upon her a knowledge of the sorrows of mankind.

[Prue Ramsay died that summer in some illness connected with childbirth, which was indeed a tragedy, people said, everything, they said, had promised so well.]

And now in the heat of summer the wind sent its spies about the house again. Flies wove a web in the sunny rooms; weeds that had grown close to the glass in the night tapped methodically at the window-pane. When darkness fell, the stroke of the Lighthouse, which had laid itself with such authority upon the carpet in the darkness, tracing its pattern, came now in the softer light of spring mixed with moonlight gliding gently as if it laid its caress and lingered stealthily and looked and came lovingly again. But in the very lull of this loving caress, as the long stroke leant upon the bed, the rock was rent asunder; another fold of the shawl loosened; there it hung, and swayed. Through the short summer nights and the long summer days, when the empty rooms seemed to murmur with the echoes of the fields and the hum of flies, the long streamer waved gently, swayed aimlessly; while the sun so striped and barred the rooms and filled them with yellow haze that Mrs. McNab, when she broke in and lurched about, dusting, sweeping, looked like a tropical fish oaring its way through sun-lanced waters.

But slumber and sleep though it might there came later in the summer ominous sounds like the measured blows of hammers dulled on felt, which, with their repeated shocks still further loosened the shawl and cracked the tea-cups. Now and again some glass tinkled in the cupboard as if a giant voice had shrieked so loud in its agony that tumblers stood inside a cupboard vibrated too. Then again silence fell; and then, night after night, and sometimes in plain mid-day when the roses were bright and light turned on the wall its shape clearly there seemed to drop into this silence, this indifference, this integrity, the thud of something falling.

[A shell exploded. Twenty or thirty young men were blown up in France, among them Andrew Ramsay, whose death, mercifully, was instantaneous.]

At that season those who had gone down to pace the beach and ask of the sea and sky what message they reported or what vision they affirmed had to consider among the usual tokens of divine bounty—the sunset on the sea, the pallor of dawn, the moon rising, fishing-boats against the moon, and children making mud pies or pelting each other with handfuls of grass, something out of harmony with this jocundity and this serenity. There was the silent apparition of an ashen-coloured ship for instance, come, gone; there was a purplish stain upon the bland surface of the sea as if something had boiled and bled, invisibly, beneath. This intrusion into a scene calculated to stir the most sublime reflections and lead to the most comfortable conclusions stayed their pacing. It was difficult blandly to overlook them; to abolish their significance in the landscape; to continue, as one walked by the sea, to marvel how beauty outside mirrored beauty within.

Did Nature supplement what man advanced? Did she complete what he began? With equal complacence she saw his misery, his meanness, and his torture. That dream, of sharing, completing, of finding in solitude on the beach an answer, was then but a reflection in a mirror, and the mirror itself was but the surface glassiness which forms in quiescence when the nobler powers sleep beneath? Impatient, despairing yet loth to go (for beauty offers her lures, has her consolations), to pace the beach was impossible; contemplation was unendurable; the mirror was broken.

[Mr. Carmichael brought out a volume of poems that spring, which had an unexpected success. The war, people said, had revived their interest in poetry.]

## VII

Night after night, summer and winter, the torment of storms, the arrow-like stillness of fine weather, held their court without interference. Listening (had there been any one to listen) from the upper rooms of the empty house only gigantic chaos streaked with lightning could have been heard tumbling and tossing, as the winds and waves disported themselves like the amorphous bulks of leviathans whose brows are pierced by no light of reason, and mounted one on top of another, and lunged and plunged in the darkness or the daylight (for night and day, month and year ran shapelessly together) in idiot games, until it seemed as if the universe were battling and tumbling, in brute confusion and wanton lust aimlessly by itself.

In spring the garden urns, casually filled with wind-blown plants, were gay as ever. Violets came and daffodils. But the stillness and the brightness of the day were as strange as the chaos and tumult of night, with the trees standing there, and the flowers standing there, looking before them, looking up, yet beholding nothing, eyeless, and so terrible.

## VIII

Thinking no harm, for the family would not come, never again, some said, and the house would be sold at Michaelmas perhaps, Mrs. McNab stooped and picked a bunch of flowers to take home with her. She laid them on the table while she dusted. She was fond of flowers. It was a pity to let them waste. Suppose the house were sold (she stood arms akimbo in front of the looking-glass) it would want seeing to—it would. There it had stood all these years without a soul in it. The books and things were mouldy, for, what with the war and help being hard to get, the house had not been cleaned as she could have wished. It was beyond one person's strength to get it straight now. She was too old. Her legs pained her. All those books needed to be laid out on the grass in the sun; there was plaster fallen in the hall; the rainpipe had blocked over the study window and let the water in; the carpet was ruined quite. But people should come themselves; they should have sent somebody down to see. For there were clothes in the cupboards; they had left clothes in all the bedrooms. What was she to do with them? They had the moth in them—Mrs. Ramsay's things. Poor lady! She would never want *them* again. She was dead, they said; years ago, in London. There was the old grey cloak she wore gardening (Mrs. McNab fingered it). She could see her, as she came up the drive with the washing, stooping over her flowers (the garden was a pitiful sight now, all run to riot, and rabbits scuttling at you out of the beds)—she could see her with one of the children by her in the grey cloak. There were boots and shoes; and a brush and comb left on the dressing-table, for all the world as if she expected to come back tomorrow. (She had died very sudden at the end, they said.) And once they had been coming, but had put off coming, what with the war, and travel being so difficult these days; they had never come all these years; just sent her money; but never wrote, never came, and expected to find things as they had left them, ah, dear! Why the dressing-table drawers were full of things (she pulled them open), handkerchiefs, bits of ribbon. Yes, she could see Mrs. Ramsay as she came up the drive with the washing.

"Good-evening, Mrs. McNab," she would say.

She had a pleasant way with her. The girls all liked her. But, dear, many things had changed since then (she shut the drawer); many families had lost their dearest. So she was dead; and Mr. Andrew killed; and Miss Prue dead too, they said, with her first baby; but every one had lost some one these years. Prices had gone up shamefully, and didn't come down again neither. She could well remember her in her grey cloak.

"Good-evening, Mrs. McNab," she said, and told cook to keep a plate of milk soup for her—quite thought she wanted it, carrying that heavy basket all the way up from town. She could see her now, stooping over her flowers; and faint and flickering, like a yellow beam or the circle at the end of a telescope, a lady in a grey cloak, stooping over her flowers, went wandering over the bedroom wall, up the dressing-table, across the wash-stand, as Mrs. McNab hobbled and ambled, dusting, straightening. And cook's name now? Mildred? Marian?—some name like that. Ah, she had forgotten—she did forget things. Fiery, like all red-haired women. Many a laugh they had had. She was always welcome in the kitchen. She made them laugh, she did. Things were better then than now.

She sighed; there was too much work for one woman. She wagged her head this side and that. This had been the nursery. Why, it was all damp in here; the plaster was falling. Whatever did they want to hang a beast's skull there? gone mouldy too. And rats in all the attics. The rain came in. But they never sent; never came. Some of the locks had gone, so the doors banged. She didn't like to be up here at dusk alone neither. It was too much for one woman, too much, too much. She creaked, she moaned. She banged the door.

She turned the key in the lock, and left the house alone, shut up, locked.

## IX

The house was left; the house was deserted. It was left like a shell on a sandhill to fill with dry salt grains now that life had left it. The long night seemed to have set in; the trifling airs, nibbling, the clammy breaths, fumbling, seemed to have triumphed. The saucepan had rusted and the mat decayed. Toads had nosed their way in. Idly, aimlessly, the swaying shawl swung to and fro. A thistle thrust itself between the tiles in the larder. The swallows nested in the drawing-room; the floor was strewn with straw; the plaster fell in shovelfuls; rafters were laid bare; rats carried off this and that to gnaw behind the wainscots. Tortoise-shell butterflies burst from the chrysalis and pattered their life out on the windowpane. Poppies sowed themselves among the dahlias; the lawn waved with long grass; giant artichokes towered among roses; a fringed carnation flowered among the cabbages; while the gentle tapping of a weed at the window had become, on winters' nights, a drumming from sturdy trees and thorned briars which made the whole room green in summer.

What power could now prevent the fertility, the insensibility of nature? Mrs. McNab's dream of a lady, of a child, of a plate of milk soup? It had wavered over the walls like a spot of sunlight and vanished. She had locked the door; she had gone. It was beyond the strength of one woman, she said. They never sent. They never wrote. There were things up there rotting in the drawers—it was a shame to leave them so, she said. The place was gone to rack and ruin. Only the Lighthouse beam entered the rooms for a moment, sent its sudden stare over bed and wall in the darkness of winter, looked with equanimity at the thistle and the swallow, the rat and the straw. Nothing now withstood them; nothing said no to them. Let the wind blow; let the poppy seed itself and the carnation mate with the cabbage. Let the swallow build in the drawing-room, and the thistle thrust aside the tiles, and the butterfly sun itself on the faded chintz of the arm-chairs. Let the broken glass and the china lie out on the lawn and be tangled over with grass and wild berries.

For now had come that moment, that hesitation when dawn trembles and night pauses, when if a feather alight in the scale it will be weighed down. One feather, and the house, sinking, falling, would have turned and pitched downwards to the depths of darkness. In the ruined room, picnickers would have lit their kettles; lovers sought shelter there, lying on the bare boards; and the shepherd stored his dinner on the bricks, and the tramp slept with his coat round him to ward off the cold. Then the roof would have fallen; briars and hemlocks would have blotted out path, step, and window; would have grown, unequally but lustily over the mound, until some trespasser, losing his way, could have told only by a red-hot poker among the nettles, or a scrap of china in the hemlock that here once some one had lived; there had been a house.

If the feather had fallen, if it had tipped the scale downwards, the whole house would have plunged to the depths to lie upon the sands of oblivion. But there was a force working; something not highly conscious; something that leered, something that lurched; something not inspired to go about its work with dignified ritual or solemn chanting. Mrs. McNab groaned; Mrs. Bast creaked. They were old; they were stiff; their legs ached. They came with their brooms and pails at last; they got to work. All of a sudden, would Mrs. McNab see that the house was ready, one of the young ladies wrote: would she get this done; would she get that done; all in a hurry. They might be coming for the summer; had left everything to the last; expected to find things as they had left them. Slowly and painfully, with broom and pail, mopping, scouring, Mrs. McNab, Mrs. Bast, stayed the corruption and the rot; rescued from the pool of Time that was fast closing over them now a basin, now a cupboard; fetched up from oblivion all the Waverley novels and a tea-set one morning; in the afternoon restored to sun and air a brass fender and a set of steel fire-irons. George, Mrs. Bast's son, caught the rats, and cut the grass. They had the builders. Attended with the creaking of hinges and the screeching of bolts, the slamming and banging of damp-swollen woodwork some rusty laborious birth seemed to be taking place, as the women, stooping, rising, groaning, singing, slapped and slammed, upstairs now, now down in the cellars. Oh, they said, the work!

They drank their tea in the bedroom sometimes, or in the study; breaking off work at mid-day with the smudge on their faces, and their old hands clasped and cramped with the broom handles. Flopped on chairs, they contemplated now the magnificent conquest over taps and bath; now the more arduous, more partial triumph over long rows of books, black as ravens once, now white-stained, breeding pale mushrooms and secreting furtive spiders. Once more, as she felt the tea warm in her, the telescope fitted itself to Mrs. McNab's eyes, and in a ring of light she saw the old gentleman, lean as a rake, wagging his head, as she came up with the washing, talking to himself, she supposed, on the lawn. He never noticed her. Some said he was dead; some said she was dead. Which was it? Mrs. Bast didn't know for certain either. The young gentleman was dead. That she was sure. She had read his name in the papers.

There was the cook now, Mildred, Marian, some such name as that—a red-headed woman, quick-tempered like all her sort, but kind, too, if you knew the way with her. Many a laugh they had had together. She saved a plate of soup for Maggie; a bite of ham, sometimes; whatever was over. They lived well in those days. They had everything they wanted (glibly, jovially, with the tea hot in her, she unwound her ball of memories, sitting in the wicker arm-chair by the nursery fender). There was always plenty doing, people in the house, twenty staying sometimes, and washing up till long past midnight.

Mrs. Bast (she had never known them; had lived in Glasgow at that time) wondered, putting her cup down, whatever they hung that beast's skull there for? Shot in foreign parts no doubt.

It might well be, said Mrs. McNab, wantoning on with her memories; they had friends in eastern countries; gentlemen staying there, ladies in evening dress; she had seen them once through the dining-room door all sitting at dinner. Twenty she dared say all in their jewellery, and she asked to stay help wash up, might be till after midnight.

Ah, said Mrs. Bast, they'd find it changed. She leant out of the window. She watched her son George scything the grass. They might well ask, what had been done to it? seeing how old Kennedy was supposed to have charge of it, and then his leg got so bad after he fell from the cart; and perhaps then no one for a year, or the better part of one; and then Davie Macdonald, and seeds might be sent, but who should say if they were ever planted? They'd find it changed.

She watched her son scything. He was a great one for work—one of those quiet ones. Well they must be getting along with the cupboards, she supposed. They hauled themselves up.

At last, after days of labour within, of cutting and digging without, dusters were flicked from the windows, the windows were shut to, keys were turned all over the house; the front door was banged; it was finished.

And now as if the cleaning and the scrubbing and the scything and the mowing had drowned it there rose that half-heard melody, that intermittent music which the ear half catches but lets fall; a bark, a bleat; irregular, intermittent, yet somehow related; the hum of an insect, the tremor of cut grass, dissevered yet somehow belonging; the jar of a dorbeetle, the squeak of a wheel, loud, low, but mysteriously related; which the ear strains to bring together and is always on the verge of harmonising, but they are never quite heard, never fully harmonised, and at last, in the evening, one after another the sounds die out, and the harmony falters, and silence falls. With the sunset sharpness was lost, and like mist rising, quiet rose, quiet spread, the wind settled; loosely the world shook itself down to sleep, darkly here without a light to it, save what came green suffused through leaves, or pale on the white flowers in the bed by the window.

(Lily Briscoe had her bag carried up to the house late one evening in September.)

## X

Then indeed peace had come. Messages of peace breathed from the sea to the shore. Never to break its sleep any more, to lull it rather more deeply to rest, and whatever the dreamers dreamt holily, dreamt wisely, to confirm—what else was it murmuring—as Lily Briscoe laid her head on the pillow in the clean still room and heard the sea. Through the open window the voice of the beauty of the world came murmuring, too softly to hear exactly what it said—but what mattered if the meaning were plain? entreating the sleepers (the house was full again; Mrs. Beckwith was staying there, also Mr. Carmichael), if they would not actually come down to the beach itself at least to lift the blind and look out. They would see then night flowing down in purple; his head crowned; his sceptre jewelled; and how in his eyes a child might look. And if they still faltered (Lily was tired out with travelling and slept almost at once; but Mr. Carmichael read a book by candlelight), if they still said no, that it was vapour, this splendour of his, and the dew had more power than he, and they preferred sleeping; gently then without complaint, or argument, the voice would sing its song. Gently the waves would break (Lily heard them in her sleep); tenderly the light fell (it seemed to come through her eyelids). And it all looked,

Mr. Carmichael thought, shutting his book, falling asleep, much as it used to look.

Indeed the voice might resume, as the curtains of dark wrapped themselves over the house, over Mrs. Beckwith, Mr. Carmichael, and Lily Briscoe so that they lay with several folds of blackness on their eyes, why not accept this, be content with this, acquiesce and resign? The sigh of all the seas breaking in measure round the isles soothed them; the night wrapped them; nothing broke their sleep, until, the birds beginning and the dawn weaving their thin voices in to its whiteness, a cart grinding, a dog somewhere barking, the sun lifted the curtains, broke the veil on their eyes, and Lily Briscoe stirring in her sleep. She clutched at her blankets as a faller clutches at the turf on the edge of a cliff. Her eyes opened wide. Here she was again, she thought, sitting bolt upright in bed. Awake.

# ZORA NEALE HURSTON
## *How It Feels to Be Colored Me*

The African-American writer Zora Neale Hurston (1891–1960) is probably the most widely read black woman writer in schools and colleges today, but her literary reputation, like her life, has been a roller-coaster. She once exulted: "I have been in Sorrow's kitchen and licked out all the pots. Then I have stood on the peaky mountain wrapped in rainbows, with a harp and a sword in my hands."

Born in Florida, poor and subjected to racism, Hurston moved North where she shone as one of the most original voices of the Harlem Renaissance. From 1925 to 1945, she was a widely acclaimed writer, author of three novels (*Jonah's Gourd Vine*, 1934; *Their Eyes Were Watching God*, 1937; and *Moses, Man of the Mountain*, 1939); two books of folklore (*Mules and Men*, 1935, and *Tell My Horse*, 1938); an autobiography (*Dust Tracks on a Road*, 1942); and many short stories, essays, and plays. After 1945, she continued to write, publishing a fourth novel (*Seraph on the Suwanee*, 1948) and a few stories and essays, but her audience lost interest and she fell into oblivion. In 1950, she worked as a maid, and, when she died, in a welfare home, she had all but been forgotten. That changed when growing interest in black culture led scholars to rediscover her works and restore her to a preeminent place in American letters.

Hurston's literary task resembled that of Hughes (see "The Negro Speaks of Rivers," etc.), her contemporary, in that both wrote about being black in a white-dominated world, expressed themselves in black vernacular speech, and drew on jazz, blues, and folk-tales. Also like Hughes, Hurston was educated; she studied at Howard University, Washington, D.C., 1921–1924, and graduated from Barnard College, New York City, in 1928, before spending some years in Columbia University's graduate program in anthropology (her books on folklore are based on research in the American South, Jamaica, Haiti, and Bermuda). Still, when compared to Hughes, Hurston was doubly disadvantaged, for, as a black and a woman writer, she had to contend with both racism and sexism. In the 1930s, most black male writers dismissed her on the grounds that her writing sounded like a minstrel show. Even Hughes, while admiring her works, found her personally too ingratiating to whites: "In her youth she was always getting scholarships and things from wealthy white people, some of whom simply paid her to sit around and represent the Negro race for them, she did it in such a racy fashion." "Representing the Negro race for whites" was, of course, the project of the Harlem Renaissance, and Hurston's genius was that, in her writings, she did it better than anyone else.

### Reading the Selection

Hurston's essay, "How It Feels to be Colored Me" (1928), registers—as if in answer to an unspoken question—her complex feelings about being born black in white America. Reviewing her life (she was 37 at the time), she offers a set of conflicting and ironic stereotypes to describe herself, "the 'happy Negro' who performed for white folks," "the exotic primitive," "the eternal feminine," "a brown bag in company with other bags, white, red, and yellow," only to dismiss all of them in the essay's last words: "Who knows?" Hurston's response affirms that identity, rather than being fixed is shape-shifting, a matter of situation and strategy.

Hurston's essay is written in mainstream English, though it is barely able to contain her irrepressible spirit, which, in later works, was more at home in the idiom of the black oral tradition.

––––––––––

I am colored but I offer nothing in the way of extenuating circumstances except the fact that I am the only Negro in the United States whose grandfather on the mother's side was *not* an Indian chief.

I remember the very day that I became colored. Up to my thirteenth year I lived in the little Negro town of Eatonville, Florida. It is exclusively a colored town. The only white people I knew passed through the town going to or coming from Orlando. The native whites rode dusty horses, the Northern tourists chugged down the sandy village road in automobiles. The town knew the Southerners and never stopped cane chewing when they passed. But the Northerners were something else again. They were peered at cautiously from behind curtains by the timid. The more venturesome would come out on the porch to watch them go past and got just as much pleasure out of the tourists as the tourists got out of the village.

The front porch might seem a daring place for the rest of the town, but it was a gallery seat for me. My favorite place was atop the gate-post. Proscenium box for a born first-nighter. Not only did I enjoy the show, but I didn't mind the actors knowing that I liked it. I usually spoke to them in passing. I'd wave at them and when they returned my salute, I would say something like this: "Howdy-do-well-I-thank-you-where-you-goin'?" Usually automobile or the horse paused at this, and after a queer exchange of compliments, I would probably "go a piece of the way" with them, as we say in farthest Florida. If one of my family happened to come to the front in time to see me, of course negotiations would be rudely broken off. But even so, it is clear that I was the first "welcome-to-our-state" Floridian, and I hope the Miami Chamber of Commerce will please take notice.

During this period, white people differed from colored to me only in that they rode through town and never lived there. They liked to hear me "speak pieces" and sing and wanted to see me dance the parse-mela, and gave me generously of their small silver for doing these things, which seemed strange to me for I wanted to do them so much that I needed bribing to stop. Only they didn't know it. The colored people gave no dimes. They deplored any joyful tendencies in me, but I was their Zora nevertheless. I belonged to them, to the nearby hotels, to the county—everybody's Zora.

But changes came in the family when I was thirteen, and I was sent to school in Jacksonville. I left Eatonville, the town of the oleanders, as Zora. When I disembarked from the river-boat at Jacksonville, she was no more. It seemed that I had suffered a sea change. I was not Zora of Orange County any more, I was now a little colored girl. I found it out in certain ways. In my heart as well as in the mirror, I became a fast brown—warranted not to rub nor run.

But I am not tragically colored. There is no great sorrow dammed up in my soul, nor lurking behind my eyes. I do not mind at all. I do not belong to the sobbing school of Negrohood who hold that nature somehow has given them a lowdown dirty deal and whose feelings are all hurt about it. Even in the helter-skelter skirmish that is my life, I have seen that the world is to the strong regardless of a little pigmentation more or less. No, I do not weep at the world—I am too busy sharpening my oyster knife.

Someone is always at my elbow reminding me that I am the granddaughter of slaves. It fails to register depression with me. Slavery is sixty years in the past. The operation was successful and the patient is doing well, thank you. The terrible struggle that made me an American out of a potential slave said "On the line!" The Reconstruction said "Get set!"; and the generation before said "Go!" I am off to a flying start and I must not halt in the stretch to look behind and weep. Slavery is the price I paid for civilization, and the choice was not with me. It is a bully adventure and worth all that I have paid through my ancestors for it. No one on earth ever had a greater chance for glory. The world to be won and nothing to be lost. It is thrilling to think—to know that for any act of mine, I shall get twice as much praise or twice as much blame. It is quite exciting to hold the center of the national stage, with the spectators not knowing whether to laugh or to weep.

The position of my white neighbor is much more difficult. No brown specter pulls up a chair beside me when I sit down to eat. No dark ghost thrusts its leg against mine in bed. The game of keeping what one has is never so exciting as the game of getting.

I do not always feel colored. Even now I often achieve the unconscious Zora of Eatonville before the Hegira. I feel most colored when I am thrown against a sharp white background.

For instance at Barnard. "Beside the waters of the Hudson" I feel my race. Among the thousand white persons, I am a dark rock surged upon, and overswept, but through it all, I remain myself. When covered by the waters, I am; and the ebb but reveals me again.

Sometimes it is the other way around. A white person is set down in our midst, but the contrast is just as sharp for me. For instance, when I sit in the drafty basement that is The New World Cabaret with a white person, my color comes. We enter chatting about any little nothing that we have in common and are seated by the jazz waiters. In the abrupt way that jazz orchestras have, this one plunges into a number. It loses no time in circumlocutions, but gets right down to business. It constricts the thorax and splits the heart with its tempo and narcotic harmonies. This orchestra grows rambunctious, rears on its hind legs and attacks the tonal veil with primitive fury, rending it, clawing it until it breaks through to the jungle beyond. I follow those heathen—follow them exultingly. I dance wildly inside myself; I yell within, I whoop; I shake my assegai above my head, I hurl it true to the mark *yeeeeooww!* I am in the jungle and living in the jungle way. My face is painted red and yellow and my body is painted blue. My pulse is throbbing like a war drum. I want to slaughter something—give pain, give death to what, I do not know. But the piece ends. The men of the orchestra wipe their lips and rest their fingers. I creep back slowly to the veneer we call civilization with the last tone and find the white friend sitting motionless in his seat, smoking calmly.

"Good music they have here," he remarks, drumming the table with his fingertips.

Music. The great blobs of purple and red emotion have not touched him. He has only heard what I felt. He is far away and I see him but dimly across the ocean and the continent that have fallen between us. He is so pale with his whiteness then and I am *so* colored.

At certain times I have no race, I am *me*. When I set my hat at a certain angle and saunter down Seventh Avenue, Harlem City, feeling as snooty as the lions in front of the Forty-Second Street Library, for instance. So far as my feelings are concerned, Peggy Hopkins Joyce on the Boule Mich with her gorgeous raiment, stately carriage, knees knocking together in a most aristocratic manner, has nothing on me. The cosmic Zora emerges. I belong to no race nor time. I am the eternal feminine with its string of beads.

I have no separate feeling about being an American citizen and colored. I am merely a fragment of the Great Soul that surges within the boundaries. My country, right or wrong.

Sometimes, I feel discriminated against, but it does not make me angry. It merely astonishes me. How *can* any deny themselves the pleasure of my company? It's beyond me.

But in the main, I feel like a brown bag of miscellany propped against a wall. Against a wall in company with other bags, white, red and yellow. Pour out the contents, and there is discovered a jumble of small things priceless and worthless. A first-water diamond, an empty spool, bits of broken glass, lengths of string, a key to a door long since crumbled away, a rusty knife-blade, old shoes saved for a road that never was and never will be, a nail bent under the weight of things too heavy for any nail, a dried flower or two still a little fragrant. In your hand is the brown bag. On the ground before you is the jumble it held—so much like the jumble in the bags, could they be emptied, that all might be dumped in a single heap and the bags refilled without altering the content of any greatly. A bit of colored glass more or less would not matter. Perhaps that is how the Great Stuffer of Bags filled them in the first place—who knows?

# WILLIAM FAULKNER
# from *The Sound and the Fury*
### April Seventh, 1928.

*The Sound and the Fury* (1929), a novel about the American South, is one of the classics of Modernism. With its stream-of-consciousness narrative, adopted from Joyce (see *Ulysses*) and Woolf (see *To the Lighthouse*), this novel introduced European-style experimentation into American letters and made its author, William Faulkner (1897–1962), a force in world literature. By 1939, for example, translations of *The Sound and the Fury* and five other novels by Faulkner were available to French writers, like Camus, who imitated their "interior monologue" technique. Largely neglected in the 1940s, Faulkner reemerged onto the international stage, in 1950, when he received the Nobel Prize for literature, a recognition of his heroic achievement.

Faulkner belonged to that species of writer who finds the world in a grain of sand, metaphorically speaking. His "grain of sand" was Yoknapatawpha, the fictional Mississippi county—based on Faulkner's own Lafayette County—whose history he wrote in the series of sixteen novels beginning with *Sartoris* (1929) and ending with *The Reivers* (1962). These novels deal with the period mainly between the end of the Civil War and the time Faulkner was writing; an old social order, characterized by a gentleman's code of behavior, was passing away, defeated from within, and a new social pattern, expressed in a code of "everyone looking out for number one," was being born. In some novels, this changing order is represented through, respectively, the Sartoris family, who are gentry in decline, and the money-grubbing Snopes clan, who are "poor whites" on the make. White society is usually the foreground, but black life, providing an element of stability, is always present, represented by black servants who hold white families together. Racism is sometimes a theme (*Light in August*, 1932), and when it is, Faulkner portrays black victims with sympathy. Yoknapatawpha functions as a symbol of the entire South, but it also stands for any place where there is a decline in old ways.

### Reading the Selection

This passage—the first few pages of *The Sound and the Fury*—shows Faulkner blending "local color" with experimental method. Tough going for a first-time Faulkner reader, the passage begins to make sense only with great difficulty. The speaker is Benjamin, the thirty-three-year-old idiot son of the Compsons, the Yoknapatawpha family gone to seed, whose history is the focus of the novel. This opening gambit, as well as the novel's title are derived from Shakespeare's famous line in *Macbeth*, Act V, Scene V: "Life's . . . a tale/Told by an idiot, full of sound and fury,/Signifying nothing." Benjamin's untrustworthy monologue runs for almost one hundred pages.

The novel is about the dissolution of the Compson family, but this theme is clouded initially, because Benjamin is the narrator, and in his disordered mind, reality and memory are merged. The full tragedy of the Compsons comes into view only later in the novel, when other family members tell their stories. When the novel opens, Benjamin is watching a golf game, while being looked after by Luster, the fourteen-year-old son of Dilsey, the black cook. At the same time, the past asserts itself in Benjamin's memories of Caddy, or Candace, his sister and protector, when he was a child. Only gradually is it learned that the family has banished the adult Candace for reasons of sexual promiscuity, and her daughter, Quentin, who lives with the Compsons, may be a child of incest.

---

Through the fence, between the curling flower spaces, I could see them hitting. They were coming toward where the flag was and I went along the fence. Luster was hunting in the grass by the flower tree. They took the flag out, and they were hitting. Then they put the flag back and they went to the table, and he hit and the other hit. Then they went on, and I went along the fence. Luster came away from the flower tree and we went along the fence and they stopped and we stopped and I looked through the fence while Luster was hunting in the grass.

"Here, caddie." He hit. They went away across the pasture. I held to the fence and watched them going away.

"Listen at you, now." Luster said. "Aint you something, thirty three years old, going on that way. After I done went all the way to town to buy you that cake. Hush up that moaning. Aint you going to help me find that quarter so I can go to the show tonight."

They were hitting little, across the pasture. I went back along the fence to where the flag was. It flapped on the bright grass and the trees.

"Come on." Luster said. "We done looked there. They aint no more coming right now. Les go down to the branch and find that quarter before them niggers finds it."

It was red, flapping on the pasture. Then there was a bird slanting and tilting on it. Luster threw. The flag flapped on the bright grass and the trees. I held to the fence.

"Shut up that moaning." Luster said. "I cant make them come if they aint coming, can I. If you dont hush up, mammy aint going to have no birthday for you. If you dont hush, you know what I going to do. I going to eat that cake all up. Eat them candles, too. Eat all them thirty three candles. Come on, les go down to the branch. I got to find my quarter. Maybe we can find one of they balls. Here. Here they is. Way over yonder. See." He came to the fence and pointed his arm. "See them. They aint coming back here no more. Come on."

We went along the fence and came to the garden fence, where our shadows were. My shadow was higher than Luster's on the fence. We came to the broken place and went through it.

"Wait a minute." Luster said. "You snagged on that nail again. Cant you never crawl through here without snagging on that nail."

*Caddy uncaught me and we crawled through. Uncle Maury said to not let anybody see us, so we better stoop over, Caddy said. Stoop over, Benjy. Like this, see. We stooped over and crossed the garden, where the flowers rasped and rattled against us. The ground was hard. We climbed the fence, where the pigs were grunting and snuffing. I expect they're sorry because one of them got killed today, Caddy said. The ground was hard, churned and knotted.*

*Keep your hands in your pockets, Caddy said. Or they'll get froze. You dont want your hands froze on Christmas, do you.*

"It's too cold out there." Versh said. "You dont want to go out doors."

"What is it now." Mother said.

"He want to go out doors." Versh said.

"Let him go." Uncle Maury said.

"It's too cold." Mother said. "He'd better stay in. Benjamin. Stop that, now."

"It wont hurt him." Uncle Maury said.

"You, Benjamin." Mother said. "If you dont be good, you'll have to go to the kitchen."

"Mammy say keep him out the kitchen today." Versh said. "She say she got all that cooking to get done."

"Let him go, Caroline." Uncle Maury said. "You'll worry yourself sick over him."

"I know it." Mother said. "It's a judgment on me. I sometimes wonder."

"I know, I know." Uncle Maury said. "You must keep your strength up. I'll make you a toddy."

"It just upsets me that much more." Mother said. "Dont you know it does."

"You'll feel better." Uncle Maury said. "Wrap him up good, boy, and take him out for a while."

Uncle Maury went away. Versh went away.

"Please hush." Mother said. "We're trying to get you out as fast as we can. I dont want you to get sick."

Versh put my overshoes and overcoat on and we took my cap and went out. Uncle Maury was putting the bottle away in the sideboard in the diningroom.

"Keep him out about half an hour, boy." Uncle Maury said. "Keep him in the yard, now."

"Yes, sir." Versh said. "We dont never let him get off the place."

We went out doors. The sun was cold and bright.

"Where you heading for." Versh said. "You dont think you going to town, does you." We went through the rattling leaves. The gate was cold. "You better keep them hands in your pockets." Versh said. "You get them froze onto that gate, then what you do. Whyn't you wait for them in the house." He put my hands into my pockets. I could hear him rattling in the leaves. I could smell the cold. The gate was cold.

"Here some hickeynuts. Whooey. Git up that tree. Look here at this squirl, Benjy."

I couldn't feel the gate at all, but I could smell the bright cold.

"You better put them hands back in your pockets."

Caddy was walking. Then she was running, her book-satchel swinging and jouncing behind her.

"Hello, Benjy." Caddy said. She opened the gate and came in and stooped down. Caddy smelled like leaves. "Did you come to meet me." she said. "Did you come to meet Caddy. What did you let him get his hands so cold for, Versh."

"I told him to keep them in his pockets." Versh said. "Holding on to that ahun gate."

"Did you come to meet Caddy." she said, rubbing my hands. "What is it. What are you trying to tell Caddy." Caddy smelled like trees and like when she says we were asleep.

*What are you moaning about, Luster said. You can watch them again when we get to the branch. Here. Here's you a jimson weed. He gave me the flower. We went through the fence, into the lot.*

"What is it." Caddy said. "What are you trying to tell Caddy. Did they send him out, Versh."

"Couldn't keep him in." Versh said. "He kept on until they let him go and he come right straight down here, looking through the gate."

"What is it." Caddy said. "Did you think it would be Christmas when I came home from school. Is that what you thought. Christmas is the day after tomorrow. Santy Claus, Benjy. Santy Claus. Come on, let's run to the house and get warm." She took my hand and we ran through the bright rustling leaves. We ran up the steps and out of the bright cold, into the dark cold. Uncle Maury was putting the bottle back in the sideboard. He called Caddy. Caddy said,

"Take him in to the fire, Versh. Go with Versh." she said. "I'll come in a minute."

We went to the fire. Mother said,

"Is he cold, Versh."

"Nome." Versh said.

"Take his overcoat and overshoes off." Mother said. "How many times do I have to tell you not to bring him into the house with his overshoes on."

"Yessum." Versh said. "Hold still, now." He took my overshoes off and unbuttoned my coat. Caddy said,

"Wait, Versh. Cant he go out again, Mother. I want him to go with me."

"You'd better leave him here." Uncle Maury said. "He's been out enough today."

"I think you'd both better stay in." Mother said. "It's getting colder, Dilsey says."

"Oh, Mother." Caddy said.

"Nonsense." Uncle Maury said. "She's been in school all day. She needs the fresh air. Run along, Candace."

"Let him go, Mother." Caddy said. "Please. You know he'll cry."

"Then why did you mention it before him." Mother said. "Why did you come in here. To give him some excuse to worry me again. You've been out enough today. I think you'd better sit down here and play with him."

"Let them go, Caroline." Uncle Maury said. "A little cold wont hurt them. Remember, you've got to keep your strength up."

"I know." Mother said. "Nobody knows how I dread Christmas. Nobody knows. I am not one of these women who can stand things. I wish for Jason's and the children's sakes I was stronger."

"You must do the best you can and not let them worry you." Uncle Maury said. "Run along, you two. But dont stay out long, now. Your mother will worry."

"Yes, sir." Caddy said. "Come on, Benjy. We're going out doors again." She buttoned my coat and we went toward the door.

"Are you going to take that baby out without his overshoes." Mother said. "Do you want to make him sick, with the house full of company."

"I forgot." Caddy said. "I thought he had them on."

We went back. "You must think." Mother said. *Hold still now* Versh said. He put my overshoes on. "Someday I'll be gone, and you'll have to think for him." *Now stomp* Versh said. "Come here and kiss Mother, Benjamin."

Caddy took me to Mother's chair and Mother took my face in her hands and then she held me against her.

"My poor baby." she said. She let me go. "You and Versh take good care of him, honey."

"Yessum." Caddy said. We went out. Caddy said,

"You needn't go, Versh. I'll keep him for a while."

"All right." Versh said. "I aint going out in that cold for no fun." He went on and we stopped in the hall and Caddy knelt and put her arms around me and her cold bright face against mine. She smelled like trees.

"You're not a poor baby. Are you. Are you. You've got your Caddy. Haven't you got your Caddy."

*Cant you shut up that moaning and slobbering, Luster said. Aint you shamed of yourself, making all this racket. We passed the carriage house, where the carriage was. It had a new wheel.*

"Git in, now, and set still until your maw come." Dilsey said. She shoved me into the carriage. T. P. held the reins.

"Clare I dont see how come Jason wont get a new surrey." Dilsey said. "This thing going to fall to pieces under you all some day. Look at them wheels."

Mother came out, pulling her veil down. She had some flowers.

"Where's Roskus." she said.

"Roskus cant lift his arms, today." Dilsey said. "T. P. can drive all right."

"I'm afraid to." Mother said. "It seems to me you all could furnish me with a driver for the carriage once a week. It's little enough I ask, Lord knows."

"You know just as well as me that Roskus got the rheumatism too bad to do more than he have to, Miss Cahline." Dilsey said. "You come on and get in, now. T. P. can drive you just as good as Roskus."

"I'm afraid to." Mother said. "With the baby."

Dilsey went up the steps. "You calling that thing a baby." she said. She took Mother's arm. "A man big as T. P. Come on, now, if you going."

"I'm afraid to." Mother said. They came down the steps and Dilsey helped Mother in. "Perhaps it'll be the best thing, for all of us." Mother said.

"Aint you shamed, talking that way." Dilsey said. "Dont you know it'll take more than a eighteen year old nigger to make Queenie run away. She older than him and Benjy put together. And dont you start no projecking with Queenie, you hear me. T. P. If you dont drive to suit Miss Cahline, I going to put Roskus on you. He aint too tied up to do that."

"Yessum." T. P. said.

"I just know something will happen." Mother said. "Stop, Benjamin."

"Give him a flower to hold." Dilsey said. "That what he wanting." She reached her hand in.

"No, no." Mother said. "You'll have them all scattered."

"You hold them." Dilsey said. "I'll get him one out." She gave me a flower and her hand went away.

"Go on now, fore Quentin see you and have to go too." Dilsey said.

"Where is she." Mother said.

"She down to the house playing with Luster." Dilsey said. "Go on, T. P. Drive that surrey like Roskus told you, now."

"Yessum." T. P. said. "Hum up, Queenie."

"Quentin." Mother said. "Dont let  "

"Course I is." Dilsey said.

The carriage jolted and crunched on the drive. "I'm afraid to go and leave Quentin." Mother said. "I'd better not go. T. P." We went through the gate, where it didn't jolt anymore. T. P. hit Queenie with the whip.

"You, T. P." Mother said.

"Got to get her going." T. P. said. "Keep her wake up till we get back to the barn."

"Turn around." Mother said. "I'm afraid to go and leave Quentin."

"Cant turn here." T. P. said. Then it was broader.

"Cant you turn here." Mother said.

"All right." T. P. said. We began to turn.

"You, T. P." Mother said, clutching me.

"I got to turn around some how." T. P. said. "Whoa, Queenie." We stopped.

"You'll turn us over." Mother said.

"What you want to do, then." T. P. said.

"I'm afraid for you to try to turn around." Mother said.

"Get up, Queenie." T. P. said. We went on.

"I just know Dilsey will let something happen to Quentin while I'm gone." Mother said. "We must hurry back."

"Hum up, there." T. P. said. He hit Queenie with the whip.

"You, T. P." Mother said, clutching me. I could hear Queenie's feet and the bright shapes went smooth and steady on both sides, the shadows of them flowing across Queenie's back. They went on like the bright tops of wheels. Then those on one side stopped at the tall white post where the soldier was. But on the other side they went on smooth and steady, but a little slower.

"What do you want." Jason said. He had his hands in his pockets and a pencil behind his ear.

"We're going to the cemetery." Mother said.

"All right." Jason said. "I dont aim to stop you, do I. Was that all you wanted with me, just to tell me that."

"I know you wont come." Mother said. "I'd feel safer if you would."

"Safe from what." Jason said. "Father and Quentin cant hurt you."

Mother put her handkerchief under her veil. "Stop it, Mother." Jason said. "Do you want to get that damn looney to bawling in the middle of the square. Drive on, T. P."

"Hum up, Queenie." T. P. said.

"It's a judgment on me." Mother said. "But I'll be gone too, soon."

"Here." Jason said.

"Whoa." T. P. said. Jason said,

"Uncle Maury's drawing on you for fifty. What do you want to do about it."

"Why ask me." Mother said. "I dont have any say so. I try not to worry you and Dilsey. I'll be gone soon, and then you  "

"Go on, T. P." Jason said.

"Hum up, Queenie." T. P. said. The shapes flowed on. The ones on the other side began again, bright and fast and smooth, like when Caddy says we are going to sleep.

*Cry baby, Luster said. Aint you shamed. We went through the barn. The stalls were all open. You aint got no spotted pony to ride now, Luster said. The floor was dry and dusty. The roof was falling. The slanting holes were full of spinning yellow. What do you want to go that way, for. You want to get your head knocked off with one of them balls.*

"Keep your hands in your pockets." Caddy said. "Or they'll be froze. You dont want your hands froze on Christmas, do you."

We went around the barn. The big cow and the little one were standing in the door, and we could hear Prince and Queenie and Fancy stomping inside the barn. "If it wasn't so cold, we'd ride Fancy." Caddy said. "But it's too cold to hold on today." Then we could see the branch, where the smoke was blowing. "That's where they are killing the pig." Caddy said. "We can come back by there and see them." We went down the hill.

"You want to carry the letter." Caddy said. "You can carry it." She took the letter out of her pocket and put it in mine. "It's a Christmas present." Caddy said. "Uncle Maury is going to surprise Mrs Patterson with it. We got to give it to her without letting anybody see it. Keep your hands in your pockets good, now." We came to the branch.

"It's froze." Caddy said. "Look." She broke the top of the water and held a piece of it against my face. "Ice. That means how cold it is." She helped me across and we went up the hill. "We cant even tell Mother and Father. You know what I think it is. I think it's a surprise for Mother and Father and Mr Patterson both, because Mr Patterson sent you some candy. Do you remember when Mr Patterson sent you some candy last summer."

There was a fence. The vine was dry, and the wind rattled in it.

"Only I dont see why Uncle Maury didn't send Versh." Caddy said. "Versh wont tell." Mrs Patterson was looking out the window. "You wait here." Caddy said. "Wait right here, now. I'll be back in a minute. Give me the letter." She took the letter out of my pocket. "Keep your hands in your pockets." She climbed the fence with the letter in her hand and went through the brown, rattling flowers. Mrs Patterson came to the door and opened it and stood there.

*Mr Patterson was chopping in the green flowers. He stopped chopping and looked at me. Mrs Patterson came across the garden, running. When I saw her eyes I began to cry. You idiot, Mrs Patterson said, I told him never to send you alone again. Give it to me. Quick. Mr Patterson came fast, with the hoe. Mrs Patterson leaned across the fence, reaching her hand. She was trying to climb the fence. Give it to me, she said. Give it to me. Mr Patterson climbed the fence. I saw her eyes again and I ran down the hill.*

"They aint nothing over yonder but houses." Luster said. "We going down to the branch."

They were washing down at the branch. One of them was singing. I could smell the clothes flapping, and the smoke blowing across the branch. . . .

---

# GERTRUDE STEIN

# from *The Autobiography of Alice B. Toklas*

---

The American expatriate Gertrude Stein (1874–1946) was a maddeningly original genius; her apartment in Paris was for more than forty years a meeting place for the avant-garde and her experimental writings helped define Modernism. Misunderstood in her own day because of the impenetrability of her prose, she earned the title of America's best-known, unread author. What was known about her was sufficient to make her a legendary character, part fraud, part genius. Stein fueled this image with her enigmatic sayings, as in this comment about America, "there is no there there," and, in her most famous remark, "a rose is a rose is a rose is a rose." Now, fifty years after her death, she is a classic, and her works, back in print, are studied in college classrooms.

A rarity in her time, Stein was an independent woman who lived her life as she pleased. Born to a wealthy Jewish family in San Francisco and trained at The Johns Hopkins University in medicine, she passed up a medical career and, instead, moved to Paris, in 1902; here she set up house, in 1910, with Alice B. Toklas (1877–1967), a fellow San Franciscan, who became her lifelong companion. Their personalities balanced one another, so that, when they entertained, the male "geniuses" sat with Stein and the "wives" were relegated to the side with Toklas. Stein, avid for life, pursued cultural lions (Picasso and Hemingway) and anyone else who amused her; she dreamed of becoming a cultural lion herself ("think of the bible and Homer think of Shakespeare and think of me"). In contrast, Toklas ran the domestic sphere (there is an *Alice B. Toklas Cookbook*, 1954), and seemed delighted to bask in Stein's reflected glory. During their lives, the Stein-Toklas household was the focus for the American love affair with France.

Stein's literary experiments bore little resemblance to Joyce's (see *Ulysses*) "interior monologues." Her literary project was to be abstract, as in Cubism. Wanting to break with all literary tradition, she slowly got rid of narrative, punctuation, logic, forms or genres, even meanings in any normal sense. She achieved a fully abstract style in *Tender Buttons* (1914), a work divided into three sections called "Objects," "Food," and "Room," marked by repetition and obscurity ("chicken"; "Alas a dirty word, alas a dirty third alas a dirty third, alas a dirty bird"). Earlier, in *Three Lives* (1909), about servant women in 1900 Baltimore, Stein was still a Realist, though experimenting with Modernist effects—especially repetition and unfocused narrative structure.

*Reading the Selection*

Who would have thought of writing the life of a cherished companion and passing it off as an autobiography? Yet, this is just what Stein did, perhaps as a stunt to make money, perhaps as just another eccentric gesture to call attention to herself. Setting aside for the moment her own abstract style, Stein wrote in a deliberate imitation of Tolkas's deadpan, slightly sour speech pattern. The popular and critical success of the book was so unexpected that Stein was unable to write for a year.

The passage, from *The Autobiography of Alice B. Toklas* (1933), is typical of the work, in the name-dropping, the provocative portraits of the famous, the highly opinionated judgments ("And so cubism is spanish"), and, above all, the centrality of Stein. In most ways, this book is a double autobiography of this eccentric couple.

---

• • •

But to return to the beginning of my life in Paris. It was based upon the rue de Fleurus and the Saturday evenings and it was like a kaleidoscope slowly turning.

What happened in those early years. A great deal happened.

As I said when I became an habitual visitor at the rue de Fleurus the Picassos were once more together, Pablo and Fernande. That summer they went again to Spain and he came back with some spanish landscapes and one may say that these landscapes, two of them still at the rue de Fleurus and the other one in Moscow in the collection that Stchoukine founded and that is now national property, were the beginning of cubism. In these there was no african sculpture influence. There was very evidently a strong Cézanne influence, particularly the influence of the late Cézanne water colours, the cutting up the sky not in cubes but in spaces.

But the essential thing, the treatment of the houses was essentially spanish and therefore essentially Picasso. In these pictures he first emphasised the way of building in spanish villages, the line of the houses not following the landscape but cutting across and into the landscape, becoming undistinguishable in the landscape by cutting across the landscape. It was the principle of the camouflage of the guns and the ships in the war. The first year of the war, Picasso and Eve, with whom he was living then, Gertrude Stein and myself, were walking down the boulevard Raspail a cold winter evening. There is nothing in the world colder than the Raspail on a cold winter evening, we used to call it the retreat from Moscow. All of a sudden down the street came some big cannon, the first any of us had seen painted, that is camouflaged. Pablo stopped, he was spell-bound. C'est nous qui avons fit ça, he said, it is we that have created that, he said. And he was right, he had. From Cézanne through him they had come to that. His foresight was justified.

But to go back to the three landscapes. When they were first put up on the wall naturally everybody objected. As it happened he and Fernande had taken some photographs of the villages which he had painted and he had given copies of these photographs to Gertrude Stein. When people said that the few cubes in the landscapes looked like nothing but cubes, Gertrude Stein would laugh and say, if you had objected to these landscapes as being too realistic there would be some point in your objection. And she would show them

the photographs and really the pictures as she rightly said might be declared to be too photographic a copy of nature. Years after Elliot Paul at Gertrude Stein's suggestion had a photograph of the painting by Picasso and the photographs of the village reproduced on the same page in transition and it was extraordinarily interesting. This then was really the beginning of cubism. The colour too was characteristically spanish, the pale silver yellow with the faintest suggestion of green, the colour afterwards so well known in Picasso's cubist pictures, as well as in those of his followers.

Gertrude Stein always says that cubism is a purely spanish conception and only spaniards can be cubists and that the only real cubism is that of Picasso and Juan Gris. Picasso created it and Juan Gris permeated it with his clarity and his exaltation. To understand this one has only to read the life and death of Juan Gris by Gertrude Stein, written upon the death of one of her two dearest friends, Picasso and Juan Gris, both spaniards.

She always says that americans can understand spaniards. That they are the only two western nations that can realise abstraction. That in americans it expresses itself by disembodiedness, in literature and machinery, in Spain by ritual so abstract that it does not connect itself with anything but ritual.

I always remember Picasso saying disgustedly apropos of some germans who said they liked bull-fights, they would, he said angrily, they like bloodshed. To a spaniard it is not bloodshed, it is ritual.

Americans, so Gertrude Stein says, are like spaniards, they are abstract and cruel. They are not brutal they are cruel. They have no close contact with the earth such as most europeans have. Their materialism is not the materialism of existence, of possession, it is the materialism of action and abstraction. And so cubism is spanish.

We were very much struck, the first time Gertrude Stein and I went to Spain, which was a year or so after the beginning of cubism, to see how naturally cubism was made in Spain. In the shops in Barcelona instead of post cards they had square little frames and inside it was placed a cigar, a real one, a pipe, a bit of handkerchief etcetera, all absolutely the arrangement of many a cubist picture and helped out by cut paper representing other objects. That is the modern note that in Spain had been done for centuries.

Picasso in his early cubist pictures used printed letters as did Juan Gris to force the painted surface to measure up to something rigid, and the rigid thing was the printed letter.

Gradually instead of using the printed thing they painted the letters and all was lost, it was only Juan Gris who could paint with such intensity a printed letter that it still made the rigid contrast. And so cubism came little by little but it came.

It was in these days that the intimacy between Braque and Picasso grew. It was in these days that Juan Gris, a raw rather effusive youth came from Madrid to Paris and began to call Picasso cher maître to Picasso's great annoyance. It was apropos of this that Picasso used to address Braque as cher maître, passing on the joke, and I am sorry to say that some foolish people have taken this joke to mean that Picasso looked up to Braque as a master.

But I am once more running far ahead of those early Paris days when I first knew Fernande and Pablo.

In those days then only the three landscapes had been painted and he was beginning to paint some heads that seemed cut out in planes, also long loaves of bread.

At this time Matisse, the school still going on, was really beginning to be fairly well known, so much so that to everybody's great excitement Bernheim jeune, a very middle class firm indeed, was offering him a contract to take all his work at a very good price. It was an exciting moment.

This was happening because of the influence of a man named Fénéon. Il est très fin, said Matisse, much impressed by Fénéon. Fénéon was a journalist, a french journalist who had invented the thing called a feuilleton en deux lignes, that is to say he was the first one to hit off the news of the day in two lines. He looked like a caricature of Uncle Sam made french and he had been painted standing in front of a curtain in a circus picture by Toulouse-Lautrec.

And now the Bernheims, how or wherefor I do not know, taking Fénéon into their employ, were going to connect themselves with the new generation of painters.

Something happened, at any rate this contract did not last long, but for all that it changed the fortunes of Matisse. He now had an established position. He bought a house and some land in Clamart and he started to move out there. Let me describe the house as I saw it.

This home in Clamart was very comfortable, to be sure the bath-room, which the family much appreciated from long contact with americans, although it must be said that the Matisses had always been and always were scrupulously neat and clean, was on the ground floor adjoining the dining room. But that was alright, and is and was a french custom, in french houses. It gave more privacy to a bath-room to have it on the ground floor. Not so long ago in going over the new house Braque was building the bath-room was again below, this time underneath the dining room. When we said, but why, they said because being nearer the furnace it would be warmer.

The grounds at Clamart were large and the garden was what Matisse between pride and chagrin called un petit Luxembourg. There was also a glass forcing house for flowers. Later they had begonias in them that grew smaller and smaller. Beyond were lilacs and still beyond a big demountable studio. They liked it enormously. Madame Matisse with simple recklessness went out every day to look at it and pick flowers, keeping a cab waiting for her. In those days only millionaires kept cabs waiting and then only very occasionally.

They moved out and were very comfortable and soon the enormous studio was filled with enormous statues and enormous pictures. It was that period of Matisse. Equally soon he found Clamart so beautiful that he could not go home to it, that is when he came into Paris to his hour of sketching from the nude, a thing he had done every afternoon of his life ever since the beginning of things, and he came in every afternoon. His school no longer existed, the government had taken over the old convent to make a Lycée of it and the school had come to an end.

These were the beginning of very prosperous days for the Matisses. They went to Algeria and they went to Tangiers and their devoted german pupils gave them Rhine wines and a very fine black police dog, the first of the breed that any of us had seen.

And then Matisse had a great show of his pictures in Berlin. I remember so well one spring day, it was a lovely day and we were to lunch at Clamart with the Matisses. When we got there they were all standing around an enormous packing case with its top off. We went up and joined them and there in the packing case was the largest laurel wreath that had ever been made, tied with a beautiful red ribbon. Matisse showed Gertrude Stein a card that had been in it. It said on it, To Henri Matisse, Triumphant on the Battlefield of Berlin, and was signed Thomas Whittemore. Thomas Whittemore was a bostonian archeologist and professor at Tufts College, a great admirer of Matisse and this was his tribute. Said Matisse, still more rueful, but I am not dead yet. Madame Matisse, the shock once over said, but Henri look, and leaning down she plucked a leaf and tasted it, it is real laurel, think how good it will be in soup. And, said she still further brightening, the ribbon will do wonderfully for a long time as a hair ribbon for Margot.

The Matisses stayed in Clamart more or less until the war. During this period they and Gertrude Stein were seeing less and less of each other. Then after the war broke out they came to the house a good deal. They were lonesome and troubled, Matisse's family in Saint-Quentin, in the north, were within the german lines and his brother was a hostage. It was Madame Matisse who taught me how to knit woollen gloves. She made them wonderfully neatly and rapidly and I learned to do so too. Then Matisse went to live in Nice and in one way and another, although remaining perfectly good friends, Gertrude Stein and the Matisses never see each other. . . .

# Chapter

# 21

## The Age of Anxiety and Beyond:
## 1945–

### GWENDOLYN BROOKS

## Poems

The African-American Gwendolyn Brooks (1917–    ) is one of the most distinguished poets today. With five major books of poetry (*A Street in Bronzeville*, 1945; *Annie Allen*, 1949; *The Bean Eaters*, 1960; *Selected Poems*, 1963; and *In the Mecca*, 1968), a novel (*Maud Martha*, 1953), and an autobiography (*Report from Part One*, 1972), she has staked out a claim to literary greatness. Her highest achievement to date has been the 1950 Pulitzer Prize for poetry, for *Annie Allen*—the first black poet to be so honored. In addition, her career has been sustained by a series of prizes and fellowships, and she has been awarded many honorary degrees for her work. Although accused of being out of touch with the black masses, her poetry is always animated by a spirit of controlled protest.

Brooks belongs to Chicago's Black Literary group, who are noted for their gritty depiction of the city's black life. Her literary task has been to chronicle the "postage stamp" world of the city's South Side, the black ghetto which was her home from the age of five weeks. Nurtured there in comfortable but by no means wealthy surroundings (during the depression, the mother held the family together while the father supported it on ten dollars a week pay), she grew to maturity believing that through her poetry she could achieve the American dream; she shared the faith of most blacks at the time that integration would eliminate racism in America.

*A Street in Bronzeville*, Brooks's first book of poetry, set the direction of her early poetry. In form, *A Street* described a South Side street lined with about thirty houses, using a series of poems to represent the lives of the inhabitants, with personality sketches or revealing vignettes. These early poems dealt with ordinary black people who simply did what was expected, which, to her, was a source of joy. A poet of obscure people, of small gestures, she wrote in standard English, rejecting the black vernacular that had been adopted by older African-American writers like Hughes (see "The Negro Speaks of Rivers," etc.).

In 1967, at a writer's conference held at Fisk University, a predominantly black school in Nashville, Brooks was confronted by student protesters, radicalized by the words of Martin Luther King, Jr., (see "I Have a Dream") and Malcolm X (see *The Autobiography of Malcolm X*); they denounced her as a "white" writer unconcerned about black issues. Afterward, her style changed, and, though she remains a gifted recorder of ordinary black people's lives expressed in mainstream English, her poetry is now addressed exclusively to the black community, as in *In the Mecca*. These poems, set in a South Side apartment complex named Mecca, teem with life and employ the revolutionary metaphors of the whirlwind and the harvest to symbolize the coming triumph of her people's struggle.

### Reading the Selection

Brooks's poem "The Mother" (1966), with its abortion theme, is her most controversial work to date. This theme appealed to her because of the common occurence of abortion in the inner city. In the poem, the poet's voice speaks as a universal mother, affirming love. In 1980, she read this poem at the Carter White House, where she was an invited guest, with other poets, to a poetry reading.

"The Bean Eaters," the title poem from a 1960 collection, reflects Brooks's poverty in the depression when there was very little to eat except beans. Optimistic in outlook, typical of her pre-1967 mood, this poem salutes black endurance in white America.

# The Mother

Abortions will not let you forget.
You remember the children you got that you did not get,
The damp small pulps with a little or with no hair,
The singers and workers that never handled the air.
You will never neglect or beat
Them, or silence or buy with a sweet.
You will never wind up the sucking-thumb
Or scuttle off ghosts that come.
You will never leave them, controlling your luscious sigh,
Return for a snack of them, with gobbling mother-eye.

I have heard in the voices of the wind the voices of my
    dim killed children.
I have contracted. I have eased
My dim dears at the breasts they could never suck.
I have said, Sweets, if I sinned, if I seized
Your luck
And your lives from your unfinished reach,
If I stole your births and your names,
Your straight baby tears and your games,

Your stilted or lovely loves, your tumults, your marriages,
    aches, and your deaths,
If I poisoned the beginnings of your breaths,
Believe that even in my deliberateness I was not
    deliberate.
Though why should I whine,
Whine that the crime was other than mine?—
Since anyhow you are dead.
Or rather, or instead,
You were never made.

But that too, I am afraid,
Is faulty: oh, what shall I say, how is the truth to be said?
You were born, you had body, you died.
It is just that you never giggled or planned or cried.

Believe me, I loved you all.
Believe me, I knew you, though faintly, and I loved, I
    loved you
All.

# The Bean Eaters

They eat beans mostly, this old yellow pair.
Dinner is a casual affair.
Plain chipware on a plain and creaking wood,
Tin flatware.

Two who are Mostly Good.
Two who have lived their day,
But keep on putting on their clothes
And putting things away.

And remembering . . .
Remembering, with twinklings and twinges,
As they lean over the beans in their rented back room
        that is full of beads and receipts and dolls and
        cloths, tobacco crumbs, vases and fringes.

## JEAN-PAUL SARTRE

## from *The Humanism of Existentialism*

France's Jean-Paul Sartre (1905–1980) was his era's greatest popularizer of existentialism, the individualistic philosophy that dominated Western thought for much of this century. Introduced to existentialism in the 1920s while studying with the German thinker Martin Heidegger (1889–1976), Sartre later developed his own ideas—freedom, choice, commitment, self-definition, and authenticity, centered around the principle of personal responsibility—all derived from Heidegger. Sartre's theoretical works make difficult reading for the layperson, but his novels, plays, and short stories, which are inseparable from his philosophy, are quite accessible and provide insight into existentialism in practice. In addition to direct influence, he also indirectly affected his age, through other writers who adopted his ideas, as in the feminist theory of Simone de Beauvoir (see *The Second Sex*), his lifelong companion, and the revolutionary thought of Frantz Fanon, a black disciple from Martinique.

The term "existentialism" derives from *existence*, one half of the pair of terms (the other is *essence*) coined by Aristotle. *Essence* means unchanging human nature, while *existence* denotes human aspects that are impermanent. Western thought from Plato to Nietzsche is essentialist, emphasizing the *essence* shared by humanity. Nietzsche begins existentialist thought, which denies human nature and stresses the human ability to change at will.

The twentieth century embraced existentialism, partly to fill the void left by the collapse of traditional religion, but mainly as a response to the period's unfolding horrors. Helplessly watching the killing inflicted during two world wars, the evil made manifest in the Holocaust, the unyielding threat of nuclear disaster, and the cruel social problems seemingly impervious to capitalistic or socialistic solutions, many Westerners came to believe, like Nietzsche, that God was dead; thus, many, including Sartre, embraced existentialism as a sort of self-help panacea. For them, existentialism was a way to remain sane, by keeping a private moral sense in a world gone mad.

### Reading the Selection

*The Humanism of Existentialism*—the source of this selection—was given first as a lecture by Sartre in 1945, as the West was trying to recover from history's most destructive war. Sartre's words, spoken amid the ruins and proclaiming a message of personal responsibility, was seen as a sign that Europe would rise again from the ashes. Issued as an essay, these words became an instant classic and made Sartre's name formidable around the world.

In this essay, Sartre explores the full meaning of atheism, starting with the idea that there is no such thing as human nature (*essence*), "since there is no God to conceive it." He then develops the Heideggerian notion that human beings are "thrust into the world" ("appear on the scene"). Thus, human beings do not choose to be born, but, having been born, they "choose" (take responsibility) for their individual existence, including sex, skin color, age, economic condition, health, disposition, and personality. In what is the shakiest part of Sartre's thought, he reasons that when human beings choose themselves, "we mean that every one of us chooses all men. . . ." This "existential condition," of "legislating" for all humankind leads to "anguish," "forlornness," and "despair"—key Sartrean concepts. Nevertheless, Sartre remains optimistic, since, in the final analysis, "man's destiny is within himself."

* * *

Atheistic existentialism, which I represent, is more coherent. It states that if God does not exist, there is at least one being in whom existence precedes essence, a being who exists before he can be defined by any concept, and that this being is man, or, as Heidegger says, human reality. What is meant here by saying that existence precedes essence? It means that, first of all, man exists, turns up, appears on the scene, and, only afterwards, defines himself. If man, as the existentialist conceives him, is indefinable, it is because at first he is nothing. Only afterwards will he be something, and he himself will have made what he will be. Thus, there is no human nature, since there is no God to conceive it. Not only is man what he conceives himself to be, but he is also only what he wills himself to be after this thrust toward existence.

Man is nothing else but what he makes of himself. Such is the first principle of existentialism. It is also what is called subjectivity, the name we are labeled with when charges are brought against us. But what do we mean by this, if not that man has a greater dignity than a stone or table? For we mean that man first exists, that is, that man first of all is the being who hurls himself toward a future and who is conscious of imagining himself as being in the future. Man is at the start a plan which is aware of itself, rather than a patch of moss, a piece of garbage, or a cauliflower; nothing exists prior to this plan; there is nothing in heaven; man will be what he will have planned to be. Not what he will want to be. Because by the word "will" we generally mean a conscious decision, which is subsequent to what we have already made of ourselves. I may want to belong to a political party, write a book, get married; but all that is only a manifestation of an earlier, more spontaneous choice that is called "will." But if existence really does precede essence, man is responsible for what he is. Thus, existentialism's first move is to make every man aware of what he is and to make the full responsibility of his existence rest on him. And when we say that a man is responsible for himself, we do not only mean that he is responsible for his own individuality, but that he is responsible for all men.

The word subjectivism has two meanings, and our opponents play on the two. Subjectivism means, on the one hand, that an individual chooses and makes himself; and, on the other, that it is impossible for man to transcend human subjectivity. The second of these is the essential meaning of existentialism. When we say that man chooses his own self, we mean that every one of us does likewise; but we also mean by that that in making this choice he also chooses all men.

In fact, in creating the man that we want to be, there is not a single one of our acts which does not at the same time create an image of man as we think he ought to be. To choose to be this or that is to affirm at the same time the value of what we choose, because we can never choose evil. We always choose the good, and nothing can be good for us without being good for all.

If, on the other hand, existence precedes essence, and if we grant that we exist and fashion our image at one and the same time, the image is valid for everybody and for our whole age. Thus, our responsibility is much greater than we might have supposed, because it involves all mankind. If I am a workingman and choose to join a Christian trade-union rather than be a communist, and if by being a member I want to show that the best thing for man is resignation, that the kingdom of man is not of this world, I am not only involving my own case—I want to be resigned for everyone. As a result, my action has involved all humanity. To take a more individual matter, if I want to marry, to have children; even if this marriage depends solely on my own circumstances or passion or wish, I am involving all humanity in monogamy and not merely myself. Therefore, I am responsible for myself and for everyone else. I am creating a certain image of man of my own choosing. In choosing myself, I choose man.

This helps us understand what the actual content is of such rather grandiloquent words as anguish, forlornness, despair. As you will see, it's all quite simple.

First, what is meant by anguish? The existentialists say at once that man is anguish. What that means is this: the man who involves himself and who realizes that he is not only the person he chooses to be, but also a lawmaker who is, at the same time, choosing all mankind as well as himself, can not help escape the feeling of his total and deep responsibility. Of course, there are many people who are not anxious; but we claim that they are hiding their anxiety, that they are fleeing from it. Certainly, many people believe that when they do something, they themselves are the only ones involved, and when someone says to them, "What if everyone acted that way?" they shrug their shoulders and answer, "Everyone doesn't act that way." But really, one should always ask himself, "What would happen if everybody looked at things that way?" There is no escaping this disturbing thought except by a kind of double-dealing. A man who lies and makes excuses for himself by saying "Not everybody does that," is someone with an uneasy conscience, because the act of lying implies that a universal value is conferred upon the lie.

Anguish is evident even when it conceals itself. This is the anguish that Kierkegaard called the anguish of Abraham.

You know the story: an angel has ordered Abraham to sacrifice his son; if it really were an angel who has come and said, "You are Abraham, you shall sacrifice your son," everything would be all right. But everyone might first wonder, "Is it really an angel, and am I really Abraham? What proof do I have?"

There was a madwoman who had hallucinations; someone used to speak to her on the telephone and give her orders. Her doctor asked her, "Who is it who talks to you?" She answered, "He says it's God." What proof did she really have that it was God? If an angel comes to me, what proof is there that it's an angel? And if I hear voices, what proof is there that they come from heaven and not from hell, or from the subconscious, or a pathological condition? What proves that they are addressed to me? What proof is there that I have been appointed to impose my choice and my conception of man on humanity? I'll never find any proof or sign to convince me of that. If a voice addresses me, it is always for me to decide that this is the angel's voice; if I consider that such an act is a good one, it is I who will choose to say that it is good rather than bad.

Now, I'm not being singled out as an Abraham, and yet at every moment I'm obliged to perform exemplary acts. For every man, everything happens as if all mankind had its eyes fixed on him and were guiding itself by what he does. And every man ought to say to himself, "Am I really the kind of man who has the right to act in such a way that humanity might guide itself by my actions?" And if he does not say that to himself, he is masking his anguish.

There is no question here of the kind of anguish which would lead to quietism, to inaction. It is a matter of a simple sort of anguish that anybody who has had responsibilities is familiar with. For example, when a military officer takes the responsibility for an attack and sends a certain number of men to death, he chooses to do so, and in the main he alone makes the choice. Doubtless, orders come from above, but they are too broad; he interprets them, and on this interpretation depend the lives of ten or fourteen or twenty men. In making a decision he can not help having a certain anguish. All leaders know this anguish. That doesn't keep them from acting; on the contrary, it is the very condition of their action. For it implies that they envisage a number of possibilities, and when they choose one, they realize that it has value only because it is chosen. We shall see that this kind of anguish, which is the kind that existentialism describes, is explained, in addition, by a direct responsibility to the other men whom it involves. It is not a curtain separating us from action, but is part of action itself.

When we speak of forlornness, a term Heidegger was fond of, we mean only that God does not exist and that we have to face all the consequences of this. The existentialist is strongly opposed to a certain kind of secular ethics which would like to abolish God with the least possible expense. About 1880, some French teachers tried to set up a secular ethics which went something like this: God is a useless and costly hypothesis; we are discarding it; but, meanwhile, in order for there to be an ethics, a society, a civilization, it is essential that certain values be taken seriously and that they be considered as having an *a priori* existence. It must be obligatory, *a priori*, to be honest, not to lie, not to beat your wife, to have children, etc., etc. So we're going to try a little device which will make it possible to show that values exist all the same, inscribed in a heaven of ideas, though otherwise God does not exist. In other words—and this, I believe, is the tendency of everything called reformism in France—nothing will be changed if God does not exist. We shall find ourselves with the same norms of honesty, progress, and humanism, and we shall have made of God an outdated hypothesis which will peacefully die off by itself.

The existentialist, on the contrary, thinks it very distressing that God does not exist, because all possibility of finding values in a heaven of ideas disappears along with Him; there can no longer be an *a priori* Good, since there is no infinite and perfect consciousness to think it. Nowhere is it written that the Good exists, that we must be honest, that we must not lie; because the fact is we are on a plane where there are only men. Dostoievsky said, "If God didn't exist, everything would be possible." That is the very starting point of existentialism. Indeed, everything is permissible if God does not exist, and as a result man is forlorn, because neither within him nor without does he find anything to cling to. He can't start making excuses for himself.

If existence really does precede essence, there is no explaining things away by reference to a fixed and given human nature. In other words, there is no determinism, man is free, man is freedom. On the other hand, if God does not exist, we find no values or commands to turn to which legitimize our conduct. So, in the bright realm of values, we have no excuse behind us, nor justification before us. We are alone, with no excuses.

That is the idea I shall try to convey when I say that man is condemned to be free. Condemned, because he did not create himself, yet, in other respects is free; because, once thrown into the world, he is responsible for everything he does. . . .

As for despair, the term has a very simple meaning. It means that we shall confine ourselves to reckoning only with what depends upon our will, or on the ensemble of probabilities which make our action possible. When we want something, we always have to reckon with probabilities. I may be counting on the arrival of a friend. The friend is coming by rail or street-car; this supposes that the train will arrive on schedule, or that the street-car will not jump the track. I am left in the realm of possibility; but possibilities are to be reckoned with only to the point where my action comports with the ensemble of these possibilities, and no further. The moment the possibilities I am considering are not rigorously involved by my action, I ought to disengage myself from them, because no God, no scheme, can adapt the world and its possibilities to my will. When Descartes said, "Conquer yourself rather than the world," he meant essentially the same thing. . . .

When all is said and done, what we are accused of, at bottom, is not our pessimism, but an optimistic toughness. If people throw up to us our works of fiction in which we write about people who are soft, weak, cowardly, and sometimes even downright bad, it's not because these people are soft, weak, cowardly, or bad; because if we were to say, as Zola did, that they are that way because of heredity, the workings of environment, society, because of biological or psychological determinism, people would be reassured. They would say, "Well, that's what we're like, no one can do anything about it." But when the existentialist writes about a coward, he says that this coward is responsible for his cowardice. . . .

What the existentialist says is that the coward makes himself cowardly, that the hero makes himself heroic. There's always a possibility for the coward not to be cowardly any more and for the hero to stop being heroic. What counts is total involvement; some one particular action or set of circumstances is not total involvement.

Thus, I think we have answered a number of the charges concerning existentialism. You see that it can not be taken for a philosophy of quietism, since it defines man in terms of action; nor for a pessimistic description of man—there is no doctrine more optimistic, since man's destiny is within himself; nor for an attempt to discourage man from acting, since it tells him that the only hope is in his acting and that action is the only thing that enables a man to live. Consequently, we are dealing here with an ethics of action and involvement. . . .

The third objection is the following: "You take something from one pocket and put it into the other. That is, fundamentally, values aren't serious, since you choose them." My answer to this is that I'm quite vexed that that's the way it is; but if I've discarded God the Father, there has to be someone to invent values. You've got to take things as they are. Moreover, to say that we invent values means nothing else but this: life has no meaning *a priori*. Before you come alive, life is nothing; it's up to you to give it a meaning, and value is nothing else but the meaning that you choose. In that

way, you see, there is a possibility of creating a human community. . . .

But it can not be granted that a man may make a judgment about man. Existentialism spares him from any such judgment. The existentialist will never consider man as an end because he is always in the making. Nor should we believe that there is a mankind to which we might set up a cult in the manner of Auguste Comte. The cult of mankind ends in the self-enclosed humanism of Comte, and, let it be said, of fascism. This kind of humanism we can do without.

But there is another meaning of humanism. Fundamentally it is this: man is constantly outside of himself; in projecting himself, in losing himself outside of himself, he makes for man's existing; and, on the other hand, it is by pursuing transcendent goals that he is able to exist; man, being this state of passing-beyond, and seizing upon things only as they bear upon this passing-beyond, is at the heart, at the center of this passing-beyond. There is no universe other than a human universe, the universe of human subjectivity. This connection between transcendency, as a constituent element of man—not in the sense that God is transcendent, but in the sense of passing beyond—and subjectivity, in the sense that man is not closed in on himself but is always present in a human universe, is what we call existentialist humanism. Humanism, because we remind man that there is no lawmaker other than himself, and that in his forlornness he will decide by himself; because we point out that man will fulfill himself as man, not in turning toward himself, but in seeking outside of himself a goal which is just this liberation, just this particular fulfillment.

# SIMONE DE BEAUVOIR
# from *The Second Sex*
## Introduction

———

Beauvoir's *The Second Sex* (1949), a treatise on female sexuality and a classic text of feminism, appeared at a time when the push for women's rights had temporarily lost forward motion. Women in most countries of the West now had voting rights (starting in Britain in 1918), thereby achieving the goal of the first phase of feminism; and no other issue drew women together as did the suffrage cause. Beauvoir's treatise did not so much offer a specific issue for women to rally around, as it constituted a more general call to action, for women to rethink the way that the sexes functioned and interacted. The burden of her message may be summed up in her bold line, "One is not born, but rather becomes a woman"—thus, she rejected innate sexual differences and proclaimed that femaleness is learned and thus subject to revision. Her message launched a second wave of feminism, revolutionizing millions of readers who have dramatically revised the way they think and act.

Simone de Beauvoir (1908–1986), this apostle of latter day feminism, was herself a contradictory figure. France's outstanding woman of letters from 1945 onward, she wrote, besides *The Second Sex*, well-received novels (*She Came to Stay,* 1943; *The Mandarins,* 1954) and books of autobiography (*Memoirs of a Dutiful Daughter,* 1958; *The Prime of Life,* 1960), and yet she was content to take second place to Sartre, her lifelong mentor and the lover with whom she was involved in an unlicensed, open "marriage." At all stages of her life with Sartre, she readily set aside her own plans to edit, sharpen, and deliver detailed responses to his writing, duties she considered an honor. Beauvoir condemned female subservience in *The Second Sex,* but, in her own life, she created a myth of Sartre's genius, apparently thinking her own fame dependent on his.

## Reading the Selection

This selection, taken from the "Introduction" to *The Second Sex,* summarizes Beauvoir's argument for sexual equality. Two of her prime analytical tools are the concepts of "the Self" and "the Other," borrowed from the German thinker George Wilhelm Friedrich Hegel (1770–1831). With these terms, she shows that, in society as currently arranged, Man is the "Self," the essential being, the necessary sex; as such, Man defines Woman as "the Other," the inessential being, "the second sex." The category of "Otherness"—which, according to Beauvoir, Woman shares with the American Negro, the Jew, and the proletariat—is a primordial way of thinking in which privileged groups distinguish themselves from those they consider inferior, mysterious, and, thus, in need of control.

Even more than Hegel, the spirit of Sartre hovers over this work. Following Sartre, Beauvoir rejects pre-existing social and moral categories, so that a woman is not "a feminine creature"; she, instead, is what she wills herself to be. Beauvoir does not claim that a woman should become a masculinized female. Indeed, she recognizes that a woman has "ovaries, a uterus [and] these . . . circumscribe her within the limits of her own nature." But a woman, just as a man, must "choose," (take responsibility) for her situation, including her sex. In Beauvoir's new social order, women will live side by side with men, economically and intellectually separate, each engaged in the project of transcendence; that is, both will work so as to leave a permanent record—such as, states, art, literature, architecture, and philosophies—when they are gone.

. . .

A man would never get the notion of writing a book on the peculiar situation of the human male. But if I wish to define myself, I must first of all say: "I am a woman"; on this truth must be based all further discussion. A man never begins by presenting himself as an individual of a certain sex; it goes without saying that he is a man. The terms *masculine* and *feminine* are used symmetrically only as a matter of form, as on legal papers. In actuality the relation of the two sexes is not quite like that of two electrical poles, for man represents both the positive and the neutral, as is indicated by the common use of *man* to designate human beings in general; whereas woman represents only the negative, defined by limiting criteria, without reciprocity. In the midst of an abstract discussion it is vexing to hear a man say: "You think thus and so because you are a woman"; but I know that my only defense is to reply: "I think thus and so because it is true," thereby removing my subjective self from the argument. It would be out of the question to reply: "And you think the contrary because you are a man," for it is understood that the fact of being a man is no peculiarity. A man is in the right in being a man; it is the woman who is in the wrong. It amounts to this: just as for the ancients there was an absolute vertical with reference to which the oblique was defined, so there is an absolute human type, the masculine. Woman has ovaries, a uterus; these peculiarities imprison her in her subjectivity, circumscribe her within the limits of her own nature. It is often said that she thinks with her glands. Man superbly ignores the fact that his anatomy also includes glands, such as the testicles, and that they secrete hormones. He thinks of his body as a direct and normal connection with the world, which he believes he apprehends objectively, whereas he regards the body of woman as a hindrance, a prison, weighed down by everything peculiar to it. "The female is a female by virtue of a certain *lack* of qualities," said Aristotle; "we should regard the female nature as afflicted with a natural defectiveness." And St. Thomas for his part pronounced woman to be an "imperfect man," an "incidental" being. This is symbolized in Genesis where Eve is depicted as made from what Bossuet called "a supernumerary bone" of Adam.

Thus humanity is male and man defines woman not in herself but as relative to him; she is not regarded as an autonomous being. Michelet writes: "Woman, the relative being. . . ." And Benda is most positive in his *Rapport d'Uriel:* "The body of man makes sense in itself quite apart from that of woman, whereas the latter seems wanting in significance by itself. . . . Man can think of himself without woman. She cannot think of herself without man." And she is simply what man decrees; thus she is called "the sex," by which is meant that she appears essentially to the male as a sexual being. For him she is sex—absolute sex, no less. She is defined and differentiated with reference to man and not he with reference to her; she is the incidental, the inessential as opposed to the essential. He is the Subject, he is the Absolute—she is the Other.

The category of the *Other* is as primordial as consciousness itself. In the most primitive societies, in the most ancient mythologies, one finds the expression of a duality—that of the Self and the Other. This duality was not originally attached to the division of the sexes; it was not dependent upon any empirical facts. It is revealed in such works as that of Granet on Chinese thought and those of Dumézil on the East Indies and Rome. The feminine element was at first no more involved in such pairs as Varuna-Mitra, Uranus-Zeus, Sun-Moon, and Day-Night than it was in the contrasts between Good and Evil, lucky and unlucky auspices, right and left, God and Lucifer. Otherness is a fundamental category of human thought.

Thus it is that no group ever sets itself up as the One without at once setting up the Other over against itself. If three travelers chance to occupy the same compartment, that is enough to make vaguely hostile "others" out of all the rest of the passengers on the train. In small-town eyes all persons not belonging to the village are "strangers" and suspect; to the native of a country all who inhabit other countries are "foreigners"; Jews are "different" for the anti-Semite, Negroes are "inferior" for American racists, aborigines are "natives" for colonists, proletarians are the "lower class" for the privileged.

Lévi-Strauss, at the end of a profound work on the various forms of primitive societies, reaches the following conclusion: "Passage from the state of Nature to the state of Culture is marked by man's ability to view biological relations as a series of contrasts; duality, alternation, opposition, and symmetry, whether under definite or vague forms, constitute not so much phenomena to be explained as fundamental and immediately given data of social reality." These phenomena would be incomprehensible if in fact human society were simply a *Mitsein* or fellowship based on solidarity and friendliness. Things become clear, on the contrary, if, following Hegel, we find in consciousness itself a fundamental hostility toward every other consciousness; the subject can be posed only in being opposed—he sets himself up as the essential, as opposed to the other, the inessential, the object.

But the other consciousness, the other ego, sets up a reciprocal claim. The native traveling abroad is shocked to find himself in turn regarded as a "stranger" by the natives of neighboring countries. As a matter of fact, wars, festivals, trading, treaties, and contests among tribes, nations, and classes tend to deprive the concept *Other* of its absolute sense and to make manifest its relativity; willy-nilly, individuals and groups are forced to realize the reciprocity of their relations. How is it, then, that this reciprocity has not been recognized between the sexes, that one of the contrasting terms is set up as the sole essential, denying any relativity in regard to its correlative and defining the latter as pure otherness? Why is it that women do not dispute male sovereignty? No subject will readily volunteer to become the object, the inessential; it is not the Other who, in defining himself as the Other, establishes the One. The Other is posed as such by the One in defining himself as the One. But if the Other is not to regain the status of being the One, he must be submissive enough to accept this alien point of view. Whence comes this submission in the case of woman?

There are, to be sure, other cases in which a certain category has been able to dominate another completely for a time.

Very often this privilege depends upon inequality of numbers—the majority imposes its rule upon the minority or persecutes it. But women are not a minority, like the American Negroes or the Jews; there are as many women as men on earth. Again, the two groups concerned have often been originally independent; they may have been formerly unaware of each other's existence, or perhaps they recognized each other's autonomy. But a historical event has resulted in the subjugation of the weaker by the stronger. The scattering of the Jews, the introduction of slavery into America, the conquests of imperialism are examples in point. In these cases the oppressed retained at least the memory of former days; they possessed in common a past, a tradition, sometimes a religion or a culture.

The parallel drawn by Bebel between women and the proletariat is valid in that neither ever formed a minority or a separate collective unit of mankind. And instead of a single historical event it is in both cases a historical development that explains their status as a class and accounts for the membership of *particular individuals* in that class. But proletarians have not always existed, whereas there have always been women. They are women in virtue of their anatomy and physiology. Throughout history they have always been subordinated to men, and hence their dependency is not the result of a historical event or a social change—it was not something that *occurred*. The reason why otherness in this case seems to be an absolute is in part that it lacks the contingent or incidental nature of historical facts. A condition brought about at a certain time can be abolished at some other time, as the Negroes of Haiti and others have proved; but it might seem that a natural condition is beyond the possibility of change. In truth, however, the nature of things is no more immutably given, once for all, than is historical reality. If woman seems to be the inessential which never becomes the essential, it is because she herself fails to bring about this change. Proletarians say "We"; Negroes also. Regarding themselves as subjects, they transform the bourgeois, the whites, into "others." But women do not say "We," except at some congress of feminists or similar formal demonstration; men say "women," and women use the same word in referring to themselves. They do not authentically assume a subjective attitude. The proletarians have accomplished the revolution in Russia, the Negroes in Haiti, the Indo-Chinese are battling for it in Indo-China; but the women's effort has never been anything more than a symbolic agitation. They have gained only what men have been willing to grant; they have taken nothing, they have only received.

The reason for this is that women lack concrete means for organizing themselves into a unit which can stand face to face with the correlative unit. They have no past, no history, no religion of their own; and they have no such solidarity of work and interest as that of the proletariat. They are not even promiscuously herded together in the way that creates community feeling among the American Negroes, the ghetto Jews, the workers of Saint-Denis, or the factory hands of Renault. They live dispersed among the males, attached through residence, housework, economic condition, and social standing to certain men—fathers or husbands—more firmly than they are to other women. If they belong to the bourgeoisie, they feel solidarity with men of that class, not with proletarian women; if they are white, their allegiance is to white men, not to Negro women. The proletariat can

propose to massacre the ruling class, and a sufficiently fanatical Jew or Negro might dream of getting sole possession of the atomic bomb and making humanity wholly Jewish or black; but woman cannot even dream of exterminating the males. The bond that unites her to her oppressors is not comparable to any other. The division of the sexes is a biological fact, not an event in human history. Male and female stand opposed within a primordial *Mitsein,* and woman has not broken it. The couple is a fundamental unity with its two halves riveted together, and the cleavage of society along the line of sex is impossible. Here is to be found the basic trait of woman: she is the Other in a totality of which the two components are necessary to one another.

One could suppose that this reciprocity might have facilitated the liberation of woman. When Hercules sat at the feet of Omphale and helped with her spinning, his desire for her held him captive; but why did she fail to gain a lasting power? To revenge herself on Jason, Medea killed their children; and this grim legend would seem to suggest that she might have obtained a formidable influence over him through his love for his offspring. In *Lysistrata* Aristophanes gaily depicts a band of women who joined forces to gain social ends through the sexual needs of their men; but this is only a play. In the legend of the Sabine women, the latter soon abandoned their plan of remaining sterile to punish their ravishers. In truth woman has not been socially emancipated through man's need—sexual desire and the desire for offspring—which makes the male dependent for satisfaction upon the female.

Master and slave, also, are united by a reciprocal need, in this case economic, which does not liberate the slave. In the relation of master to slave the master does not make a point of the need that he has for the other; he has in his grasp the power of satisfying this need through his own action; whereas the slave, in his dependent condition, his hope and fear, is quite conscious of the need he has for his master. Even if the need is at bottom equally urgent for both, it always works in favor of the oppressor and against the oppressed. That is why the liberation of the working class, for example, has been slow.

Now, woman has always been man's dependent, if not his slave; the two sexes have never shared the world in equality. And even today woman is heavily handicapped, though her situation is beginning to change. Almost nowhere is her legal status the same as man's, and frequently it is much to her disadvantage. Even when her rights are legally recognized in the abstract, long-standing custom prevents their full expression in the mores. In the economic sphere men and women can almost be said to make up two castes; other things being equal, the former hold the better jobs, get higher wages, and have more opportunity for success than their new competitors. In industry and politics men have a great many more positions and they monopolize the most important posts. In addition to all this, they enjoy a traditional prestige that the education of children tends in every way to support, for the present enshrines the past—and in the past all history has been made by men. At the present time, when women are beginning to take part in the affairs of the world, it is still a world that belongs to men—they have no doubt of it at all and women have scarcely any. To decline to be the Other, to refuse to be a party to the deal—this would be for women to renounce all the advantages conferred upon them by their alliance with the superior caste. Man-the-sovereign will provide woman-the-liege with material protection and will undertake the moral justification of her existence; thus she can evade at once both economic risk and the metaphysical risk of a liberty in which ends and aims must be contrived without assistance. Indeed, along with the ethical urge of each individual to affirm his subjective existence, there is also the temptation to forgo liberty and become a thing. This is an inauspicious road, for he who takes it—passive, lost, ruined—becomes henceforth the creature of another's will, frustrated in his transcendence and deprived of every value. But it is an easy road; on it one avoids the strain involved in undertaking an authentic existence. When man makes of woman the *Other*, he may, then, expect her to manifest deep-seated tendencies toward complicity. Thus, woman may fail to lay claim to the status of subject because she lacks definite resources, because she feels the necessary bond that ties her to man regardless of reciprocity, and because she is often very well pleased with her role as the *Other*.

But it will be asked at once: how did all this begin? It is easy to see that the duality of the sexes, like any duality, gives rise to conflict. And doubtless the winner will assume the status of absolute. But why should man have won from the start? It seems possible that women could have won the victory; or that the outcome of the conflict might never have been decided. How is it that this world has always belonged to the men and that things have begun to change only recently? Is this change a good thing? Will it bring about an equal sharing of the world between men and women?

These questions are not new, and they have often been answered. But the very fact that woman *is the Other* tends to cast suspicion upon all the justifications that men have ever been able to provide for it. These have all too evidently been dictated by men's interest. A little-known feminist of the seventeenth century, Poulain de la Barre, put it this way: "All that has been written about women by men should be suspect, for the men are at once judge and party to the lawsuit." Everywhere, at all times, the males have displayed their satisfaction in feeling that they are the lords of creation. "Blessed be God . . . that He did not make me a woman," say the Jews in their morning prayers, while their wives pray on a note of resignation: "Blessed be the Lord, who created me according to His will." The first among the blessings for which Plato thanked the gods was that he had been created free, not enslaved; the second, a man, not a woman. But the males could not enjoy this privilege fully unless they believed it to be founded on the absolute and the eternal; they sought to make the fact of their supremacy into a right. "Being men, those who have made and compiled the laws have favored their own sex, and jurists have elevated these laws into principles," to quote Poulain de la Barre once more.

Legislators, priests, philosophers, writers, and scientists have striven to show that the subordinate position of woman is willed in heaven and advantageous on earth. The religions invented by men reflect this wish for domination. In the legends of Eve and Pandora men have taken up arms against women. They have made use of philosophy and theology, as the quotations from Aristotle and St. Thomas have shown. Since ancient times satirists and moralists have delighted in showing up the weaknesses of women. We are familiar with the savage indictments hurled against women throughout French literature. Montherlant, for example, follows the tradition of Jean de Meung, though with less gusto. This hostility may at times be well founded, often it is gratuitous; but in truth it more or less successfully conceals a desire for self-justification. As Montaigne says, "It is easier to accuse one sex than to excuse the other." Sometimes what is going on is clear enough. For instance, the Roman law limiting the rights of woman cited "the imbecility, the instability of the sex" just when the weakening of family ties seemed to threaten the interests of male heirs. And in the effort to keep the married woman under guardianship, appeal was made in the sixteenth century to the authority of St. Augustine, who declared that "woman is a creature neither decisive nor constant," at a time when the single woman was thought capable of managing her property. Montaigne understood clearly how arbitrary and unjust was woman's appointed lot: "Women are not in the wrong when they decline to accept the rules laid down for them, since the men make these rules without consulting them. No wonder intrigue and strife abound." But he did not go so far as to champion their cause.

It was only later, in the eighteenth century, that genuinely democratic men began to view the matter objectively. Diderot, among others, strove to show that woman is, like man, a human being. Later John Stuart Mill came fervently to her defense. But these philosophers displayed unusual impartiality. In the nineteenth century the feminist quarrel became again a quarrel of partisans. One of the consequences of the industrial revolution was the entrance of women into productive labor, and it was just here that the claims of the feminists emerged from the realm of theory and acquired an economic basis, while their opponents became the more aggressive. Although landed property lost power to some extent, the bourgeoisie clung to the old morality that found the guarantee of private property in the solidity of the family. Woman was ordered back into the home the more harshly as her emancipation became a real menace. Even within the working class the men endeavored to restrain woman's liberation, because they began to see the women as dangerous competitors—the more so because they were accustomed to work for lower wages. . . .

So it is that many men will affirm as if in good faith that women *are* the equals of man and that they have nothing to clamor for, while *at the same time* they will say that women can never be the equals of man and that their demands are in vain. It is, in point of fact, a difficult matter for man to realize the extreme importance of social discriminations which seem outwardly insignificant but which produce in women moral and intellectual effects so profound that they appear to spring from her original nature. The most sympathetic of men never fully comprehend woman's concrete situation. And there is no reason to put much trust in the men when they rush to the defense of privileges whose full extent they can hardly measure. We shall not, then, permit ourselves to be intimidated by the number and violence of the attacks launched against women, nor to be entrapped by the self-seeking eulogies bestowed on the "true woman," nor to profit by the enthusiasm for woman's destiny manifested by men who would not for the world have any part of it. . . .

What peculiarly signalizes the situation of woman is that she—a free and autonomous being like all human creatures—nevertheless finds herself living in a world where men compel her to assume the status of the Other. They propose to stabilize her as object and to doom her to immanence since her transcendence is to be overshadowed and forever transcended by another ego (*conscience*) which is essential and sovereign. The drama of woman lies in this conflict between the fundamental aspirations of every subject (ego)—who always regards the self as the essential—and the compulsions of a situation in which she is the inessential. How can a human being in woman's situation attain fulfillment? What roads are open to her? Which are blocked? How can independence be recovered in a state of dependency? What circumstances limit woman's liberty and how can they be overcome? These are the fundamental questions on which I would fain throw some light. This means that I am interested in the fortunes of the individuals as defined not in terms of happiness but in terms of liberty. . . .

---

# W. H. AUDEN
## *The Shield of Achilles*

---

Britain's W. H. Auden (1907–1973) is generally considered the best poet writing in English in the middle of this century. He began his studies at Oxford University, 1925–1928, in the sciences, but soon changed to poetry, which presented him with a dilemma. Two paths beckoned. Modernist poetry, represented by Eliot (see "The Love Song of J. Alfred Prufrock"), with its deeply personal and original voice, and "civic" poetry, represented by the dead Tennyson (see "Ulysses"), which addressed a wide public on civic and moral themes. Auden chose "civic" poetry; over the course of his life, he became the poet of the *Zeitgeist* (German, for "spirit of the times"), registering shifts in the collective unconscious of the moment, though he also alienated some readers, who could not tolerate his comic, even flippant, manner of speech.

In his poems, Auden was always at ease with other people's ideas, freely drawing from wide-ranging sources, including science, politics, psychology, religion, and poetry, wherever his poetic muse led. Soon after entering Oxford, he became committed generally to left-wing causes, supporting Britain's General Strike in 1926, and siding with the Spanish republic against the Fascists in the 1930s. Many at the time thought him a communist and a Freudian, but he only lifted ideas from Marx and Freud to suit his needs. Never afraid to contradict himself, he, after 1940, grew more conservative and adopted a private version of the Anglican faith, which he had abandoned at Oxford. His reconversion to Christianity enabled him to accept his homosexuality, for he lived by the Anglican belief that all persons sin, as he acknowledged his homosexual acts to be, and thus all can be forgiven.

The most controversial aspect of Auden's life swirls around his decision in 1939 to emigrate to America (where, in 1946, he became a citizen), just as World War II was beginning in Europe. Having encouraged readers in the 1930s to identify him with left-wing causes, as in the *New Country* poems (1933), Auden by this step seemed to betray both his country and himself; British readers cooled to his later poetry. All seemed forgiven when Auden returned to Oxford, 1956–1961, as professor of poetry. Still, Auden's post-1939 works are not as highly regarded as his earlier poems, though *The Age of Anxiety* (1944–1946) (which inspired a ballet and a symphony) is ranked among his most accomplished works.

### Reading the Selection

Auden's "The Shield of Achilles" (1952) is a commentary on the disquieting scene that emerged after World War II. In form, it adopts the approach used by Tennyson in "Ulysses," in that both poems derive their impact from the reader's familiarity with Homer. Auden's poem is based on Homer's *Iliad*, Book XVIII, where the goddess Thetis inspects her son Achilles' new shield and finds signs of good government, religious piety, and artistic life. Auden's Thetis, similarly engaged in an inspection of Achilles' shield, sees only negative images: standardized totalitarianism ("A million eyes, a million boots in line/Without expression, waiting for a sign"), a military parody of Christ's crucifixion ("three pale figures were led forth and bound/To three posts"), and, random, senseless violence ("ragged urchin . . . girls are raped . . . boys knife a third"). Unlike Homer, Auden suggests that the doomed Achilles will die in vain since his cause, as symbolized by these negative images, is not worth fighting for.

---

She looked over his shoulder
  For vines and olive trees.
Marble well-governed cities
  And ships upon untamed seas,
But there on the shining metal
  His hands had put instead
An artificial wilderness
  And a sky like lead.

A plain without a feature, bare and brown,
  No blade of grass, no sign of neighborhood,
Nothing to eat and nowhere to sit down,
  Yet, congregated on its blankness, stood
  An unintelligible multitude,
A million eyes, a million boots in line,
Without expression, waiting for a sign.

Out of the air a voice without a face
  Proved by statistics that some cause was just
In tones as dry and level as the place:
  No one was cheered and nothing was discussed;
  Column by column in a cloud of dust
They marched away enduring a belief
Whose logic brought them, somewhere else, to grief.

She looked over his shoulder
  For ritual pieties,
White flower-garlanded heifers,
  Libation and sacrifice,
But there on the shining metal
  Where the altar should have been,
She saw by his flickering forge-light
  Quite another scene.

Barbed wire enclosed an arbitrary spot
  Where bored officials lounged (one cracked a joke)
And sentries sweated for the day was hot:
  A crowd of ordinary decent folk

Watched from without and neither moved nor spoke
As three pale figures were led forth and bound
To three posts driven upright in the ground.

The mass and majesty of this world, all
  That carries weight and always weighs the same
Lay in the hands of others; they were small
  And could not hope for help and no help came:
  What their foes liked to do was done, their shame
Was all the worst could wish; they lost their pride
And died as men before their bodies died.

She looked over his shoulder
  For athletes at their games,
Men and women in a dance
  Moving their sweet limbs
Quick, quick, to music
  But there on the shining shield
His hands had set no dancing-floor
  But a weed-choked field.

A ragged urchin, aimless and alone,
  Loitered about that vacancy; a bird
Flew up to safety from his well-aimed stone:
  That girls are raped, that two boys knife a third,
  Were axioms to him, who'd never heard
Of any world where promises were kept,
Or one could weep because another wept.

The thin-lipped armorer,
  Hephaestos, hobbled away,
Thetis of the shining breasts
  Cried out in dismay
At what the god had wrought
  To please her son, the strong
Iron-hearted man-slaying Achilles
  Who would not live long.

ALBERT CAMUS

# The Myth of Sisyphus

When Albert Camus was killed in an automobile crash in 1960, he was a living legend, the West's most famous contemporary literary and philosophical figure. Then, and even now, his untimely end seemed an ironically fitting climax to the life of the founder of Absurdism— the philosophy that proclaimed that human beings are alone in an absurd universe, compelled to act but lacking any reasonable grounds for doing so. Within his brief life, Camus won the 1957 Nobel Prize for literature and composed a dazzling array of novels (*The Stranger*, 1942; *The Plague*, 1947), plays (*Caligula*, 1942) and philosophical essays (*The Myth of Sisyphus*, 1943). Reflecting his Absurdism, these collected works defined and helped propagate a twentieth-century sensibility of uncomplaining stoicism.

Despite the stoic message of his writings, Camus, as a man, did not watch idly as life passed by but, instead, immersed himself in left-wing causes, hoping to make the world a better place. He aspired to be his generation's conscience, and thus he wrote many letters to journal and newspaper editors and signed protest petitions, taking sides in the political quarrels that raged during this period. History has justified many of his causes, such as his rejection of capital punishment, his 1940s leadership in the French Resistance against Nazi occupation, and his 1952 break with the Marxists, as set forth in his philosophical essay, *The Rebel*; this book sparked a rupture between Camus and the existentialist Sartre, who remained friendly to communism.

Camus's only major moral failure involved his indecisiveness during Algeria's civil war. Having been born into a settler family in France's colony of Algeria, he refused to side with either the Arab Muslims, who wanted to rid their land of foreigners, or the French colonists, who preferred a multiethnic state; instead, he joined Arab liberals, appearing on platforms with them to appeal to reason, and was howled down by all sides. Recognizing the futility of his position, Camus was led to write *The Fall* (1956), a novel in which he revealed painful self-doubt and led some critics to predict his reconversion to the Christian faith he had earlier abandoned.

Algeria left its stamp on Camus in other ways. Reared in poverty by a barely literate mother with a severe hearing disability (his father was killed in 1914), he remained sensitive to the plight of the oppressed. The local Mediterranean coast made him into a sensualist, in love with the sun and sea, and he delighted in contrasting Mediterranean with Nordic culture, which he associated with the coldness and guilt of northern Europe.

## Reading the Selection

This selection contains the last part of *The Myth of Sisyphus*. In it, Camus reinterprets the Greek tale of Sisyphus, who revealed divine secrets to mortals, and, in retribution, the gods condemned him to an eternity of work, ceaselessly pushing a rock up a mountain. In Camus's version, Sisyphus is an absurd hero, a "modern everyman," a symbol of the meaningless (in the face of death) yet necessary tasks that ordinary men and women are daily "condemned" to perform. Sisyphus's triumph—for, indeed, Sisyphus is victorious over his "rock"—lies in his consciousness, his double awareness that he is superior to his fate and that he is sensually linked to the earth, the only heaven that exists. This upbeat conclusion affirms the quiet stoicism at the heart of Camus's philosophy.

---

The gods had condemned Sisyphus to ceaselessly rolling a rock to the top of a mountain, whence the stone would fall back of its own weight. They had thought with some reason that there is no more dreadful punishment than futile and hopeless labor.

If one believes Homer, Sisyphus was the wisest and most prudent of mortals. According to another tradition, however, he was disposed to practice the profession of highwayman. I see no contradiction in this. Opinions differ as to the reasons why he became the futile laborer of the underworld. To begin with, he is accused of certain levity in regard to the gods. He stole their secrets. Aegina, the daughter of Aesopus, was carried off by Jupiter. The father was shocked by that disappearance and complained to Sisyphus. He, who knew of the abduction, offered to tell about it on condition that Aesopus would give water to the citadel of Corinth. To the celestial thunderbolts he preferred the benediction of water. He was punished for this in the underworld. Homer tells us also that Sisyphus had put Death in chains. Pluto could not endure the sight of his deserted, silent empire. He dispatched the god of war, who liberated Death from the hands of her conqueror.

It is said also that Sisyphus, being near to death, rashly wanted to test his wife's love. He ordered her to cast his unburied body into the middle of the public square. Sisyphus woke up in the underworld. And there, annoyed by an obedience so contrary to human love, he obtained from Pluto permission to return to earth in order to chastise his wife. But when he had seen again the face of this world, enjoyed water and sun, warm stones and the sea, he no longer wanted to go back to the infernal darkness. Recalls, signs of anger, warnings were of no avail. Many years more he lived facing the curve of the gulf, the sparkling sea, and the smiles of earth. A decree of the gods was necessary. Mercury came and seized the impudent man by the collar and, snatching him from his joys, led him forcibly back to the underworld, where his rock was ready for him.

You have already grasped that Sisyphus is the absurd hero. He *is*, as much through his passions as through his torture. His scorn of the gods, his hatred of death, and his passion for life won him that unspeakable penalty in which the whole being is exerted toward accomplishing nothing. This is the price that must be paid for the passions of this earth. Nothing is told us about Sisyphus in the underworld. Myths are made for the imagination to breathe life into them. As for this myth, one sees merely the whole effort of a body straining to raise the huge stone, to roll it and push it up a slope a hundred times over; one sees the face screwed up, the cheek tight against the stone, the shoulder bracing the clay-covered mass, the foot wedging it, the fresh start with arms outstretched, the wholly human security of two earth-clotted hands. At the very end of his long effort measured by skyless space and time without depth, the purpose is achieved. Then Sisyphus watches the stone rush down in a few moments toward that lower world whence he will have to push it up again toward the summit. He goes back down to the plain.

It is during that return, that pause, that Sisyphus interests me. A face that toils so close to stones is already stone itself! I see that man going back down with a heavy yet measured step toward the torment of which he will never know the end. That hour like a breathing-space which returns as surely as his suffering, that is the hour of consciousness. At each of those moments when he leaves the heights and gradually sinks toward the lairs of the gods, he is superior to his fate. He is stronger than his rock.

If this myth is tragic, that is because its hero is conscious. Where would his torture be, indeed, if at every step the hope of succeeding upheld him? The workman of today works every day in his life at the same tasks, and this fate is no less absurd. But it is tragic only at the rare moments when it becomes conscious. Sisyphus, proletarian of the gods, powerless and rebellious, knows the whole extent of his wretched condition: it is what he thinks of during his descent. The lucidity that was to constitute his torture at the same time crowns his victory. There is no fate that cannot be surmounted by scorn.

If the descent is thus sometimes performed in sorrow, it can also take place in joy. This word is not too much. Again I fancy Sisyphus returning toward his rock, and the sorrow was in the beginning. When the images of earth cling too tightly to memory, when the call of happiness becomes too insistent, it happens that melancholy rises in man's heart: this is the rock's victory, this is the rock itself. The boundless grief is too heavy to bear. These are our nights of Gethsemane. But crushing truths perish from being acknowledged. Thus, Oedipus at the outset obeys fate without knowing it. But from the moment he knows, his tragedy begins. Yet at the same moment, blind and desperate, he realizes that the only bond linking him to the world is the cool hand of a girl. Then a tremendous remark rings out: "Despite so many ordeals, my advanced age and the nobility of my soul make me conclude that all is well." Sophocles' Oedipus, like Dostoevsky's Kirilov, thus gives the recipe for the absurd victory. Ancient wisdom confirms modern heroism.

One does not discover the absurd without being tempted to write a manual of happiness. "What! by such narrow ways—?" There is but one world, however. Happiness and the absurd are two sons of the same earth. They are inseparable. It would be a mistake to say that happiness necessarily springs from the absurd discovery. It happens as well that the feeling of the absurd springs from happiness. "I conclude that all is well," says Oedipus, and that remark is sacred. It echoes in the wild and limited universe of man. It teaches that all is not, has not been, exhausted. It drives out of this world a god who had come into it with dissatisfaction and a preference for futile sufferings. It makes of fate a human matter, which must be settled among men.

All Sisyphus' silent joy is contained therein. His fate belongs to him. His rock is his thing. Likewise, the absurd man, when he contemplates his torment, silences all the idols. In the universe suddenly restored to its silence, the myriad wondering little voices of the earth rise up. Unconscious, secret calls, invitations from all the faces, they are the necessary reverse and price of victory. There is no sun without shadow, and it is essential to know the night. The absurd man says yes and his effort will henceforth be unceasing. If there is a personal fate, there is no higher destiny, or at least there is but one which he concludes is inevitable and despicable. For the rest, he knows himself to be the master of his days. At that subtle moment when man glances backward over his life, Sisyphus returning toward his rock, in that slight pivoting he contemplates that series of unrelated actions which becomes his fate, created by him, combined under his memory's eye and soon sealed by his death. Thus, convinced of the wholly human origin of all that is human, a blind man eager to see who knows that the night has no end, he is still on the go. The rock is still rolling.

I leave Sisyphus at the foot of the mountain! One always finds one's burden again. But Sisyphus teaches the higher fidelity that negates the gods and raises rocks. He too concludes that all is well. This universe henceforth without a master seems to him neither sterile nor futile. Each atom of that stone, each mineral flake of that nightfilled mountain, in itself forms a world. The struggle itself toward the heights is enough to fill a man's heart. One must imagine Sisyphus happy.

---

# ALLEN GINSBERG

## *A Supermarket in California*

---

The American Allen Ginsberg (1926–    ) is the best-known poet writing in English to appear after 1945. He was the voice of the Beat Generation, the group of writers and artists who dropped out of the "rat-race" during Truman's and Eisenhower's presidencies (1945–1961); the "beats" sought alternative styles of living through drugs, drink, casual sex, Buddhism, jazz, long car trips, and identification with society's "beaten-down" fringes. Bursting on the world like a bombshell, Ginsberg's poem titled *Howl* (1956), glorified and, at the same time, lamented the "destruction by madness" of his fellow "beats," at the hands of capitalist America. *Howl* became the subject of an obscenity trial, though found not to be obscene. The furor caused it to become a bestseller and made Ginsberg a celebrity. In the 1960s, he cemented his place in the counterculture when he wrote poems protesting the Vietnam War ("Pentagon Exorcism," 1967) and the arms race ("War Profit Litany," 1967).

Critics tend to read Ginsberg's poetry as sections of an ongoing autobiography. Thus, two key events in the Ginsberg saga are the death of his mother, Naomi (1894–1956), in a mental ward, and his mystical visions of the poet William Blake (1757–1827), which he experienced in 1948–1949. His mother's death led him to write *Kaddish*, 1958–1960, based on the Jewish prayer for the dead but cleansed of its religious affirmations; it is, except for *Howl*, his most successful work. The Blakean visions caused him to organize his poetry around them for about fifteen years. Also influencing Ginsberg's poetry was Whitman (see "When Lilacs Last in the Dooryard Bloom'd"), whose democratic spirit and bohemianism seemed to anticipate the Beat Generation.

### Reading the Selection

The theme of "A Supermarket in California" (1955) is the contrast between Whitman's nineteenth-century and Ginsberg's twentieth-century America. As if in a dream, Ginsberg moves through a supermarket, "aisles full of husbands! Wives in the avocados, babies in the tomatoes!" checking out the produce and fantasizing about Whitman shopping too: "I saw you . . . childless, lonely old grubber, poking among the meats in the refrigerator and eyeing the grocery boys." Ginsberg, homosexual and lonely, shares Whitman's marginal social status. He also stresses the poet's disquieting role in society, when he imagines that he and Whitman are followed by the store detective. The poem ends with a question (paraphrased here): What America did you leave behind when you died, Walt Whitman?

Typical of Ginsberg's works, this poem seems to express his artistic freedom and love of whimsy, relying, he says, on his own "neural" (nerve) and writing impulses, rather than trying to fill in the pattern of a preexisting plan. Despite its spontaneous feel, however, this poem is carefully worked out and is firmly rooted in literary tradition. It does not unfold logically or tell a story but depends for its effect on the accumulation of parallel words and sounds, in the repetition of "what" and "I" and in the refrain of words beginning with "w"; this constitutes a blending of the devices of accumulation and parallelism, used by Whitman, developed in Hebrew poetry (see *The New English Bible*), and rooted in Egyptian models (see *The Great Hymn to the Aten*). Whitman is also the inspiration for the poem's basic unit, the unaccented line; there are twelve lines altogether, each line constituting a single thought.

"Garcia Lorca" refers to the Spanish poet of the same name, 1898–1936, one of whose poems about Whitman was translated by Ginsberg.

What thoughts I have of you tonight, Walt Whitman,
for I walked down the sidestreets under the trees with a
headache self-conscious looking at the full moon.

In my hungry fatigue, and shopping for images, I
went into the neon fruit supermarket, dreaming of your
enumerations!

What peaches and what penumbras! Whole
families shopping at night! Aisles full of husbands!
Wives in the avocados, babies in the tomatoes!—and
you, García Lorca, what were you doing down by the
watermelons?

I saw you, Walt Whitman, childless, lonely old
grubber, poking among the meats in the refrigerator and
eyeing the grocery boys.

I heard you asking questions of each: Who killed the
pork chops? What price bananas? Are you my Angel?

I wandered in and out of the brilliant stacks of cans
following you, and followed in my imagination by the
store detective.

We strode down the open corridors together in our
solitary fancy tasting artichokes, possessing every frozen
delicacy, and never passing the cashier.

Where are we going, Walt Whitman? The doors close
in an hour. Which way does your beard point tonight?

(I touch your book and dream of our odyssey in the
supermarket and feel absurd.)

Will we walk all night through solitary streets? The
trees add shade to shade, lights out in the houses, we'll
both be lonely.

Will we stroll dreaming of the lost America of love
past blue automobiles in driveways, home to our silent
cottage?

Ah, dear father, graybeard, lonely old courage-
teacher, what America did you have when Charon quit
poling his ferry and you got out on a smoking bank and
stood watching the boat disappear on the black waters
of Lethe?

# ELIE WIESEL

# from *Night*

Of all the moral dilemmas raised by World War II, including America's dropping of atomic
bombs on non-strategic cities, and air attacks on civilian populations by both Allied and Axis
forces, the dominant issue in the postwar world has been the Holocaust—Nazi Germany's
master plan. Termed by its leaders the Final Solution, it was intended to eliminate the Jewish
people, which involved the murder of six million Jews out of a population of nine million, along
with perhaps six million other people deemed undesirable, such as gypsies, handicappers, and
homosexuals. In a sense it was the German people who provided the terrifying vision of the
Holocaust; race paranoia, especially anti-Semitism, or hatred of Jews, was deeply embedded in
German culture, fostered by generations of nationalist-minded intellectuals since the dawn of
the Romantic era in about 1800. It was only during World War II, as part of a national response
to war, that the Nazis provided the means to carry out this colossal crime.

Since World War II, in an effort to come to terms with these senseless killings, a vast
Holocaust literature has emerged; it consists of novels, short stories, plays, essays, memoirs,
histories, anthropological studies, sociological analyses, and theological treatises, not to mention
countless films and TV productions, dealing, in part or in whole, with this theme. In the
forefront of Holocaust literature has been the Hungarian writer, Elie Wiesel (1928–    ), himself
a survivor of a Nazi death camp. As a writer of international stature, Wiesel has adopted the
literary task of keeping the world's attention focused unflinchingly on the Holocaust, lest it be
forgotten and history repeat itself.

Wiesel, first interned by the Nazis in 1944, when he lost his sisters and parents, was
eventually transferred to the camp in Buchenwald, Germany. Here typhus-vaccine experiments
were conducted on inmates; he survived to be freed by American troops during the war's final
days. After the war, he became part of the homeless refugee population, called displaced
persons, or "D.P.'s," roaming over Europe, until he settled in Paris to study philosophy and
literature. From Paris he traveled to Asia, where he shifted his interest to comparative
mysticism, a project which led him to make the Holocaust his lifelong literary project.

*Reading the Selection*

Wiesel's novel *Night* (1960) belongs to Holocaust literature, the genre whose central concern is the question of how a beneficent God could have allowed the Final Solution. One of the first and, in many ways, the most powerful of the Holocaust's accounts, it not only chronicles the atrocities inflicted on the Jews but raises the question of God's apparent indifference to human suffering.

In *Night*, prior to this selection, the scholarly narrator, living in an isolated village, near the end of World War II, when Russian invaders appeared to have the Germans on the run, tells of the disruption of his biblical study; a fellow Jew, fleeing from the Nazis, warns him and the rest of the village about mass killings. The villagers fail to heed this warning, only to fall victim to a last ditch Nazi effort; it results in shipping the entire village to a death camp. In this selection, the Holocaust's horror is personalized in scenes of humiliation, deprivation, and murder—with the ending being that the narrator's spirit is crushed, as he questions God's existence.

———

The cherished objects we had brought with us thus far were left behind in the train, and with them, at last, our illusions.

Every two yards or so an SS man held his tommy gun trained on us. Hand in hand we followed the crowd.

An SS noncommissioned officer came to meet us, a truncheon in his hand. He gave the order:

"Men to the left! Women to the right!"

Eight words spoken quietly, indifferently, without emotion. Eight short, simple words. Yet that was the moment when I parted from my mother. I had not had time to think, but already I felt the pressure of my father's hand: we were alone. For a part of a second I glimpsed my mother and my sisters moving away to the right. Tzipora held Mother's hand. I saw them disappear into the distance; my mother was stroking my sister's fair hair, as though to protect her, while I walked on with my father and the other men. And I did not know that in that place, at that moment, I was parting from my mother and Tzipora forever. I went on walking. My father held onto my hand.

Behind me, an old man fell to the ground. Near him was an SS man, putting his revolver back in its holster.

My hand shifted on my father's arm. I had one thought not to lose him. Not to be left alone.

The SS officers gave the order:

"Form fives!"

Commotion. At all costs we must keep together.

"Here, kid, how old are you?"

It was one of the prisoners who asked me this. I could not see his face, but his voice was tense and weary.

"I'm not quite fifteen yet."

"No. Eighteen."

"But I'm not," I said. "Fifteen."

"Fool. Listen to what *I* say."

Then he questioned my father, who replied:

"Fifty."

The other grew more furious than ever.

"No, not fifty. Forty. Do you understand? Eighteen and forty."

He disappeared into the night shadows. A second man came up, spitting oaths at us.

"What have you come here for, you sons of bitches? What are you doing here, eh?"

Someone dared to answer him.

"What do you think? Do you suppose we've come here for our own pleasure? Do you think we asked to come?"

A little more, and the man would have killed him.

"You shut your trap, you filthy swine, or I'll squash you right now! You'd have done better to have hanged yourselves where you were than come here. Didn't you know what was in store for you at Auschwitz? Haven't you heard about it? In 1944?"

No, we had not heard. No one had told us. He could not believe his ears. His tone of voice became increasingly brutal.

"Do you see that chimney over there? See it? Do you see those flames? (Yes, we did see the flames.) Over there—that's where you're going to be taken. That's your grave, over there. Haven't you realized it yet? You dumb bastards, don't you understand anything? You're going to be burned. Frizzled away. Turned into ashes."

He was growing hysterical in his fury. We stayed motionless, petrified. Surely it was all a nightmare? An unimaginable nightmare?

I heard murmurs around me.

"We've got to do something. We can't let ourselves be killed. We can't go like beasts to the slaughter. We've got to revolt."

There were a few sturdy young fellows among us. They had knives on them, and they tried to incite the others to throw themselves on the armed guards.

One of the young men cried:

"Let the world learn of the existence of Auschwitz. Let everybody hear about it, while they can still escape. . . ."

But the older ones begged their children not to do anything foolish:

"You must never lose faith, even when the sword hangs over your head. That's the teaching of our sages. . . ."

The wind of revolt died down. We continued our march toward the square. In the middle stood the notorious Dr. Mengele (a typical SS officer: a cruel face, but not devoid of intelligence, and wearing a monocle); a conductor's baton in his hand, he was standing among the other officers. The baton moved unremittingly, sometimes to the right, sometimes to the left.

I was already in front of him:

"How old are you?" he asked, in an attempt at a paternal tone of voice.

"Eighteen." My voice was shaking.

"Are you in good health?"

"Yes."

"What's your occupation?"

Should I say that I was a student?

"Farmer," I heard myself say.

This conversation cannot have lasted more than a few seconds. It had seemed like an eternity to me.

The baton moved to the left. I took half a step forward. I wanted to see first where they were sending my father. If he went to the right, I would go after him.

The baton once again pointed to the left for him too. A weight was lifted from my heart.

We did not yet know which was the better side, right or left; which road led to prison and which to the crematory. But for the moment I was happy; I was near my father. Our procession continued to move slowly forward.

Another prisoner came up to us:

"Satisfied?"

"Yes," someone replied.

"Poor devils, you're going to the crematory."

He seemed to be telling the truth. Not far from us, flames were leaping up from a ditch, gigantic flames. They were burning something. A lorry drew up at the pit and delivered its load—little children. Babies! Yes, I saw it—saw it with my own eyes . . . those children in the flames. (Is it surprising that I could not sleep after that? Sleep had fled from my eyes.)

So this was where we were going. A little farther on was another and larger ditch for adults.

I pinched my face. Was I still alive? Was I awake? I could not believe it. How could it be possible for them to burn people, children, and for the world to keep silent? No, none of this could be true. It was a nightmare. . . . Soon I should wake with a start, my heart pounding, and find myself back in the bedroom of my childhood, among my books. . . .

My father's voice drew me from my thoughts:

"It's a shame . . . a shame that you couldn't have gone with your mother. . . . I saw several boys of your age going with their mothers. . . ."

His voice was terribly sad. I realized that he did not want to see what they were going to do to me. He did not want to see the burning of his only son.

My forehead was bathed in cold sweat. But I told him that I did not believe that they could burn people in our age, that humanity would never tolerate it. . . .

"Humanity? Humanity is not concerned with us. Today anything is allowed. Anything is possible, even these crematories. . . ."

His voice was choking.

"Father," I said, "if that is so, I don't want to wait here. I'm going to run to the electric wire. That would be better than slow agony in the flames."

He did not answer. He was weeping. His body was shaken convulsively. Around us, everyone was weeping. Someone began to recite the Kaddish, the prayer for the dead. I do not know if it has ever happened before, in the long history of the Jews, that people have ever recited the prayer for the dead for themselves.

*"Yitgadal veyitkadach shmé raba.* . . . May His name be blessed and magnified. . . ." whispered my father.

For the first time, I felt revolt rise up in me. Why should I bless His name? The Eternal, Lord of the Universe, the All-Powerful and Terrible, was silent. What had I to thank Him for?

We continued our march. We were gradually drawing closer to the ditch, from which an infernal heat was rising. Still twenty steps to go. If I wanted to bring about my own death, this was the moment. Our line had now only fifteen paces to cover. I bit my lips so that my father would not hear my teeth chattering. Ten steps still. Eight. Seven. We marched slowly on, as though following a hearse at our own funeral. Four steps more. Three steps. There it was now, right in front of us, the pit and its flames. I gathered all that was left of my strength, so that I could break from the ranks and throw myself upon the barbed wire. In the depths of my heart, I bade farewell to my father, to the whole universe; and, in spite of myself, the words formed themselves and issued in a whisper from my lips: *Yitgadal veyitkadach shmé raba.* . . . May His name be blessed and magnified. . . . My heart was bursting. The moment had come. I was face to face with the Angel of Death. . . .

No. Two steps from the pit we were ordered to turn to the left and made to go into a barracks.

I pressed my father's hand. He said:

"Do you remember Madame Schächter, in the train?"

Never shall I forget that night, the first night in camp, which has turned my life into one long night, seven times cursed and seven times sealed. Never shall I forget that smoke. Never shall I forget the little faces of the children, whose bodies I saw turned into wreaths of smoke beneath a silent blue sky.

Never shall I forget those flames which consumed my faith forever.

Never shall I forget that nocturnal silence which deprived me, for all eternity, of the desire to live. Never shall I forget those moments which murdered my God and my soul and turned my dreams to dust. Never shall I forget these things, even if I am condemned to live as long as God Himself. Never.

The barracks we had been made to go into was very long. In the roof were some blue-tinged skylights. The antechamber of Hell must look like this. So many crazed men, so many cries, so much bestial brutality!

There were dozens of prisoners to receive us, truncheons in their hands, striking out anywhere, at anyone, without reasons. Orders:

"Strip! Fast! *Los!* Keep only your belts and shoes in your hands. . . ."

We had to throw our clothes at one end of the barracks. There was already a great heap there. New suits and old, torn coats, rags. For us, this was the true equality, nakedness. Shivering with the cold.

Some SS officers moved about in the room, looking for strong men. If they were so keen on strength, perhaps one should try and pass oneself off as sturdy? My father thought the reverse. It was better not to draw attention to oneself. Our fate would then be the same as the others. (Later, we were to learn that he was right. Those who were selected that day were enlisted in the *Sonder-Kommando,* the unit which worked in the crematories. Bela Katz—son of a big trades-man from our town—had arrived at Birkenau with the first transport, a week before us. When he heard of our arrival, he managed to get word to us that, having been chosen for his strength, he had himself put his father's body into the crematory oven.)

Blows continued to rain down.

"To the barber!"

Belt and shoes in hand, I let myself be dragged off to the barbers. They took our hair off with clippers, and shaved off all the hair on our bodies. The same thought buzzed all the time in my head—not to be separated from my father.

Freed from the hands of the barbers, we began to wander in the crowd, meeting friends and acquaintances. These meetings filled us with joy—yes, joy—"Thank God! You're still alive!"

But others were crying. They used all their remaining strength in weeping. Why had they let themselves be brought here? Why couldn't they have died in their beds? Sobs choked their voices.

Suddenly, someone threw his arms round my neck in an embrace: Yechiel, brother of the rabbi of Sighet. He was sobbing bitterly. I thought he was weeping with joy at still being alive.

"Don't cry, Yechiel," I said. "Don't waste your tears. . . ."

"Not cry? We're on the threshold of death. . . . Soon we shall have crossed over. . . . Don't you understand? How could I not cry?"

Through the blue-tinged skylights I could see the darkness gradually fading. I had ceased to feel fear. And then I was overcome by an inhuman weariness.

Those absent no longer touched even the surface of our memories. We still spoke of them—"Who knows what may have become of them?"—but we had little concern for their fate. We were incapable of thinking of anything at all. Our senses were blunted; everything was blurred as in a fog. It was no longer possible to grasp anything. The instincts of self-preservation, of self-defense, of pride, had all deserted us. In one ultimate moment of lucidity it seemed to me that we were damned souls wandering in the half-world, souls condemned to wander through space till the generations of man came to an end, seeking their redemption, seeking oblivion—without hope of finding it.

Toward five o'clock in the morning, we were driven out of the barracks. The Kapos beat us once more, but I had ceased to feel any pain from their blows. An icy wind envel-oped us. We were naked, our shoes and belts in our hands. The command: "Run!" And we ran. After a few minutes of racing, a new barracks.

A barrel of petrol at the entrance. Disinfection. Everyone was soaked in it. Then a hot shower. At high speed. As we came out from the water, we were driven outside. More run-ning. Another barracks, the store. Very long tables. Mountains of prison clothes. On we ran. As we passed, trousers, tunic, shirt, and socks were thrown to us.

Within a few seconds, we had ceased to be men. If the situation had not been tragic, we should have roared with laughter. Such outfits! Meir Katz, a giant, had a child's trousers,

and Stern, a thin little chap, a tunic which completely swamped him. We immediately began the necessary exchanges.

I glanced at my father. How he had changed! His eyes had grown dim. I would have liked to speak to him, but I did not know what to say.

The night was gone. The morning star was shining in the sky. I too had become a completely different person. The student of the Talmud, the child that I was, had been con-sumed in the flames. There remained only a shape that looked like me. A dark flame had entered into my soul and devoured it.

So much had happened within such a few hours that I had lost all sense of time. When had we left our houses? And the ghetto? And the train? Was it only a week? One night—*one single night?*

How long had we been standing like this in the icy wind? An hour? Simply an hour? Sixty minutes?

Surely it was a dream.

Not far from us there were some prisoners at work. Some were digging holes, others carrying sand. None of them so much as glanced at us. We were so many dried-up trees in the heart of a desert. Behind me, some people were talking. I had not the slightest desire to listen to what they were saying, to know who was talking or what they were talking about. No one dared to raise his voice, though there was no supervisor near us. People whispered. Perhaps it was because of the thick smoke which poisoned the air and took one by the throat. . . .

We were made to go into a new barracks, in the "gypsies' camp." In ranks of five.

"And now stay where you are!"

There was no floor. A roof and four walls. Our feet sank into the mud.

Another spell of waiting began. I went to sleep standing up. I dreamed of a bed, of my mother's caress. And I woke up: I was standing, my feet in the mud. Some people collapsed and lay where they were. Others cried:

"Are you mad? We've been told to stay standing. Do you want to bring trouble on us all?"

As if all the trouble in the world had not descended already upon our heads! Gradually, we all sat down in the mud. But we had to jump up constantly, every time a Kapo came in to see if anybody had a pair of new shoes. If so, they had to be given up to him. It was no use opposing this: blows rained down and in the final reckoning you had lost your shoes anyway.

I had new shoes myself. But as they were coated with a thick layer of mud, no one had noticed them. I thanked God, in an improvised prayer, for having created mud in His infinite and wonderful universe.

Suddenly the silence grew oppressive. An SS officer had come in and, with him, the odor of the Angel of Death. We stared fixedly at his fleshy lips. From the middle of the barracks, he harangued us:

"You're in a concentration camp. At Auschwitz. . . ."

A pause. He observed the effect his words had produced. His face has stayed in my memory to this day. A tall man, about thirty, with crime inscribed upon his brow and in the pupils of his eyes. He looked us over as if we were a pack of leprous dogs hanging onto our lives.

"Remember this," he went on. "Remember it forever. Engrave it into your minds. You are at Auschwitz. And Auschwitz is not a convalescent home. It's a concentration camp. Here, you have got to work. If not, you will go straight to the furnace. To the crematory. Work or the crematory—the choice is in your hands."

We had already lived through so much that night, we thought nothing could frighten us any more. But his clipped words made us tremble. Here the word "furnace" was not a word empty of meaning: it floated on the air, mingling with the smoke. It was perhaps the only word which did have any real meaning here. He left the barracks. Kapos appeared, crying:

"All skilled workers—locksmiths, electricians, watch-makers—one step forward!"

The rest of us were made to go to another barracks, a stone one this time. With permission to sit down. A gypsy deportee was in charge of us.

My father was suddenly seized with colic. He got up and went toward the gypsy, asking politely, in German:

"Excuse me, can you tell me where the lavatories are?"

The gypsy looked him up and down slowly, from head to foot. As if he wanted to convince himself that this man addressing him was really a creature of flesh and bone, a living being with a body and a belly. Then, as if he had suddenly woken up from a heavy doze, he dealt my father such a clout that he fell to the ground, crawling back to his place on all fours.

I did not move. What had happened to me? My father had just been struck, before my very eyes, and I had not flickered an eyelid. I had looked on and said nothing. Yesterday, I should have sunk my nails into the criminal's flesh. Had I changed so much, then? So quickly? Now

remorse began to gnaw at me. I thought only: I shall never forgive them for that. My father must have guessed my feelings. He whispered in my ear, "It doesn't hurt." His cheek still bore the red mark of the man's hand.

"Everyone outside!"

Ten gypsies had come and joined our supervisor. Whips and truncheons cracked round me. My feet were running without my being aware of it. I tried to hide from the blows behind the others. The spring sunshine.

"Form fives!"

The prisoners whom I had noticed in the morning were working at the side. There was no guard near them, only the shadow of the chimney. . . . Dazed by the sunshine and by my reverie, I felt someone tugging at my sleeve. It was my father. "Come on, my boy."

We marched on. Doors opened and closed again. On we went between the electric wires. At each step, a white placard with a death's head on it stared us in the face. A caption: "Warning. Danger of death." Mockery: was there a single place here where you were not in danger of death?

The gypsies stopped near another barracks. They were replaced by SS, who surrounded us. Revolvers, machine guns, police dogs.

The march had lasted half an hour. Looking around me, I noticed that the barbed wires were behind us. We had left the camp.

It was a beautiful April day. The fragrance of spring was in the air. The sun was setting in the west.

But we had been marching for only a few moments when we saw the barbed wire of another camp. An iron door with this inscription over it:

*"Work is liberty!"*

Auschwitz.

•  •  •

# MARTIN LUTHER KING, JR.

## *I Have a Dream*

From 1862 when Lincoln issued the Emancipation Proclamation ending slavery to the 1963 March on Washington, D.C., where Martin Luther King, Jr. (1929-1968) delivered his "I Have a Dream" speech, African-Americans suffered legal and informal segregation from mainstream society; they were exploited economically by capitalist forces and were denied nearly all of the basic civil rights guaranteed by law and tradition to other groups in the United States. Emerging after World War II as the leader of the so-called Free World, the United States entered into an economic boom, lasting until about 1970, which provided many opportunities for its citizens; African-Americans, however, until the early 1960s, remained marginalized, unable to take advantage of the expanding economy and shut out of the political process. However, starting around 1955, black Americans, led by homegrown black leaders and joined by many white

Americans, began a series of marches, legal challenges, and political maneuverings; these were aimed at eliminating racial discrimination and integrating blacks into America's political, social, and economic mainstream. Thus, the civil rights movement was born.

In the mid-1950s, the Protestant pastor Martin Luther King, Jr. stepped forward to become the civil rights movement's most forceful and eloquent voice. The son of a prominent Atlanta preacher, King attended college, seminary, and graduate school before taking a church in Montgomery, Alabama; here, in 1956, he led a successful boycott against the local bus company's segregated seating policy. Within three years King was a national figure, and during the Kennedy-Johnson era, he became the most powerful black leader in the nation, indeed in its history. From 1967 onward, he headed a coalition linking the cause of poverty, the Vietnam War, and the civil rights movement; while trying to unite his followers on these three issues, he was assassinated in Memphis, Tennessee.

## Reading the Selection

King's leadership was rooted in the Judeo-Christian tradition of personal salvation and the social gospel. Understanding also that southern blacks derived strength from church membership, he built a national movement, the Southern Christian Leadership Conference, centered around America's black churches. Gifted with wise political instincts, he inspired those around him to hold to the policy of passive resistance as an agent of change, rather than resorting to violence. King's tactic proved most effective, for it won the sympathy of most Americans, white and black, as well as of peoples across the world. The idea of "passive resistance" was based on the example of two figures he admired—Thoreau, who defied his state government over what he deemed an immoral law; and Gandhi, the Indian leader, who used nonviolent civil disobedience in his drive for his country's independence from Britain.

At the March on Washington in August, 1963, 250,000 people crowded before the Lincoln Memorial to hear King and others speak. Using his superb command of English, his biblical knowledge, which infused the structure of his speech with repetition and parallelism, and his ability to voice the unconscious feelings of his race, King gave what is now recognized as the speech of his life. The civil rights movement reached new heights that day from which it went on to more triumphs, but, after his assassination in 1968, the movement never recovered its direction.

---

I am happy to join with you today in what will go down in history as the greatest demonstration for freedom in the history of our nation.

Five score years ago, a great American, in whose symbolic shadow we stand today, signed the Emancipation Proclamation. This momentous decree came as a great beacon light of hope to millions of Negro slaves, who had been seared in the flames of withering injustice. It came as a joyous daybreak to end the long night of their captivity.

But one hundred years later, the Negro still is not free. One hundred years later, the life of the Negro is still sadly crippled by the manacles of segregation and the chains of discrimination. One hundred years later, the Negro lives on a lonely island of poverty in the midst of a vast ocean of material prosperity. One hundred years later, the Negro is still languished in the corners of American society and finds himself an exile in his own land. And so we've come here today to dramatize a shameful condition.

In a sense we've come to our nation's Capitol to cash a check. When the architects of our republic wrote the magnificent words of the Constitution and the Declaration of Independence, they were signing a promissory note to which every American was to fall heir. This note was a promise that all men—yes, black men as well as white men—would be guaranteed the unalienable rights of life, liberty, and the pursuit of happiness.

It is obvious today that America has defaulted on this promissory note insofar as her citizens of color are concerned. Instead of honoring this sacred obligation, America has given the Negro people a bad check—a check which has come back marked "insufficient funds."

But we refuse to believe that the bank of justice is bankrupt. We refuse to believe that there are insufficient funds in the great vaults of opportunity of this nation. And so we've come to cash this check—a check that will give us upon demand the riches of freedom and the security of justice.

We have also come to this hallowed spot to remind America of the fierce urgency of now. This is no time to engage in the luxury of cooling off or to take the tranquillizing drug of gradualism. Now is the time to make real the promises of democracy. Now is the time to rise from the dark and desolate valley of segregation to the sunlit path of racial justice. Now is the time to lift our nation from the quicksands of racial injustice to the solid rock of brotherhood. Now is the time to make justice a reality for all of God's children.

It would be fatal for the nation to overlook the urgency of the moment. This sweltering summer of the Negro's legitimate discontent will not pass until there is an invigorating autumn of freedom and equality. Nineteen sixty-three is not an end, but a beginning. Those who hope that the Negro needed to blow off steam and will now be content will have a rude awakening if the nation returns to business as usual. There will be neither rest nor tranquillity in America until the Negro is granted his citizenship rights. The whirlwinds of revolt will continue to shake the foundations of our nation until the bright day of justice emerges.

But there is something that I must say to my people, who stand on the warm threshold which leads into the palace of justice. In the process of gaining our rightful place, we must not be guilty of wrongful deeds. Let us not seek to satisfy our thirst for freedom by drinking from the cup of bitterness and hatred.

We must forever conduct our struggle on the high plane of dignity and discipline. We must not allow our creative protest to degenerate into physical violence. Again and again we must rise to the majestic heights of meeting physical force with soul force.

The marvelous new militancy which has engulfed the Negro community must not lead us to a distrust of all white people. For many of our white brothers, as evidenced by their presence here today, have come to realize that their destiny is tied up with our destiny. They have come to realize that their freedom is inextricably bound to our freedom. We cannot walk alone.

As we walk, we must make the pledge that we shall always march ahead. We cannot turn back. There are those who are asking the devotees of civil rights, "When will you be satisfied?" We can never be satisfied as long as the Negro is the victim of the unspeakable horrors of police brutality. We can never be satisfied as long as our bodies, heavy with the fatigue of travel, cannot gain lodging in the motels of the highways and the hotels of the cities. We cannot be satisfied as long as a Negro in Mississippi cannot vote and a Negro in New York believes he has nothing for which to vote. No, no, we are not satisfied, and we will not be satisfied until justice rolls down like waters, and righteousness like a mighty stream.

I am not unmindful that some of you have come here out of great trials and tribulations. Some of you have come fresh from narrow jail cells. Some of you have come from areas where your quest for freedom left you battered by the storms of persecution and staggered by the winds of police brutality. You have been the veterans of creative suffering. Continue to work with the faith that unearned suffering is redemptive.

Go back to Mississippi, go back to Alabama, go back to South Carolina, go back to Georgia, go back to Louisiana, go back to the slums and ghettos of our Northern cities, knowing that somehow this situation can and will be changed. Let us not wallow in the valley of despair.

I say to you today, my friends, so even though we face the difficulties of today and tomorrow, I still have a dream. It is a dream deeply rooted in the American dream.

I have a dream that one day this nation will rise up and live out the true meaning of its creed, "We hold these truths to be self-evident, that all men are created equal."

I have a dream that one day on the red hills of Georgia the sons of former slaves and the sons of former slaveowners will be able to sit down together at the table of brotherhood.

I have a dream that one day even the state of Mississippi, a state sweltering with the heat of injustice, sweltering with the heat of oppression, will be transformed into an oasis of freedom and justice.

I have a dream that my four little children will one day live in a nation where they will not be judged by the color of their skin but by the content of their character. I have a dream today.

I have a dream that one day, down in Alabama, with its vicious racists, with its governor having his lips dripping with the words of interposition and nullification, one day right there in Alabama little black boys and black girls will be able to join hands with little white boys and white girls as sisters and brothers. I have a dream today.

I have a dream that one day every valley shall be exalted, every hill and mountain shall be made low, the rough places will be made plane and the crooked places will be made straight, and the glory of the Lord shall be revealed, and all flesh shall see it together.

This is our hope. This is the faith that I go back to the South with. With this faith we will be able to hew out of the mountain of despair a stone of hope. With this faith we will be able to transform the jangling discords of our nation into a beautiful symphony of brotherhood. With this faith we will be able to work together, to pray together, to struggle together, to go to jail together, to stand up for freedom together, knowing that we will be free one day.

This will be the day—this will be the day when all of God's children will be able to sing with new meaning, "My country 'tis of thee, sweet land of liberty, of thee I sing. Land where my fathers died, land of the piligrim's pride, from every mountainside, let freedom ring." And if America is to be a great nation, this must become true.

So let freedom ring from the prodigious hilltops of New Hampshire. Let freedom ring from the mighty mountains of New York. Let freedom ring from the heightening Alleghenies of Pennsylvania!

Let freedom ring from the snowcapped Rockies of Colorado! Let freedom ring from the curvaceous slopes of California!

But not only that. Let freedom ring from Stone Mountain of Georgia!

Let freedom ring from Lookout Mountain of Tennessee!

Let freedom ring from every hill and molehill of Mississippi. From every mountainside, let freedom ring.

And when this happens, when we allow freedom ring—when we let it ring from every village and every hamlet, from every state and every city—we will be able to speed up that day when all of God's children, black men and white men, Jews and Gentiles, Protestants and Catholics, will be able to join hands and sing in the words of the old Negro spiritual, "Free at last! Free at last! Thank God almighty, we are free at last!"

# JAMES BALDWIN

## from *The Fire Next Time*

### My Dungeon Shook: A Letter to My Nephew on the One Hundredth Anniversary of the Emancipation

---

The writer James Baldwin (1926–1987) aspired to be the voice of his generation of African-Americans, the ones who came of age, in 1954, when the U.S. Supreme Court made segregation unconstitutional. To this end, he produced a body of works, including five novels (*Another Country,* 1962), two plays (*Blues for Mr. Charlie,* 1964), and five books of essays (*Nobody Knows My Name,* 1961); these made him a major figure in world letters and brought him prizes, honorary degrees, and France's Legion of Honor—a rare honor for a non-Frenchman. But his dream of becoming a leading advocate of his race eluded him, because religious groups within the black community were offended by his homosexuality, which he did not bother to conceal (his 1956 novel, *Giovanni's Room,* is a pioneering study of gay life). Baldwin's reception in black America can be illustrated by two contrasting events in 1963: On May 24, he was among the black leaders who met with Robert Kennedy, the federal attorney general, to discuss racial matters; in August, he was excluded from the roster of black speakers who addressed the March on Washington, D.C. Thus, Baldwin throughout his career was forced to labor under the double burden of being black *and* homosexual.

Born in Harlem, the illegitimate son of a cleaning woman, James Baldwin knew what it was like to be black and poor. Times were not easy, living with his stepfather, David Baldwin, a laborer and storefront preacher; movies and secular music were strictly forbidden, and education was suspect as a delusion devised by whites to confuse black men. After high school, James Baldwin's life turned more sour as he encountered racism in menial jobs, sparking a "rage in the blood," a fever that, he thought, finally infected all black people. At the same time, he was struggling with his sexual identity. He began to think of himself as a writer, publishing a few reviews and essays; but feeling alienated from America, he exiled himself to Paris (1948–1958), the traditional haven for American expatriates, black and white, straight and gay. In Paris, Baldwin flourished, learning to accept his homosexuality and launching his writing career with the novel, *Go Tell It on the Mountain* (1953), and the essay collection, *Notes of a Native Son* (1955); these books united autobiographical material with social issues.

## Reading the Selection

Baldwin wrote "My Dungeon Shook" to flesh out *The Fire Next Time* (1963), a volume named for its single long essay. The volume created a sensation when published in hardcover (the long essay had earlier received national attention when it was printed in *The New Yorker,* November 17, 1962). In hardcover, it was at the top of the bestseller lists for more than a year. Paperback rights earned $65,000 for Baldwin, then an amazing sum. Baldwin was now a media star, and his face graced the cover of *Time* magazine.

The purpose of "My Dungeon Shook" is explained by its subtitle: "A Letter to My Nephew on the One Hundredth Anniversary of the Emancipation"—a reference to Lincoln's 1862 Proclamation which ended slavery in America. The letter's language is vintage Baldwin, angry and pained by racism, steeped in revolutionary rhetoric, and yet hopeful, as he envisions an integrated society in America's future; he invokes Homer and Dickens, thereby aligning himself with the West's traditional culture rather than calling for a separatist African-American tradition.

Now, my dear namesake, these innocent and well-meaning people, your countrymen, have caused you to be born under conditions not very far removed from those described for us by Charles Dickens in the London of more than a hundred years ago. (I hear the chorus of the innocents screaming, "No! This is not true! How *bitter* you are!"—but I am writing this letter to *you*, to try to tell you something about how to handle *them*, for most of them do not yet really know that you exist. I *know* the conditions under which you were born, for I was there. Your countrymen were *not* there, and haven't made it yet. Your grandmother was also there, and no one has ever accused her of being bitter. I suggest that the innocents check with her. She isn't hard to find. Your countrymen don't know that *she* exists, either, though she has been working for them all their lives.)

Well, you were born, here you came, something like fifteen years ago; and though your father and mother and grandmother, looking about the streets through which they were carrying you, staring at the walls into which they brought you, had every reason to be heavyhearted, yet they were not. For here you were, Big James, named for me— you were a big baby, I was not—here you were: to be loved. To be loved, baby, hard, at once, and forever, to strengthen you against the loveless world. Remember that: I know how black it looks today, for you. It looked bad that day, too, yes, we were trembling. We have not stopped trembling yet, but if we had not loved each other none of us would have survived. And now you must survive because we love you, and for the sake of your children and your children's children.

This innocent country set you down in a ghetto in which, in fact, it intended that you should perish. Let me spell out precisely what I mean by that, for the heart of the matter is here, and the root of my dispute with my country. You were born where you were born and faced the future that you faced because you were black and *for no other reason*. The limits of your ambition were, thus, expected to be set forever. You were born into a society which spelled out with brutal clarity, and in as many ways as possible, that you were a worthless human being. You were not expected to aspire to excellence: you were expected to make peace with mediocrity. Wherever you have turned, James, in your short time on this earth, you have been told where you could go and what you could do (and *how* you could do it) and where you could live and whom you could marry. I know your countrymen do not agree with me about this, and I hear them saying, "You exaggerate." They do not know Harlem, and I do. So do you. Take no one's word for anything, including mine—but trust your experience. Know whence you came. If you know whence you came, there is really no limit to where you can go. The details and symbols of your life have been deliberately constructed to make you believe what white people say about you. Please try to remember that what they believe, as well as what they do and cause you to endure, does not testify to your inferiority but to their inhumanity and fear. Please try to be clear, dear James, through the storm which rages about your youthful head today, about the reality which lies behind the words *acceptance* and *integration*. There is no reason for you to try to become like white people and there is no basis whatever for their impertinent assumption that *they* must accept *you*. The really terrible thing, old buddy, is that *you* must accept *them*. And I mean that very seriously. You must accept them and accept them with love. For these innocent people have no other hope. They are, in effect, still trapped in a history which they do not understand; and until they understand it, they cannot be released from it. They have had to believe for many years, and for innumerable reasons, that black men are inferior to white men. Many of them, indeed, know better, but, as you will discover, people find it very difficult to act on what they know. To act is to be committed, and to be committed is to be in danger. In this case, the danger, in the minds of most white Americans, is the loss of their identity. Try to imagine how you would feel if you woke up one morning to find the sun shining and all the stars aflame. You would be frightened because it is out of the order of nature. Any upheaval in the universe is terrifying because it so profoundly attacks one's sense of one's own reality. Well, the black man has functioned in the white man's world as a fixed star, as an immovable pillar: and as he moves out of his place, heaven and earth are shaken to their foundations. You, don't be afraid. I said that it was intended that you should perish in the ghetto, perish by never being allowed to go behind the white man's definitions, by never being allowed to spell your proper name. You have, and many of us have, defeated this intention; and by a terrible law, a terrible paradox, those innocents who believed that your imprisonment made them safe are losing their grasp of reality. But these men are your brothers—your lost, younger brothers. And if the word *integration* means anything, this is what it means: that we, with love, shall force our brothers to see themselves as they are, to cease fleeing from reality and begin to change it. For this is your home, my friend, do not be driven from it; great men have done great things here, and will again, and we can make America what America must become. It will be hard, James, but you come from sturdy, peasant stock, men who picked cotton and dammed rivers and built railroads, and, in the teeth of the most terrifying odds, achieved an unassailable and monumental dignity. You come from a long line of great poets, some of the greatest poets since Homer. One of them said, *The very time I thought I was lost, My dungeon shook and my chains fell off.*

You know, and I know, that the country is celebrating one hundred years of freedom one hundred years too soon. We cannot be free until they are free. God bless you, James, and Godspeed.

*Your uncle,*
*James*

MALCOLM X AND ALEX HALEY

## from *The Autobiography of Malcolm X*

Chapter 11: Saved

———

In the 1950s, most African-American leaders, rallying around King, adopted the political agenda of racial integration into the American mainstream; however, there also began to emerge more militant leaders who saw the future of their race as separate from white culture and society. Believing whites to be basically against full integration, these latter leaders argued that blacks should strive to become independent from white control; to this end, they advocated the use of violence, if conditions called for it. The militant agenda of these leaders appealed to the minority of blacks on the margin of black society, particularly those who had run afoul of the white justice system or those who believed, for whatever reason, that black separatism was necessary.

Malcolm X (born Malcolm Little, 1925–1965) was the most charismatic of these militant black leaders of the 1950s; his ideas are enjoying a renaissance today among a large group of African-Americans, his life having become the subject of a major film. Malcolm X came from a poor midwestern family who suffered at the hands of white racists, their home being burned and the father brutally murdered. His mentally unstable mother, unable to care for eight children, allowed them to be assigned to relatives' homes and state institutions. The teenage Malcolm wound up first in Boston and then New York, where he became a hustler and petty thief. Prison became his school. There, he learned about the Black Muslims, an American version of the Islamic religion, which gave him a new purpose in life. His name change, from Little to X, reflected the new direction he intended to take. Released from prison in the 1950s, he became a leader of the Black Muslims, calling on African-Americans, in striking and bold language, to separate themselves completely from white society. His militancy alarmed most whites and upset many black leaders at the time. However, his pleas for self-respect attracted young blacks in the 1960s. After a trip to Mecca, Malcolm X worked for closer co-operation with whites, but before he could launch his new program he was assassinated in 1965.

### Reading the Selection

The record of Malcolm X's struggle for both his own identity and that of his fellow African-Americans was made possible by the patience and writing skills of Alex Haley (1921–1992); Haley was a black writer who later achieved fame with his book *Roots*, which was a search for Haley's African and slave forebears. During the writing of the book, Haley interviewed Malcolm X at length and accompanied him on speaking engagements where he could observe his personality, his oratorical skills, and the reactions of admirers and detractors.

This selection, from Chapter 11, entitled "Saved," of *The Autobiography of Malcolm X*, recounts Malcolm X's prison days, as he began to educate himself, learning to read and studying books in the prison library. Earlier chapters had detailed his criminal past, and later chapters laid out his triumphs as a black leader; this chapter, then, represents the turning point of his life. In prison, he studied the teachings of Elijah Muhammad, the founder of the Black Muslims; from him he learned that white writers leave "the black man" out of history books, a fact which reinforced his growing conviction that whites could not be trusted and that blacks must recover their own history as a first step to gaining self-respect.

• • •

I became increasingly frustrated at not being able to express what I wanted to convey in letters that I wrote, especially those to Mr. Elijah Muhammad. In the street, I had been the most articulate hustler out there—I had commanded attention when I said something. But now, trying to write simple English, I not only wasn't articulate, I wasn't even functional. How would I sound writing in slang, the way I would *say* it, something such as "Look, daddy, let me pull your coat about a cat, Elijah Muhammad—"

Many who today hear me somewhere in person, or on television, or those who read something I've said, will think I went to school far beyond the eighth grade. This impression is due entirely to my prison studies.

It had really begun back in the Charlestown Prison, when Bimbi first made me feel envy of his stock of knowledge. Bimbi had always taken charge of any conversation he was in, and I had tried to emulate him. But every book I picked up had few sentences which didn't contain anywhere from one to nearly all of the words that might as well have been in Chinese. When I just skipped those words, of course, I really ended up with little idea of what the book said. So I had come to the Norfolk Prison Colony still going through only book-reading motions. Pretty soon, I would have quit even these motions, unless I had received the motivation that I did.

I saw that the best thing I could do was get hold of a dictionary—to study, to learn some words. I was lucky enough to reason also that I should try to improve my penmanship. It was sad. I couldn't even write in a straight line. It was both ideas together that moved me to request a dictionary along with some tablets and pencils from the Norfolk Prison Colony school.

I spent two days just riffling uncertainly through the dictionary's pages. I'd never realized so many words existed! I didn't know *which* words I needed to learn. Finally, just to start some kind of action, I began copying.

In my slow, painstaking, ragged handwriting, I copied into my tablet everything printed on that first page, down to the punctuation marks.

I believe it took me a day. Then, aloud, I read back, to myself, everything I'd written on the tablet. Over and over, aloud, to myself, I read my own handwriting.

I woke up the next morning, thinking about those words—immensely proud to realize that not only had I written so much at one time, but I'd written words that I never knew were in the world. Moreover, with a little effort, I also could remember what many of these words meant. I reviewed the words whose meanings I didn't remember. Funny thing, from the dictionary first page right now, that "aardvark" springs to my mind. The dictionary had a picture of it, a long-tailed, long-eared, burrowing African mammal, which lives off termites caught by sticking out its tongue as an anteater does for ants.

I was so fascinated that I went on—I copied the dictionary's next page. And the same experience came when I studied that. With every succeeding page, I also learned of people and places and events from history. Actually the dictionary is like a miniature encyclopedia. Finally the dictionary's A section had filled a whole tablet—and I went on into the B's. That was the way I started copying what eventually became the entire dictionary. It went a lot faster after so much practice helped me to pick up handwriting speed. Between what I wrote in my tablet, and writing letters, during the rest of my time in prison I would guess I wrote a million words.

I suppose it was inevitable that as my word-base broadened, I could for the first time pick up a book and read and now begin to understand what the book was saying. Anyone who has read a great deal can imagine the new world that opened. Let me tell you something: from then until I left that prison, in every free moment I had, if I was not reading in the library, I was reading on my bunk. You couldn't have gotten me out of books with a wedge. Between Mr. Muhammad's teachings, my correspondence, my visitors—usually Ella and Reginald—and my reading of books, months passed without my even thinking about being imprisoned. In fact, up to then, I never had been so truly free in my life.

The Norfolk Prison Colony's library was in the school building. A variety of classes was taught there by instructors who came from such places as Harvard and Boston universities. The weekly debates between inmate teams were also held in the school building. You would be astonished to know how worked up convict debaters and audiences would get over subjects like "Should Babies Be Fed Milk?"

Available on the prison library's shelves were books on just about every general subject. Much of the big private collection that Parkhurst had willed to the prison was still in crates and boxes in the back of the library—thousands of old books. Some of them looked ancient: covers faded, old-time parchment-looking binding. Parkhurst, I've mentioned, seemed to have been principally interested in history and religion. He had the money and the special interest to have a lot of books that you wouldn't have in general circulation. Any college library would have been lucky to get that collection.

As you can imagine, especially in a prison where there was heavy emphasis on rehabilitation, an inmate was smiled upon if he demonstrated an unusually intense interest in books. There was a sizable number of well-read inmates, especially the popular debaters. Some were said by many to be practically walking encyclopedias. They were almost celebrities. No university would ask any student to devour literature as I did when this new world opened to me, of being able to read and *understand*.

I read more in my room than in the library itself. An inmate who was known to read a lot could check out more than the permitted maximum number of books. I preferred reading in the total isolation of my own room.

When I had progressed to really serious reading, every night at about ten P.M. I would be outraged with the "lights out." It always seemed to catch me right in the middle of something engrossing.

Fortunately, right outside my door was a corridor light that cast a glow into my room. The glow was enough to read by, once my eyes adjusted to it. So when "lights out" came, I would sit on the floor where I could continue reading in that glow.

At one-hour intervals the night guards paced past every room. Each time I heard the approaching footsteps, I jumped into bed and feigned sleep. And as soon as the guard passed, I got back out of bed onto the floor area of that light-glow, where I would read for another fifty-eight minutes—until the guard approached again. That went on until three or four every morning. Three or four hours of sleep a night was enough for me. Often in the years in the streets I had slept less than that.

The teachings of Mr. Muhammad stressed how history had been "whitened"—when white men had written history books, the black man simply had been left out. Mr. Muhammad couldn't have said anything that would have struck me much harder. I had never forgotten how when my class, me and all of those whites, had studied seventh-grade United States history back in Mason, the history of the Negro had been covered in one paragraph, and the teacher had gotten a big laugh with his joke, "Negroes' feet are so big that when they walk, they leave a hole in the ground."

This is one reason why Mr. Muhammad's teachings spread so swiftly all over the United States, among *all* Negroes, whether or not they became followers of Mr. Muhammad. The teachings ring true—to every Negro. You can hardly show me a black adult in America—or a white one, for that matter—who knows from the history books anything like the truth about the black man's role. In my own case, once I heard of the "glorious history of the black man," I took special pains to hunt in the library for books that would inform me on details about black history.

I can remember accurately the very first set of books that really impressed me. I have since bought that set of books and have it at home for my children to read as they grow up. It's called *Wonders of the World*. It's full of pictures of archeological finds, statues that depict, usually, non-European people.

I found books like Will Durant's *Story of Civilization*. I read H. G. Wells' *Outline of History*. *Souls Of Black Folk* by W. E. B. Du Bois gave me a glimpse into the black people's history before they came to this country. Carter G. Woodson's *Negro History* opened my eyes about black empires before the black slave was brought to the United States, and the early Negro struggles for freedom.

J. A. Rogers' three volumes of *Sex and Race* told about race-mixing before Christ's time; about Aesop being a black man who told fables; about Egypt's Pharaohs; about the great Coptic Christian Empires; about Ethiopia, the earth's oldest continuous black civilization, as China is the oldest continuous civilization.

Mr. Muhammad's teachings about how the white man had been created led me to *Findings In Genetics* by Gregor Mendel. (The dictionary's G section was where I had learned what "genetics" meant.) I really studied this book by the Austrian monk. Reading it over and over, especially certain sections, helped me to understand that if you started with a black man, a white man could be produced; but starting with a white man, you never could produce a black man—because the white gene is recessive. And since no one disputes that there was but one Original Man, the conclusion is clear.

During the last year or so, in the *New York Times*, Arnold Toynbee used the word "bleached" in describing the white man. (His words were: "White (i.e. bleached) human beings of North European origin. . . .") Toynbee also referred to the European geographic area as only a peninsula of Asia. He said there is no such thing as Europe. And if you look at the globe, you will see for yourself that America is only an extension of Asia. (But at the same time Toynbee is among those who have helped to bleach history. He has written that Africa was the only continent that produced no history. He won't write that again. Every day now, the truth is coming to light.)

I never will forget how shocked I was when I began reading about slavery's total horror. It made such an impact upon me that it later became one of my favorite subjects when I became a minister of Mr. Muhammad's. The world's most monstrous crime, the sin and the blood on the white man's hands, are almost impossible to believe. Books like the one by Frederick Olmstead opened my eyes to the horrors suffered when the slave was landed in the United States. The European woman, Fannie Kimball, who had married a Southern white slaveowner, described how human beings were degraded. Of course I read *Uncle Tom's Cabin*. In fact, I believe that's the only novel I have ever read since I started serious reading.

Parkhurst's collection also contained some bound pamphlets of the Abolitionist Anti-Slavery Society of New England. I read descriptions of atrocities, saw those illustrations of black slave women tied up and flogged with whips; of black mothers watching their babies being dragged off, never to be seen by their mothers again; of dogs after slaves, and of the fugitive slave catchers, evil white men with whips and clubs and chains and guns. I read about the slave preacher Nat Turner, who put the fear of God into the white slavemaster. Nat Turner wasn't going around preaching pie-in-the-sky and "non-violent" freedom for the black man. There in Virginia one night in 1831, Nat and seven other slaves started out at his master's home and through the night they went from one plantation "big house" to the next, killing, until by the next morning 57 white people were dead and Nat had about 70 slaves following him. White people, terrified for their lives, fled from their homes, locked themselves up in public buildings, hid in the woods, and some even left the state. A small army of soldiers took two months to catch and hang Nat Turner. Somewhere I have read where Nat Turner's example is said to have inspired John Brown to invade Virginia and attack Harper's Ferry nearly thirty years later, with thirteen white men and five Negroes.

I read Herodotus, "the father of History," or, rather, I read about him. And I read the histories of various nations, which opened my eyes gradually, then wider and wider, to how the whole world's white men had indeed acted like devils, pillaging and raping and bleeding and draining the whole world's non-white people. I remember, for instance, books such as Will Durant's story of Oriental civilization, and Mahatma Gandhi's accounts of the struggle to drive the British out of India.

Book after book showed me how the white man had brought upon the world's black, brown, red, and yellow peoples every variety of the sufferings of exploitation. I saw how since the sixteenth century, the so-called "Christian trader" white man began to ply the seas in his lust for Asian and African empires, and plunder, and power. I read, I saw, how the white man never has gone among the non-white peoples bearing the Cross in the true manner and spirit of Christ's teachings—meek, humble, and Christ-like.

I perceived, as I read, how the collective white man had been actually nothing but a piratical opportunist who used Faustian machinations to make his own Christianity his initial wedge in criminal conquests. First, always "religiously," he branded "heathen" and "pagan" labels upon ancient non-white cultures and civilizations. The stage thus set, he then turned upon his non-white victims his weapons of war.

I read how, entering India—half a *billion* deeply religious brown people—the British white man, by 1759, through promises, trickery and manipulations, controlled much of

India through Great Britain's East India Company. The parasitical British administration kept tentacling out to half of the subcontinent. In 1857, some of the desperate people of India finally mutinied—and, excepting the African slave trade, nowhere has history recorded any more unnecessary bestial and ruthless human carnage than the British suppression of the non-white Indian people.

Over 115 million African blacks—close to the 1930's population of the United States—were murdered or enslaved during the slave trade. And I read how when the slave market was glutted, the cannibalistic white powers of Europe next carved up, as their colonies, the richest areas of the black continent. And Europe's chancelleries for the next century played a chess game of naked exploitation and power from Cape Horn to Cairo.

Ten guards and the warden couldn't have torn me out of those books. Not even Elijah Muhammad could have been more eloquent than those books were in providing indisputable proof that the collective white man had acted like a devil in virtually every contact he had with the world's collective non-white man. I listen today to the radio, and watch television, and read the headlines about the collective white man's fear and tension concerning China. When the white man professes ignorance about why the Chinese hate him so, my mind can't help flashing back to what I read, there in prison, about how the blood forebears of this same white man raped China at a time when China was trusting and helpless. Those original white "Christian traders" sent into China millions of pounds of opium. By 1839, so many of the Chinese were addicts that China's desperate government destroyed twenty thousand chests of opium. The first Opium War was promptly declared by the white man. Imagine! Declaring *war* upon someone who objects to being narcotized! The Chinese were severely beaten, with Chinese-invented gunpowder.

The Treaty of Nanking made China pay the British white man for the destroyed opium; forced open China's major ports to British trade; forced China to abandon Hong Kong; fixed China's import tariffs so low that cheap British articles soon flooded in, maiming China's industrial development.

After a second Opium War, the Tientsin Treaties legalized the ravaging opium trade, legalized a British-French-American control of China's customs. China tried delaying that Treaty's ratification; Peking was looted and burned.

"Kill the foreign white devils!" was the 1901 Chinese war cry in the Boxer Rebellion. Losing again, this time the Chinese were driven from Peking's choicest areas. The vicious, arrogant white man put up the famous signs, "Chinese and dogs not allowed."

Red China after World War II closed its doors to the Western white world. Massive Chinese agricultural, scientific, and industrial efforts are described in a book that *Life* magazine recently published. Some observers inside Red China have reported that the world never has known such a hate-white campaign as is now going on in this non-white country where, present birth-rates continuing, in fifty more years Chinese will be half the earth's population. And it seems that some Chinese chickens will soon come home to roost, with China's recent successful nuclear tests.

Let us face reality. We can see in the United Nations a new world order being shaped, along color lines—an alliance among the non-white nations. America's U.N. Ambassador Adlai Stevenson complained not long ago that in the United Nations "a skin game" was being played. He was right. He was facing reality. A "skin game" *is* being played. But Ambassador Stevenson sounded like Jesse James accusing the marshal of carrying a gun. Because who in the world's history ever has played a worse "skin game" than the white man?

Mr. Muhammad, to whom I was writing daily, had no idea of what a new world had opened up to me through my efforts to document his teachings in books.

When I discovered philosophy, I tried to touch all the landmarks of philosophical development. Gradually, I read most of the old philosophers, Occidental and Oriental. The Oriental philosophers were the ones I came to prefer; finally, my impression was that most Occidental philosophy had largely been borrowed from the Oriental thinkers. Socrates, for instance, traveled in Egypt. Some sources even say that Socrates was initiated into some of the Egyptian mysteries. Obviously Socrates got some of this wisdom among the East's wise men.

I have often reflected upon the new vistas that reading opened to me. I knew right there in prison that reading had changed forever the course of my life. As I see it today, the ability to read awoke inside me some long dormant craving to be mentally alive. I certainly wasn't seeking any degree, the way a college confers a status symbol upon its students. My homemade education gave me, with every additional book that I read, a little bit more sensitivity to the deafness, dumbness, and blindness that was afflicting the black race in America. Not long ago, an English writer telephoned me from London, asking questions. One was, "What's your alma mater?" I told him, "Books." You will never catch me with a free fifteen minutes in which I'm not studying something I feel might be able to help the black man.

Yesterday I spoke in London, and both ways on the plane across the Atlantic I was studying a document about how the United Nations proposes to insure the human rights of the oppressed minorities of the world. The American black man is the world's most shameful case of minority oppression. What makes the black man think of himself as only an internal United States issue is just a catch-phrase, two words, "civil rights." How is the black man going to get "civil rights" before first he wins his *human* rights? If the American black man will start thinking about his *human* rights, and then start thinking of himself as part of one of the world's great peoples, he will see he has a case for the United Nations.

I can't think of a better case! Four hundred years of black blood and sweat invested here in America, and the white man still has the black man begging for what every immigrant fresh off the ship can take for granted the minute he walks down the gangplank.

But I'm digressing. I told the Englishman that my alma mater was books, a good library. Every time I catch a plane, I have with me a book that I want to read—and that's a lot of books these days. If I weren't out here every day battling the white man, I could spend the rest of my life reading, just satisfying my curiosity—because you can hardly mention anything I'm not curious about. I don't think anybody ever got more out of going to prison than I did. In fact, prison enabled me to study far more intensively than I would have if my life had gone differently and I had attended some college. I imagine that one of the biggest troubles with colleges is there are too many distractions, too much panty-raiding, fraternities,

and boola-boola and all of that. Where else but in a prison could I have attacked my ignorance by being able to study intensely sometimes as much as fifteen hours a day? . . .

---

# GABRIEL GARCÍA MÁRQUEZ
## from *One Hundred Years of Solitude*
### Chapter 1

---

The Colombian author García Márquez's *One Hundred Years of Solitude* is arguably the most important novel to appear since 1945. When published in Buenos Aires in 1967, it provoked a literary earthquake across the Hispanic world. Critics hailed it as a masterpiece and the public quickly agreed, buying up copies so fast that, at one point, new editions were appearing weekly. Its spectacular success made García Márquez into a celebrity on the order of a great soccer player or a pop music star. Similar critical and public acclaim resulted when the novel was translated into other languages around the world, winning literary prizes in many countries and rocketing to the top of bestseller lists, where it stayed for months. In 1982, García Márquez was awarded the Nobel Prize for literature, the first Latin American novelist to be so honored.

García Márquez's book was responsible for putting the Spanish-American novel on the international map. Since 1945, a literary explosion—called "El Boom"—had been under way in Latin America, with the result that the region's writers turned away from the realist tradition that had dominated their literature since about 1870; instead, they adopted Modernist methods, learned from reading Woolf and others. The defining feature of this new type of fiction in Spanish America was its insistence on the right of invention, resulting in what has been called "magic realism," a genre which mixes realistic and supernatural elements. García Márquez's novel, rather than pioneering "magic realism," simply brought this already successful Spanish-American genre to the world's notice.

Gabriel García Márquez (1929–    ) gives credit to Faulkner for his becoming a writer, and this influence is felt in *One Hundred Years of Solitude.* Inspired by Faulkner's fictional county of Yoknapatawpha, Mississippi, García Márquez invented the town of Macondo to serve as a symbol of his Colombian birthplace, Aracataca; in this small town near the Caribbean coast, he spent the first eight years of his life with his grandparents, the rest of his family living elsewhere. The grandparents are the source of the fantastic events that unfold in the novel; for in García Márquez's years with them, both grandparents, who were superstitious and impressionable, delighted in evenings of storytelling about local history and legends and unexplained mysteries— nothing was too strange for them. García Márquez has written many other novels, including the well-received *The Autumn of the Patriarch* (1976)—but none has the compelling fascination of this work.

## Reading the Selection

This selection contains the opening pages of *One Hundred Years of Solitude,* in which the intertwined histories of the Buendía family and the town of Macondo are introduced. A hallucinatory mood is created in the first sentence; the reader is plunged into the middle of the story, and future ("many years later"), present, and past ("that distant afternoon") are co-mingled and then left obscure, at least for the moment. Adding to the sense of fantasy is this description of Macondo's early years: "the world was so recent that many things lacked names," thus suggesting a biblical paradise. Holding this sprawling work together is the narrative voice—an attitude of naturalness and indifference toward absolutely everything—a Modernist device but one which was also inspired by the voice of García Márquez's grandmother in Aracataca.

Many years later, as he faced the firing squad, Colonel Aureliano Buendía was to remember that distant afternoon when his father took him to discover ice. At that time Macondo was a village of twenty adobe houses, built on the bank of a river of clear water that ran along a bed of polished stones, which were white and enormous, like prehistoric eggs. The world was so recent that many things lacked names, and in order to indicate them it was necessary to point. Every year during the month of March a family of ragged gypsies would set up their tents near the village, and with a great uproar of pipes and kettledrums they would display new inventions. First they brought the magnet. A heavy gypsy with an untamed beard and sparrow hands, who introduced himself as Melquíades, put on a bold public demonstration of what he himself called the eighth wonder of the learned alchemists of Macedonia. He went from house to house dragging two metal ingots and everybody was amazed to see pots, pans, tongs, and braziers tumble down from their places and beams creak from the desperation of nails and screws trying to emerge, and even objects that had been lost for a long time appeared from where they had been searched for most and went dragging along in turbulent confusion behind Melquíades' magical irons. "Things have a life of their own," the gypsy proclaimed with a harsh accent. "It's simply a matter of waking up their souls." José Arcadio Buendía, whose unbridled imagination always went beyond the genius of nature and even beyond miracles and magic, thought that it would be possible to make use of that useless invention to extract gold from the bowels of the earth. Melquíades, who was an honest man, warned him: "It won't work for that." But José Arcadio Buendía at that time did not believe in the honesty of gypsies, so he traded his mule and a pair of goats for the two magnetized ingots. Úrsula Iguarán, his wife, who relied on those animals to increase their poor domestic holdings, was unable to dissuade him. "Very soon we'll have gold enough and more to pave the floors of the house," her husband replied. For several months he worked hard to demonstrate the truth of his idea. He explored every inch of the region, even the riverbed, dragging the two iron ingots along and reciting Melquíades' incantation aloud. The only thing he succeeded in doing was to unearth a suit of fifteenth-century armor which had all of its pieces soldered together with rust and inside of which there was the hollow resonance of an enormous stone-filled gourd. When José Arcadio Buendía and the four men of his expedition managed to take the armor apart, they found inside a calcified skeleton with a copper locket containing a woman's hair around its neck.

In March the gypsies returned. This time they brought a telescope and a magnifying glass the size of a drum, which they exhibited as the latest discovery of the Jews of Amsterdam. They placed a gypsy woman at one end of the village and set up the telescope at the entrance to the tent. For the price of five reales, people could look into the telescope and see the gypsy woman an arm's length away. "Science has eliminated distance," Melquíades proclaimed. "In a short time, man will be able to see what is happening in any place in the world without leaving his own house." A burning noonday sun brought out a startling demonstration with the gigantic magnifying glass: they put a pile of dry hay in the middle of the street and set it on fire by concentrating the sun's rays. José Arcadio Buendía, who had still not been consoled for the failure of his magnets, conceived the idea of using that invention as a weapon of war. Again Melquíades tried to dissuade him, but he finally accepted the two magnetized ingots and three colonial coins in exchange for the magnifying glass. Úrsula wept in consternation. That money was from a chest of gold coins that her father had put together over an entire life of privation and that she had buried underneath her bed in hopes of a proper occasion to make use of it. José Arcadio Buendía made no attempt to console her, completely absorbed in his tactical experiments with the abnegation of a scientist and even at the risk of his own life. In an attempt to show the effects of the glass on enemy troops, he exposed himself to the concentration of the sun's rays and suffered burns which turned into sores that took a long time to heal. Over the protests of his wife, who was alarmed at such a dangerous invention, at one point he was ready to set the house on fire. He would spend hours on end in his room, calculating the strategic possibilities of his novel weapon until he succeeded in putting together a manual of startling instructional clarity and an irresistible power of conviction. He sent it to the government, accompanied by numerous descriptions of his experiments and several pages of explanatory sketches, by a messenger who crossed the mountains, got lost in measureless swamps, forded stormy rivers, and was on the point of perishing under the lash of despair, plague, and wild beasts until he found a route that joined the one used by the mules that carried the mail. In spite of the fact that a trip to the capital was little less than impossible at that time, José Arcadio Buendía promised to undertake it as soon as the government ordered him to so that he could put on some practical demonstrations of his invention for the military authorities and could train them himself in the complicated art of solar war. For several years he waited for an answer. Finally, tired of waiting, he bemoaned to Melquíades the failure of his project and the gypsy then gave him a convincing proof of his honesty: he gave him back the doubloons in exchange for the magnifying glass, and he left him in addition some Portuguese maps and several instruments of navigation. In his own handwriting he set down a concise synthesis of the studies by Monk Hermann, which he left José Arcadio so that he would be able to make use of the astrolabe, the compass, and the sextant. José Arcadio Buendía spent the long months of the rainy season shut up in a small room that he had built in the rear of the house so that no one would disturb his experiments. Having completely abandoned his domestic obligations, he spent entire nights in the courtyard watching the course of the stars and he almost contracted sunstroke from trying to establish an exact method to ascertain noon. When he became an expert in the use and manipulation of his instruments, he conceived a notion of space that allowed him to navigate across unknown seas, to visit uninhabited territories, and to establish relations with splendid beings without having to leave his study. That was the period in which he acquired the habit of talking to himself, of walking through the house without paying attention to anyone, as Úrsula and the children broke their backs in the garden, growing banana and caladium, cassava and yams, ahuyama roots and eggplants. Suddenly, without warning, his feverish activity was interrupted and was replaced by a kind of fascination. He spent several days as if he were bewitched, softly repeating to himself a string of fearful conjectures without giving credit to his own understanding. Finally, one Tuesday in December, at lunchtime, all at once he released the whole weight of his torment. The children would remember for the rest of their lives the august solemnity with which their father, devastated by his prolonged vigil and by the wrath of his imagination, revealed his discovery to them:

"The earth is round, like an orange."

Úrsula lost her patience. "If you have to go crazy, please go crazy all by yourself!" she shouted. "But don't try to put your gypsy ideas into the heads of the children." José Arcadio Buendía, impassive, did not let himself be frightened by the desperation of his wife, who, in a seizure of rage, smashed the astrolabe against the floor. He built another one, he gathered the men of the village in his little room, and he demonstrated to them, with theories that none of them could understand, the possibility of returning to where one had set out by consistently sailing east. The whole village was convinced that José Arcadio Buendía had lost his reason, when Melquíades returned to set things straight. He gave public praise to the intelligence of a man who from pure astronomical speculation had evolved a theory that had already been proved in practice, although unknown in Macondo until then, and as a proof of his admiration he made him a gift that was to have a profound influence on the future of the village: the laboratory of an alchemist.

By then Melquíades had aged with surprising rapidity. On his first trips he seemed to be the same age as José Arcadio Buendía. But while the latter had preserved his extraordinary strength, which permitted him to pull down a horse by grabbing its ears, the gypsy seemed to have been worn down by some tenacious illness. It was, in reality, the result of multiple and rare diseases contracted on his innumerable trips around the world. According to what he himself said as he spoke to José Arcadio Buendía while helping him set up the laboratory, death followed him everywhere, sniffing at the cuffs of his pants, but never deciding to give him the final clutch of its claws. He was a fugitive from all the plagues and catastrophes that had ever lashed mankind. He had survived pellagra in Persia, scurvy in the Malayan archipelago, leprosy in Alexandria, beriberi in Japan, bubonic plague in Madagascar, an earthquake in Sicily, and a disastrous ship-wreck in the Strait of Magellan. That prodigious creature, said to possess the keys of Nostradamus, was a gloomy man, enveloped in a sad aura, with an Asiatic look that seemed to know what there was on the other side of things. He wore a large black hat that looked like a raven with widespread wings, and a velvet vest across which the patina of the centuries had skated. But in spite of his immense wisdom and his mysterious breadth, he had a human burden, an earthly condition that kept him involved in the small problems of daily life. He would complain of the ailments of old age, he suffered from the most insignificant economic difficulties, and he had stopped laughing a long time back because scurvy

had made his teeth drop out. On that suffocating noontime when the gypsy revealed his secrets, José Arcadio Buendía had the certainty that it was the beginning of a great friendship. The children were startled by his fantastic stories. Aureliano, who could not have been more than five at the time, would remember him for the rest of his life as he saw him that afternoon, sitting against the metallic and quivering light from the window, lighting up with his deep organ voice the darkest reaches of the imagination, while down over his temples there flowed the grease that was being melted by the heat. José Arcadio, his older brother, would pass on that wonderful image as a hereditary memory to all of his descendants. Úrsula, on the other hand, held a bad memory of that visit, for she had entered the room just as Melquíades had carelessly broken a flask of bichloride of mercury.

"It's the smell of the devil," she said.

"Not at all," Melquíades corrected her. "It has been proven that the devil has sulphuric properties and this is just a little corrosive sublimate."

Always didactic, he went into a learned exposition of the diabolical properties of cinnabar, but Úrsula paid no attention to him, although she took the children off to pray. That biting odor would stay forever in her mind linked to the memory of Melquíades.

The rudimentary laboratory—in addition to a profusion of pots, funnels, retorts, filters, and sieves—was made up of a primitive water pipe, a glass beaker with a long, thin neck, a reproduction of the philosopher's egg, and a still the gypsies themselves had built in accordance with modern descriptions of the three-armed alembic of Mary the Jew. Along with those items, Melquíades left samples of the seven metals that corresponded to the seven planets, the formulas of Moses and Zosimus for doubling the quantity of gold, and a set of notes and sketches concerning the processes of the Great Teaching that would permit those who could interpret them to undertake the manufacture of the philosopher's stone. Seduced by the simplicity of the formulas to double the quantity of gold, José Arcadio Buendía paid court to Úrsula for several weeks so that she would let him dig up her colonial coins and increase them by as many times as it was possible to subdivide mercury. Úrsula gave in, as always, to her husband's unyielding obstinacy. Then José Arcadio Buendía threw three doubloons into a pan and fused them with copper filings, orpiment, brimstone, and lead. He put it all to boil in a pot of castor oil until he got a thick and pestilential syrup which was more like common caramel than valuable gold. In risky and desperate processes of distillation, melted with the seven planetary metals, mixed with hermetic mercury and vitriol of Cyprus, and put back to cook in hog fat for lack of any radish oil, Úrsula's precious inheritance was reduced to a large piece of burnt hog cracklings that was firmly stuck to the bottom of the pot.

When the gypsies came back, Úrsula had turned the whole population of the village against them. But curiosity was greater than fear, for that time the gypsies went about the town making a deafening noise with all manner of musical instruments while a hawker announced the exhibition of the most fabulous discovery of the Naciancenes. So that everyone went to the tent and by paying one cent they saw a youthful Melquíades, recovered, unwrinkled, with a new and flashing set of teeth. Those who remembered his gums that had been destroyed by scurvy, his flaccid cheeks, and his withered lips trembled with fear at the final proof of the gypsy's supernatural power. The fear turned into panic when Melquíades took out his teeth, intact, encased in their gums, and showed them to the audience for an instant—a fleeting instant in which he went back to being the same decrepit man of years past—and put them back again and smiled once more with the full control of his restored youth. Even José Arcadio Buendía himself considered that Melquíades' knowledge had reached unbearable extremes, but he felt a healthy excitement when the gypsy explained to him alone the workings of his false teeth. It seemed so simple and so prodigious at the same time that overnight he lost all interest in his experiments in alchemy. He underwent a new crisis of bad humor. He did not go back to eating regularly, and he would spend the day walking through the house. "Incredible things are happening in the world," he said to Úrsula. "Right there across the river there are all kinds of magical instruments while we keep on living like donkeys." Those who had known him since the foundation of Macondo were startled at how much he had changed under Melquíades' influence. . . .

# ADRIENNE RICH

# *The Burning of Paper Instead of Children*

Adrienne Rich (1929–    ) is one of the most honored American poets since 1945. Noted for angry feminist works, she has won some of America's most prestigious prizes, including the National Book Award for *Diving into the Wreck: Poems, 1971–1972*, in 1974. The way she chose to receive this honor shows the centrality of feminism to her life and work: Refusing the award as an individual, calling it "tokenism", Rich, joined by two other of that year's nominees, Audre Lord and Alice Walker, accepted it in the name of all women.

Along with Beat Generation and African-American poets, Rich and feminist poets in general were part of a broad-based assault on Modernism—the reigning literary style since about 1900. Radicalized by the social upheavals of the 1950s and 1960s, these three groups of poets focused on different though overlapping problems; still, they shared the view that Modernism, with its stress on experimentation to the exclusion of meaning, was at a dead end because of its irrelevance to real life. Dedicated to the ideal that poetry should reflect reality, these poets wrote poems of protest against the existing social order. Not making a complete break with Modernism, however, they combined its free spirit with topical themes. When new to the scene, these poets seemed outside the mainstream, but, today, it is clear that they were the vanguard of Post-Modernism, the contemporary movement that embraces the works of women and minorities and is committed to a global culture.

Because Rich's writings are openly autobiographical (she once wrote: "We're living through a time/that needs to be lived through us"), her life and poetic interests tend to reflect the general changes that have coursed through American society in the last fifty years. Her moral courage in opening herself in her poems has touched the lives of a generation of women readers, mainly white, relatively privileged, both heterosexual and homosexual, and mostly now thirty-something and up, who identify with her private hardships and her public concerns. These readers have watched as she changed from a woman of privilege, to domestic partner with an upwardly mobile husband and three small children, to engaged activist who redefined herself as a lesbian and political radical.

## Reading the Selection

"The Burning of Paper Instead of Children" reflects the social upheavals of the 1960s, which radically changed Rich's life and poetry. In theme, the poem identifies four areas of concern: the victimization of children; the age's general immorality; the sense that sex no longer is able to dispel human loneliness; and, the view that the first three problems are caused by patriarchy (male rule).

In stream-of-consciousness fashion, the poem explores Rich's mood at a moment frozen in time. The triggering event for her mood is a prank played by her son and a friend who burn their schoolbooks at the end of term; the prank is blown out of proportion by the friend's father, who calls bookburning a fascist gesture, evoking "memories of Hitler," and demands that Rich, as he has with his son, punish her son. Thinking this demand a form of child abuse, or, rather, patriarchal "oppression," Rich refuses his request, saying, better to burn books than "burn" children. While working out her thoughts, she widens her list of charges against patriarchy; she concludes that books themselves are images of rule by the fathers, just as is the male-planned and -fought Vietnam War.

---

*I was in danger of*
*verbalizing my moral*
*impulses out of existence.*

—DANIEL BERRIGAN,
on trial in Baltimore.

1. My neighbor, a scientist and art-collector, telephones me in a state of violent emotion. He tells me that my son and his, aged eleven and twelve, have on the last day of school burned a mathematics textbook in the backyard. He has forbidden my son to come to his house for a week, and has forbidden his own son to leave the house during that time. "The burning of a book," he says, "arouses terrible sensations in me, memories of Hitler; there are few things that upset me so much as the idea of burning a book."

Back there: the library, walled
with green Britannicas
Looking again
in Dürer's *Complete Works*
for MELANCOLIA, the baffled woman

the crocodiles in Herodotus
the Book of the Dead

the *Trial of Jeanne d'Arc,* so blue
I think, It is her color

and they take the book away
because I dream of her too often

love and fear in a house
knowledge of the oppressor
I know it hurts to burn

2. To imagine a time of silence
or few words
a time of chemistry and music

the hollows above your buttocks
traced by my hand
or, *hair is like flesh,* you said

an age of long silence

relief

from this tongue      this slab of limestone
or reinforced concrete
fanatics and traders
dumped on this coast wildgreen clayred
that breathed once
in signals of smoke
sweep of the wind

knowledge of the oppressor
this is the oppressor's language

yet I need it to talk to you

•

3. *People suffer highly in poverty and it takes dignity and intelligence to overcome this suffering. Some of the suffering are: a child did not had dinner last night: a child steal because he did not have money to buy it: to hear a mother say she do not have money to buy food for her children and to see a child without cloth it will make tears in your eyes.*

(the fracture of order
the repair of speech
to overcome this suffering)

4. We lie under the sheet
after making love, speaking
of loneliness
relieved in a book
relived in a book
so on that page
the clot and fissure
of it appears
words of a man
in pain
a naked word
entering the clot
a hand grasping
through bars:

deliverance

What happens between us
has happened for centuries
we know it from literature

still it happens

sexual jealousy
outflung hand
beating bed

dryness of mouth
after panting

•

there are books that describe all this
and they are useless

You walk into the woods behind a house
there in that country
you find a temple
built eighteen hundred years ago
you enter without knowing
what it is you enter

so it is with us

no one knows what may happen
though the books tell everything

*burn the texts*    said Artaud

5. I am composing on the typewriter late at night, thinking of today. How well we all spoke. A language is a map of our failures. Frederick Douglass wrote an English purer than Milton's. People suffer highly in poverty. There are methods but we do not use them. Joan, who could not read, spoke some peasant form of French. Some of the suffering are: it is hard to tell the truth; this is America; I cannot touch you now. In America we have only the present tense. I am in danger. You are in danger. The burning of a book arouses no sensation in me. I know it hurts to burn. There are flames of napalm in Catonsville, Maryland. I know it hurts to burn. The typewriter is overheated, my mouth is burning, I cannot touch you and this is the oppressor's language.

---

# ALICE WALKER
## *Everyday Use*

---

Alice Walker (1944–     ) is the most honored and widely read African-American writer of her generation, the one which grew to maturity after 1954 when the Supreme Court handed down its ruling outlawing separate but equal schools. A prolific author who writes in varied genres, she has produced five books of poetry, two books of essays, two collections of short stories, and five novels. A measure of the quality of her work is that her books appeal to mainstream audiences while remaining true to the black experience. Her most celebrated novel, *The Color Purple* (1982), won both the Pulitzer Prize for fiction and the National Book Award, in 1983, a rarity in the annals of publishing; when made into a film, it became one of the most popular movies of the 1980s—a record unmatched by any other black author at work today.

Among black writers, Walker is distinctive because of her brand of feminism. She has made her literary project the reclaiming of the matrilineal (tracing ancestry through the mothers) dimension in African-American life. To this end, she has researched the female goddesses of Africa and interwoven them and their history into the texture of her novels, the genre for which she is best known. In her novels, such as *The Temple of My Familiar* (1989), she explores the black women's collective subconscious, using dreams, imaginings, rituals, and legends. She also furthered black feminism by editing an anthology of works by Zora Neale Hurston, thus restoring this neglected author to a central place in black women's writing.

Walker came of age in the social upheavals of the 1950s. Born in Georgia, the eighth child in a family of sharecroppers, she grew up, in her words, "poor [and] dusty"; she received a privileged education, however, at predominantly black Spelman College in Atlanta and mainly white Sarah Lawrence College in Massachusetts. Radicalized by the civil rights movement, she registered black voters in Georgia, assisted with the Head Start program in Mississippi, and worked for the department of welfare in New York City. In her writings, Walker draws on her experience in this movement, but she refuses to deal in simple propaganda. She does portray the sufferings of blacks at the hands of whites, but she is equally interested in showing hypocrisy and cruelty within black life, disguised as militancy in support of a worthy cause.

### Reading the Selection

Walker's "Everyday Use," set within today's black community, is a short story with the theme of culture clash, old versus new. In the story, two sisters with little in common are reunited after many years, only to discover that they do not like one another. In the style of a parable, the sisters represent two aspects of black culture: Sister Dee is educated, wealthy, and into trendy "blackness," as evidenced by her African name Wangero; sister Maggie is scarred, mentally slow, poor, and untouched by civil rights advances. For a moment, a battle looms between the sisters over ownership of quilts—made by a grandmother and thus symbolic of black heritage. Dee wants the quilts for wall hangings; Maggie needs them for everyday use. Rather than fight, though, Maggie nobly agrees to give them up. At which point the mother (the narrator) "snatche[s] the quilts out of Miss Wangero's hands and dump[s] them into Maggie's lap." Thus, in this culture clash, the mother sides with Maggie and the ancestral tradition.

---

*For Your Grandmama*

I will wait for her in the yard that Maggie and I made so clean and wavy yesterday afternoon. A yard like this is more comfortable than most people know. It is not just a yard. It is like an extended living room. When the hard clay is swept clean as a floor and the fine sand around the edges lined with tiny, irregular grooves anyone can come and sit and look up into the elm tree and wait for the breezes that never come inside the house.

Maggie will be nervous until after her sister goes: she will stand hopelessly in corners homely and ashamed of the burn scars down her arms and legs, eyeing her sister with a mixture of envy and awe. She thinks her sister has held life always in the palm of one hand, that "no" is a word the world never learned to say to her.

You've no doubt seen those TV shows where the child who has "made it" is confronted, as a surprise, by her own mother and father, tottering in weakly from backstage. (A pleasant surprise, of course: What would they do if parent and child came on the show only to curse out and insult each other?) On TV mother and child embrace and smile into each other's faces. Sometimes the mother and father weep, the child wraps them in her arms and leans across the table to tell how she would not have made it without their help. I have seen these programs.

Sometimes I dream a dream in which Dee and I are suddenly brought together on a TV program of this sort. Out of a dark and soft-seated limousine I am ushered into a bright room filled with many people. There I meet a smiling, gray, sporty man like Johnny Carson who shakes my hand and tells me what a fine girl I have. Then we are on the stage and Dee is embracing me with tears in her eyes. She pins on my dress a large orchid, even though she has told me once that she thinks orchids are tacky flowers.

In real life I am a large, big-boned woman with rough, man-working hands. In the winter I wear flannel nightgowns to bed and overalls during the day. I can kill and clean a hog as mercilessly as a man. My fat keeps me hot in zero weather. I can work outside all day, breaking ice to get water for washing; I can eat pork liver cooked over the open fire minutes after it comes steaming from the hog. One winter I knocked a bull calf straight in the brain between the eyes with a sledge hammer and had the meat hung up to chill before nightfall. But of course all this does not show on television. I am the way my daughter would want me to be: a hundred pounds lighter, my skin like an uncooked barley pancake. My hair glistens in the hot bright lights. Johnny Carson has much to do to keep up with my quick and witty tongue.

But that is a mistake. I know even before I wake up. Who ever knew a Johnson with a quick tongue? Who can even imagine me looking a strange white man in the eye? It seems to me I have talked to them always with one foot raised in flight, with my head turned in whichever way is farthest from them. Dee, though. She would always look anyone in the eye. Hesitation was no part of her nature.

"How do I look, Mama?" Maggie says, showing just enough of her thin body enveloped in pink shirt and red blouse for me to know she's there, almost hidden by the door.

"Come out into the yard," I say.

Have you ever seen a lame animal, perhaps a dog run over by some careless person rich enough to own a car, sidle up to someone who is ignorant enough to be kind to him? That is the way my Maggie walks. She has been like this, chin on chest, eyes on ground, feet in shuffle, ever since the fire that burned the other house to the ground.

Dee is lighter than Maggie, with nicer hair and a fuller figure. She's a woman now, though sometimes I forget. How long ago was it that the other house burned? Ten, twelve years? Sometimes I can hear the flames and feel Maggie's arms sticking to me, her hair smoking and her dress falling off her in little black papery flakes. Her eyes seemed stretched open, blazed open by the flames reflected in them. And Dee. I see her standing off under the sweet gum tree she used to dig gum out of; a look of concentration on her face as she watched the last dingy gray board of the house fall in toward the red-hot brick chimney. Why don't you do a dance around the ashes? I'd wanted to ask her. She had hated the house that much.

I used to think she hated Maggie, too. But that was before we raised the money, the church and me, to send her to Augusta to school. She used to read to us without pity; forcing words, lies, other folks' habits, whole lives upon us two, sitting trapped and ignorant underneath her voice. She washed us in a river of make-believe, burned us with a lot of knowledge we didn't necessarily need to know. Pressed us to her with the serious way she read, to shove us away at just the moment, like dimwits, we seemed about to understand.

Dee wanted nice things. A yellow organdy dress to wear to her graduation from high school; black pumps to match a green suit she'd made from an old suit somebody gave me. She was determined to stare down any disaster in her efforts. Her eyelids would not flicker for minutes at a time. Often I fought off the temptation to shake her. At sixteen she had a style of her own: and knew what style was.

I never had an education myself. After second grade the school was closed down. Don't ask me why: in 1927 colored asked fewer questions than they do now. Sometimes Maggie reads to me. She stumbles along good-naturedly but can't see well. She knows she is not bright. Like good looks and money, quickness passed her by. She will marry John Thomas (who has mossy teeth in an earnest face) and then I'll be free to sit here and I guess just sing church songs to myself. Although I never was a good singer. Never could carry a tune. I was always better at a man's job. I used to love to milk till I was hooked in the side in '49. Cows are soothing and slow and don't bother you, unless you try to milk them the wrong way.

I have deliberately turned my back on the house. It is three rooms, just like the one that burned, except the roof is tin; they don't make shingle roofs any more. There are no real windows, just some holes cut in the sides, like the portholes in a ship, but not round and not square, with rawhide holding the shutters up on the outside. This house is in a pasture, too, like the other one. No doubt when Dee sees it she will want to tear it down. She wrote me once that no matter where we "choose" to live, she will manage to come see us. But she will never bring her friends. Maggie and I thought about this and Maggie asked me, "Mama, when did Dee ever *have* any friends?"

She had a few. Furtive boys in pink shirts hanging about on washday after school. Nervous girls who never laughed. Impressed with her they worshiped the well-turned phrase, the cute shape, the scalding humor that erupted like bubbles in lye. She read to them.

When she was courting Jimmy T she didn't have much time to pay to us, but turned all her faultfinding power on

him. He *flew* to marry a cheap gal from a family of ignorant flashy people. She hardly had time to recompose herself.

When she comes I will meet—but there they are!

Maggie attempts to make a dash for the house, in her shuffling way, but I stay her with my hand. "Come back here," I say. And she stops and tries to dig a well in the sand with her toe.

It is hard to see them clearly through the strong sun. But even the first glimpse of leg out of the car tells me it is Dee. Her feet were always neat-looking, as if God himself had shaped them with a certain style. From the other side of the car comes a short, stocky man. Hair is all over his head a foot long and hanging from his chin like a kinky mule tail. I hear Maggie suck in her breath. "Uhnnnh," is what it sounds like. Like when you see the wriggling end of a snake just in front of your foot on the road. "Uhnnnh."

Dee next. A dress down to the ground, in this hot weather. A dress so loud it hurts my eyes. There are yellows and oranges enough to throw back the light of the sun. I feel my whole face warming from the heat waves it throws out. Earrings gold, too, and hanging down to her shoulders. Bracelets dangling and making noises when she moves her arm up to shake the folds of the dress out of her armpits. The dress is loose and flows, and as she walks closer, I like it. I hear Maggie go "Uhnnnh" again. It is her sister's hair. It stands straight up like the wool on a sheep. It is black as night and around the edges are two long pigtails that rope about like small lizards disappearing behind her ears.

"Wa-su-zo-Tean-o!" she says, coming on in that gliding way the dress makes her move. The short stocky fellow with the hair to his navel is all grinning and he follows up with "Asalamalakim, my mother and sister!" He moves to hug Maggie but she falls back, right up against the back of my chair. I feel her trembling there and when I look up I see the perspiration falling off her chin.

"Don't get up," says Dee. Since I am stout it takes something of a push. You can see me trying to move a second or two before I make it. She turns, showing white heels through her sandals, and goes back to the car. Out she peeks next with a Polaroid. She stoops down quickly and lines up picture after picture of me sitting there in front of the house with Maggie cowering behind me. She never takes a shot without making sure the house is included. When a cow comes nibbling around the edge of the yard she snaps it and me and Maggie *and* the house. Then she puts the Polaroid in the back seat of the car, and comes up and kisses me on the forehead.

Meanwhile Asalamalakim is going through the motions with Maggie's hand. Maggie's hand is as limp as a fish, and probably as cold, despite the sweat, and she keeps trying to pull it back. It looks like Asalamalakim wants to shake hands but wants to do it fancy. Or maybe he don't know how people shake hands. Anyhow, he soon gives up on Maggie.

"Well," I say. "Dee."

"No, Mama," she says. "Not 'Dee,' Wangero Leewanika Kemanjo!"

"What happened to 'Dee'?" I wanted to know.

"She's dead," Wangero said. "I couldn't bear it any longer being named after the people who oppress me."

"You know as well as me you was named after your aunt Dicie," I said. Dicie is my sister. She named Dee. We called her "Big Dee" after Dee was born.

"But who was *she* named after?" asked Wangero.

"I guess after Grandma Dee," I said.

"And who was she named after?" asked Wangero.

"Her mother," I said, and saw Wangero was getting tired. "That's about as far back as I can trace it," I said. Though, in fact, I probably could have carried it back beyond the Civil War through the branches.

"Well," said Asalamalakim, "there you are."

"Uhnnnh," I heard Maggie say.

"There I was not," I said, "before 'Dicie' cropped up in our family, so why should I try to trace it that far back?"

He just stood there grinning, looking down on me like somebody inspecting a Model A car. Every once in a while he and Wangero sent eye signals over my head.

"How do you pronounce this name?" I asked.

"You don't have to call me by it if you don't want to," said Wangero.

"Why shouldn't I?" I asked. "If that's what you want us to call you, we'll call you."

"I know it might sound awkward at first," said Wangero.

"I'll get used to it," I said. "Ream it out again."

Well, soon we got the name out of the way. Asalamalakim had a name twice as long and three times as hard. After I tripped over it two or three times he told me to just call him Hakim-a-barber. I wanted to ask him was he a barber, but I didn't really think he was, so I didn't ask.

"You must belong to those beef-cattle peoples down the road," I said. They said "Asalamalakim" when they met you, too, but they didn't shake hands. Always too busy: feeding the cattle, fixing the fences, putting up salt-lick shelters, throwing down hay. When the white folks poisoned some of the herd the men stayed up all night with rifles in their hands. I walked a mile and a half just to see the sight.

Hakim-a-barber said, "I accept some of their doctrines, but farming and raising cattle is not my style." (They didn't tell me, and I didn't ask, whether Wangero [Dee] had really gone and married him.)

We sat down to eat and right away he said he didn't eat collards and pork was unclean. Wangero, though, went on through the chitlins and corn bread, the greens and everything else. She talked a blue streak over the sweet potatoes. Everything delighted her. Even the fact that we still used the benches her daddy made for the table when we couldn't afford to buy chairs.

"Oh, Mama!" she cried. Then turned to Hakim-a-barber. "I never knew how lovely these benches are. You can feel the rump prints," she said, running her hands underneath her and along the bench. Then she gave a sigh and her hand closed over Grandma Dee's butter dish. "That's it!" she said. "I knew there was something I wanted to ask you if I could have." She jumped up from the table and went over in the corner where the churn stood, the milk in it clabber by now. She looked at the churn and looked at it.

"This churn top is what I need," she said. "Didn't Uncle Buddy whittle it out of a tree you all used to have?"

"Yes," I said.

"Uh huh," she said happily. "And I want the dasher, too."

"Uncle Buddy whittle that, too?" asked the barber.

Dee (Wangero) looked up at me.

"Aunt Dee's first husband whittled the dash," said Maggie so low you almost couldn't hear her. "His name was Henry, but they called him Stash."

"Maggie's brain is like an elephant's," Wangero said, laughing. "I can use the churn top as a centerpiece for the alcove table," she said, sliding a plate over the churn, "and I'll think of something artistic to do with the dasher."

When she finished wrapping the dasher the handle stuck out. I took it for a moment in my hands. You didn't even have to look close to see where hands pushing the dasher up and down to make butter had left a kind of sink in the wood. In fact, there were a lot of small sinks; you could see where thumbs and fingers had sunk into the wood. It was beautiful light yellow wood, from a tree that grew in the yard where Big Dee and Stash had lived.

After dinner Dee (Wangero) went to the trunk at the foot of my bed and started rifling through it. Maggie hung back in the kitchen over the dishpan. Out came Wangero with two quilts. They had been pieced by Grandma Dee and then Big Dee and me had hung them on the quilt frames on the front porch and quilted them. One was in the Lone Star pattern. The other was Walk Around the Mountain. In both of them were scraps of dresses Grandma Dee had worn fifty and more years ago. Bits and pieces of Grandpa Jarrell's paisley shirts. And one teeny faded blue piece, about the size of a penny matchbox, that was from Great Grandpa Ezra's uniform that he wore in the Civil War.

"Mama," Wangero said sweet as a bird. "Can I have these old quilts?"

I heard something fall in the kitchen, and a minute later the kitchen door slammed.

"Why don't you take one or two of the others?" I asked. "These old things was just done by me and Big Dee from some tops your grandma pieced before she died."

"No," said Wangero. "I don't want those. They are stitched around the borders by machine."

"That'll make them last better," I said.

"That's not the point," said Wangero. "These are all pieces of dresses Grandma used to wear. She did all this stitching by hand. Imagine!" She held the quilts securely in her arms, stroking them.

"Some of the pieces, like those lavender ones, come from old clothes her mother handed down to her," I said, moving up to touch the quilts. Dee (Wangero) moved back just enough so that I couldn't reach the quilts. They already belonged to her.

"Imagine!" she breathed again, clutching them closely to her bosom.

"The truth is," I said, "I promised to give them quilts to Maggie, for when she marries John Thomas."

She gasped like a bee had stung her.

"Maggie can't appreciate these quilts!" she said. "She'd probably be backward enough to put them to everyday use."

"I reckon she would," I said. "God knows I been saving 'em for long enough with nobody using 'em. I hope she will!" I didn't want to bring up how I had offered Dee (Wangero) a quilt when she went away to college. Then she had told me they were old-fashioned, out of style.

"But they're *priceless!*" she was saying now, furiously; for she has a temper. "Maggie would put them on the bed and in five years they'd be in rags. Less than that!"

"She can always make some more," I said. "Maggie knows how to quilt."

Dee (Wangero) looked at me with hatred. "You just will not understand. The point is these quilts, *these* quilts!"

"Well," I said, stumped. "What would *you* do with them?"

"Hang them," she said. As if that was the only thing you *could* do with quilts.

Maggie by now was standing in the door. I could almost hear the sound her feet made as they scraped over each other.

"She can have them, Mama," she said, like somebody used to never winning anything, or having anything reserved for her. "I can 'member Grandma Dee without the quilts."

I looked at her hard. She had filled her bottom lip with checkerberry snuff and it gave her face a kind of dopey, hangdog look. It was Grandma Dee and Big Dee who taught her how to quilt herself. She stood there with her scarred hands hidden in the folds of her skirt. She looked at her sister with something like fear but she wasn't mad at her. This was Maggie's portion. This was the way she knew God to work.

When I looked at her like that something hit me in the top of my head and ran down to the soles of my feet. Just like when I'm in church and the spirit of God touches me and I get happy and shout. I did something I never had done before: hugged Maggie to me, then dragged her on into the room, snatched the quilts out of Miss Wangero's hands and dumped them into Maggie's lap. Maggie just sat there on my bed with her mouth open.

"Take one or two of the others," I said to Dee.

But she turned without a word and went out to Hakim-a-barber.

"You just don't understand," she said, as Maggie and I came out to the car.

"What don't I understand?" I wanted to know.

"Your heritage," she said. And then she turned to Maggie, kissed her, and said, "You ought to try to make something of yourself, too, Maggie. It's really a new day for us. But from the way you and Mama still live you'd never know it."

She put on some sunglasses that hid everything above the tip of her nose and her chin.

Maggie smiled; maybe at the sunglasses. But a real smile, not scared. After we watched the car dust settle I asked Maggie to bring me a dip of snuff. And then the two of us sat there just enjoying, until it was time to go in the house and go to bed.

---

# MAXINE HONG KINGSTON

## from *The Woman Warrior*

### No Name Woman

---

Maxine Hong Kingston (1940–    ) is one of the most talented and original Chinese-American writers in this nation's history. Through her critically acclaimed and popular writings, she has put the Chinese-American experience into American literature. Her literary project is to "claim America," meaning to show that the Chinese have the right to belong through their labor in building the country and supporting themselves. In staking out this claim, she has been influenced by the poet William Carlos Williams (1883–1963), who envisioned an American culture distinct from Europe and built from indigenous materials and forms. On another level, she wants to combat Sinophobia, fear of the "yellow race," which has been a marked feature of American life since the first wave of Chinese immigrants in the late nineteenth century. Thus, Kingston not only celebrates Chinese achievement but she also avenges past wrongs—by calling exploitation, racism, and ignorance by their true names.

As the first generation daughter of immigrants, Kingston uses her own life as a paradigm of Chinese-American culture. A graduate of an American university and a high-school teacher, from 1965–1977, Kingston nevertheless feels a need to explore her ancestral roots. In China, both her parents were engaged in promising careers, the father as a school teacher and the mother as a midwife; both left their jobs to seek their fortunes in "Gold Mountain," their overly optimistic name for California. Once in Stockton's Chinatown, they could only find work in a laundry. The parents' fall in the world plunged her father into black moods during much of Maxine's childhood; in contrast, her mother kept her good humor by telling stories, in the peasant talk-story Cantonese tradition, which is the heritage of most Chinese-Americans.

Talk-stories are moral tales of ancient heroes and family secrets. It is these stories, reworked from those Kingston's mother told, written in an artful combination of Chinese rhythms and

American slang, which provide the narrative structure of Kingston's best-known works: *The Woman Warrior: Memoirs of a Girlhood Among Ghosts* (1976), dealing with matriarchal influence, and *China Men* (1980), telling of the patriarchal side. Partly written to come to terms with her family, both books have the broader aim of describing the Chinese-American predicament—being caught in a double bind between two proud, often mutually antagonistic cultures.

## Reading the Selection

"No Name Woman," the first episode in *The Woman Warrior*, is the talk-story of Kingston's paternal aunt, a "ghost" who haunts the author's past. The aunt's name is unmentionable, because she disgraced the family in China by becoming pregnant—perhaps by rape—while her husband was in America. When her illegitimate baby was born, villagers destroyed the family compound. In despair, "No Name" aunt drowned herself and her child in the family well.

The talk-story of "No Name" sets the tone for *The Woman Warrior*, establishing that traditional Chinese culture has a low opinion of women. It is this oppression against which the heroic deeds of the idealized female warriors, treated in later chapters, can be judged. The "No Name" episode also reflects Kingston's self-identification as a woman warrior. Her sympathetic portrait of the aunt whom the family deliberately forgot is an act of rebellion against tradition and a vindication of the wronged relative.

---

"You must not tell anyone," my mother said, "what I am about to tell you. In China your father had a sister who killed herself. She jumped into the family well. We say that your father has all brothers because it is as if she had never been born.

"In 1924 just a few days after our village celebrated seventeen hurry-up weddings—to make sure that every young man who went 'out on the road' would responsibly come home—your father and his brothers and your grandfather and his brothers and your aunt's new husband sailed for America, the Gold Mountain. It was your grandfather's last trip. Those lucky enough to get contracts waved goodbye from the decks. They fed and guarded the stowaways and helped them off in Cuba, New York, Bali, Hawaii. 'We'll meet in California next year,' they said. All of them sent money home.

"I remember looking at your aunt one day when she and I were dressing; I had not noticed before that she had such a protruding melon of a stomach. But I did not think, 'She's pregnant,' until she began to look like other pregnant women, her shirt pulling and the white tops of her black pants showing. She could not have been pregnant, you see, because her husband had been gone for years. No one said anything. We did not discuss it. In early summer she was ready to have the child, long after the time when it could have been possible.

"The village had also been counting. On the night the baby was to be born the villagers raided our house. Some were crying. Like a great saw, teeth strung with lights, files of people walked zigzag across our land, tearing the rice. Their lanterns doubled in the disturbed black water, which drained away through the broken bunds. As the villagers closed in, we could see that some of them, probably men and women we knew well, wore white masks. The people with long hair hung it over their faces. Women with short hair made it stand up on end. Some had tied white bands around their foreheads, arms, and legs.

"At first they threw mud and rocks at the house. Then they threw eggs and began slaughtering our stock. We could

hear the animals scream their deaths—the roosters, the pigs, a last great roar from the ox. Familiar wild heads flared in our night windows; the villagers encircled us. Some of the faces stopped to peer at us, their eyes rushing like searchlights. The hands flattened against the panes, framed heads, and left red prints.

"The villagers broke in the front and the back doors at the same time, even though we had not locked the doors against them. Their knives dripped with the blood of our animals. They smeared blood on the doors and walls. One woman swung a chicken, whose throat she had slit, splattering blood in red arcs about her. We stood together in the middle of our house, in the family hall with the pictures and tables of the ancestors around us, and looked straight ahead.

"At that time the house had only two wings. When the men came back, we would build two more to enclose our courtyard and a third one to begin a second courtyard. The villagers pushed through both wings, even your grandparents' rooms, to find your aunt's, which was also mine until the men returned. From this room a new wing for one of the younger families would grow. They ripped up her clothes and shoes and broke her combs, grinding them underfoot. They tore her work from the loom. They scattered the cooking fire and rolled the new weaving in it. We could hear them in the kitchen breaking our bowls and banging the pots. They overturned the great waist-high earthenware jugs; duck eggs, pickled fruits, vegetables burst out and mixed in acrid torrents. The old woman from the next field swept a broom through the air and loosed the spirits-of-the-broom over our heads. 'Pig.' 'Ghost.' 'Pig,' they sobbed and scolded while they ruined our house.

"When they left, they took sugar and oranges to bless themselves. They cut pieces from the dead animals. Some of them took bowls that were not broken and clothes that were not torn. Afterward we swept up the rice and sewed it back up into sacks. But the smells from the spilled preserves lasted. Your aunt gave birth in the pigsty that night. The next morning when I went for the water, I found her and the baby plugging up the family well.

"Don't let your father know that I told you. He denies her. Now that you have started to menstruate, what happened to her could happen to you. Don't humiliate us. You wouldn't like to be forgotten as if you had never been born. The villagers are watchful."

Whenever she had to warn us about life, my mother told stories that ran like this one, a story to grow up on. She tested our strength to establish realities. Those in the emigrant generations who could not reassert brute survival died young and far from home. Those of us in the first American generations have had to figure out how the invisible world the emigrants built around our childhoods fits in solid America.

The emigrants confused the gods by diverting their curses, misleading them with crooked streets and false names. They must try to confuse their offspring as well, who, I suppose, threaten them in similar ways—always trying to get things straight, always trying to name the unspeakable. The Chinese I know hide their names; sojourners take new names when their lives change and guard their real names with silence.

Chinese-Americans, when you try to understand what things in you are Chinese, how do you separate what is peculiar to childhood, to poverty, insanities, one family, your mother who marked your growing with stories, from what is Chinese? What is Chinese tradition and what is the movies?

If I want to learn what clothes my aunt wore, whether flashy or ordinary, I would have to begin, "Remember Father's drowned-in-the-well sister?" I cannot ask that. My mother has told me once and for all the useful parts. She will add nothing unless powered by Necessity, a riverbank that guides her life. She plants vegetable gardens rather than lawns; she carries the odd-shaped tomatoes home from the fields and eats food left for the gods.

Whenever we did frivolous things, we used up energy; we flew high kites. We children came up off the ground over the melting cones our parents brought home from work and the American movie on New Year's Day—*Oh, You Beautiful Doll* with Betty Grable one year, and *She Wore a Yellow Ribbon* with John Wayne another year. After the one carnival ride each, we paid in guilt; our tired father counted his change on the dark walk home.

Adultery is extravagance. Could people who hatch their own chicks and eat the embryos and the heads for delicacies and boil the feet in vinegar for party food, leaving only the gravel, eating even the gizzard lining—could such people engender a prodigal aunt? To be a woman, to have a daughter in starvation time was a waste enough. My aunt could not have been the lone romantic who gave up everything for sex. Women in the old China did not choose. Some man had commanded her to lie with him and be his secret evil. I wonder whether he masked himself when he joined the raid on her family.

Perhaps she had encountered him in the fields or on the mountain where the daughters-in-law collected fuel. Or perhaps he first noticed her in the marketplace. He was not a stranger because the village housed no strangers. She had to have dealings with him other than sex. Perhaps he worked an adjoining field, or he sold her the cloth for the dress she sewed and wore. His demand must have surprised, then terrified her. She obeyed him; she always did as she was told.

When the family found a young man in the next village to be her husband, she had stood tractably beside the best rooster, his proxy, and promised before they met that she would be his forever. She was lucky that he was her age and she would be the first wife, an advantage secure now. The night she first saw him, he had sex with her. Then he left for America. She had almost forgotten what he looked like. When she tried to envision him, she only saw the black and white face in the group photograph the men had had taken before leaving.

The other man was not, after all, much different from her husband. They both gave orders: she followed. "If you tell your family, I'll beat you. I'll kill you. Be here again next week." No one talked sex, ever. And she might have separated the rapes from the rest of living if only she did not have to buy her oil from him or gather wood in the same forest. I want her fear to have lasted just as long as rape lasted so that the fear could have been contained. No drawn-out fear. But women at sex hazarded birth and hence lifetimes. The fear did not stop but permeated everywhere. She told the man, "I think I'm pregnant." He organized the raid against her.

On nights when my mother and father talked about their life back home, sometimes they mentioned an "outcast table" whose business they still seemed to be settling, their voices tight. In a commensal tradition, where food is precious, the powerful older people made wrongdoers eat alone. Instead of letting them start separate new lives like the Japanese, who could become samurais and geishas, the Chinese family, faces averted but eyes glowering sideways, hung on to the offenders and fed them leftovers. My aunt must have lived in the same house as my parents and eaten at an outcast table. My mother spoke about the raid as if she had seen it, when she and my aunt, a daughter-in-law to a different household, should not have been living together at all. Daughters-in-law lived with their husbands' parents, not their own; a synonym for marriage in Chinese is "taking a daughter-in-law." Her husband's parents could have sold her, mortgaged her, stoned her. But they had sent her back to her own mother and father, a mysterious act hinting at disgraces not told me. Perhaps they had thrown her out to deflect the avengers.

She was the only daughter; her four brothers went with her father, husband, and uncles "out on the road" and for some years became western men. When the goods were divided among the family, three of the brothers took land, and the youngest, my father, chose an education. After my grandparents gave their daughter away to her husband's family, they had dispensed all the adventure and all the property. They expected her alone to keep the traditional ways, which her brothers, now among the barbarians, could fumble without detection. The heavy, deep-rooted women were to maintain the past against the flood, safe for returning. But the rare urge west had fixed upon our family, and so my aunt crossed boundaries not delineated in space.

The work of preservation demands that the feelings playing about in one's guts not be turned into action. Just watch their passing like cherry blossoms. But perhaps my aunt, my forerunner, caught in a slow life, let dreams grow and fade and after some months or years went toward what persisted. Fear at the enormities of the forbidden kept her desires delicate, wire and bone. She looked at a man because she liked the way the hair was tucked behind his ears, or she liked the question-mark line of a long torso curving at the shoulder and straight at the hip. For warm eyes or a soft voice or a slow walk—that's all—a few hairs, a line, a brightness, a sound, a pace, she gave up family. She offered us up for a charm that vanished with tiredness, a pigtail that didn't toss when the wind died. Why, the wrong lighting could erase the dearest thing about him.

It could very well have been, however, that my aunt did not take subtle enjoyment of her friend, but, a wild woman, kept rollicking company. Imagining her free with sex doesn't fit, though. I don't know any women like that, or men either. Unless I see her life branching into mine, she gives me no ancestral help.

To sustain her being in love, she often worked at herself in the mirror, guessing at the colors and shapes that would interest him, changing them frequently in order to hit on the right combination. She wanted him to look back.

On a farm near the sea, a woman who tended her appearance reaped a reputation for eccentricity. All the married women blunt-cut their hair in flaps about their ears or pulled it back in tight buns. No nonsense. Neither style blew easily into heart-catching tangles. And at their weddings they displayed themselves in their long hair for the last time. "It brushed the backs of my knees," my mother tells me. "It was braided, and even so, it brushed the backs of my knees."

At the mirror my aunt combed individuality into her bob. A bun could have been contrived to escape into black streamers blowing in the wind or in quiet wisps about her face, but only the older women in our picture album wear buns. She brushed her hair back from her forehead, tucking the flaps behind her ears. She looped a piece of thread, knotted into a circle between her index fingers and thumbs, and ran the double strand across her forehead. When she closed her fingers as if she were making a pair of shadow geese bite, the string twisted together catching the little hairs. Then she pulled the thread away from her skin, ripping the hairs out neatly, her eyes watering from the needles of pain. Opening her fingers, she cleaned the thread, then rolled it along her hairline and the tops of her eyebrows. My mother did the same to me and my sisters and herself. I used to believe that the expression "caught by the short hairs" meant a captive held with a depilatory string. It especially hurt at the temples, but my mother said we were lucky we didn't have to have our feet bound when we were seven. Sisters used to sit on their beds and cry together, she said, as their mothers or their slaves removed the bandages for a few minutes each night and let the blood gush back into their veins. I hope that the man my aunt loved appreciated a smooth brow, that he wasn't just a tits-and-ass man.

Once my aunt found a freckle on her chin, at a spot that the almanac said predestined her for unhappiness. She dug it out with a hot needle and washed the wound with peroxide.

More attention to her looks than these pullings of hairs and pickings at spots would have caused gossip among the villagers. They owned work clothes and good clothes, and they wore good clothes for feasting the new seasons. But since a woman combing her hair hexes beginnings, my aunt rarely found an occasion to look her best. Women looked like great sea snails—the corded wood, babies, and laundry they carried were the whorls on their backs. The Chinese did not admire a bent back; goddesses and warriors stood straight. Still there must have been a marvelous freeing of beauty when a worker laid down her burden and stretched and arched.

Such commonplace loveliness, however, was not enough for my aunt. She dreamed of a lover for the fifteen days of New Year's, the time for families to exchange visits, money, and food. She plied her secret comb. And sure enough she cursed the year, the family, the village, and herself.

Even as her hair lured her imminent lover, many other men looked at her. Uncles, cousins, nephews, brothers would have looked, too, had they been home between journeys. Perhaps they had already been restraining their curiosity, and they left, fearful that their glances, like a field of nesting birds, might be startled and caught. Poverty hurt, and that was their first reason for leaving. But another, final reason for leaving the crowded house was the never-said.

She may have been unusually beloved, the precious only daughter, spoiled and mirror gazing because of the affection the family lavished on her. When her husband left, they welcomed the chance to take her back from the in-laws; she could live like the little daughter for just a while longer. There are stories that my grandfather was different from other people, "crazy ever since the little Jap bayoneted him in the head." He used to put his naked penis on the dinner table, laughing. And one day he brought home a baby girl, wrapped up inside his brown western-style greatcoat. He had traded one of his sons, probably my father, the youngest, for her. My grandmother made him trade back. When he finally got a daughter of his own, he doted on her. They must have all loved her, except perhaps my father, the only brother who never went back to China, having once been traded for a girl.

Brothers and sisters, newly men and women, had to efface their sexual color and present plain miens. Disturbing hair and eyes, a smile like no other, threatened the ideal of five generations living under one roof. To focus blurs, people shouted face to face and yelled from room to room. The immigrants I know have loud voices, unmodulated to American tones even after years away from the village where they called their friendships out across the fields. I have not been able to stop my mother's screams in public libraries or over telephones. Walking erect (knees straight, toes pointed forward, not pigeon-toed, which is Chinese-feminine) and speaking in an inaudible voice, I have tried to turn myself American-feminine. Chinese communication was loud, public. Only sick people had to whisper. But at the dinner table, where the family members came nearest one another, no one could talk, not the outcasts nor any eaters. Every word that falls from the mouth is a coin lost. Silently they gave and accepted food with both hands. A preoccupied child who took his bowl with one hand got a sideways glare. A complete moment of total attention is due everyone alike. Children and lovers have no singularity here, but my aunt used a secret voice, a separate attentiveness.

She kept the man's name to herself throughout her labor and dying; she did not accuse him that he be punished with her. To save her inseminator's name she gave silent birth.

He may have been somebody in her own household, but intercourse with a man outside the family would have been no less abhorrent. All the village were kinsmen, and the titles shouted in loud country voices never let kinship be forgotten. Any man within visiting distance would have been neutralized as a lover—"brother," "younger brother," "older brother"—one hundred and fifteen relationship titles. Parents researched birth charts probably not so much to assure good fortune as to circumvent incest in a population that has but one hundred surnames. Everybody has eight million relatives. How useless then sexual mannerisms, how dangerous.

As if it came from an atavism deeper than fear, I used to add "brother" silently to boys' names. It hexed the boys, who would or would not ask me to dance, and made them less scary and as familiar and deserving of benevolence as girls.

But, of course, I hexed myself also—no dates. I should have stood up, both arms waving, and shouted out across libraries, "Hey, you! Love me back." I had no idea, though, how to make attraction selective, how to control its direction and magnitude. If I made myself American-pretty so that the five or six Chinese boys in the class fell in love with me, everyone else—the Caucasian, Negro, and Japanese boys—would too. Sisterliness, dignified and honorable, made much more sense.

Attraction eludes control so stubbornly that whole societies designed to organize relationships among people cannot keep order, not even when they bind people to one another from childhood and raise them together. Among the very poor and the wealthy, brothers married their adopted sisters, like doves. Our family allowed some romance, paying adult brides' prices and providing dowries so that their sons and daughters could marry strangers. Marriage promises to turn strangers into friendly relatives—a nation of siblings.

In the village structure, spirits shimmered among the live creatures, balanced and held in equilibrium by time and land. But one human being flaring up into violence could open up a black hole, a maelstrom that pulled in the sky. The frightened villagers, who depended on one another to maintain the real, went to my aunt to show her a personal, physical representation of the break she had made in the "roundness." Misallying couples snapped off the future, which was to be embodied in true offspring. The villagers punished her for acting as if she could have a private life, secret and apart from them.

If my aunt had betrayed the family at a time of large grain yields and peace, when many boys were born, and wings were being built on many houses, perhaps she might have escaped such severe punishment. But the men—hungry, greedy, tired of planting in dry soil—had been forced to leave the village in order to send food-money home. There were ghost plagues, bandit plagues, wars with the Japanese, floods. My Chinese brother and sister had died of an unknown sickness. Adultery, perhaps only a mistake during good times, became a crime when the village needed food.

The round moon cakes and round doorways, the round tables of graduated sizes that fit one roundness inside another, round windows and rice bowls—these talismans had lost their power to warn this family of the law: a family must be whole, faithfully keeping the descent line by having sons to feed the old and the dead, who in turn look after the family.

The villagers came to show my aunt and her lover-in-hiding a broken house. The villagers were speeding up the circling of events because she was too shortsighted to see that her infidelity had already harmed the village, that waves of consequences would return unpredictably, sometimes in disguise, as now, to hurt her. This roundness had to be made coin-sized so that she would see its circumference: punish her at the birth of her baby. Awaken her to the inexorable. People who refused fatalism because they could invent small resources insisted on culpability. Deny accidents and wrest fault from the stars.

After the villagers left, their lanterns now scattering in various directions toward home, the family broke their silence and cursed her. "Aiaa, we're going to die. Death is coming. Death is coming. Look what you've done. You've killed us. Ghost! Dead ghost! Ghost! You've never been born." She ran out into the fields, far enough from the house so that she could no longer hear their voices, and pressed herself against the earth, her own land no more. When she felt the birth coming, she thought that she had been hurt. Her body seized together. "They've hurt me too much," she thought. "This is gall, and it will kill me." With forehead and knees against the earth, her body convulsed and then relaxed. She turned on her back, lay on the ground. The black well of sky and stars went out and out and out forever; her body and her complexity seemed to disappear. She was one of the stars, a bright dot in blackness, without home, without a companion, in eternal cold and silence. An agoraphobia rose in her, speeding higher and higher, bigger and bigger; she would not be able to contain it; there would no end to fear.

Flayed, unprotected against space, she felt pain return, focusing her body. This pain chilled her—a cold, steady kind of surface pain. Inside, spasmodically, the other pain, the pain of the child, heated her. For hours she lay on the ground, alternately body and space. Sometimes a vision of normal comfort obliterated reality: she saw the family in the evening gambling at the dinner table, the young people massaging their elders' backs. She saw them congratulating one another, high joy on the mornings the rice shoots came up. When these pictures burst, the stars drew yet further apart. Black space opened.

She got to her feet to fight better and remembered that old-fashioned women gave birth in their pigsties to fool the jealous, pain-dealing gods, who do not snatch piglets. Before the next spasms could stop her, she ran to the pigsty, each step a rushing out into emptiness. She climbed over the fence and knelt in the dirt. It was good to have a fence enclosing her, a tribal person alone.

Laboring, this woman who had carried her child as a foreign growth that sickened her every day, expelled it at last. She reached down to touch the hot, wet, moving mass, surely smaller than anything human, and could feel that it was human after all—fingers, toes, nails, nose. She pulled it up on to her belly, and it lay curled there, butt in the air, feet precisely tucked one under the other. She opened her loose shirt and buttoned the child inside. After resting, it squirmed and thrashed and she pushed it up to her breast. It turned its head this way and that until it found her nipple. There, it made little snuffling noises. She clenched her teeth at its preciousness, lovely as a young calf, a piglet, a little dog.

She may have gone to the pigsty as a last act of responsibility: she would protect this child as she had protected its father. It would look after her soul, leaving supplies on her grave. But how would this tiny child without family find her grave when there would be no marker for her anywhere, neither in the earth nor the family hall? No one would give her a family hall name. She had taken the child with her into the wastes. At its birth the two of them had felt the same raw pain of separation, a wound that only the family pressing tight could close. A child with no descent line would not soften her life but only trail after her, ghostlike, begging her to give it purpose. At dawn the villagers on their way to the fields would stand around the fence and look.

Full of milk, the little ghost slept. When it awoke, she hardened her breasts against the milk that crying loosens. Toward morning she picked up the baby and walked to the well.

Carrying the baby to the well shows loving. Otherwise abandon it. Turn its face into the mud. Mothers who love their children take them along. It was probably a girl; there is some hope of forgiveness for boys.

"Don't tell anyone you had an aunt. Your father does not want to hear her name. She has never been born." I have believed that sex was unspeakable and words so strong and fathers so frail that "aunt" would do my father mysterious harm. I have thought that my family, having settled among immigrants who had also been their neighbors in the ancestral land, needed to clean their name, and a wrong word would incite the kinspeople even here. But there is more to this silence: they want me to participate in her punishment. And I have.

In the twenty years since I heard this story I have not asked for details nor said my aunt's name; I do not know it. People who can comfort the dead can also chase after them to hurt them further—a reverse ancestor worship. The real punishment was not the raid swiftly inflicted by the villagers, but the family's deliberately forgetting her. Her betrayal so maddened them, they saw to it that she would suffer forever, even after death. Always hungry, always needing, she would have to beg food from other ghosts, snatch and steal it from those whose living descendants give them gifts. She would have to fight the ghosts massed at crossroads for the buns a few thoughtful citizens leave to decoy her away from village and home so that the ancestral spirits could feast unharassed. At peace, they could act like gods, not ghosts, their descent lines providing them with paper suits and dresses, spirit money, paper houses, paper automobiles, chicken, meat, and rice into eternity—essences delivered up in smoke and flames, steam and incense rising from each rice bowl. In an attempt to make the Chinese care for people outside the family, Chairman Mao encourages us now to give our paper replicas to the spirits of outstanding soldiers and workers, no matter whose ancestors they may be. My aunt remains forever hungry. Goods are not distributed evenly among the dead.

My aunt haunts me—her ghost drawn to me because now, after fifty years of neglect, I alone devote pages of paper to her, though not origamied into houses and clothes. I do not think she always means me well. I am telling on her, and she was a spite suicide, drowning herself in the drinking water. The Chinese are always very frightened of the drowned one, whose weeping ghost, wet hair hanging and skin bloated, waits silently by the water to pull down a substitute.

---

# MILAN KUNDERA
## from *The Unbearable Lightness of Being*

---

The Czech writer Milan Kundera (1929–    ) is one of Europe's most important authors working today. Short story writer, essayist, playwright, and poet, he is best known for his novels, which embody his aesthetic theories, as set forth in *The Art of the Novel* (1990), a work of literary criticism. What is most striking about Kundera's novels is their lack of obedience to the rule of unity of action; instead of traditional narrative structures, they present parallel stories on related themes. The result is a type of novel that (in his words): "searches and poses questions. I don't know which of my characters is right. I invent stories, confront one with the other, and by this means I ask questions." The roots of this type of novel are in Cervantes and Kafka; however, the disorienting methods—patterns based on musical forms and disjointed time frames—reflect Kundera's training in music and film.

In the 1960s, Kundera was often grouped with the East European "dissident" writers, a coterie of writers who used their fiction to play secret games against the communist regimes then in power in Poland, Hungary, Czechoslovakia, and East Germany. Hating the term "dissident," he always rejected it as a label, for he claimed that his writings were not innately political. Still, his early works challenged the authorities with sly humor, as in *The Joke* (1967), his first novel; in it, the student hero is sent to work in the mines because he mailed a postcard bearing a joke about Lenin. When Russian troops invaded Czechoslovakia in 1968, local leaders, who previously distrusted Kundera, expelled him from the communist party and fired him from his teaching post. His works were removed from libraries and bookstores, and he was forbidden to publish in his own country. In 1976, invited to teach at a French university, he escaped to France where he lives in permanent exile. The Czech government canceled his citizenship upon publication of the novel, *The Book of Laughter and Forgetting,* in 1979.

The novel which made Kundera a world literary figure was *The Unbearable Lightness of Being* (1984), whose success was partly due to the popularity of the erotic movie based on it. In theme, the novel argues that keeping a clear memory is a way to protect oneself in a world where history is daily distorted, whether for ideological reasons under socialism or out of indifference under capitalism. To explore this theme, he presented two couples—Tomas and Tereza, and Franz and Sabina—portraying their doomed affairs with ironic humor and brutal eroticism. Situated mainly in Czechoslovakia during the 1968 Russian invasion, but with scenes set in Switzerland, this novel suggests the hopelessness of life under modern conditions.

### Reading the Selection

This selection—the first six episodes of *The Unbearable Lightness of Being*—introduces two of the novel's main characters, Tomas and Tereza. Unlike in conventional novels, these characters seem to be an afterthought: "I have been thinking about Tomas for many years. But only in the light of these reflections did I see him clearly." They appear after a digression on the Nietzschean idea of "the eternal return"—that is, history repeats itself endlessly with no moral lessons learned. Framed within this idea, the novel seems destined to portray (as it does) the futility of trying to be moral under the hostile conditions of modern life—an existential view shared with Sartre (see *The Humanism of Existentialism*).

---

### 1

The idea of eternal return is a mysterious one, and Nietzsche has often perplexed other philosophers with it: to think that everything recurs as we once experienced it, and that the recurrence itself recurs ad infinitum! What does this mad myth signify?

Putting it negatively, the myth of eternal return states that a life which disappears once and for all, which does not return, is like a shadow, without weight, dead in advance, and whether it was horrible, beautiful, or sublime, its horror, sublimity, and beauty mean nothing. We need take no more note of it than of a war between two African kingdoms in the fourteenth century, a war that altered nothing in the destiny of the world, even if a hundred thousand blacks perished in excruciating torment.

Will the war between two African kingdoms in the fourteenth century itself be altered if it recurs again and again, in eternal return?

It will: it will become a solid mass, permanently protuberant, its inanity irreparable.

If the French Revolution were to recur eternally, French historians would be less proud of Robespierre. But because they deal with something that will not return, the bloody years of the Revolution have turned into mere words, theories, and discussions, have become lighter than feathers, frightening no one. There is an infinite difference between a Robespierre who occurs only once in history and a Robespierre who eternally returns, chopping off French heads.

Let us therefore agree that the idea of eternal return implies a perspective from which things appear other than as we know them: they appear without the mitigating circumstance of their transitory nature. This mitigating circumstance prevents us from coming to a verdict. For how can we condemn something that is ephemeral, in transit? In the sunset of dissolution, everything is illuminated by the aura of nostalgia, even the guillotine.

Not long ago, I caught myself experiencing a most incredible sensation. Leafing through a book on Hitler, I was touched by some of his portraits: they reminded me of my childhood. I grew up during the war; several members of my family perished in Hitler's concentration camps; but what were their deaths compared with the memories of a lost period in my life, a period that would never return?

This reconciliation with Hitler reveals the profound moral perversity of a world that rests essentially on the nonexistence of return, for in this world everything is pardoned in advance and therefore everything cynically permitted.

### 2

If every second of our lives recurs an infinite number of times, we are nailed to eternity as Jesus Christ was nailed to the cross. It is a terrifying prospect. In the world of eternal return the weight of unbearable responsibility lies heavy on every move we make. That is why Nietzsche called the idea of eternal return the heaviest of burdens (*das schwerste Gewicht*).

If eternal return is the heaviest of burdens, then our lives can stand out against it in all their splendid lightness.

But is heaviness truly deplorable and lightness splendid?

The heaviest of burdens crushes us, we sink beneath it, it pins us to the ground. But in the love poetry of every age, the woman longs to be weighed down by the man's body. The heaviest of burdens is therefore simultaneously an image of life's most intense fulfillment. The heavier the burden, the closer our lives come to the earth, the more real and truthful they become.

Conversely, the absolute absence of a burden causes man to be lighter than air, to soar into the heights, take leave of the earth and his earthly being, and become only half real, his movements as free as they are insignificant.

What then shall we choose? Weight or lightness?

Parmenides posed this very question in the sixth century before Christ. He saw the world divided into pairs of opposites: light/darkness, fineness/coarseness, warmth/cold, being/non-being. One half of the opposition he called positive (light, fineness, warmth, being), the other negative. We might find this division into positive and negative poles childishly simple except for one difficulty: which one is positive, weight or lightness?

Parmenides responded: lightness is positive, weight negative.

Was he correct or not? That is the question. The only certainty is: the lightness/weight opposition is the most mysterious, most ambiguous of all.

### 3

I have been thinking about Tomas for many years. But only in the light of these reflections did I see him clearly. I saw him standing at the window of his flat and looking across the courtyard at the opposite walls, not knowing what to do.

He had first met Tereza about three weeks earlier in a small Czech town. They had spent scarcely an hour together. She had accompanied him to the station and waited with him until he boarded the train. Ten days later she paid him a visit. They made love the day she arrived. That night she came down with a fever and stayed a whole week in his flat with the flu.

He had come to feel an inexplicable love for this all but complete stranger; she seemed a child to him, a child someone had put in a bulrush basket daubed with pitch and sent downstream for Tomas to fetch at the riverbank of his bed.

She stayed with him a week, until she was well again, then went back to her town, some hundred and twenty-five miles from Prague. And then came the time I have just spoken of and see as the key to his life: Standing by the window, he looked out over the courtyard at the walls opposite him and deliberated.

Should he call her back to Prague for good? He feared the responsibility. If he invited her to come, then come she would, and offer him up her life.

Or should he refrain from approaching her? Then she would remain a waitress in a hotel restaurant of a provincial town and he would never see her again.

Did he want her to come or did he not?

He looked out over the courtyard at the opposite walls, seeking an answer.

He kept recalling her lying on his bed; she reminded him of no one in his former life. She was neither mistress nor wife.

She was a child whom he had taken from a bulrush basket that had been daubed with pitch and sent to the riverbank of his bed. She fell asleep. He knelt down next to her. Her feverous breath quickened and she gave out a weak moan. He pressed his face to hers and whispered calming words into her sleep. After a while he felt her breath return to normal and her face rise unconsciously to meet his. He smelled the delicate aroma of her fever and breathed it in, as if trying to glut himself with the intimacy of her body. And all at once he fancied she had been with him for many years and was dying. He had a sudden clear feeling that he would not survive her death. He would lie down beside her and want to die with her. He pressed his face into the pillow beside her head and kept it there for a long time.

Now he was standing at the window trying to call that moment to account. What could it have been if not love declaring itself to him?

But was it love? The feeling of wanting to die beside her was clearly exaggerated: he had seen her only once before in his life! Was it simply the hysteria of a man who, aware deep down of his inaptitude for love, felt the self-deluding need to simulate it? His unconscious was so cowardly that the best partner it could choose for its little comedy was this miserable provincial waitress with practically no chance at all to enter his life!

Looking out over the courtyard at the dirty walls, he realized he had no idea whether it was hysteria or love.

And he was distressed that in a situation where a real man would instantly have known how to act, he was vacillating and therefore depriving the most beautiful moments he had ever experienced (kneeling at her bed and thinking he would not survive her death) of their meaning.

He remained annoyed with himself until he realized that not knowing what he wanted was actually quite natural.

We can never know what to want, because, living only one life, we can neither compare it with our previous lives nor perfect it in our lives to come.

Was it better to be with Tereza or to remain alone?

There is no means of testing which decision is better, because there is no basis for comparison. We live everything as it comes, without warning, like an actor going on cold. And what can life be worth if the first rehearsal for life is life itself? That is why life is always like a sketch. No, "sketch" is not quite the word, because a sketch is an outline of something, the groundwork for a picture, whereas the sketch that is our life is a sketch for nothing, an outline with no picture.

*Einmal ist keinmal*, says Tomas to himself. What happens but once, says the German adage, might as well not have happened at all. If we have only one life to live, we might as well not have lived at all.

### 4

But then one day at the hospital, during a break between operations, a nurse called him to the telephone. He heard Tereza's voice coming from the receiver. She had phoned him from the railway station. He was overjoyed. Unfortunately, he had something on that evening and could not invite her to his place until the next day. The moment he hung up, he reproached himself for not telling her to go straight there. He had time enough to cancel his plans, after all! He tried to imagine what Tereza would do in Prague during the thirty-six long hours before they were to meet, and had half a mind to jump into his car and drive through the streets looking for her.

She arrived the next evening, a handbag dangling from her shoulder, looking more elegant than before. She had a thick book under her arm. It was *Anna Karenina*. She seemed in a good mood, even a little boisterous, and tried to make him think she had just happened to drop in, things had just worked out that way: she was in Prague on business, perhaps (at this point she became rather vague) to find a job.

Later, as they lay naked and spent side by side on the bed, he asked her where she was staying. It was night by then, and he offered to drive her there. Embarrassed, she answered that she still had to find a hotel and had left her suitcase at the station.

Only two days ago, he had feared that if he invited her to Prague she would offer him up her life. When she told him her suitcase was at the station, he immediately realized that the suitcase contained her life and that she had left it at the station only until she could offer it up to him.

The two of them got into his car, which was parked in front of the house, and drove to the station. There he claimed the suitcase (it was large and enormously heavy) and took it and her home.

How had he come to make such a sudden decision when for nearly a fortnight he had wavered so much that he could not even bring himself to send a postcard asking her how she was?

He himself was surprised. He had acted against his principles. Ten years earlier, when he had divorced his wife, he celebrated the event the way others celebrate a marriage. He understood he was not born to live side by side with any woman and could be fully himself only as a bachelor. He tried to design his life in such a way that no woman could move in with a suitcase. That was why his flat had only the one bed. Even though it was wide enough, Tomas would tell his mistresses that he was unable to fall asleep with anyone next to him, and drive them home after midnight. And so it was not the flu that kept him from sleeping with Tereza on her first visit. The first night he had slept in his large armchair, and the rest of that week he drove each night to the hospital, where he had a cot in his office.

But this time he fell asleep by her side. When he woke up the next morning, he found Tereza, who was still asleep, holding his hand. Could they have been hand in hand all night? It was hard to believe.

And while she breathed the deep breath of sleep and held his hand (firmly: he was unable to disengage it from her grip), the enormously heavy suitcase stood by the bed.

He refrained from loosening his hand from her grip for fear of waking her, and turned carefully on his side to observe her better.

Again it occurred to him that Tereza was a child put in a pitch-daubed bulrush basket and sent downstream. He couldn't very well let a basket with a child in it float down a stormy river! If the Pharaoh's daughter hadn't snatched the basket carrying little Moses from the waves, there would have been no Old Testament, no civilization as we now know it! How many ancient myths begin with the rescue of an abandoned child! If Polybus hadn't taken in the young Oedipus, Sophocles wouldn't have written his most beautiful tragedy!

Tomas did not realize at the time that metaphors are dangerous. Metaphors are not to be trifled with. A single metaphor can give birth to love.

### 5

He lived a scant two years with his wife, and they had a son. At the divorce proceedings, the judge awarded the infant to its mother and ordered Tomas to pay a third of his salary for its support. He also granted him the right to visit the boy every other week.

But each time Tomas was supposed to see him, the boy's mother found an excuse to keep him away. He soon realized that bringing them expensive gifts would make things a good deal easier, that he was expected to bribe the mother for the son's love. He saw a future of quixotic attempts to inculcate his views in the boy, views opposed in every way to the mother's. The very thought of it exhausted him. When, one Sunday, the boy's mother again canceled a scheduled visit, Tomas decided on the spur of the moment never to see him again.

Why should he feel more for that child, to whom he was bound by nothing but a single improvident night, than for any other? He would be scrupulous about paying support; he just didn't want anybody making him fight for his son in the name of paternal sentiments!

Needless to say, he found no sympathizers. His own parents condemned him roundly: if Tomas refused to take an interest in his son, then they, Tomas's parents, would no longer take an interest in theirs. They made a great show of maintaining good relations with their daughter-in-law and trumpeted their exemplary stance and sense of justice.

Thus in practically no time he managed to rid himself of wife, son, mother, and father. The only thing they bequeathed to him was a fear of women. Tomas desired but feared them. Needing to create a compromise between fear and desire, he devised what he called "erotic friendship." He would tell his mistresses: the only relationship that can make both partners happy is one in which sentimentality has no place and neither partner makes any claim on the life and freedom of the other.

To ensure that erotic friendship never grew into the aggression of love, he would meet each of his long-term mistresses only at intervals. He considered this method flawless and propagated it among his friends: "The important thing is to abide by the rule of threes. Either you see a woman three times in quick succession and then never again, or you maintain relations over the years but make sure that the rendezvous are at least three weeks apart."

The rule of threes enabled Tomas to keep intact his liaisons with some women while continuing to engage in short-term affairs with many others. He was not always understood. The woman who understood him best was Sabina. She was a painter. "The reason I like you," she would say to him, "is you're the complete opposite of kitsch. In the kingdom of kitsch you would be a monster."

It was Sabina he turned to when he needed to find a job for Tereza in Prague. Following the unwritten rules of erotic friendship, Sabina promised to do everything in her power, and before long she had in fact located a place for Tereza in the darkroom of an illustrated weekly. Although her new job did not require any particular qualifications, it raised her status from waitress to member of the press. When Sabina herself introduced Tereza to everyone on the weekly, Tomas knew he had never had a better friend as a mistress than Sabina.

## 6

The unwritten contract of erotic friendship stipulated that Tomas should exclude all love from his life. The moment he violated that clause of the contract, his other mistresses would assume inferior status and become ripe for insurrection.

Accordingly, he rented a room for Tereza and her heavy suitcase. He wanted to be able to watch over her, protect her, enjoy her presence, but felt no need to change his way of life. He did not want word to get out that Tereza was sleeping at his place: spending the night together was the corpus delicti of love.

He never spent the night with the others. It was easy enough if he was at their place: he could leave whenever he pleased. It was worse when they were at his and he had to explain that come midnight he would have to drive them home because he was an insomniac and found it impossible to fall asleep in close proximity to another person. Though it was not far from the truth, he never dared tell them the whole truth: after making love he had an uncontrollable craving to be by himself; waking in the middle of the night at the side of an alien body was distasteful to him, rising in the morning with an intruder repellent; he had no desire to be overheard brushing his teeth in the bathroom, nor was he enticed by the thought of an intimate breakfast.

That is why he was so surprised to wake up and find Tereza squeezing his hand tightly. Lying there looking at her, he could not quite understand what had happened. But as he ran through the previous few hours in his mind, he began to sense an aura of hitherto unknown happiness emanating from them.

From that time on they both looked forward to sleeping together. I might even say that the goal of their lovemaking was not so much pleasure as the sleep that followed it. She especially was affected. Whenever she stayed overnight in her rented room (which quickly became only an alibi for Tomas), she was unable to fall asleep; in his arms she would fall asleep no matter how wrought up she might have been. He would whisper impromptu fairy tales about her, or gibberish, words he repeated monotonously, words soothing or comical, which turned into vague visions lulling her through the first dreams of the night. He had complete control over her sleep: she dozed off at the second he chose.

While they slept, she held him as on the first night, keeping a firm grip on wrist, finger, or ankle. If he wanted to move without waking her, he had to resort to artifice. After freeing his finger (wrist, ankle) from her clutches, a process which, since she guarded him carefully even in her sleep, never failed to rouse her partially, he would calm her by slipping an object into her hand (a rolled-up pajama top, a slipper, a book), which she then gripped as tightly as if it were a part of his body.

Once, when he had just lulled her to sleep but she had gone no farther than dream's antechamber and was therefore still responsive to him, he said to her, "Good-bye, I'm going now." "Where?" she asked in her sleep. "Away," he answered sternly. "Then I'm going with you," she said, sitting up in bed. "No, you can't. I'm going away for good," he said, going out into the hall. She stood up and followed him out, squinting. She was naked beneath her short nightdress. Her face was blank, expressionless, but she moved energetically. He walked through the hall of the flat into the hall of the building (the hall shared by all the occupants), closing the door in her face. She flung it open and continued to follow him, convinced in her sleep that he meant to leave her for good and she had to stop him. He walked down the stairs to the first landing and waited for her there. She went down after him, took him by the hand, and led him back to bed.

Tomas came to this conclusion: Making love with a woman and sleeping with a woman are two separate passions, not merely different but opposite. Love does not make itself felt in the desire for copulation (a desire that extends to an infinite number of women) but in the desire for shared sleep (a desire limited to one woman).

# TIM O'BRIEN

# from *The Things They Carried*

## How to Tell a True War Story

War novels, usually based on the author's experiences, have been popular for more than a century in American literature, going back to Stephen Crane's *The Red Badge of Courage*, about the Civil War. Crane's realistic treatment of the common soldier's reaction to battle and his fear of dying set a pattern for the war novel genre. Books on World War I often followed this model but with more of an emphasis on the futility of conflict and the senseless loss of human life for "causes" that could not be justified in the author's opinion. The war novels coming out of World War II continued along these same lines but were much more explicit; they used a great deal of profanity and detailed the fighting and killing. Post-World-War-II authors also brought in Freud and stream-of-consciousness narration techniques; further, they were influenced by Kafka (see *The Metamorphosis*) and Sartre (see *The Humanism of Existentialism*) about the absurdity of human existence, especially in situations in which normal values and human relationships seemed irrelevant, as in combat. Since the Vietnam War, a handful of veterans and writers have begun to emerge, taking the war novel in a somewhat different direction; they are trying to come to grips with their own experiences, in America's most controversial war, one whose moral ambiguity remains a factor in American political life.

The best of the new wave of war novelists is Tim O'Brien (1946–    ), the author of three novels based on his experiences as a foot soldier in Vietnam. After graduation from college in Minnesota in the late 1960s, he was drafted to fight in a war of which he did not approve; he felt compelled to serve out of fear of family and social pressure. After his return, O'Brien went to graduate school and wrote for a newspaper before starting his career as a full-time writer, which is now his chief occupation.

### Reading the Selection

This selection is taken from O'Brien's third novel, *The Things They Carry* (1990), a collection of "stories" about the war and its combatants. In a lecture he once said, "Everything I write is made up, but that doesn't mean it's not true." Thus, when he begins with these words, "This is true," he is being playfully ironic; in a sense, he is trying to catch the mood of the war, which he claimed, among soldiers, was dominated by an overwhelming feeling of monotony.

O'Brien's literary style is sort of a pastiche, a patchwork of other writers' methods; this technique is often used in Post-Modernism, the post-1970 movement that seeks not to obliterate Modernism but to take it to a higher level. In O'Brien's writing, there are echoes of Hemingway, for example, in the "tough guy voice," the stripped-down prose, and the general air of midwestern muscularity. There is also something of the absurdity of Joseph Heller, author of *Catch 22*; for example, in the off-the-wall things the soldiers are willing to do in order to escape the system, either by direct action or through flights of the imagination. Lastly, there is a "magic realist" quality, in the manner of García Márquez (see *One Hundred Years of Solitude*); for example, when the same scene—the precise moment of Lemon's death—gets replayed in the "story." O'Brien also repeats the traditional war novel's themes of bravery, comradeship, and the transformation of young boys into men. Perhaps the major issue in O'Brien's work is, what is war really like? Although he approaches this issue from many angles, ultimately the reader must conclude that it is not possible to represent war in words.

This is true.

I had a buddy in Vietnam. His name was Bob Kiley, but everybody called him Rat.

A friend of his gets killed, so about a week later Rat sits down and writes a letter to the guy's sister. Rat tells her what a great brother she had, how together the guy was, a number one pal and comrade. A real soldier's soldier, Rat says. Then he tells a few stories to make the point, how her brother would always volunteer for stuff nobody else would volunteer for in a million years, dangerous stuff, like doing recon or going out on these really badass night patrols. Stainless steel balls, Rat tells her. The guy was a little crazy, for sure, but crazy in a good way, a real daredevil, because he liked the challenge of it, he liked testing himself, just man against gook. A great, great guy, Rat says.

Anyway, it's a terrific letter, very personal and touching. Rat almost bawls writing it. He gets all teary telling about the good times they had together, how her brother made the war seem almost fun, always raising hell and lighting up villes and bringing smoke to bear every which way. A great sense of humor, too. Like the time at this river when he went fishing with a whole damn crate of hand grenades. Probably the funniest thing in world history, Rat says, all that gore, about twenty zillion dead gook fish. Her brother, he had the right attitude. He knew how to have a good time. On Halloween, this real hot spooky night, the dude paints up his body all different colors and puts on this weird mask and hikes over to a ville and goes trick-or-treating almost stark naked, just boots and balls and an M-16. A tremendous human being, Rat says. Pretty nutso sometimes, but you could trust him with your life.

And then the letter gets very sad and serious. Rat pours his heart out. He says he loved the guy. He says the guy was his best friend in the world. They were like soul mates, he says, like twins or something, they had a whole lot in common. He tells the guy's sister he'll look her up when the war's over.

So what happens?

Rat mails the letter. He waits two months. The dumb cooze never writes back.

A true war story is never moral. It does not instruct, nor encourage virtue, nor suggest models of proper human behavior, nor restrain men from doing the things men have always done. If a story seems moral, do not believe it. If at the end of a war story you feel uplifted, or if you feel that some small bit of rectitude has been salvaged from the larger waste, then you have been made the victim of a very old and terrible lie. There is no rectitude whatsoever. There is no virtue. As a first rule of thumb, therefore, you can tell a true war story by its absolute and uncompromising allegiance to obscenity and evil. Listen to Rat Kiley. Cooze, he says. He does not say bitch. He certainly does not say woman, or girl. He says cooze. Then he spits and stares. He's nineteen years old—it's too much for him—so he looks at you with those big sad gentle killer eyes and says *cooze*, because his friend is dead, and because it's so incredibly sad and true: she never wrote back.

You can tell a true war story if it embarrasses you. If you don't care for obscenity, you don't care for the truth; if you don't care for the truth, watch how you vote. Send guys to war, they come home talking dirty.

Listen to Rat: "Jesus Christ, man, I write this beautiful fuckin' letter, I slave over it, and what happens? The dumb cooze never writes back."

The dead guy's name was Curt Lemon. What happened was, we crossed a muddy river and marched west into the mountains, and on the third day we took a break along a trail junction in deep jungle. Right away, Lemon and Rat Kiley started goofing. They didn't understand about the spookiness. They were kids; they just didn't know. A nature hike, they thought, not even a war, so they went off into the shade of some giant trees—quadruple canopy, no sunlight at all—and they were giggling and calling each other yellow mother and playing a silly game they'd invented. The game involved smoke grenades, which were harmless unless you did stupid things, and what they did was pull out the pin and stand a few feet apart and play catch under the shade of those huge trees. Whoever chickened out was a yellow mother. And if nobody chickened out, the grenade would make a light popping sound and they'd be covered with smoke and they'd laugh and dance around and then do it again.

It's all exactly true.

It happened, to *me*, nearly twenty years ago, and I still remember that trail junction and those giant trees and a soft dripping sound somewhere beyond the trees. I remember the smell of moss. Up in the canopy there were tiny white blossoms, but no sunlight at all, and I remember the shadows spreading out under the trees where Curt Lemon and Rat Kiley were playing catch with smoke grenades. Mitchell Sanders sat flipping his yo-yo. Norman Bowker and Kiowa and Dave Jensen were dozing, or half dozing, and all around us were those ragged green mountains.

Except for the laughter things were quiet.

At one point, I remember, Mitchell Sanders turned and looked at me, not quite nodding, as if to warn me about something, as if he already *knew*, then after a while he rolled up his yo-yo and moved away.

It's hard to tell you what happened next.

They were just goofing. There was a noise, I suppose, which must've been the detonator, so I glanced behind me and watched Lemon step from the shade into bright sunlight. His face was suddenly brown and shining. A handsome kid, really. Sharp gray eyes, lean and narrow-waisted, and when he died it was almost beautiful, the way the sunlight came around him and lifted him up and sucked him high into a tree full of moss and vines and white blossoms.

In any war story, but especially a true one, it's difficult to separate what happened from what seemed to happen. What seems to happen becomes its own happening and has to be told that way. The angles of vision are skewed. When a booby trap explodes, you close your eyes and duck and float outside yourself. When a guy dies, like Curt Lemon, you look away and then look back for a moment and then look away again. The pictures get jumbled; you tend to miss a lot. And then afterward, when you go to tell about it, there is always that surreal seemingness, which makes the story seem untrue, but which in fact represents the hard and exact truth as it *seemed*.

• • •

In many cases a true war story cannot be believed. If you believe it, be skeptical. It's a question of credibility. Often the crazy stuff is true and the normal stuff isn't, because the normal stuff is necessary to make you believe the truly incredible craziness.

In other cases you can't even tell a true war story. Sometimes it's just beyond telling.

I heard this one, for example, from Mitchell Sanders. It was near dusk and we were sitting at my foxhole along a wide muddy river north of Quang Ngai. I remember how peaceful the twilight was. A deep pinkish red spilled out on the river, which moved without sound, and in the morning we would cross the river and march west into the mountains. The occasion was right for a good story.

"God's truth," Mitchell Sanders said. "A six-man patrol goes up into the mountains on a basic listening-post operation. The idea's to spend a week up there, just lie low and listen for enemy movement. They've got a radio along, so if they hear anything suspicious—anything—they're supposed to call in artillery or gunships, whatever it takes. Otherwise they keep strict field discipline. Absolute silence. They just listen."

Sanders glanced at me to make sure I had the scenario. He was playing with his yo-yo, dancing it with short, tight little strokes of the wrist.

His face was blank in the dusk.

"We're talking regulation, by-the-book LP. These six guys, they don't say boo for a solid week. They don't got tongues. *All ears*."

"Right," I said.

"Understand me?"

"Invisible."

Sanders nodded.

"Affirm," he said. "Invisible. So what happens is, these guys get themselves deep in the bush, all camouflaged up, and they lie down and wait and that's all they do, nothing else, they lie there for seven straight days and just listen. And man, I'll tell you—it's spooky. This is mountains. You don't *know* spooky till you been there. Jungle, sort of, except it's way up in the clouds and there's always this fog—like rain, except it's not raining—everything's all wet and swirly and tangled up and you can't see jack, you can't find your own pecker to piss with. Like you don't even have a body. Serious spooky. You just go with the vapors—the fog sort of takes you in . . . And the sounds, man. The sounds carry forever. You hear stuff nobody should *ever* hear."

Sanders was quiet for a second, just working the yo-yo, then he smiled at me.

"So after a couple days the guys start hearing this real soft, kind of wacked-out music. Weird echoes and stuff. Like a radio or something, but it's not a radio, it's this strange gook music that comes right out of the rocks. Faraway, sort of, but right up close, too. They try to ignore it. But it's a listening post, right? So they listen. And every night they keep hearing that crazyass gook concert. All kinds of chimes and xylophones. I mean, this is wilderness—no way, it can't be real—but there it *is*, like the mountains are tuned in to Radio fucking Hanoi. Naturally they get nervous. One guy sticks Juicy Fruit in his ears. Another guy almost flips. Thing is, though, they can't report music. They can't get on the horn and call back to base and say, 'Hey, listen, we need some firepower, we got to blow away this weirdo gook rock band.' They can't do that. It wouldn't go down. So they lie there in the fog and keep their mouths shut. And what makes it extra bad, see, is the poor dudes can't horse around like normal. Can't joke it away. Can't even talk to each other except maybe in whispers, all hush-hush, and that just revs up the willies. All they do is listen."

Again there was some silence as Mitchell Sanders looked out on the river. The dark was coming on hard now, and off to the west I could see the mountains rising in silhouette, all the mysteries and unknowns.

"This next part," Sanders said quietly, "you won't believe."

"Probably not," I said.

"You won't. And you know why?" He gave me a long, tired smile. "Because it happened. Because every word is absolutely dead-on true."

Sanders made a sound in his throat, like a sigh, as if to say he didn't care if I believed him or not. But he did care. He wanted me to feel the truth, to believe by the raw force of feeling. He seemed sad, in a way.

"These six guys," he said, "they're pretty fried out by now, and one night they start hearing voices. Like at a cocktail party. That's what it sounds like, this big swank gook cocktail party somewhere out there in the fog. Music and chitchat and stuff. It's crazy, I know, but they hear the champagne corks. They hear the actual martini glasses. Real hoity-toity, all very civilized, except this isn't civilization. This is Nam.

"Anyway, the guys try to be cool. They just lie there and groove, but after a while they start hearing—you won't believe this— they hear chamber music. They hear violins and cellos. They hear this terrific mama-san soprano. Then after a while they hear gook opera and a glee club and the Haiphong Boys Choir and a barbershop quartet and all kinds of weird chanting and Buddha-Buddha stuff. And the whole time, in the background, there's still that cocktail party going on. All these different voices. Not human voices, though. Because it's the mountains. Follow me? The rock—it's *talking*. And the fog, too, and the grass and the goddamn mongooses. Everything talks. The trees talk politics, the monkeys talk religion. The whole country. Vietnam. The place talks. It talks. Understand? Nam—it truly *talks*.

"The guys can't cope. They lose it. They get on the radio and report enemy movement—a whole army, they say—and they order up the firepower. They get arty and gunships. They call in air strikes. And I'll tell you, they fuckin' crash that cocktail party. All night long, they just smoke those mountains. They make jungle juice. They blow away trees and glee clubs and whatever else there is to blow away. Scorch time.

They walk napalm up and down the ridges. They bring in the Cobras and F-4s, they use Willie Peter and HE and incendiaries. It's all fire. They make those mountains burn.

"Around dawn things finally get quiet. Like you never even *heard* quiet before. One of those real thick, real misty days—just clouds and fog, they're off in this special zone—and the mountains are absolutely dead-flat silent. Like Brigadoon—pure vapor, you know? Everything's all sucked up inside the fog. Not a single sound, except they still *hear* it.

"So they pack up and start humping. They head down the mountain, back to base camp, and when they get there they don't say diddly. They don't talk. Not a word, like they're deaf and dumb. Later on this fat bird colonel comes up and asks what the hell happened out there. What'd they hear? Why all the ordnance? The man's ragged out, he gets down tight on their case. I mean, they spent six trillion dollars on firepower, and this fatass colonel wants answers, he wants to know what the fuckin' story is.

"But the guys don't say zip. They just look at him for a while, sort of funny like, sort of amazed, and the whole war is right there in that stare. It says everything you can't ever say. It says, man, you got *wax* in your ears. It says, poor bastard, you'll never know—wrong frequency—you don't *even* want to hear this. Then they salute the fucker and walk away, because certain stories you don't ever tell."

You can tell a true war story by the way it never seems to end. Not then, not ever. Not when Mitchell Sanders stood up and moved off into the dark.

It all happened.

Even now, at this instant, I remember that yo-yo. In a way, I suppose, you had to be there, you had to hear it, but I could tell how desperately Sanders wanted me to believe him, his frustration at not quite getting the details right, not quite pinning down the final and definitive truth.

And I remember sitting at my foxhole that night, watching the shadows of Quang Ngai, thinking about the coming day and how we would cross the river and march west into the mountains, all the ways I might die, all the things I did not understand.

Late in the night Mitchell Sanders touched my shoulder.

"Just came to me," he whispered. "The moral, I mean. Nobody listens. Nobody hears nothin'. Like that fatass colonel. The politicians, all the civilian types. Your girlfriend. My girlfriend. Everybody's sweet little virgin girlfriend. What they need is to go out on LP. The vapors, man. Trees and rocks—you got to *listen* to your enemy."

And then again, in the morning, Sanders came up to me. The platoon was preparing to move out, checking weapons, going through all the little rituals that preceded a day's march. Already the lead squad had crossed the river and was filing off toward the west.

"I got a confession to make," Sanders said. "Last night, man, I had to make up a few things."

"I know that."

"The glee club. There wasn't any glee club."

"Right."

"No opera."

"Forget it, I understand."

"Yeah, but listen, it's still true. Those six guys, they heard wicked sound out there. They heard sound you just plain won't believe."

Sanders pulled on his rucksack, closed his eyes for a moment, then almost smiled at me. I knew what was coming.

"All right," I said, "what's the moral?"

"Forget it."

"No, go ahead."

For a long while he was quiet, looking away, and the silence kept stretching out until it was almost embarassing. Then he shrugged and gave me a stare that lasted all day.

"Hear that quiet, man?" he said. "That quiet—just listen. There's your moral."

In a true war story, if there's a moral at all, it's like the thread that makes the cloth. You can't tease it out. You can't extract the meaning without unraveling the deeper meaning. And in the end, really, there's nothing much to say about a true war story, except maybe "Oh."

True war stories do not generalize. They do not indulge in abstraction or analysis.

For example: War is hell. As a moral declaration the old truism seems perfectly true, and yet because it abstracts, because it generalizes, I can't believe it with my stomach. Nothing turns inside.

It comes down to gut instinct. A true war story, if truly told, makes the stomach believe.

• • •

This one does it for me. I've told it before—many times, many versions—but here's what actually happened.

We crossed that river and marched west into the mountains. On the third day, Curt Lemon stepped on a booby-trapped 105 round. He was playing catch with Rat Kiley, laughing, and then he was dead. The trees were thick; it took nearly an hour to cut an LZ for the dustoff.

Later, higher in the mountains, we came across a baby VC water buffalo. What it was doing there I don't know—no farms or paddies—but we chased it down and got a rope around it and led it along to a deserted village where we set up for the night. After supper Rat Kiley went over and stroked its nose.

He opened up a can of C rations, pork and beans, but the baby buffalo wasn't interested.

Rat shrugged.

He stepped back and shot it through the right front knee. The animal did not make a sound. It went down hard, then got up again, and Rat took careful aim and shot off an ear. He shot it in the hindquarters and in the little hump at its back. He shot it twice in the flanks. It wasn't to kill; it was to hurt. He put the rifle muzzle up against the mouth and shot the mouth away. Nobody said much. The whole platoon stood there watching, feeling all kinds of things, but there wasn't a great deal of pity for the baby water buffalo. Curt Lemon was dead. Rat Kiley had lost his best friend in the world. Later in the week he would write a long personal letter to the guy's sister, who would not write back, but for now it was a question of pain. He shot off the tail. He shot away chunks of meat below the ribs. All around us there was the smell of smoke and filth and deep greenery, and the evening was humid and very hot. Rat went to automatic. He shot randomly, almost casually, quick little spurts in the belly and butt. Then he reloaded, squatted down, and shot it in the left front knee. Again the animal fell hard and tried to get up, but this time it couldn't quite make it. It wobbled and went down sideways. Rat shot it in the nose. He bent forward and whispered something, as if talking to a pet, then he shot it in the throat. All the while the baby buffalo was silent, or almost silent, just a light bubbling sound where the nose had been. It lay very still. Nothing moved except the eyes, which were enormous, the pupils shiny black and dumb.

Rat Kiley was crying. He tried to say something, but then cradled his rifle and went off by himself.

The rest of us stood in a ragged circle around the baby buffalo. For a time no one spoke. We had witnessed something essential, something brand-new and profound, a piece of the world so startling there was not yet a name for it.

Somebody kicked the baby buffalo.

It was still alive, though just barely, just in the eyes.

"Amazing," Dave Jensen said. "My whole life, I never seen anything like it."

"Never?"

"Not hardly. Not once."

Kiowa and Mitchell Sanders picked up the baby buffalo. They hauled it across the open square, hoisted it up, and dumped it in the village well.

Afterward, we sat waiting for Rat to get himself together.

"Amazing," Dave Jensen kept saying. "A new wrinkle. I never seen it before."

Mitchell Sanders took out his yo-yo. "Well, that's Nam," he said. "Garden of Evil. Over here, man, every sin's real fresh and original."

How do you generalize?

War is hell, but that's not the half of it, because war is also mystery and terror and adventure and courage and discovery and holiness and pity and despair and longing and love. War is nasty; war is fun. War is thrilling; war is drudgery. War makes you a man; war makes you dead.

The truths are contradictory. It can be argued, for instance, that war is grotesque. But in truth war is also beauty. For all its horror, you can't help but gape at the awful majesty of combat. You stare out at tracer rounds unwinding through the dark like brilliant red ribbons. You crouch in ambush as a cool, impassive moon rises over the nighttime paddies. You admire the fluid symmetries of troops on the move, the harmonies of sound and shape and proportion, the great sheets of metal-fire streaming down from a gunship, the illumination rounds, the white phosphorus, the purply orange glow of napalm, the rocket's red glare. It's not pretty, exactly. It's astonishing. It fills the eye. It commands you. You hate it, yes, but your eyes do not. Like a killer forest fire, like cancer under a microscope, any battle or bombing raid or artillery barrage has the aesthetic purity of absolute moral indifference—a powerful, implacable beauty—and a

true war story will tell the truth about this, though the truth is ugly.

To generalize about war is like generalizing about peace. Almost everything is true. Almost nothing is true. At its core, perhaps, war is just another name for death, and yet any soldier will tell you, if he tells the truth, that proximity to death brings with it a corresponding proximity to life. After a firefight, there is always the immense pleasure of aliveness. The trees are alive. The grass, the soil—everything. All around you things are purely living, and you among them, and the aliveness makes you tremble. You feel an intense, out-of-the-skin awareness of your living self—your truest self, the human being you want to be and then become by the force of wanting it. In the midst of evil you want to be a good man. You want decency. You want justice and courtesy and human concord, things you never knew you wanted. There is a kind of largeness to it, a kind of godliness. Though it's odd, you're never more alive than when you're almost dead. You recognize what's valuable. Freshly, as if for the first time, you love what's best in yourself and in the world, all that might be lost. At the hour of dusk you sit at your foxhole and look out on a wide river turning pinkish red, and at the mountains beyond, and although in the morning you must cross the river and go into the mountains and do terrible things and maybe die, even so, you find yourself studying the fine colors on the river, you feel wonder and awe at the setting of the sun, and you are filled with a hard, aching love for how the world could be and always should be, but now is not.

Mitchell Sanders was right. For the common soldier, at least, war has the feel—the spiritual texture—of a great ghostly fog, thick and permanent. There is no clarity. Everything swirls. The old rules are no longer binding, the old truths no longer true. Right spills over into wrong. Order blends into chaos, love into hate, ugliness into beauty, law into anarchy, civility into savagery. The vapors suck you in. You can't tell where you are, or why you're there, and the only certainty is overwhelming ambiguity.

In war you lose your sense of the definite, hence your sense of truth itself, and therefore it's safe to say that in a true war story nothing is ever absolutely true.

Often in a true war story there is not even a point, or else the point doesn't hit you until twenty years later, in your sleep, and you wake up and shake your wife and start telling the story to her, except when you get to the end you've forgotten the point again. And then for a long time you lie there watching the story happen in your head. You listen to your wife's breathing. The war's over. You close your eyes. You smile and think, Christ, what's the *point?*

This one wakes me up.

In the mountains that day, I watched Lemon turn sideways. He laughed and said something to Rat Kiley. Then he took a peculiar half step, moving from shade into bright sunlight, and the booby-trapped 105 round blew him into a tree. The parts were just hanging there, so Dave Jensen and I were ordered to shinny up and peel him off. I remember the white bone of an arm. I remember pieces of skin and something wet and yellow that must've been the intestines.

The gore was horrible, and stays with me. But what wakes me up twenty years later is Dave Jensen singing "Lemon Tree" as we threw down the parts.

You can tell a true war story by the questions you ask. Somebody tells a story, let's say, and afterward you ask, "Is it true?" and if the answer matters, you've got your answer.

For example, we've all heard this one. Four guys go down a trail. A grenade sails out. One guy jumps on it and takes the blast and saves his three buddies.

Is it true?

The answer matters.

You'd feel cheated if it never happened. Without the grounding reality, it's just a trite bit of puffery, pure Hollywood, untrue in the way all such stories are untrue. Yet even if it did happen—and maybe it did, anything's possible—even then you know it can't be true, because a true war story does not depend upon that kind of truth. Absolute occurrence is irrelevant. A thing may happen and be a total lie; another thing may not happen and be truer than the truth. For example: Four guys go down a trail. A grenade sails out. One guy jumps on it and takes the blast, but it's a killer grenade and everybody dies anyway. Before they die, though, one of the dead guys says, "The fuck you do *that* for?" and the jumper says, "Story of my life, man," and the other guy starts to smile but he's dead.

That's a true story that never happened.

Twenty years later, I can still see the sunlight on Lemon's face. I can see him turning, looking back at Rat Kiley, then he laughed and took that curious half step from shade into sunlight, his face suddenly brown and shining, and when his foot touched down, in that instant, he must've thought it was the sunlight that was killing him. It was not the sunlight. It was a rigged 105 round. But if I could ever get the story right, how the sun seemed to gather around him and pick him up and lift him high into a tree, if I could somehow recreate the fatal whiteness of that light, the quick glare, the

obvious cause and effect, then you would believe the last thing Curt Lemon believed, which for him must've been the final truth.

Now and then, when I tell this story, someone will come up to me afterward and say she liked it. It's always a woman. Usually it's an older woman of kindly temperament and humane politics. She'll explain that as a rule she hates war stories; she can't understand why people want to wallow in all the blood and gore. But this one she liked. The poor baby buffalo, it made her sad. Sometimes, even, there are little tears. What I should do, she'll say, is put it all behind me. Find new stories to tell.

I won't say it but I'll think it.

I'll picture Rat Kiley's face, his grief, and I'll think, *You dumb cooze.*

Because she wasn't listening.

It *wasn't* a war story. It was a *love* story.

But you can't say that. All you can do is tell it one more time, patiently, adding and subtracting, making up a few things to get at the real truth. No Mitchell Sanders, you tell her. No Lemon, no Rat Kiley. No trail junction. No baby buffalo. No vines or moss or white blossoms. Beginning to end, you tell her, it's all made up. Every goddamn detail— the mountains and the river and especially that poor dumb baby buffalo. None of it happened. *None* of it. And even if it did happen, it didn't happen in the mountains, it happened in this little village on the Batangan Peninsula, and it was raining like crazy, and one night a guy named Stink Harris woke up screaming with a leech on his tongue. You can tell a true war story if you just keep on telling it.

And in the end, of course, a true war story is never about war. It's about sunlight. It's about the special way that dawn spreads out on a river when you know you must cross the river and march into the mountains and do things you are afraid to do. It's about love and memory. It's about sorrow. It's about sisters who never write back and people who never listen.